TOTAL RECALL

The Evolution of Memory

Edited by / *Herausgegeben von*
Hannes Leopoldseder / Gerfried Stocker / Christine Schöpf

Ars Electronica 2013
Festival für Kunst, Technologie und Gesellschaft
Festival for Art, Technology, and Society

5. – 9. September 2013 / September 5 – 9, 2013
Ars Electronica, Linz

Herausgeber / *Editors:* Hannes Leopoldseder,
Christine Schöpf, Gerfried Stocker

Redaktion / *Editing:* Jutta Schmiederer

Übersetzungen / *Translations:*
(Englisch-Deutsch / English-German): Martina Bauer,
Ingrid Fischer-Schreiber, Michael Kaufmann, Wilfried Prantner
(Deutsch-Englisch / German-English, all texts unless
otherwise indicated): Mel Greenwald
(Spanisch-Deutsch / Spanish-German): Jutta Schmiederer

Lektorat / *Copyediting:* Ingrid Fischer-Schreiber,
Catherine M. Lewis, Jutta Schmiederer

Grafische Gestaltung und Produktion /
Graphic design and production: Gerhard Kirchschläger

Schrift / *Typeface:* Klavika

Druck / *Printed by:* Gutenberg Werbering GmbH, Linz

Papier / *Paper:* BVS matt, 135 g/m²
Galerie Vision, 285 g/m²

Erschienen im / *Published by*
Hatje Cantz Verlag
Zeppelinstrasse 32
73760 Ostfildern
Deutschland / *Germany*
Tel. +49 711 4405-200
Fax +49 711 4405-220
www.hatjecantz.com
Ein Unternehmen der Ganske Verlagsgruppe
A Ganske Publishing Group company

Informationen zu dieser oder zu anderen
Ausstellungen finden Sie unter www.kq-daily.de
*You can find information on this exhibition
and many others at www.kq-daily.de*

Hatje Cantz books are available internationally at
selected bookstores. For more information about our
distribution partners please visit our homepage at
www.hatjecantz.com.

ISBN 978-3-7757-3630-5

Printed in Austria

Umschlagabbildung / *Cover illustration:*
Textur: grungetextures.com
Illustration: Nicolas Naveau, Ars Electronica Futurelab

PEFC
PEFC/06-39-27
Dieses Produkt stammt aus
nachhaltig bewirtschafteten
Wäldern und kontrollierten Quellen.

klimaneutral gedruckt CP IKS-Nr.: 53401-1308-1001

ARS ELECTRONICA

HATJE
CANTZ

Ars Electronica 2013

Festival für Kunst, Technologie und Gesellschaft
Festival for Art, Technology and Society

Organization
Ars Electronica Linz GmbH

Managing Directors
Gerfried Stocker, Diethard Schwarzmair
Ars-Electronica-Straße 1, 4040 Linz, Austria
Tel: +4373272720
Fax: +4373272722
info@aec.at

Co-organizers

ORF Oberösterreich
Director: Kurt Rammerstorfer

LIVA – Veranstaltungsgesellschaft m.b.H.
Directors: Hans-Joachim Frey, Wolfgang Lehner

OK Offenes Kulturhaus im OÖ Kulturquartier
Directors: Martin Sturm, Gabriele Daghofer

Partners
LENTOS Kunstmuseum Linz
Kunstuniversität Linz – Universität für künstlerische und industrielle Gestaltung
Tabakfabrik Linz
afo – architekturforum oberösterreich
MAERZ
Mariendom Linz
KIAVE
Bezalel Academy of Arts and Design, Jerusalem
Hamidrasha Art School am Beit Berl College
H.I.T – Holon Institute of Technology
Kibbutzim College of Art & Education, Tel Aviv
Shenkar College of Engineering and Design, Ramat Gan
Media Innovation Lab (miLAB) am IDC Herzliya
Musrara School, Jerusalem
Neri Bloomfield School of Design and Education, Haifa
Hadassah Academic College, Jerusalem
The College of Management – Academic Studies (COMAS)
FH Oberösterreich – Campus Hagenberg
Diakoniewerk
Japan Media Arts Festival
ikono.tv
Ministry of Culture, Republic of China (Taiwan)
中華民國文化部
The Association of the Visual Arts in Taiwan (AVAT)
SideBySide Studio e.V.
La Maison Laurentine
Ministry of Foreign Affairs, Republic of China (Taiwan)
中華民國外交部
Quanta Arts Foundation
MEGA - Museum of Electronic Games & Art
Austria Game Jam, Verein für Innovative Unterhaltungssoftware
Andranik Ghalustians, Bildschirmsprünge

Directors Ars Electronica: Gerfried Stocker, Christine Schöpf
Head of Festival: Martin Honzik
Technical Head: Karl Julian Schmidinger
Internal Organization: Veronika Liebl

Production Team: Liam Achaibou, Laura Baumann, Katharina Bienert, Sigrid Blauensteiner, Stefan Brandmayr, Katharina Edlmair, Marlene Eggenreich, Hannes Franks, Stephanie Fuchs, Evi Garsleitner, Carmen Grabuschnig, Rosi Grillmair, Sarah Hellwagner, Simon Kopfberger, Alex Marasescu, Hans Christian Merten, Gerald Moser, Franziska Mucha, Kathrin Obernhumer, Emiko Ogawa, Maria Ogawa, Maria Pfeifer, Roland Ploner, Georg Pühringer, Miriam Schmeikal, Jutta Schmiederer, Florian Sedmak, Joschi Viteka, Susi Windischbauer, Michaela Wimplinger

Co-curators
Ars Electronica Animation Festival: Christine Schöpf, Jürgen Hagler
Big Concert Night: Dennis Russell Davies, Hans-Joachim Frey, Heribert Schröder
Campus Exhibition: Lila Chitayat, Yael Eylat Van-Essen, Sayfan G. Borghini, Oren Zuckerman, Eyal Vexler
Featured Artist HR Giger: Andreas Hirsch
Interface Cultures Exhibition: Faculty – Christa Sommerer, Laurent Mignonneau, Martin Kaltenbrunner, Michaela Ortner, Marlene Hochrieser, Georg Russegger
Pixelspaces: Horst Hörtner, Roland Haring, Veronika Pauser, Matthew Gardiner, Kristefan Minski, Johanna Mathauer, Michael Badics, Gabriele Purdue, Roland Reiter
Wir sind Hier: Salvatore Vanasco, Claudius Brodmann

Prix Ars Electronica 2013

Co-organizers

ORF Oberösterreich
Director: Kurt Rammerstorfer

LIVA – Veranstaltungsgesellschaft m.b.H.
Directors: Hans-Joachim Frey, Wolfgang Lehner

OK Offenes Kulturhaus im OÖ Kulturquartier
Directors: Martin Sturm, Gabriele Daghofer

Idea: Hannes Leopoldseder
Conception: Christine Schöpf, Gerfried Stocker
Coordination: Martin Honzik, Emiko Ogawa
Technical Management: Karl Julian Schmidinger

Production Team: Florian Bauböck, Bernhard Böhm, Viktor Delev, Stefan Dorn, Marlene Eggenreich, Christoph Einfalt, Ingrid Fischer-Schreiber, Gregor Göttfert, Sarah Stefanie Hellwagner, Michael Lettner, Veronika Liebl, Johanna Mathauer, Manuela Naveau, Kathrin Obernhumer, Johannes Ramsl, Remo Rauscher, Miriam Schmeikal, Florian Voggeneder, Susi Windischbauer

Press: Christopher Sonnleitner, Robert Bauernhansl, Michael Knoll, Raphael Gierlinger

Marketing: Sina Balke-Juhn, Cornelia Erber, Isabella Grünauer, Martina Huber

Ars Electronica Archive: Martina Hechenberger, Elvis Pavic, Christina Radner, Heinz Sambs, Jutta Schmiederer

Ars Electronica Linz GmbH

Ars Electronica Center: Andreas Bauer, Christoph Kremer, Renata Aigner, Viktoria Aistleitner, Reinhard Bengesser, Tamara Böhm, Sarah Breinbauer, Blanka Denkmaier, Wolfgang Deutsch, Hans Peter Ecker, Johannes Egler, Erika Eiter, Stefanie Farkashazy, Karl Federspiel, Julia Felberbauer, Melinda File, Evelyn Fränzl, Anna Friedinger, Andrea Fröhlich, Mitra Gazvini-Zateh, Christian Gerber, Elisabeth Gerhard-Mayrhofer, Nicole Grüneis, Ulrike Gschwandtner, Harald Haas, Gerid Maria Hager, Birgit Hartinger, Gerlinde Hauder, Florian Heiml, Martin Hieslmair, Thomas Hillinger, Denise Hinger, Gerold Hofstadler, Sri Rahayu Hofstadler, Katharina Hoffelner, Klaus Hollinetz, Lorena Höllrigl, Philip Huemer, Thomas Jannke, Erika Jungreithmayr, Elisabeth Kattner, Daniel Kern, Herwig Kerschner, Viktoria Klepp, Eva Klimesova, Michael Koller, Thomas Kollmann, Wolfgang König, Kristýna Krabatschová, David Lang, Andreas Leeb, Sabine Leidlmair, Juliane Leitner, Dominic Lengauer, Anna Katharina Link, Ulrike Mair, Reingard Medicus, Kathrin Meyer, Clemens Mock, Horst Morocutti, Marc Mühlberger, Daniel Murina, Heinrich Niederhuber, Michaela Obermayer, Benjamin Perndl, Svetlana Petrovic, Katharina Pilar, Armin Pils, Victoria Pilz, Andreas Plakolm, Anna Polewiak, Mathias Pöschko, Ulrike Rieseneder, Karl Hans Rois, Andreas Roth, Petra Saubolle-Hofmann, Alina Sauter, Birgitt Schäffer, Johann Schauer, Barbara Schmidt, Nina Schönberger, Markus Schwarzmair, Stefan Schwarzmair, Elio Seidl, Manfred Seifriedsberger, Margarete Stöttner-Breuer, Johannes Strasser, Lioubov Studener, Johannes Stürzlinger, Istvan Szabo, Bhoomesh Tak, Kerstin Tak-Wakolbinger, Michaela Maria Tanzer, Michael Thaler, Michael Trebo, Clarissa Ujvari, Linda Vankova, Thomas Viehböck, Florian Voggeneder, Karin Wabro, Florian Wanninger, Sebastian Zach, Silvia Zainzinger

Ars Electronica Futurelab: Horst Hörtner, Christopher Lindinger, Roland Haring, Roland Aigner, Tamer Aslan, Florian Berger, Bhavanesh Chamdal, Manuel Dobusch, Barbara Erlinger, Maria Eschlböck, Peter Freudling, Matthew Gardiner, Peter Holzkorn, Andreas Jalsovec, Michael Knoll, Anna Lucia Kuthan, Martina Mara, Johanna Mathauer, Benjamin Mayr, Michael Mayr, Kristefan Minski, Stefan Mittlböck-Jungwirth-Fohringer, Patrick Müller, Otto Naderer, Nicolas Naveau, Hideaki Ogawa, Veronika Pauser, Michael Platz, Erwin Reitböck, Deniz Saglam

Ars Electronica Festival: Martin Honzik, Karl Julian Schmidinger, Florian Bauböck, Laura Baumann, Katharina Bienert, Sigrid Blauensteiner, Stefan Brandmayr, Marlene Eggenreich, Stephanie Fuchs, Carmen Grabuschnig, Rosi Grillmair, Sarah Stefanie Hellwagner, Veronika Liebl, Michael Lettner, Hans Christian Merten, Franziska Mucha, Manuela Naveau, Kathrin Obernhumer, Emiko Ogawa, Maria Ogawa, Maria Pfeifer, Georg Pühringer, Miriam Schmeikal, Jutta Schmiederer, Susi Windischbauer

Ars Electronica Management Services: Elisabeth Kapeller, Markus Jandl, Sina Balke-Juhn, Sebastian Bauböck, Robert Bauernhansl, Bettina Danninger, Barbara Diesenreither, Bettina Gahleitner, Gerhard Grafinger, Michael Grausgruber, Isabella Grünauer, Martina Hechenberger, Gerald Hochhauser, Gerold Hofstadler, Martina Huber, Andrea Huemer, Heinrich Klambauer, Martin Kneidinger, Stephan Kobler, Zulfija Magomedova, Michaela Neunherz, Peter -J. Nitzschmann,- Elvis Pavic, Julia Rabeder, Christina Radner, Christopher-Sonnleitner, Heinz Sambs, David Starzengruber, Michaela Wimplinger

Ars Electronica Solutions: Bernd Albl, Michael Badics, Lukas Bischof, Chris Bruckmayr, Cecile Bucher, Stefan Dorn, Stefan Fuchs, David Gann, My-Trinh Gardiner, Imanol Gomez, Yvonne Hauser, Barbara Hinterleitner, Christoph Hofbauer, Martina Karrer, Petros Kataras, Fadil Kujundzic, Kathrin Agnes Meyer, Harald Moser, Ali Nikrang, Benjamin Olsen, Dietmar Peter, Andreas Pramböck, Gerald Priewasser, Stephan Pointner, Gabriele Purdue, Roland Reiter, Vanessa Schauer, Markus Wipplinger, Claus Zweythurm

Spaxels Task Force: Horst Hörtner, Daniel Aigenbauer, Florian Berger, Chris Bruckmayr, Andreas Jalsovec, Martin Mörth, Benjamin Olsen, Michael Platz

OK Offenes Kulturhaus im OÖ Kulturquartier

OK CyberArts Team
Artistic Director: Martin Sturm
Commercial Director: Gabriele Daghofer
Curator: Genoveva Rückert
Public Relations: Maria Falkinger
Technical Manager: Rainer Jessl
Production: Martina Rauschmayer, Aron Rynda
Technical Head: Markus Wallner

Production Team: Jarno Bachheimer, Attila Ferenczi, Alfred Fürholzer, Martin Haselsteiner, Bernhard Kitzmüller, Andreas Kurz, Daniel Mandel, Gerald Schreilechner, Andreas Steindl, André Tschinder, Tom Vens, Hans-Jörg Weidinger, Gerhard Wörnhörer, Simon Wilhelm

Team: Verena Atteneder, Johann Aufreiter, Erika Baldinger, Renate Berger, Julia Brunner, Michael Dalpiaz, Walter Eckerstorfer, Max Fabian, Michaela Fröhlich, Andrea Gintner, Manuela Gruber, Dominik Harrer, Sabine Haunschmid, Evi Heininger, Robert Herbst, Maximilian Höglinger, Fritz Holzinger, Verena, Karner, Simon Lachner, -Katharina Lackner, Elisabeth Lehner, Judith Maule, Franz Minichberger, Walter Mühlböck, Wolfgang Nagl, Josef Pfarrhofer, Franz -Pfifferling, Wilhelm Pichler, Angelika Pöschl, Franz Quirchtmayr, Brigitte Rosenthaler, Gerda Sailer, Markus Schiller, Ulrike Schimpl, Alexandra Schlager, Helene Schoißengeyr, Ulrike Seelmann, Barbara Steindl, Marlies Stöger

Brucknerhaus

Wolfgang Scheibner, Wolfgang Schützeneder, Ursula Kislinger

afo – architekturforum oberösterreich

Architektur und Klang
Curatorial Head: Andre Zogholy
Co-Curator: Elmecker Ewald
Technical Team: Dietmar Elmecker Ewald, Hannes Franks

ORGANIZATION / VERANSTALTER

ARS ELECTRONICA

Ars Electronica Linz GmbH is a company of the city of Linz.
Ars Electronica Linz GmbH ist ein Unternehmen der Stadt Linz.

COOPERATION PARTNERS / KOOPERATIONSPARTNER

LENTOS Kunstmuseum Linz
Kunstuniversität Linz – Universität für künstlerische und industrielle Gestaltung
Tabakfabrik Linz
afo – architekturforum oberösterreich
MAERZ
Mariendom Linz
KIAVE
Bezalel Academy of Arts and Design, Jerusalem
Hamidrasha Art School, Beit Berl College
H.I.T – Holon Institute of Technology
Kibbutzim College of Art & Education, Tel Aviv
Shenkar College of Engineering and Design, Ramat Gan
Media Innovation Lab (miLAB), IDC Herzliya
Musrara School, Jerusalem
Neri Bloomfield School of Design and Education, Haifa
Hadassah Academic College, Jerusalem
College of Management – Academic Studies (COMAS)
FH Oberösterreich – Campus Hagenberg
Diakoniewerk
Japan Media Arts Festival
ikono.tv
Ministry of Culture, Republic of China (Taiwan) 中華民國文化部
The Association of the Visual Arts in Taiwan (AVAT)
SideBySide Studio e.V.
La Maison Laurentine
Ministry of Foreign Affairs, Republic of China (Taiwan) 中華民國外交部
Quanta Arts Foundation
MEGA – Museum of Electronic Games & Art
Austria Game Jam, Verein für Innovative Unterhaltungssoftware
Andranik Ghalustians, Bildschirmsprünge
Kinderfreunde Oberösterreich
LIFEtool gemeinnützige GmbH
LEGO
REHA SERVICE GmbH

ARS ELECTRONICA RECEIVES SUPPORT FROM / ARS ELECTRONICA WIRD UNTERSTÜTZT VON:

Stadt Linz

Land Oberösterreich

Bundesministerium für Unterricht, Kunst und Kultur

Bundesministerium für Wissenschaft und Forschung

voestalpine

bfi

Hutchison 3

Linz AG

Mercedes-Benz

SSI Schäfer Shop

Liwest

ARS ELECTRONICA RECEIVES SUPPORT FROM / ARS ELECTRONICA WIRD UNTERSTÜTZT VON:

Sparkasse OÖ

Wirtschaftskammer OÖ

Ton + Bild

ÖBB

OÖ Nachrichten

Kronen Zeitung

Ö1

FM4

Standard

Arte

Smurfit Kappa

Casino Linz

Japan Foundation

EU-Japan Fest Japan Committee

Quanta Arts Foundation

Messe Linz

LIVA

NTS

Trotec

Screenteam

Kuka

Studiolab

European Union

7th Framework Programme

Diakoniewerk

Pro Helvetia

Mondriaan Fonds

Jugend in Aktion

PH Oberösterreich

Rotes Kreuz

Cordial

USP

Triple A

Phoenics

Sony DADC

Sampad

Akademie des österreichischen Films

Additional Support: KulturKontakt Austria, Cubus

CONTENTS

Gerfried Stocker
12 **TOTAL RECALL – The Evolution of Memory**

TOTAL RECALL

John-Dylan Haynes
18 **Mindreading in Modern Neuroscience**

Rodrigo Quian Quiroga
25 **Funes and Other Cases of Extraordinary Memory**

Helga Rohra
33 **Dementia exists everywhere**

Nick Goldman, Charlotte Jarvis
35 **The DNA Chronicles**

Frank Hartmann
38 **Paul Otlet and the Logic of the Database**

Michael K. Buckland
46 **Recorded is not remembered: The case of Emanuel Goldberg**

Claudia Schmölders
54 **The Female Voice in Acoustic Archives**

TOTAL RECALL EXHIBITION

62 Ei Wada, **Falling Records**

64 Dimension+, **Device Playing Cassette Recorder (II)**

66 Yuri Suzuki, **The Sound of the Earth**

68 Brian House, **Quotidian Record**

70 Patrick Feaster, **The oldest recorded sounds**

72 Social Fabrication Center SFC (SFC*SFC), **Wave Form Media**

74 Oliver Bimber, **Light-Field Technology**

76 Reinhard Nestlbacher, **Cell Camera**

78 Daniel Reetz, **DIY Book Scanner**

80 Hiroshi Ishiguro, **Beicho Android**

82 Hiroto Ikeuchi, **Fantasy Captured in Plastic Model**

84 Doris Graf, **Pikträt**

86 Mariano Sardón, Mariano Sigman **The Table of Gazes**

88 Benjamin Pollach, **The World Map Archive**

90 Theresa Schubert, **bodymetries**

92 Heather Dewey-Hagborg, **Stranger Visions**

94 Paul Vanouse, **Suspect Inversion Center**

96 Joaquin Fargas, BioArt Lab–Maimonides University **Big Brain Project**

100 Michael Madsen, **Into Eternity**

102 Markus Schmidt, Camillo Meinhart, **Diverseeds**

105 MEGA e.V., **Ludic Memento**

106 A. Ghalustian, J. Diephuis, S. Schraml **Retro/per/spectives**

108 Austria Game Jam, **Game Jam**

110 ikono, **ikono On Air Festival**

114 Alexander Schellow, **Drawing**

116 **Mobiles Ö1 Atelier – Projekt Bienenstock**

TOTAL RECALL EVENTS

120 Opening Project Ars Electronica 2013 **Wir sind hier**

138 Wolfgang "Fadi" Dorninger **The Aural Memory Machine**

140 **Huang Yi & KUKA**

144 Die Große Konzertnacht, **Welcome Transients**

146 Roberto Paci Dalò, **Ye Shanghai** 夜上海

148 **voestalpine Klangwolke 2013:** Bruckner lebt!

152 **Ars Electronica Music Day**

155 Werner Jauk, **Pop: music + media / art**

160 Station Rose, **Digital Quarter Century << ShelTeR >>**

162 Andre Zogholy, **Architecture and Sound**

FEATURED ARTIST

166 **HR Giger, Featured Artist Ars Electronica 2013**

INTERNATIONAL GUESTS

176 **Schizophrenia Taiwan 2.0**

184 **Japan Media Arts Festival**

CAMPUS

192 **Ars Campus Israel**

214 **Interface Cultures at Ars Electronica 2013**

ARS ELECTRONICA EXPORT

224 **External Exhibitions 2012/2013**
- 224 Ars Electronica – Wie eine zweite Natur, Berlin
- 227 Artists as Catalysts, Bilbao

230 Donumenta Regensburg, Germany
230 Possible Futures, São Paulo
231 TEA Collective Wisdom, Taiwan
232 Ars Electronica Animation Festival On Tour

ARS ELECTRONICA CENTER

236 **Project Genesis - Life from the Lab**
236 Matthew Gardiner, Yours Synthetically
245 Project Genesis - The Exhibition

252 **Like a Second Nature**
254 Yasuhiro Suzuki, Blinking Leaves
255 Rejane Cantoni & Leonardo Crescenti , Wall
256 Alistair McClymont, The Limitations of Logic and the Absence of Absolute Certainty
257 Keiko Takahashi, Meter Crawler
258 David Bowen, Tele-Present Wind
259 Ivan Henriques, Prototype for a New Biomachine
260 Hiroshi Ishiguro, Geminoid HI-4

262 **Zeit ist Held**

264 Kurt Hörbst, **people_scans**

268 Erika Jungreithmayr, g.tec, **Faces in the MatriX**

ARS ELECTRONICA CENTER - DEEP SPACE

272 Maki Namekawa, Dennis Russell Davies **The Memory of Le sacre du printemps**

276 Ina Conradi Chavez, **Elysian Fields**

280 University of Applied Sciences Upper Austria **Mind Games**

282 Alan Kwan, **Bad Trip**

283 ITAF 2013, **International Teletext Art Festival**

ARS ELECTRONICA FUTURELAB PIXELSPACES

288 **Pixelspaces 2013**

289 **Inside Ars Electronica Futurelab**
290 Horst Hörtner, SPAXEL - embodied spaces
298 phase7 Murmuration
299 TOSCA, Visualizations for TOSCA's Odeon
300 ELEKIT Japan Co., LTD Candlescape - Create a world in the light
301 Radio FRO openAIR - Accessibility in Radio Production
302 nitsch museum Hermann Nitsch - SINNE UND SEIN
303 Overview—In Touch with the Earth

304 **Ars Electronica Residency Network**
305 [the next idea] voestalpine Art and Technology Grant
307 Prix Ars Electronica Collide@CERN
309 Queensland University of Technology, Inter-virtual
310 The OHMI Ars Electronica Competition

311 **Ars Electronica Futurelab Academy**
312 Queensland University of Technology, QUT
314 Queensland University of Technology Project Bee Hive
315 University of Newcastle Imagination, Collaboration and Innovation
316 Connecting Cities: A European Network of Media Façades
320 Studiolab / Sphæræ
322 Fachhochschule Salzburg, CADET
323 Aakash Odedra, Lewis Major, Resonate
324 Hakuhodo Inc., Innovation Catalyst
325 OK Go, The Future Rock Show
326 Miraikan, Cultural Communication Program
330 Knowledge Capital Osaka, Ars Electronica Creative Cloud

332 **Inside Ars Electronica Solutions**
334 From Austria to the World Gigapixel Images of New York City at Vienna International Airport
338 MED-EL, Audioversum
341 GeoPulse - Ars Electronica Center
342 Musiktheater Linz, Interactive Installations
344 Stadt Linz, Linz verändert
346 Digital World by Schattdecor
347 Österreich Werbung, The atb experience
348 Umdasch Shopfitting, RAG Wall
349 Liebherr, Slide Presenter

ARS ELECTRONICA ANIMATION

352 Jürgen Hagler, **Expanded Digital Animation**

354 **Ars Electronica Animation Festival 2013**

362 **Prix Ars Electronica 2013**

u19 - CREATE YOUR WOLRD

370 **u19 - CREATE YOUR WORLD**
371 **u19 - CREATE YOUR WOLRD** - Projects 2013

376 **Biographies**

Gerfried Stocker

TOTAL RECALL

The Evolution of Memory

One of science's most coveted secrets and one of humankind's greatest technological challenges will occupy the focal point of the next Ars Electronica Festival September 5-9, 2013: memory and its storage. What is remembrance? How is information saved to memory and how is it lost—in nature, in technology, in the future?

TOTAL RECALL is the theme of Ars Electronica 2013, a search for the perfect memory. We'll ask neuroscientists and computer engineers, artists and philosophers about their approaches, about the latest findings and their interpretations of them, and about their plans and visions of a future in which we'll be able to save everything to memory.

But just how does one go about performing research on recollection, and how much progress have we made? What's connectome research, and what in the world is a Jennifer Aniston neuron? How is a memory formed in the human brain and how is it lost? Are there prospects of someday being able to heal or even prevent dementia and Alzheimer's disease?

How far have we come in finally delivering on the promise of mapping the human brain and creating artificial intelligence? When we do succeed in developing artificial intelligence, what will we

Vom 5. bis 9. September stehen eines der größten Geheimnisse der Wissenschaft und eine der größten technischen Herausforderungen im Mittelpunkt von Ars Electronica 2013: Erinnerung und ihre Speicherung – was ist Erinnerung, wie entsteht Gedächtnis und wie geht es verloren? In der Natur, in der Technologie, in der Zukunft.

Unter dem Titel *TOTAL RECALL* begibt sich Ars Electronica 2013 auf die Suche nach dem perfekten Gedächtnis, befragt HirnforscherInnen und ComputerwissenschaftlerInnen, KünstlerInnen und PhilosophInnen nach ihren Zugängen, nach neuesten Erkenntnissen und Interpretationen, nach ihren Plänen und Visionen für eine Zukunft, in der wir alles speichern können.

Doch wie erforscht man das Erinnern? Wie weit verstehen wir es überhaupt schon? Was ist Konnektom-Forschung und was ist ein Jennifer-Aniston-Neuron? Wie entsteht Erinnerung in unserem Gehirn und wie geht sie verloren? Besteht die Aussicht, dass Demenz und Alzheimer irgendwann geheilt oder zumindest verhindert werden können?

Wie steht es mit dem schon so lange anstehenden Versprechen, das menschliche Gehirn nachzubilden und künstliche Intelligenz zu schaffen? Und wenn wir künstliche Intelligenz zustande bringen,

actually do with it, and what TV shows will these artificial intelligences spend their spare time watching?
What techniques will dominate the future of data storage? Will we ever be able to reevaluate the vast quantities of information we're generating? And what happens when, suddenly, there's no more electricity?
When everything about us is saved to memory, interlinked and accessible to everyone 24/7, what sort of society will be the upshot of this? And to whom will all these memories then belong, and who will be earning a fortune with them? Will forgetting be a human right someday? Which policies of remembrance will we institute and enforce?
What are the most important current projects and visions to save humankind's cultural heritage and to conserve it for posterity? What methods will be used in the future to accomplish this?
Is it possible to implement a storage method that's reliable not just for centuries but for millennia, and why do we actually want to do this?
Here are a few facts & figures and comparisons as a sort of lead-in to our dealings with this topic:
This is a byte: 01000001–eight combinations of 0 and 1 yield 256 permutations. This one, for instance, represents the number 65 and is ascribed to the letter A. This binary method of expression–one that's been known since the 3rd century–is a simple, efficient means of storing any type of information in digital circuits.
There are 1,048,576 such bytes in a megabyte. Writing a megabyte of text takes no fewer than 8,388,608 keystrokes. With an average-sized font (like the one you're reading now), you can get about 5,500 characters onto a standard A4 page, so printing out that text would take 1,525

was fangen wir dann damit an? Mit welchen Fernsehsendungen werden sich diese künstlichen Intelligenzen dann die Zeit vertreiben?
Welche Techniken sind die Zukunft der Datenspeicherung? Werden wir die unvorstellbaren Mengen an Information jemals wieder auswerten können? Und was passiert, wenn es plötzlich keinen Strom mehr gibt?
Wenn alles über uns gespeichert und verknüpft wird und von jedem jederzeit abrufbar ist, welche Gesellschaft wird daraus entstehen? Wem gehören dann all diese Erinnerungen und wer wird damit viel Geld verdienen? Wird es ein Menschenrecht auf Vergessen geben? Welche Erinnerungspolitik werden wir pflegen?
Welche sind die aktuellen Projekte und Visionen, um das menschliche Kulturerbe zu speichern und für die Nachwelt zu erhalten, welche Methoden werden in Zukunft dafür zum Einsatz kommen? Kann man eine verlässliche Speicherung nicht nur für Jahrhunderte, sondern für Jahrtausende überhaupt bewerkstelligen, und warum wollen wir das eigentlich?
Ein paar Zahlenspiele und Vergleiche als Einstimmung auf das Thema:
Das ist ein Byte: 01000001. Acht Kombinationen von 0 und 1 erlauben 256 verschiedene Kombinationen. Damit kann man wie in diesem Fall die Zahl 65 darstellen und ihr den Buchstaben A zuordnen. Mit dieser seit dem 3. Jh. bekannten binären Darstellung kann jede Information einfach und effizient in digitalen Schaltkreisen gespeichert werden.
1.048.576 solcher Bytes ergeben ein MegaByte. Das aufzuschreiben, würde bereits 8.388.608 Zeichen benötigen. Mit einer durchschnittlichen Schriftgröße, wie sie für diesen Text verwendet wird, bringt man etwa 5.500 Zeichen auf eine DIN-A4-Seite und würde somit 1.525 Seiten dafür benötigen – aber das wäre gerade mal 1 MB, also viel weniger als jedes

pages. And that's all of 1 MB, which is much less than any cell phone photo and no more than six seconds of music on a CD.

6 MB was the size of the programs written at IBM for the moon landing ("the most complex software ever written"), and thus the equivalent of two snapshots taken by a modern smartphone.

The human genome constitutes 800 MB of data; a clever programmer could express the portions that differentiate individual humans from one another in 4 MB.

The quantity of data that humankind has stored to memory so far (i.e. not just created but saved to some medium that still makes it accessible, and yes, including the clay tablets that are still around) is estimated at 2.7 zettabytes, and of course it goes without saying that less than 1% of it is in non-digital form. 2.7 zettabytes has 21 zeroes on the end; connecting the sheets of standard paper needed to print it out would produce a band that could be wrapped around the world 500 times.

In 2007, the number was a mere 295 exabytes; the breakthrough of the 1 zettabyte mark is reported to have occurred in 2010; and the prognosis for 2015 is 8 zettabytes. By 2016, there'll be so many videos put online every month that it would take 6 million years to view them, and the amount of data put online in that year alone will exceed the total amount stored to date.

The latest methods in biotechnology have already successfully been used to store digital information in DNA. This will make it possible to store 100 million hours of high-definition videos in a single cup of DNA.

But what are we going to do with all this data, and what differentiates saved data from remembrance, from memory? What is memory, actually? How do neuronal networks function—from the simplest forms of life to the super-brain of Homo sapiens? Nature's perfect memory is DNA, which it uses not only for self-replication but also for evolution.

Handyfoto benötigt bzw. gerade mal 6 Sekunden Musik auf einer CD.

6 MB groß waren die Programme, die bei IBM für die Mondlandung geschrieben wurden („the most complex software ever written") – so viel wie gerade mal zwei Schnappschüsse mit einem modernen Smartphone.

Das menschliche Genom repräsentiert eine Datenmenge von 800 MB. Die Teile davon, die uns Menschen voneinander unterscheiden, kann man mit ein wenig Geschick auf 4 MB unterbringen. Die Menge an Daten, die von der Menschheit bis dato gespeichert wurde (also nicht bloß erzeugt, sondern gespeichert wurde und nach wie vor abrufbar ist – ja, inklusive der noch erhaltenen Schrifttafeln), wird auf 2,7 ZettaByte geschätzt Es erübrigt sich wohl darauf hinzuweisen, dass weniger als ein Prozent davon nicht digital sind. 2,7 ZettaByte – das ist eine Zahl mit 21 Nullen, und mit den DIN-A4-Seiten, die man dafür benötigen würde, könnte man die Erde 500 Mal umwickeln. 2007 waren es noch 295 ExaByte, 2010 berichtete man vom Überschreiten der 1-Zettabyte-Grenze, und bis 2015, wird die Datenmenge, so schätzt man, auf 8 ZettaByte anwachsen. Bis 2016 werden so viele Videos pro Monat im Netz zirkulieren, dass man 6 Millionen Jahre bräuchte, um sie zu sehen. Dann werden in allein diesem Jahr so viele Daten durchs Internet laufen, wie bislang überhaupt jemals gespeichert wurden. Mit den neuesten Möglichkeiten der Biotechnologie ist es bereits erfolgreich gelungen, digitale Informationen in DNA abzuspeichern. Damit lassen sich in Zukunft 100 Millionen Stunden HD-Videomaterial in einer einzigen Tasse DNA speichern.

Doch was tun wir mit all diesen Daten? Was unterscheidet gespeicherte Daten von Erinnerung und Gedächtnis? Was ist eigentlich Gedächtnis? Wie funktionieren neuronale Netzwerke, von den einfachsten Lebensformen bis zum Superhirn des Homo Sapiens?

But isn't every hydrogen atom ultimately a 100% exact and perfectly accessible memory that preserves the moment immediately after the Big Bang (380,000 years ago, scientists say) when the universe had cooled down sufficiently so that elementary particles could coalesce into atoms and everything began to take shape? Or perhaps it's the case that language is the basis for the transmission of knowledge and the preservation of memory?

"Recording," our term for registering information, comes from two syllables, "re" and "cor," and thus reminds us that people used to believe that we preserved memories in our heart. This might be a helpful association as we increasingly face the decision of what among this endless deluge of data actually interests or moves us. But where exactly is recollection located now? We don't know.

There's a story told about Ronald Reagan that during his 1980 presidential campaign he related with complete conviction a wartime experience that, although he seemed to have believed that it had really happened, turns out to have been merely the plot of a Hollywood film that he had internalized and made into a reminiscence. In numerous experiments, scientists have proved that our memories are anything but objective recordings of events that actually occurred. Accordingly, they're not something that's been put away for future reference like a book on a shelf, but rather a construction repeatedly regenerated in real time in our brain. Thus, the brain doesn't play the role of a repository or even of consciousness itself; rather, it's the interface between the individual and his/her environment, and memory and consciousness are constantly being created anew from the processes of this connection.

http://www.aec.at/totalrecall

Das perfekte Gedächtnis der Natur ist die DNA, mit der sich die Natur nicht nur selbst repliziert, sondern auch weiterentwickelt. Aber ist nicht letztlich jedes Wasserstoffatom ein hundertprozentig exaktes und abrufbares Gedächtnis, in dem der Moment kurz nach dem Urknall (380.000 Jahren danach, glauben die WissenschaftlerInnen) festgehalten ist, als das Universum erstmals soweit abgekühlt war, dass sich die Elementarteilchen zu Atomen zusammenfinden konnten und alles begann, Form anzunehmen? Oder ist doch erst die Sprache der Grundstein für die Weitergabe von Wissen und die Bewahrung von Erinnerung?

„Recording", unser technischer Begriff für das Aufzeichnen von Informationen, kommt von den zwei Silben „re" und „cor" und erinnert daran, dass man einst glaubte, Erinnerungen wären in unserem Herzen gespeichert – eventuell eine hilfreiche Assoziation, wenn es immer mehr darum geht zu entscheiden, was uns aus der unendlichen Datenflut tatsächlich interessieren, berühren soll. Doch wo sitzt Erinnerung nun wirklich? Wir wissen es nicht.

Von Ronald Reagan weiß man, dass er in seinem Wahlkampf 1980 immer wieder mit großer Überzeugung ein Kriegserlebnis schilderte, das aber, obwohl er selbst anscheinend fest daran glaubte, bloß die Handlung eines Hollywoodfilms war, die er aber für sich verinnerlicht und zu seiner Erinnerung gemacht hatte. WissenschaftlerInnen haben mittlerweile mit vielen Experimenten nachgewiesen, dass unsere Erinnerungen alles andere als objektive Aufzeichnungen des tatsächlich Geschehenen sind. Sie sind auch nichts, das abgelegt ist wie ein Buch in einem Regal, sondern jedes Mal wieder ein in Echtzeit entstehendes Konstrukt unseres Gehirns. Das Gehirn spielt also nicht die Rolle einer Lagerstätte oder gar des Bewusstseins selbst. Vielmehr ist das Gehirn der Verbindungspunkt zwischen dem Individuum und seinem Umfeld, und aus den Prozessen dieser Verbindung entstehen Erinnerung und Bewusstsein andauernd neu.

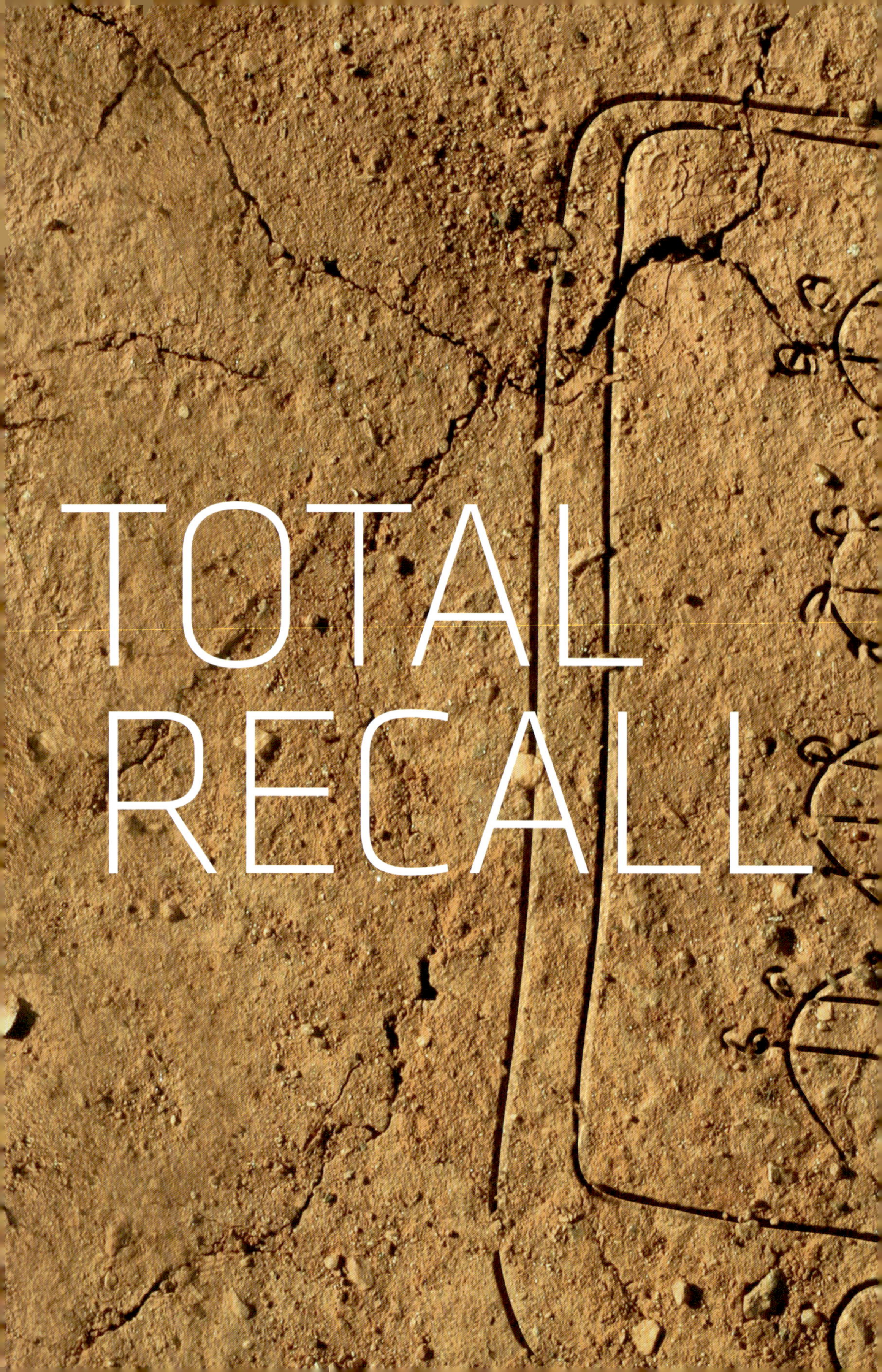
TOTAL
RECALL

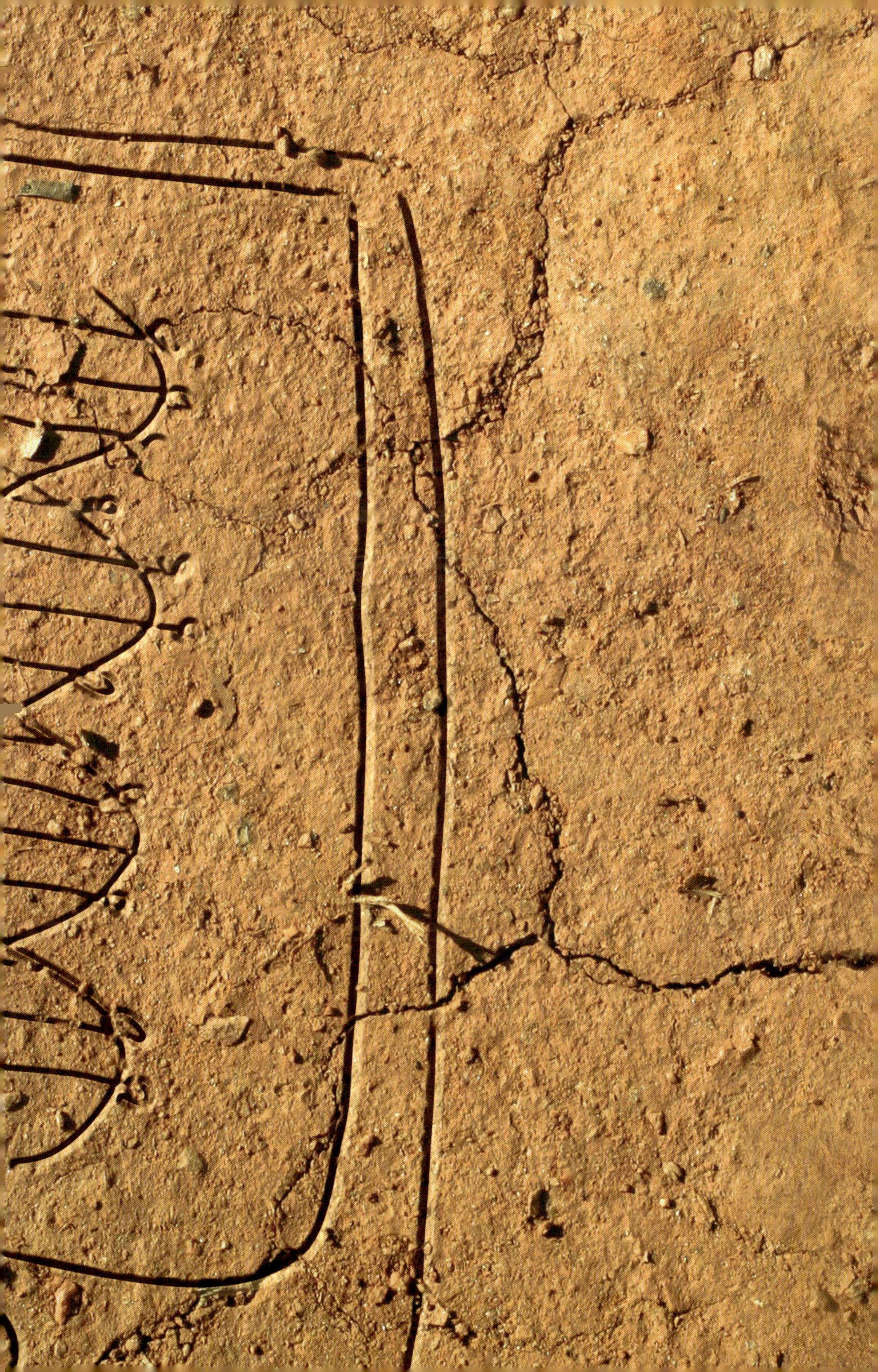

John-Dylan Haynes

Mindreading in Modern Neuroscience

Gedankenlesen in der modernen Hirnforschung*

Bernstein Center for Computational Neuroscience, Charité – Universitätsmedizin Berlin

A machine that can read a person's mind has long been considered pure science fiction. However, recent research has made impressive progress towards turning this vision into a reality, at least to some degree. Sophisticated computer programs can extract a surprising amount of information about a person's thoughts from their brain scans. Although a universal mind reading machine that can read any thought of any person will still remain a dream, at least in the near future, there are several simple applications, ranging from brain games to lie detection and market research, that might enter our lives. This poses several cultural and ethical challenges, especially regarding the "privacy" of our minds.

In everyday life, we can learn a lot about what people are thinking from their facial expressions, gestures and body language. For example, facial expressions tell us whether a person is happy, sad or angry. But our capacity to find out what's really going on in a person's mind is very limited. We are often deceived in our readings of people's thoughts and feelings, and it's difficult to know what a person is thinking based on their facial expressions and behavior alone. This led neuroscientists to consider whether it would be possible to derive this information directly from a person's brain activity. An illustration of a hypothetical mind reading technology can be seen in the film *Future World,* a 1976 U.S. science fiction film featuring a machine that can read thoughts from brain activity. A female journalist dons a helmet that looks like a cross between a beauty salon hair dryer and a modern magnetencephalograph machine—a device to measure the magnetic fields that form as a result of signal currents in the brain (Figure 1, top). In the film, the brain activity recorded in this way is depicted as complex, superimposed wave patterns that are read out and interpreted by computers. The journalist's thoughts are then displayed on a screen in real time as a video—a colorful dream-

Maschinen, die Gedanken lesen können, galten bislang als reine Science-Fiction. Sind es auch – noch. Dennoch haben Forscher bereits eindrucksvolle Schritte in Richtung Umsetzung dieser Vision unternommen: Mithilfe ausgeklügelter Computerprogramme lassen sich MRT-Scans erstaunlich viel Information darüber entlocken, was die jeweilige Person zum Zeitpunkt der Aufnahme dachte. Die Anwendungsfelder sind umfangreich und reichen vom Lügendetektor bis zur Werbeforschung.

Im Alltag können wir aus Mimik, Gestik oder Körperhaltung viel über die Gedanken eines Menschen erfahren. Am Gesichtsausdruck lässt sich beispielsweise ablesen, ob er fröhlich, traurig oder wütend ist. Trotzdem ist unsere Fähigkeit, die Innenwelt anderer zu erkennen, sehr begrenzt. Oft täuschen wir uns in ihren Gedanken und Gefühlen und können auch deren Gründe anhand der Mimik nur schwer erkennen. Für Neurowissenschaftler liegt da der Gedanke nahe, dass sich diese Informationen vielleicht direkt der Hirnaktivität entnehmen lassen.

Ein Beispiel dafür liefert etwa der amerikanische Science-Fiction-Film *Future World* aus dem Jahr 1976, in dem eine Maschine vorgestellt wird, die Gedanken aus der Hirnaktivität auslesen kann. Eine Journalistin setzt sich unter einen Helm, der aussieht wie eine Kombination aus Trockenhaube und modernem Magnetenzephalograf – einem Gerät zur Messung der magnetischen Felder, die auf Grund der Signalströme im Gehirn entstehen (siehe Bild 1, oben). Im Film zeigt sich die so aufgenommene Hirnaktivität in Form von komplexen überlagerten Wellenmustern, die mit Hilfe von Computern ausgelesen und interpretiert werden. Die Gedanken der Journalistin zeigt ein Bildschirm dann in Echtzeit als Video: Man sieht eine

* Gekürzte Fassung aus: Haynes, J.-D.: Der Traum vom Gedankenlesen. In: *Spektrum der Wissenschaft Extra*, in Kooperation mit der Volkswagenstiftung 2011, S. 4–11, in *Spektrum der Wissenschaft* September 2011; mit freundlicher Genehmigung der Spektrum der Wissenschaft Verlagsgesellschaft mbH Heidelberg 2013

like journey back to her childhood, with pictures of birthday parties, pets and friends.

Of course, such a machine is still science fiction today. Nevertheless, researchers have taken amazing strides in recent years to read a person's experiences, thoughts, plans, memories and feelings from the activity of his/her brain.

Most neuroscientists today are guided by the assumption that the brain is the sole basis of all our thoughts, memories and feelings. Research has shown that a single, distinctive pattern of brain activity is associated with every specific thought. Two different thoughts—for instance, about a dog and a cat—have different brain activity patterns (Figure 1). If one can learn to recognize these patterns of brain activity then it should be possible, at least theoretically, to infer from a person's brain activity what he/she is thinking at the moment.

bunte Traumreise zurück in ihre Kindheit, mit Bildern von Geburtstagen, Haustieren und Freunden.

Solch eine Maschine ist natürlich auch heute noch Science-Fiction. Doch haben Forscher in den letzten Jahren erstaunliche Fortschritte darin gemacht, aus der Aktivität eines Gehirns Erlebnisse, Gedanken, Pläne, Erinnerungen und Gefühle auslesen.

Heute gehen die meisten Neurowissenschaftler davon aus, dass das Gehirn die alleinige Grundlage des Denkens ist. Demnach sollte mit jedem Gedanken ein einzigartiges, unverwechselbares Muster der Hirnaktivität einhergehen. Zwei verschiedene mentale Vorstellungen, etwa von einem Hund und einer Katze, haben also unterschiedliche Muster – und wenn ich zweimal an denselben Hund denke, ergibt sich jeweils dasselbe Muster (siehe Bild 1). Sollte dies zutreffen, müsste es zumindest theoretisch möglich sein, allein aus der Hirnaktivität einer Person herauszulesen, was sie gerade denkt.

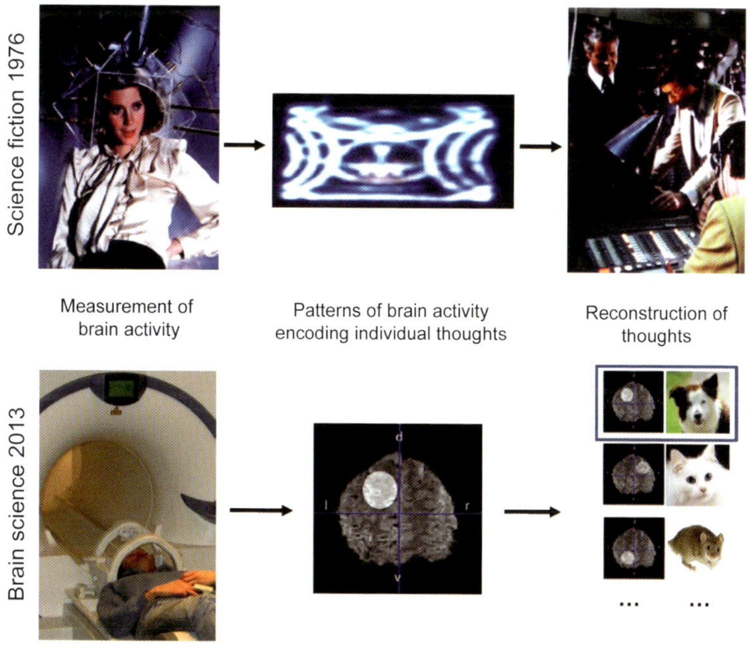

Figure 1: The 1976 movie *Future World* shows a science fiction account of a brain-based mind-reading machine. The idea is to measure the patterns of brain activity and then to make a "videotape" of a person's thoughts that can be viewed by others on a computer screen. Current mind-reading technology based on brain scanners has made rapid progress in recent years. By measuring the patterns of brain activity associated with different thoughts (shown here schematically) and by training computers to recognize these patterns it is possible—at least to some degree—to read out simple thoughts, such as about a dog, cat or mouse.

To accomplish this, researchers use mathematical pattern recognition algorithms. This is somewhat comparable to identifying an individual based on their fingerprints. If every person's fingerprints are stored in a file, then, when an unknown fingerprint is found, it can be compared to all those on file to determine whose it is. Similarly, the pattern of brain activity that occurs with a particular thought can be defined as the thought's "fingerprint" in the brain.

First of all, a test subject's brain activity during various different thoughts has to be registered. For healthy subjects of course one is restricted to so-called "noninvasive" measurement techniques—that is, scanners that can measure brain activity from outside a person's body without penetrating or harming it. Typical methods are electroencephalography (EEG), which records electrical brain activity by means of an electrode-studded cap, and functional magnetic resonance imaging (fMRI) that registers cerebral metabolism. In a typical study, the subject is, for example, shown alternating images of dogs and cats, or is requested to imagine these animals alternately. The resulting brain activity patterns that occur for each thought can then be used to train a computer. With the help of pattern recognition algorithms, the computer learns to optimally recognize the activity patterns and match them to the corresponding thoughts.

In the next step, brain scans of a test subject thinking about either a dog or a cat are fed into the computer, which then has to determine which animal it was. This procedure cannot literally "read" a person's mind; it merely assigns brain activity patterns based on brute-force statistical techniques. This number-crunching does not care with the question of *why* the respective pattern is associated with a particular thought.

With the help of these pattern recognition approaches in recent years, researchers have already succeeded in reading various types of thoughts from brain activity. The first images they used for testing purposes were of animals, household objects, faces and works of art. Once the computer had been familiarized with the test subject's brain activity while he/she was viewing or visualizing the respective images, it could suc-

Zu diesem Zweck benutzen Forscher mathematische Verfahren zur Mustererkennung. Das ist in etwa vergleichbar mit der Identifikation von Personen anhand von Fingerabdrücken: Ist in einer Kartei für jeden Menschen der zugehörige Fingerabdruck gespeichert, kann man einen gefundenen Abdruck mit der Kartei abgleichen und so den Besitzer bestimmen. In diesem Sinne lässt sich das Muster der Hirnaktivität, das sich bei einem bestimmten Gedanken einstellt, als Fingerabdruck des Gedankens im Gehirn auffassen.

Zunächst muss man die Hirnaktivität eines Probanden bei verschiedenen Gedanken registrieren. Bei gesunden Untersuchungspersonen kommen dafür nur so genannte nichtinvasive Messverfahren in Betracht – also solche, bei denen man von außen die Hirnaktivität der Versuchsperson misst, ohne diese zu verletzen. Gängige Methoden sind die Elektroenzephalografie (EEG), welche die elektrische Hirnaktivität mit Hilfe von Elektrodenhauben aufzeichnet, und die funktionelle Magnetresonanztomografie (fMRT), die den Hirnstoffwechsel registriert. Während der Messung würde man beispielsweise dem Probanden entweder abwechselnd Bilder von Hunden und Katzen zeigen oder ihn bitten, sich diese Tiere nacheinander vorzustellen. Anhand der sich dabei ergebenden Hirnaktivitätsmuster lässt sich dann ein Computer trainieren. Er lernt mit Hilfe spezieller, von Experten für Maschinelles Lernen entwickelter Algorithmen, die Aktivitätsmuster optimal zu erkennen und den entsprechenden Gedanken zuzuordnen.

Jetzt kommt die entscheidende Phase: Der Computer erhält Aufnahmen der Hirnaktivität des entweder an einen Hund oder eine Katze denkenden Probanden und soll daraus bestimmen, um welches Tier es sich handelte. Dieses Verfahren liest nicht Gedanken im wörtlichen Sinne, sondern ordnet sie schlicht Hirnaktivitätsmustern zu, ohne sich darum zu kümmern, warum gerade ein bestimmtes Muster mit einem Gedanken einhergeht.

Nun zeichnen Forscher schon länger Bilder der Hirnaktivität bei allerlei komplexen mentalen Vorgängen auf, etwa romantischer Liebe oder religiösen Empfindungen. Allerdings stellen diese in der Regel Mittelwerte der Hirnaktivität von sehr vielen Probanden dar. In den Bildern einer einzelnen Person sind die Effekte zu schwach und verrauscht, um zu Tage zu treten. Bei den neuen Mustererkennungsverfahren stellt sich nun zum ersten Mal die Frage, wie genau man die Gedan-

cessfully recognize which image the test subject was thinking about at a particular instant solely on the basis of the measurement data.
A team of researchers in Japan headed by Yukiyasu Kamitani presented an especially good example in 2009. Using a customized mathematical model, they were able to decode any visual image the test subject saw from that person's brain activity. They could even recognize letters of the alphabet. This raises the prospect of someday even being able to reconstruct the visual world of dreams.
In 2005, we showed that it's even possible to read subliminal perceptions. To achieve this, we present extremely brief glimpses of images amidst a series of diversionary stimuli so that the test subject isn't consciously aware of the images. Nevertheless, with these pattern recognition algorithms, it's possible to find traces of the brain's processing of these invisible images.
In the meantime, we've also learned to recognize more abstract and more complex thoughts. In 2007, our working group at the Charité Berlin's Bernstein Center was able to uncover hidden intentions from a person's brain activity. To do so, we had the test subjects choose between various simple intentions: They could either choose to add or subtract two numbers. The question was: Is it possible to read out the decision from brain activity after subjects had made up their mind but before they had started executing the chosen task? We trained the computer with examples of brain activity when test subjects had opted for addition or subtraction. It turned out that activity patterns in the so-called prefrontal cortex made it possible to reconstruct the test subject's intentions with 70% reliability. Located behind the forehead, this region of the brain is responsible for, among other things, storing and recalling plans for complex actions.
In a subsequent study, our test subjects were requested to spontaneously use either their left or right hand to press a button. Parallel to this, they had to report when exactly they had the impression of having made up their mind. This allowed us to test whether it is possible to predict the outcome of the decision even *before the subjects believed to be making up their mind*. Once again, we achieved an above-chance prediction and, indeed, up to seven seconds before the decision (Figure 2). The accu-

kenwelt eines bestimmten Menschen aus seiner Hirnaktivität ablesen kann und welche Verfahren dafür optimal geeignet sind.
Mit Hilfe solcher Mustererkennungsansätze haben Forscher in den letzten Jahren bereits verschiedene Arten von Gedanken aus der Hirnaktivität ausgelesen. Als erstes testeten sie Bilder von Tieren, Haushaltsgegenständen, Gesichtern oder auch Kunstwerken. Sofern der Computer zuvor die Hirnaktivität des Probanden beim Betrachten oder beim Visualisieren der einzelnen Bilder gelernt hatte, konnte er allein aus den Messdaten sehr gut erkennen, an welches Bild die Person gerade dachte.
Ein besonders schönes Beispiel präsentierte ein Forscherteam um Yukiyasu Kamitani aus Japan 2009. Sie dekodierten mit einem maßgeschneiderten mathematischen Modell beliebige visuelle Bilder, die eine Person sah, aus ihrer Hirnaktivität. Sogar Buchstaben konnten sie erkennen. Auf diese Weise ließe sich eines Tages vielleicht auch die Bilderwelt von Träumen rekonstruieren.
Wir haben 2005 gezeigt, dass es sogar möglich ist, unterschwellige Wahrnehmungen auszulesen. Hierfür präsentieren wir Bilder extrem kurz in einer Reihe von Ablenkreizen, so dass die Probanden sie nicht bewusst erkennen können. Dennoch ist es möglich, mit den Mustererkennungsalgorithmen Spuren der Verarbeitung dieser unsichtbaren Bilder im Gehirn zu finden.
Auch abstraktere und komplexere Gedanken lassen sich inzwischen erkennen. Im Jahr 2007 registrierten wir in unserer Arbeitsgruppe am Bernstein Center der Charité Berlin in der Hirnaktivität verdeckte Absichten – sogar mehrere Sekunden, bevor sie in die Tat umgesetzt wurden. Dazu ließen wir die Probanden zwischen verschiedenen möglichen Intentionen wählen. Sie mussten zwei Zahlen, die sie erst später sehen würden, entweder addieren oder subtrahieren. Die Frage lautete: Ist es nach der Entscheidung, aber noch vor der Handlung, möglich, aus ihrer Hirnaktivität zu bestimmen, was sie gleich machen würden? Um sie zu beantworten, trainierten wir den Computer mit Beispielen der Hirnaktivität, wenn Probanden sich für Addition oder Subtraktion entschieden hatten. Es zeigte sich, dass die Aktivitätsmuster im so genannten präfrontalen Kortex erlaubten, die Absichten mit 70-prozentiger Zuverlässigkeit zu rekonstruieren. Diese Hirnregion liegt hinter der Stirn und ist unter

racy was far from perfect, possibly reflecting the limitations of current brain scanning technology. Our findings suggest that, in certain situations, the brain can start to prepare a decision even before one is consciously aware of the choice. Since then, researchers have used brain activity as a basis to successfully reconstruct many other complex mental processes—for instance, memories and feeling, but also purchasing decisions and lies.

anderem zuständig für das Speichern und Abrufen von komplexen Handlungsplänen.

In einer späteren Studie sollten Probanden spontan entweder mit der linken oder der rechten Hand einen Knopf drücken. Parallel dazu berichteten sie, wann genau sie den Eindruck hatten, sich entschieden zu haben. Somit war es möglich zu testen, ob sich bereits vor dem subjektiv wahrgenommenen Entscheidungszeitpunkt vorhersagen lässt, wie sich der Proband gleich entscheiden wird. Wieder konnten wir die Entscheidung überzufällig häufig richtig vorhersagen, und zwar bis zu sieben Sekunden vor der Entscheidung, wenn auch insgesamt nur mit einer niedrigen Trefferquote (siehe Bild 2). Dies zeigt, dass das Gehirn in gewissen Situationen Entscheidungen vorbereitet, bevor man sich dessen klar wird. Inzwischen haben Forscher noch viele andere komplexe mentale Vorgänge aus der Hirnaktivität rekonstruiert – etwa Erinnerungen und Gefühle, aber auch Kaufabsichten und Lügen.

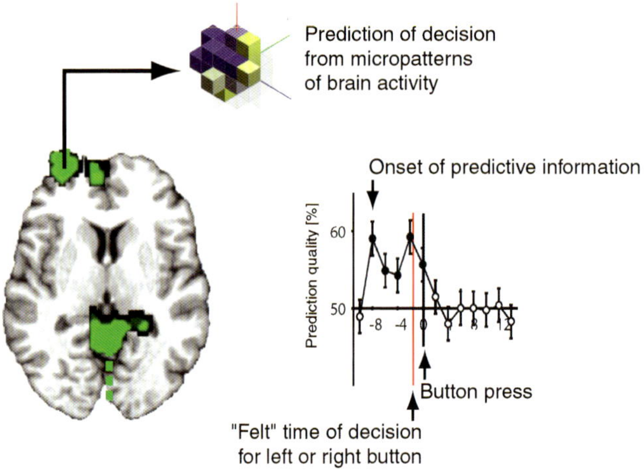

Figure 2: In one study we were able to predict a person's decisions several seconds before they themselves even knew which option they were going to choose (Soon, Brass, Heinze & Haynes, *Nature Neuroscience* 2008). This might appear like "magic", but instead it reflects the fact that decisions can build up slowly and unconsciously in the brain.

But even in light of all the breakthroughs achieved in this field in recent years, we're still far from a universal mindreading machine. A machine that can precisely read any person's arbitrary thoughts will presumably remain science fiction for a long time to come. But what exactly are the difficulties now facing developers?

One of the crucial problems is the limited precision of the methods now used to measure brain activity. Of all the noninvasive procedures, fMRI

Bei allen Erfolgen auf diesem Gebiet in den letzten Jahren ist man natürlich trotzdem noch sehr weit von einer universellen Gedankenlesemaschine entfernt. Eine Maschine, die beliebige Gedanken von beliebigen Personen präzise auslesen kann, wird voraussichtlich noch auf lange Zeit Zukunftsmusik bleiben. Doch vor welchen Schwierigkeiten stehen die Entwickler im Detail?

Eines der Kernprobleme ist die begrenzte Genauigkeit der Methoden, mit denen man heute die Hirnaktivität currently provides the highest spatial resolution; nevertheless, its resolution is still rather limited. This is because it registers the activity of nerve cells only indirectly by measuring the oxygen content of the blood in the thin vessels of the brain's vascular system. Since it is impossible to increase the resolution of these veins and arteries, this technique is limited by both technical as well as biological constraints.

Brain activity patterns also vary considerably from person to person. Of course, roughly speaking, auditory experiences or memories are stored in the same regions of every person's brain, but test subjects' brains differ from each other significantly in numerous details. Only slightly dissimilar intentions can be associated with totally dissimilar patterns on the part of different test subjects, which is why it's not yet possible to train a computer with one person's data and then use the algorithm derived in this way on another person—at least not for the purpose of reading their minds in detail.

Furthermore, it's quite difficult to ascertain what a person is thinking about at a particular point in time. Let's assume, for example, that we were to measure the brain activity of a test subject continuously for an hour while he lies in a scanner daydreaming. Now, what thoughts are we supposed to input into the computer together with the images of the brain activity for training purposes? Certainly, we could ask the test subject to think aloud, but then the recorded data that we fed into our computer would be contaminated by language. That is why current research uses such simplified situations in which test subjects are given instructions as to what they should think about at particular time intervals. Obviously, the complexity of the thoughts that can be registered in this way is quite limited.

The biggest obstacle, however, is human creativity—we're able to think many, many different things. You have to plan for even the most improbably bizarre constructions—"My hovercraft is full of eels" from the famous Monty Python sketch, for instance. So, are we supposed to have a test subject lie in an MRI machine and systematically go through countless possible thoughts while we measure the brain activity associated with each one? Although the problem at first seems unsolvable,

misst. Die funktionelle Magnetresonanztomografie hat zwar derzeit von allen nicht-invasiven Verfahren die höchste räumliche Auflösung, aber diese ist trotzdem begrenzt. Denn sie erfasst die Aktivität von Nervenzellen nur indirekt, indem sie den Sauerstoffgehalt des Blutes in den feinen Verästelungen des Gefäßsystems im Gehirn misst. Da man die Auflösung der Gefäße nicht erhöhen kann, stößt das Verfahren nicht nur an technische Grenzen, sondern auch an biologische.

Auch unterscheiden sich die Hirnaktivitätsmuster von Person zu Person erheblich. Grob betrachtet sind zwar die Regionen, in denen etwa Hörerlebnisse oder Erinnerungen gespeichert sind, bei allen Menschen gleich. Aber in den Details unterscheiden sich die Gehirne von Probanden doch erheblich. Nur leicht unterschiedliche Absichten können bei verschiedenen Probanden mit ganz anderen Mustern verbunden sein. Daher ist es heute noch nicht möglich, einen Computer mit den Daten einer Person zu trainieren und den so gewonnen Algorithmus bei einer anderen Person anzuwenden – zumindest nicht, wenn es um Einzelheiten ihrer Gedankenwelt geht.

Zudem ist es überhaupt schwierig zu erfassen, was ein Mensch zu einem bestimmten Zeitpunkt denkt. Angenommen, wir würden eine Stunde lang kontinuierlich die Hirnaktivität eines Probanden messen, während er tagträumend im Scanner liegt. Welche Gedanken sollen wir nun dem Computer zusammen mit Beispielen der Hirnaktivität eingeben, um ihn zu trainieren? Wir könnten den Probanden zwar bitten, laut zu denken, allerdings wären dann die Messdaten, mit dem wir unseren Computer füttern, mit Sprache kontaminiert. Zurzeit untersucht man deshalb vereinfachte Situationen, bei denen man dem Probanden vorgibt, woran er in einem bestimmten Zeitintervall denken soll. Allerdings ist die Komplexität der Gedanken, die man so erfassen kann, erheblich eingeschränkt.

Das größte Hindernis liegt jedoch in der menschlichen Kreativität – wir können unglaublich viele verschiedene Dinge denken. Selbst die ausgefallensten Konstrukte müsste man einplanen, wie etwa den Satz „mein Luftkissenboot ist voller Aale" aus einem Sketch von Monty Python. Soll man etwa einen Menschen in einen Magnetresonanztomografen legen und systematisch alle unendlich vielen möglichen Gedanken durchgehen und die zugehörige Hirnaktivität messen? Obwohl das Problem zunächst unlösbar scheint, gibt es doch zumindest einen ersten Ansatz:

there is nevertheless at least one initial approach: Taking advantage of the similarity between the brain activities associated with different thoughts (Figure 3). A team of researchers headed by Tom Mitchell at Carnegie Mellon University in the U.S. very recently demonstrated that it is indeed possible to differentiate among a great many thoughts even when only a few training examples are available.

Man kann sich die Ähnlichkeit zwischen der Hirnaktivität verschiedener Gedanken zunutze machen (siehe Bild 3). Erst jüngst zeigten Forscher um Tom Mitchell von der amerikanischen Carnegie Mellon University, dass man so sehr viele verschiedene Gedanken unterscheiden kann, selbst wenn man nur eine Handvoll Trainingsbeispiele zur Verfügung hat.

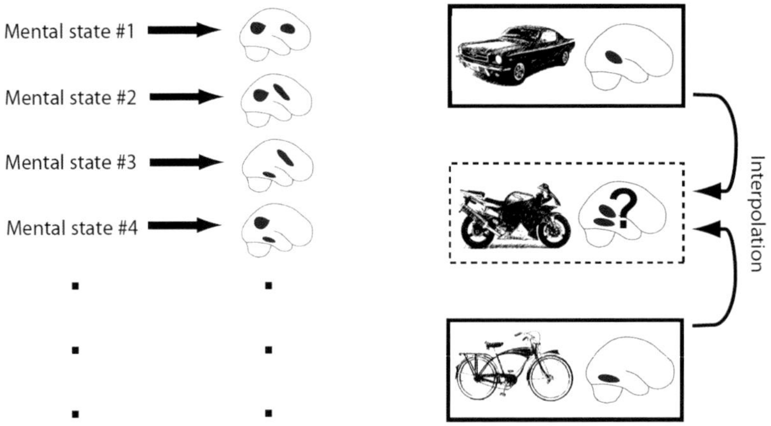

Figure 3: One problem for mind-reading machines is that they need to know which pattern of brain activity is associated with each different thought. How could one ever measure all these brain responses? One solution is to exploit the similarities between different thoughts. For example, if the computer knows the patterns associated with thoughts about cars and bicycles, it might be able to guess that if it sees a pattern that is a little like a car and a little like a bicycle, that it must be a motorbike.

Although it will presumably take a long time until we're in a position to build a universal mindreading machine, even today's simple techniques are already yielding initial applications—for instance, in the medical field, where pattern recognition is being used to control prostheses. For some time now, innovative EEG caps have also been developed for the computer gaming industry. Players put them on and, after a brief calibration process, they can operate a computer game using their thoughts alone. There are also controversial applications, such as detecting lies or predicting decisions to purchase merchandise. Perhaps the future will confront the users of such neurotechnology with similar awkward decisions as with Facebook, Google & Co: How much of our mental privacy do we really want to surrender in return for new technologies?

Obwohl wir vermutlich noch lange nicht dazu in der Lage sein werden, eine universelle Gedankenlesemaschine zu bauen, entstehen bereits mit den heutigen einfachen Techniken erste Anwendungen – so etwa für den medizinischen Bereich, wo Mustererkennung genutzt wird, um Prothesen zu steuern. Für die Gaming-Industrie werden seit einiger Zeit innovative EEG-Kappen entwickelt. Sie werden einfach aufgesetzt und nach einer kurzen Kalibrierung kann mit Gedankenkraft ein Spiel gesteuert werden. Aber es gibt auch umstrittenere Anwendungen, zum Beispiel in der Erkennung von Lügen oder in der Vorhersage von Kaufentscheidungen. Möglicherweise stehen wir in Zukunft vor einer ähnlichen Entscheidung wie bei der Datensicherheit von Facebook und Co: Wie viel unserer mentalen Privatsphäre wollen wir für neue Techniken wirklich preisgeben?

Rodrigo Quian Quiroga

Funes and Other Cases of Extraordinary Memory*

Funes und andere Fälle eines ungewöhnlichen Gedächtnisses*

June 7, 1942, was a Sunday like any other amid the altered routine of the Second World War. The front page of the newspaper *La Nación*[1] reported on the British onslaught, which continued with a bombing campaign over the German industrial area in the Ruhr. On the same page one could read about the casualties inflicted on the Japanese fleet at Midway and about British infantry tanks attacking German positions in the desert. Pages 5 and 6 of the paper, in between advertisements for Eno's "Fruit Salt" (a digestive aid selling at $0.70 per vial) and Fernet Branca (a beverage that should be brought home as one brings a friend), give an account of an earthquake without victims in Mendoza and announce that tire factories can start restoring used tires. In sports, Argentinos Juniors beat Sportivo Alsina by 4 goals to 1 in their campaign to reach the premier league, and the entertainment pages promote *Pirates of the Caribbean,* in Technicolor, and a new movie starring Olivia de Havilland and Henry Fonda at $1.50 a *super pullman* seat. June 7, 1942, a day like any other according to *La Nación,* except for a short story appearing in the Arts and Letters section that would turn this issue of the newspaper into a historic document. The first page of this Sunday supplement features a story by Stefan Zweig; the second page contains an essay by Ernesto Sabato praising Galileo; and on the third page, almost hidden in plain sight, for the first time appears "Funes the Memorious," Jorge Luis Borges's monumental short story, with an illustration by Alejandro Sirio.

"Funes the Memorious" tells the vicissitudes of Ireneo Funes, a peasant from Fray Bentos, who after falling off a horse and hitting his head hard recovers consciousness with the incredible skill—or perhaps curse—of remembering absolutely everything.

Says Borges of Funes:

Der 7. Juni 1942 war, gemessen am veränderten Alltag des Zweiten Weltkriegs, ein ganz gewöhnlicher Sonntag. Die Tageszeitung *La Nación*[1] berichtete auf der Titelseite von der Fortsetzung der britischen Offensive mit der Bombardierung des Ruhrgebiets. Dazu erfuhr man von den Verlusten, die die japanische Flotte bei Midway erlitten hatte, und den Angriffen britischer Infanteriepanzer auf deutsche Wüstenstellungen. Auf den Seiten 5 und 6 befand sich, zwischen Anzeigen für „Eno Fruit Salt" (ein Mittel gegen Sodbrennen für 0,70 Dollar pro Fläschchen) und Fernet Branca (ein Getränk zum Mitnachhausenehmen wie einen Freund), ein Bericht von einem Erdbeben ohne Todesopfer in Mendoza sowie die Meldung, dass Reifenfabriken nun auch Gebrauchtreifen wiederaufbereiten können. Im Sportteil war zu lesen, dass die Argentinos Juniors über Sportivo Alsina mit 4:1 gewonnen hatten, und die Unterhaltungsseiten bewarben einen Technicolor-Schinken über Piraten im karibischen Meer und einen neuen Film mit Olivia de Havilland und Henry Fonda für 1,50 Dollar auf dem „Super-Pullmann-Sitz". Der 7. Juni 1942 war also laut *La Nación* ein Tag wie jeder andere, wäre da nicht eine Kurzgeschichte im Kulturteil erschienen, die diese Ausgabe der Zeitung zu einem historischen Dokument machen sollte. Die erste Seite der Sonntagskulturbeilage zierte eine Geschichte von Stefan Zweig, auf der zweiten stimmte Ernesto Sabato ein essayistisches Loblied auf Galileo an; und auf der dritten war, vor aller Augen verborgen, erstmals Jorge Luis Borges' denkwürdige Kurzgeschichte „Funes el memorioso" (deutsch: „Das unerbittliche Gedächtnis") abgedruckt, illustriert von Alejandro Sirio.

Die Geschichte erzählt vom Schicksal des Ireneo Funes, einem Farmarbeiter aus Fray Bentos, der, als er nach einem schweren Sturz vom Pferd sein Bewusstsein wiedererlangt, mit der unglaublichen Fähigkeit begabt – oder dem Fluch geschlagen – ist, sich an absolut alles erinnern zu können. Borges über Funes:

* Reprinted from *Borges and Memory: Encounters with the Human Brain*, by Rodrigo Quian Quiroga. Copyright © 2013, by Massachusetts Institute of Technology. Used with permission of the publisher The MIT Press.

* Exzerpt aus *Borges and Memory: Encounters with the Human Brain*, von Rodrigo Quian Quiroga. Copyright © 2013, Massachusetts Institute of Technology. Abdruck mit freundlicher Genehmigung des Verlags The MIT Press.

Nosotros, de un vistazo, percibimos tres copas en una mesa; Funes, todos los vástagos y racimos y frutos que comprende una parra. Sabía las formas de las nubes australes del amanecer del 30 de abril de 1882 y podía compararlas en el recuerdo con las vetas de un libro en pasta española que sólo había mirado una vez y con las líneas de la espuma que un remo levantó en el Río Negro la víspera de la acción del Quebracho.[2]

"We, at a stroke, perceive three cups lying on a table; Funes would see all the shoots and clusters and fruit comprised by a vine. He knew the shapes of the southern clouds at dawn on April 30, 1882, and could compare them in his memory with the streaks on a book of Spanish cover that he had seen only once and with the swirls on the foam raised by an oar in the Río Negro on the eve of the battle of the Quebracho."

Jorge Luis Borges (1899–1986) has received universal acclaim for the depth with which he approached matters of philosophic and scientific import in his writings. In Borges's hands, the topic of infinity comes alive either as a point that contains the universe ("The Aleph"), impregnable labyrinths ("The Two Kings and the Two Labyrinths"), a library that is eternally repeated ("The Library of Babel"), stories that subdivide into innumerable possibilities ("The Garden of Forking Paths"), or an imperial map so perfectly detailed that it ends up having the size of the empire itself ("Of Rigor in Science"). In "Funes the Memorious," a story of barely 12 pages that was eventually published as part of *Ficciones* (1944), Borges again plays with the infinite in a context no less fascinating: the vast labyrinths of memory and the consequences of having an unlimited capacity to remember.

Funes is first mentioned in an obituary of James Joyce, "A Fragment on Joyce," published in 1941 in the magazine *Sur.*[3] There, with some measure of sarcasm, Borges says that to read straight through a "monster" like Joyce's *Ulysses*—a 400,000-word reconstruction of a single day in Dublin—requires another monster able to remember an infinite number of details. The strange thing about the obituary is that Borges barely refers to Joyce or his work and instead describes Ireneo Funes, the main character of the story he was writing at the time.

„Wir nehmen mit einem Blick drei Gläser auf einem Tisch wahr; Funes alle Triebe, Trauben und Beeren, die zu einem Rebstock gehören. Er kannte genau die Formen der südlichen Wolken des Sonnenaufgangs vom 30. April 1882 und konnte sie in der Erinnerung mit der Maserung auf einem Pergamentband vergleichen, den er nur ein einziges Mal angeschaut hatte, und mit den Linien der Gischt, die ein Ruder auf dem Río Negro am Vorabend des Quebracho-Gefechtes aufgewühlt hatte."

Jorge Luis Borges (1899–1986) ist heute allgemein für seine tiefgründige Behandlung von philosophisch und wissenschaftlich bedeutsamen Sachverhalten bekannt. In Borges' Händen wird das Thema Unendlichkeit lebendig, sei es in Gestalt eines Punkts, der das ganze Universum enthält („Das Aleph"), undurchdringlicher Labyrinthe („Die zwei Könige und die zwei Labyrinthe"), einer sich ewig wiederholenden Bibliothek („Die Bibiothek von Babel"), in unzählige Möglichkeiten zerfallende Geschichten („Der Garten der Pfade, die sich verzweigen") oder einer kaiserlichen Landkarte, die so genau ist, dass sie am Ende die gleiche Größe wie das Reich besitzt („Von der Strenge der Wissenschaft"). In „Funes el memorioso", einer kaum zwölf Seiten langen Geschichte, die schließlich in den Erzählband *Ficciones* (1944) aufgenommen wurde, spielt Borges in einem nicht minder faszinierenden Zusammenhang mit der Idee des Unendlichen: dem weiten Labyrinth des Gedächtnisses und den Folgen eines unbeschränkten Erinnerungsvermögens.

Erstmals erwähnt wird Funes in einem 1941 in der Zeitschrift *Sur*[3] erschienenen Nachruf auf James Joyce, „Fragment über Joyce". Darin schreibt Borges leicht sarkastisch, um ein „Ungeheuer" wie Joyce' *Ulysses* – eine 400.000 Wörter zählende Rekonstruktion eines einzigen Tages in Dublin – auf einen Sitz zu lesen, bedürfe es eines anderen Ungeheuers, das in der Lage ist, sich unendlich viele Einzelheiten zu merken. Das Eigenartige an diesem Nachruf ist, dass Borges kaum auf Joyce und sein Werk eingeht, sondern stattdessen Ireneo Funes schildert, die Hauptfigur der Geschichte, an der er damals gerade schrieb.

Entre las obras que no he escrito ni escribiré (pero que de alguna manera me justifican, siquiera misteriosa y rudimental) hay un relato de unas ocho o diez páginas cuyo profuso borrador se titula "Funes el memorioso". ... Del compadrito mágico de mi cuento cabe afirmar que es un precursor de los superhombres, un Zaratustra suburbano y parcial; lo indiscutible es que es un monstruo. Lo he recordado porque la consecutiva y recta lectura de las cuatrocientas mil palabras de Ulises exigiría monstruos análogos.[4]

"Among the works that I have not written and will never write (but that somehow justify me, in however mysterious and rudimentary a way) there is a short story, some eight to ten pages long, whose copious draft is entitled "Funes the Memorious." Of the magical *compadrito* of my story I can state that he is a precursor to supermen, a suburban, incomplete Zarathustra; what cannot be denied is that he is a monster. I have remembered him because a straight, uninterrupted reading of *Ulysses's* four hundred thousand words would require similar monsters."

In the preface to "Artifices," the second part of *Ficciones,* Borges argues that "Funes the Memorious" is a long metaphor of insomnia. In fact, toward the end of the story he mentions that Funes found sleeping difficult, because to sleep is to get distracted from the world. Borges gives more details on the way he conceived Funes during his own sleepless nights (perhaps during a sticky summer night at the *quinta* in Adrogué), in an interview published in the United States:

"When I suffered from insomnia I tried to forget myself, to forget my body, the position of my body, the bed, the furniture, the three gardens of the hotel, the eucalyptus tree, the books on the shelf, all the streets of the village, the station, the farmhouses. And since couldn't forget, I kept on being conscious and couldn't fall asleep. Then I said to myself, let us suppose there was a person who couldn't forget anything he had perceived, and it's well known that this happened to James Joyce, who in the course of a single day could have brought out Ulysses, a day in which thousands of things happened. I thought of someone who couldn't forget those events and who in the end dies swept away by his infinite memory. In a word that fragmentary hoodlum is me, or is an *image I stole for literary purposes but which corresponds to my own insomnia.*"[5]

"Unter den Werken, die ich nicht geschrieben habe und nie schreiben werde (die mich aber, wie mysteriös und rudimentär auch immer, irgendwie rechtfertigen) ist eine etwa acht oder zehn Seiten lange Kurzgeschichte, deren allzu üppiger erster Entwurf den Titel „Funes el memorioso" trägt. ... Den magischen *compadrito* meiner Geschichte könnte man einen Vorläufer der künftigen Rasse von Übermenschen nennen, einen partiellen Vorstadt-Zarathustra; unbestreitbar ist er ein Ungeheuer. Ich habe ihn erwähnt, weil die konsekutive, geradlinige Lektüre der vierhundertausend Wörter des *Ulysses* eines ähnlichen Ungeheuers bedürfte."

Im Vorwort zu den „Kunststücken", dem zweiten Teil der *Ficciones,* behauptet Borges, dass es sich bei „Funes el memorioso" um eine lange Metapher der Schlaflosigkeit handle. Und tatsächlich erfährt man gegen Ende der Geschichte, dass Funes das Schlafen schwer fiel, weil Schlafen bedeute, sich von der Welt abzulenken. In einem in den USA publizierten Interview beschreibt Borges ausführlicher, wie er während seiner eigenen schlaflosen Nächte (z. B. in einer feuchtheißen Sommernacht auf der *quinta* in Adrogué) auf Funes kam:

„Wenn ich unter Schlaflosigkeit litt, versuchte ich mich zu vergessen, versuchte, meinen Körper, seine Position, das Bett, die Möbel, die drei Gärten des Hotels, den Eukalyptusbaum, die Bücher auf dem Regal, sämtliche Straßen des Dorfes, den Bahnhof, die Bauernhöfe zu vergessen. Und da ich nicht vergessen konnte, blieb ich wach und fand keinen Schlaf. Da sagte ich mir, stell dir jemanden vor, der nichts von dem, was er je wahrgenommen hat, vergessen kann, und bekanntlich war ja James Joyce so jemand, der hätte den *Ulysses* an einem einzigen Tag hervorbringen können, einem Tag, an dem Tausende Dinge passiert sind. Ich dachte an jemanden, der all diese Ereignisse nicht mehr vergessen kann und schließlich von diesem unendlichen Gedächtnis überwältigt wird. Kurzum, dieser fragmentarische Gauner, das bin ich, oder ein für literarische Zwecke geborgtes Bild meiner eigenen Schlaflosigkeit."[5]

Already in the literature of the first millennium there are references to people with prodigious memory, particularly in the *Naturalis historia (Natural History)* of Pliny the Elder (Gaius Plinius Secundus, 23–79 A.D.), a sort of encyclopedia that in 37 books describes everything from the geography, science, and technology to the agriculture, medicinal herbs, and insects of ancient Rome. In chapter 24 of book VII, on the topic of memory, Pliny mentions King Cyrus of Persia, who knew the names of all his soldiers; Scipio, who knew the names of all in Rome; Cineas, King Pyrrhus's ambassador, who learned the names of all the Roman senators just one day after arriving in Rome; Mithridates Eupator, who administered justice in the 22 languages spoken in his empire; Simonides, inventor of mnemonics; or Charmadas the Greek, who could recite by heart any book from a library as though he were reading it.[6]

Pliny considers it a blessing to possess an extraordinary memory. In fact, he starts chapter 24 of book VII saying:

Memoria necessarium maxime vitae bonum cui praecipua fuerit, haut facile dictu est, tam multis eius gloriam adeptis ["As to memory, the boon most necessary for life, it is not easy to say who most excelled in it, so many men having gained renown for it"].[7]

Pliny also describes the fragility of memory, arguing that it can be lost, in whole or in part, due to illness, injury, and even panic. As an example he tells the story of a man who lost the capacity to name letters after being struck by a stone, and of another who forgot certain people after falling from a roof. He also mentions Messala Corvinus, the orator, who lost recollection of even his own name.

Borges, it is known, was fascinated by encyclopedias and by the *Naturalis historia*[8] (perhaps the first encyclopedia in history), which in fact he mentions in "Funes the Memorious": Funes asks the narrator (Borges) for any Latin text, and Borges obliges with volume VII of Pliny's encyclopedia and Quicherat's *Thesaurus*, just so the rube will be rudely disappointed upon finding out that one cannot learn such a complicated language using only a book and a dictionary. On their next meeting, however, Funes welcomes Borges by reciting,

Schon in der Literatur des ersten Jahrtausends unserer Zeitrechnung finden sich Hinweise auf Menschen mit erstaunlichen Gedächtnisleistungen, vor allem in der *Naturalis historia (Naturgeschichte)* des älteren Plinius (Gaius Plinius Secundus, 23–79 n. Chr.), einer Art Enzyklopädie in 37 Bänden, die von der Geografie, Wissenschaft und Technologie bis zur Landwirtschaft, den Heilpflanzen und Insekten die gesamte römische Welt beschreibt. Im 24. Kapitel von Buch VII, das vom Gedächtnis handelt, erwähnt Plinius den Perserkönig Kyros, der alle Soldaten seines Heeres beim Namen nennen konnte; Scipio, der die Namen aller Römer kannte; Kineas, den Gesandten des Königs Pyrrhos, der nur einen Tag nach seiner Ankunft in Rom die Namen aller Senatoren wusste; Mithridates Eupator, der in allen 22 Sprachen seines Reichs Recht sprach; Simonides, den Erfinder der Gedächtniskunst; oder den Griechen Charmadas, der jedes Buch seiner Bibliothek hersagen konnte, als wenn er es vorläse.[6]

Plinius betrachtet ein vorzügliches Gedächtnis als Segen. Er beginnt das Kapitel 24 des siebten Buchs mit den Worten:

Memoria necessarium maxime vitae bonum cui praecipua fuerit, haut facile dictu est, tam multis eius gloriam adeptis [„Wer das beste Gedächtnis, dieses im Leben am meisten notwendige Gut, besessen hat, lässt sich nicht leicht sagen, da so viele dadurch Ruhm erlangt haben"].[7]

Plinius beschreibt aber auch, wie anfällig das Gedächtnis ist, dass es aufgrund von Krankheiten, Unfällen und sogar Furcht ganz oder teilweise verloren gehen kann. Als Beispiele führt er einen Mann an, der keine Buchstaben mehr kannte, nachdem er von einem Stein getroffen worden war, und einen anderen, der sich nicht mehr an die Namen gewisser Menschen erinnern konnte, nachdem er vom Dach gefallen war. Außerdem erwähnt er noch den Redner Messala Corvinus, der sogar seinen eigenen Namen vergaß.

Borges begeisterte sich bekanntlich für Enzyklopädien und für die *Naturalis historia*[8] (die wahrscheinlich erste Enzyklopädie der Geschichte). Diese kommt denn auch in „Funes el memorioso" vor: Funes bittet den Erzähler (Borges) um einen lateinischen Text, und Borges entspricht seinem Wunsch mit dem Buch VII der Plinius'schen Enzyklopädie und Quicherats *Gradus ad Parnassum*, nur um dem Landei zu zeigen, dass man eine so komplizierte Sprache nicht bloß mit einem mockingly, in perfect Latin: *"ut nihil non iisdem verbis redderetur auditum"* (which, literally translated, means: "Nothing that has been heard can be repeated with the same words").[9]

Through Funes, Borges, just like Pliny, enters the realm of memory, though his reaction differs from the Roman's in a crucial regard: while Pliny considers it a virtue to have a prodigious capacity to remember, Borges looks beyond and argues that an extraordinary memory can become a curse. Says Funes, midway through the story:

Más recuerdos tengo yo solo que los que habrán tenido todos los hombres desde que el mundo es mundo... . Mi memoria, señor, es como un vaciadero de basura. ["I alone have more memories than all men may have ever had since the world exists... . My memory, sir, is like a rubbish heap."]

Given their historical significance, Pliny's stories are of undeniable value. It is, nonetheless, impossible to judge their veracity, and in fact the characters described in the *Naturalis historia* seem more legendary than real (perhaps arousing Borges's curiosity even more). To a large extent this is due to the fact that many of Pliny's descriptions are based on word-of-mouth information, inevitably altered in the telling. For example, when he describes cases of astonishing eyesight in chapter 21 of book VII, Pliny writes that Homer's *Iliad* was written in such small script that the complete manuscript could fit in a nutshell; he also mentions a man called Strabo, who could recognize objects 135 miles away and who, during the Punic Wars, could sight and even count the enemy ships docked in Carthage from a promontory in Sicily.

The first properly documented case of extraordinary memory is that of Solomon Shereshevskii, studied by the celebrated Russian psychologist Alexander Luria starting in the 1920s. As Luria reports in his book *The Mind of a Mnemonist: A Little Book about a Vast Memory,* subject S. (as he refers to Shereshevskii to protect his name), unlike everyone else, had to make an effort if he wished to forget something. As we shall see in the following chapters, Shereshevskii possessed a very strong synesthesia—an involuntary link between different senses, like associating numbers with colors— that gave his memories a much richer content and thus

Buch und einem Lexikon erlernen könne. Bei ihrem nächsten Treffen aber empfängt ihn Funes höhnisch mit den in vollkommenem Latein rezitierten Worten: *ut nihil non iisdem verbis redderetur auditum* (was wörtlich heißt: „dass nichts Gehörtes mit denselben Worten wiedergegeben werden kann").[9]

Mit Funes betritt Borges – wie Plinius – die Welt des Gedächtnisses, fasst diese aber in einem wesentlichen Punkt ganz anders auf als der Römer: Betrachtet Plinius ein großes Erinnerungsvermögen als Vorzug, so erkennt Borges, dass ein außerordentliches Gedächtnis auch ein Fluch sein kann. O-Ton Funes, etwa in der Mitte der Geschichte:

Más recuerdos tengo yo solo que los que habrán tenido todos los hombres desde que el mundo es mundo... . Mi memoria, señor, es como un vaciadero de basura. [„Ich allein habe mehr Erinnerungen, als alle Menschen zusammen je gehabt haben, solange die Welt besteht. ... Mein Gedächtnis, Herr, ist wie eine Abfalltonne."]

Plinius' Geschichten sind historisch zweifellos von großer Bedeutung. Allerdings ist ihr Wahrheitsgehalt kaum zu überprüfen, und tatsächlich erscheinen die in der *Naturalis historia* beschriebenen Figuren eher als sagenhaft denn real (was Borges' Neugierde wohl umso mehr geweckt haben dürfte). Das hat weitgehend damit zu tun, dass Plinius' Geschichten auf mündlicher Überlieferung beruhen, beim Weitererzählen also unvermeidlich verändert wurden. So schreibt er zum Beispiel in Kapitel 21 des siebten Buchs, das von Fällen außergewöhnlicher Sehkraft handelt, die *Ilias* des Homer sei in einer so kleinen Schrift verfasst worden, dass das gesamte Manuskript in eine Nuss gepasst habe, und erwähnt einen Mann namens Strabo, der 135 Meilen weit sehen konnte und im Punischen Krieg von einem sizilianischen Vorgebirge aus die Flotte im Hafen von Karthago erkennen und sogar die Anzahl der Schiffe angeben konnte.

Der erste sachkundig dokumentierte Fall eines außerordentlichen Gedächtnisses ist der von Solomon Šereševskij, den der bekannte russische Neuropsychologe Alexander Lurija ab den frühen 1920er Jahren studierte. In seinem Aufsatz „Kleines Porträt eines großen Gedächtnisses"[10] berichtet Lurija, dass sich Š. (wie er seinen Probanden anonymisierend nennt) im Gegensatz zu uns anderen bewusst anstrengen musste, um etwas zu vergessen. Šereševskij war ein sehr starker Synästhesiker, d. h. er verband unwillmade them easier to recollect. These associations, as well as the use of simple mnemonics, allowed Shereshevskii to remember long sequences of numbers and letters many years after first hearing them. After studying Shereshevskii for more than 30 years, Luria confessed his inability to find a limit to S.'s memory, a surprising statement considering that it comes not from an amateur but from one of the foremost psychologists of his time.

There are clear parallels between Shereshevskii and Funes, despite the fact that the former trained his memory based on his synesthesia while for the latter to remember everything was completely natural. It is, however, unlikely that Borges knew of Luria's work, since Luria published his book (in English) only in 1968, more than 25 years after Borges wrote the story of Funes.

"Funes the Memorious" shows Nietzsche's influence as well (as Roxana Kreimer describes in an interesting essay);[10] in particular, Borges calls Funes "a precursor to supermen, a suburban, incomplete Zarathustra." In a brilliant piece on the importance of forgetting, Nietzsche writes:

"Imagine the most extreme example, a human being who does not possess the power to forget, who is damned to see becoming everywhere; such a human being would no longer believe in his own being, would no longer believe in himself, would see everything flow apart in turbulent particles, and would lose himself in this stream of becoming; like the true student of Heraclitus, in the end he would hardly even dare to lift a finger. All action requires forgetting, just as the existence of all organic things requires not only light, but darkness as well." [11]

kürlich verschiedene Sinnesbereiche wie z. B. Farben und Zahlen miteinander, wodurch seine Erinnerungen inhaltsreicher und damit einprägsamer wurden. Mithilfe dieser Assoziationen, aber auch durch den Einsatz einfacher Mnemotechniken, konnte sich Šereševskij oft noch viele Jahre, nachdem er sie zum ersten Mal gehört hatte, an lange Zahlen- und Buchstabenreihen erinnern. Nach über 30jähriger Beschäftigung mit Šereševskij bekannte Lurija, er habe nicht feststellen können, dass Š.'s Gedächtnis irgendeine Grenze gesetzt sei – eine erstaunliche Aussage, wenn man bedenkt, dass sie von keinem Laien, sondern von einem der führenden Psychologen seiner Zeit stammt.

Zwischen Šereševskij und Funes bestehen deutliche Parallelen, auch wenn ersterer sein Gedächtnis auf der Basis seiner Synästhesie trainierte, während es für letzteren etwas völlig Natürliches war, sich zu erinnern. Allerdings ist unwahrscheinlich, dass Borges von Lurijas Studie wusste, weil diese erst 1968 – über 25 Jahre nach der Niederschrift des „Funes" – veröffentlicht wurde.

Dafür zeigt sich bei „Funes el memorioso" auch der Einfluss Nietzsches (wie Roxana Kreimer in einem interessanten Essay darlegt[11]), vor allem an der Stelle, wo Borges seinen Helden einen „Vorläufer [...] des Übermenschen" und „partiellen Vorstadt-Zarathustra" nennt. In einem brillanten Text über die Notwendigkeit des Vergessens schrieb Nietzsche:

„Denkt euch das äusserste Beispiel, einen Menschen, der die Kraft zu vergessen gar nicht besässe, der verurtheilt wäre, überall ein Werden zu sehen: ein Solcher glaubt nicht mehr an sein eigenes Sein, glaubt nicht mehr an sich, sieht alles in bewegte Punkte auseinander fliessen und verliert sich in diesem Strome des Werdens: er wird wie der rechte Schüler Heraklits zuletzt kaum mehr wagen den Finger zu heben. Zu allem Handeln gehört Vergessen: wie zum Leben alles Organischen nicht nur Licht, sondern auch Dunkel gehört."[12]

Aus dem Englischen von Wilfried Prantner

1. One of the main newspapers in Argentina.
2. Jorge Luis Borges, "Funes el memorioso," in *Obras completas* (Buenos Aires: Emecé, 2007), vol. 1, pp. 583–590; subsequent quotations from this story are from the same source. Except where otherwise specified, all English translations of Borges in this book are by Juan Pablo Fernández.
3. I am not the first to reflect on the roots of "Funes the Memorious" and its possible interpretations. In fact, I would like to give credit to those who have previously written on this topic (many of them cited in subsequent footnotes), and although any list I make will end up being unfair, since I will surely forget more than one reference, I would like to mention the essays by Víctor Zonana ("Memoria del mundo clásico en 'Funes el memorioso'" ["Remembrance of the classical world in 'Funes the Memori-ous'"], whose introduction includes an excellent summary of related work); Roxana Kreimer ("Nietzsche, autor de 'Funes el memorioso': Crítica al saber residual de la modernidad" ["Nietzsche, author of "Funes the Memorious": A critique of modernity's residual knowledge"]); Eduardo Mizraji ("Memoria y pensamiento" ["Memory and thought"], among other essays in the book *Borges y la ciencia* ["Borges and science"]); Patricia Novillo-Corvalán ("James Joyce, Author of 'Funes the Memorious'"); Carlos Baratti ("'Funes el memorioso': Ficción que invita a ref lexionar acerca de la neurobiología de la memoria" ["'Funes the Memorious': A fiction that invites reflection on the neurobiology of memory"]); and the books by Iván Izquierdo *(El arte de olvidar [The art of forgetting])*, Guillermo Martínez *(Borges y la matemática [Borges and mathematics])*, and Diego Golombek *(Cavernas y palacios: En busca de la conciencia en el cerebro [Caverns and palaces: Searching for consciousness in the brain])*. Funes is, I would say, a classic reference in any book by an Argentine author on the topic of memory.
4. Jorge Luis Borges, "Fragmento sobre Joyce," in *Jorge Luis Borges en Sur*, 1931–1980 (Buenos Aires: Emecé, 1999), pp. 167–169.
5. *Jorge Luis Borges: Conversations*, ed. Richard Burgin (Jackson: University Press of Mississippi, 1998), p. 166. This passage of the interview has been cited by Patricia Novillo-Corvalán in "James Joyce, Author of 'Funes the Memorious'."
6. Most of these characters had been earlier described by Cicero in his *Tusculan Disputations*. See Cicero, *Tusculan Disputations*, rev. ed., trans. J. E. King (Cambridge, MA: Harvard University Press; London: Heinemann, 1960).
7. Pliny, *Natural History*, vol. 2, trans. Harris Rackham (Cambridge, MA: Harvard University Press, 1942; London: Heinemann, 1947), pp. 562, 563.

1. Eine der wichtigsten argentinischen Tageszeitungen.
2. Jorge Luis Borges, „Funes el memorioso", in: *Obras completas*, Buenos Aires: Emecé, 2007, Bd. 1, S. 583–590; alle Zitate aus der Geschichte stammen vom angegebenen Ort. (Die deutschen Übersetzungen des Textes sind Band 5 der deutschen Werkausgabe entnommen: Jorge Luis Borges, Fiktionen: Erzählungen 1939–1944, übers. v. K.A. Horst, W. Luchting u. Gisbert Haefs, Frankfurt am Main: Fischer 2013; da die deutsche Übersetzung der Erzählung die Hauptfigur aus dem Titel verbannt, wird hier durchgehend dem spanischen Originaltitel der Vorzug gegeben. A. d. Ü.)
3. Ich bin nicht der erste, der sich Gedanken über die Ursprünge von „Funes el memorioso" und die mögliche Bedeutung der Geschichte macht. Ich möchte hier denen Anerkennung zollen, die sich vor mir mit diesem Thema befasst haben (auf viele davon verweisen auch die folgenden Fußnoten). Auch wenn jede Auflistung letztlich ungerecht ist, weil ich zwangsläufig mehrere vergessen werde, seien hier doch die Aufsätze von Víctor Zonana ("Memoria del mundo clásico en ‚Funes el memorioso'", in dessen Einleitung sich eine hervorragende Zusammenfassung einschlägiger Arbeiten findet), Roxana Kreimer („Nietzsche, autor de ‚Funes el memorioso': Crítica al saber residual de la modernidad"), Eduardo Mizraji („Memoria y pensamiento", nebst anderen Aufsätzen in dem Buch *Borges y la ciencia)*, Patricia Novillo-Corvalán („James Joyce, Author of ‚Funes the Memorious'"), Carlos Baratti („‚Funes el memorioso': Ficción que invita a reflexionar acerca de la neurobiología de la memoria"; sowie die Bücher von Iván Izquierdo *(El arte de olvidar)*, Guillermo Martínez *(Borges y la matemática)* und Diego Golombek *(Cavernas y palacios: En busca de la conciencia en el cerebro)* zu nennen. Funes ist sicher der klassische Bezugspunkt eines jeden von einem Argentinier verfassten Buchs zum Thema Gedächtnis.
4. Jorge Luis Borges, „Fragmento sobre Joyce," in *Jorge Luis Borges en Sur*, 1931–1980, Buenos Aires: Emecé, 1999, S. 167–169 (Dt. „Fragment über Joyce", in: ders., Eine neue Widerlegung der Zeit und 66 andere Essays, übers. v. Gisbert Haefs, Frankfurt am Main: Eichborn 2003, S. 175ff.)
5. *Jorge Luis Borges: Conversations*, hg. v. Richard Burgin, Jackson: University Press of Mississippi, 1998, S. 166. Patricia Novillo-Corvalán zitiert diesen Ausschnitt aus dem Interview in ihrem Aufsatz „Nietzsche, autor de ‚Funes el memorioso'".
6. Die meisten dieser Personen waren schon früher von Cicero in den *Tusculanae disputationes* beschrieben worden. Vgl. Cicero, *Tusculan Disputations*, rev. Ausg., Übers. J. E. King, Cambridge, MA: Harvard University Press; London: Heinemann, 1960.
7. C. Plinius Secundus d. Ä., *Naturkunde*, Lateinisch – Deutsch, Buch VII: Anthropologie, übers. v. R. König et al., 2. Aufl., Zürich/Düsseldorf: Artemis und Winkler 1996, S. 67.

8. Upon receiving the Cervantes Prize in 1979 ("a generous blunder that I shamelessly accept," he said), Borges commented in an interview that with the prize money—a million pesetas, to be shared with Spanish poet Gerardo Diego—he planned to buy the *Espasa Calpe* encyclopedia, which he eventually received as a present from the publishers. Borges also had several editions of the *Naturalis historia* in his library, along with a 1907 edition of Sir Francis Galton's *Inquiries into Human Faculty and Its Development*, on whose final page Borges transcribed chapter 24 of book VII of the *Naturalis historia* in the original Latin (along with a French translation on the first page).
9. In the context of Pliny's paragraph this phrase can also be translated as "[Through memory] it is possible to repeat with the same words what has been heard."
10. Roxana Kreimer, "Nietzsche, autor de 'Funes el memorioso': Crítica al saber residual de la modernidad" ("Nietzsche, author of "Funes the Memori- ous": A critique of modernity's residual knowledge"), in *Jorge Luis Borges: Intervenciones sobre pensamiento y literatura* (Buenos Aires: Paidós, 2000).
11. Friedrich Nietzsche, "On the Utility and Liability of History for Life," in *Unfashionable Observations*, trans. Richard T. Gray (Stanford: Stanford University Press, 1995). In this essay Nietzsche refers to forgetting in a historical context, suggesting that man should not tie himself to the prejudices of History (a fundamental requirement for the creation of his famous "superman").

8. Nach der Verleihung des Cervantespreises 1979 (die er als „großzügigen Missgriff, den ich schamlos annehme", bezeichnete) sagte Borges in einem Interview, er plane mit dem Preisgeld – eine Million Peseten, die er mit dem spanischen Dichter Gerardo Diego teilen musste – die *Enciclopedia Espasa-Calpe* zu kaufen, welche ihm die Herausgeber schließlich schenkten. Borges hatte in seiner Bibliothek auch mehrere Ausgaben der *Naturalis historia* stehen, nebst einer Ausgabe von Sir Frances Galtons *Inquiries into Human Faculty and Its Development*, auf dessen letzter Seite er sich das Kapitel 24 aus dem Buch VII der *Naturalis historia* auf Latein abgeschrieben hatte (mit einer französischen Übersetzung auf der ersten).
9. Im Kontext von Plinius' Kapitel wird die Passage mit „[die Gedächtniskunst macht es möglich], alles Gehörte mit denselben Worten wiederzugeben" übersetzt.
10. Dt. in: Alexander Lurija, *Der Mann, dessen Welt in Scherben ging. Zwei neurologische Geschichten*, Reinbeck: Rowohlt 1991, S. 151-249. (A.d.Ü.)
11. Roxana Kreimer, „Nietzsche, autor de ‚Funes el memorioso': Crítica al saber residual de la modernidad", in: *Jorge Luis Borges: Intervenciones sobre pensamiento y literatura*, Buenos Aires: Paidós 2000.
12. Friedrich Nietzsche, „Vom Nutzen und Nachteil der Historie für das Leben", in: ders., *Die Geburt der Tragödie. Unzeitgemäße Betrachtungen*, Kritische Studienausgabe, München: Deutscher Taschenbuch Verlag; Berlin: De Gruyter 1999, S. 250. Nietzsche betrachtet hier das Vergessen im Zusammenhang mit der Geschichte, wobei er dazu rät, dass sich der Mensch nicht an die Vorurteile der Historie binden sollte (eine wesentliche Voraussetzung für die Schaffung des „Übermenschen").

Helga Rohra

Dementia exists everywhere
Demenz existiert überall

Dementia exists everywhere. People get diagnosed at quite a young age. This syndrome called dementia can start at 30 years of age or 40 or 50. It is the new generation of PWD (people with dementia) who are prepared to encounter the different attitudes in society. People who do not want to be victims of this disease but victors in their new life, even living with dementia.

I myself got diagnosed with DLB (Dementia with Lewy Bodies) at 54 years of age. As a former interpreter I started to accept my new situation—an everlasting process. But also a way of personal maturity of standing up again and again.

Imagine, you have been working in 5 foreign languages, your PC and I-phone are tolls in your tight timetable. Social and political involvement are a part of your life. Sports, painting, music, social gatherings are highlights. You never miss anything! And day after day some new signs turn up: you forget first some vocabulary, the way a PC works. Driving your car gets impossible as road signs and sceneries are unknown to you. Social involvement as well as political gets tough: you forget in the mid of the sentence what you wanted to point at. Your language gets a problem even in the mother tongue. You cannot work anymore. The foreign languages disappear daily. It seems like a wet sponge that wipes slowly and steadily away my knowledge. You need not only the medical, pharmaceutical treatment but even more the non-pharmaceutical. You realize that you are left alone in society. First you get frozen, what really means that depression is added to dementia.

I myself started MY WAY. Self-analysis, celebrating myself. Even with dementia I am a valuable human being. I decided to teach everyone that dementia has so many faces and we ourselves make the difference! My doctor got amazed how demanding I am: speech therapy, new diet, physical and mental exercise. No, you cannot bring back memory loss, nor can you stop dementia. But essential is the active part the patient plays, the feeling of being a winner, not always the loser!

Demenz existiert überall. Bei manchen Menschen wird die Krankheit schon in relativ jungen Jahren diagnostiziert. Das „Demenz" genannte Syndrom kann schon mit 30 Jahren beginnen, oder mit 40 oder 50. Es ist die neue Generation der PWD (*People with dementia*, Menschen mit Demenz), die darauf gefasst sind, auf sehr unterschiedliche Reaktionen ihrer Umwelt zu treffen. Menschen, die nicht Opfer dieser Krankheit sein wollen, sondern Sieger in ihrem neuen Leben, auch wenn sie an Demenz leiden.

Bei mir wurde LBD (Lewy-Body-Demenz) diagnostiziert, als ich 54 Jahre alt war. Als frühere Dolmetscherin begann ich meine neue Situation zu akzeptieren – ein nie endender Prozess. Aber auch eine Möglichkeit, immer wieder einen kleinen Sieg zu erringen und so persönlich zu reifen.

Stellen Sie sich vor, dass Sie mit fünf Fremdsprachen arbeiten, Ihr PC, Ihr iPhone sind Ihre Gefährten in Ihrem gedrängten Alltag. Soziales und politisches Engagement sind Teil Ihres Lebens. Sport, Malerei, Musikveranstaltungen sind Highlights. Sie versäumen nie etwas! Und Tag für Tag tauchen neue Anzeichen auf: Zuerst vergessen Sie einige Vokabel und wie ein PC funktioniert. Auto fahren wird unmöglich, weil Sie Straßenschilder und Umgebung nicht mehr erkennen. Soziales und politisches Engagement wird schwieriger: Sie vergessen mitten im Satz, worauf Sie eigentlich hinaus wollten. Die Sprache funktioniert nicht mehr, nicht einmal Ihre Muttersprache. Sie können nicht mehr arbeiten. Die Fremdsprachen verschwinden langsam. Es scheint, als würde ein nasser Schwamm langsam und stetig das ganze Wissen wegwischen. Sie brauchen nicht nur medizinische und medikamentöse Behandlung, sondern vor allem nicht-medikamentöse. Sie erkennen, dass Sie allein gelassen sind in der Gesellschaft. Zuerst erstarren Sie: In Wirklichkeit kommt zur Demenz auch noch eine Depression.

Ich selbst begann mich auf MEINE ART damit auseinanderzusetzen. Selbstanalyse, ein Zelebrieren meiner selbst. Auch mit Demenz bin ich ein wertvoller Mensch. Ich beschloss, allen zu erklären, dass Demenz so viele Gesichter hat und wir selbst einen Unter-

Doctors have to get used to this new type of patient, who stands up and speaks up. Society and so-called integrational services are not prepared for us: people with onset dementia. No opportunities, no advice, no competence programs. We are forgotten, we are classified as the final stage of dementia and advised to go to self-support groups. Of course, a good Idea I must confess at the very beginning after getting diagnosed. But believe me, after some years I know the best way is inclusion. All those millions of young people diagnosed with early dementia in Europe cannot be mistaken. We need a new approach in different ways.

I started 5 years ago to raise my voice. I wrote a book: *Stepping out of the shadow–Why I am a dementia campaigner.* The mass media reacted shortly. My interviews on TV stations in different countries, my lecture tours. My voice, as the Chair of the first EWGPD (European working group of people with dementia), under the umbrella association of AE (Alzheimer Europe–Luxembourg) is heard even in the EU Parliament. I meet politicians and doctors, carers, journalists, relatives and all my friends with dementia–they support me in raising awareness: dementia is not the end of life. No, dementia is a new beginning.

Ask us, people with dementia (pwd) must be included in planning dementia-friendly societies. We are the experts. Take us into your programs: either in assistive technologies, the influence of music and art. Nothing is more amazing than the human brain. We pwd all know: more research to find a cure for this new epidemic called dementia, more inclusion but mainly: a new way of communicating in society–we are all a part of society–with or without impairment.

Helga Rohra, a native speaker of German, wrote her text for this catalog in English because, in her words, "I'm still as fluent as I was back when I worked as an interpreter." Due to her professional training as an interpreter, she has a more solid command of (written?) English than she does of her mother tongue.

Helga Rohra, deren Muttersprache Deutsch ist, hat den Text für diesen Katalog auf Englisch geschrieben, weil, wie sie selbst meinte, „da noch top ist, wie zu meiner Berufszeit als Dolmetscherin". Durch das Dolmetsch-Training ist die (geschriebene?) englische Sprache gefestigter als die deutsche Muttersprache.

schied machen! Mein Arzt konnte es nicht fassen, wie anspruchsvoll ich war: Sprachtherapie, eine neue Diät, körperliches und mentales Training. Nein, den Gedächtnisverlust kann man nicht ausgleichen, und man kann die Demenz auch nicht aufhalten. Aber wesentlich ist, wie aktiv der Patient ist, dass er das Gefühl hat, ein Gewinner und nicht immer nur ein Verlierer zu sein!

Die Ärzte müssen sich an diesen neuen Typus von Patient gewöhnen, der sich auf seine Beine stellt und sich engagiert. Die Gesellschaft und sogenannte Integrationsservices sind auf uns nicht vorbereitet: Menschen mit beginnender Demenz. Keine Chancen, kein Rat, keine Kompetenzprogramme. Wir sind vergessen, uns wird das Etikett einer Demenz im Endstadium umgehängt, man rät uns, Selbsthilfegruppen zu besuchen. Natürlich ist das eine gute Idee, das muss ich zugeben, vor allem am Anfang, gleich nach der Diagnose. Aber glauben Sie mir, nach ein paar Jahren weiß ich, dass Inklusion die beste Methode ist. All die Millionen junger Menschen in Europa, bei denen Demenz diagnostiziert wird, können nicht falsch liegen. Wir müssen in vielerlei Hinsicht neue Wege gehen.

Vor fünf Jahren begann ich, meine Stimme zu erheben. Ich schrieb ein Buch: *Aus dem Schatten treten – Warum ich mich für unsere Rechte als Demenzbetroffene einsetze.* Die Massenmedien reagierten schnell: Interviews im Fernsehen verschiedener Länder, eine Lesereise. Meine Stimme als Vorsitzende der ersten europäischen Arbeitsgruppe für Menschen mit Demenz *EWGPD (European working group of people with dementia),* die Mitglied der Dachorganisation Alzheimer Europe (Luxemburg) ist, findet sogar im EU-Parlament Gehör. Ich traf Politiker und Ärzte, Pflegekräfte, Journalisten, Angehörige und alle meine Freunde mit PWD – sie unterstützen mich bei meiner Sensibilisierungsarbeit: Demenz ist nicht das Ende des Lebens. Nein, Demenz ist ein neuer Anfang.

Wenn man uns fragt: PWDs müssen in die Planung einer Demenz-freundlichen Gesellschaft einbezogen werden. Wir sind die Experten. Nehmt uns in eure Programme auf: wenn es um technische Hilfsmittel oder den Einfluss von Musik und Kunst geht. Nichts ist erstaunlicher als das menschliche Gehirn. Wir PWDs wissen: mehr Forschung, um eine Heilung dieser neuen, Demenz genannten Epidemie zu finden, mehr Integration, aber vor allem: eine neue Art und Weise, in der Gesellschaft zu kommunizieren: Wir alle sind ein Teil davon – mit oder ohne Behinderung.

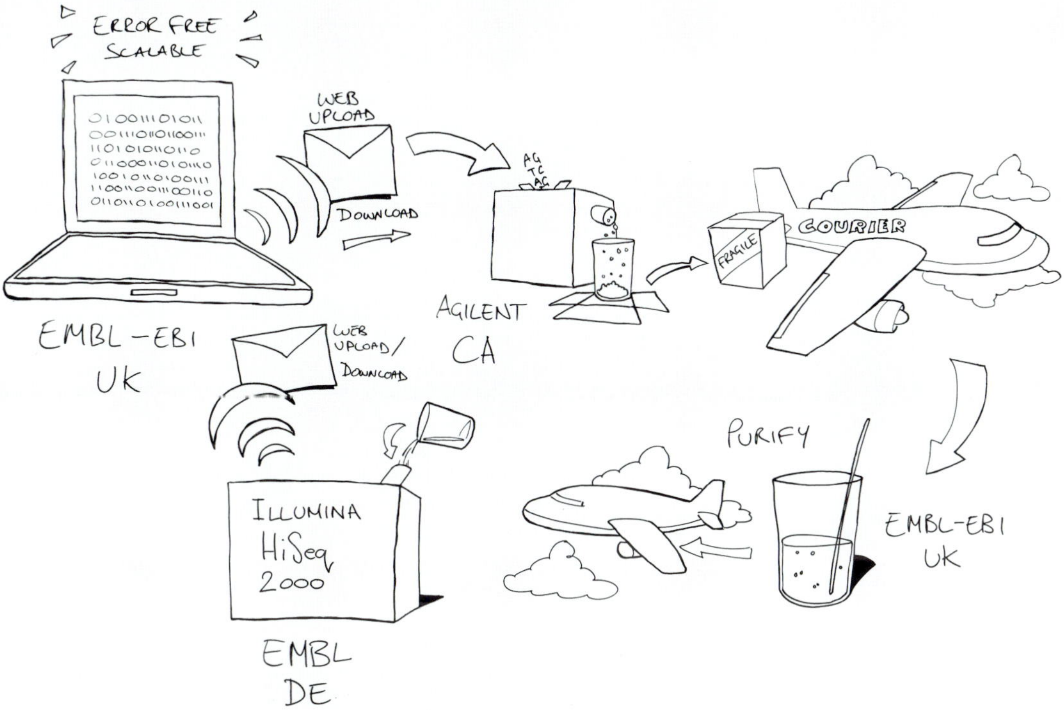

Nick Goldman, Charlotte Jarvis

The DNA Chronicles

The amount of information humans produce and want to store digitally is increasing exponentially, and is currently measured in zettabytes: thousands of billions of billions of bytes. The amount that people want to store safely and in an easily recoverable manner for long periods of time—with minimal effort and expense—is also growing. Why? And how?
At present there is no genuinely long-term archiving of digital information taking place. That's mainly because the available storage media—CDs, DVDs, hard disk drives, magnetic tapes, etc.—are fairly high maintenance. Both the storage medium itself and the machines that read it require constant refreshing, because no technology is trusted to survive beyond a few years.
Think about what happened to your floppy disks, your Betamax tapes, or even your VHSs: even if you had kept them safe, they would eventually

Die Informationsmenge, die Menschen produzieren und digital speichern wollen, steigt exponentiell an und wird derzeit in Zettabytes gemessen: etwa einer Billion Gigabytes. Das Datenvolumen, das Menschen sicher und auf eine einfach wieder auszulesende Weise – mit minimalem Aufwand und niedrigen Kosten – über eine lange Zeitspanne speichern wollen, steigt ebenfalls. Warum? Und wie?
Derzeit gibt es keine wirklich langfristige Archivierung digitaler Information. Das liegt vor allem daran, dass die üblichen Speichermedien – CDs, DVDs, Festplattenlaufwerke, Magnetbänder etc. – relativ wartungsintensiv sind. Sowohl das Speichermedium selbst als auch die Maschinen zu ihrer Auslesung müssen ständig aktualisiert werden, weil man bei keiner dieser Technologien darauf vertrauen kann, dass sie länger als ein paar Jahre hält.
Man denke nur daran, was mit den Disketten, den

decay and become unreadable, and the hardware for reading them would vanish. Digital archiving requires considerable investments in time, space and technology.

A proven medium

One storage medium has truly stood the test of time: DNA. Life on Earth has been successfully passing information from one generation to the next for 3.5 billion years using deoxyribonucleic acid, the chemical molecule that holds the instructions for life, located in each cell of every living organism. A DNA molecule consists of a long chain of nucleotides, which are usually abbreviated A, C, G and T. Nucleotides can be joined in any order to form a compact and highly stable structure, including the famous "double helix" adopted by pairs of complementary, anti-parallel DNA molecules. A DNA sequence can be very short, like ATGGTGCTGTCT at the beginning of a human gene, or mind-bogglingly long, like the 3 billion that form a human genome. Every one of us carries all of this information in each of the cells in our bodies.

Scientists have worked to piece together the genomes of wooly mammoths (20,000 years old), Neanderthals (40,000 years old), bison (60,000 years) and even a prehistoric horse that had been frozen in the Arctic permafrost for 700,0000 years. Clearly, DNA does pretty well if it is kept cold, dark and dry: conditions that are relatively simple and inexpensive to achieve. And it's a fair assumption that as long as humans remain curious about what makes life work, they will keep developing technologies for reading and writing DNA.

Translating human-designed information

DNA has many features that make it ideal for storing digital information. Our research team recently showed that DNA sequences can be formed that represent large quantities of human-designed information.

We used standard DNA synthesis and DNA sequencing to store and then recover five computer files, totaling 750 kb: all of Shakespeare's sonnets (a text file), an excerpt from Martin Luther King's "I Have a Dream" speech (mp4), a photograph (jpeg), Wat-

Betamax- oder auch den VHS-Kassetten geschah: Auch wenn man sie sicher aufbewahrte, hatten sie ein Ablaufdatum und wurden mit der Zeit unlesbar, die Hardware zu ihrer Auslesung verschwand. Die digitale Archivierung erfordert einen beträchtlichen Aufwand an Zeit, Raum und Technologie.

Ein bewährtes Medium

Ein Speichermedium hat die Prüfung der Zeit wirklich bestanden: die DNA. Das Leben auf der Erde hat mithilfe der Desoxyribonukleinsäure, dem chemischen Molekül, das Träger der Erbinformation ist und in jeder Zelle eines lebenden Organismus vorkommt, erfolgreich über 3,5 Milliarden Jahre lang Informationen von einer Generation an die nächste weitergegeben.

Ein DNA-Molekül besteht aus einer langen Kette von Nukleotiden, die im Allgemeinen abgekürzt mit den Buchstaben A, C, G und T bezeichnet werden. Nukleotide können in beliebigen Abfolgen zu einer kompakten und äußerst stabilen Struktur kombiniert werden, so auch zur berühmten „Doppelhelix", die aus komplementären, gegenläufigen DNA-Doppelsträngen aufgebaut ist. Eine DNA-Sequenz kann sehr kurz sein, wie etwa ATGGTGCTGTCT am Anfang eines menschlichen Gens oder verblüffend lang sein und drei Milliarden Buchstaben bzw. Basenpaare umfassen wie das menschliche Genom. Jeder von uns trägt diese Informationen in jeder einzelnen Körperzelle. Wissenschaftler haben daran gearbeitet, die Genome der Wollhaarmammuts (20.000 Jahre alt), der Neandertaler (40.000 Jahre), der Bisons (60.000 Jahre) und sogar eines prähistorischen Pferdes, das 700.0000 Jahre lang im Permafrost der Arktis konserviert war, zusammenzusetzen. Bei kühler, dunkler und trockener Lagerung ist die DNA offenbar gut haltbar: Bedingungen, die relativ einfach und kostengünstig herzustellen sind. Und man kann auch davon ausgehen, dass weiterhin Technologien zum Lesen und Schreiben der DNA entwickelt werden, solange die Menschheit neugierig darauf ist, wie das Leben funktioniert.

Die Übertragung menschengemachter Informationen

Die DNA hat viele Merkmale, die sie für die Speicherung digitaler Informationen prädestinieren. Unser Forschungsteam hat kürzlich gezeigt, dass DNA-son and Crick's seminal paper on the structure of DNA (a PDF) and, just for fun, the code/decode file (don't ask). The experiment was 100% successful, and the methods we used, after a little refinement, could be scaled up to archive the world's digital information.

Nature's (delicious) shorthand

The idea of placing human-designed information into the natural world's information medium is intriguing on both technological and artistic levels. Ars Electronica has been the natural home for artists grappling with the subject for many years, notably Eduardo Kac *(Genesis,* 1999) and Joe Davis *(Bacterial Radio,* Golden Nica award 2012).

In 2012, Charlotte Jarvis *(http://www.artforeating.com)* designed the project *Blighted by Kenning,* in which the Universal Declaration of Human Rights was encoded into the genome of a bacterium. The DNA was extracted, and in a performance piece the artist "contaminated" apples grown near The Hague (home of the International Court of Justice) with the synthetic DNA. These "forbidden fruit" were then sent to laboratories around the world, whose scientists were asked to "sequence the declaration" and also to eat the fruit.

Nick Goldman and Charlotte Jarvis are collaborating on further projects based on the storage of digital information using DNA. They will jointly present their science and art, and will offer audience members a chance to take away a new and original artwork.

Nick Goldman is affiliated with the European Molecular Biology Laboratory-European Bioinformatics Institute (EMBL-EBI).

Sequenzen gebildet werden können, die große Informationsmengen repräsentieren können.

Wir verwendeten die standardmäßige DNA-Synthese und DNA-Sequenzierung, um fünf Computerdateien (insgesamt 750 kb) zu speichern und dann auszulesen: sämtliche Sonette Shakespeares (eine Textdatei), einen Ausschnitt aus Martin Luther Kings berühmter Rede „I Have a Dream" (mp4), eine Fotografie (jpg), die bahnbrechende Studie der Genetik-Pioniere Watson und Crick über die Struktur der DNA (ein pdf) und, nur zum Spaß, eine Beschreibung der Kodierung und Dekodierung (Details erspare ich Ihnen). Das Experiment war zu hundert Prozent erfolgreich und die von uns verwendeten Methoden könnten mit etwas Optimierung in einem größeren Maßstab eingesetzt werden, um die digitalen Informationen der Welt zu speichern.

Die (wunderbare) Kurzschrift der Natur

Die Idee, menschliches Wissen in das Informationsmedium der Natur einzuschleusen, ist sowohl in technischer als auch in künstlerischer Hinsicht faszinierend. Ars Electronica ist seit vielen Jahren die erste Adresse für Künstler, die sich seit Langem mit diesem Thema beschäftigen, beispielsweise für Eduardo Kac *(Genesis,* 1999) und Joe Davis *(Bacterial Radio,* Goldene Nica 2012).

2012 entwickelte Charlotte Jarvis *(http://www.artforeating.com)* das Projekt *Blighted by Kenning,* bei dem die Allgemeine Erklärung der Menschenrechte im Genom einer Bakterie kodiert wurde. Die DNA wurde extrahiert und die synthetische DNA in einer Performance der Künstlerin unweit von Den Haag (dem Sitz des Internationalen Gerichtshofs) in geerntete Äpfel eingeschleust. Sie schickte diese „verbotene Frucht" an Labors auf der ganzen Welt und forderte die Wissenschaftler auf, die „Menschenrechtserklärung zu sequenzieren" und auch die Frucht zu essen.

Nick Goldman und Charlotte Jarvis arbeiten an weiteren Projekten, die auf der Speicherung digitaler Informationen mithilfe der DNA basieren. Sie werden ihre wissenschaftlichen und künstlerischen Arbeiten gemeinsam präsentieren und dem Publikum die Möglichkeit bieten, ein neues und originelles Kunstwerk zu erstehen.

Aus dem Englischen von Martina Bauer

Frank Hartmann

Paul Otlet and the Logic of the Database
Paul Otlet und die Logik der Datenbank

Books and libraries as means of storing knowledge were already targets of criticism a century ago. To Paul Otlet (1868–1944), an independent scholar in Belgium, these data storage media seemed no longer suitable for representing knowledge that was relevant to humankind at the turn of the 20th century. Accordingly, he focused all his intellectual energy on restructuring the *documentation* of information and knowledge. In light of the various problems caused by the industrialization of commercial printing, what was called for was a paradigm shift that went beyond the principle of monography. For Otlet, this was the logic of the databank, as it would later be called.[1]
The elaboration of this new logic would become his life's work: revamping the decimal classification of library holdings into the *classification décimale universelle,* professionalization of the system of documentation via index cards and microfilm in his Mundaneum, and the design of a global network of knowledge and communication (though one that was, of course, still technically premature).[2]
Following the publication of his thoughts in 1934, all of this sunk into complete oblivion until 1968, when Australian scholar W. Boyd Rayward began to do research in Brussels on the Mundaneum's long-since-forgotten inventory. He went on to publish an intellectual biography of Paul Otlet and later edited a collection of his essays translated into English.[3]
Together with Henri La Fontaine, Otlet founded the *Office International de Bibliographie* in 1895 and launched the ambitious project of indexing all sorts of facts gleaned from and about publications by means of a system of index cards, the so-called *Répertoire Bibliographique Universel.* This was conceived as a place to store the entire accumulated knowledge of humankind, and thus the very concept itself reveals the intention of superseding the book format and the monographic principle by

Bücher und Bibliotheken als Wissensspeicher fanden schon vor einem Jahrhundert ihre Kritiker. Diese Datenträger schienen dem belgischen Privatgelehrten Paul Otlet (1868–1944) nicht länger angemessen, um im anbrechenden 20. Jahrhundert das relevante Wissen zu repräsentieren. Er wandte deshalb seine gesamte intellektuelle Energie dafür auf, die *Dokumentation* von Information und Wissen neu zu strukturieren. Angesichts vielfältiger Problemlagen, die mit der Industrialisierung des Druckwesens begannen, musste ein neues Paradigma jenseits des Prinzips der Monografie her, und für Otlet war das *avant le mot* die Logik der Datenbank.[1]
Die Klärung dieser neuen Logik wurde zu seinem Lebenswerk: von der Überarbeitung der Dezimalklassifikation für Bibliotheksbestände zur *Classification décimale universelle* über die Professionalisierung des Dokumentationswesens mittels Karteikarten und Mikrofilm im Mundaneum bis hin zum technisch natürlich noch unausgereiften Entwurf eines weltweiten Wissens- und Kommunikationsnetzes.[2]
Nach der Publikation seiner Gedanken im Jahr 1934 geriet dies alles jedoch völlig in Vergessenheit, bis 1968 der australische Wissenschaftler W. Boyd Rayward in Brüssel die verlassenen Bestände des Mundaneums zu erforschen begann, eine intellektuelle Biografie Paul Otlets publizierte und später auch die englische Übersetzung einer Auswahl seiner Essays besorgte.[3]
Mit Henri La Fontaine gründete Otlet 1895 das *Office International de Bibliographie* und begann mit dem ambitionierten Projekt einer Indizierung aller möglichen „Fakten" aus und über Publikationen mittels eines Karteikartensystems, dem sogenannten *Répertoire Bibliographique Universel.* Dies sollte ein Aufbewahrungsort des gesamten bekannten Wissensbestandes werden, an dem bereits die Absicht erkennbar wird, das Buchformat bzw. das monografische Prinzip zugunsten eines flexiblen Wissensbestandes aufzulösen. Dieses Projekt besetzte jene technologische

instituting a flexible mode of storing knowledge. This project occupied the technological void produced by a new culture of knowledge that had emerged in the 19th century. The project's mission: terminating the typographical epoch.
At this time, however, virtually no one had come up with a concept for an alternative to libraries and encyclopedias. The dissemination of knowledge presupposed its storage, and the crucial element in storing bodies of knowledge is its classification. Classifying knowledge according to particular criteria gives rise to taxonomies or systems of categories that can assume highly diverse forms and may be weighted much differently in various cultures and at different times. Things that one might think had been around for ages often turn out to be of rather recent provenance—and so it is with respect to systematic ordering in the domain of books. It wasn't until the end of the 17th century that Gottfried Wilhelm Leibniz developed his "Plan for Arranging a Library" *(Idea bibliothecae ordinande)* that went beyond the scope of an individual collection of books. And a general system of classification in libraries had to wait for the work of American librarian Melvil Dewey towards the end of the 19th century.
Knowledge requires classification as well as organization in physical structures such as archives and libraries—and ultimately databanks and networks—in order to be culturally operational beyond the subjective, limited capacities of individuals. Now, it is surely appropriate to apply the term visionary to someone who anticipates the significance of a technical development while others have not yet even gotten as far as recognizing the problem. In this sense, Paul Otlet was a visionary of a knowledge-based society that a series of media revolutions would ultimately endow with an unprecedented new technical foundation: for one, actually registering what transpired in the world, as paradigmatically enabled by photography; for another, wiring the world for the purpose of telecommunications.[4]
Otlet recognized this mediatized modernity as the opportunity to solve those problems that had been created by the proliferation of printed publications, and saw that responses to them would have to be methodological, technical and institutional. In all

Leerstelle, die eine im 19. Jahrhundert beginnende, die typografische Epoche aufsprengende neue Wissenskultur produziert hat.
Für die Vision einer Alternative zu Bibliotheken und Enzyklopädien gab es aber damals noch kaum eine Vorstellung. Die Verbreitung von Wissen setzt dessen Aufbereitung voraus, und das wichtigste Element der Aufbereitung von Wissensbeständen ist deren Klassifikation. Wird Wissen nach bestimmten Kriterien klassifiziert, dann entstehen Taxonomien oder Kategoriensysteme, die in unterschiedlichen Kulturen und zu verschiedenen Zeiten höchst differente Formen und Gewichtungen annehmen können. Wovon man denken möchte, es hätte seit langer Zeit Bestand, ist tatsächlich oft eher jüngeren Datums – so die systematische Ordnung im Reich der Bücher. Erst Gottfried Wilhelm Leibniz entwickelte gegen Ende des 17. Jahrhunderts einen über die einzelne Bücheransammlung hinausgehenden „Plan zur Anordnung einer Bibliothek" *(Idea bibliothecae ordinande)*, und erst der amerikanische Bibliothekar Melvil Dewey etablierte gegen Ende des 19. Jahrhunderts ein allgemeines System zur Klassifikation in Bibliotheken.
Wissen braucht Klassifikation sowie Organisation in materiellen Strukturen wie Archiven und Bibliotheken, schließlich Datenbanken und Netzwerken, um über die subjektiv beschränkten Kapazitäten von Individuen hinaus kulturell wirksam werden zu können. Nun mag als Visionär bezeichnet werden, wem die Antizipation der Bedeutung einer technischen Entwicklung schon gelingt, wenn andere noch nicht einmal die Problemlage zu erkennen vermögen. Paul Otlet war in diesem Sinne Visionär einer Wissensgesellschaft, die aufgrund unterschiedlicher Medienrevolutionen neue technische Grundlagen als die bislang bekannten erhalten sollte: Zum einen war dies die Realaufzeichnung von Weltgeschehen, wie sie paradigmatisch die Fotografie ermöglicht hat, zum anderen die Verkabelung der Welt zu Zwecken der Telekommunikation.[4]
In dieser Medienmoderne erkannte Otlet die Chance, jene Probleme zu lösen, die sich mit der Proliferation gedruckter Publikationen ergaben: Man würde methodisch, technisch und institutionell darauf reagieren müssen. In allen drei Bereichen leistete er Grundlegendes, vor allem die Einrichtung der Ebene von Metadaten in Form von Karteikarten und deren Verwaltung. Eine Weltstadt des Wissens, das Mundaneum, sollte als Zentrum einer globalen Wissensbasis in

three areas, he made fundamental contributions, above all the implementation of the level of metadata in the form of index cards and the administration of them. A cosmopolis of knowledge, the Mundaneum, was conceived as the global center of knowledge in Geneva, Rome or Brussels. Thus, Otlet was conceptualizing the end of the bourgeois Age of the Book in terms of a databank or a *universal* book while others were still thinking in categories like national museums and national libraries. In Mons, Belgium, it's still possible to view what's left of his lifelong mission: setting up a world databank that integrated all information that could be documented. These remains—in the form of enormous index card catalogs—clearly show what a laborious job it must have been then to interlink knowledge in a network of paper.

One of the defining events of the second half of the 19th century was the commencement of construction of international transportation and communications infrastructure. World's fairs, launched in London in 1851, culminated in the *Exposition Universelle* in Paris in 1889 and the idea that the world is a generalizable, homogenous place of experience. This event attracted 32 million visitors, and the Eiffel Tower erected in conjunction with it remains the city's most eye-catching landmark. The catalog of this world's fair, illustrated by numerous engravings portraying its sensational attractions, gave the global village a much higher profile while simultaneously endowing it with the polished appearance of a social utopia.[5] The influence exerted on Paul Otlet's project by this world's fair and the one later held in Brussels should not be underestimated.

Beginning with the idea of maintaining the availability of information about individual countries, he spent the following decades in the intense pursuit of institutionalizing his obsession: documenting the world's entire published knowledge in a new form to thereby enhance its utility. Today, accessing all sorts of content regardless of the data storage media to which this material was originally saved is something we take completely for granted, but back then, the very idea of an approach to knowledge management that went beyond the purview of the exclusive routines of a book & library culture was completely unheard of. Paradoxically, though, the terminology continued to be derived from library

Genf, Rom oder Brüssel angesiedelt werden. So begriff Otlet das Ende des bürgerlichen Buchzeitalters im Geiste der Datenbank oder des *universellen* Buches, während die Allgemeinheit noch in den Kategorien von Nationalmuseen und Nationalbibliotheken dachte. Heute noch sind im belgischen Mons die Überreste seiner lebenslangen Anstrengung zu sehen, eine Weltdatenbank einzurichten, die alle dokumentierbaren Informationen integriert. Sie führen in Form eines immensen Zettelkastens deutlich vor Augen, wie mühsam es einst gewesen sein muss, Wissensvernetzung im Papierformat zu betreiben.

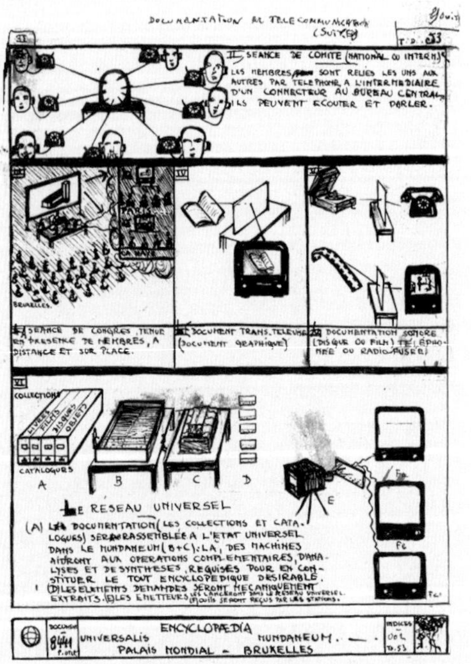

Documentation et Télécommunication:
Visualization of a hypermedial fusion of documentation and telecommunications according to a server-client architecture. Paul Otlet: *Encyclopedia Universalis,* circa 1934

Documentation et Télécommunication:
Visualisierung einer hypermedialen Verschmelzung von Dokumentation und Telekommunikation nach einer Server-Client-Architektur. Paul Otlet: *Encyclopedia Universalis,* ca. 1934

Source © Mundaneum, Mons, Belgium

science. Nevertheless, Otlet's magnum opus, his *Traité de documentation* published in 1934, speculatively elaborated on how written culture could be definitively superseded by the amalgamation of all storage & transmission media on an integrated systemic level that was said to be the only way to manage the documented knowledge of humankind. In fact, he already dubbed it the "hypermedium." It's not very productive to argue about whether this anticipated the World Wide Web (interlinking documents online) or Google (as a search engine to locate documents online). But it certainly can be asserted that Otlet was already dealing with what was called for to implement technically supported knowledge management on the basis of networked resources, and thus with issues that simply had to emerge in the wake of technology from the Gutenberg Age, and to which today's responses are the extended Web with its search engines and social networks.

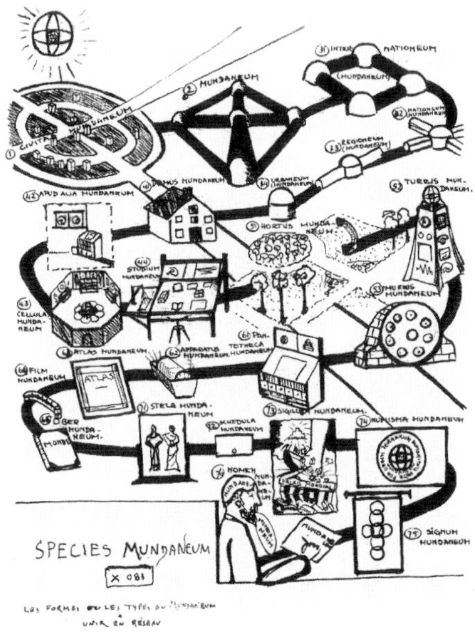

Source © Mundaneum, Mons, Belgium

Species Mundaneum. Les formes ou les types du Mundaneum à unir en réseau: Sketch of a networked architecture of a unified space containing the knowledge of the world. Paul Otlet: *Encyclopedia Universalis*, circa 1934

Species Mundaneum. Les formes ou les types du Mundaneum à unir en réseau: Skizze einer vernetzten Architektur des vereinten Weltwissensraums. Paul Otlet: *Encyclopedia Universalis*, ca. 1934

Die zweite Hälfte des 19. Jahrhunderts war bestimmt vom Ausbau einer erstmals internationalen Infrastruktur im Verkehrs- und Kommunikationswesen. Die 1851 in London begonnenen Weltausstellungen kulminierten in der Pariser Weltausstellung von 1889 *(L'Exposition Universelle)* und der Idee, die Welt wäre ein verallgemeinerbar homogener Ort der Erfahrung: Sie wurde von 32 Millionen Menschen besucht, und der damals errichtete Eiffelturm wurde zum weithin bekannten Wahrzeichen der Stadt. Das Journal dieser Weltausstellung, mit vielen Stahlstichen von den Sensationen illustriert, sorgte für eine erweiterte Wahrnehmbarkeit und zugleich den Vorschein einer gesellschaftlichen Utopie vom *Global Village.*[5] Der Einfluss dieser Weltausstellung und der späteren in Brüssel auf Paul Otlets Projekt einer Weltdatenbank ist wohl nicht zu unterschätzen.

Beginnend mit der Idee, die Länderinformationen verfügbar zu halten, war er in den nun folgenden Jahrzehnten intensiv mit der Institutionalisierung seiner Obsession beschäftigt, sämtliches publizierte Wissen der Welt in neuer Form zu dokumentieren und damit besser nutzbar zu machen. So selbstverständlich uns heute die Tatsache scheint, auf alle möglichen Inhalte unabhängig von ihren Datenträgern zugreifen zu können, so unerhört war damals allein schon die Idee, Fragen des Wissensmanagements außerhalb der exklusiven Routinen einer Buch- und Bibliothekskultur anzusiedeln. Paradoxerweise blieb die Terminologie vorerst aber noch dem Bibliothekarischen angelehnt. Otlets Opus Magnum jedoch, sein 1934 publizierter *Traité de documentation,* handelt in spekulativen Ausführungen vom definitiven Jenseits der Schriftkultur, von der Zusammenführung aller Speicher- und Übertragungsmedien auf einer integrierten systemischen Ebene, die allein ein Management des dokumentierten Weltwissens erlauben würde. Er nannte es schon damals „Hypermedium". Es ist wenig fruchtbar, darüber zu streiten, ob dies eine Vorwegnahme des World Wide Web (als Verbindung von Dokumenten im Internet) oder von Google (als Suchmaschine im Web der Dokumente) gewesen ist. Mit Sicherheit lässt sich sagen, dass Otlet sich bereits mit den Erfordernissen eines technisch gestützten Wissensmanagements auf der Grundlage vernetzter Ressourcen beschäftigt hat, also mit Fragen, die nach dem Zeitalter der Gutenberg-Technologie einfach auftauchen mussten und auf die heute das erweiterte

The traditional mode in which knowledge manifests itself in book form was challenged not only by the tele-technologies developed in the 19th century on the basis of electricity, but also by the methods of technical mass production with which industrialization massively impacted and reconfigured cultural products. The process developed by Friedrich G. Keller in 1843 to produce paper from wood pulp reduced the cost of paper by more than half. This meant that more could be printed and distributed at a lower price, and newspapers were transformed from reading matter for the intelligentsia into the first mass medium. The construction of a worldwide telegraph network made possible the growth of press agencies and a market for news. Tickers reporting securities prices fed the growth of a global financial market. Industrial repro technology automated by fast, steam-driven printing presses and the rotary printing process, led to vastly higher print runs.

In addition to the hardware, this also had an effect on the "software" of the media world that was still organized along analog, mechanical lines. Noteworthy developments were Mergenthaler's 1886 linotype machine that used line-cast typesetting to greatly increase the speed at which the printing industry could turn out content, as well as distribution logistics facilitated by networked infrastructure for communication (telegraph lines) and transportation (railway lines). With media redefining space and time, the world became accessible to modern men and women in unprecedented new ways—a world perceived as increasingly spherical, as a supranational entity. The founding of the International Telegraph Union in 1865 and the Universal Postal Union in 1874 were key milestones on this route. This was the time of the emergence of a synchronized world as a realm of the imagination of the impresarios of countless global projects,[6] as a cabled sphere of communication through the nascent infrastructure of globalized media culture, as the international inner sanctum of capital, a huge amenity of the globalized world of commerce and finance celebrated at world's fairs held at regular intervals.[7]

A short while later in the 1930s, author and socialist H. G. Wells postulated the emergence of a *World Brain*, the cells of which were such facilities as

Web mit seinen Suchmaschinen und sozialen Netzwerken eine Antwort ist.

Die traditionelle Weise, mit der sich Wissen in Buchform manifestiert, wird nicht nur durch die im 19. Jahrhundert auf Basis der Elektrizität entwickelten Teletechnologien herausgefordert, sondern ebenso durch die technische Massenproduktion, mit der die Industrialisierung auf die Kulturprodukte übergreift und sie überformt. Mit dem von Friedrich G. Keller 1843 entwickelten Verfahren zur Herstellung von Holzschliffpapier reduzierten sich die Papierpreise um mehr als die Hälfte, es konnte also zu geringeren Kosten mehr gedruckt und mehr vertrieben werden, die Zeitung wandelt sich vom „Intelligenzblatt" zum ersten Massenmedium. Bedingt durch die weltweiten Telegrafennetze entstanden die Presseagenturen und der Nachrichtenmarkt, mit dem Kursticker wuchs der globale Finanzmarkt heran. Die industrielle Reproduktionstechnik, deren Rationalisierung mittels dampfgetriebener Schnellpressen und dem Rotationsdruckverfahren ließ die Auflagen von Druckerzeugnissen in die Höhe schnellen.

Und neben der „Hardware" betrifft es weiter die „Software" der freilich noch analog und mechanisch organisierten Medienwelt. Zu nennen sind Mergenthalers Setzmaschine (Linotype, 1886), die mit dem Letternlinienguss die Verarbeitungsgeschwindigkeit der Inhalte im Druckwesen erhöhte, sowie die Vertriebslogistik durch eine vernetzte Infrastruktur der Kommunikation (Telegrafennetze) und des Transports (Eisenbahn). *Welt* erschloss sich für den modernen Menschen nun, da Medien Raum und Zeit neu definierten, ganz anders als je zuvor. Sie wird zunehmend sphärisch wahrgenommen, als ein supranationales Gebilde. Darauf lässt nicht zuletzt die 1865 erfolgte Gründung des Welttelegrafenvereins sowie 1874 des Weltpostvereins *(Union postale universelle)* schließen. Jetzt entstand die Synchronwelt als Imaginationsraum der zahlreichen Weltprojektemacher[6], als verkabelter Kommunikationsraum einer sich infrastrukturell formierenden globalen Medienkultur, als jener Weltinnenraum des Kapitals, ein von nun an mit regelmäßig stattfindenden internationalen Weltausstellungen zelebriertes Komfortgebilde der globalisierten Handels- und Finanzwelt.[7]

Einige Zeit später, in den 1930er-Jahren, sah der Schriftsteller und Sozialist H. G. Wells ein *World Brain* im Entstehen, wobei Bibliotheken, Archive, Universilibraries, archives and universities that in time would be ever-more-efficiently interlinked. Wells as well enlisted the metaphor of the world encyclopedia when it came to describing the overall organization:

"The phrase 'Permanent World Encyclopaedia' conveys the gist of these ideas. As the core of such an institution would be a world synthesis of bibliography and documentation with the indexed archives of the world. A great number of workers would be engaged perpetually in perfecting this index of human knowledge and keeping it up to date. Concurrently, the resources of micro-photography, as yet only in their infancy, will be creating a concentrated visual record."[8]

Both the formal organization as well as the technical structure of this world encyclopedia would take their leave of the Gutenberg Galaxy, the world of printed books. A new ontological form of knowledge, the concentrated visual record, was said to be called for. Otlet's conception of an integrative medium beyond the book also evoked the possibilities of new data storage media such as microfilm as well as new data transmission media like telegraphy, telephony, radio and television:

"Film, phonograph, radio, TV: regarded as substitutes for the book, these instruments have indeed become the new book, the technologies with the highest degree of effectiveness in propagating human thought. Thanks to radio, one will be able to not only hear everywhere, but speak from everywhere too. Television will not only enable you to see what's going on all around; no matter where you happen to be, you'll be able to make anything you want visible by others. Addresses, music, theater, exhibitions, demonstrations—they'll let anyone hear, see and participate from the comfort of an easy chair, and at the same time applaud, cheer, sing along, and display approbation together with all the others. [...] After all, empowered by these instruments of ubiquity, universality and eternity, human beings can approach the divine state, [...] which means all-encompassing consideration of reality as a whole. All of this, no less and perhaps more, is what the universal book [Livre] shall have wrought!"[9]

täten etc. dessen einzelne Zellen bilden, die zunehmend besser vernetzt werden würden. Auch Wells bemühte die Metapher der Welt-Enzyklopädie, wenn es um die Organisation des Ganzen ging:

„The phrase ‚Permanent World Encyclopaedia' conveys the gist of these ideas. As the core of such an institution would be a world synthesis of bibliography and documentation with the indexed archives of the world. A great number of workers would be engaged perpetually in perfecting this index of human knowledge and keeping it up to date. Concurrently, the resources of micro-photography, as yet only in their infancy, will be creating a concentrated visual record."[8]

Die Welt-Enzyklopädie würde in ihrer formalen Organisation ebenso wie in ihrer technischen Struktur die Gutenberg-Galaxis, die Welt der gedruckten Bücher, hinter sich lassen: Eine neue ontologische Form des Wissens *(concentrated visual record)* ist angedacht. Auch Otlets Vorstellung von einem integrativen Medium jenseits des Buches bemühte die Möglichkeiten neuer Datenträger wie Mikrofilm sowie neuer Übertragungsmedien wie Telegrafie, Telefonie, Radio und Fernsehen:

„Kino, Phono, Radio, Tele: als Substitute für das Buch genommen, sind diese Instrumente in der Tat das neue Buch geworden, die Werke mit dem höchsten Wirkungsgrad zur Verbreitung menschlichen Denkens. Durch das Radio wird man nicht nur überall hören können, sondern man wird von überall her sprechen können. Durch Television wird man nicht allein sehen können, was sich überall tut, sondern jedermann wird von dem Ort aus, wo er ist, sehbar machen können, was er will. Ansprachen, Musik, Theater, Schaustellung, Kundgebung, jeder wird sie auf diese Weise von seinem Lehnstuhl aus hören, sehen, an ihnen teilhaben können, und zugleich applaudieren, bejubeln, mitsingen, seine Zustimmung abgeben, zusammen mit all den anderen. [...] Durch diese Instrumente der Allgegenwart, der Universalität und der Ewigkeit wird der Mensch sich doch dem göttlichen Zustand nähern, [...] das heißt einer allumfassenden Betrachtung der Gesamtwirklichkeit. Dies alles, nichts weniger, mehr vielleicht, findet sich in der Leistung des universellen Buches [Livre]!"[9]

It is essential to point out that what Paul Otlet saw as being in the process of emerging was a new multimedial tool that goes beyond the book's traditional form. As befitting this meta-medium, he suggested interlinking all elements of this body of knowledge and making them available via telecommunications channels. Not only would telephone, radio and TV expand the possibilities of providing access to documents and disseminating them; they could also serve the purpose of disassembling this body of knowledge into its component parts and enriching these with additional information in order to interlink documents and other content via such additional information. New links would be engendered on the semantic level. And Otlet was undoubtedly aware of the fact that the interlinkages of meanings would mean a qualitative quantum leap not only in the organization of knowledge but also in knowledge formation itself. If media organize people's cognitive capacities, then this media-based reorganization of a culture's accumulated knowledge would bring about a *cerveau mécanique,* a sort of artificial intelligence, but above all a qualitatively new dimension of global knowledge. This is what H. G. Wells called the *World Brain,* which Teilhard de Chardin's Noosphere then took to the next spiritual level.[10]

In the "Inventions à faire" section of his *Traité de documentation,* Otlet formulated a sort of specifications manual for engineers, whereby the automation of information processing is presented as something extraordinarily desirable. Taking the place of the writing surface and paper as storage medium would be a universally accessible data space, and work at a desk would be replaced by an innovative device: "La machinerie qui réaliserait ces [...] desiderata serait un véritable cerveau mécanique et collectif."[11] In several detailed points, he proclaimed the reformation of intellectual work as the outcome of telematic cultural technology, mechanical artifices—this is what it's all been about ever since Leibniz—as well as, of course, their automation. Thus, computing devices are not meant to express thoughts; rather, they're for elucidating and systematizing thinking beyond metaphysical speculation.

Wesentlich festzuhalten bleibt, dass Paul Otlet ein neues, multimediales „Buch" jenseits seiner traditionellen Form im Entstehen begriffen sah, und zwar als Meta-Medium: Er schlug denn auch vor, den Wissensbestand mittels Telekommunikation zugänglich zu machen und zu vernetzen. Nicht nur würden Telefon, Radio und Fernsehen erweiterte Möglichkeiten bieten, auf Dokumente zuzugreifen und sie zu verbreiten, auch könnte die Zerlegung des Wissensbestandes in seine Elemente dazu dienen, eben diese mit Informationen anzureichern, um Dokumente bzw. Inhalte über solche Zusatzinformation zu verbinden. Neue Verknüpfungen auf semantischer Ebene würden entstehen. Dass mit der Verknüpfung von Bedeutungen ein qualitativer Sprung nicht nur in der Wissensorganisation, sondern auch in der Wissensformation selbst erreicht wäre, dessen war Otlet sich wohl bewusst. Wenn Medien das kognitive Vermögen von Menschen organisieren, dann entstünde mit dieser medientechnischen Reorganisation des kulturellen Wissensbestandes ein *cerveau mécanique,* eine Art künstlicher Intelligenz, vor allem aber eine qualitativ neue Dimension von globalem Wissen – von H. G. Wells als *World Brain* gefasst und von Teilhard de Chardin dann als Noosphäre spiritualistisch überhöht.[10]

Im Abschnitt „Inventions à faire" seines *Traité de documentation* formulierte Otlet eine Art Pflichtenheft für Ingenieure, wobei die Automatisierung der Informationsarbeit als Desideratum vorgestellt wird: An die Stelle der Schreibfläche und des Datenträgers Papier träte dann ein universell zugänglicher Datenraum, die Arbeit am Schreibtisch würde durch eine neuartige Apparatur ersetzt: „La machinerie qui réaliserait ces [...] desiderata serait un véritable cerveau mécanique et collectif."[11] In mehreren detaillierten Punkten wird die Reformation der intellektuellen Arbeit angekündigt, als Vorstellung einer telematischen Kulturtechnik. Mechanische Kunstgriffe – darum geht es seit Leibniz, und freilich auch darum, diese zu automatisieren: Rechenapparate nicht zum Ausdruck von Gedanken, sondern zur Klärung und Systematisierung eines Denkens jenseits metaphysischer Spekulation.

1 Frank Hartmann (Ed.): *Vom Buch zur Datenbank. Paul Otlets Utopie der Wissensvisualisierung*, Berlin 2012

2 "Réseau de communication, de coopération et d'echanges à l'intervention d'un Centre Mondial," Paul Otlet: *Traité de Documentation. Le livre sur le livre. Théorie et pratique*, Brüssel 1934, p.420.

3 W. Boyd Rayward: The Universe of Information. The Work of Paul Otlet for Documentation and International Organisation, Moscow 1975 (FID 520). Boyd Rayward (Ed.): *International Organisation and Dissemination of Knowledge. Selected Essays of Paul Otlet*, Amsterdam, New York 1990 (FID 684).

4 Frank Hartmann: *Globale Medienkultur. Technik, Geschichte, Theorien*, Vienna 2006.

5 Beat Wyss: *Die Pariser Weltausstellung 1889: Bilder von der Globalisierung*, Berlin 2010.

6 Markus Krajewski: *Restlosigkeit. Weltprojekte um 1900*, Frankfurt am Main 2006.

7 Peter Sloterdijk: *Im Weltinnenraum des Kapitals*, Frankfurt am Main 2005.

8 H.G. Wells: World Brain. The Idea of a Permanent World Encyclopedia, in: *Encyclopédie Française*, 1937.

9 "Ciné, phono, radio, télé: ces instruments tenus par les substituts du livre sont devenus en fait le livre nouveau, les oeuvres au degré le plus puissant pour la diffusion de la pensée humaine. Par radio, on ne pourra pas seulement entendre partout, mais on pourra parler de partout. Par télévision, on pourra non seulement voir ce qui se passe partout, mais chacun pourra faire voir ce qu'il voudra du point où il est. Ainsi, discours, musique, théâtre, musée, spectacle, manifestation, de son fauteuil chacun les entendra, les verra, y assistera et même pourra applaudir, ovationner, chanter en choer, clamer ses cris de participation, ensemble, avec tous les autres. [...] Par ces instruments d'ubiquité, d'universalité et d'éternité, l'homme se sera donc rapproche de l'état de divinité, de l'état présumé être celui des élus devant Dieu, c'est à dire la contemplation radieuse de la Réalité Totale. Tout cela, rien moins, plus peut-être, se trouve en puissance dans le Livre!" – Paul Otlet: *Traité de Documentation. Le livre sur le livre, théorie et pratique*, Brussels 1934, p. 431.

10 Wells, *World Brain*, loc. cit.; Pierre Teilhard de Chardin: *Der Mensch im Kosmos*, Munich 1959.

11 Otlet, *Traité*, loc. cit., p. 391.

1 Frank Hartmann (Hrsg.): *Vom Buch zur Datenbank. Paul Otlets Utopie der Wissensvisualisierung*, Berlin 2012

2 „Réseau de communication, de coopération et d'echanges à l'intervention d'un Centre Mondial", in Paul Otlet: *Traité de Documentation. Le livre sur le livre. Théorie et pratique*, Brüssel 1934, S.420.

3 W. Boyd Rayward: *The Universe of Information. The Work of Paul Otlet for Documentation and International Organisation*, Moskau 1975 (FID 520). Boyd Rayward (Hrsg.): *International Organisation and Dissemination of Knowledge. Selected Essays of Paul Otlet*, Amsterdam, New York 1990 (FID 684).

4 Frank Hartmann: *Globale Medienkultur. Technik, Geschichte, Theorien*, Wien 2006.

5 Beat Wyss: *Die Pariser Weltausstellung 1889: Bilder von der Globalisierung*, Berlin 2010.

6 Markus Krajewski: *Restlosigkeit. Weltprojekte um 1900*, Frankfurt am Main 2006.

7 Peter Sloterdijk: *Im Weltinnenraum des Kapitals*, Frankfurt am Main 2005.

8 H.G. Wells: World Brain. The Idea of a Permanent World Encyclopedia, in: *Encyclopédie Française*, 1937.

9 „Ciné, phono, radio, télé: ces instruments tenus par les substituts du livre sont devenus en fait le livre nouveau, les oeuvres au degré le plus puissant pour la diffusion de la pensée humaine. Par radio, on ne pourra pas seulement entendre partout, mais on pourra parler de partout. Par télévision, on pourra non seulement voir ce qui se passe partout, mais chacun pourra faire voir ce qu'il voudra du point où il est. Ainsi, discours, musique, théâtre, musée, spectacle, manifestation, de son fauteuil chacun les entendra, les verra, y assistera et même pourra applaudir, ovationner, chanter en choer, clamer ses cris de participation, ensemble, avec tous les autres. [...] Par ces instruments d'ubiquité, d'universalité et d'éternité, l'homme se sera donc rapproche de l'état de divinité, de l'état présumé être celui des élus devant Dieu, c'est à dire la contemplation radieuse de la Réalité Totale. Tout cela, rien moins, plus peut-être, se trouve en puissance dans le Livre!" – Paul Otlet: *Traité de Documentation. Le livre sur le livre, théorie et pratique*, Brüssel 1934, S. 431.

10 Wells, *World Brain*, a. a. O.; Pierre Teilhard de Chardin: *Der Mensch im Kosmos*, München 1959.

11 Otlet, *Traité*, a.a.O., S. 391.

Michael K. Buckland

Recorded is not remembered: The case of Emanuel Goldberg*

Gespeichert ist nicht (gleich) erinnert: Der Fall Emanuel Goldberg

The history of recall technology has been largely forgotten! Fortunately the lives and achievements of forgotten pioneers can provide an introduction. Prehistoric societies used speech, dance, and gesture to communicate, and drawings to record. Since then, four vectors of technology have developed, each extending the other: writing, printing, telecommunication and copying.

Writing provides an alternative to speech. It can record something that has happened or that should be done. Writing can "re-mediate" speech, which is local and ephemeral, into an enduring form and, being portable, it resists the effects of both distance and time. Printing provides an extreme multiplication of writing and so amplifies its effects. Telecommunication used to mean someone travelling on foot, by horse, or by ship to bring good news or bad. The semaphore, telegraph, telephone, radio, television and the Internet have speeded up communication across space, thereby reducing the effects of distance.

Substantial use of document copying technologies developed only in the twentieth century, with specialized cameras copying directly on to photographic paper (photostat), then microfilm and its variants, and later electrostatic copying (xerography).

A key result of these technologies is to reduce the effects of both time and space. Records have become increasingly accessible in any place and at any time, making it easier to read what would otherwise have been forgotten. Each technology amplifies the effects of the others, resulting also in an explosion of documents and creating the need for additional technology for finding the suitable records for our needs. Together these technologies

* Revised 9 July 2013 for Ars Electronica 2013

Die Geschichte der Abruftechnologie ist größtenteils in Vergessenheit geraten! Glücklicherweise können das Leben und die Leistungen vergessener Pioniere Licht in die Thematik bringen.

In prähistorischen Gesellschaften erfolgte Kommunikation über die gesprochene Sprache sowie nonverbal über Mimik, Tanz und Gestik, für die Aufzeichnung und Überlieferung wurden Zeichnungen verwendet. Seither haben sich vier technologische Vektoren entwickelt, die einander jeweils erweitern: Schrift, Druck, Telekommunikation und Kopierverfahren.

Die Schrift wird komplementär zur Rede verstanden. In Schriftform lässt sich festhalten, was geschehen ist oder zu tun wäre. Die Schrift vermag die Rede, die an einen Ort gebunden und flüchtig ist, in eine dauerhafte Form zu übertragen; dank ihrer Mobilität entfallen räumliche und zeitliche Beschränkung. Der Druck ermöglicht eine schier endlose Vervielfältigung der Schrift und potenziert deren Möglichkeiten und Wirkungen. Die Fernkommunikation wurde ursprünglich durch Boten gewährleistet, die zu Fuß, per Pferd oder mit dem Schiff gute oder schlechte Nachrichten überbrachten. Semaphor, Telegraf, Telefon, Radio, Fernsehen und Internet haben die Kommunikation über Entfernungen hinweg beschleunigt und räumliche Distanzen aufgehoben.

Der Einsatz von Kopiertechnologien für Dokumente hat sich erst im 20. Jahrhundert durch die Entwicklung spezieller Kameras, die direkt auf Fotopapier (Photostat) kopieren, durchgesetzt; es folgte der Mikrofilm mit seinen Varianten und später das elektrostatische Kopieren (Xerografie).

Die wesentliche Wirkung dieser Technologien ist, dass sie raumzeitliche Distanzen überwinden. Aufzeichnungen sind nahezu überall und jederzeit verfügbar, wodurch einfacher auf Wissen zugegriffen werden kann, das sonst leicht in Vergessenheit geriete. Jede constitute an artificial, external memory. We often speak of the growth of an "information society," but all communities, including prehistoric societies, depend or depended on information. The real change is in the increase of records. It would more fitting to speak of an emerging "document society." The historical development and social impacts of writing, of printing, and of telecommunications have been studied and discussed extensively. In contrast the history and consequences of copying and of finding systems, especially during the critical period from the late nineteenth to mid-twentieth century, have received much less attention.

Some pioneers

Martin Schrettinger, a Bavarian monk turned librarian, asserted the need for formal systems for finding and retrieving documents to replace the fallible memories of scholarly librarians who could forget things, move away, or simply die. Schrettinger coined the term *Bibliothek-Wissenschaft* ("library science") for his textbook of 1808. The techniques of modern librarianship were well developed by the end of the nineteenth century.

Libraries, however, deal with a limited range of published documents and pay limited attention to the details of their contents. So in 1895 two Belgians, Paul Otlet and Henri La Fontaine, decided to solve the recall problem. They started a complete and detailed index, the Universal Bibliographic Repertory, of everything, in every medium, everywhere, for everyone, anywhere: texts, images, maps, government records, statistical data, manuscripts, films, museum objects, everything. They used the best available technology of the time: standard cards, 125 mm x 75 mm, for random access storage and an elaborate artificial language, the Universal Decimal Classification, to describe each item in detail and to show how each is related by topic, date, and origin to each other item. The result was a kind of hypertextual network and a search service was offered. Card technology, however, becomes increasingly labor-intensive with scale. After decades of work and many millions of cards later this system could no longer be supported. What remains of the Repertory at the Mundaneum in Mons, Belgium, was recently added to UNESCO's Memory of the World Register.

dieser Technologien erweitert die Möglichkeiten und Wirkungen der anderen. Dies führte zu einer wahren Dokumentenflut, die nach einer weiteren Technologie zur Wiederauffindung der benötigten Aufzeichnungen verlangte. Gemeinsam stellen diese Technologien ein externes künstliches Gedächtnis dar. Immer wieder ist vom Zeitalter der „Informationsgesellschaft" die Rede, wobei aber zu bedenken ist, dass alle Gemeinschaften, einschließlich prähistorische, von Information abhängig waren und sind. Die wirkliche Veränderung besteht in der Zunahme von Aufzeichnungen, weshalb man besser von einer sich formierenden „Dokumentgesellschaft" sprechen sollte.

Die historische Entwicklung und die gesellschaftlichen Auswirkungen der Schrift, des Drucks und der Telekommunikation wurden umfassend analysiert und erörtert. Der Geschichte von Kopier- und Suchsystemen und ihrer Konsequenzen hingegen wurde, insbesondere im Zeitraum ihrer maßgeblichen Entwicklung vom späten 19. bis zur Mitte des 20. Jahrhunderts, bedeutend weniger Aufmerksamkeit zuteil.

Einige Pioniere

Martin Schrettinger, ein bayrischer Mönch und Bibliothekar, betonte die Notwendigkeit von Systemen zur Bestandserschließung, um nicht auf das fehlbare Gedächtnis der Bibliothekare angewiesen zu sein, da Wissen definitiv verloren ging, wenn diese etwas vergaßen, die Bibliothek verließen oder starben. In einem Text aus dem Jahr 1808 prägte Schrettinger den Begriff „Bibliothekswissenschaft". Die Techniken der modernen Bibliothekswissenschaft waren Ende des 19. Jahrhunderts bereits hoch entwickelt. Bibliotheken haben allerdings nur mit einer begrenzten Anzahl an Publikationen zu tun und auch das Interesse an deren inhaltlichen Details war begrenzt. 1895 beschlossen zwei Belgier, Paul Otlet und Henri La Fontaine, das Problem der Dokumentation zu lösen. Sie begannen einen vollständigen, detaillierten Index zu entwickeln, das *Répertoire Bibliographique Universel*, in dem alles Wissen – von jedem Medium, jedem Ort und für jeden Nutzer – aufgenommen werden sollte: Texte, Bilder, Landkarten, amtliche Unterlagen, statistische Daten, Manuskripte, Filme, museale Objekte, einfach alles. Sie verwendeten dafür die beste Technik ihrer Zeit: Karteikarten, 125 mm x 75 mm, einen Informationsspeicher mit direktem Zugriff, und ein elaboriertes alphanumerisches System, die universelle Dezimal-

The chemist Wilhelm Ostwald was inspired by Otlet to use most of his Nobel prize money to establish an institute in Munich named The Bridge *(Die Brücke)* to develop technology for intellectual work *(Technik der geistigen Arbeit)*. Ostwald wanted to extract facts and concepts from books and periodicals in order to create efficient recall of knowledge. New concepts and facts would be added and each element updated as needed. By 1912 he and his colleagues were writing lyrically about this "World Brain" *(Das Gehirn der Welt)*. H. G. Wells promoted the same "World Brain" idea. Imagine a rigorously edited Wikipedia on cards or microfiche. "World Memory" would have been more accurate, but Ostwald wanted more. Associating concepts combinatorially could form new knowledge, he hoped, just

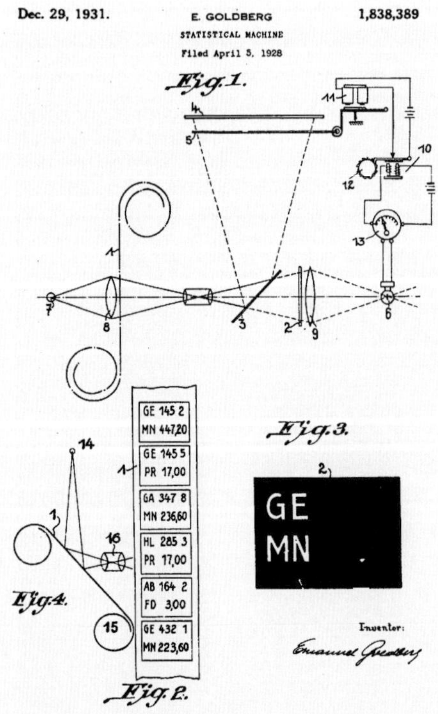

Image of the diagram from Goldberg's 1931 US patent for his "Statistical Machine"
Diagramm von Goldbergs US Patent aus dem Jahr 1931 für seine „Statistical Machine"

klassierung, um jedes Element im Detail zu beschreiben und aufzuzeigen, wie es thematisch, chronologisch und ursächlich mit allen anderen zusammenhängt. Das Ergebnis war eine Art Hypertext-System, auch ein Suchservice wurde angeboten. Die Karteikartentechnik wurde jedoch mit ihrem Anwachsen immer arbeitsintensiver. Nach jahrzehntelanger Arbeit und Millionen von Kärtchen später war dieses System nicht länger aufrechtzuerhalten. Was vom Repertorium und vom Mundaneum im belgischen Mons erhalten blieb, wurde kürzlich in das UNESCO-Register „Memory of the World" aufgenommen.

Der Chemiker Wilhelm Ostwald wurde von Otlet inspiriert, den Großteil seines Nobelpreisgelds für die Gründung eines Instituts namens „Die Brücke" zu verwenden, in dem eine „Technik der geistigen Arbeit" entwickelt werden sollte. Ostwald wollte Fakten und Ideen aus Büchern und Zeitschriften exzerpieren, um Wissen effizient abrufen zu können. Es sollten laufend neue Ideen und Fakten hinzukommen und jedes Element nach Bedarf aktualisiert werden. 1912 verfassten er und seine Kollegen eine poetische Schrift über dieses „Gehirn der Welt". Auch H. G. Wells träumte von einem Weltgehirn. Man kann sich darunter eine streng redigierte Wikipedia auf Karteikarten oder Mikrofiche vorstellen. „Gedächtnis der Welt" wäre wohl eine genauere Bezeichnung gewesen, aber Ostwald wollte mehr. Die kombinatorische Verknüpfung von Ideen würde, so hoffte er, neues Wissen hervorbringen, ähnlich wie die einzelnen Buchstaben von Gutenbergs beweglichen Lettern zu neuen Worten angeordnet werden konnten.

Ostwald und Otlet hatten einen modernen Ansatz, der auf Systemen, Logik, Normen, Maschinen, Effizienz und Fortschritt basierte. Bedauerlicherweise war die vorhandene Technologie damals noch nicht ausreichend entwickelt. Auch war ihre Utopie etwas naiv und basierte auf einem begrenzten Verständnis von Wissen. Selbst wissenschaftliche Fakten können ohne Kontext nicht richtig verstanden werden, wie Ludwig Fleck in seinem Werk *Entstehung und Entwicklung einer wissenschaftlichen Tatsache* 1935 ausführte. Es gab immer schon drei wesentliche Voraussetzungen für das Verständnis: den Leser, die Aufzeichnung und den kulturellen Kontext des Lesers. Dies sollte sich jeder vor Augen führen, der meint, dass die totale Erinnerung durch ein technisches System gewährleistet werden könnte.

as individual letters in Gutenberg's moveable type could be rearranged to form new words.
Ostwald and Otlet represented a modernist view based on systems, logic, standards, machinery, efficiency, and progress. Sadly, existing technology was inadequate. It was also a naïve, utopian view based on a limited understanding of knowledge. Even scientific facts cannot be properly understood out of context, as Ludwig Fleck explained in his *Entstehung und Entwicklung einer wissenschaftlichen Tatsache (The Genesis and Development of a Scientific Fact)* in 1935. There were always three elements: the reader, the record, and the cultural context of the reader. This has enormous consequences for anyone imagining that a technological system of total recall could be sufficient.
These writings by Schrettinger, Otlet, Ostwald, and Fleck were forgotten for many years until rediscovered by specialists.

The Case of Emanuel Goldberg

Born in 1881, Emanuel Goldberg grew up in Moscow. His father was a colonel in the Tsar's army medical corps. Extreme restrictions on the admission of Jews prevented Goldberg from studying engineering in Moscow, so he studied chemistry instead. In 1906 he received his Ph.D. from Wilhelm Ostwald's Institute in Leipzig. In Germany Goldberg was very successful as an academic, an inventor, and an industrialist. He contributed to many different

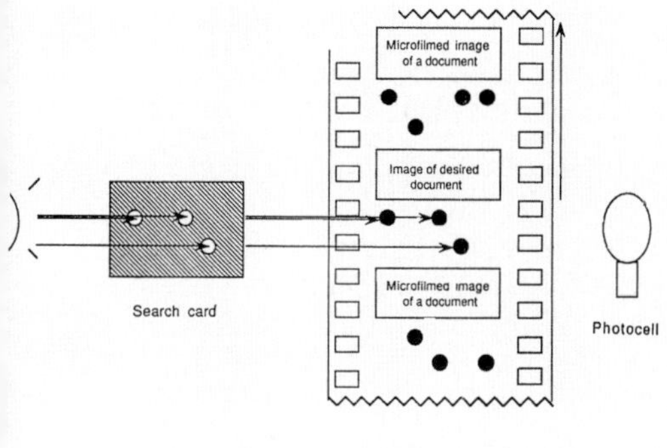

Simplified schema of the design by Michael Buckland

Die Schriften von Schrettinger, Otlet, Oswald und Fleck waren über viele Jahre vergessen, bis sie von Experten wiederentdeckt wurden.

Der Fall Emanuel Goldberg

Emanuel Goldberg wurde 1881 geboren und wuchs in Moskau auf. Sein Vater war Offizier im medizinischen Dienst des Zaren. Rigide Zugangsbeschränkungen für die Aufnahme von Juden verhinderten, dass Goldberg Ingenieurswissenschaft in Moskau studieren konnte, weshalb er sich der Chemie zuwandte. 1906 promovierte er am von Wilhelm Ostwald geleiteten Institut in Leipzig. In Deutschland war Goldberg als Wissenschaftler, Erfinder und Unternehmer sehr erfolgreich. Er leistete zahlreiche Beiträge in unterschiedlichen Bereichen der Bildtechnologie: fotografische Sensitometrie, Reprotechnik, Druck, Mikrofilm mit extremem Verkleinerungsmaßstab (Mikropunkte), Kameradesign (Contax), Filmkameras (Kinamo) und frühe Fernsehtechnologie. In den späten 1920ern kündigte er die erste elektronische Suchmaschine an. Die „Statistische Maschine", wie er sie nannte, durchsuchte mithilfe von Mustererkennung Metadaten auf Mikrofilmrollen. Er gab die Suchanfragen per Telefon auf seinem Schreibtisch ein, die abgerufenen Dokumente erschienen auf einem Bildschirm.
Goldberg war 1926 Gründungsdirektor von Zeiss Ikon in Dresden. 1933 wurde er von SA-Schergen entführt, konnte jedoch nach Frankreich fliehen. 1937 emigrierte er nach Palästina. Er half mit, die Hightechindustrie in Israel aufzubauen, 1970 starb er in Tel Aviv.
Bei einem internationalen Fotografiekongress 1925 in Paris verteilte Goldberg Erinnerungsbilder: das „Mikrat nach Goldberg". In einer kleinen Schachtel befand sich ein Mikroskop-Objektträger mit einem Porträt von Nicéphore Niépce, das so stark verkleinert war, dass der Abstand zwischen den Linien nur einen Tausendstelmillimeter betrug. Bei einer solchen Verkleinerung fände eine gewöhnliche Seite auf einem Hundertstel eines Quadratmillimeters Platz, 100 Seiten könnten auf einem Quadratmillimeter und 64.500 Seiten auf etwa 6 Quadratzentimeter untergebracht werden. Diese extreme Verkleinerung wurde durch die Verwendung eines umgedrehten Mikroskops als Kamera erzielt. Goldberg beschrieb dieses Verfahren in führenden englischen, französischen und deutschen Publikationen. In den letzten fünfzig Jahren wurde die Erfindung der Mikropunkt-Technik mit wenigen Aus-

aspects of imaging technology: photographic sensitometry, reprographics, printing, extreme reduction microphotography (microdots), camera design (the Contax), movie cameras (the Kinamo), and early television. In the late 1920s he announced the first electronic search engine. Named the "Statistical Machine" it used pattern recognition to match queries against metadata encoded next to images of documents on rolls of microfilm. He would dial queries on a telephone on his desk and retrieved documents would appear in a screen.

Goldberg became the founding director of Zeiss Ikon, in Dresden, in 1926, but in 1933 he was kidnapped by Nazis and fled to France. In 1937, he went to Palestine and helped build the high tech industry in Israel where he died in 1970.

At an International Congress of Photography in Paris in 1925, Goldberg distributed a souvenir: a "Goldberg microdot" *(Mikrat nach Goldberg)*. A small box contained a microscope slide bearing a portrait of Nicéphore Niépce so reduced that the interval between lines was about one-thousandth of a millimeter. At this reduction an ordinary page would occupy 0.01 of a square millimeter, hence 100 pages per square millimeter or 64,500 pages per square inch. This extreme reduction was achieved by using a microscope in reverse as a camera. He described this process in prominent English, French and German publications. But for the past fifty years, the invention of this microdot technology has, with rare exceptions, been attributed instead to a mythical Professor Zapp. What happened?

During the same fifty years a distinguished American engineer, Vannevar Bush was famous as a pioneer of recall because in a famous essay, "As We May Think", he imagined a personal desktop retrieval system, the Memex. Published in 1945 and cited ever since, Bush's Memex fantasy was based on his *Rapid Selector* machine, a microfilm reader with a search mechanism that scanned index terms encoded as opaque marks on the film next to each document image. It was pattern recognition using a light, an encoded search card, and a photoelectric cell. But Bush's patent application was denied by the US Patent Office, citing a prior patent issued to Goldberg in 1931. Descriptions of Goldberg's

nahmen jedoch einem mysteriösen Professor Zapp zugeschrieben. Was war geschehen?

In ebendiesen fünfzig Jahren hatte ein angesehener amerikanischer Ingenieur namens Vannevar Bush als Wegbereiter der Informationsverarbeitung Berühmtheit erlangt, weil er in einem viel beachteten Aufsatz mit dem Titel „As We May Think" ein Wissensfindungs- und -verwertungssystem in Form eines Schreibtischs, den sogenannten Memex, beschrieben hatte. Bushs 1945 veröffentlichte und seither immer wieder zitierte Memex-Fantasie basierte auf einer Maschine namens „Rapid Selector", einem Mikrofilmlesegerät mit Suchmechanismus, das Schlagworte scannte, die als lichtundurchlässige Zeichen auf dem Film neben jedem Bilddokument kodiert waren. Das System basierte auf einer Mustererkennung mithilfe von Licht, einer kodierten Suchkarte und einer Fotozelle. Bushs Patentansuchen wurde jedoch vom amerikanischen Patentamt mit dem Verweis auf ein früheres Patent, das Goldberg 1931 erhalten hatte, abgelehnt. Goldberg erhielt zahlreiche Patente, seine Maschine wurde auf Tagungen in Berlin, Dresden, London und Paris vorgeführt und in englisch- und deutschsprachigen Publikationen beschrieben. Seine Schriften scheinen jedoch nach 1938 außerhalb Israels nicht zitiert worden zu sein, und die wenigen Erwähnungen seiner Suchmaschine scheinen wenig oder kein Interesse geweckt zu haben.

In den frühren 1930ern war Goldberg eine bekannte Persönlichkeit. 1990 jedoch waren er und seine Arbeit fast spurlos von der Bildfläche verschwunden und seine beiden wichtigsten Erfindungen wurden anderen zugeschrieben.

Politische und persönliche Agenden

Als 1933 die Nazis an die Macht kamen, bedeutete dies für Juden, insbesondere für jene aus Osteuropa, das Ende ihrer beruflichen Karriere. Ab März 1933 wurden illegale Verhaftungen durch Mitglieder der NSDAP nicht mehr dokumentiert. Aus Angst vor Repressionen wurde über die Opfer nicht gesprochen. Leistungen von Juden wurden im Dritten Reich nicht anerkannt; in der kommunistischen DDR wurden später jene „jüdischer Kapitalisten" in Abrede gestellt. Nicht zuletzt war die Geschichte Goldbergs auch von drei mächtigen und ehrgeizigen Männern beeinflusst.

machine had been widely patented, demonstrated at meetings in Berlin, Dresden, London, and Paris, and described in English and German publications. Yet Goldberg's papers seem not to have been cited, outside of Israel, after 1938, and the very few mentions of his retrieval machine seem to have aroused little or no interest.

In the early 1930s, Goldberg was a well-known figure. But by 1990, he and his work had disappeared with little trace and these two major innovations were attributed to others.

Political and personal agendas

When the Nazis came to power in 1933, the careers of Jews, especially Jews from Eastern Europe, ended. From March 1933, illegal arrests by Nazi party members went unreported. Discussion of the victims was discouraged. The achievements of Jews were not recognized. Nor, during the Communist period, were those of a Jewish capitalist. The Goldberg story was also impacted by the actions of three powerful and ambitious men.

J. Edgar Hoover

In 1946 a *Readers Digest* article, "The Enemy's masterpiece of espionage," by J. Edgar Hoover, Director of the U.S. Federal Bureau of Investigation, boasted that the FBI discovered microdots sent by German spies. Hoover stated, correctly, that microdot technology was developed by a professor at the Technical University in Dresden, but he substituted the name Zapp for Goldberg and described the process incorrectly. Any expert would have recognized both errors. There never was a Professor Zapp in Dresden, but the mythical Professor Zapp lives on as the inventor of the microdot in the literature of espionage.

Heinz Küppenbender

Zeiss Ikon was founded in Dresden in 1926, under Goldberg's leadership, through the merger of four existing firms. A leader in precision engineering, Zeiss Ikon was the world's largest camera company and it needed a new 35 mm camera to compete with the Leica. Goldberg's response was the famous Contax. Heinz Küppenbender, a young engineer,

J. Edgar Hoover

Im Jahr 1946 behauptete J. Edgar Hoover, der Begründer des FBI, in einem Artikel in *Readers Digest* mit dem Titel „The Enemy's masterpiece of espionage", dass das FBI Mikropunkte entdeckt hätte, mit deren Hilfe deutsche Spione korrespondiert hätten. Hoover erwähnte korrekterweise, dass die Mikropunkt-Technologie von einem Professor der Technischen Universität in Dresden entwickelt worden war, ersetzte aber den Namen Goldbergs durch jenen Zapps und beschrieb das Verfahren falsch. Ein Experte hätte beide Fehler sofort erkannt. Es gab nie einen Professor Zapp in Dresden, in der Spionageliteratur aber lebt der geheimnisvolle Professor als Erfinder des Mikropunkts weiter.

Heinz Küppenbender

Zeiss Ikon wurde 1926 in Dresden unter Goldbergs Leitung durch die Fusion von vier Firmen gegründet. Zeiss Ikon war führend im Bereich Präzisionstechnologie und der größte Kamerahersteller der Welt. Um mit Leica konkurrieren zu können, brauchte das Unternehmen eine neue 35-mm-Kamera. Goldbergs Antwort war die berühmte Contax. Heinz Küppenbender, ein junger Ingenieur, arbeitete unter Goldbergs Leitung an den technischen Details. Nach Goldbergs Verschwinden war Küppenbender während des Dritten Reichs sehr erfolgreich. Er wurde Leiter des Zeiss-Kartells, war für die nationale Zuteilung von Rohmaterialien für die optische Industrie verantwortlich und trat für den Einsatz von Fremd- und Zwangsarbeitern ein. Nach der kurzen Zeit der Entnazifizierung in der Nachkriegszeit wurde Küppenbender Leiter der westdeutschen Zeiss Ikon. Er betonte seine eigenen Leistungen und strich jene Goldbergs aus den Annalen. Küppenbenders Darstellung hat sich durch die Veröffentlichungen des Unternehmens verfestigt und wurde in Texten über Zeiss Ikon unkritisch wiederholt. Selbst im Jahr 2000 wurde Goldbergs Rolle in der Unternehmensgeschichte von Zeiss noch nicht anerkannt.

Vannevar Bush

Vannevar Bush publizierte 1945 in der Zeitschrift *Atlantic Monthly* den Aufsatz „As we may think". Dieser wurde im Magazin *Life* mit dem Untertitel „Ein amerikanischer Top-Wissenschaftler antizipiert worked on the technical details under Goldberg's direction. After Goldberg departed, Küppenbender flourished during the Third Reich. He became head of the Zeiss cartel, was responsible for the national allocation of raw materials for the optical industry, and advocated the use of imported forced labor. After a brief postwar process of denazification, Küppenbender headed the West German Zeiss Ikon. He emphasized his own achievements and minimized Goldberg's. Küppenbender's narrative was amplified in corporate publicity and was repeated uncritically in writings about Zeiss Ikon. Corporate histories of Zeiss did not acknowledge Goldberg's role, even in 2000.

Vannevar Bush

Vannevar Bush published his essay "As we may think" in the *Atlantic Monthly* in 1945. It was reprinted in *Life* magazine with the subtitle: "A Top U.S. Scientist Foresees a Possible Future World In Which Man-Made Machine Will Start To Think." The ideas in it were not new, but it is well written and stimulates the imagination with the mythical Memex as a symbol of what might one day be achieved. It has been reprinted frequently and cited ever since. Bush led the U.S. scientific effort to win the Second World War and his personal prestige gave legitimacy to those who invoked his name. What reveals the popular invocation of the Memex to have been a cultural and political gesture rather than an ordinary technical acknowledgment, is the striking absence of accompanying references to any of the many people who had expressed the same or similar ideas before Bush. Bush did not acknowledged Goldberg's priority. Others did not have enough curiosity to look.

What is recalled is accidental

Several factors appear to have contributed to the erasure of Emanuel Goldberg. The history of technology tends to be nation-based, so the history of German technology is neglected elsewhere. The history of photography has concentrated on the nineteenth century. Nazis would not recognize Jewish achievements. The communist German

eine mögliche Zukunft, in der Maschinen zu denken beginnen" nachgedruckt. Die Ideen, die er darin vertrat, waren nicht neu, aber gut formuliert, und der geheimnisvolle Memex beflügelte als Symbol künftiger Möglichkeiten die Fantasie. Der Artikel wurde häufig nachgedruckt und zitiert. Bush koordinierte die wissenschaftlichen Forschungsprogramme der USA während des Zweiten Weltkriegs und sein Renommee verlieh jenen, die ihn zitierten, Legitimität. Dass die verbreitete Beschwörung des Memex eher eine kulturelle und politische Geste als ein Zeichen der Anerkennung war, zeigt sich im auffälligen Fehlen begleitender Hinweise auf eine der vielen Personen, die dieselbe oder ähnliche Ideen schon vor Bush hatten. Bush hat Goldbergs Vorreiterrolle nie anerkannt. Andere waren nicht neugierig genug, um intensiver nachzuforschen.

Was in Erinnerung bleibt, ist auch Zufall

Dass Emanuel Goldbergs Name aus den Annalen der Wissenschaftsgeschichte gelöscht wurde, ist vermutlich auf mehrere Faktoren zurückzuführen: Die Geschichte der Technologie scheint einzelstaatlich aufgearbeitet zu werden, weshalb die Geschichte der deutschen Technologie anderenorts vernachlässigt wird. Die Geschichte der Fotografie ist auf das neunzehnte Jahrhundert konzentriert. Die Nazis haben jüdische Errungenschaften nicht anerkannt und in der kommunistischen DDR wurden jene von jüdischen Kapitalisten in Abrede gestellt. Drei mächtige, ehrgeizige Männer (Bush, Hoover und Küppenbender) verbreiteten Geschichten, in denen Goldberg ausgeblendet wurde. In drei von vier Unternehmensgeschichten von Zeiss wird Goldbergs Arbeit nicht erwähnt. Die vierte, aus einer marxistischen Perspektive geschrieben, wurde nicht berücksichtigt. Goldbergs Schriften wurden fast vollständig von Bomben, Überschwemmungen und Feuer zerstört. Historiker ziehen es vor, über gut dokumentierte Themen zu forschen. Goldberg lebte in der zweiten Hälfte seines Lebens sehr zurückgezogen. Auch wer sich dazu entschließt, ein Thema historisch aufzuarbeiten, ist oft vom Zufall abhängig. Niemand scheint Interesse, die Motivation oder die Zeit gehabt zu haben, über Goldberg zu schreiben, bis auf einen Historiker, der eine Biografie

Democratic Republic would not honor the work of a Jewish capitalist. Three powerful, ambitious men (Bush, Hoover, and Küppenbender) promoted narratives which eclipsed Goldberg. Three out of four Zeiss corporate histories omit Goldberg's work. The fourth, with a Marxist perspective, has been discounted. Goldberg's papers were almost entirely destroyed by bombs, flood, and burning. Historians prefer to research well documented topics. Goldberg lived the latter part of his life in relative obscurity. Who decides to write a history of any topic is largely accidental. Nobody seems to have had the interest, the motivation or the time to write about Goldberg. One historian wanted to write a biography, but died before he could get round to it. In Information Science, interest in history has been limited, uncritical, and accepting of myth.

This combination of reasons helps explain why Goldberg remained so unknown. They are quite diverse and they are also accidental in several senses. It could easily have been otherwise. If the bombs in Dresden had fallen differently; if Bush, Hoover, or Küpperbender had given Goldberg his due; if the Zeiss corporate histories had been more complete; and so on. If any one of these factors had been otherwise, the received history would probably have been significantly different. What we know of the past is not simply a matter of recall.

The future of recall long-term

Projecting these technologies forward, we can envisage writing evolving into the *recording* of everything; printing becoming the *representation* of anything; and telecommunication achieving, in effect, *simultaneous interaction.* Copying depends on sensitivity to the characteristics of what is to be copied and so leads to the *analysis* of a resource, with a visual likeness being just one option. Changes in technology enable new genres. Advancing technologies lead to an environment in which different genres can be woven together into a new tapestry. The technology for finding records will involve the building of endless connections, but a greater emphasis on cultural context will be needed for effective recall.

beabsichtigt hatte, aber starb, bevor er sein Projekt verwirklichen konnte. In der Informationswissenschaft ist das Interesse an Geschichte begrenzt und unkritisch, Mythen werden gerne aufgegriffen.

In der Kombination erklären diese Faktoren, warum Goldberg so unbekannt ist. Sie sind recht unterschiedlich und in mehrerer Hinsicht vom Zufall bestimmt. Es hätte leicht anders kommen können. Wenn die Bomben in Dresden anders gefallen wären, wenn Bush, Hoover oder Küppenbender Goldberg die ihm zustehende Anerkennung zuteil werden hätten lassen, wenn die Firmengeschichte von Zeiss exakter gewesen wäre usw. Wäre nur einer dieser Faktoren nicht gegeben oder anders gewesen, wäre vermutlich auch die historische Überlieferung eine andere gewesen. Was wir über die Vergangenheit wissen, ist nicht nur eine Frage des Gedächtnisses und der Erinnerung.

Die langfristige Zukunft der Abruftechnologien

Projiziert man die gegenwärtigen Trends dieser Technologien in die Zukunft, ist vorstellbar, dass sich Schrift zur „Aufzeichnung" von allem entwickelt, Druck zur „Repräsentation" von allem und Telekommunikation tatsächlich zu einer „simultanen Interaktion" wird. Der Kopiervorgang hängt von der Empfindlichkeit gegenüber den Eigenschaften der Vorlage ab und führt so zur „Analyse" der Quelle, wobei optische Ähnlichkeit nur eine der möglichen Optionen ist. Technologische Veränderungen ermöglichen neue Entwicklungen. Der technische Fortschritt führt zu einem Umfeld, in dem verschiedene Entwicklungen zu einem neuen Ganzen verwoben werden können.

Die Zukunft der Abruftechnologien für das Auffinden von Dokumenten impliziert den Aufbau endloser Verbindungen, für die Trefferquote des externalisierten Gedächtnisses ist jedoch unablässig, dass dem kulturellen Kontext eine höhere Bedeutung zugemessen wird.

Aus dem Englischen von Martina Bauer

Michael Buckland. *Emanuel Goldberg and his Knowledge Machine: Information, Invention, and Political Forces,* by (Libraries Unlimited, 2006). German edition: *Vom Mikrofilm zur Wissensmaschine: Emanuel Goldberg zwischen Medientechnik und Politik.* Avinus Verlag, Berlin, 2010.

Claudia Schmölders

The Female Voice in Acoustic Archives
Female Voice in akustischen Archiven

When someone endeavors to write history on the basis of acoustic sources, his statements depend on the existence of such source material just like an old-school historian's conclusions depend on his sources. And just like the conventional colleague does, the acoustic historian has to consider the contingency of his claims, and differentiate between first-hand and second-hand sources. First-hand sources are actually audible experiences; second-hand sources are accounts of audible experiences and, thus, accounts of human voices as well. One of the most interesting interpretational nodes in this matrix has been, since the beginning of the 20th century, the female voice, and not only in German-speaking Europe. As women gradually got to have a say—that is, began to get the right to vote—following World War I, the word "voice" (Stimme, voce, voix, etc.) became metaphorical in almost all political-judicial as well as cultural contexts and was no longer operational in strictly a physical sense. One might tend to think that the fact that women were granted a "voice" in all purviews of intellectual life would have meant that their opinions were heard, that it was desirable that they would speak their mind, whether physically or in print or even solely in the field of their own ideas like those that a man could also have articulated. Language rules and regulations were instituted on such a massive scale by feminists themselves that it was possible, even as late as the early 1990s, for a book to be published with a foreword complaining about this very state of affairs. One found oneself in the grotesque situation in which everyone was talking about the "female voice" but nobody really heard what "female voices" were saying. Though, it must be noted, with one exception: the cinema beginning in 1928.[1]

Let's go a little deeper into this. Of course, the acoustic storage of voices—or sounds of any kind, for that matter—became a reality long before wom-

Wer sich anschickt, Geschichte / Historie aufgrund akustischer Quellen zu schreiben, hängt in seinen Aussagen von der Existenz solcher Quellen genauso ab wie ein Historiker alter Schule von den seinen. Wie dieser, so muss auch der Klanghistoriker die Kontingenz seiner Aussagen bedenken, und wie dieser muss er zwischen Quellen erster und zweiter Ordnung unterscheiden. Die erste Ordnung besteht in wirklich hörbaren Ereignissen, die zweite in *Berichten* über hörbare Ereignisse, also auch über Menschenstimmen. Einen der interessantesten Deutungsknoten in diesem Feld liefert seit Beginn des letzten Jahrhunderts die Frauenstimme, und dies nicht nur im deutschen Sprachraum. Indem man den Frauen nach dem Ersten Weltkrieg allmählich das Stimm-Recht verlieh, wurde das Wort „Stimme" *(voice, voce, voix* etc.) in fast allen politisch juristischen, aber auch kulturellen Kontexten metaphorisch und nicht mehr in seiner physischen Bedeutung virulent. Dass man den Frauen, in welchem geistigen Bezirk auch immer, eine „Stimme" zubilligte, sollte in aller Regel bedeuten, dass man ihre Meinung hören, dass man sie zu Wort kommen lassen wollte, ob physisch oder im Print oder überhaupt nur im Feld ihrer Ideen, die auch ein Mann hätte artikulieren können. So massiv wurde die Sprachregelung von den Feministinnen selber betrieben, dass noch Anfang der 1990er Jahre ein Buch erscheinen konnte, dessen Vorwort eben diesen Umstand beklagt. Man fand sich in der grotesken Lage, dass alle Welt von *female voice* sprach, aber *female voices (voix, voce* etc.) nicht wirklich vernahm. Freilich muss man hinzusetzen: mit Ausnahme der Welt des Films seit 1928.[1]

Gehen wir der Sache etwas nach. Die akustische Speicherung von Stimmen und Klängen überhaupt hat sich natürlich viel früher als das politische Stimmrecht der Frau durchgesetzt, und Frauen waren offenbar durchaus vertreten. Schon 1860 gab es angeblich eine erste Aufnahme mit einer Singstimme, die *Au clair de la lune* sang; man entdeckte das 10-Sekundenstück 2008 und hält es heute für eine Frauenstimme.[2]

en's suffrage, and women, obviously, were very much represented here. The very first recording of a human voice—singing "Au Clair de la Lune," by the way—is said to have been made in 1860. This 10-second fragment discovered in 2008 is presumed to be a female voice.[2] According to Friedrich Kittler, even Thomas Edison's first recording in 1877 was of him declaiming "Mary had a little lamb," a nursery rhyme about a little girl. In the first decades of the 20th century, most recordings of women's voices were of them singing or speaking dramatically on the stage or for a radio broadcast—thus, as vocalists, poets or actresses such as Sarah Bernhardt on 1910–vintage wax cylinders, of Ricarda Huch in 1908, or of soprano Nellie Melba singing three minutes of a famous aria in Donizetti's opera *Lucia di Lammermoor* recorded in 1904. At the turn of the 20th century, there quickly emerged a recording industry that, on one hand, made use of the available wax cylinders but also, of course, purveyed more and more original recordings.

On the other hand, what hardly (if at all) went down in acoustic history was the female prose voice, women who neither acted nor sang nor recited poetry but, rather, made political utterances. Be that as it may: the first recording of a suffragette was of a woman named Cristabel Pankhurst following her release from prison. This was made in 1908, 10 years before women started to get the right to vote in Europe and the USA.

This gap in the acoustic record got even wider the more powerfully acoustic communication came to dominate everyday life. With the advent of radio broadcasting in 1923, women were indeed increasingly engaged as announcers for women's programming or as readers of fairy tales on kiddie shows, but serious stuff—the political news of the day—remained tightly in the grasp of males. British men in particular used arguments that were nothing less than hysterical in rejecting women as newsreaders.

Auch Thomas Edison hat 1877, wie Friedrich Kittler berichtet, bei seiner ersten Aufnahme immerhin ein Mädchenkinderlied in den Trichter geschrieben – *Mary had a little lamb.* In den ersten Jahrzehnten des 20. Jahrhunderts wurden Frauenstimmen in aller Regel als singende oder auf der Bühne oder für das Radio theatralisch sprechende gespeichert, also als Sängerinnen oder Dichterinnen oder Schauspielerinnen, wie etwa Sarah Bernhardt auf Wachswalzen 1910, Ricarda Huch 1908 oder die Sopranistin Nellie Melba mit drei Minuten aus der Donizetto-Oper *Lucia di Lammermoor,* die berühmte Wahnsinnsarie, aufgenommen 1904. Seit der vorletzten Jahrhundertwende gab es ja eine aufschäumende Schallplattenindustrie, die sich einerseits der vorhandenen Wachswalzen bediente, aber natürlich auch mehr und mehr Originalaufnahmen lieferte.

Was hingegen nicht oder fast nicht in die akustische Erinnerung eindrang, war die Frau mit einer Prosastimme, die weder schauspielerte noch dichtete noch sang, sondern politische Inhalte sprach. Immerhin stammt die erste Aufnahme einer Suffragette namens Cristabel Pankhurst aus dem Jahr 1908, aufgenommen nach ihrer Entlassung aus dem Gefängnis – zehn Jahre, bevor sich das Wahlrecht in Europa und den USA durchsetzte.

Diese Lücke im Feld der akustischen Erinnerung vergrößerte sich, je mächtiger die akustische Kommunikation den Alltag beherrschte. Mit der Erfindung des Radios 1923 wurden zwar immer mehr Frauen als Ansagerinnen in Frauensendungen oder als Vorleserinnen für die Märchenstunde eingesetzt, aber das Heiligtum der politischen Nachrichten blieb fest in männlicher Hand. Besonders in Großbritannien wurden Frauen als Sprecherinnen von Nachrichten geradezu hektisch abgelehnt; und in Deutschland gab es, vor allem nach der Radioreform unter Propagandaminister Goebbels, eigentlich nur noch eine einzige herrschende männliche Stimme, die Adolf Hitlers.[3]

Mit Ausbruch des Krieges änderten sich die Einschät-

In Germany, especially after Propaganda Minister Goebbels' radio reform, there was actually only one prevailing male voice: that of Adolf Hitler.[3]
Assessments changed following the outbreak of war. Then, women had to substitute for male newsreaders, at least in England, whereas their male counterparts in Nazi Germany became key protagonists of propaganda dissemination. Nothing was more essential than a confident, energetic male voice that didn't get all weepy when reporting things like defeats on the battlefield. Research done by Hans-Ulrich Wagner documents how these men remained on the airwaves after 1945,[4] and accordingly, their mellifluous, sometimes celebratory, sometimes comforting wartime voices went on to narrate Germany's postwar reconstruction. But were these facts recorded and stored to the acoustic memory, or was it rather the case that precisely this material had become obsolete?
In any case, the commemoration of the tonal configuration of 20th-century Germany has since been established in the form of several solid sets of data. The German Broadcasting Archive's collection, "Voices of the 20th Century," for example, has existed since 1997. It currently consists of 35 CDs, most treating a particular theme such as "Prussia in Weimar," "The Sound of the '20s," "Capitulation and Reconstruction," and "Survival in Postwar Germany."
In this sector in the 1990s, gender-oriented thinking was probably not yet high on the agenda. Accordingly, physical voices of women were so minimally represented in this assortment that the editors thought it appropriate to bring out a collection devoted to precisely this theme. So, CD #9 contains 41 speeches by women on the subject of emancipation. The judicial idea of a woman possessing the right to vote was paired, as it were, with heeding women's physical voices, whereby the collection's few other female voices are generally those of singers and actresses not speaking their own minds but rather performing works written by others. Even the 28 cuts on the "Survival in Postwar Germany" CD include recordings of only two female voices, only one of which was that of a so-called rubble woman to whom, after all, West German society actually owed its survival.
But the editors of the sound archive weren't the

zungen. Nun mussten die Frauen Nachrichtensprecher ersetzen, jedenfalls in England, während die männlichen Kollegen in Nazideutschland zu Schlüsselfiguren der Propaganda wurden. Nichts war wichtiger als eine zuversichtliche, energische Männerstimme, die auch Nachrichten über Niederlagen nicht etwa weinerlich vortrug. Der Forschung von Hans-Ulrich Wagner kann man die Weiterbeschäftigung dieser Sprecher auch nach 1945 entnehmen;[4] und einleuchtend ist natürlich, dass die teils fanfarenartigen, teils tröstlich sonoren Stimmen der Kriegszeit den Aufbau einer Bundesrepublik begleiten mussten. Aber hat man das ins akustische Gedächtnis aufgenommen – oder war nicht gerade dieses Material obsolet geworden?
Die Memorierung der Klanggestalt des 20. Jahrhunderts in Deutschland hat jedenfalls inzwischen mehrere feste Datensätze erhalten. Die Sammlung des deutschen Rundfunkarchivs, „Stimmen des 20. Jahrhunderts" zum Beispiel, gibt es seit 1997, sie umfasst inzwischen 35 CDs, von denen die meisten thematisch orientiert sind und Titel tragen wie etwa: „Preußen in Weimar", „Der Klang der Zwanziger Jahre", „Kapitulation und Wiederaufbau" oder „Überleben im Nachkriegsdeutschland".
Genderorientiertes Denken war in den 1990er Jahren in dieser Branche wohl noch nicht wirklich aktuell. So hatte man physische „Frauenstimmen" in dieser Auswahl so minimal repräsentiert, dass sich die Redaktion entschloss, eine eigene CD unter eben diesem Titel herauszubringen, die Nummer 9. Es wurde eine Sammlung mit 41 verschiedenen Reden von Frauen zum Thema Emanzipation. Die juristische Idee der Frau, die ein Stimmrecht hat, wurde also mit der physischen Stimmgebung gleichsam zusammengelegt, während die übrigen wenigen Frauenstimmen in der Sammlung meist von Sängerinnen oder Schauspielerinnen stammten, die nicht ihre eigenen, sondern fremde Werke vortrugen. Selbst die CD „Überleben im Nachkriegsdeutschland" lässt in 28 Takes nur zwei Frauen zu Wort kommen, davon nur eine aus der Welt der „Trümmerfrauen", denen die westdeutsche Gesellschaft immerhin ihr Überleben verdankt.
Es waren aber nicht nur die Redakteure des Lautarchivs vorurteilsbehaftet. Dieselbe Lücke findet man auch an anderen Orten der Medienhistorik. Bis zur Jahrhundertmitte sind die weiblichen Stimmen fast überall unterrepräsentiert, gemessen an der Rolle, welche Frauen längst in Wirklichkeit kulturell und politisch

only biased ones. Similar gaps are widespread throughout the field of media history. Until mid-century, female voices were underrepresented almost everywhere judging from the cultural and political roles that women had long since assumed in reality. For instance, one of Germany's foremost archives of the voice of the people (in Freiburg) responded to a query with the information that there were no notations on early phonographic recordings as to whether the voices were feminine or masculine. The difference was obviously unimportant. The same goes for international collections of the spoken word—a "female voice" is practically never saved for posterity, though for a variety of reasons. For example, the three departments of the Berlin Sound Archive—Voices of the Peoples, German Dialects, and Voices of Famous Persons—are collections of almost exclusively male voices. Of course, this is understandable when one considers that what are euphemistically referred to here as voices of the peoples are, in fact, recordings made in POW camps during the First and Second World Wars. The prominent personages, on the other hand, are without exception politicians and scientists, who always did tend to outshine housewives and suffragettes when it came to occupying the spotlight of public attention. The Sound Archive of the Province of Baden-Württem-

spielten. So etwa teilt eines der bekanntesten Archive für Volksstimmen (in Freiburg) auf Anfrage mit, dass auf den frühen phonographischen Aufnahmen nicht notiert wurde, ob es sich um weibliche oder männliche Stimmen handelt. Der Unterschied war offenbar unwichtig. Auch in internationalen Sammlungen zur Sprechstimme ist eine *female voice* so gut wie nicht überliefert, wenn auch aus unterschiedlichen Gründen. Das Berliner Lautarchiv zum Beispiel hat in seinen drei Abteilungen „Stimmen der Völker", „Deutsche Mundarten" und „Stimmen berühmter Persönlichkeiten" nahezu ausschließlich Männerstimmen gesammelt – verständlich, denn was hier euphemistisch „Stimmen der Völker" genannt wird, sind in Wahrheit Aufnahmen aus Kriegsgefangenenlagern des Ersten und Zweiten Weltkriegs. Bei den „berühmten Persönlichkeiten" wiederum handelt es sich ausschließlich um Politiker und Wissenschaftler, die schon immer in der Öffentlichkeit eher Gehör fanden als Hausfrauen oder Suffragetten. Auch das Tonarchiv des Landesmedienzentrums Baden-Württemberg hat nur Männerreden weltweit gespeichert: de Gaulle, Kennedy, Weizsäcker, Obama. Keine Margret Thatcher, keine Golda Meir, keine Benazir Bhutto, keine Indira Ghandi. Selbst die hauseigene Website für Poesie kennt nur männliche Stimmen.

Derselbe Befund gilt für das österreichische Pendant, die akustische Chronik der Mediathek. Hier fügen sich

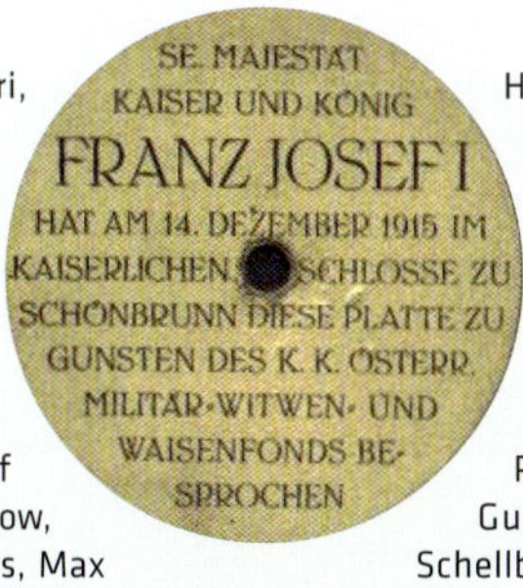

Contents: Rosa Albach-Retty, Dino Alfieri, Robert Allmers, Josef Altmann, Achim von Arnim, Siegfried Aufhäuser, Ludwig Friedrich Barthel, Bernhard Baumeister, Ernst von Bergmann, Theobald von Bethmann-Hollweg, Rudolf G. Binding, Wilhelm von Bode, Hans Bodenstedt, Andreas Bolek, Alois Brandl, Alfred Braun, Otto Braun, Paul von Breitenbach, Rudolf Breitscheid, Lujo Brentano, Bernhard von Bülow, Galeazzo Ciano di Cortelazzo, Alfred Daniels, Max Devrient, Erich Drach, Friedrich Ebert, Hugo Eckener, Arthur Eddington, Rudolf Eucken, Konstantin Fehrenbach, Lion Feuchtwanger, Bogdan Filoff, Emil Fischer, Käthe Franck-Witt, Franz Josef I, Heinrich George, Otto von Gierke, Friedrich Grimm, Wilhelm Groener, Gustaf Gründgens, Theo Habicht, Ernst Haeckel, Adolf von Harnack, Rudolf Havenstein, Sven Hedin, Richard Hertwig, Paul von Hindenburg, Adalbert Houben, Johannes Kaempf, Josef Kainz, Jacobus C. Kapteyn, Kienzle Uhren A.G., Hermann Köhl, Paul König, Josef Lewinsky, Carl von Linde, Alexander von Linsingen, Theodor Loos, Ludwig III, Heinrich Lüders, August von Mackensen, Alexander Moissi, Heinrich Morf, Gustav Noske, Wilhelm Pfeffer, Erich Raeder, Joachim von Ribbentrop, Gustav Roethe, Philipp Scheidemann, Oscar Schellbach, Joachim Schepke, Arthur Schmidt, Jacob Gould Schurman, Gustav Schweinfurth, Hans von Schwerin-Löwitz, Kurt Schwitters, Adolf von Sonnenthal, Elis Strömgren, Rabindranath Tagore, Alfred von Tirpitz, Ernst Toller, Leo Tolstoi, Karl Valentin, Wilhelm Voigt, Ulrich von Wilamowitz-Moellendorf, Wilhelm II, Richard Willstätter, Alexander Wulff, Wilhelm Wundt, Ferdinand von Zeppelin.

www.lotz-verlag.de/series4.html

Can you find the woman's voice?

Finden Sie die Frauenstimme?

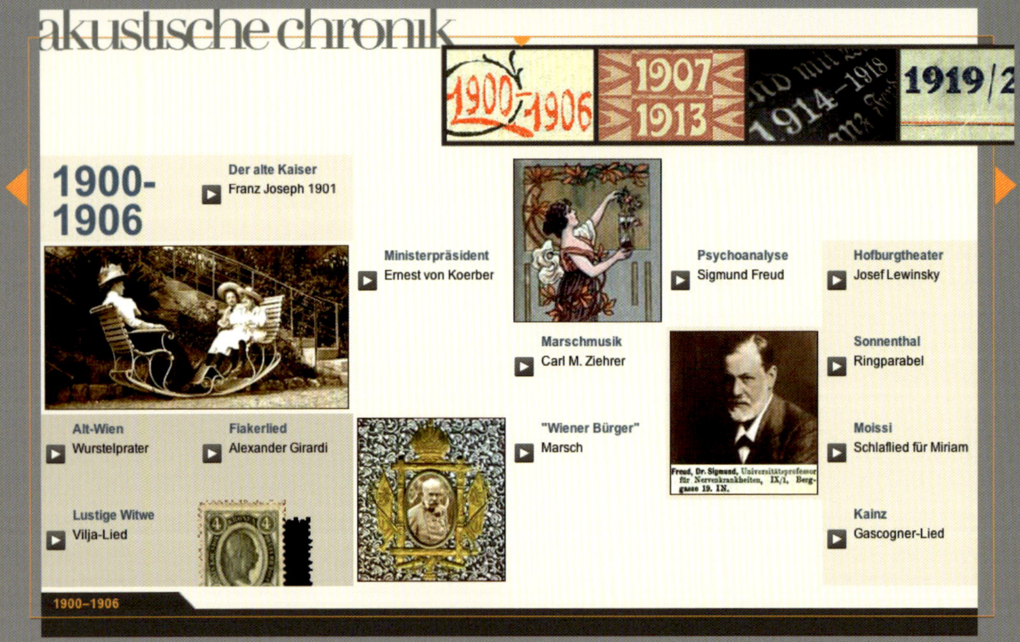

www.akustische-chronik.at/1900-1906

berg's Media Center includes speeches by men only: de Gaulle, Kennedy, Weizsäcker, Obama. No Margaret Thatcher, no Golda Meir, no Benazir Bhutto, no Indira Ghandi. Not surprisingly, its poetry website as well is strictly a mouthpiece for male voices.

The same applies to the facility's Austrian counterpart, the Mediathek's acoustic chronicle, in which audio and video material from the period between 1900 and about 1970 coalesces into an almost exclusively male tradition—perhaps because there's a lack of recordings of female voices; maybe because curators don't deem them important enough. In fact, the first female voice we ever encounter here was recorded in 1932, a speech delivered by Alma Motzko in front of Parliament, an inflammatory address about the current economic crisis. Of the 44 authors in the Phonogram Archive's Acoustic Literature collection, eight are women, who thus constitute a rather minor factor in this audible historiography. Ilse Aichinger, Ingeborg Bachmann and Barbara Frischmuth are distributed over about 40 years. It's not until 1972 that a woman is heard uttering a political statement.

Male editors do not, as a matter of fact, comprise the decisive filter. After all, 80% of the many audio

Ton- und Bildstücke aus der Zeit zwischen 1900 und etwa 1970 zu einer fast ausschließlich männlichen Tradition zusammen, sei es, weil Aufnahmen weiblicher Stimmen fehlen, sei es, weil sie von den Redaktoren nicht für genügend wichtig erachtet wurde. Die erste weibliche Sprechstimme taucht hier überhaupt erst im Jahr 1932 auf in Gestalt einer Rede von Alma Motzko vor dem Parlament, einer Brandrede zur Weltwirtschaftskrise. Das akustische Literaturarchiv innerhalb des Phonogrammarchivs zählt insgesamt 44 Autoren, davon acht Frauen, die bei einer akustischen Geschichtsschreibung wohl nicht wirklich ins Gewicht fallen würden. Ilse Aichinger, Ingeborg Bachmann, Barbara Frischmuth sind auf etwa 40 Jahre verteilt, in denen bis 1972 ansonsten kein politisches Statement aus Frauenmund zu hören ist.

Tatsächlich bilden aber die männlichen Redakteure nicht wirklich den entscheidenden Filter. Denn auch die vielen Hörbücher der letzten zwanzig Jahre werden zu 80 Prozent von Männerstimmen bestritten, selbst wenn es das Buch einer Autorin ist und eine weibliche Hauptfigur hat. Warum? Eine einfache Erklärung wäre, dass so, wie die meisten Buchkäufer und Leser weiblichen Geschlechts sind, so auch die Hörer von Hörbüchern – und Frau hören eben viel-books published over the last 20 years feature the voice of a man, and that is so even if a woman authored the work and its chief protagonist is female. Why? A simple explanation would be that just like most booksellers and readers are women, most listeners of audio books are too, and thus, perhaps for erotic reasons, they prefer to hear male voices. Or maybe there are just good ol' fashioned authoritarian reasons for this? Of course, public broadcasting companies have always assumed what amounts to governmental significance, and radio and TV news are still an outgrowth of the official communiqués issued by the official speakers of political life.

When, as an upshot of the protests of 1968, women finally achieved a presence in the media worldwide—in 1972, when Wibke Bruhns debuted on the German Public Broadcasting Company's Channel 2 news; in 1976 with Dagmar Berghoff on Channel 1; and the BBC finally followed suit in 1986—this was in no small measure attributable to the visual desirability of attractive women, whose images and voices had been a staple in the public consciousness since the arrival of talkies in 1928. Thus, right from its inception, the format named TV news became a piece of fiction, a sequence from a dramatic film, an imaginary event, and something very different from the radio voice that, although disembodied and dislocated, could nevertheless come across as all the more intellectual. The media history of the Soviet Union since 1917—another story altogether—illustrates, in turn, how women speaking and singing in filmed musicals could be used as the very personification of the revolution and, not least of all, as counter-propaganda to male-dominated German society. But that's quite another story.

1 1994 Leslie C. Dunn and Nancy A. Jones (Eds.): *Embodied Voices: Representing Female Vocality in Western Culture.* Cambridge: Cambridge UP 1994

2 Jody Rosen: Researchers Play Tune Recorded Before Edison, *New York Times,* March 27, 2008

3 On this subject, see Claudia Schmölders, Die Stimme des Bösen. Zur Klanggestalt des Dritten Reiches. In *MERKUR* 581 (1997), 681–893.

4 Hans-Ulrich Wagner, Sounds like the Fifties. Zur Klangarchäologie der Stimme im Westdeutschen Rundfunk der Nachkriegszeit. In: *Zeithistorische Forschungen/Studies in Contemporary History 2* (2011), 266–284

leicht aus erotischen Gründen lieber männliche als weibliche Stimmen. Oder eben doch aus altbekannten autoritären Gründen? Natürlich hat der Rundfunk als öffentlich-rechtliche Anstalt von Anfang an eine quasi gouvernmentale Bedeutung erlangt; Radio- oder TV-Nachrichten verlängern sich noch heute zu den offiziellen Verlautbarungen der offiziellen Sprecher des politischen Lebens zurück.

Als in der Folge der 68er-Bewegung endlich Frauen weltweit die Medien eroberten – 1972 Wibke Bruhns die *heute*-Sendung des ZDF, 1976 Dagmar Berghoff die *Tagesthemen* der ARD, 1986 dann endlich auch Frauen die BBC – war dies nicht zuletzt der visuellen Existenz hübscher Frauen geschuldet, die seit Entstehung des Tonfilms 1928 im öffentlichen Bewusstsein bekannt waren, mit Bild und Stimme. So wurde das Format namens „Nachrichten" im TV auf Anhieb zu einem Stück Fiktion, einem Stück Spielfilm, zu einer imaginären Veranstaltung, ganz anders als die Radiostimme, die zwar ortlos und körperlos, aber dafür umso intellektueller wirken konnte. Die ebenfalls ganz andere Mediengeschichte der Sowjetunion seit 1917 zeigt andererseits, wie sich die im Film (Musical) singende und sprechende Frau als Verkörperung der Revolution einsetzen ließ: nicht zuletzt als Gegenpropaganda zur deutschen Männergesellschaft. Aber das ist eben auch eine andere Geschichte.

1 1994 Leslie C. Dunn and Nancy A. Jones (Hrsg.): *Embodied Voices: Representing Female Vocality in Western Culture.* Cambridge: Cambridge UP 1994

2 Jody Rosen: Researchers Play Tune Recorded Before Edison, *New York Times,* 27 März 2008

3 Vgl. dazu Claudia Schmölders, Die Stimme des Bösen. Zur Klanggestalt des Dritten Reiches. In *MERKUR 581* (1997), 681–893.

4 Hans-Ulrich Wagner, Sounds like the Fifties. Zur Klangarchäologie der Stimme im Westdeutschen Rundfunk der Nachkriegszeit. In: *Zeithistorische Forschungen / Studies in Contemporary History 2* (2011), 266-284

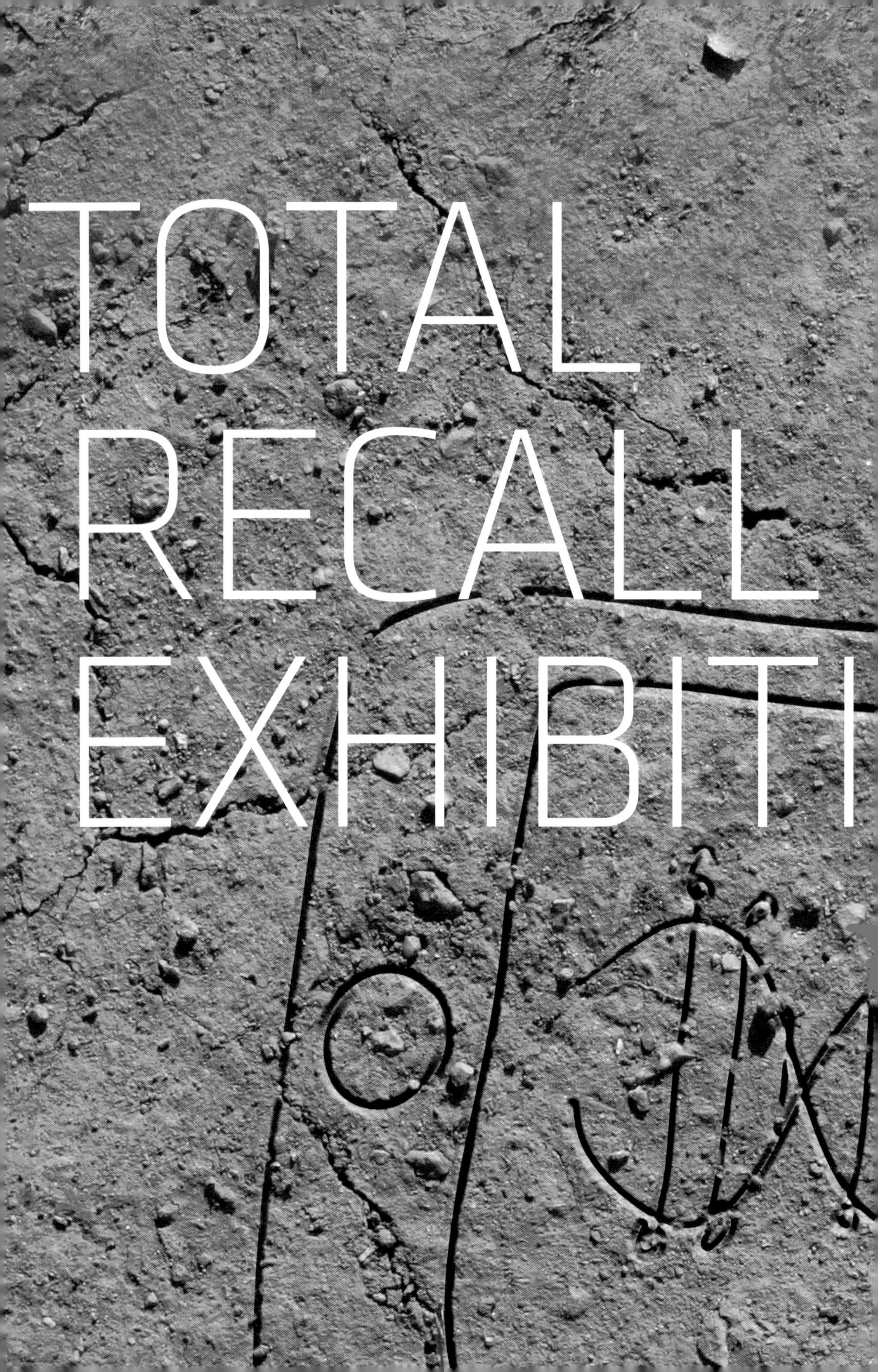
TOTAL
RECALL
EXHIBITI

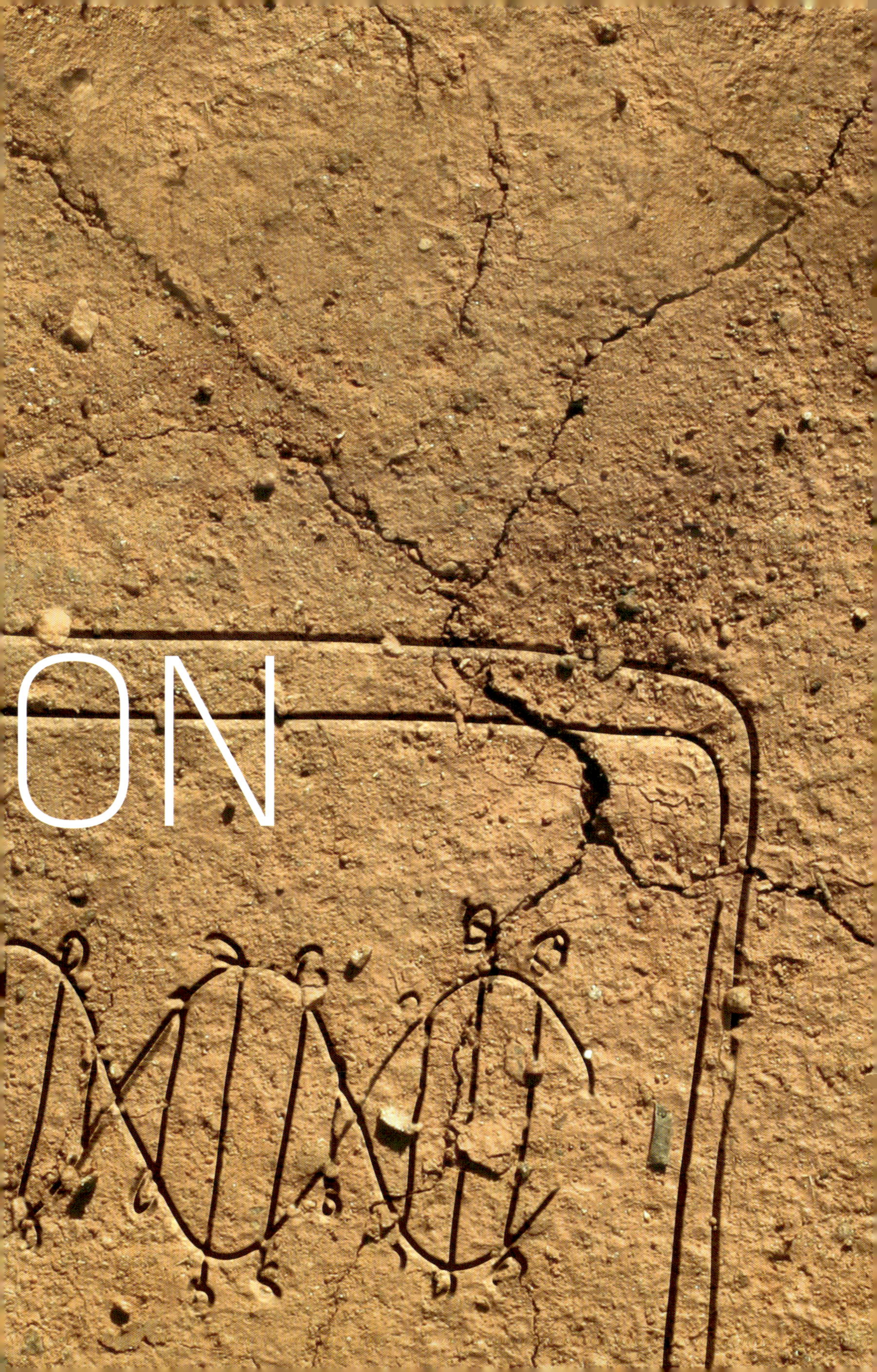
ON

Ei Wada

Toki Ori Ori Nasu
Falling Records

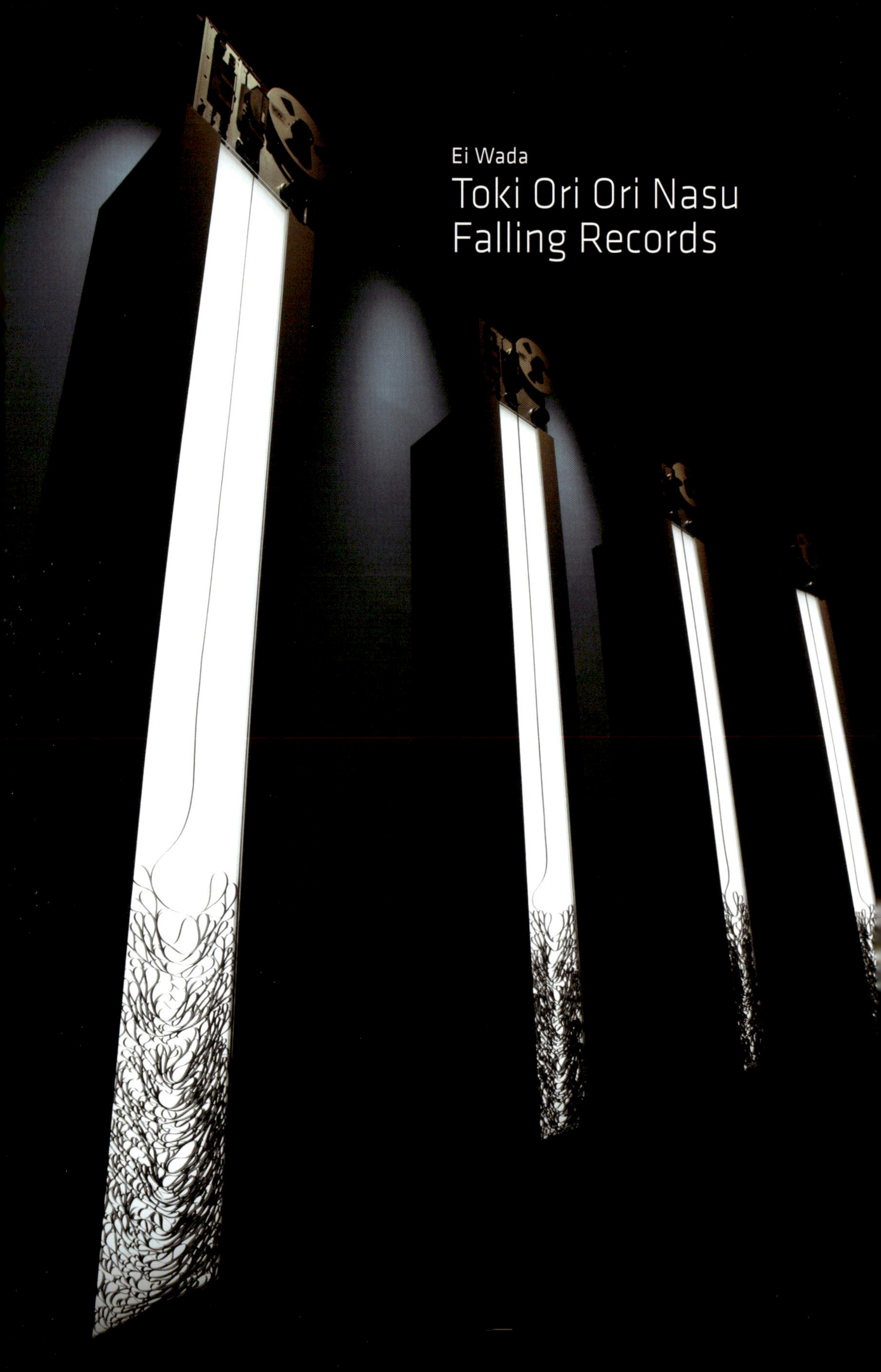

Reel-to-reel tape recorders, playback apparatus of yesteryear, are turned on their sides and displayed on high pedestals. As they play from single reels, their magnetic tapes unwind and drop down into clear acrylic cases. The tapes are thrown in folds, filling the cases, weaving unique and intricate patterns in the space. Each resembles a woven picture or drawing, representing the passing of time. Once the cases are filled with tape, they are rewound at high speed. The old patterns vanish, to be replaced by new ones...

The sounds recorded on the tapes are output in totally distinct ways as they fall and as they rewind, with different rotation rates and in different directions. As the tape rolls up, one can recognize the same sounds recorded there and simultaneously recall the sounds and the visual spectacle during the time the tape was falling, but in a completely different way.

This work is based on my notion of *Electronicostic Imagination*. *Electronicos* is a word I coined that means something old has been transformed from its original purpose into a new contemporary paradigm. The work was inspired by a real incident in which I observed a tape dropping and piling up on a floor.

At a certain point of time in the future, inhabitants of some unknown culture, who have never seen a tape recorder before, may discover this machine with its one broken reel and try to play back the tape ... And because of their fascination with the phenomenon of music visually piling-up, they may build a huge tower of *Electronicos* in some public space. In the evening they will look at the tower, at the magnetic materials falling, the rotational movement, the rewinding. And, over time, the sounds and vision will become indelibly inscribed on their memories.

My concept of *Electronicostic Imagination* will continue to grow and its whispering voice will be heard: *"Look! The 20th century is falling down like a waterfall..."*

www.facebook.com/OpenReelEnsembleBraunTubeJazzBand
www.steamblue.net/

Tonbandmaschinen, die Wiedergabegeräte vergangener Jahre, stehen hochkant auf hohen Stelen. Die Geräte sind nur mit einer Spule ausgestattet, sodass die Bänder beim Abspielen lose nach unten fallen – hinein in durchscheinende Acrylglasvitrinen. Während sich diese füllen, legen sich die Bänder in Falten und bilden einzigartige, verschlungene Muster, die Geweben oder Kritzelzeichnungen gleichen und das Vergehen der Zeit räumlich darstellen. Sind die Vitrinen voll, werden die Bänder im Schnelllauf zurückgespult, die Muster verschwinden und machen Platz für neue...

Die auf den Bändern gespeicherten Töne werden auf immer andere Weise wiedergegeben, da sie mit wechselnden Geschwindigkeiten und Richtungen abgespielt und zurückgespult werden. Auch wenn die auf den Bändern gespeicherten Töne nun ganz anders klingen, erkennt man sie beim Zurückspulen wieder und erinnert sich dabei an das akustische und visuelle Geschehen beim Abspielvorgang.

Dies ist eine der Arbeiten, die auf meinem Konzept der *Electronicostic Imagination* beruhen. *Electronicos* ist ein von mir geprägter Begriff für etwas Altes, dessen einstige Verwendungsweise in eine neue, zeitgenössische überführt wurde. Die Idee verdankt sich der zufälligen Beobachtung eines zu Boden rieselnden und dort zum Berg anwachsenden Tonbands.

Irgendwann in der Zukunft werden Angehörige einer unbekannten Kultur, die noch nie ein Tonbandgerät gesehen haben, vielleicht diese einspulige Maschine entdecken und das Band abzuspielen versuchen... Und weil sie diese sich buchstäblich auftürmende Musik so faszinierend finden, werden sie vielleicht an einem öffentlichen Platz einen mächtigen *Electronicos*-Turm errichten. An den Abenden werden sie vor dem Turm sitzen und das Fallen der Magnetbänder, die Drehbewegungen, den Rückspulvorgang beobachten, und mit der Zeit werden die Töne und der Anblick sich unauslöschlich in ihr Gedächtnis eingraben.

Mein Konzept der *Electronicostic Imagination* wird sich weiterentwickeln und ich und andere werden eine Stimme vernehmen, die uns zuflüstert: „Schau! Das 20. Jahrhundert stürzt herab wie ein Wasserfall..."

Aus dem Englischen von Wilfried Prantner

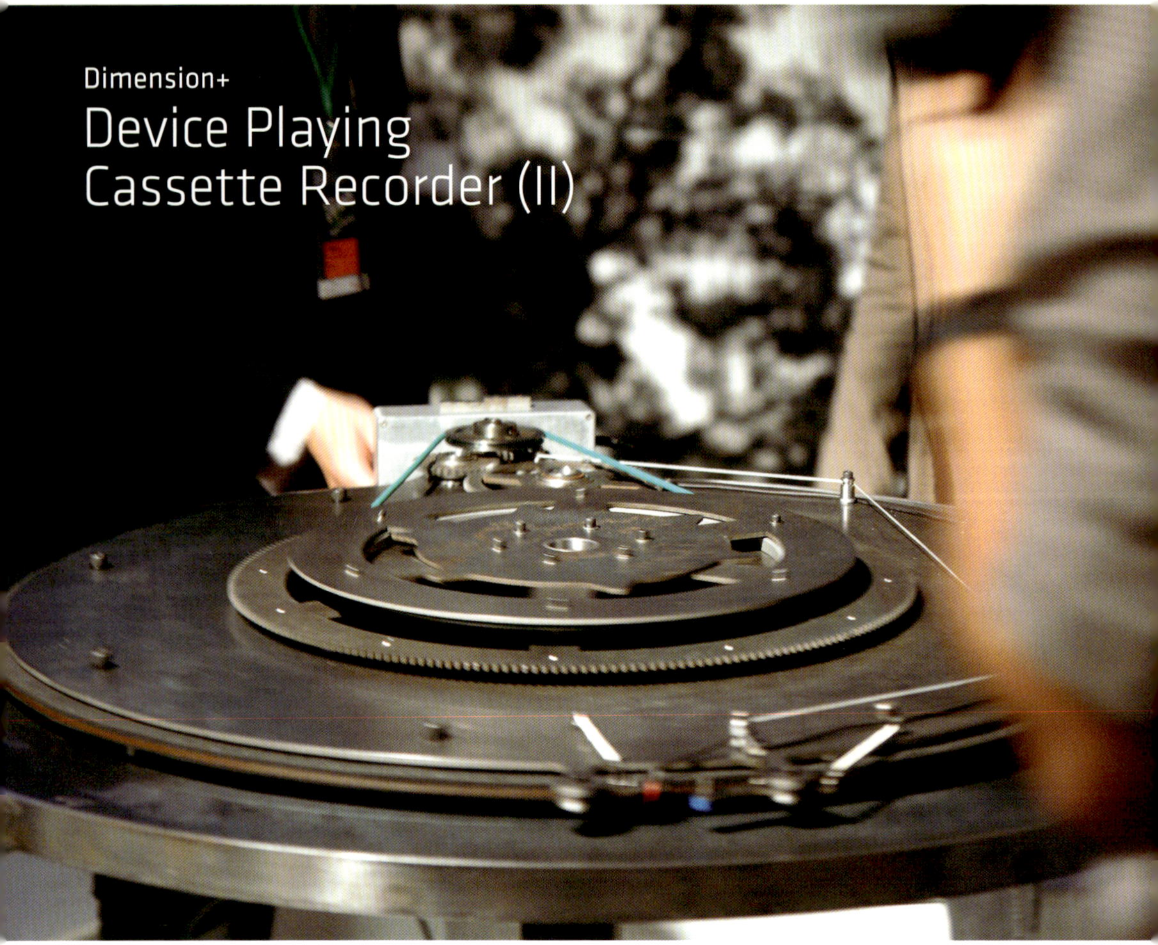

Dimension+

Device Playing Cassette Recorder (II)

Device Playing is a series of works that takes a medium back to its origins, observing and discovering the original mechanism. The audience can rediscover the re-constructed medium during the performance, reflect upon its origins and upon the role of digital media in our daily lives.

Device Playing–Cassette Recorder II is all about the medium of sound. Nowadays it is digital music and sound from your iPod that enter your ear and your brain. Through the process of deconstruction and the "rediscovery" of a past generation of portable music sound and devices–the cassette recorder,

Die Werkreihe *Device Playing* führt uns zu den Anfängen eines Mediums zurück und ermöglicht die Beobachtung und Entdeckung seiner ursprünglichen Mechanismen. Das Publikum kann das re-konstruierte Medium während der Performance neu erschließen, sich über dessen Ursprünge und die Rolle digitaler Medien in unserem Alltag Gedanken machen.

Bei *Device Playing – Cassette Recorder* dreht sich alles um das Medium Klang. Heute gelangt digitale Musik vom iPod zum Ohr und ins Gehirn. Durch Dekonstruktion und „Neu-Entdeckung" einer früheren Generation portabler Musik und ihrer Abspielgeräte – dem the *Device Playing–Cassette Recorder* takes the audience back to the analog medium of sound. The basic cassette recorder mechanism: there's an analog relationship between magnetic tape and magnetic heads, and music is generated according to the varying magnetic field. By preserving the mechanical operation of cassette recorder/player, this work gives all the control power back to the audience. The round-shaped platform represents the inter-mechanics of traditional cassette recording technology, and extends the fixed-length medium to infinity. During the spinning of the device on the track when listening to or recording sound, the audience experiences the linear movement of this medium with their body, and rediscovers the analog medium of sound.

http://www.dimensionplus.co

Dimension+, Bi-city New Media Arts Team based in Hong Kong and Taipei, founded by Keith Lam (HK) and Escher Tsai (TW), Original Concept of *Device Playing: Cassette Recorder:* Michelle Ngai

Kassettenrecorder– nimmt *Device Playing – Cassette Recorder* die Zuschauer mit in die Vergangenheit analoger Klangmedien.
Die Funktionsweise eines Kassettenrecorders basiert auf dem analogen Verhältnis zwischen Magnetband und Tonköpfen, wobei die aufgezeichnete Musik entsprechend dem sich verändernden Magnetfeld wiederhergestellt wird. Die Arbeit legt die mechanische Bedienung eines Kassettenaufnahme- und -wiedergabegeräts in die Hände des Publikums und gibt ihm damit die volle Kontrolle über diese Prozesse zurück. Die kreisrunde Plattform entspricht der Mechanik eines traditionellen Kassettenrecorders und erweitert die durch das Medium Tonband vorgegebene Spieldauer ins Unendliche. Dreht man an der Kurbel, um eine Tonspur abzuspielen oder aufzunehmen, nimmt man die lineare Bewegung des Mediums mit dem eigenen Körper wahr und entdeckt so dieses analoge Klangmedium neu.

Aus dem Englischen von Michael Kaufmann

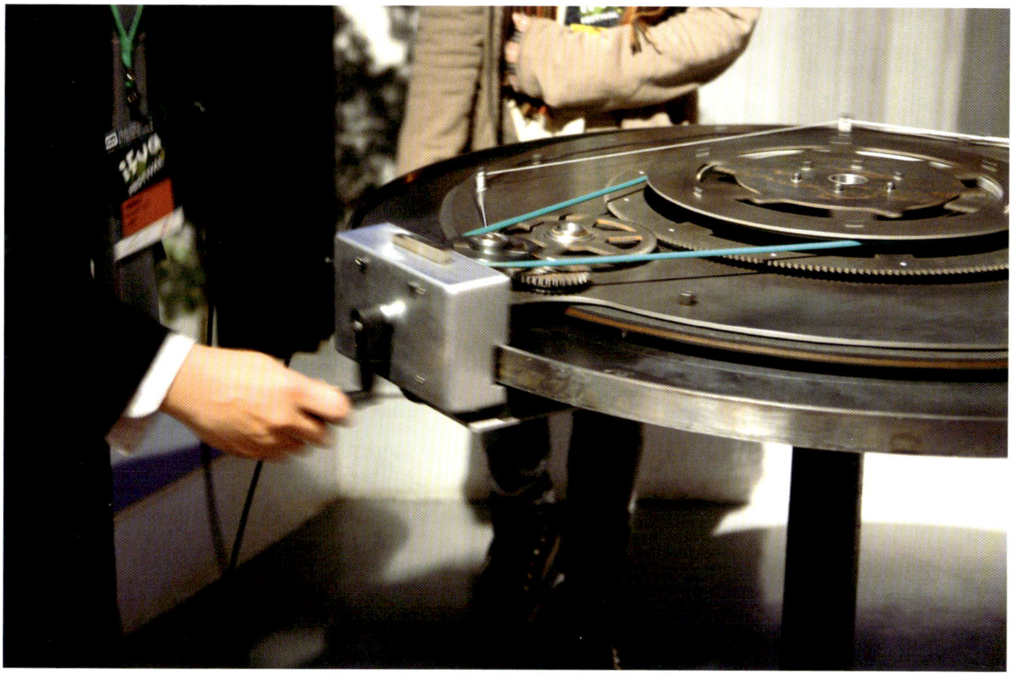

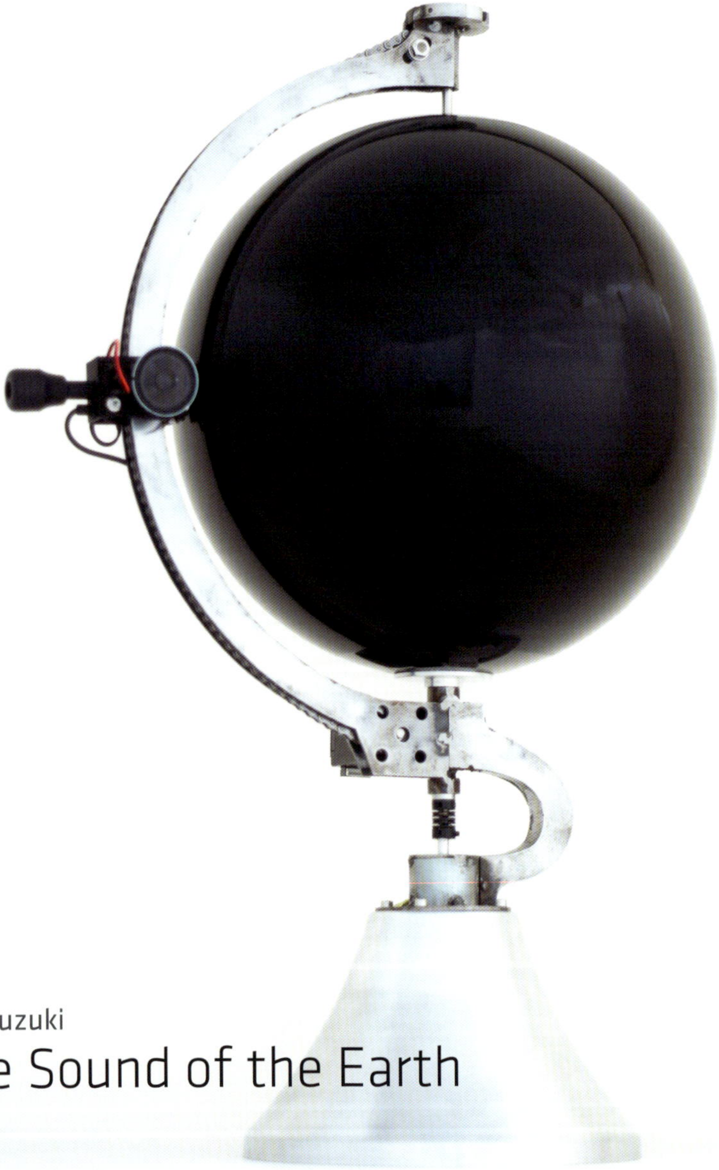

Yuri Suzuki

The Sound of the Earth

The Sound of the Earth is a spherical vinyl record and record player that can play back the sounds stored on it. The surface of the globe is engraved just like a normal vinyl but recording the sound in 3D instead of a flat surface—the grooves representing the outlines of the geographic land mass. Each country on the disc is engraved with a differ-

The Sound of the Earth besteht aus einem Schallplatten-Globus und einem Plattenspieler, der die darauf gespeicherten Klänge wiedergibt. Die Oberfläche des Globus ist wie eine Vinylschallplatte geprägt, wobei die Signale auf einer dreidimensionalen statt einer flachen Oberfläche gespeichert sind. Die Rillen repräsentieren die Umrisse der geografischen Gebiete.

ent sound; as the needle passes over it plays field recordings collected by Yuri Suzuki from around the world over the course of four years—traditional folk music, national anthems, popular music and spoken broadcasts.

The record player uses bush roller chain to move the stylus from the North Pole to the South Pole. A full journey across the earth takes around 30 minutes. The stylus has a small speaker and an amplifier to generate sound. As the record player moves across the earth in a spiral, the *Sounds of the Earth* are split into fragments which you hear as the stylus moves over the seas and borders of the world.

Concept collaboration: Yoshihiro Katsumata; hardware development: KIMURA (Tasco Inc) / Akichika Tanaka; sound programming: Bengt Sjölén. Special thanks to Vestax.

http://yurisuzuki.com/works/the-sound-of-the-earth-2/

Honorary Mention Digital Musics & Sound Art, Prix Ars Electronica 2013

Jedes Land auf der Schallplatte ist mit einem anderen Sound vertreten. Wenn die Nadel das jeweilige Land passiert, werden Feldaufnahmen abgespielt, die Yuri Suzuki auf der ganzen Welt im Lauf von vier Jahren aufgenommen hat: traditionelle Volksmusik, Nationalhymnen, Straßenmusik und Gesprächsaufnahmen. Der Plattenspieler verfügt über eine Rollenkette, um die Nadel vom Nord- zum Südpol zu bewegen. Eine Reise rund um den Globus dauert etwa dreißig Minuten. Die Nadel hat einen kleinen Lautsprecher und Verstärker integriert, die die Klänge wiedergeben. Da sich der Plattenspieler in einer Spirale um die Erde bewegt, werden „die Klänge der Erde" in Fragmente aufgesplittert, die man hören kann, wenn die Nadel über den jeweiligen Breitengrad läuft.

Aus dem Englischen von Martina Bauer

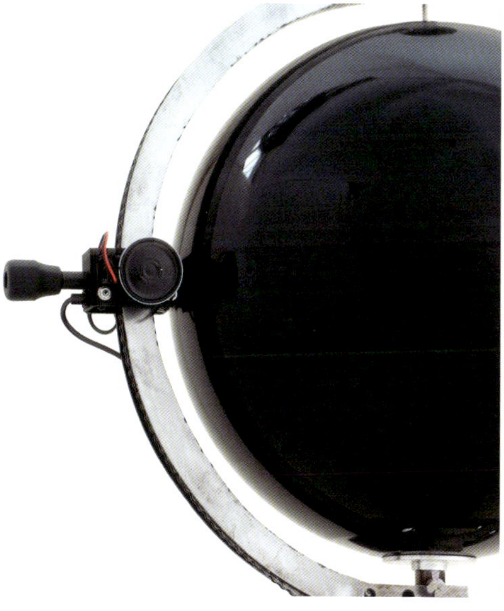

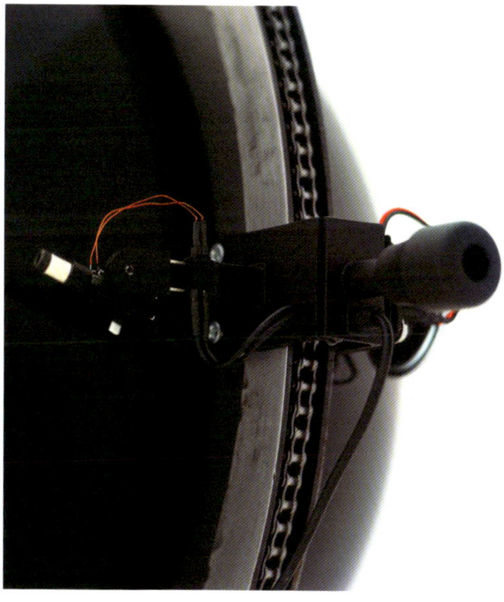

Brian House
Quotidian Record

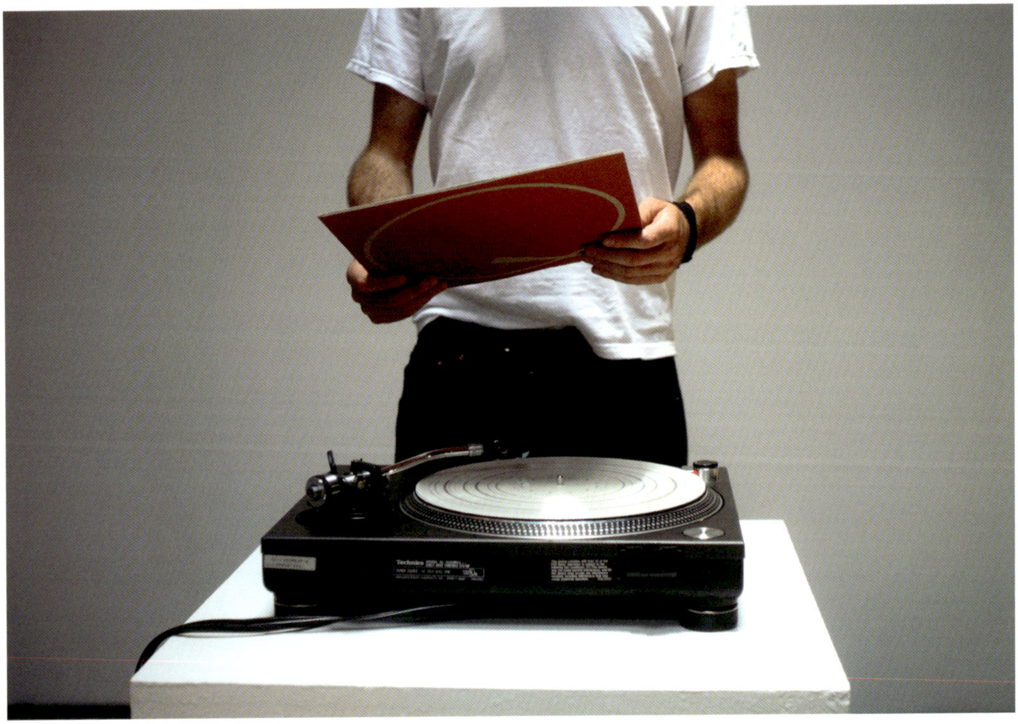

We spend a lot of time taking photos of exceptional events and posting them online. These are reified moments, and a little false, in that they leave out the gaps that are more truly the material of the everyday. *Quotidian Record* is meant to propose one alternative method for archiving our experience.

The project builds off of a year's worth of my personal location data collected via the OpenPaths platform. The points are clustered in order to enumerate the different places in my life. Each place is assigned a step of the scale in the music, and each city is allocated a key. What you hear are the motifs that I cycle through over the course of my movements day-to-day—a personal rhythmic signature. One rotation of the record corresponds to one day of lived time. As the record turns, it functions as

Wir verbringen viel Zeit damit, Fotos von außergewöhnlichen Ereignissen zu schießen, um sie dann zu posten. Diese erstarrten Momente verzerren die Realität, da die Zeit dazwischen ausgelassen wird, die viel eher unseren Alltag ausmacht. *Quotidian Record* stellt eine Möglichkeit dar, alle unsere Erfahrungen zu archivieren.

Meine im Lauf eines Jahrs auf OpenPaths gesammelten Ortsdaten bilden den Grundstock dieses Projekts. Die Punkte sind gebündelt und stellen die verschiedenen Orte dar, an denen ich mich aufgehalten habe. Jeder Örtlichkeit ist ein Ton auf der Tonleiter zugeordnet und jeder Stadt eine Tonart. Die zu hörenden Motive geben meine tagtäglichen Wege wieder – sind eine persönliche rhythmische Signatur.

Eine Umdrehung der Schallplatte entspricht einem Tag meines Lebens und fungiert damit als 24-Stunden-a 24-hour clock. A year becomes about 11 minutes, which is the length of the piece. The markings indicate when I travel—the background is New York City, but you can see where I take off to Colorado or Korea, and if you move the stylus to those rings, you'll hear the change.

Mapping information to something physical emphasizes that it is lived, subjective data. The piece is intended to be experienced tactilely by placing the record on the turntable, seeing its rotation, and selecting into it with the stylus. The back of the sleeve shows the score—for each city, it depicts the network of places that I travel between. *Quotidian Record* may be collected and fetishized, connecting the value of data today with the history of popular music culture. It points out that data are always qualitative and mean different things depending on how they are cast—a critical gesture in a world in which the collection of personal data has become inescapable.

Concept, data performance, code, and audio: Brian House
Design and production: Greg Mihalko / Partner & Partners
Vinyl production: Ted Riederer / Never Records
Mastering: Nik Levinsky
Data gathered via: OpenPaths
Supported by: Eyebeam Art and Technology Center
Thanks: The New York Times Company Research and Development Lab

Uhr. So wird ein Jahr auf elf Minuten komprimiert, die Länge des Musikstücks. Ausgehend von New York City zeigen die Markierungen meine Reisen nach Colorado oder Korea an; setzt man die Nadel in diesen Rillen ab, wird die Ortsveränderung sofort hörbar.

Durch die Kartierung dieser Daten in einem physischen Medium wird deren persönlicher Hintergrund betont. Das Stück soll taktil erfahren werden, indem man die Schallplatte auf den Plattenspieler legt, ihre Drehung beobachtet und die Nadel an ausgewählten Stellen absetzt. Die Rückseite der Hülle zeigt die Partitur – für jede Stadt das Netzwerk der Orte, die ich aufsuche.

Quotidian Record kann gesammelt und zum Kult erhoben werden, indem es den heutigen Wert von Daten mit der Geschichte der Populärmusikkultur verbindet. Das Projekt unterstreicht, dass Daten immer eine bestimmte Qualität haben und je nach Betrachtungsweise eine unterschiedliche Bedeutung haben – eine kritische Geste in einer Welt, in der das Sammeln persönlicher Daten unvermeidbar geworden ist.

Aus dem Englischen von Michael Kaufmann

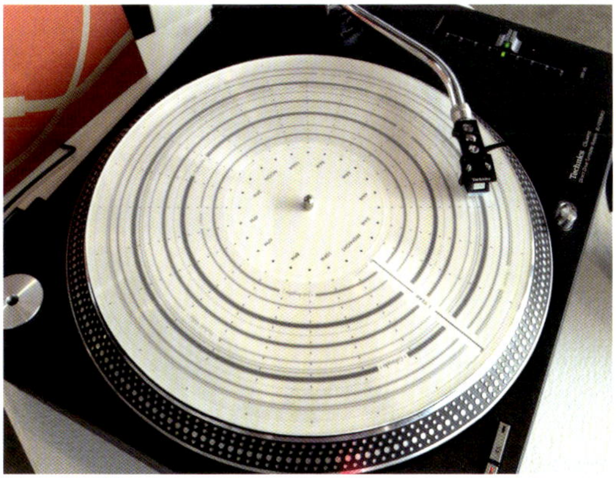

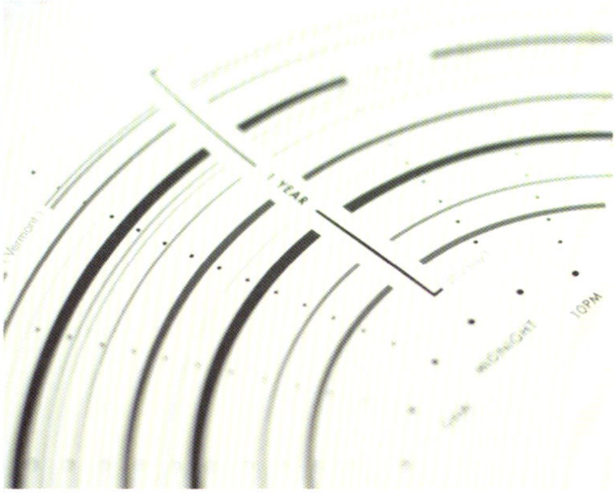

Patrick Feaster

The oldest recorded sounds
Die ältesten aufgenommenen Klänge

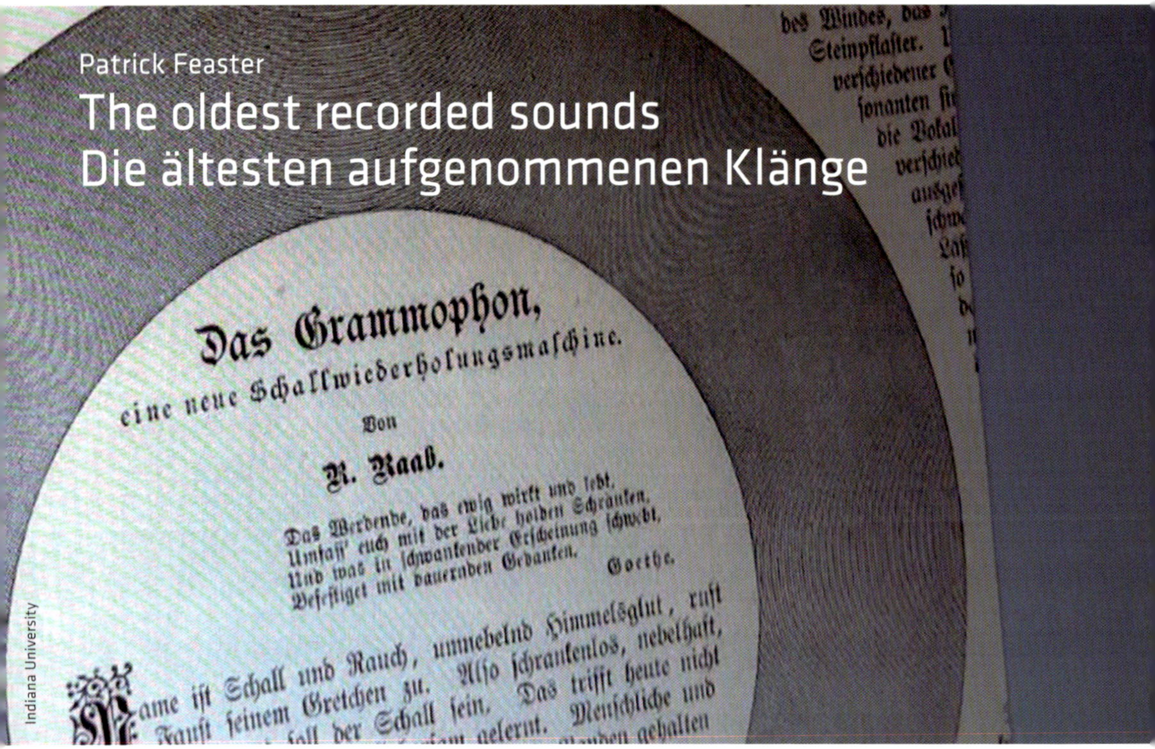

Indiana University

A printed replica of the early gramophone disc "Der Handschuh"
Eine photographische Abbildung der frühen Grammophonplatte „Der Handschuh" von Friedrich Schiller

Many of the world's earliest sound recordings, dating from the nineteenth century, have survived into the present only as images on sheets of paper.
In some cases, the playable media—such as gramophone discs—from which these images were made, were lost long ago, leaving little hope that their sounds could ever be heard again. In other cases, there had never been any intention of playing the records back; the goal had been merely to fix sound waves for visual study.
But sound media historian Patrick Feaster has developed a method for extracting sound from these images, bringing to life rare audio content thought lost to history. He discovered one print in a German periodical, housed in the stacks at Indiana University Bloomington's Wells Library, which represents the oldest gramophone-type recording

Viele der frühen Tonaufzeichnungen aus dem 19. Jahrhundert haben nur als gedruckte Bilder auf Papier bis in die Gegenwart überlebt. In einigen Fällen gingen schon vor langer Zeit die abspielbaren Medien – z. B. Grammophonplatten – verloren, von denen diese Bilder gemacht wurden, und es bestand wenig Hoffnung, sie jemals wieder hören zu können. In anderen Fällen waren die Aufzeichnungen nie zur Wiedergabe gedacht, sondern die Schallwellen sollten lediglich für optische Studien festgehalten werden.
Doch der Ton-Archäologe Patrick Feaster hat ein Verfahren zur Extraktion des Tons aus diesen Bildern entwickelt, das seltene und verloren geglaubte historische Tonaufnahmen zu neuem Leben erweckt. In den Magazinen der Wells Library an der Indiana University Bloomington entdeckte er in einer deutschen Zeitschrift einen Abdruck der ältesten, Ende

available anywhere for listening today. Created in late 1889, it is the earliest audible ancestor of the world's vintage vinyl. By "playing" the inked spiral, we can again hear the voice of gramophone inventor Emile Berliner as he recites the poem "Der Handschuh" ("The Glove") by Friedrich Schiller.

Together with his associates in the First Sounds Initiative, he has also recovered the world's oldest known "sound recordings"—in the sense of sound vibrations automatically recorded out of the air. These are the groundbreaking phonautograms recorded in Paris by Édouard-Léon Scott de Martinville in the 1850s and 1860s as wavy lines scratched on soot-blackened paper—humanity's first-ever recordings of its own voice.

In addition to playing back the oldest recorded sounds captured automatically from life, Feaster has recently pursued the thread even further into the past by using innovative digital techniques to play (or "educe") a variety of other early efforts to depict sound—ranging from medieval music manuscripts to eighteenth-century notations of Shakespearean recitation—just as though they were modern sound recordings.

1889 entstandenen Aufnahme nach dem Grammophon-Prinzip, die man heute noch anhören kann – wohl der älteste noch tönende Urahn der klassischen Vinylplatte. Durch „Abspielen" der in Tinte verewigten Spirale ertönt heute wieder die Stimme von Emil Berliner, dem Erfinder des Grammophons, beim Rezitieren von Friedrich Schillers Ballade „Der Handschuh".

Gemeinsam mit seinen Kollegen von der First Sounds Initiative stellte er auch der Welt älteste „Tonaufnahmen" – im Sinn einer automatischen Aufzeichnung von Schallwellen oder Luftschwingungen – wieder her. Es handelt sich um die bahnbrechenden Phonautogramme, die Édouard-Léon Scott de Martinville zwischen 1850 und 1860 in Paris anfertigte: in rußgeschwärztes Papier gekratzte Wellenlinien, die allerersten Aufnahmen einer menschlichen Stimme.

Doch Feaster begnügt sich nicht mit der Wiedergabe der ältesten automatisch aufgezeichneten Tondokumente, sondern stößt seit Neustem noch tiefer in die Vergangenheit vor, indem er mithilfe innovativer Digitaltechniken eine Reihe früher Klangdarstellungsversuche abspielt (oder „ableitet"), als seien es moderne Tonaufnahmen – z. B. mittelalterliche Musikmanuskripte oder Notationen von Shakespeare-Rezitationen aus dem 18. Jahrhundert.

Aus dem Englischen von Michael Kaufmann

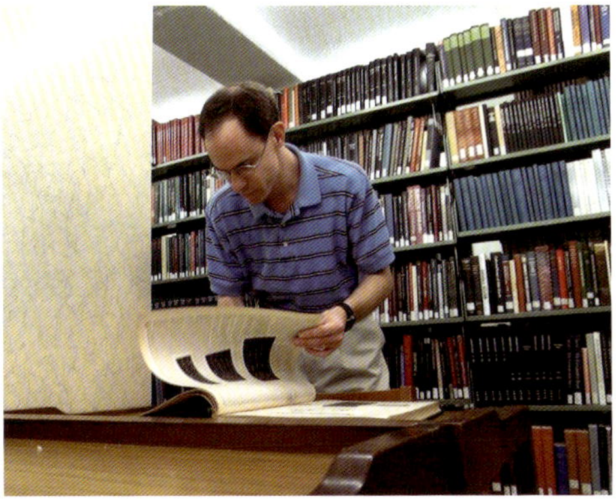

Indiana University

Patrick Feaster looks through an item in the collection at Indiana University Bloomington's Wells Library, where he discovered a print of an early sound recording in a German periodical, and was able to play it.

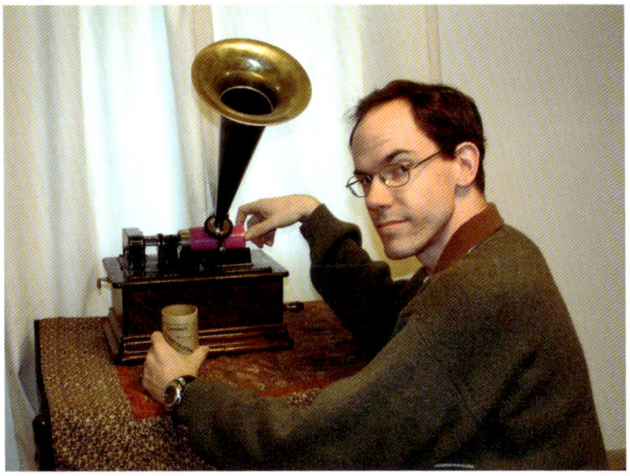

Patrick Feaster beim Stöbern in der Sammlung der Bloomington Wells Library an der Indiana University, wo er in einer deutschen Zeitschrift die Abbildung einer frühen Tonaufnahme entdeckte und es schaffte, diese auch abzuspielen.

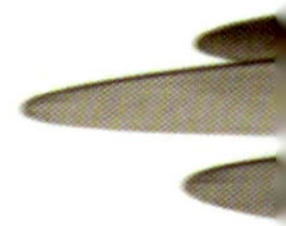

Social Fabrication Center SFC (SFC*SFC)

Wave Form Media

Sound is produced by air vibrating, and these vibrations are called waves. *Wave Form Media* is a physical object that shows the form of sound data. In other words, it works like a music record, but it's mobile, wearable and customizable. It can be produced directly from digital sound data using digital fabrication tools such as a laser cutter.

One of our products, the *Sound Accessory*, is a mixture between a fashionable accessory and a music record. You can wear the sound message recorded by your ancestor, by your grandmother or by another loved one. Whenever you wear it, you are physically reminded of their heartfelt message. Our *Wave Form* software can also "play back" the message by capturing the images of the *Wave Form Media* with a Web camera.

Another product, the *Sound Block*, is a new toy that enables us to play with *Wave Form Media*. You can easily make your own original *Wave Form* by changing the combinations of small sound blocks.

The technologies we use are all simple and low-tech in comparison with other music formats like mp3, wav and compressed data. We believe that this extremely simple format of *Wave Form Media* could outlive all other formats, and possibly still be around in 1000 years time. Media becomes memory.

Social Fabrication Center SFC (SFC*SFC): Yusuke Tominaka, Shigeki Shimizu, Yusuke Nakamura, Hiroya Tanaka Hiroya Tanaka Laboratory

Ein Ton entsteht durch die Übertragung von Schwingungen in der Luft, die man als Schallwellen bezeichnet. *Wave Form Media* ist ein Objekt, das die Wellen eines Klangs physisch darstellt. Mit anderen Worten, es ist eine Musikaufnahme, darüber hinaus aber mobil, tragbar und individuell gestaltbar. Das Objekt kann mit computergesteuerten Werkzeugen, wie etwa einem Laserschneidgerät, direkt aus digitalen Tonaufnahmen hergestellt werden.

Eines unserer Produkte, das *Sound Accessory*, ist eine Kombination aus modischem Accessoire und Musikaufnahme. Damit kann man Klangbotschaften von Angehörigen und anderen nahestehenden Personen wie ein Schmuckstück tragen und spürbar an ihre von Herzen kommenden Worte erinnert werden. Die *Wave Form*-Software kann diese Botschaften auch wieder abspielen, indem man das Programm mit einem Foto des *Sound Accessory* füttert.

Ein weiteres Produkt, *Sound Block* genannt, ist ein neues Gadget, das dem Benutzer einen spielerischen Umgang mit *Wave Form*-Medien ermöglicht. Man kann auf einfache Weise eine eigene *Wave Form* erstellen, indem man kleine Klangblöcke neu kombiniert.

Verglichen mit anderen Musikformaten wie mp3, wav oder komprimierten Daten ist unsere Lösung eine Lowtech-Variante. Wir glauben, dass *Wave Form Media* aufgrund seiner einfachen Struktur und Handhabung alle anderen Formate überdauern wird und auch in tausend Jahren noch abgespielt werden kann. Medien werden unser Gedächtnis.

Aus dem Englischen von Martina Bauer

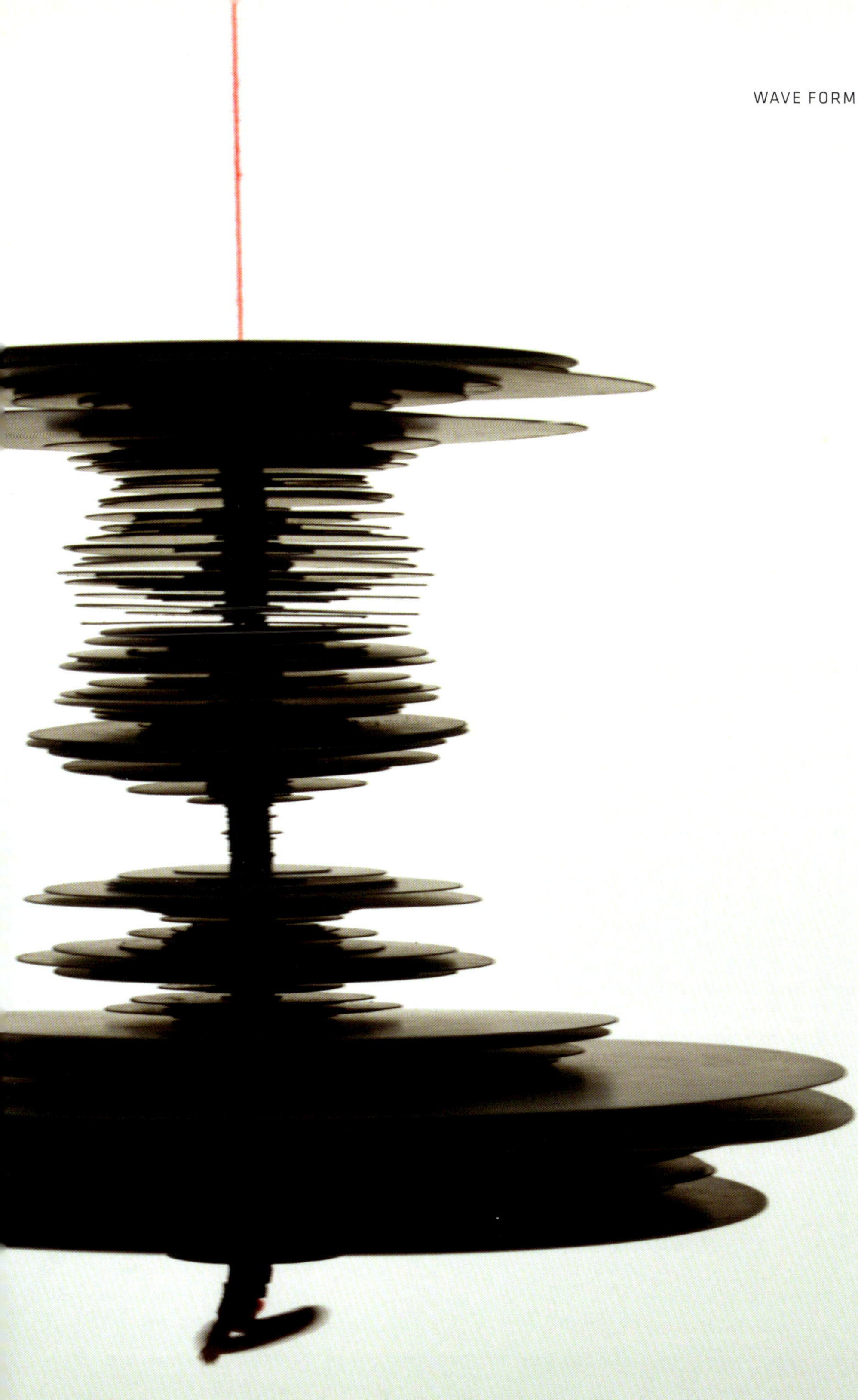

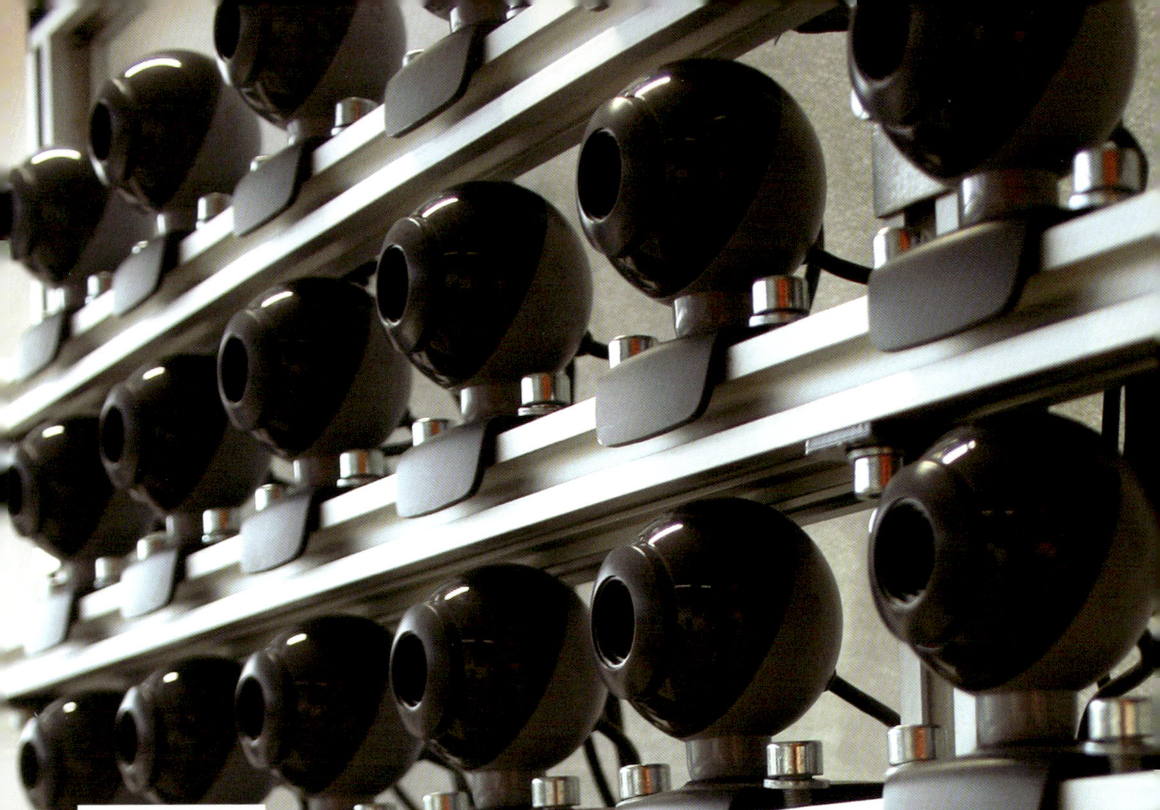

Oliver Bimber

Light-Field Technology
Lichtfeldtechnologie

Light-field photography has the potential to radically revolutionize everything that we associate with digital imaging today.

Our three-dimensional world is usually depicted two-dimensionally now. This is the case, for instance, in display systems like television, imaging systems like photography, and digital image processing. But two-dimensional images don't deliver an ideal representation of our world. So, if representing a real scene accurately and completely is what you'd like to do, then you have to consider the scene's entire light transport process. That is, you have to know the brightness and color of the light that's reflected from any three-dimensional point in the scene in any direction whatsoever. A camera able to capture all that light transports (also known as the 5-D plenoptic function) would be a perfect imaging system. Unfortunately, it's impossible

In Lichtfeldern steckt das Potenzial, all das radikal zu revolutionieren, was man heute mit digitalen Bildern in Verbindung bringt.

Unsere dreidimensionale Welt wird in vielen Fällen zweidimensional abgebildet. Das ist zum Beispiel bei Displays, in der Fotografie oder der digitalen Bildverarbeitung der Fall. Zweidimensionale Bilder sind keine optimale Repräsentation unserer Welt. Wenn man eine reale Umgebung in geeigneter und vollständiger Form repräsentieren möchte, dann müsste man den gesamten Lichttransport im Raum betrachten. Man müsste also wissen, welche Helligkeit und Farbe das Licht hat, das von jedem Punkt im Raum in eine beliebige Richtung abgestrahlt wird. Eine Kamera, die den gesamten Lichttransport (auch 5-D-plenoptische Funktion genannt) aufnimmt, wäre ein perfektes Imaging-System. Leider ist es nicht möglich, die plenoptische Funktion vollständig mit Kameras to completely capture the plenoptic function with cameras or to reproduce it on displays. Light fields are 4D excerpts of the 5D plenoptic function and thus the closest approximation of them. They contain considerably more information than 2-D images or the 3-D data of a depth sensor. A problem that's still holding back this technology is the enormous quantity of data produced when it's used.

During the Ars Electronica Festival, light-field photography will be explained and illustrated on the basis of three concrete examples. Visitors will be able to see how light-field data can be recorded and processed. The project features applications in the areas of light-field photography, processing and microscopy, and also offers interaction possibilities to Festival visitors, who will have a chance to shoot images with a compact, commercially available light-field camera and then view them online. A camera matrix illustrates another use of light-field photography—visitors can use it to take self-portraits and see themselves stereoscopically. A light-field microscope will also be on hand to show a potential application beyond the realm of photography.

abzutasten oder mit Displays wiederzugeben. Lichtfelder sind ein 4D-Auszug der plenoptischen Funktion und dabei ihre bestmögliche Annäherung. Sie enthalten um einiges mehr Informationen, als Bilder (2D) oder Daten eines Tiefensensors (3D). Ein Problem, das diese Technologie derzeit noch zurückhält, sind die hohen Datenmengen, die bei ihrem Einsatz erzeugt werden.

Während des Ars Electronica Festivals werden Lichtfelder erklärt und anhand von drei konkreten Beispielen veranschaulicht. Besucher sehen, wie Lichtfelddaten aufgenommen und weiterverarbeitet werden können. Das Projekt zeigt Anwendungen in den Bereichen Lichtfeld-Fotografie, -Verarbeitung und -Mikroskopie und bietet den Besuchern Möglichkeiten zur Interaktion: Mit einer kompakten Consumer-Lichtfeldkamera können Festivalbesucher Lichtfeldaufnahmen machen und diese auch später online ansehen. Eine Kameramatrix zeigt eine weitere Möglichkeit, Lichtfelder aufzunehmen. Besucher können sich damit ablichten lassen und sich stereoskopisch betrachten. Ein Lichtfeldmikroskop zeigt ein Anwendungsbeispiel für Lichtfelder jenseits von Fotografie.

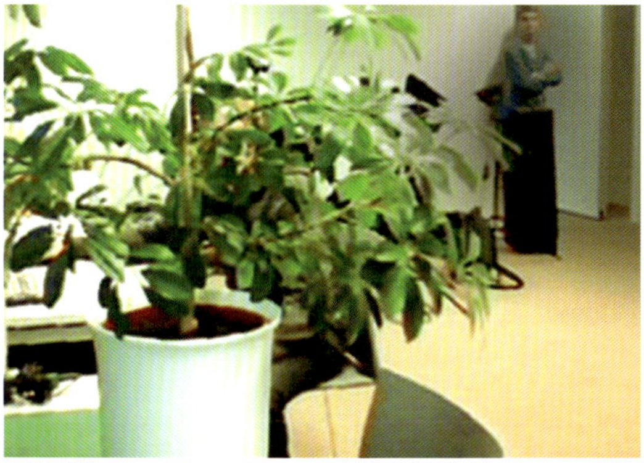

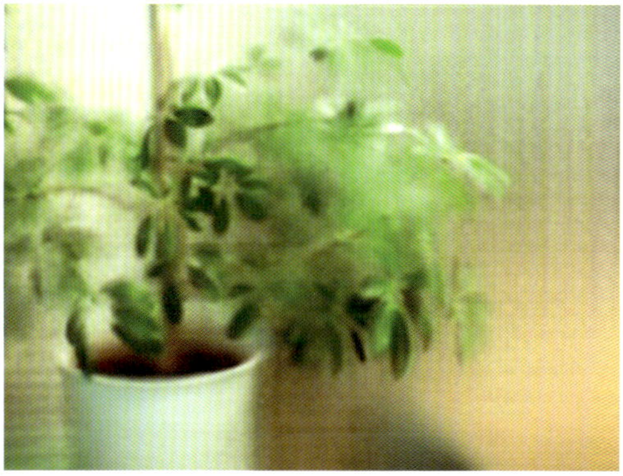

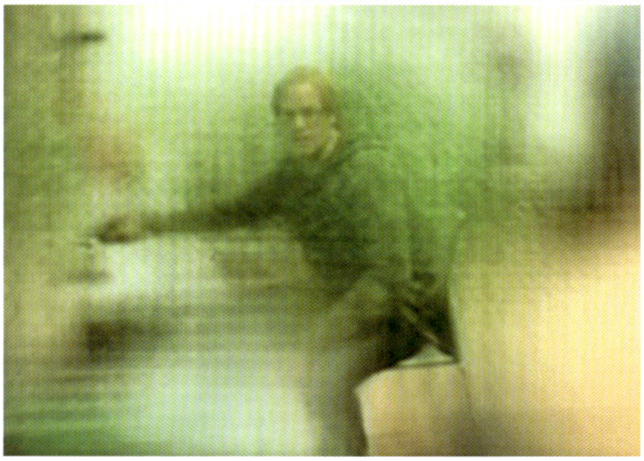

Reinhard Nestlbacher

Cell Camera

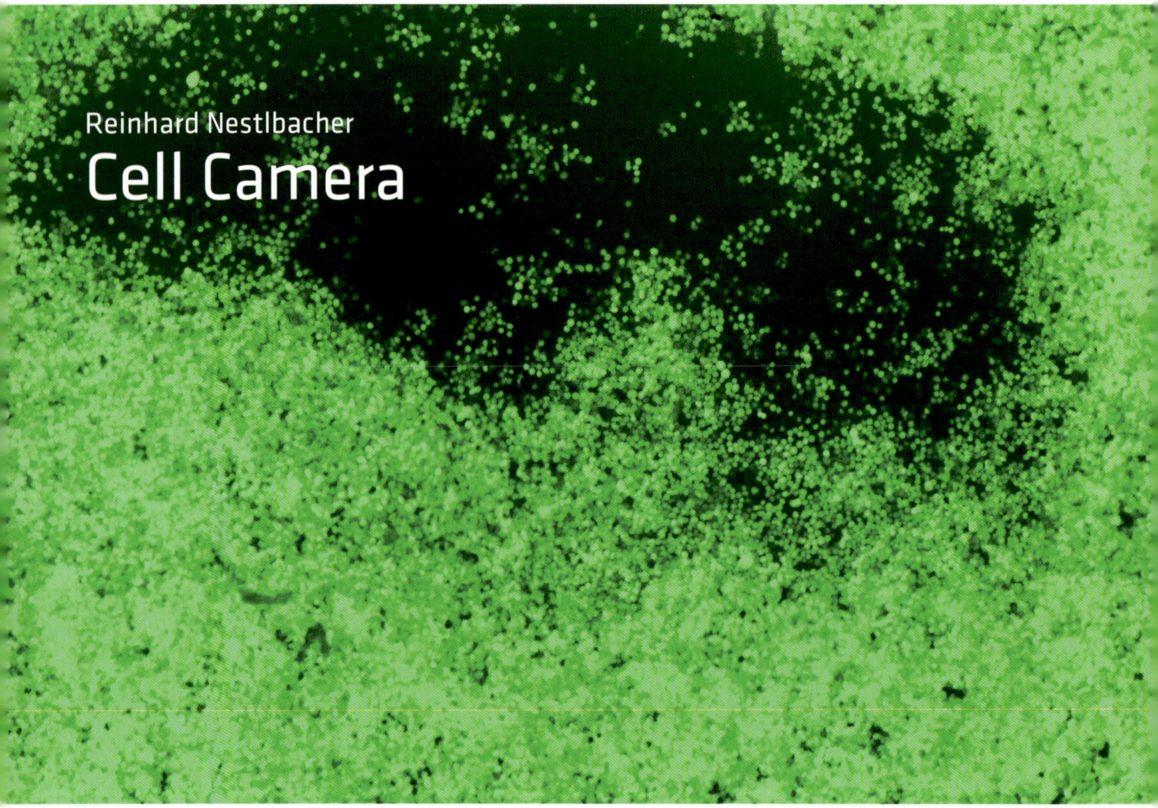

For this BioArt project, cells from the artist's body were technically modified in such a way that, as fluorescent cancer cells, they can live "forever" in a culture medium and can thus be continuously cultivated. The cells are sensitized to light with special chemicals used in photodynamic cancer therapy. The cell culture modified in this way is transferred onto a 9x7-centimeter-format plate in a foil frame and forms a layer of light-sensitive cells on it. For the artistic work, this living photographic paper is affixed inside a plate camera and exposed to light. An alternative to this procedure would be for the exposure to occur in a classic darkroom setting via photo-negative process. Once

Für das BioArt-Projekt *Cell Camera* werden Zellen des Künstlers technisch so modifiziert, dass sie als fluoreszierende Krebszellen in Kultur „ewig" leben und dadurch laufend gezüchtet werden können. Mit Spezialchemikalien aus der photodynamischen Krebstherapie werden die Zellen auf Licht sensibilisiert. Die so veränderte Zellkultur wird im Kleinbildformat (9 mal 7 Zentimeter) in Folien-Rähmchen überführt und bildet dort eine lichtempfindliche Zellschicht. Für die künstlerische Arbeit wird dieses lebende Fotopapier in eine Plattenkamera eingespannt und belichtet. Alternativ dazu kann die Belichtung wie in der klassischen Dunkelkammer über ein Fotonegativ erfolgen. Nach einer weiteren Behandlung kann die Platte it's treated, the plate can be photographed and viewed directly for a couple of days, but the cells are alive and uncontrollably change the depiction. For the actual panel image, the layer of living cells that were exposed to light is scanned with a special microscope and this scanned image is used to produce a large-scale print. Here, it's possible to recognize how the cells—and thus the artist's own biological system—function as an "image-generating apparatus" that forms and modifies the picture. Using this procedure, a single image can never be reproduced in the exact same form.

Modern technology operates on the edge. Little glitches can cause a system to break down and lead to a catastrophe. This also applies to the extremely fragile image of the cell camera. One false move working with his own cultivated cells could endanger the artist's health. The cell camera images that will be presented at Ars Electronica depict events that were not only burned into his memory but also into his cells: the Fukushima disaster, the series of screw-ups that led to the Deepwater Horizon oil spill, the explosion of the Challenger, or the failure of a single wheel that derailed a high-speed train near Eschede, Germany.

Team: Kristjan Plaetzer & Verena Ziegler (Universität Salzburg), Arbeitsgruppe Fatima Ferreira (Universität Salzburg), Zeiss (Mikroskopie) & Lotus View Kamera / Günter Ströbele

nun fotografiert und ein paar Tage direkt betrachtet werden – die Zellen leben aber und verändern unkontrollierbar das Bild. Für das eigentliche Tafelbild wird die belichtete lebende Zellschicht mit einem Spezialmikroskop abgerastert und daraus ein großflächiger Druck erstellt. Nun ist erkennbar, wie die Zellen – und damit das biologische System des Künstlers selbst – als „bilderzeugender Apparat" das Bild formen und verändern. Dadurch kann ein Bild nicht in identer Form reproduziert werden.

Die moderne Technologie bewegt sich an Grenzen. Kleine Fehler können zum Kippen eines Systems und zur Katastrophe führen. Dies gilt auch für das äußerst fragile Bild der *Cell Camera*. Die eigenen kultivierten Zellen können für den Künstler bei falscher Handhabung zu einem gesundheitlichen Risiko führen. Die bei Ars Electronica präsentierten Motive von *Cell Camera* stellen Ereignisse dar, die sich nicht nur im Gedächtnis des Künstlers, sondern nun auch in seinen Zellen eingebrannt haben: das Desaster von Fukushima, die Versagenskette bei der Ölpest der Deepwater Horizon, die Explosion der Challenger oder der Bruch eines einzelnen Rads, der den ICE-Zug bei Eschede zerstört hat.

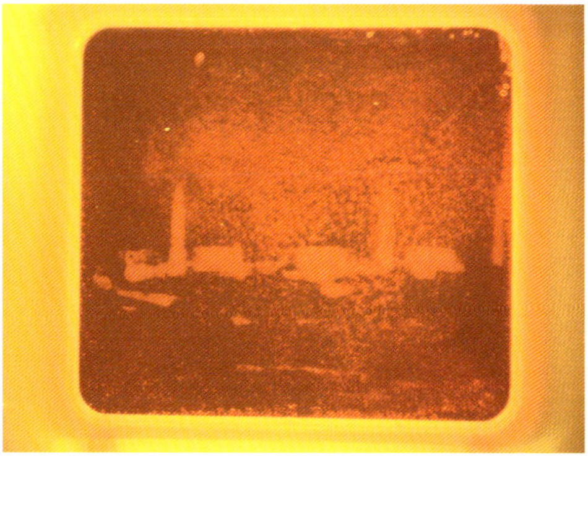

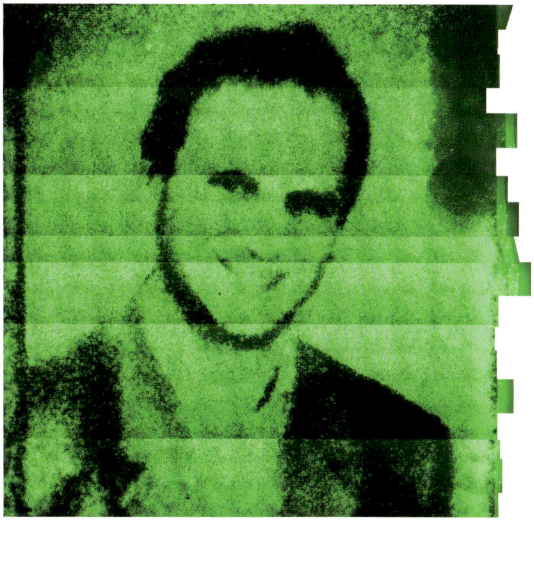

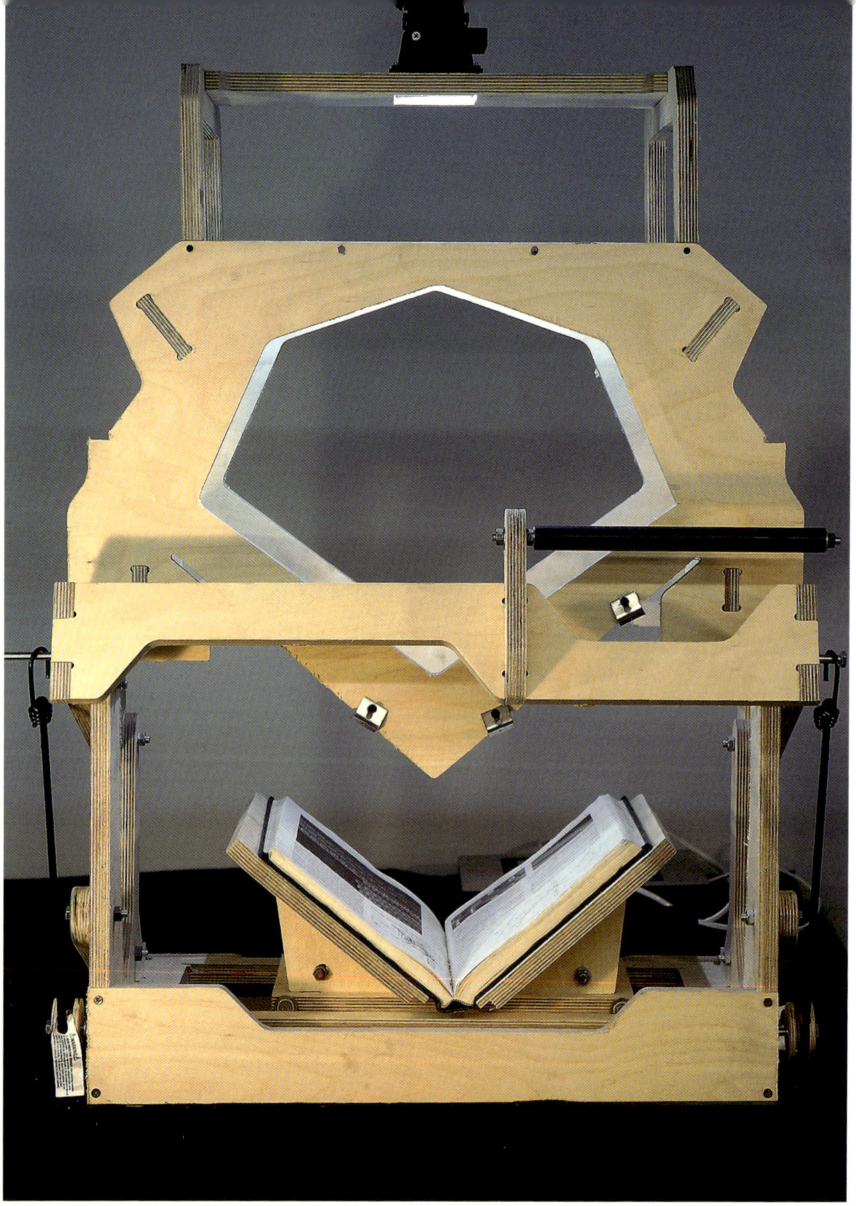

Daniel Reetz

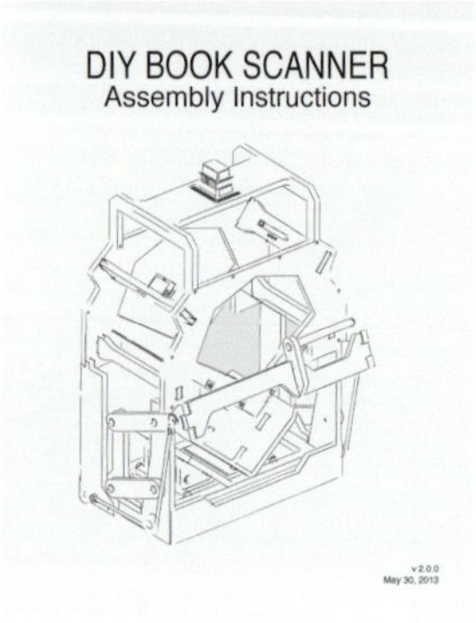

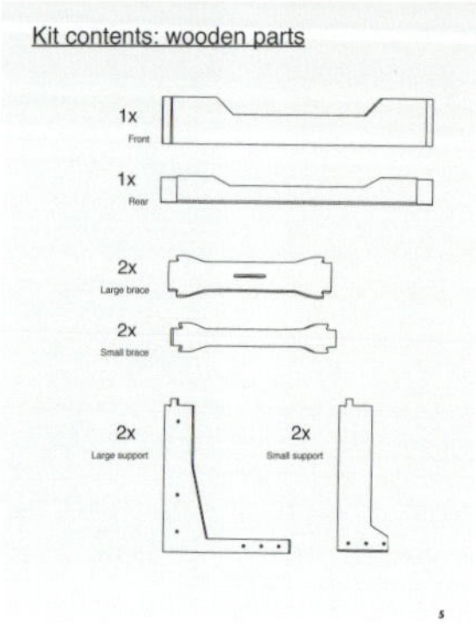

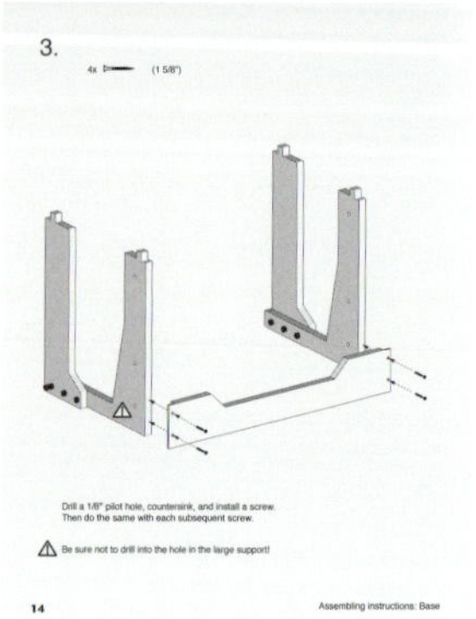

Robert Baruch and Dario DeMoura

Daniel Reetz

DIY Book Scanner

Two years ago the cheapest cameras were cheaper than textbooks, but today the cheapest cameras are cheaper than beer. This community-developed Open Source *Do It Yourself Book Scanner* takes advantage of cheap cameras to bridge the gap between your bookshelf and your e-reader. It was designed to be made from a single sheet of plywood, on the same kind of machine that produces IKEA furniture. Hackerspaces and community workshops around the world have the equipment and expertise to affordably replicate this machine. It is made from common parts—skateboard bearings, bicycle parts, cheap cameras, bungee cords, and fasteners that work in both metric and imperial sizes (5/16" and 8 mm). This particular machine was prototype #13 of the 21 prototypes that went into the final design.

The fundamental idea of *DIY Book Scanning* technology is to point a camera at a document and to digitize it. People have been doing this forever. But only now do we have such cheap and powerful cameras. The remainder of the hardware in this machine is designed to make scanning easy and repeatable, and to handle the enormous variety of problems encountered in book scanning.

DIY Book Scanners are appropriate technology—they are not intended for industrial scale scanning, but rather for scanning books quickly where traditional scanning is unaffordable, impossible, or inappropriate. Over the years, we have learned that not everybody needs a book scanner in their home, but everybody needs access to a book scanner. The *DIY Book Scanner* community is about access AND ownership, and we aim to put a book scanner in every Hackerspace on earth. Ideally, they will be loaned out like books, so that books that are too private, too precious, and too personal can be scanned in a private place.

Daniel Reetz, Robert Baruch, Dario DeMoura, Mark Van Den Borre, the *DIY Book Scanner* Community

Vor zwei Jahren waren die billigsten Kameras günstiger als Lehrbücher, aber heute kosten sie bereits weniger als ein Bier. Der via Open Source gemeinschaftlich entwickelte *Do-it-Yourself Book Scanner* nützt diese billigen Kameras, um die Lücke zwischen Bücherregal und E-Reader zu schließen. Das Gerät ist so konzipiert, dass es aus einer einzigen Sperrholzplatte auf den gleichen Maschinen wie die IKEA-Möbel hergestellt werden kann. Hackerspaces und Community Workshops auf der ganzen Welt verfügen über die Werkzeuge und das Wissen, um dieses Gerät kostengünstig nachbauen zu können. Es wird aus handelsüblichen Teilen gefertigt – Kugellager von Skateboards, Ersatzteile für Fahrräder, billige Kameras, Gummispanner und Befestigungselemente mit metrischem oder Zollgewinde (5/16" bzw. 8 mm). Das hier ausgestellte Gerät ist die Nr. 13 der 21 gebauten Prototypen.

Der Grundgedanke hinter der *DIY Book Scanning*-Technologie ist es, Dokumente mithilfe einer Kamera zu digitalisieren. Diese Idee ist nicht neu, aber erst heute verfügen wir über entsprechend leistungsfähige Billigkameras. Die restliche Hardware des Geräts soll das Scannen von Büchern so einfach wie möglich machen und die vielfachen Probleme, die dabei auftreten können, im Zaum halten.

Die Technologie der *DIY Book Scanner* ist nicht für gewerbsmäßiges Scannen gedacht, sondern soll helfen, Bücher zu digitalisieren, wo herkömmliche Methoden zu teuer, unmöglich oder ungeeignet sind. Mit den Jahren haben wir erkannt, dass nicht jedes Zuhause einen Buchscanner benötigt, aber jeder braucht Zugang zu einem solchen. Bei der *DIY Book Scanner*-Community geht es um Zugang UND Besitz; jeder Hackerspace auf dieser Welt soll einen Buchscanner sein eigen nennen. Sie sollten idealerweise wie Bücher entlehnbar sein, damit man Bücher, die zu privat, zu wertvoll und zu persönlich sind, an einem Ort fernab der Öffentlichkeit scannen kann.

Aus dem Englischen von Michael Kaufmann

Hiroshi Ishiguro
Beicho Android

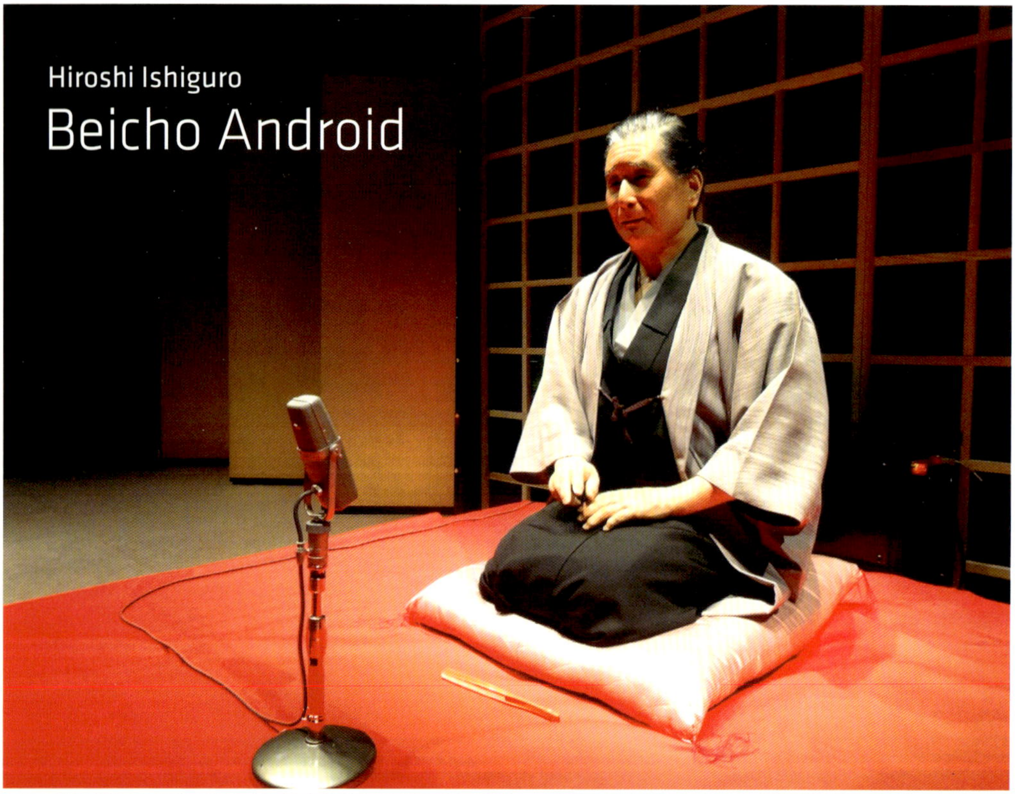

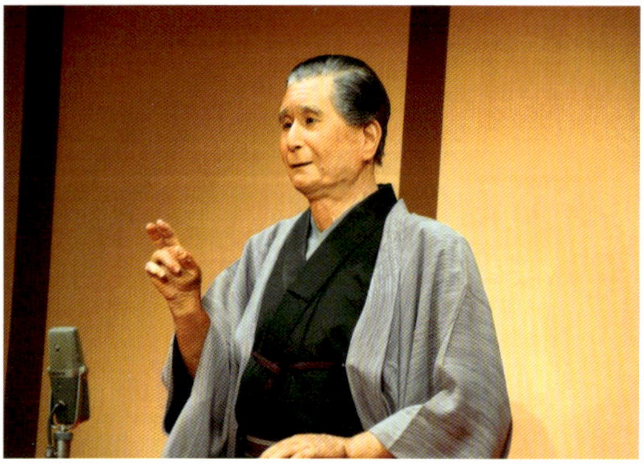

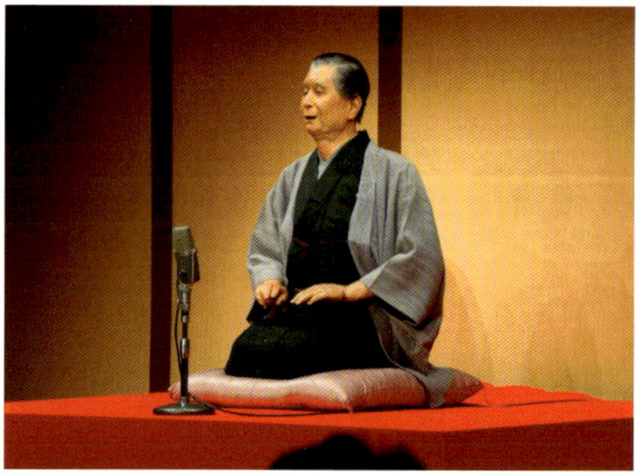

Japanese rakugo storyteller and "Living National Treasure" Beicho is immortalized by android technology.
Durch Androidentechnologie wurde der als „Lebender Nationalschatz" geltende japanische Rakugo-Erzähler Beicho unsterblich.

Beicho Katsura III is the most important performer alive of the traditional Japanese art of comic storytelling, *rakugo,* and the Japanese government bestowed him with the "Living National Treasure" title in 2012. However, Beicho is now an old man and can no longer perform... So his son, Yonedanji, Hiroshi Ishiguro (as representative of the creator team) and the sponsor, Breeze Arts Co., Ltd., decided to create an android copy of him, so that young people who have never seen Beicho perform can experience one of his professional performances. Video cannot convey the sensation of an actual human presence, but an android can indeed give the audience this experience.

There were three steps in the creative process. The first step was to scan Beicho's body using a laser scanner to obtain 3D data of his body. The second step was to develop and create his android based on the 3D data. However, the android was modeled on a younger version of Beicho in his fifties, when he was at the prime of his *rakugo* career. First we made a clay model of his face and then we made it younger by removing wrinkles and lifting the cheekbones. This is the Beicho people remember from his active storytelling days. The final step was to create the movement. But Beicho can no longer perform, so his son, Yonedanji, imitated his performance after studying videos of his father. We recorded the movement using a motion capture system and then programmed the android.

However memorable a professional artistic performance may be, someday it will be forgotten. But Beicho's performance will never be forgotten, as it is immortalized by his android counterpart, *Beicho Android.*

Developed by Hiroshi Ishiguro (Osaka University) and BREEZE ARTS CO., Ltd.

Beicho Katsura III ist der bedeutendste noch lebende Vertreter des *Rakugo,* der traditionellen japanischen Kunstform des Erzählens komischer Geschichten. Deshalb hat ihm die japanische Regierung den Titel „lebender Nationalschatz" verliehen.

Allerdings ist er schon in die Jahre gekommen und kann keine komischen Geschichten mehr vor Publikum erzählen... Daher besprachen sein Sohn Yonedanji, Hiroshi Ishiguro (als Vertreter des Entwicklungsteams) und der Sponsor Breeze Arts Co., Ltd. die Möglichkeit, einen Androiden zu entwickeln. Sie wollten diese außergewöhnlichen Darbietungen auch jungen Menschen zeigen, die sie noch nie gesehen hatten. Ein Video kann die Präsenz eines Menschen nicht ersetzen – aber ein Androide ist dazu imstande und kann dem Publikum die einzigartige Erfahrung einer solchen Performance näherbringen.

Die Herstellung umfasste drei Phasen. Im ersten Schritt wurde Beichos Körper mittels eines Laserscanners abgetastet, um dessen 3D-Daten zu erhalten. In der zweiten Stufe wurde aus den 3D-Daten der Androide modelliert, allerdings nach Beichos Aussehen in seinen Fünfzigern, am Höhepunkt seiner *Rakugo*-Karriere. Zuerst erstellten wir ein Tonmodell seines Gesichts, anschließend verjüngten wir es, indem wir Falten glätteten und die Wangen anhoben. So haben die Menschen Beicho, den Geschichtenerzähler, in Erinnerung.

In der letzten Phase mussten wir dem Androiden beibringen, wie er sich bewegt. Aber Beicho kann nicht mehr spielen. Daher ahmte sein Sohn Yonedanji ihn nach, indem er sich Videoaufzeichnungen von seinem Vater ansah. Wir haben die Bewegungsmuster per Motion-Capture-System aufgezeichnet und daraus die Bewegungen des Androiden programmiert.

Viele erinnern sich an beeindruckende Darbietungen von Künstlern, vergessen sie später aber dann doch. Beichos Erzählweise wird Unsterblichkeit erlangen, denn sein Androide wird sie immer wieder zum Besten geben.

Aus dem Englischen von Michael Kaufmann

Hiroto Ikeuchi

Fantasy Captured in Plastic Model: A Desk Diorama

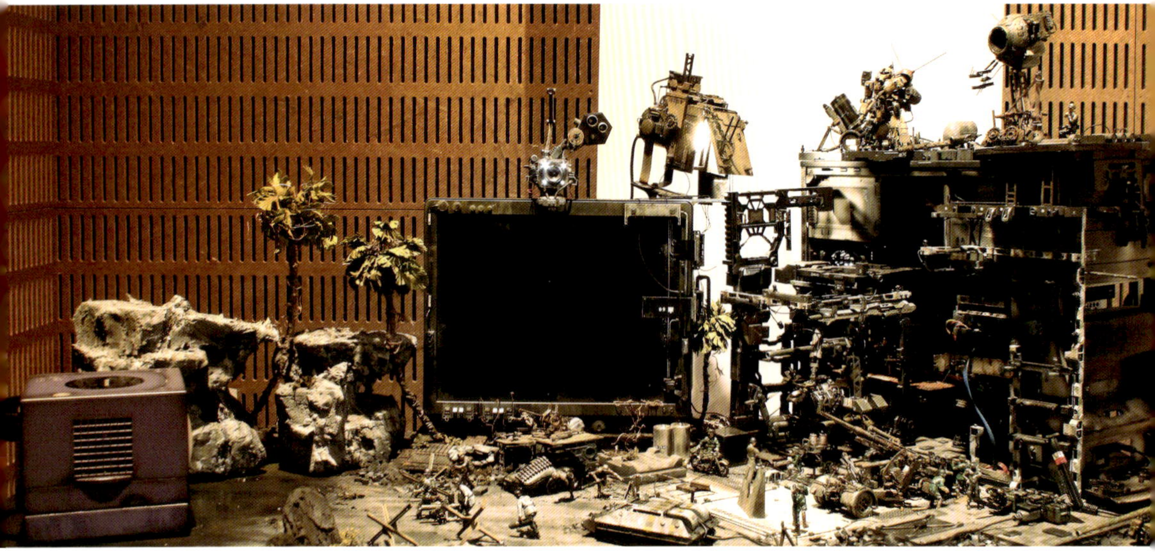

In the diorama you find what looks like a secret military base. But the scale is obviously different to that of the diorama world. Gradually people will notice that what looks like a building in the miniature diorama world is actually a PC, and that it is on a normal desk. The computer components have been transformed into buildings that are closely guarded by toy soldiers. The wiring and the electronic circuits are intact, so the equipment can still be used.

The theme of the diorama is "storage base". The armed plastic toy figures are there to protect a PC full of records and experiences, and so protect the author's memory, from hacking and computer regulations.

Das Diorama sieht nach einem geheimen Militärstützpunkt aus. Aber sein Maßstab passt nicht so richtig zur restlichen Welt des Dioramas. Allmählich erkennt man, dass es sich bei dem vermeintlichen Gebäude in der Miniaturwelt eigentlich um einen PC handelt, der auf einem ganz normalen Schreibtisch steht. Die verschiedenen Komponenten des Computers sind zu Bauten mutiert, die von Spielzeugsoldaten scharf bewacht werden. Die Verkabelung und die Schaltkreise sind intakt, so dass man den Rechner weiter benutzen kann.

Thema des Dioramas ist „das Depot". Die Spielzeugsoldaten bewachen einen PC voller Aufzeichnungen und Erfahrungen, beschützen also die Erinnerung des Autors vor Hackerangriffen und softwarebedingten Einschränkungen.

Aus dem Englischen von Wilfried Prantner

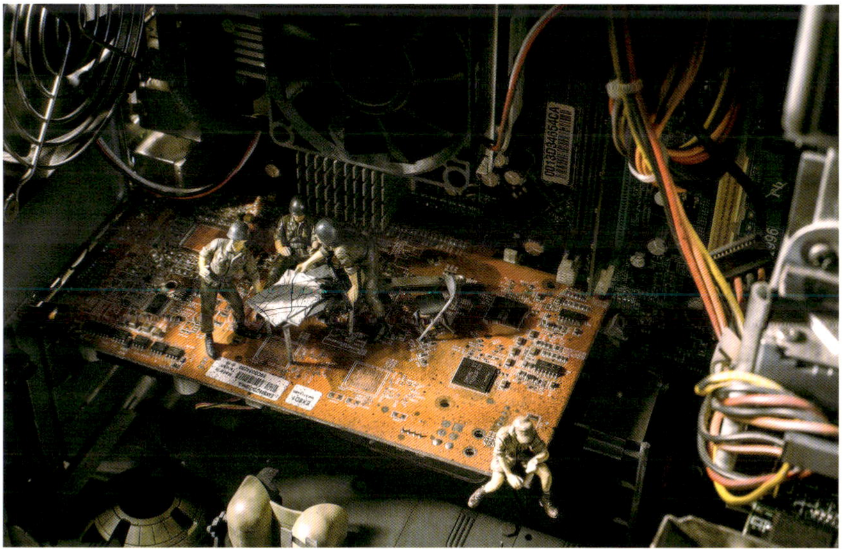

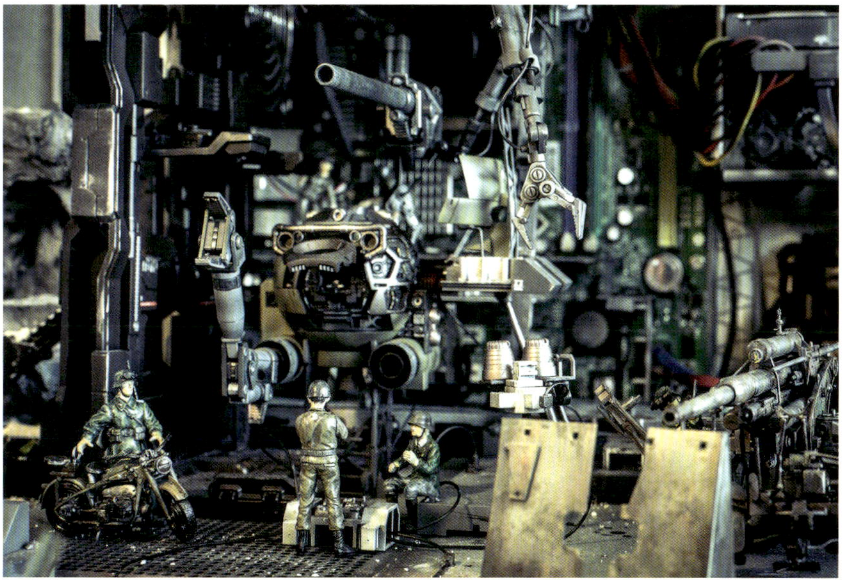

Doris Graf

Pikträt

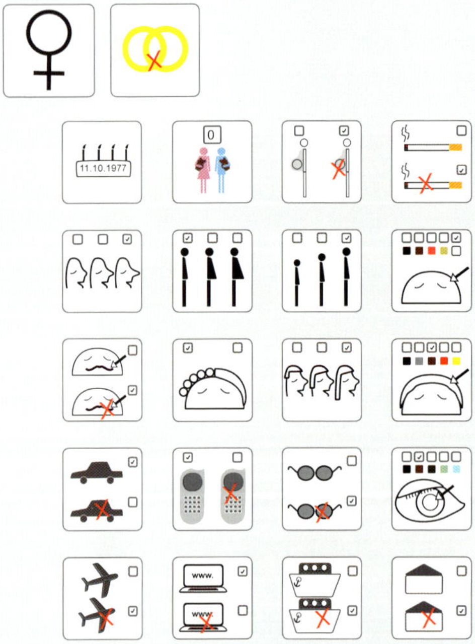

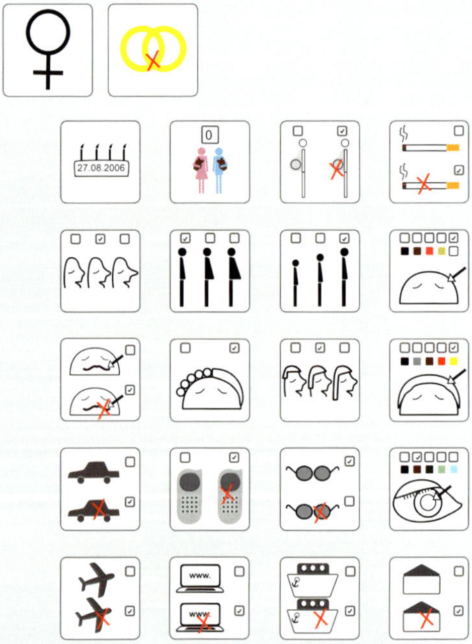

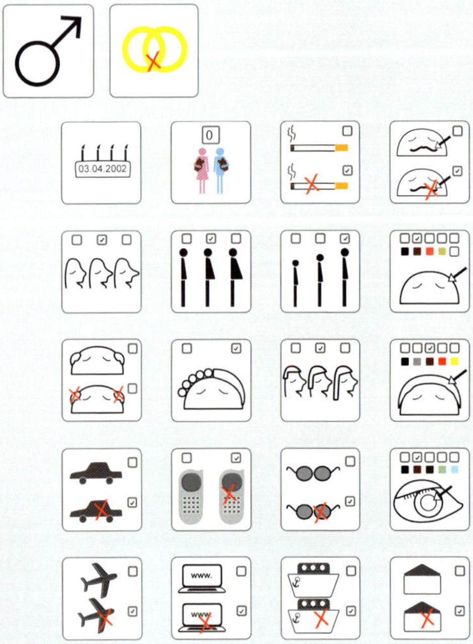

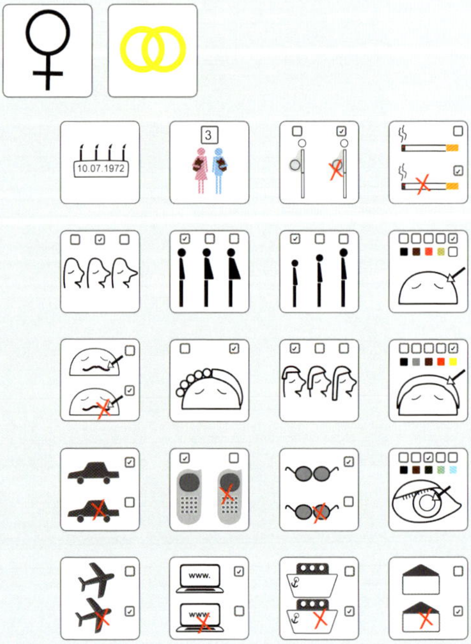

Pictures of the Disappearance of the Individual in Virtual Domains

Lots of networking enthusiasts who are active in the virtual spheres of Facebook, YouTube or Google regard this as a promising option to expand the reach of their own personality and the latitude of real life. That these activities are also accompanied by careless dealings with one's personal data and, in many cases, an almost obsessive urge to expose one's private affairs in public is only a part of the downside of a development that deeply concerns Doris Graf in these times of post-privacy. Topping her agenda, though, is an effort to use artistic means to unmask the empty promises of purported personality development. Let's face it: instead of diversity, internet users generally expect standardization and the reduction of individuality down to a few facts for the sake of economic utility.

This phenomenon is portrayed in especially vivid fashion by Doris Graf's *Pikträts,* standard-format computer printouts in which individuals' qualities and characteristics are visualized in the form of pictograms. The *Pikträts* are the visible end result of a process in which the artist simulates, so to speak, data acquisition methods used on the internet. In so-called Pikträt sessions, she questions her interviewees, gathering personal information about their physical attributes and character traits, family life and possessions, all of which she tallies on data sheets. Actually, this face-to-face encounter with the interviewer is designed to trigger a flash of awareness, as the interview subject is unexpectedly overcome by a feeling of reserve and caution, which is actually what's called for when that same person is confronted with the seemingly so straightforward, everyday questionnaires proffered by the industrious data collectors online.

Framed and arranged in rows and columns, an exhibition of *Pikträts* is a particularly striking illustration of the standardization mechanisms at work on the Web. The individual computer printouts do indeed differ in terms of their varying combination of pictograms; all the same, the overall visual impression they create is one of comparability and homogeneity of the personality profiles.

Bilder vom Verschwinden des Individuums in virtuellen Sphären

Als verheißungsvolle Option zur Erweiterung der eigenen Persönlichkeit und des realen Lebens empfinden es viele, die sich in den virtuellen Räumen von Facebook, YouTube oder Google tummeln. Dass damit auch der sorglose Umgang mit persönlichen Daten und vielfach der fast schon zwanghafte Drang zur Selbstentblößung einhergehen, ist nur eine der Schattenseiten der Entwicklung, die Doris Graf in Zeiten der Post-Privacy umtreiben. Vor allem aber ist ihr daran gelegen, mit künstlerischen Mitteln die leeren Versprechungen vorgeblicher Persönlichkeitsentfaltung zu entlarven. Denn anstelle von Vielfalt erwarten den Internetnutzer zumeist Standardisierung und die Reduktion von Individualität auf wenige Fakten zum Zwecke der ökonomischen Verwertbarkeit.

Besonders anschaulich greifbar wird das Phänomen in Doris Grafs *Pikträts* – DIN-A4-Computerausdrucke, in denen Eigenschaften und Charakteristika einzelner Personen in Form von Piktogrammen visualisiert werden. Die *Pikträts* sind das sichtbare Ergebnis eines Verfahrens, in dem die Künstlerin die Methoden der Datenerhebungen im Internet gleichsam simuliert. In sogenannten „Pikträtsitzungen" erfragt sie von ihrem Gegenüber persönliche Angaben zu körperlichen und charakterlichen Merkmalen ebenso wie zu Familien- und Besitzstand, die sie in Datenblättern erfasst. Es ist diese unmittelbare Begegnung mit der Interviewerin, die idealerweise den Prozess des Bewusstwerdens in Gang setzt: Unerwartet beschleicht den Befragten jenes Gefühl der Scheu und Vorsicht, das eigentlich geboten wäre, wenn man sich den so nüchtern anmutenden Formularen der fleißigen Datensammler im Internet anvertraut.

In der Zusammenschau der gerahmten und in Reih und Glied arrangierten *Pikträts* werden die Standardisierungsmechanismen des Internet besonders augenfällig. Die einzelnen Computerausdrucke unterscheiden sich zwar in der variierenden Kombination von Piktogrammen, der visuelle Gesamteindruck ist aber der von Vergleichbarkeit und Homogenität der Persönlichkeitsprofile.

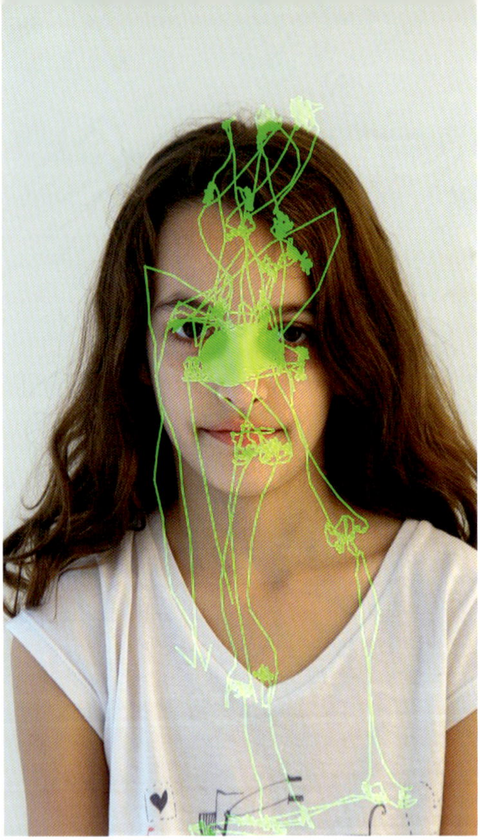

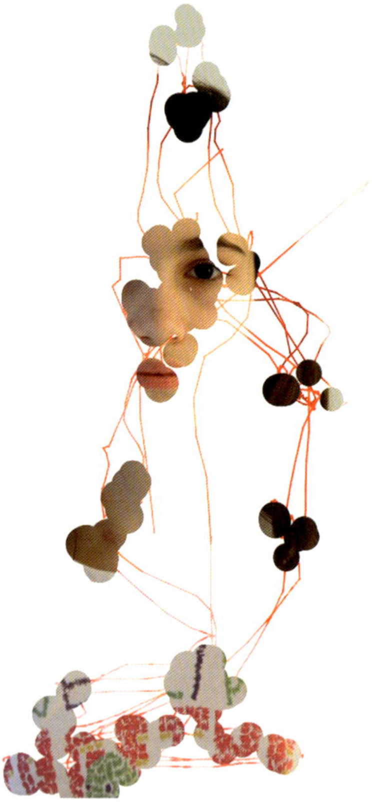

Mariano Sardón, Mariano Sigman

The Table of Gazes

The Table of Gazes is a project that relates art and neuroscience. It consists of a table with several screens on which visitors can see how images of portraits are created over time by the gazes of Ars Electronica Festival visitors. The visitors can participate in two ways: their gaze can be captured by the eye tracker experimental setup or they can contribute a portrait picture of themselves.

Participants sit in front of a screen that shows images of portraits for several seconds. An eye tracker device follows the movement of their eyes, locating the places on the image where the eyes rest for a while ("fixations"), and their trajectories ("saccades").

The gaze of the people who participate in the experiment are recorded and stored. Numerous visitors view the same portraits time and time again and each particular "gaze tour" is added to those of previous participants.

The trajectories of the eyes on a portrait of all viewers are added together and then visualized on the

The Table of Gazes ist ein Projekt, das Kunst und Neurowissenschaft verbindet. Auf einem Tisch mit mehreren Screens kann man verfolgen, wie durch die Blicke der Ars-Electronica-Besucher nach und nach Porträts aufgebaut werden. Besucher können auf zweierlei Weise an dem Projekt teilnehmen: indem sie mit der experimentellen Eyetracking-Vorrichtung andere betrachten oder indem sie das eigene Gesicht als Porträt zur Verfügung stellen.

Die Teilnehmer sitzen vor einem Bildschirm, auf dem sie jeweils einige Sekunden lang verschiedene Porträts zu sehen bekommen. Eine Eyetracking-Vorrichtung erfasst ihre Augenbewegungen und zeichnet ihre Fixationen (das Verweilen des Blicks auf bestimmten Stellen) und Sakkaden (rasche Blickbewegungen) auf. Auf diese Weise werden die Blickbahnen aller an dem Experiment teilnehmenden Personen aufgezeichnet und gespeichert. Jedes Porträt wird also immer wieder von neuen Personen betrachtet und jede Blickbahn denen der früheren Teilnehmer hinzugefügt. Die Blickbahnen aller Betrachter auf dem jeweiligen Porträt

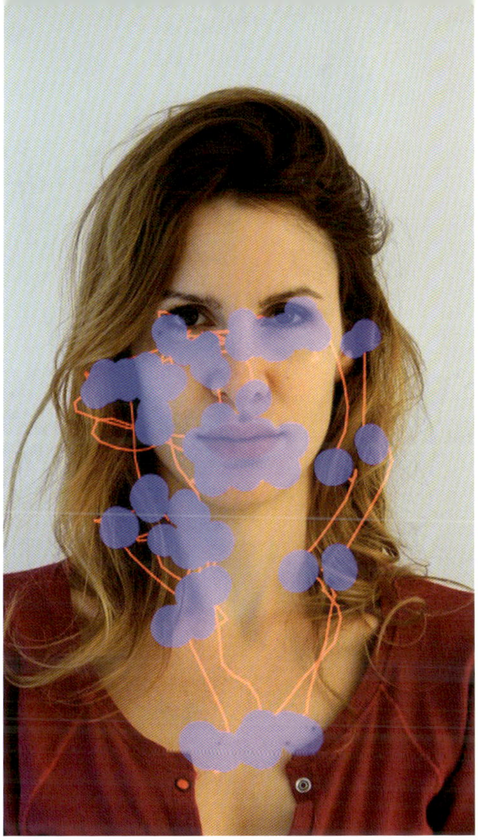

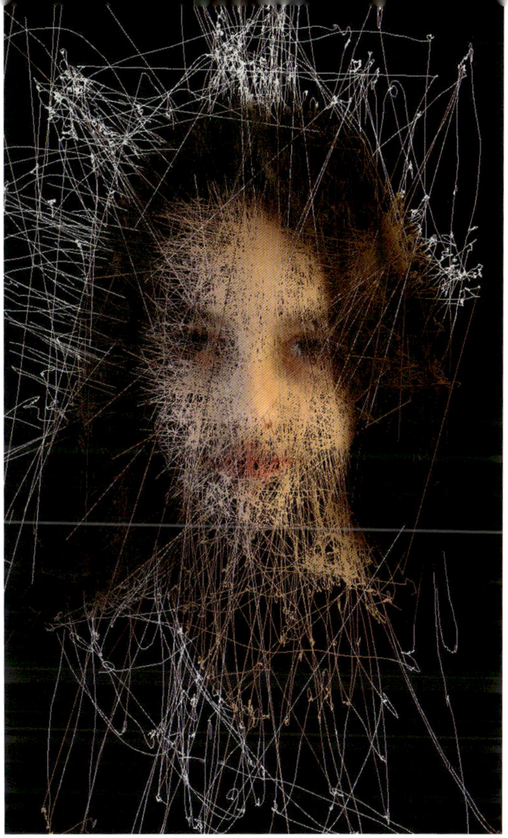

screens in *The Table of Gazes*. The generated image shows the way the face is uncovered by the gazes of many people at the same time.

The Table of Gazes aims to engage people with those parts of a portrait that are really seen and with those parts that remain "unseen" while attention is focused elsewhere on the portrait.

The project investigates what we see and what we focus on when we create our own image of a person. The countenance and hence the identity result from the combined gazes of many different visitors.

The act of "looking at" something reflects a particular way of interacting with the world and with other people, and in this sense it can be understood as being characteristic of a particular time in human history. For this reason, day after day, a large database of visitors' gazes at portraits will be generated as a memory collection of gazes that reflect a particular aspect of our times.

Electronic Art Degree Universidad Nacional de Tres de Febrero, Buenos Aires – Integrative Neuroscience Laboratory, Universidad de Buenos Aires
Team: Germán Ito, Ivan Lengyel, Laila Kazimierski
Acknowledgment: Joaquín Ais

werden übereinander gelegt und auf den Bildschirmen am „Tisch der Blicke" dargestellt. Das so generierte Bild zeigt, wie das Gesicht nach und nach von mehreren Personen „freigelegt" wird.

The Table of Gazes inspiriert die Besucher, sich damit auseinanderzusetzen, welche Teile eines Gesichts wirklich gesehen und welche ausgeblendet werden, wenn wir andere betrachten. Das Projekt erkundet, was wir sehen und worauf wir achten, wenn wir uns ein Bild von einer Person machen. Das Gesicht einer Person, und damit ihre Identität, kommt durch die Blicke vieler zustande.

Der Vorgang des „Blickens" steht für eine bestimmte Art der Interaktion mit der Welt und mit anderen und kann insofern als ein epochentypisches Merkmal betrachtet werden. Wenn wir daher die Blicke, die die Besucher Tag für Tag über die Porträts schweifen lassen, in einer großen Datenbank sammeln, generieren wir damit auch eine Art Blickgedächtnis, ein spezifisches Residuum unserer Zeit.

Aus dem Englischen von Wilfried Prantner

http://marianosardon.com.ar
http://neurociencia.df.uba.ar/

Benjamin Pollach

The World Map Archive

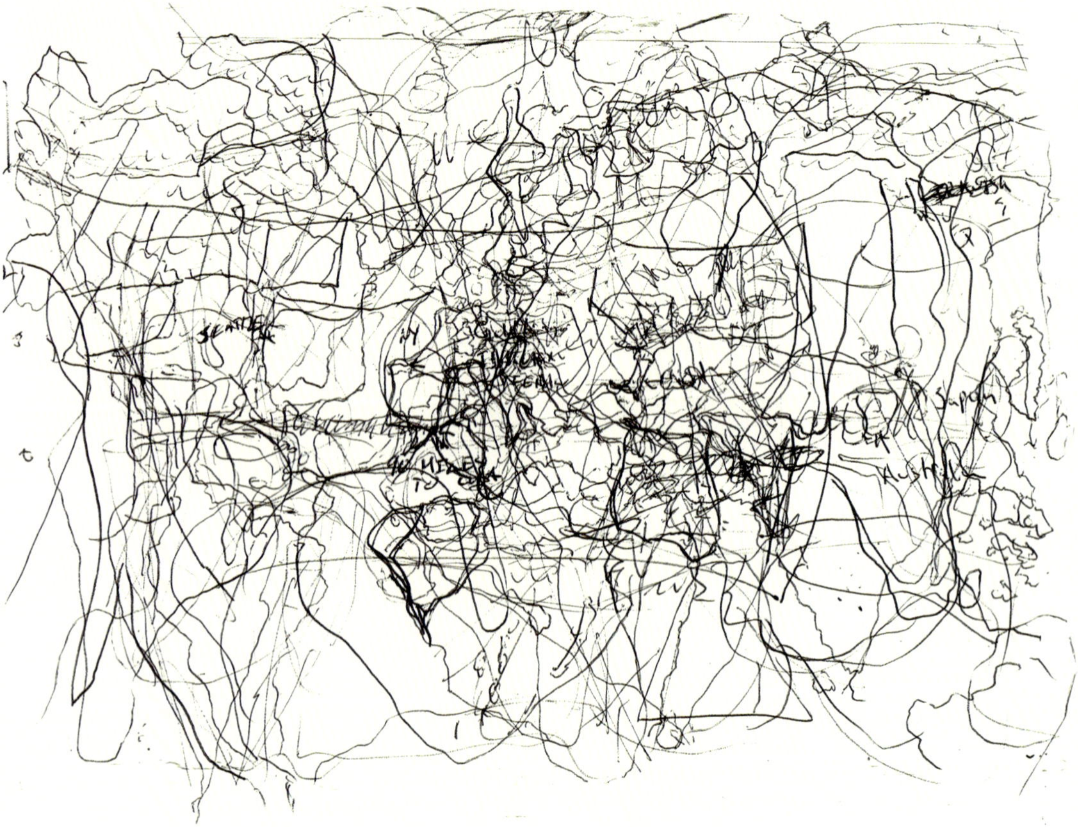

The *World Map Archive* is the only—and therefore also the biggest—archive for first-try world mappings.

What started as a mere doodle many years ago, when founder Benjamin Pollach sketched a world map on a napkin, has since grown into an ever expanding collection of such maps from all over the globe. Friends and friends of friends from such far-flung places as Peru, Mexico, California, Germany, Bangladesh, Ireland and New York have already participated and contributed their first-try maps to the *World Map Archive.*

Das *World Map Archive* ist das einzige und damit größte Archiv für erste Versuche von Zeichnungen der Weltkarte.

Vor vielen Jahren von Benjamin Pollach ins Leben gerufen, sind mittlerweile viele Weltkarten aus aller Welt, zum Beispiel aus Peru, Bangladesch, Mexiko und Kalifornien eingetroffen, die jetzt der Öffentlichkeit präsentiert werden sollen.

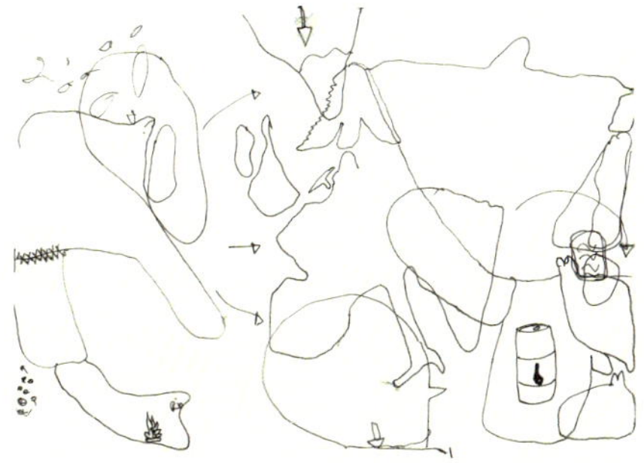

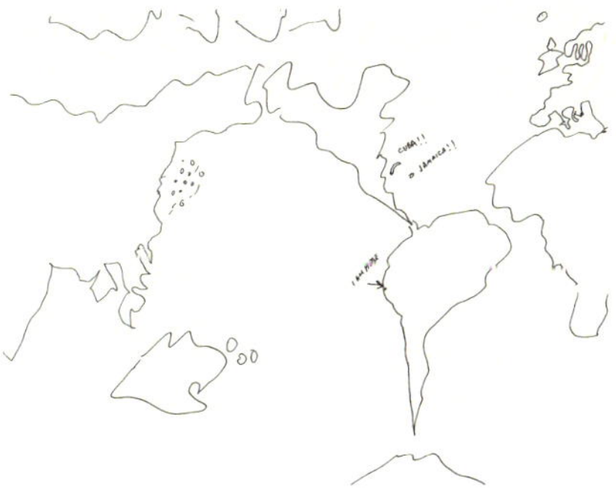

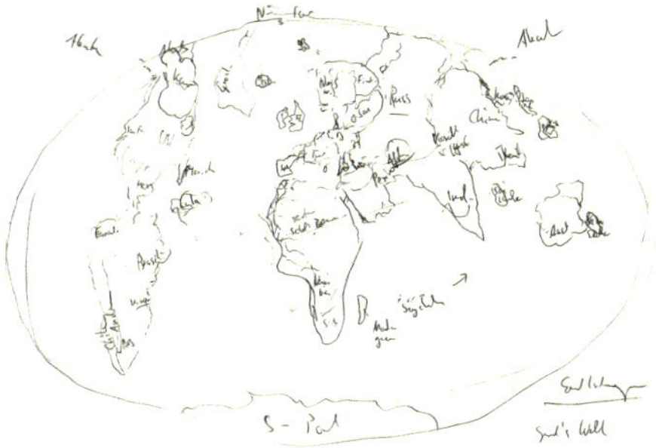

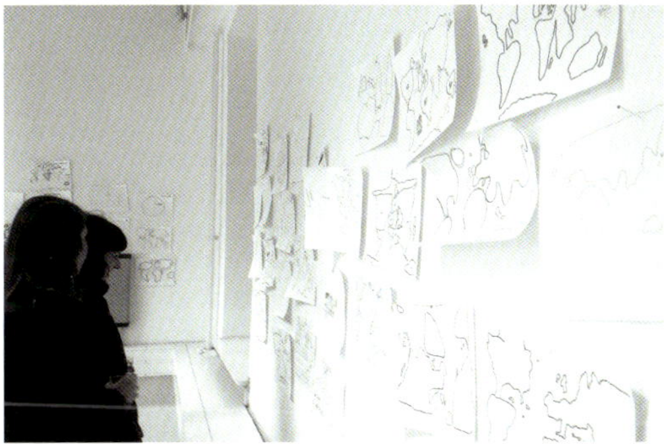

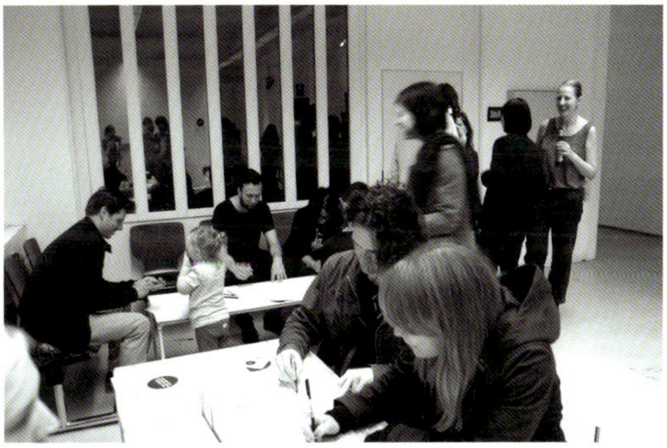

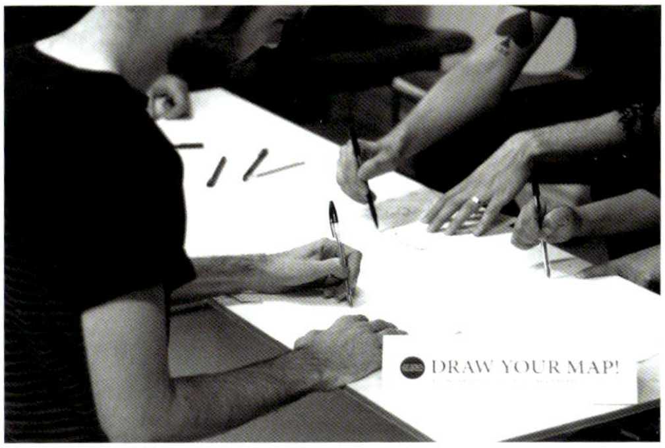

Despite all being maps of the world, each map is unique. As the World Map Archive grows, it becomes more and more apparent just how different people's perception of the world is. The ultimate goal of this project is to collect a first-try sketch of the world map from every world citizen. The Archive is planning on releasing volume 1 of this collected material to date in book form by Winter 2013, with proceeds going to help an educational organization.

Nachdem bis jetzt hauptsächlich nur Freunde und Bekannte beteiligt waren, soll nun jeder Weltbürger eine Karte beisteuern. Je größer das Archiv wird, umso deutlicher wird, wie unterschiedlich die Welt gesehen wird. Keine Karte gleicht der anderen!
Aus dem Archiv soll im Winter 2013 ein Buch entstehen, mit dessen Ertrag verschiedene Bildungsprojekte unterstützt werden sollen.

http://www.worldmaparchive.com

Theresa Schubert

bodymetries

mapping the human body through amorphous intelligence

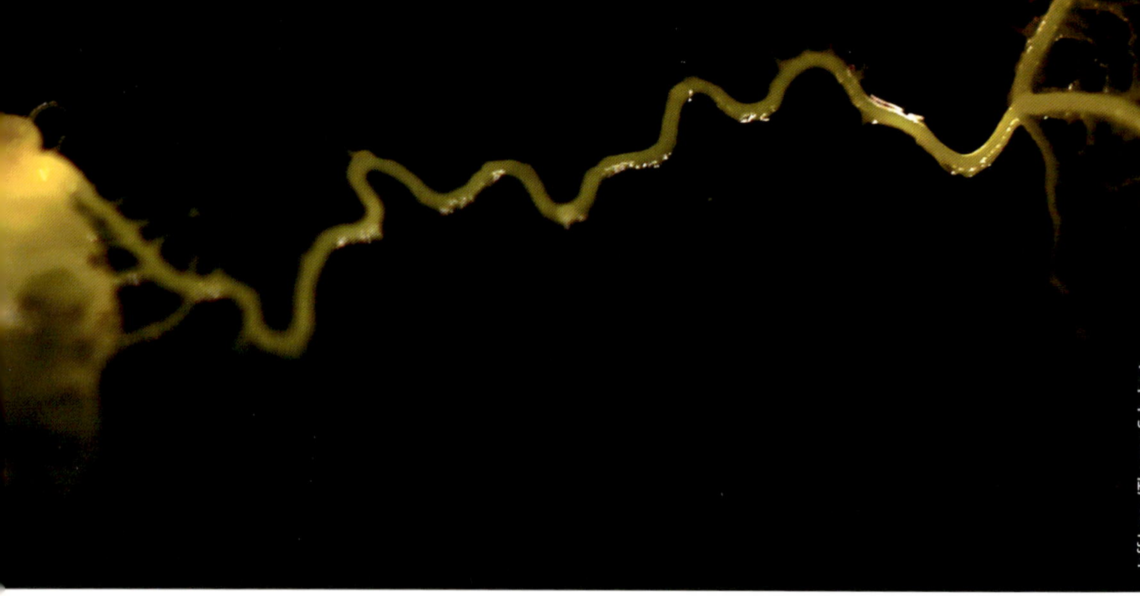

Jeff Jones/Theresa Schubert

bodymetries explores possibilities of mapping the human body using the spatial logic of the acellular slime mold *Physarum polycephalum*. It is a generative projection environment and interactive application for body-morphology computation based on the behavior of this amorphous organism.
Skin is the largest perceptual organ of our body, which marks the frontier between the inner and the outer world. Skin is more than a mere surface, it is also an interface that connects and communicates. Inspired by Marshall McLuhan's vision of the human body as "a laboratory for experiments" (*Culture is our Business*, 1970), *bodymetries* re-maps configurations of melanin spots to the protoplasmic network of *Physarum*.
The genesis of melanin spots is governed by interplay between melanin concentrations, innervation and immune system. Based on a series of lab experiments, this interaction was imitated with the living organism *P. polycephalum*. A multi-agent framework for network visualizations simulates slime mold behavior rules and human body morphology. *Physarum* is an experimental substrate for network optimization and an "agent" for solving

Das Projekt *bodymetries* untersucht Kartographien des menschlichen Körpers, die mit der räumlichen Logik des azellulären Schleimpilz *Physarum polycephalum* in Beziehung gesetzt werden. Es ist eine generative Projektionsumgebung mit Computersimulationen, die auf dem Verhalten dieses amorphen Organismus basieren, und eine interaktive Anwendung für die Berechnung von Körpermorphologien.
Haut ist das größte Wahrnehmungsorgan unseres Körpers. Sie markiert die Grenze zwischen innerer und äußerer Welt, aber ändert sich auch im Laufe der Zeit. Haut ist mehr als eine bloße Oberfläche, sie ist auch Schnittstelle, die verbindet und kommuniziert. Inspiriert von McLuhans Vision des menschlichen Körpers als „Labor für Experimente" (*Culture is Our Business*, 1970), ordnet *bodymetries* Konfigurationen von Leberflecken dem protoplasmischen Gewebe von *Physarum* zu. Aus Sicht von *P. polycephalum* besteht die Welt aus positiven und negativen Reizen. Er reagiert auf bestimmte Stimuli ähnlich wie die menschliche Haut, z. B. bei Schäden durch übermäßige Sonneneinstrahlung. Leberflecke entstehen durch das Zusammenwirken von Pigmentkonzentration, Innervation und Immunsystem. Basierend auf Laborexperimenten

geometrical problems using distributive law. It sees the world as attractants and repellents, providing an experimental analogue for many abstract and physical models. It reacts to stimuli similarly to human skin, e.g. damage by excessive sun exposure = negative phototaxis.
In *bodymetries* visitors can interact with the model by adding moles and other parameters, thus determining the morphology of the generative mesh. Parameters are fed into the simulation engine, which learns the structure of the environment and integrates it into a communal network of participants. The project applies a different method of de-centralized cell organization to the human body by letting people be involved in the morphogenesis of *Physarum polycephalum* and melanin spots. It challenges the way we perceive our bodies through bio-inspired computing.

wurde diese Interaktion mit dem lebenden Organismus *P. polycephalum* imitiert. Er ist ein experimentelles Substrat für Netzwerkoptimierung und ein „Agent“, um geometrische Probleme distributiv zu lösen. Daraus entstehende Algorithmen eines Multi-Agent-Frameworks simulieren Verhaltensregeln des Einzellers und visualisieren Körperstrukturen.
In *bodymetries* können Besucher mit dem Modell durch die Eingabe von Pigmentierungen und anderen Parametern interagieren und so die Morphologie des generativen Netzwerks bestimmen. Die Parameter werden der Simulation hinzugefügt, die die Struktur der Umgebung lernt und diese in ein gemeinsames Netz der Teilnehmer integriert. Das Projekt überträgt eine alternative Methode der dezentralen Zellorganisation auf den menschlichen Körper und hinterfragt die Art, wie wir unseren Körper wahrnehmen.

Collaborators: Moritz Dreßler, Michael Markert, Jeff Jones, Karthik Revendraan, David Stolarsky
Scientific Advisor: Andrew Adamatzky
Partly supported by EU research project *PhyChip: Growing Computers from Slime Mould* (FP7 ICT Ref 316366) and Kreativfonds Bauhaus-Universität Weimar.

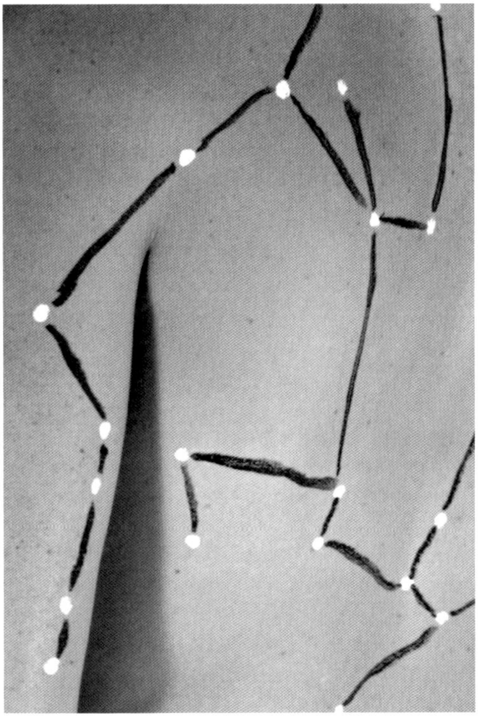

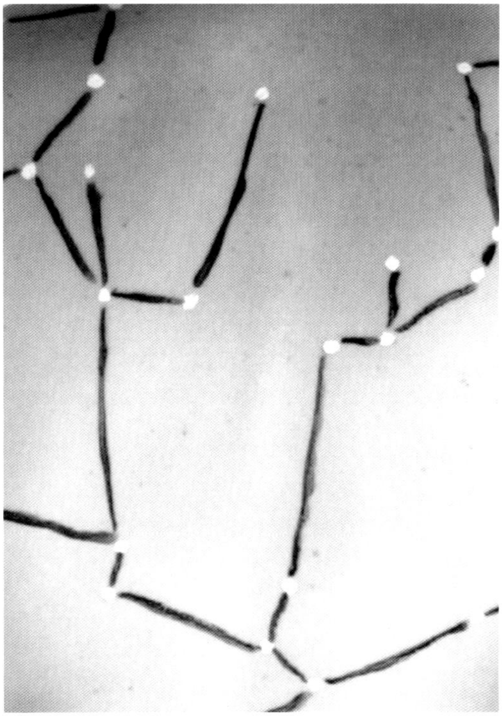

Andy Adamatzky/Theresa Schubert

Heather Dewey-Hagborg

Stranger Visions

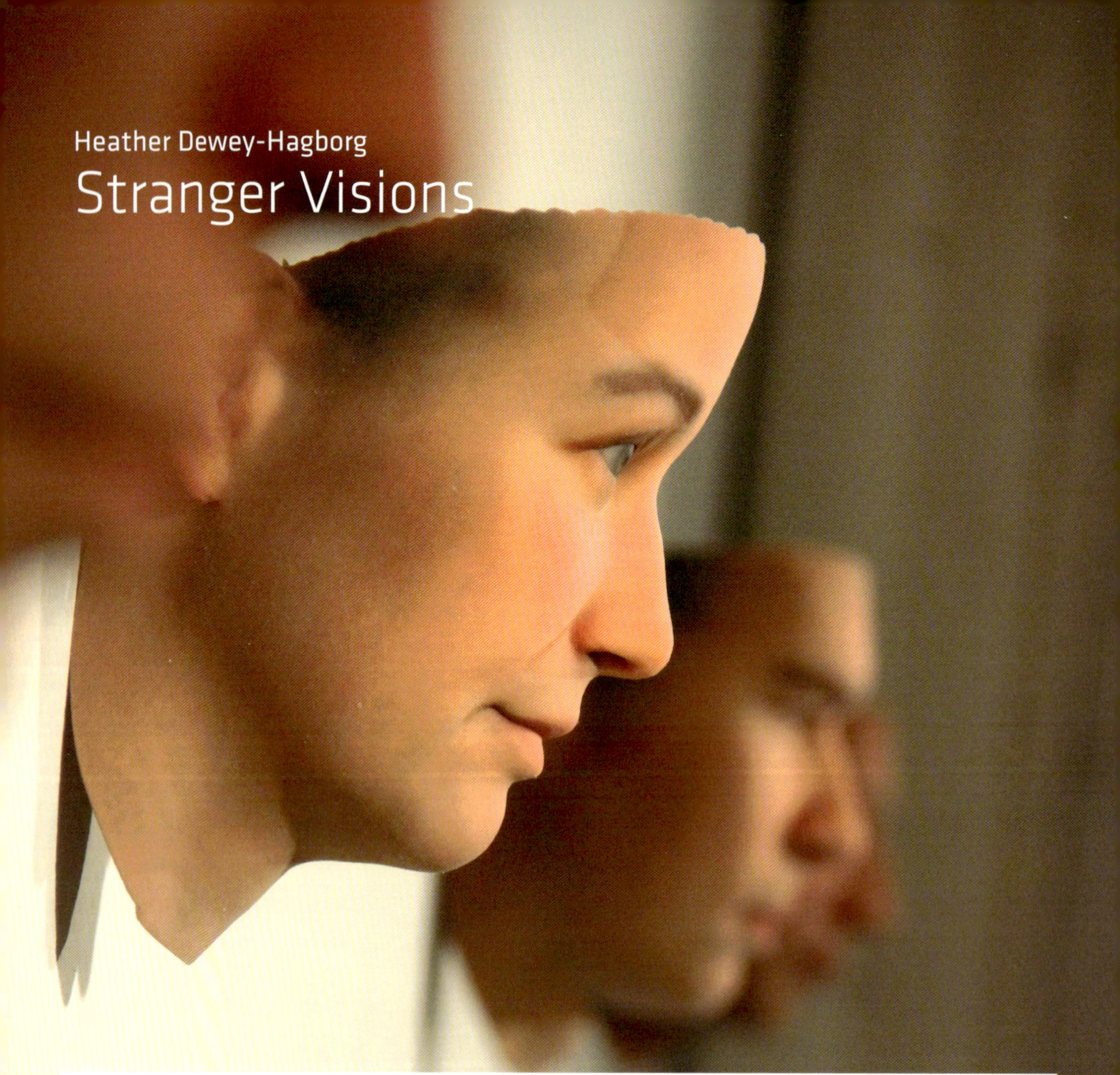

In my artwork *Stranger Visions* I create portrait sculptures from analyses of genetic material collected in public spaces. Working with artifacts that strangers unwittingly leave behind, this work demonstrates the possible future of forensic DNA phenotyping (determining appearance from DNA), and points to the emerging privacy issues related to the increasing accessibility and decreasing costs of biotechnology.

Much of my work begins with a question. In past works I have asked questions about language, AI, creativity and machines. The question behind *Stranger Visions* came to me as I was sitting in a therapy session, ostensibly with the purpose of introspecting and reflecting on myself. Staring at a generic print on the wall, I noticed that the glass covering the print was

Im Rahmen meines Kunstprojekts *Stranger Visions* gestalte ich Porträtskulpturen aus Analysen genetischen Materials, das ich im öffentlichen Raum gesammelt habe. Die Arbeit mit Fundstücken, mit Dingen, die Fremde ungewollt zurücklassen, verweist auf die mögliche Zukunft der forensischen DNA-Phänotypisierung (Bestimmung der Erscheinungsbilds durch die DNA) und wirft Fragen zum Schutz der Privatsphäre auf, die sich mit der wachsenden Zugänglichkeit zur Biotechnologie und deren sinkenden Kosten stellen.

Fragen bilden den Ausgangspunkt vieler meiner Arbeiten – früher etwa zur Sprache, zur Künstlichen Intelligenz, zur Kreativität und zu Maschinen. Die Frage, von der *Stranger Visions* ausgeht, kam mir in den Sinn, als ich – vorgeblich zum Zweck der Selbsterkundung – bei einem Therapeuten war. Als

cracked and in that crack was lodged a single hair. I became fascinated by this hair. Who did it belong to? What did they look like? How did they act? What did they think about? How much could I find out about a person from a single hair? I became entranced by this question of what I could learn about a person from a carelessly shed hair—like a detective story unfolding before me. On my way home that afternoon I began to notice all these genetic artifacts, all these *clues*, littered on the sidewalks, subway benches and streets. It occurred to me that if I could extract DNA from these kinds of items, I would have a pretty good indication as to who left them.
So I began collecting "samples"—traces of human DNA that I found on my travels. I brought the samples into a lab and performed DNA extraction. I amplify certain regions of the DNA using a technique called PCR—Polymerase Chain Reaction. This allows me to study certain regions of the genome that tend to vary from person to person, known as SNPs or Single Nucleotide Polymorphisms. I determine what allele is present for a particular SNP on each sample, and then feed this information into a custom computer program I wrote which takes all these values that correlate with physical genetic traits and parameterizes a 3D model of a face to represent them. I export the model and send it to a rapid prototyping machine that prints the model in full color 3D.
It is important to remember that this is art, not the development of a new product or company.
Stranger Visions is meant as a provocation, a confrontation of the viewer with the possibility that someone might be able to examine their DNA, inspect their identity, from detritus they didn't even notice that they had left behind. The point isn't that I know *everything* about a person from a piece of chewing gum, rather that I, an amateur, know as much as I do. And I can potentially find out a whole lot more.

Supported by: Eyebeam, Genspace, Clocktower Gallery

ich einen dieser 08/15-Drucke an der Wand anstarrte, bemerkte ich, dass das Glas, das ihn schützte, einen Sprung hatte, aus dem ein einzelnes Haar hing. Dieses Haar faszinierte mich. Wessen Haar war es? Wie könnte die Person, der es gehörte, aussehen, handeln, denken? Wie viel kann man ausgehend von einem Haar über eine Person wissen?
Wie ein Detektiv in einem Kriminalroman war ich von der Frage besessen, was ich durch ein achtlos zurückgelassenes Haar über eine Person erfahren könnte. Als ich an diesem Nachmittag nach Hause ging, fielen mir plötzlich all diese genetischen Fundstücke auf, all diese „Indizien", die auf Gehsteigen, Straßen, auf Bänken in der U-Bahn herumlagen. Es kam mir der Gedanke, dass ich einen ziemlich guten Anhaltspunkt hätte, von wem diese Dinge stammen, wenn ich die DNA aus ihnen extrahieren könnte.
So begann ich „Proben" zu sammeln – Spuren menschlicher DNA, die ich auf meinen Reisen fand. Diese Proben bringe ich dann in ein Labor und nehme eine DNA-Extraktion vor. Ich vergrößere bestimmte Regionen der DNA mithilfe einer Technik namens Polymerase-Kettenreaktion. Auf diese Weise kann ich bestimmte Regionen des Genoms studieren, die gewöhnlich von Person zu Person variieren: die sogenannten Einzelnukleotid-Polymorphismen (SNP). Ich bestimme, welches Allel für einen bestimmten SNP in jeder Probe vorhanden ist und gebe diese Information in eine spezielle selbst programmierte Software ein, die alle mit physischen genetischen Zügen korrelierenden Werte erfasst und ein 3D-Modell eines Gesichts parametriert. Dieses Modell exportiere ich und schicke es an eine Rapid-Prototyping-Maschine, die das Modell in 3D und Farbe ausdruckt.
Zu beachten ist, dass es sich bei alldem um Kunst handelt und nicht um die Entwicklung eines neuen Produkts oder eines Unternehmens.
Stranger Visions ist als Provokation gedacht, die den Betrachter mit der Möglichkeit konfrontiert, dass man aus achtlos zurückgelassenen Überbleibseln seine DNA entnehmen und damit seine Identität entschlüsseln könnte. Es geht darum, dass ich aus einem Stück Kaugummi *alles* über eine Person erfahren kann und nicht auf mein Wissen und meine Wahrnehmung beschränkt bin. Und theoretisch lässt sich noch viel mehr herausfinden.

Aus dem Englischen von Martina Bauer

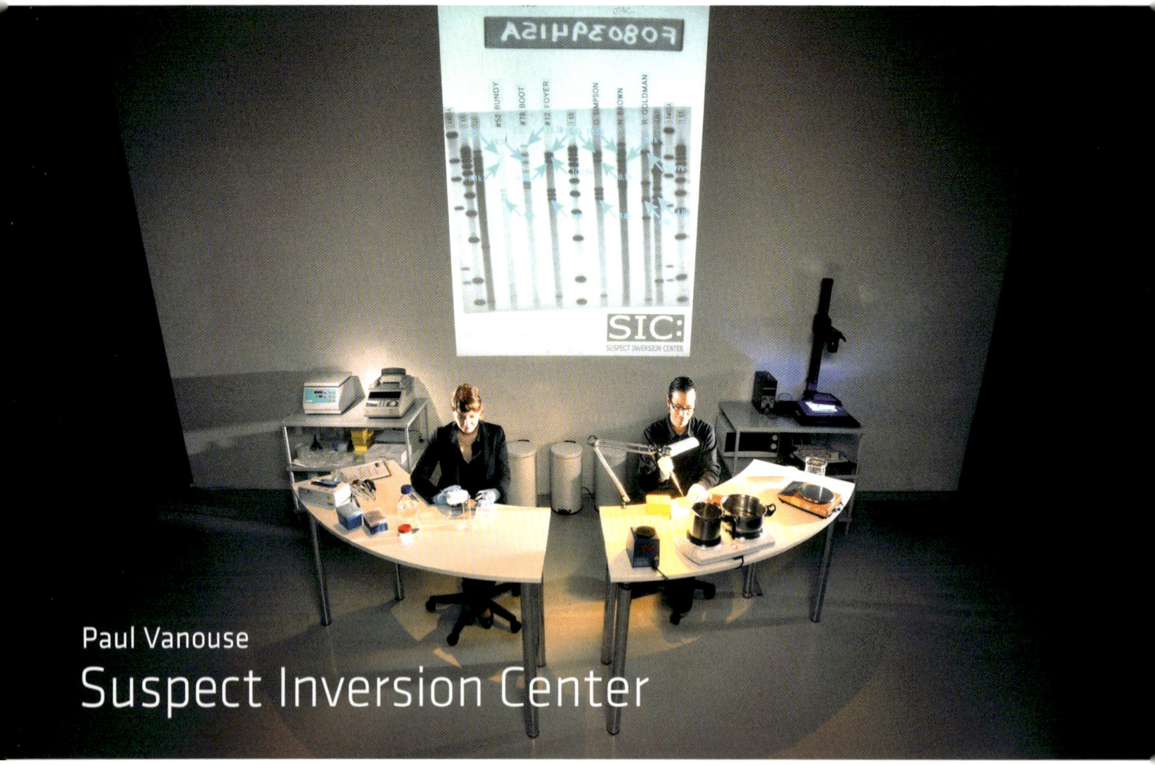

Paul Vanouse

Suspect Inversion Center

Suspect Inversion Center (SIC) is an open working laboratory where artist Paul Vanouse and assistant Kerry Sheehan recreate DNA evidence from the 1995 O. J. Simpson murder trial: using the artist's own DNA. The installation consists of semicircular lab tables and shelves containing all the necessary equipment to perform the activities of the *Suspect Inversion Center.* Vanouse and Sheehan continuously perform the work, during daily gallery operations, witnessed by visitors to the exhibition. When the work is complete and the original DNA image has been reasonably accurately reproduced, the "reverse-engineered" copy and the original are displayed side by side, along with the full chemical "recipes" used to create the images. SIC invites the audience to observe each step of the laboratory process and interact with the experimenters. After more than two years of working to reproduce this

Das *Suspect Inversion Center* (SIC) ist ein offenes Arbeitslabor, in dem der Künstler Paul Vanouse und seine Assistentin Kerry Sheehan DNA-Beweismaterial vom Mordprozess gegen O. J. Simpson aus dem Jahr 1995 nachbilden – und zwar aus der DNA des Künstlers. Die Installation besteht aus zwei halbkreisförmig angeordneten Labortischen und Regalen mit allen notwendigen Utensilien für die Tätigkeit des *Suspect Inversion Center*. Vanouse und Sheehan gehen während der gesamten Galerieöffnungszeiten unter den Augen des Publikums ihrer Arbeit nach. Ist diese abgeschlossen und das Bild der Original-DNA einigermaßen genau rekonstruiert, werden die nachgebaute Kopie und das Original nebeneinander ausgestellt, zusammen mit den chemischen „Rezepten" zur Erzeugung dieser Bilder. Das SIC lädt das Publikum ein, sämtliche Schritte der Laborarbeit mitzuverfolgen und mit den Experimentatoren zu interagieren. Nach image the first success took place in March 2013. We will be continuing this month to make additional reproductions with alternate imaging technologies, with the aim of improving even further—I will be posting these on the website.

In *Suspect Inversion Center,* Vanouse is not simply making his DNA look like the original suspect DNA, but using his own DNA to recreate an entire historical DNA document by scrutinizing every component of the authoritative DNA artifact. The history of art is replete with such intentional reproduction: from students' copying a master's painting, to art forgeries, to pop and postmodern appropriation, but of course each has radically different connotations and effects upon the "original".

http://www.paulvanouse.com/sic.html

Honorary Mention Hybrid Art, Prix Ars Electronica 2013

über zwei Jahren Arbeit an der Reproduktion dieses Bildes hat sich nun im März 2013 ein erster Erfolg eingestellt. Wir wollen weitere Reproduktionen mit anderen Bildgebungsverfahren herstellen und noch bessere Ergebnisse erzielen, die wir dann auf der Website veröffentlichen .

Mit dem *Suspect Inversion Center* verleiht Vanouse seiner DNA nicht nur das Aussehen der ursprünglichen DNA des mutmaßlichen Täters, sondern bildet mit ihr das gesamte historische DNA-Dokument nach, wobei er jede Komponente des offiziellen DNA-Artefakts einer genauen Prüfung unterzieht. Die Geschichte der Kunst ist voll von solchen bewussten Reproduktionen: von Kopien alter Meister zu Studienzwecken, über Kunstfälschungen bis zu den Appropriationen der Pop Art und der Postmoderne, die natürlich alle ganz anders konnotiert sind und sich ganz unterschiedlich auf das „Original" auswirken.

Aus dem Englischen von Wilfried Prantner

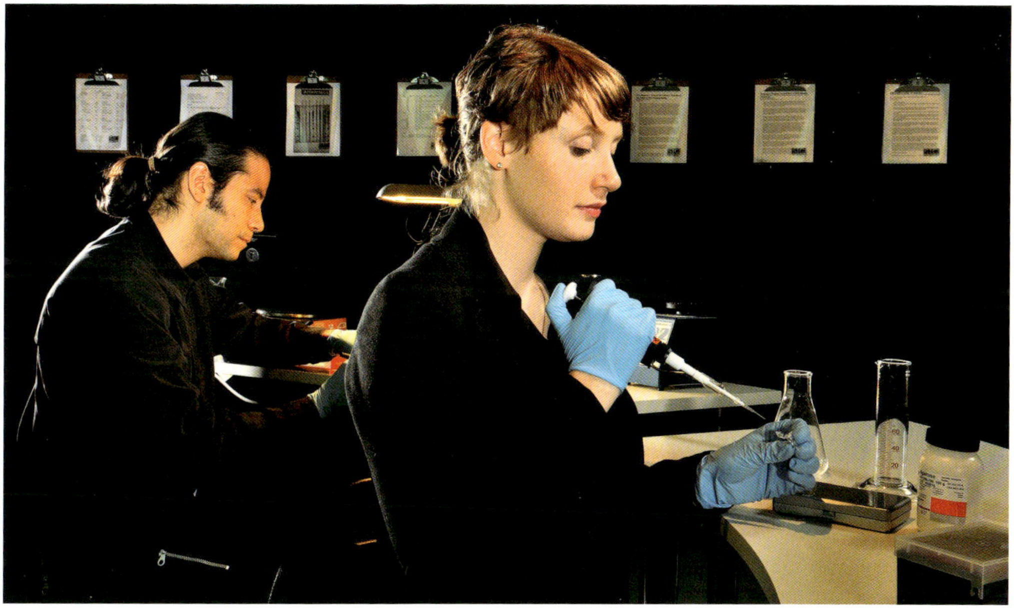

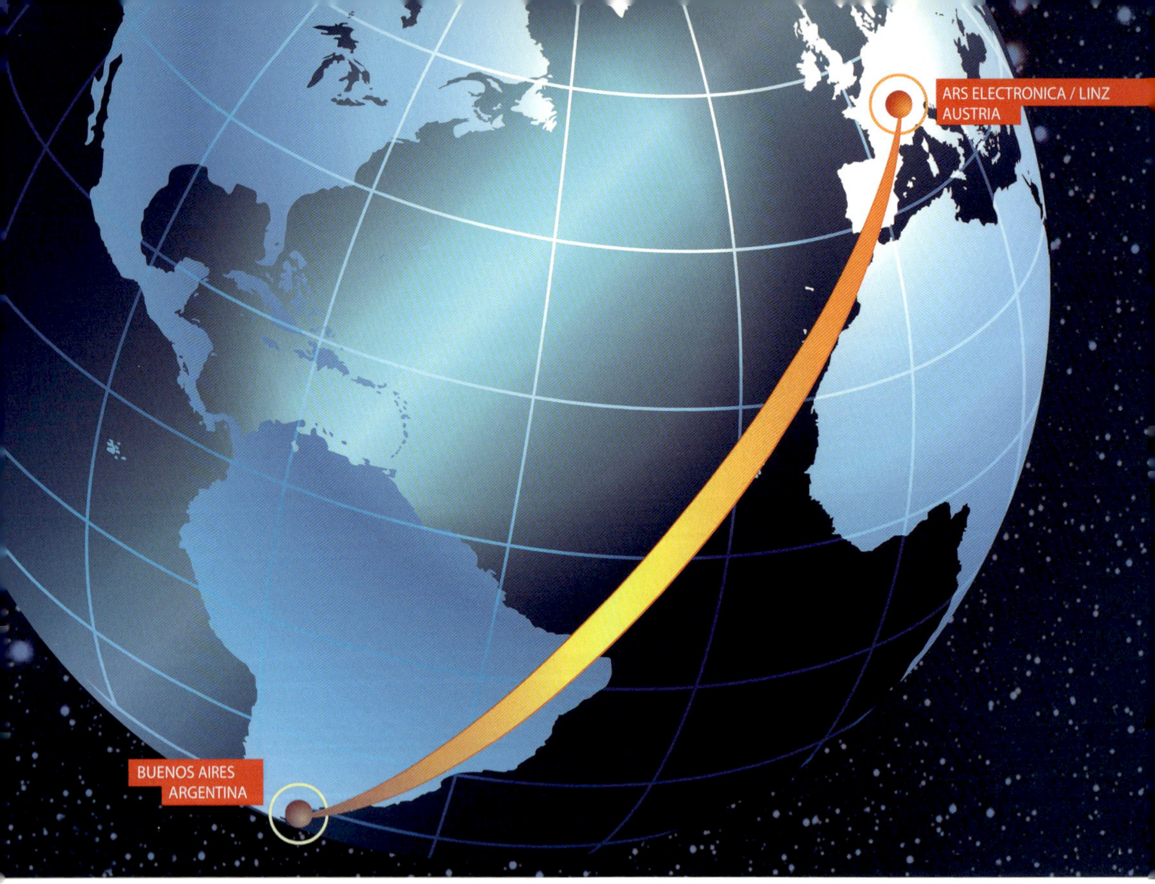

Joaquin Fargas, BioArt Lab–Maimonides University

Big Brain Project

Big Brain Project is a hybrid universal net consisting of cultures of nerve cells spread around the world and interconnected through the web.
The genesis of *Big Brain Project* underlies the birth of a systemic universe in which all its parts communicate and interconnect as a large synaptic network. *Big Brain Project* consists of a series of nerve cell cultures which, located at remote sites, interconnects through the web and constitutes a sort of neuronal network, a universal brain.

Das *Big Brain Projekt* ist ein hybrides globales Netzwerk, bestehend aus neuronalen Zellkulturen, die auf der ganzen Welt verteilt und über das Web miteinander verbunden sind.
Der Entstehung des *Big Brain Projekts* liegt die Idee eines systemischen Universums zu Grunde, in dem alle Teile miteinander kommunizieren und untereinander verbunden sind, wie in einem großen synaptischen Netzwerk. Das *Big Brain Projekt* besteht aus einer Reihe von an entfernten Orten befindlichen Nervenzellkulturen, die über das Internet miteinander verbunden sind und eine Art neuronales Netzwerk, ein globales Gehirn bilden.

A global world: a boundless body

The project shows new communication possibilities comparing the concept of synapsis with digital connection. In a first stage, it questions how the introduction of communication means in social life gave birth to the concept of a global world that challenges the concept of limitation as a spatial category, changes the perception of distance and redefines the notion of living being. According to this concept, *Big Brain Project*, suggests the experience of a technologically boundless, fragmented and recomposed being, thus questioning the limits of the individual. A global brain transcends the boundaries of its own organic being and is part of multiple simultaneous realities.

Artificial Intelligence

The brain is considered the nucleus of intelligence. In *Big Brain* this quality does not lie within the biological substratum, but is provided by electronic and artificial means. The sensors and transducers located in the terminals of *Big Brain* turn into the intelligence of the brain.

This universal and hybrid brain combines nervous cells tissue cultures with an artificial neuronal system, which facilitate remote interconnection and communication with all its nodes through Internet. This big network feeds on the surrounding experience and stimulus, providing as a result collective brain waves.

Universal brain waves

The whole range of interactions in the network may be summarized in waves that can be caught in different places, showing the concept of a unique system in which all of its parts link and produce a common effect.

New Interfaces of communication

However, the Internet and neuronal tissue are selected as materials due to their communicative capacity. Both the brain and the Internet are enormous networks resulting in complex dynamic systems and they have unique emerging properties. *Big Brain Project* shows communication as a common factor capable of linking the natural and the artificial within a single system, in a new communication entity in which what matters is that it goes through linked information such as chemical,

Eine globale Welt: Der entgrenzte Körper

Das Projekt zeigt neue Möglichkeiten der Kommunikation auf, indem es eine Analogie zwischen Synapsen und digitaler Vernetzung herstellt. In einem ersten Ansatz wirft es die Frage auf, inwieweit mit dem Vordringen der Kommunikationsmedien in unseren Alltag das Konzept einer globalen Welt entstanden ist, die den Begriff der Grenze als räumliche Kategorie in Frage stellt, den Begriff von Ferne verändert und den des Menschseins neu definiert. Ausgehend von dieser Überlegung regt das *Big Brain Projekt* die Auseinandersetzung mit einem technologisch entgrenzten, fragmentierten und neu konfigurierten Körper an und stellt so die Grenzen des Individuums in Frage. Ein globales Hirn überwindet die Einschränkung seines organischen Daseins und ist Teil multipler und simultaner Realitäten.

Künstliche Intelligenz

Das Gehirn gilt als Zentrum der Intelligenz. Bei *Big Brain* liegt diese Qualität nicht im biologischen Substrat, sondern wird durch elektronische und künstliche Mittel hervorgebracht. Die Sensoren und Wandler an den Terminals des *Big Brain* werden zur Intelligenz des Gehirns. Dieses globale und hybride Gehirn verbindet Nervenzellkulturen mit einem künstlichen neuronalen System, wodurch die Vernetzung und die Kommunikation mit all seinen Knotenpunkten über das Internet möglich werden. Der Output dieses umfassenden Netzwerkes, das sich aus den Erfahrungen und Stimuli seiner Umgebung speist, sind kollektive Gehirnströme.

Globale Gehirnströme

Die gesamte Bandbreite an Interaktion in diesem Netzwerk könnte man als Ströme, die an verschiedenen Orten gemessen werden, begreifen, die die Idee eines einzigartigen Systems verdeutlichen, in dem alle Teile zusammenwirken und einen gemeinsamen Effekt produzieren.

Neue Kommunikationsschnittstellen

Das Internet und das neuronale Gewebe wurden aufgrund ihrer Kommunikationsfähigkeit als Materialien ausgewählt. Beide, Gehirn wie auch Internet, sind gigantische Netzwerke, die komplexe dynamische Systeme bilden und einzigartige emergente Eigenschaften besitzen.

Das *Big Brain Projekt* zeigt Kommunikation als einen gemeinsamen Faktor, der das Natürliche und das Künstliche innerhalb eines einzigen Systems zu einer

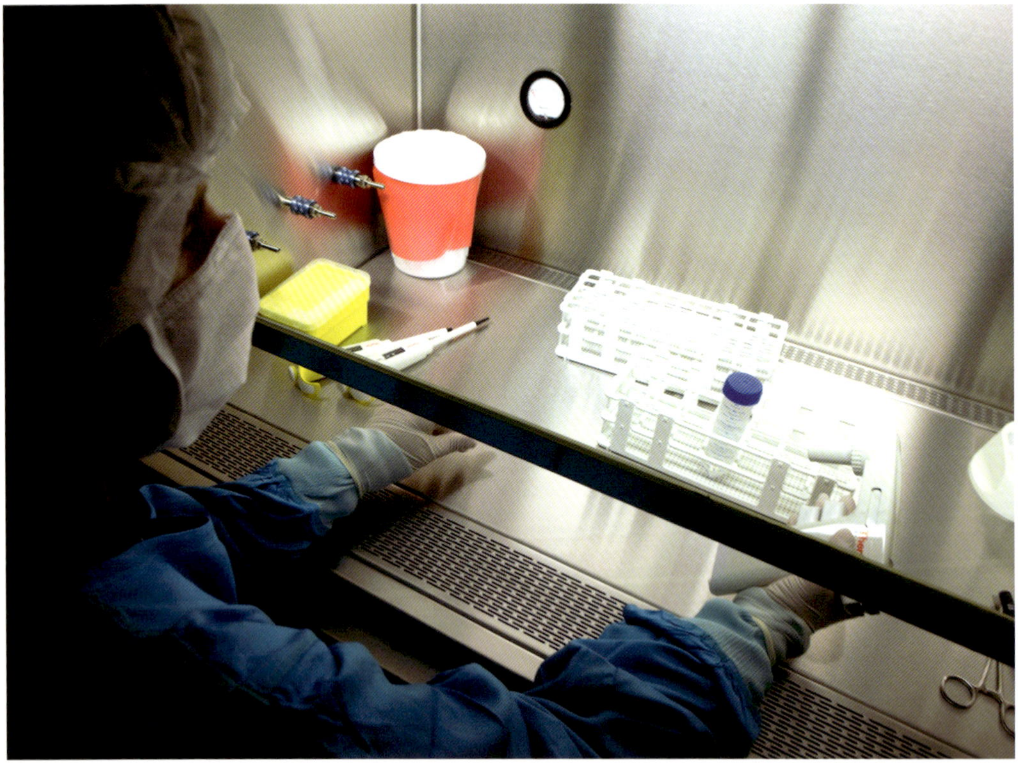

mechanical, optical, sounding stimuli, bits and electrical impulses that feed this huge organic/artificial network. In this way technology and nature make up a parallel interaction as a bio-electronic interface that represents the surrounding world.

Technical Description

Big Brain Project is a bio-telematics installation in which biological processes are joined with technological means of information transmission.
In several cities of the world a culture of brain cells is grown in Petri dishes kept in a bioreactor, which allows its survival and development.
Each capsule, where the biological system lives, receives information from each city's environment, from different sensors such as light, sound, temperature, movement and activity in the Internet. Information enters the capsule, which becomes a Bio-Opto-Electronic system, turning the data into electric impulses. The synapse, the structure through which the brain cells send signals to each

neuen Kommunikationseinheit zu verbinden vermag, in der es um die Verteilung vernetzter Information geht, gewonnen z. B. aus chemischen, mechanischen, optischen, akustischen Stimuli, Bits und elektrischen Impulsen, mit denen dieses gigantische organisch/künstliche Netzwerk gespeist wird. Auf diese Weise treten Technologie und Natur in gleichzeitige Interaktion als bio-elektronisches Interface der sie umgebenden Welt.

Technische Details

Das *Big Brain Projekt* ist eine bio-telematische Installation, in der biologische Prozesse mit technologischen Mitteln der Informationsübertragung verbunden werden. In verschiedenen Städten der Erde werden in Bioreaktoren (Kapseln), die das Wachstum und Überleben der Zellen sicherstellen, neuronale Zellkulturen in Petrischalen mit 50 Zentimeter Durchmesser gezüchtet. Jedes in einer dieser Kapseln befindliche biologische System erhält Umweltdaten aus den einzelnen Städten, über verschiedenste Sen-other, connects to the Internet in order to send a stimulus to emerge from the biological system. The connection receives the electric impulses sent by the brain cells and sends them through the artificial neuronal system, towards the other neural culture fragments. The artificial neuronal network helps conceptualize the different collective neuronal answers, generating a series of behavioral patterns of the neuronal tissues.

In this way a big network is formed, a sort of global brain, through which flow the signals of each group experiment activity. Each part of the brain sends what it perceives from the environment to the system—and this information feeds *Big Brain.*

The activity within each group reflects in waves what can be measured and visualized. *Big Brain*'s activity results in a unique, collective, universal wave, the sum of all waves.

Eventually the signals that circulate through *Big Brain* are again decoded in each terminal, as light and sound, suggesting to the spectator an experience of what happens in *Big Brain* in real time.

Translated from Spanish by Maie Bonfiglio, Florencia Battiti

General Production: Alejandra Marinaro, BioArt Lab and Multimedia design career Director at Maimónides University
Scientific consultant BioArt Lab: Jorge Genovese, Regenerative Medicine and Biomaterials Research Center Director at Maimónides University
Coordination and Management: Tomas Outon, Objeto A Gallery Director
Graphic and Interactive Interface Development: Proyecto Untitled – Maimónides University
Programming: Fabricio Mouzo Lema, Mariano Makedonsky, Escuela de Comunicación y Diseño Multimedial at Universidad Maimónides
General Project Assistant: Gabriela Munguía
Galileo Galilei Planetarium of Buenos Aires Director: Lucía Sendón
Image Design Development: Mariano Mendoca
With the support of: Maimónides University, Maimónides University BioArt Lab, Objeto A Gallery, Planetarium *Galileo Galilei* from Buenos Aires, Argentina

soren, wie etwa Licht-, Geräusch-, Temperatur- und Bewegungssensoren sowie der Auswertung des Internettraffic. Diese Daten werden in elektrische Impulse umgewandelt und in das neuronale Netzwerk eingespeist. Die Synapse, also jene Struktur, über die die neuronalen Zellen Signale untereinander übertragen, wird an das Internet angeschlossen, um Stimuli aus dem biologischen System zu senden. Die Verbindung empfängt die von den neuronalen Zellen ausgesandten elektrischen Impulse und sendet sie durch das künstliche neuronale System an die anderen Zellkulturbehälter. Das künstliche neuronale Netzwerk ist selbstlernend und ermöglicht die Konzeptualisierung der verschiedenen kollektiven neuronalen Antworten, indem es eine Reihe von Verhaltensmustern neuronaler Zellen generiert. Auf diese Weise wird ein riesiges Netzwerk gebildet, eine Art „Global Brain", durch das die Signale der Aktivitäten fließen, die an jedem Standort stattfinden. Jeder Teil des Gehirns kommuniziert dem System seine Wahrnehmungen der Umwelt und belebt mit diesen Informationen das *Big Brain.*

Die Aktivität des *Big Brain,* die Interaktion aller Gehirnteile, kann von jedem einzelnen Ort aus konsultiert und die Gehirnströme können visualisiert werden. Die Summe aller einzelnen Gehirnströme mündet schließlich in einem einzigen, kollektiven globalen Strom.

Die Signale, die durch das *Big Brain* zirkulieren, werden schließlich wieder an jedem Terminal decodiert und als Licht und Ton ausgegeben, um den BesucherInnen ein Gefühl dafür zu vermitteln, was im *Big Brain* in Echtzeit passiert.

Aus dem Spanischen von Jutta Schmiederer

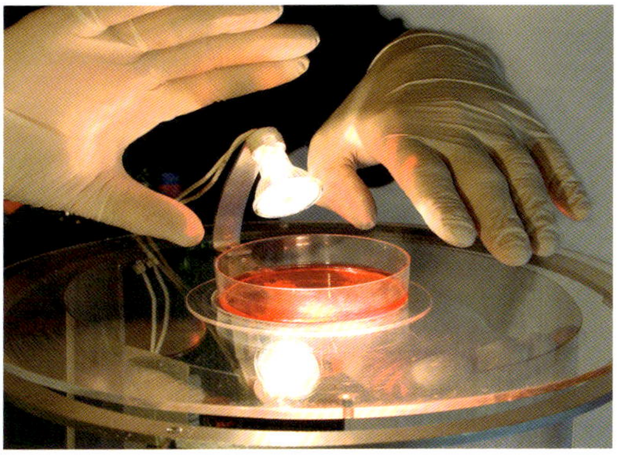

Michael Madsen

Into Eternity

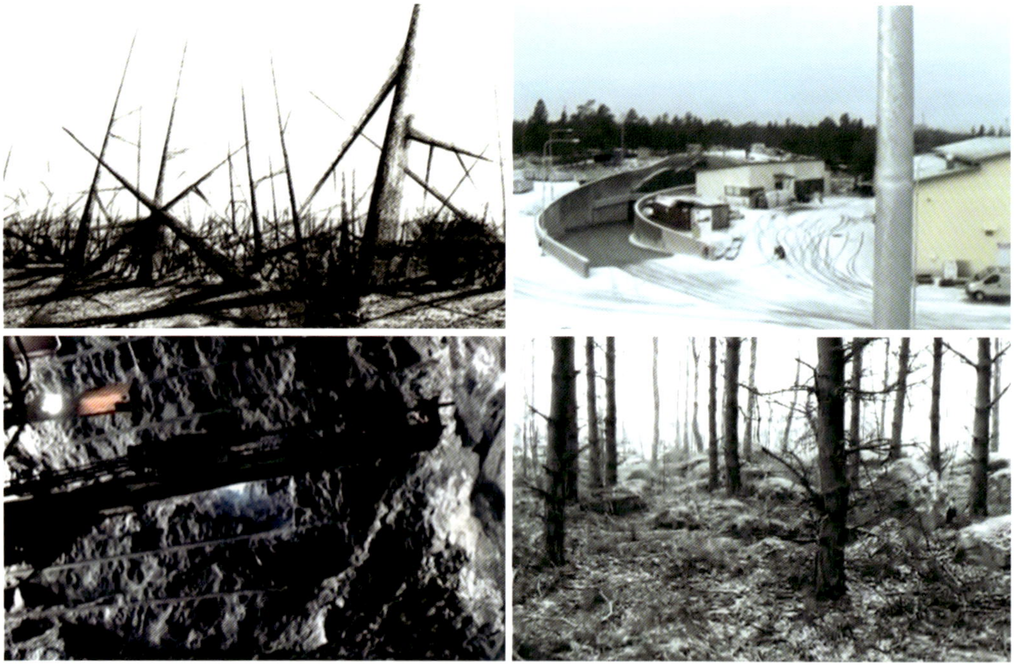

"This place is not a place of honour. No esteemed deeds are commemorated here. This is not a place for you. What is here is dangerous and repulsive. The danger will still be present in your time, as it is in ours."

These are the sentences that future man will meet, if he finds and opens the gigantic network of underground tunnels, which presently are hewn out of the bedrock in Finland. The tunnels will be filled with high-level radioactive waste, which must be kept isolated from human beings and other live organisms for at least 100.000 years into the future, not to render large areas uninhabitable.
Not only must the facility last 10 times longer than any manmade construction ever, it must also be able to resist all thinkable climate changes, erosion, evolution. The real challenge, however, is to secure the facility from human intrusion. To succeed with that is vital in order to keep future man safe and prevent the waste from escaping into the biosphere. When the waste has been deposited, the facility will be sealed off, never to be opened again. But can we ensure that? How is it possible to

Ein epischer Thriller über den weltweit ersten Versuch, nuklearen Abfall für alle Ewigkeit zu verstecken.
Es ist ein Ort, der für immer verschlossen bleiben muss, gefährlich und abstoßend. Niemand soll ihn jemals betreten. Doch wie lange wird er sicher sein?
„Wir nennen ihn Onkalo – Onkalo bedeutet Versteck. Wir bauen ihn, um uns selbst zu schützen. Die Arbeiten an Onkalo haben im 20. Jahrhundert begonnen, als wir Kinder waren, und werden im 22. Jahrhundert vollendet sein, lange nach unserem Tod. Für 100.000 Jahre soll hier etwas versteckt werden, was nirgendwo anders versteckt werden kann. Nichts von Menschen je Erbautes hat auch nur ein Zehntel dieser Zeitspanne überdauert. Unsere ältesten Bauwerke, die Pyramiden, wurden vor 5.000 Jahren errichtet. Onkalo muss für die Ewigkeit gebaut werden."
Into Eternity nimmt die Zuseher mit auf eine Reise in die Tiefe – und in eine ungewisse Zukunft.

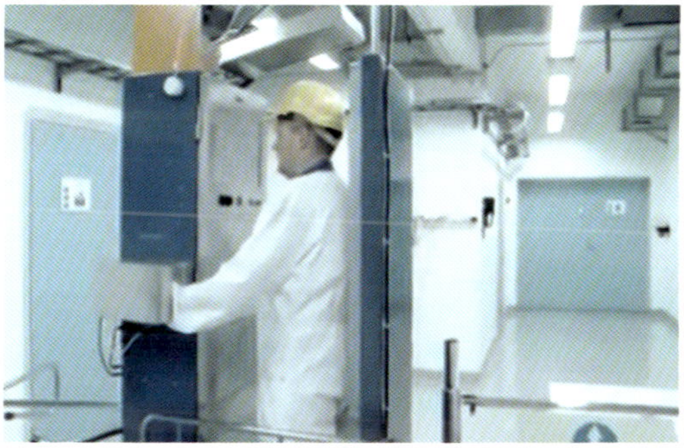

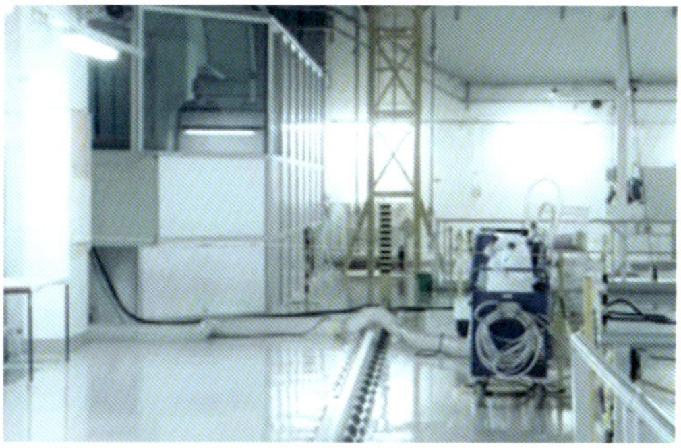

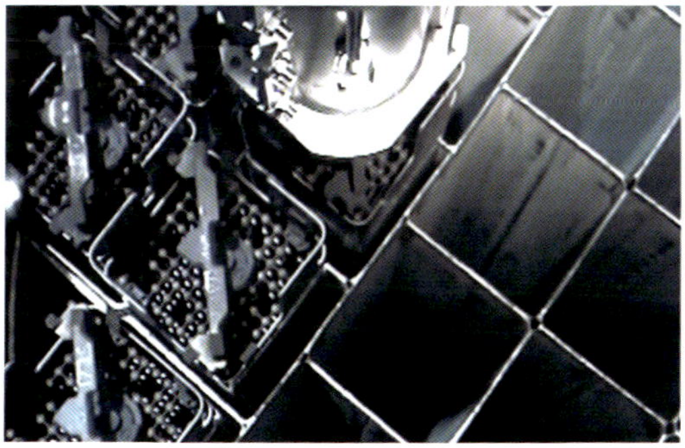

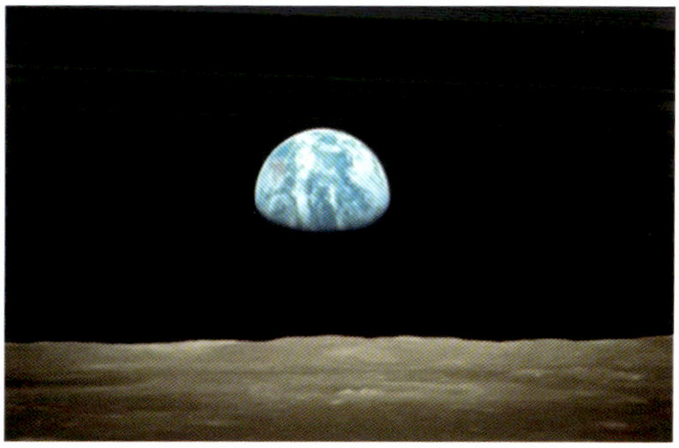

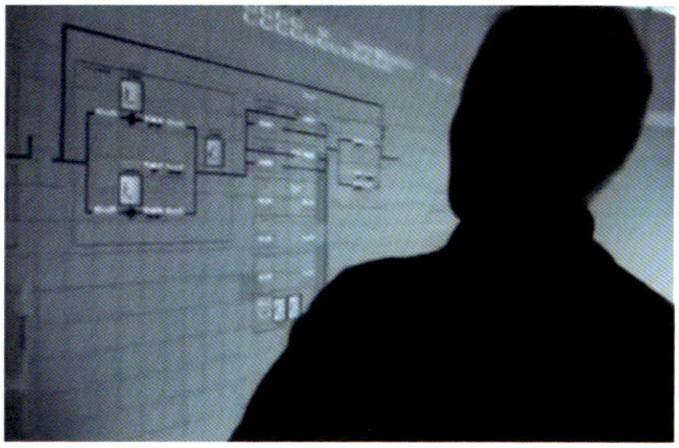

Poool Filmverleih

warn future man of the waste we left behind? How do we prevent them from thinking they have found the pyramids of our time, mystical burial grounds, hidden treasures? Which languages and signs will they understand, and if they understand, will they respect our instructions?

Hopefully these questions will have found answers before the facility is finished 120 years from now. At that time it will contain max. 1 % of the world's nuclear waste, which today is kept in interim storages on the surface, and cannot be secured against societal breakdowns, natural or manmade disasters. While gigantic monster machines dig deeper and deeper into the dark, experts above ground strive to find solutions to the radioactive waste issue, solutions which can secure mankind now and in the future.

A documentary time capsule, a wondrous and frightening journey into the underworld and into the future.

Documentary 2009
75 min
HD 16:9
DK 2010
directed by Michael Madsen

Markus Schmidt, Camillo Meinhart

Diverseeds

Plant Genetic Resources for Food and Agriculture
Documentary Film

In agriculture, the widespread adoption of a few improved varieties has narrowed the genetic base of important food crops and led to the disappearance of hundreds of landraces. Conserving and using plant genetic diversity is vital in meeting the world's future development needs in Europe, Asia and elsewhere. This documentary shows why biodiversity is important for agriculture and how it is conserved and used in many different locations in Europe and Asia.

The film describes, with splendid pictures from Europe and Asia and insights from leading international scientists, the relevance of traditional landraces, crop wild relatives, gene banks, and civil society movements in the global challenge to preserve and use plant genetic resources for food and agriculture. The film takes us from the cradle of agriculture in the "fertile crescent", all the way up to the Svalbard Global Seed Vault that serves as a frozen Garden of Eden in the Arctic North.

The film was part of the activities carried out in the 2-year EC funded project *DIVERSEEDS* enhancing networking activities on conservation and use of plant genetic resources between Europe and Asia. The film was made to document the importance of seed biodiversity, its decline and countermeasures to safeguard agro-biodiversity for future generations.

http://www.diverseeds.eu/DVD

In der Landwirtschaft haben Monokulturen in den letzten Jahrzehnten zu einer dramatischen Reduktion der Saatgutvielfalt geführt. Der Schutz und die nachhaltige Nutzung der pflanzengenetischen Vielfalt ist aber wesentlich, um auch in Zukunft den globalen Nahrungsmittelbedarf decken zu können. Der Film erklärt, warum die Artenvielfalt so wichtig für die Landwirtschaft ist und wie sie geschützt werden kann. *Diverseeds* zeigt nicht nur eindrucksvolle Bilder aus Europa und Asien, sondern lässt auch führende internationale Wissenschaftler zu Wort kommen, um die Bedeutung von traditionellen Landrassen, den wilden Verwandten unserer Nutzpflanzen, von Gen-Banken und zivilgesellschaftlichen Bewegungen für den Schutz und die nachhaltige Nutzung der landwirtschaftlichen Vielfalt auf globaler Ebene zu erläutern. Der Film nimmt uns auf eine Reise von der Wiege der Landwirtschaft im „fruchtbaren Halbmond" bis hin zur *Global Seed Vault* in Spitzbergen, der als gefrorener Garten Eden im arktischen Norden dient.

Der Film war Teil eines zweijährigen Networking-EU-Projekts zum Schutz und zur nachhaltigen Nutzung pflanzen-genetischer Vielfalt in Europa und Asien. *Diverseeds* wurde gedreht, um die Wichtigkeit der Saatgutvielfalt, deren Verlust und aktuelle Gegenmaßnahmen zum Schutz derselben für zukünftige Generationen zu dokumentieren.

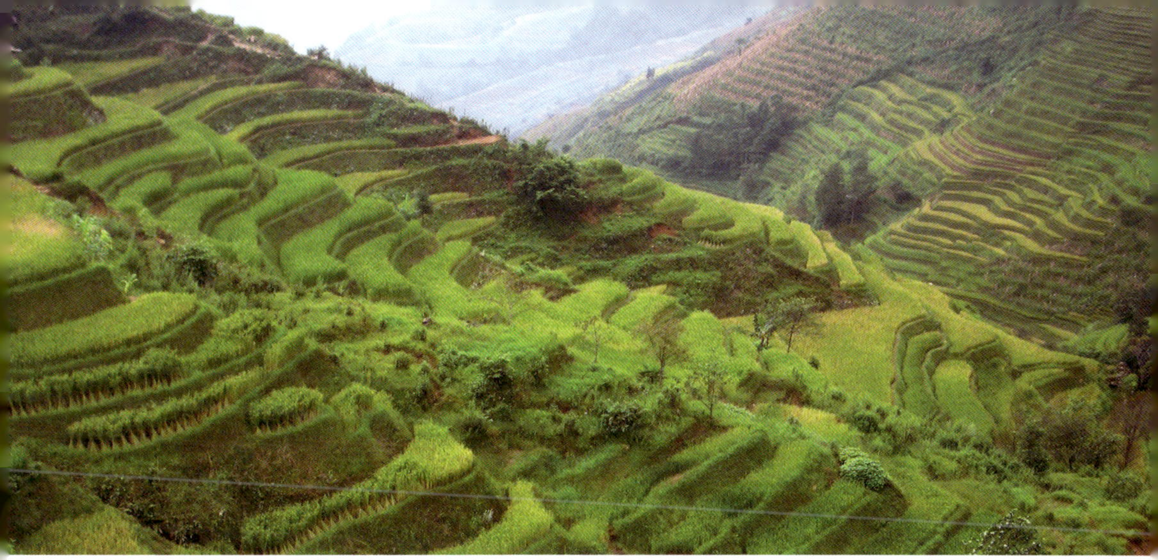
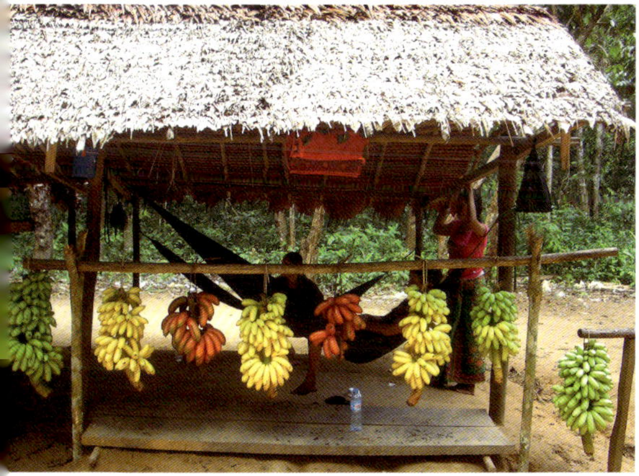
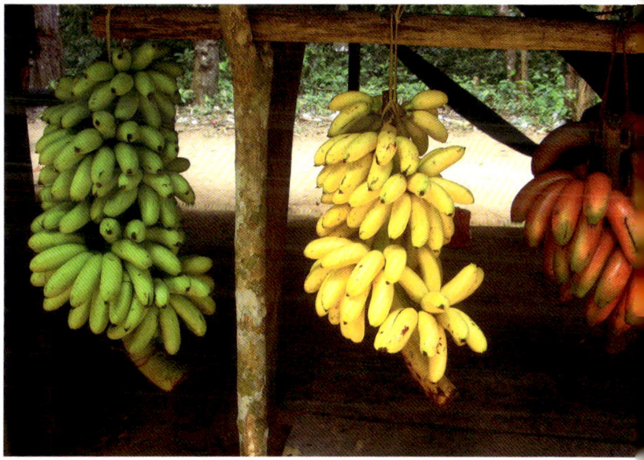
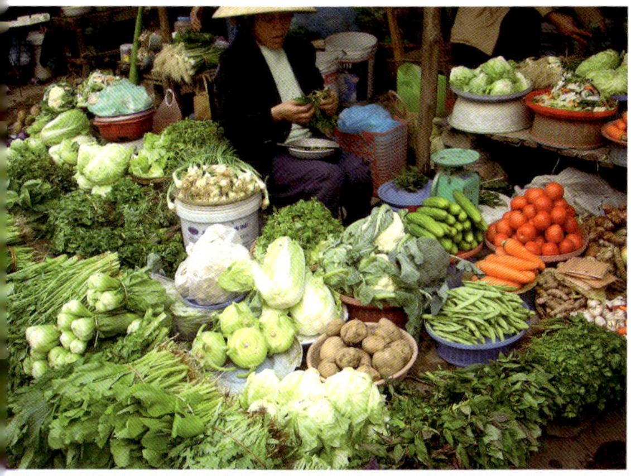
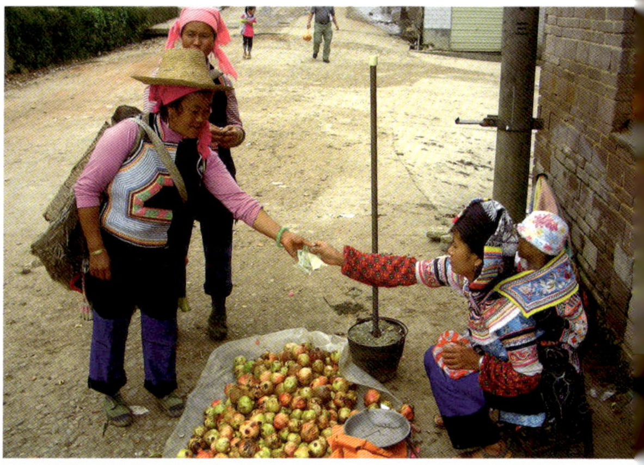
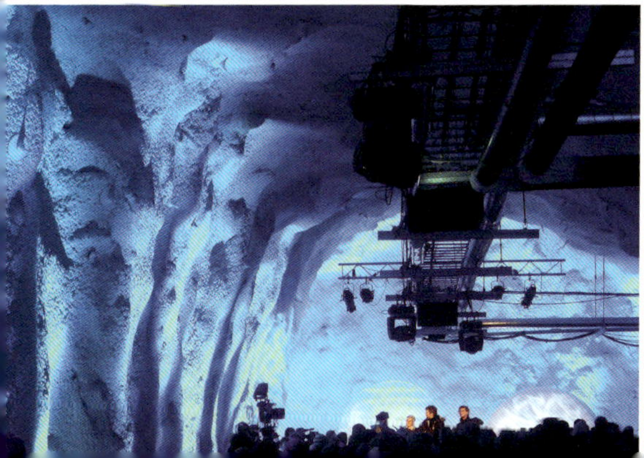
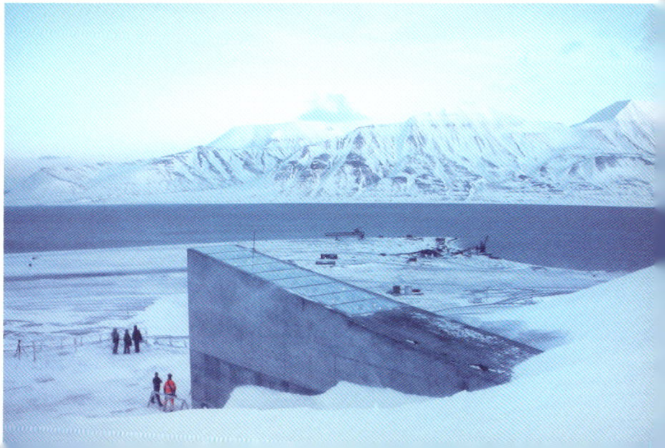

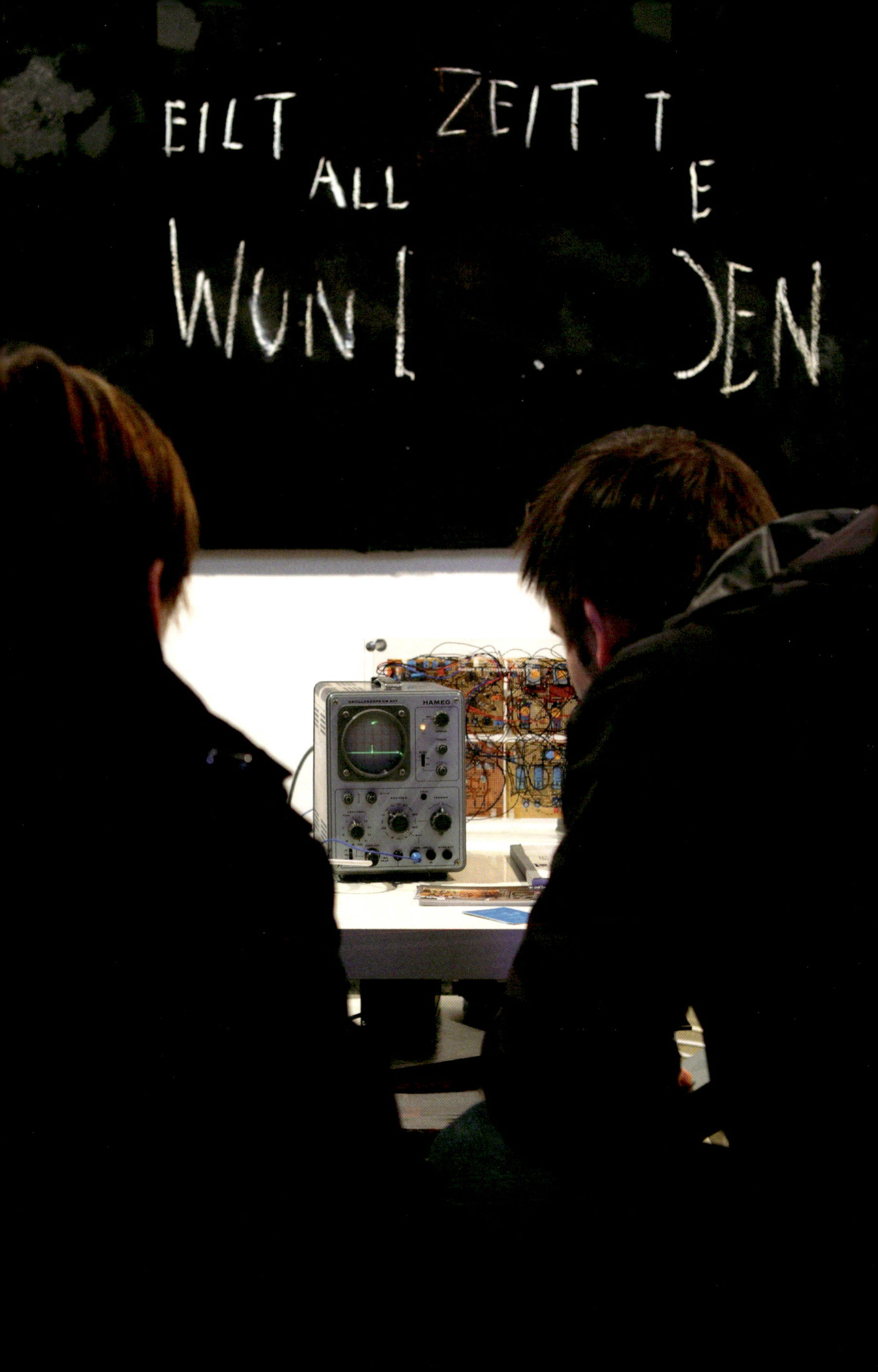
EILT
ZEIT
T
ALL
E
WUN
DEN
HAMEG

MEGA e.V. – Museum of Electronic Games & Art

Ludic Memento

On Fleeting Remembrance and Digital Forgetting

Von flüchtigen Erinnerungen und digitalem Vergessen

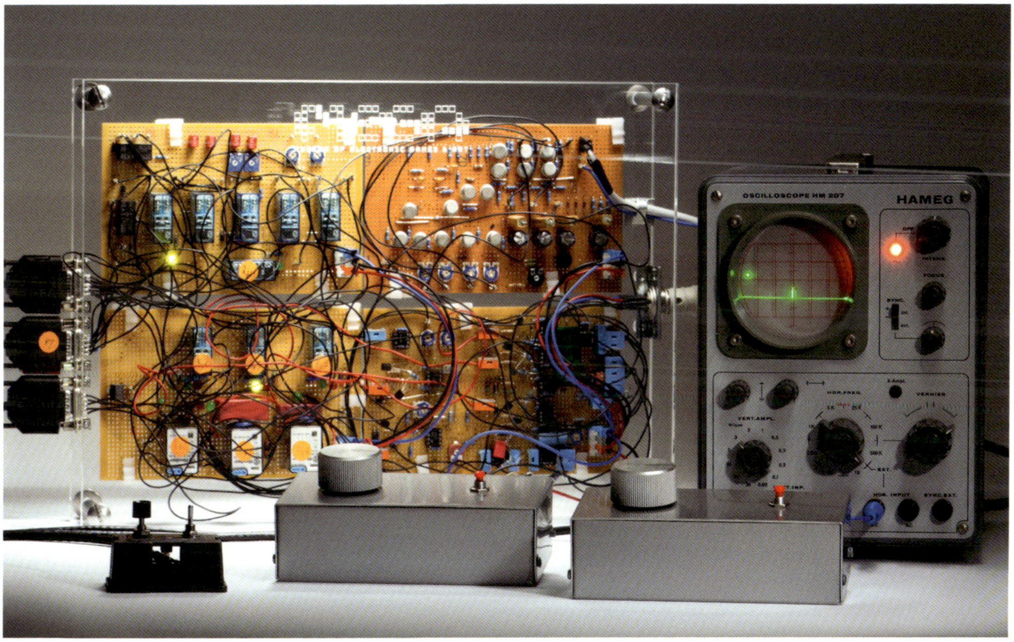

Martin Streit

Media assume an important role as bearers of cultural memory. Along with changes in these media come transformations to traditions and spaces of commemoration. Now that the electronic game has advanced to the status of core medium and leading-edge cultural technology, its multifarious technical manifestations and cultural practices are already establishing a presence across the spectrum of the contemporary culture of remembrance. Now MEGA presents *Ludic Memento*, an exhibition dealing with the evolution of digital forgetting in the context of an event-oriented commemoration culture. *Ludic Memento* shows how memories, fragments of recollections, and digital forgetting are to be understood. The reciprocal relationship between technology and society occupies the focal point of attention, while permitting multiple interpretations.

Traveling through time from the infancy of the electronic game to the present makes it clear how

Medien nehmen eine wichtige Rolle als Träger des kulturellen Gedächtnisses ein. Mit dem Wandel dieser Medien ändern sich Erinnerungsräume und Traditionen. Das zu einem Leitmedium und einer prägenden Kulturtechnik avancierte elektronische Spiel findet durch seine technologische Verfasstheit und seine kulturellen Praktiken bereits Ausdruck in einem vielfältigen Spektrum gegenwärtiger Erinnerungskultur. Mit *Ludic Memento* präsentiert MEGA e.V. eine Ausstellung über die Evolution des digitalen Vergessens im Kontext eventorientierter Erinnerungskultur. Das Projekt zeigt, wie Erinnerungen, Erinnerungsstücke und das digitale Vergessen einzuordnen sind. Die wechselseitige Beziehung von Technik und Gesellschaft steht dabei im Vordergrund der Betrachtung und lässt viele Lesarten zu.

In einer Zeitreise von den Anfängen des elektronischen Spiels bis in die Gegenwart wird deutlich, wie wichtig es ist, Abspielsysteme zu konservieren, zu restaurieren und zu rekonstruieren, um dem digita-

important it is to preserve, restore and reconstruct game-playing systems in order to thwart digital forgetting. The exhibits permit visitors to immerse themselves as deeply as they care to go in the history of technology, imparting visual, auditory and haptic elements to their substantive considerations.
Those beholding the installations arrayed along this journey into the past can refresh long-forgotten childhood memories. Either the medium itself triggers the awakening, or the visitor can opt for an active gaming experience and choose from a whole library to make it happen. Interpretations clarify the media shift and call the status quo into question in a quest to see how things actually are.
In the spirit of Thomas More's insight that "Tradition is not holding on to the ashes but passing on the flame," the *Ludic Memento* exhibition establishes a new form of cultural conservation, and, together with the *Retro/per/spectives* exhibition, clearly demonstrates that this is no longer only a matter for society's institutions of memory. It remains to be seen whether the outcome will be to briefly jog event-oriented short-term memory or whether enduring recollections will take hold.

len Vergessen entgegenzuwirken. Die Exponate lassen nach Belieben eine inhaltliche Vertiefung in die Technikgeschichte zu, indem sie visuell, auditiv und haptisch das Erlebnis prägen.
Der Rezipient frischt an den Stationen in dieser Zeitreise längst vergessene Kindheitserinnerungen auf. Entweder wirkt das Medium selbst als Pille zum Erwachen, oder der Besucher kann in einer Bibliothek aktiv Spielerlebnisse auswählen. Interpretationen machen den Medienwandel deutlich und hinterfragen den Status quo auf der Suche nach Wirklichkeit.
Frei nach Thomas Morus' Ausspruch „Tradition ist nicht das Bewahren der Asche, sondern das Weitergeben der Flamme" etabliert die Ausstellung *Ludic Memento* eine neue Form der kulturellen Überlieferung und macht zusammen mit der Ausstellung *Retro/per/spektiven* deutlich, dass dies nicht mehr reine Angelegenheit von Gedächtnisinstitutionen ist. Ob dabei nur das eventorientierte Kurzzeitgedächtnis strapaziert wird oder gar bleibende Erinnerungen entstehen, bleibt abzuwarten.
Text: Canan Hastik

Andranik Ghalustian, Jeremiah Diephuis, Stefan Schraml

Retro/per/spectives

Computer games have undergone a considerable metamorphosis over the past 40 years of their digital existence, progressing from moving points of light as an entertaining test of dexterity to complex and artistically interesting interactive productions.
Technological constraints imposed by the respective hardware have played a significant role in the conception and implementation of novel game ideas. At the same time, there has always been a constant demand for higher-performance hardware that effectively redefines the bounds of the possible. Thus, yesterday's devices incessantly become

In den bisherigen 40 Jahren seiner digitalen Existenz hat sich das Medium Computerspiel inhaltlich von bewegten Bildpunkten als unterhaltsames Geschicklichkeitsspiel zu komplexen und künstlerisch relevanten interaktiven Produktionen gewandelt.
Die technologischen Einschränkungen durch die jeweilige Hardware spielten eine wesentliche Rolle bei der Konzeption und Umsetzung von neuartigen Spielideen. Umgekehrt wird stets nach leistungsfähigerer Hardware verlangt, um die Grenzen des Möglichen immer wieder neu zu definieren. Die Geräte von gestern werden somit kontinuierlich überholt und in

obsolete, ending up in a drawer, the basement or the trash can. They may be gone, but they're not forgotten ...

As a mass medium, computer games have become sustainably entrenched in the collective memory. Contemporary game culture and other forms of media frequently reference a rich stock of game-related memes, visual codes and narrative recollections. Thus, the purportedly outmoded continues to provide new perspectives and serves as a source of inspiration for current and future works.

Retro/per/spectives examines the evolution of the medium of computer games on the basis of its hardware and technological developments over the last four decades. Due to frequent media discontinuities and the failures of technical innovations, many of these devices have morphed into artifacts. Arranged on a timeline, the items on display—classics such as Pong, original arcade games, and the first networked home consoles—can be experienced and played. For selected games, the exhibition offers the authentic experience of playing on the original device, and also juxtaposes it to playing an emulated version on a modern processor. Thus, every player can decide for him/herself to what degree a contemporary knockoff retains the significance of the original or whether all that these digital duplicates constitute are decontextualized relics.

Retro/per/spectives is presented as the historical counterpart of *Ludic Memento,* an exhibition from MEGA—the Museum for Electronic Games and Art.

Schränke, Keller oder auf den Schrotthaufen versetzt. Dennoch sind sie nicht vergessen ...

Als Massenmedium haben sich Computerspiele nachhaltig ins kollektive Gedächtnis eingegraben – die heutige „Game Culture" referenziert einen reichen Fundus an Memen, visuellen Codes und narrativen Erinnerungen. Somit bekommt auch das vermeintlich Obsolete neue Perspektiven und wird zur Inspirationsquelle für gegenwärtige und zukünftige Werke.

Retro/per/spektiven untersucht die Evolution des Mediums Computerspiel anhand dessen Hardware und technologischer Entwicklungen im Verlauf der letzten vier Jahrzehnte. Durch häufige Medienbrüche und den Misserfolg von technischen Innovationen sind viele dieser Geräte zu Artefakten geworden. Auf einer Zeitachse werden die Exponate neben Klassikern wie Pong, originalen Arcade-Automaten und den ersten vernetzten Heimkonsolen erleb- und spielbar. Für ausgesuchte Titel wird der authentischen Erfahrung auf dem originalen Gerät eine emulierte Version auf modernen Rechnern gegenüber gestellt. Somit kann jeder für sich entscheiden, bis zu welchem Grad eine digitale Emulation die Bedeutung des Originals behält oder ob von digitalen Abbildern nur kontextlose Relikte überbleiben.

Retro/per/spektiven wird als historisches Gegenstück zur Ausstellung *Ludic Memento* vom MEGA – Museum for Electronic Games and Art angeboten.

Team: Andranik Ghalustians / Bildschirmsprünge; Jeremiah Diephuis / Fachhochschule Hagenberg; Stefan Schraml / GameStage

Teresa Timelthaler

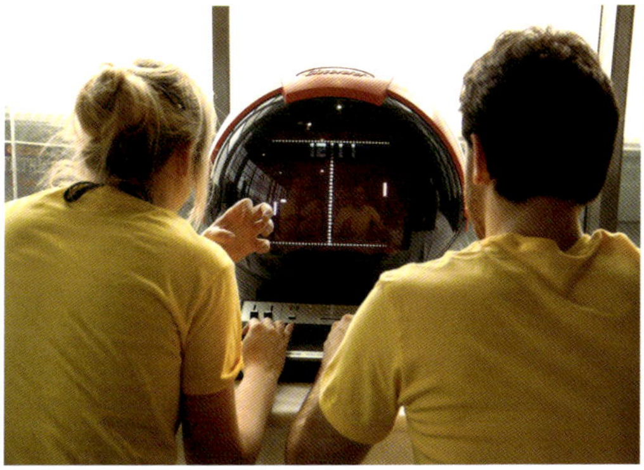

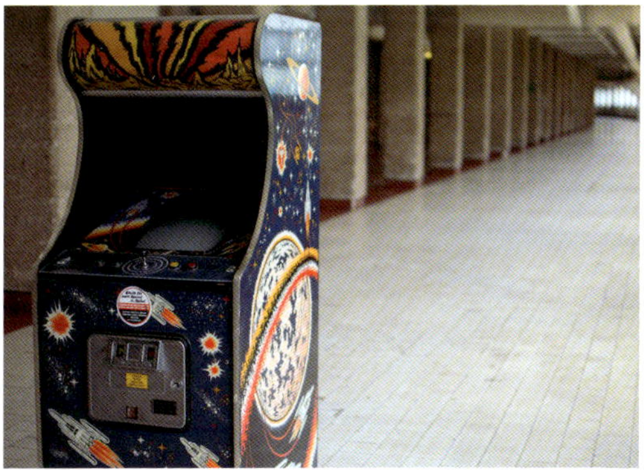

Austria Game Jam

Game Jam

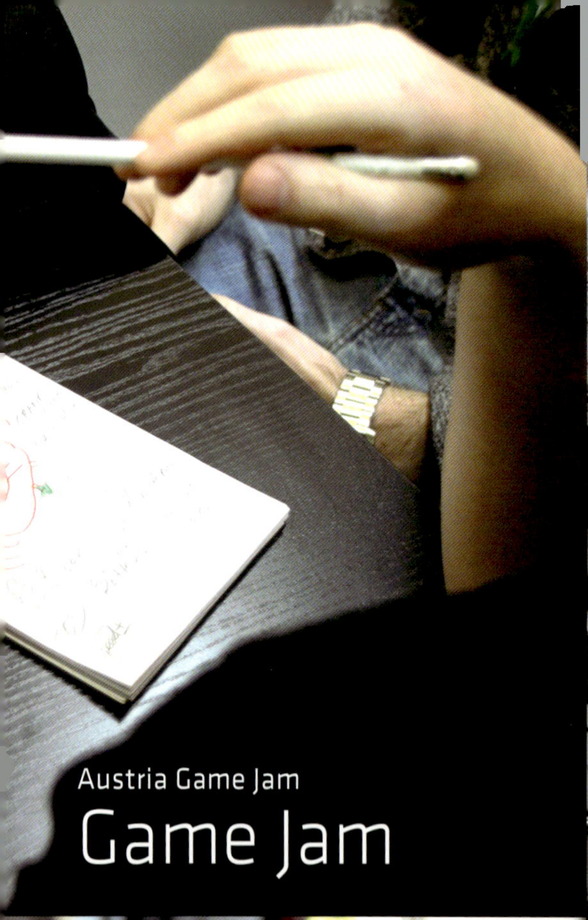

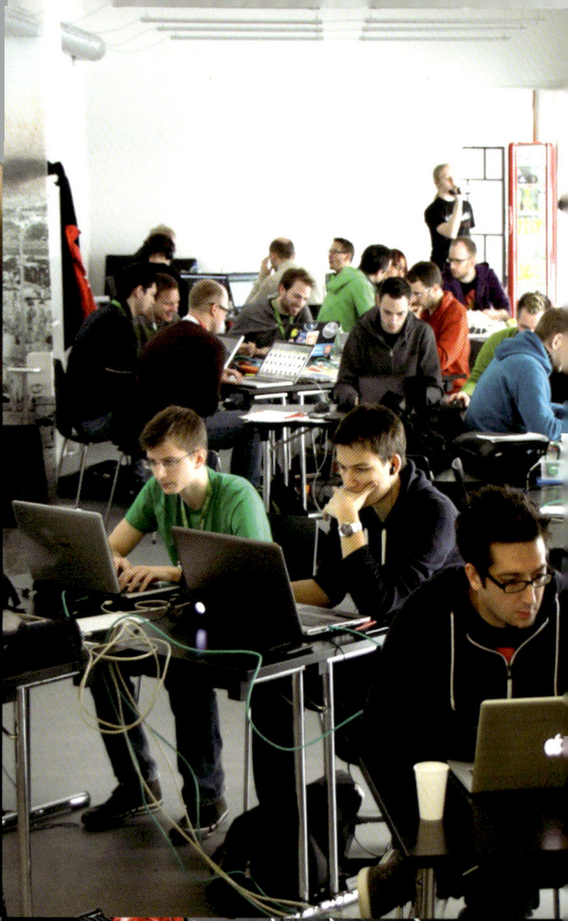

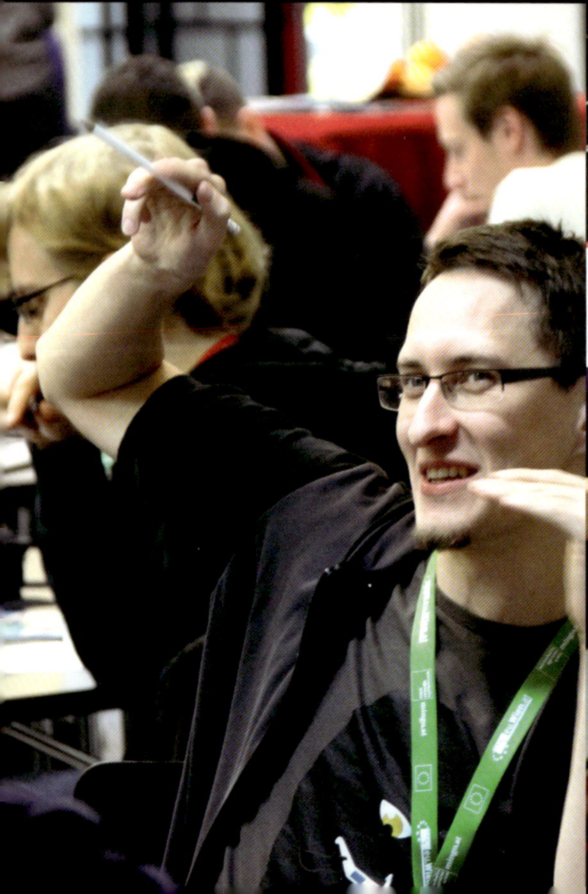

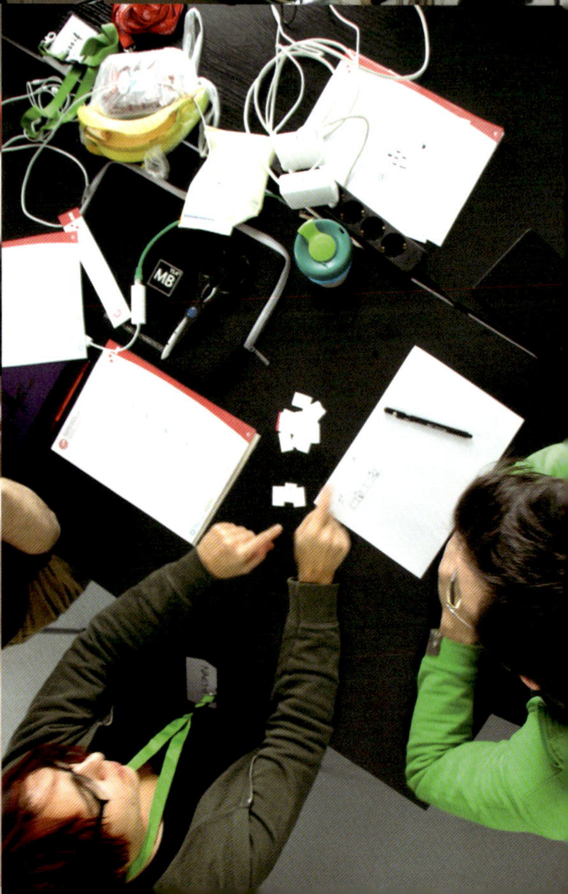

Just like with a musical jam session, the goal of a game jam is at its core about being spontaneously creative together—in this case, the chosen medium is Computer Games. Limited to only 48 hours, the teams have to decide quickly on the main phases of the game development process. This provides a great opportunity to observe on a small scale how digital games are made, and how the in-between steps from the initial idea to the playable prototype look like.

Game jams bring together participants with different experience levels (professionals, students, hobbyists) and from multiple disciplines, including visual arts, audio and interaction design and software development. A game jam aims to create an open, cooperative environment and is thus the ideal place to experiment with new tools and production techniques, as well as to experience working in an interdisciplinary team. Exploring creative ways to work with the given constraints, finding the right balance between arts and technology and swift teamwork are central aspects of the game jam spirit. It is a free-for-all where everything is allowed if it allows you to reach your goal faster.

A special theme, that is kept secret until the beginning, acts as overall conceptual guidance for the entire game jam. Its announcement marks the opening of the jam with the participants diving into an initial brainstorming session. Ad-hoc teams, which group around the brainstormed ideas, then start to design, implement and refine the game prototypes until the end of the jam.

The game jam theme will reflect the overall festival theme *TOTAL RECALL*. But the interpretation space, however, is vast and it is up to the teams to creatively transform this design constraint into a captivating game prototype.

Ars Electronica Festival visitors are welcome to take a look behind the scenes and try out the work-in-progress prototypes during the jam.

Austria Game Jam *(http://austriagamejam.org)*,
Verein für Innovative Unterhaltungssoftware
(http://innovativesoftware.at) Roland Moritz,
Jürgen Musil, David Schwingenschlögl, Simon Wallner

Wie bei einer musikalischen Jam-Session geht es bei einer Game-Jam darum, spontan gemeinsam kreativ zu sein – als Medium dient in diesem Fall das Computerspiel. Innerhalb von nur wenigen Tagen, z. B. über ein Wochenende, werden neue Spielideen als Prototypen umgesetzt. Eine Game-Jam zeigt im Kleinen, wie digitale Spiele entstehen und wie die Zwischenschritte von der ersten Idee bis hin zu einem spielbaren Prototypen aussehen.

Eine Jam vereint TeilnehmerInnen aus unterschiedlichen Disziplinen, wobei die Spanne von den visuellen Künsten und Audio über Interaktionsdesign bis hin zu den softwaretechnischen Bereichen der konkreten Umsetzung reicht. Game-Jams bieten immer eine gute Gelegenheit, um mit neuen Technologien und Arbeitstechniken zu experimentieren und in einem interdisziplinären Umfeld zu arbeiten.

Kreatives Arbeiten mit den gegebenen Einschränkungen, Spontaneität und Teamarbeit sind zentrale Elemente einer Game-Jam. Durch die meist auf nur 48 Stunden beschränkte Dauer müssen die Teams improvisieren und ihre Ideen sowie deren Umsetzung mit einem opportunistischen Ansatz verfolgen. Alles ist erlaubt, was zum Ziel führt und einen schnellen Fortschritt verspricht.

Den kreativen Startimpuls der Jam stellt das bis zum Beginn geheime Thema dar. Es gibt eine grobe Richtung vor und dient den TeilnehmerInnen als Ausgangspunkt für ein Brainstorming. Um die hieraus resultierenden Ideen bilden sich dann Ad-hoc-Gruppen, die bis zum Ende der Jam an deren prototypischer Umsetzung arbeiten.

Die Themenvorgabe der Game-Jam wird das Festivalthema *TOTAL RECALL* reflektieren. Die dabei entstehenden Spieleprototypen werden darauf Bezug nehmen und somit in den Gesamtkontext des Festivals eingebunden. Die Interpretationsspielräume sind dabei groß, und es steht den Teams frei, bei der Umsetzung der konzeptuellen Vorgaben ihrer Kreativität freien Raum zu lassen.

Während des Ars Electronica Festivals haben die FestivalbesucherInnen die Möglichkeit, beim Game-Jam einen Einblick in die Spieleentwicklung zu bekommen, den Spielen bei ihrer Entstehung zuzusehen und sie auch selbst auszuprobieren.

ikono

ikono On Air Festival

ikono is delighted to be invited by Ars Electronica to launch the first edition of the ikono On Air Festival, drawing together an international selection of moving images, installation and performance artworks. This includes over 100 artists from over 30 nationalities. Launching on September 6th 2013, the ikono On Air Festival will present a three-week program of works by established artists who have shaped today's contemporary art landscape, and will be joined by emerging contemporary artists forging new ground in artistic production. Innovative in approach, this international art event will be broadcast on TV in over 30 countries, streamed online in HD and accompanied by public events in 12 cities. Exclusive premieres, unique 24-hour events, and curated selections by some of the world's leading art professionals and institutions will create a rich and diverse program.

The ikono On Air Festival will focus on non-narrative and time-based artworks, which employ intuitive and often purely visual structures that challenge conventional connections with the audience. The inclusion of time in artistic practice persuades the viewer into an active and participatory role challenging traditional gallery and museum environments. Time will form one of the four main programmed sections during the ikono On Air Festival. A number of artists will respond to, reference and explore this complex and hard-to-define element in unconventional ways. Other sections include *(Un)Boxed,* which is a discovery of the changing aesthetic and progressive nature of video and media art focusing on how and where it is seen, as well as what it looks like, and how this has evolved, *(Re)Animate,* which focuses on artists working with existing, found and archival material as well as popular visual languages and clichés to create independent new artworks and *Sublime,* which showcases works seeking a per-

Die erste Ausgabe des ikono On Air Festivals findet im Rahmen des Ars Electronica Festival 2013 statt und präsentiert vom 6. bis 29. September eine internationale Auswahl an filmischen Arbeiten, Installationen und performativen Kunstwerken von über 100 Künstlern aus 30 Nationen. Über einen Zeitraum von drei Wochen wird ein Programm ausgestrahlt, das Werke etablierter Künstler, die die zeitgenössische Kunstlandschaft entscheidend geprägt und mitbestimmt haben, neben aufstrebenden, jungen Positionen zeigt. Erstmalig wird dabei ein internationales Kunstfestival ausschließlich über Fernsehen in über 30 Ländern sowie via globalem HD-Livestream ausgestrahlt und von öffentlichen Veranstaltungen in 12 Städten weltweit begleitet. Exklusive Premieren, einzigartige 24-Stunden-Events und Beiträge, die von einigen der weltweit renommiertesten Kunstexperten und -institutionen kuratiert werden, garantieren ein reiches und vielfältiges Programm.

Das ikono On Air Festival richtet seinen Fokus auf nicht-narrative und zeitbasierte Kunstwerke, die intuitive und häufig rein visuelle Strukturen einsetzen und konventionelle Beziehungen zum Betrachter hinterfragen. So verlangt die Einbindung von Zeit in die künstlerische Praxis vom Betrachter eine aktive, partizipatorische Rolle und fordert zugleich die traditionelle Struktur von Galerien und Museen heraus. *Time* überschreibt somit auch eines der vier Themen des Hauptprogramms des ikono On Air Festivals, dem jene Künstler zugeordnet sind, die auf Zeit reagieren, verweisen oder das komplexe und schwer beschreibbare Element künstlerisch zu erkunden suchen.

Zu den anderen Sektionen: *(Un)Boxed* nimmt sich der Enthüllung einer sich wandelnden ästhetischen und progressiven Natur von Video- und Medienkunst an, wobei sich der Fokus auf die Art und Weise und den Ort der Ausstrahlung richtet sowie auf ihre äußerliche Erscheinung und deren jeweilige Entwicklung. *(Re)Animate* wiederum widmet sich jenen Künstlern,

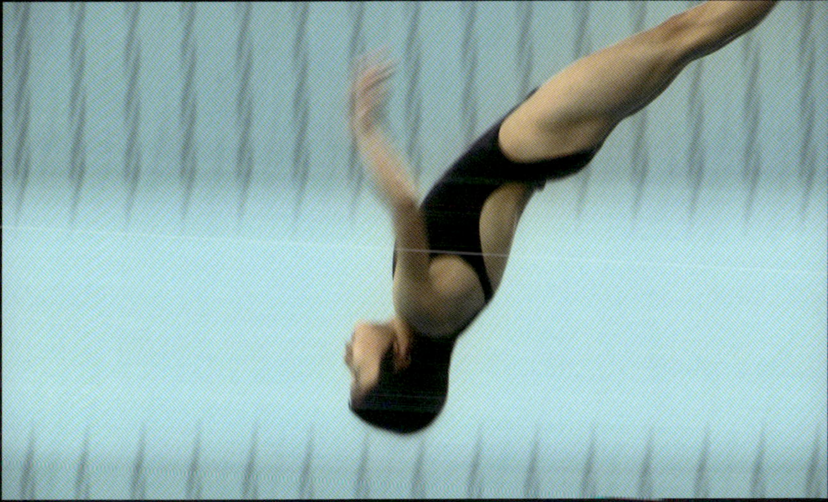

Ma Qiusha
Embrace, 2011
single-channel video, 2'36'' (still)

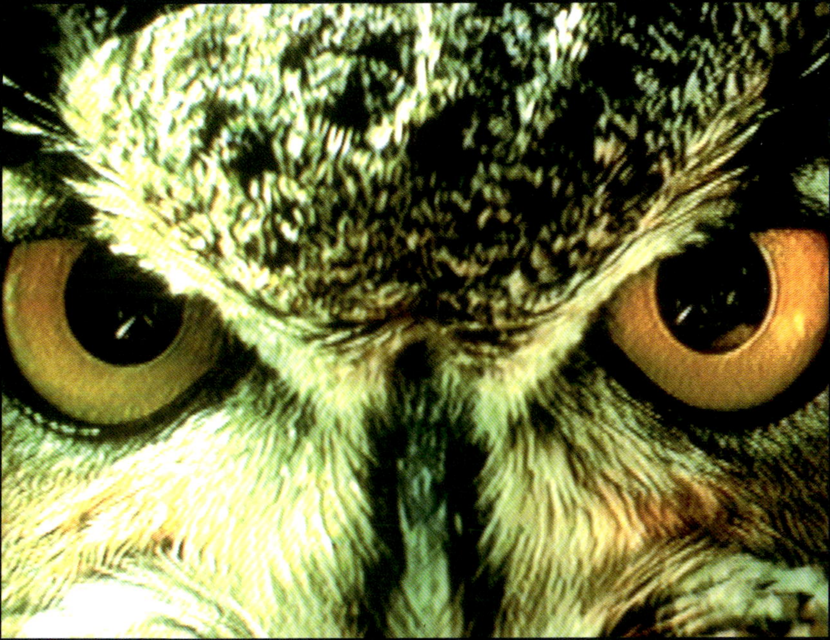

Bill Viola
I Do Not Know What It Is I Am Like, 1986

sonal, emotional and often long-lasting response through pure aesthetic seduction.
Complementing these four main programs will be a series of specials focusing on different artists, techniques, periods and concepts, as well as a selection of ikono's highlights from recent years.

About ikono

ikono is an international media platform dedicated to democratizing art through the production and broadcasting of short films that present art to the wider public sphere. The program is created in cooperation with artists, archives, collections and art institutions from all over the world. Through ikono's website and online social platforms, the television broadcast program is supported with immediately accessible in-depth information aimed at continuing the audience's journey with a particular artist or artwork.
The ikono On Air Festival follows ikono's vision of creating visual bridges between epochs and styles throughout art history. It hopes to foster a greater appreciation of time-based and non-narrative artworks by increasing its accessibility to the general public. Breaking new ground with the ikono On Air Festival, ikono brings a truly democratic art experience via TV, the Internet and public events. It celebrates new ways for art to live in our lives, while also giving a large and diverse audience the opportunity to see artworks that are too often confined to physical locations for fleeting moments in gallery and museum circuits.

die mit vorhandenen Dingen, Fundstücken oder Archivmaterialien arbeiten oder sich populären visuellen Sprachen oder Klischees bedienen um neue, unabhängige Kunstwerke zu schaffen. *Sublime* schließlich zeigt Arbeiten, die durch rein ästhetische Verführung eine persönliche, emotionale und häufig lang anhaltende Wirkung erzielen.
Die vier Sektionen des Hauptprogramms werden durch eine Serie an Themen-Specials ergänzt, die sich unterschiedlichen Künstlern, Techniken, Epochen und Konzepten widmen sowie eine Auswahl aus ikonos-Höhepunkten der letzten Jahre präsentieren.

Über ikono

ikono ist eine internationale Medienplattform, die sich der Demokratisierung von Kunst verschrieben hat: Über die Produktion und Ausstrahlung von kurzen Filmen wird Kunst aller Stile und Epochen einem internationalen Publikum zugänglich gemacht. Das Programm wird in Kooperation mit Künstlern, Archiven, Sammlungen und Kunstinstitutionen aus aller Welt gestaltet. Über die ikonos-Webseite und soziale Onlineplattformen wird das ausgestrahlte Fernsehprogramm von unmittelbar zugänglicher Hintergrundinformation begleitet, die dem Publikum die weiterführende Auseinandersetzung mit einzelnen Künstlern, Kunstwerken oder Ausstellungen ermöglicht.
Das ikono On Air Festival folgt ikonos Vision, visuelle Brücken zwischen Zeiten und Strömungen innerhalb der Kunstgeschichte zu kreieren – mit dem Ziel, über die internationale Zugänglichmachung der künstlerischen Positionen eine breitere öffentliche Aufmerksamkeit für zeitbasierte und nicht-narrative Kunstwerke zu schaffen. Mit dem ikono On Air Festival betritt ikono neuen Boden und lädt über Fernsehen, Internet und öffentliche Veranstaltungen zu einem wahrhaft demokratischen Kunsterleben ein. Es feiert neue Wege, Kunst im alltäglichen Leben Raum zu schenken, während es gleichzeitig einem großen und vielfältigen Publikum ermöglicht, jene Kunstwerke zu erleben, denen aufgrund der physischen Beschränkung von Galerie- oder Museumsräumen zu häufig nur ein flüchtiger Moment der Betrachtung vergönnt ist.

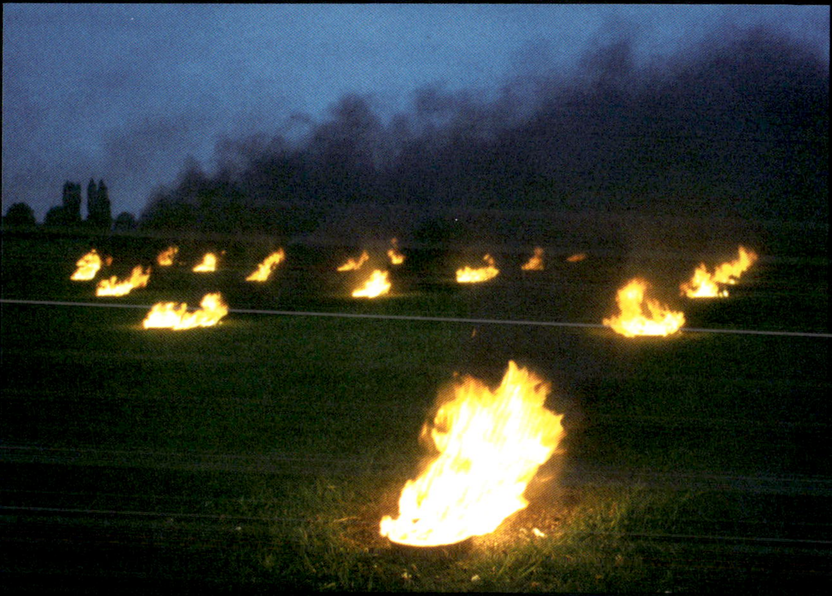

Anthony McCall
Landscape for Fire, 1972
16mm Film, 6'55'' (still)

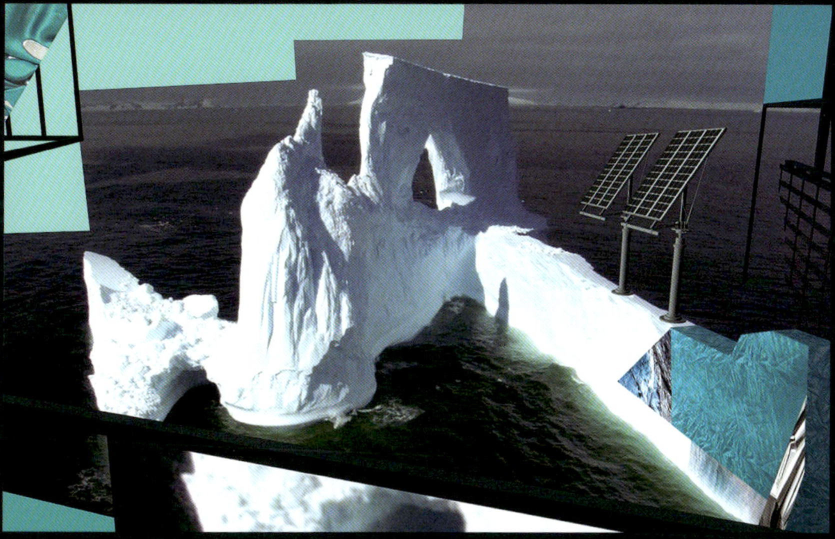

Joe Hamilton
Hyper Geography, 2011
Video, 1'00'' (still)

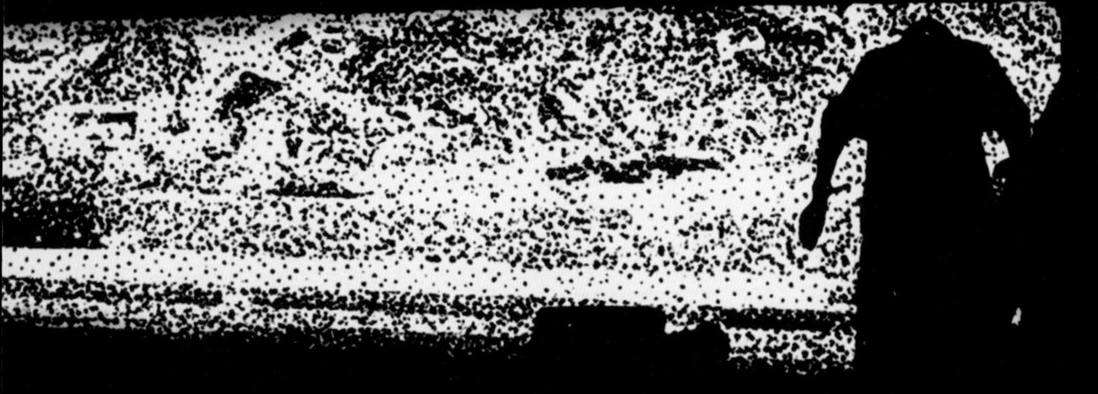

Alexander Schellow

Drawing

Frame from NERO [open archive of drawings, animations, texts / production: MELD / since 2011] 21x30cm / Filzstift auf Transparentpapier, 2013

The individual drawing is realized through a strictly regimented process that I developed over a long period of time and in constant reference to the materiality of the drawing process.
With the help of this process and with a predetermined temporal and spatial distance to that which has been seen, I can gain a certain access to visual memory. This access shifts between the processes of perception and memory (as the intentional (re-)activation of the perceived in the memory of the moment).
The process of reconstruction through drawing does not function as the reproduction of a remembered object. Instead it is the development and revision of this object as a visual constellation in the drawing.
The drawing method of a work point by point requires a continual comparison between the drawn visual surface and the remembered. Ultimately, the visual overwrites the memory itself, overtaking it and then completely replacing it in its capacity as representation.
Within the development of the method, many projects were realized in response to a concrete context raising an urgent question concerning visibility and possible participation in a preexisting political and social order (see Bolzano/Italy 2008, Tirana/Albania 2009–2013, NERO–Athens/Greece, since 2011), in order to question a reciprocal inscription of individual and collective memory-related practices and forms.

Die Einzelzeichnung entsteht in einem streng geregelten Verfahren, das über einen langen Zeitraum und mit ständigem Bezug auf die Materialität des Zeichnens entwickelt wurde.
Mithilfe dieses Verfahrens und mit einem vorgegebenen zeitlichen und räumlichen Abstand zum Gesehenen ist es mir möglich, einen gewissen Zugang zum visuellen Gedächtnis zu erlangen. Dieser Zugang schwankt zwischen Wahrnehmungs- und Erinnerungsprozessen (der intentionalen (Re-)Aktivierung des Wahrgenommenen in der Erinnerung des jeweiligen Augenblicks).
Bei diesem zeichnerischen Rekonstruktionsverfahren handelt es sich nicht um die Reproduktion eines erinnerten Objekts, sondern um die Entwicklung und Neubearbeitung desselben als eine visuelle Konstellation innerhalb der Zeichnung.
Die Punkt-für-Punkt-Zeichnung eines Werks erfordert den fortwährenden Vergleich der gezeichneten visuellen Oberfläche mit dem Erinnerten. Am Ende überlagert das Visuelle die eigentliche Erinnerung, übernimmt und ersetzt sie in ihrer Eigenschaft als Repräsentation.
Im Lauf der Entwicklung dieser Methode wurden zahlreiche Projekte realisiert, die immer in Zusammenhang mit einer konkreten Situation standen, in der es um Sichtbarkeit und eine mögliche Partizipation in einer bestehenden politischen und sozialen Ordnung ging (z. B. Bozen/Italien 2008; Tirana/Albanien 2009–2013, NERO – Athen/Griechenland, seit 2011), wobei jeweils die reziproke Einschreibung

The work on drawings becomes relevant as an activity that must constantly negotiate its place between the political, as the manifestation of that which is always excluded from the existing dominant order, and the policy of any conceivable regime of representation.
Instead of the representation of a figure within the drawing as image, the focus thus lies on the activity of image production as a form of "realization".

Animation

The development from drawing to animation first started with large groups of images in installations, coming together in serial patterns and visual surfaces according to various regulating principles. These led to the repeated reconstruction of the same image lined up as still animation and finally to entire filmic sequences.
This resulted organically from an ongoing confrontation with the potential of the interstice (in the image between two points / in the installation between two pictures / in film between two frames—and in any case between image and viewer) as the space in which perception and recollection become fundamentally intertwined.
The work with filmic animation is driven by an investigation into how a procedural notion of imagery can be conceived with animation, and how, through the process of memory-based reconstruction, this can be perceived and reflected as such by the viewer, who observes not as recipient but rather as (re)-constructor.
Animation is seen as a kind of imaging process, through which not only classical parameters of drawing such as "perspective" and "object" may be addressed and observed, but also their (and other) implementations within perception- and memory-processes as policies of reality construction.
As the drawings are composed of dots and spotted structures, a general movement within the picture results from the combination of continuous position shifts of the numerous markings from sheet to sheet—caused by the impossibility of repeating an exact image-structure from memory.

individueller und kollektiver gedächtnisbezogener Praktiken und Formen untersucht werden sollte.
Die Arbeit an den Zeichnungen wird relevant als Aktivität, die sich unablässig ihren Platz zwischen dem Politischen als Ausdruck dessen, was immer aus der herrschenden Ordnung ausgeschlossen ist, und der konkreten Politik – oder Methode – eines möglichen Repräsentationsregimes suchen muss.
Statt auf der Repräsentation einer Figur als Bild liegt der Fokus beim Zeichnen also auf der Aktivität der Bildproduktion als einer Form der „Realisierung".

Animation

Die Entwicklung von der Zeichnung zur Animation begann mit großen Bildgruppierungen in Installationen, die sich nach verschiedenen Ordnungsprinzipien zu seriellen Mustern und visuellen Oberflächen fügten. Dies führte immer häufiger zu Rekonstruktionen ein- und desselben Bildes, die zu einem animierten Standbild aneinandergereiht wurden, und schließlich zur Verfertigung richtiger Filmsequenzen.
All das ergab sich organisch aus der ständigen Beschäftigung mit dem Potenzial des Zwischenraums (im Bild zwischen zwei Punkten / in der Installation zwischen zwei Bildern / im Film zwischen zwei Frames – und in all diesen Fällen zwischen Bild und Betrachter) als dem Ort, an dem sich Wahrnehmung und Erinnerung fundamental verschränken.
Mit der Arbeit an der Filmanimation versuche ich herauszufinden, inwieweit sich damit eine prozedurale Bildauffassung umsetzen lässt und inwieweit diese – durch das Verfahren der gedächtnisgestützten Rekonstruktion – auch von einem nicht mehr rezipierenden, sondern (re-)konstruierenden Betrachter wahrgenommen und reflektiert werden könnte.
Die Animation wird als eine Art Bildgebungsverfahren gesehen, mit dem nicht nur klassische Parameter des Zeichnens wie „Perspektive" und „Objekt", sondern auch die Implementierung dieser (und anderer) Parameter als Mittel der Realitätskonstruktion in Wahrnehmungs- und Erinnerungsprozessen thematisiert und beobachtet werden können.
Da die Zeichnungen aus Punkten und Fleckenstrukturen bestehen, kommt es aufgrund der Positionsverschiebungen dieser Vielzahl an Elementen zwischen den einzelnen Blättern zu einer ständigen Bewegung innerhalb des Bildes. Sie ergibt sich aus der Unmöglichkeit einer exakten Wiedergabe der Bildstruktur aus dem Gedächtnis.

Aus dem Englischen von Wilfried Prantner

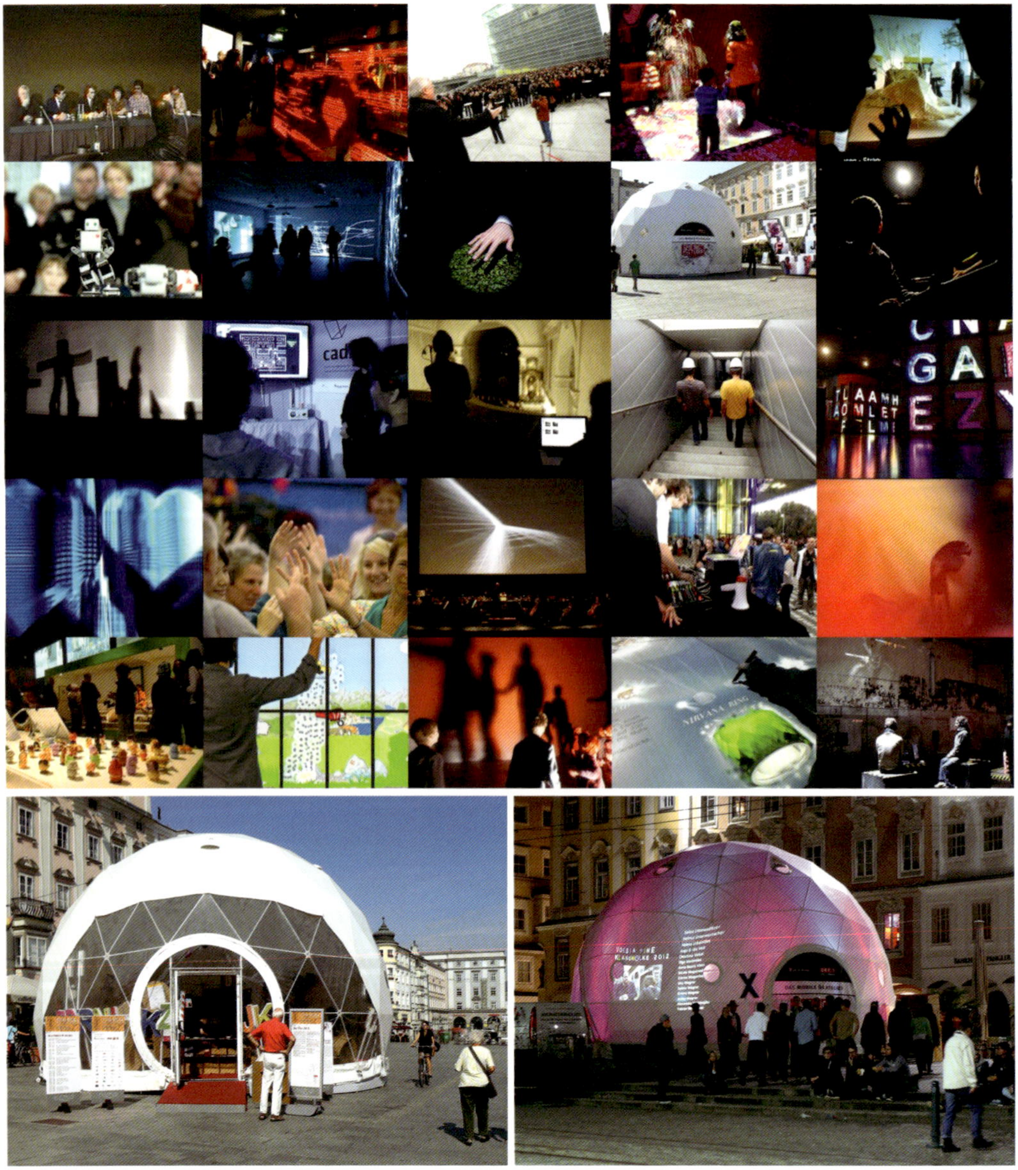

AEC, rubra, Kristefan Minski

Mobile Ö1 Atelier–Project Beehive
Mobiles Ö1 Atelier – Projekt Bienenstock

In the spirit of this year's festival theme, we're going to try out a new and different form of festival documentation on Linz's Hauptplatz. Instead of filming the goings-on at the festival as neutrally, as objectively as possible, and then storing the categorized material in our in-house archive, we're going to be focusing on a subjective festival experience this time.

A team of students from Queensland University of Technology, a group of youngsters from u19 – CREATE YOUR WORLD and "normal, everyday" festival visitors will be equipped with wide-angle Action Cams and sent out into the hustle and bustle for the length of one battery charge. What they cover and how they do it is completely up to them. What they most definitely shouldn't film is the stuff that producers, curators and artists consider interesting and worthy of digital immortality. Instead, they should go out and capture what appeals to them. Once each swarm has scoured the festival grounds for sweet images, it's time to buzz back to the Beehive, the Mobile Ö1 Atelier on Hauptplatz. Here, they can turn in their SD cards, download all the data, and finally view their material on a jumbo wall tiled with screens. This kaleidoscope juxtaposes a whole array of perspectives and angles and thus opens up insights into festival life that differ significantly from what's to be gleaned from archive footage. So, the point isn't to document what happened at the 2013 Ars Electronica Festival, but to portray how it was experienced.

http://oe1.orf.at

Als Reaktion auf das diesjährige Thema des Ars Electronica Festivals wird auf dem Linzer Hauptplatz eine andere, neue Art der „Festivaldokumentation" erprobt: Anstatt das Festivalgeschehen so neutral, so „objektiv" wie möglich abzufilmen und das verschlagwortete Rohmaterial im hauseigenen Archiv zu sichern, rückt diesmal das subjektive Festivalerleben in den Fokus.

Ein Team von Studierenden der Queensland University of Technology, Youngsters aus dem Umfeld von u19 – CREATE YOUR WORLD und ganz „normale" FestivalbesucherInnen werden dafür mit weitwinkeligen Actioncams ausgerüstet und für eine Akkulänge durchs Festivalgeschehen geschickt. Und das ohne jede Vorgabe, versteht sich. Gefilmt werden soll nicht das, was Veranstalter, KuratorInnen oder KünstlerInnen interessant und deswegen dokumentationswürdig finden, sondern das, was sie selbst als aufzeichnungswürdig erachten. Wenn der Schwarm an allen Ecken und Enden seine Festivalbilder eingesammelt hat, geht's zurück zum *Bienenstock,* zum Mobilen Ö1 Atelier am Linzer Hauptplatz. Hier werden die SD-Karten abgegeben, alle Daten heruntergeladen und die Bilder schließlich auf einer mehrere Meter langen und hohen Wand aus Screens abgespielt. Dieses Kaleidoskop stellt verschiedene Perspektiven und Blickwinkel gleichberechtigt nebeneinander und eröffnet so Einblicke in das Festival, die sich gänzlich von jenen unterscheiden, die in einem Archiv gewonnen werden können. Weil es nicht darum geht, das festzuhalten, was 2013 bei der Ars Electronica passiert ist, sondern zu dokumentieren, wie dies erlebt worden ist.

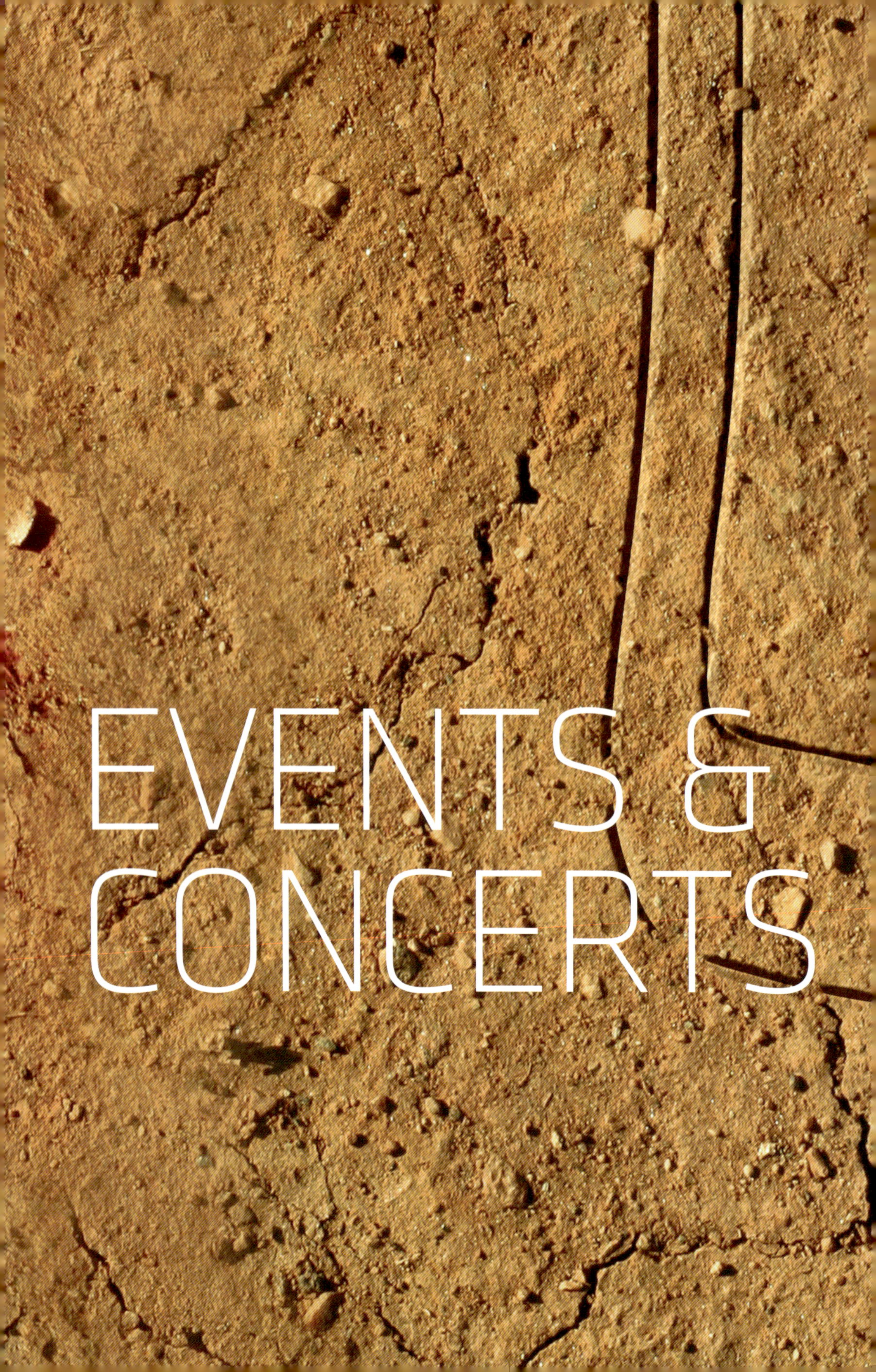

EVENTS & CONCERTS

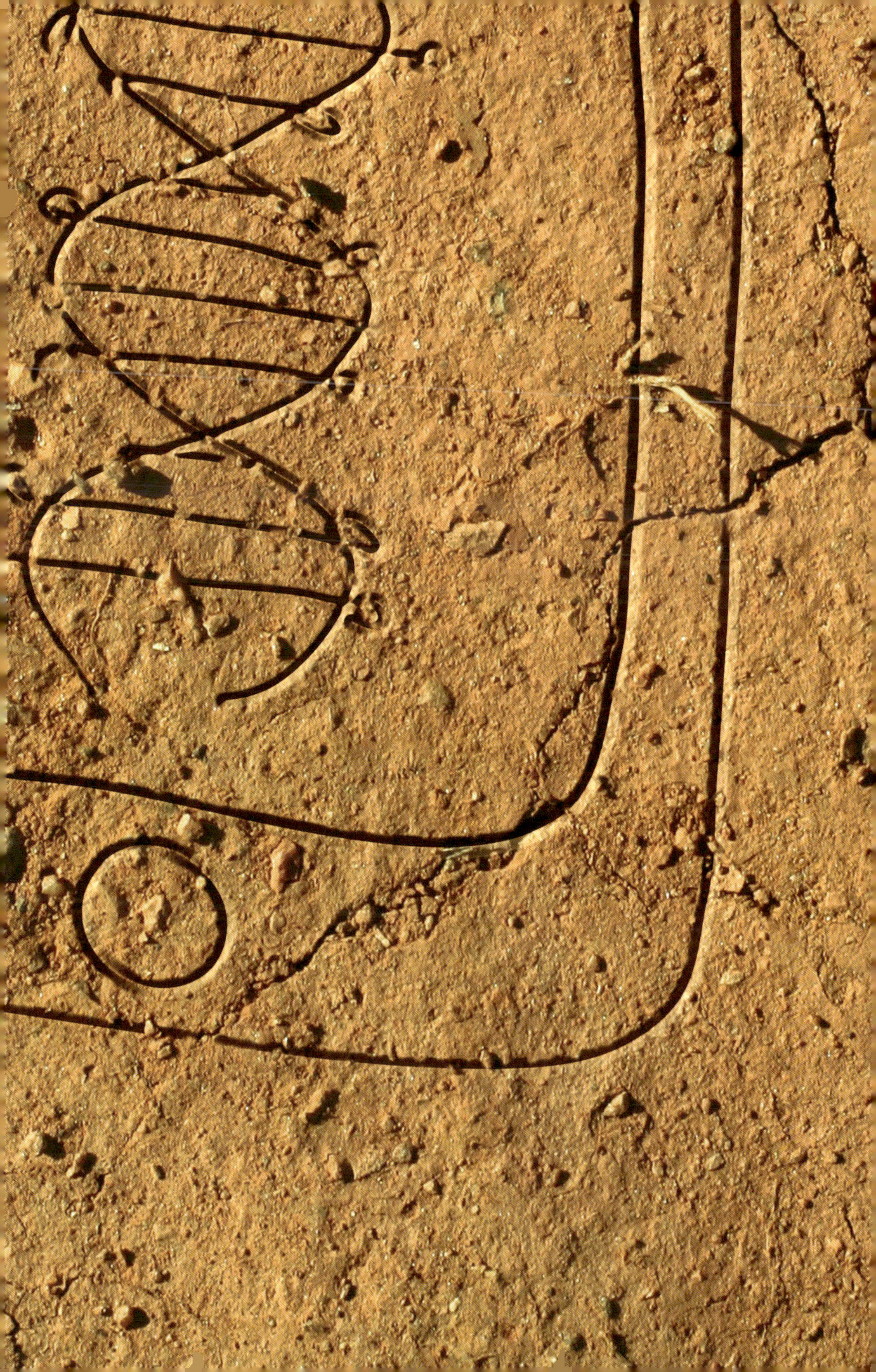

Wir sind hier

Book Burning, Surveillance and Interaction

Bücherverbrennung, Überwachung und Interaktion

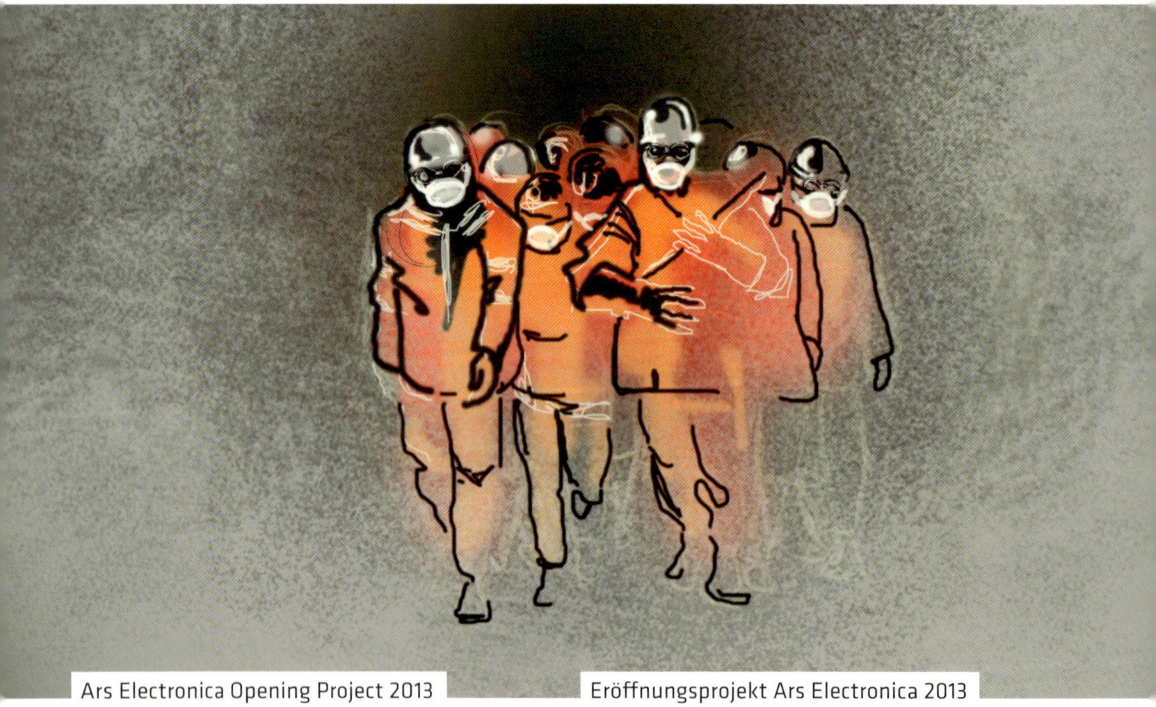

Ars Electronica Opening Project 2013

Eröffnungsprojekt Ars Electronica 2013

Whoever takes part in the Ars Electronica opening ceremony on 5 September 2013 at the grounds of the Tabakfabrik in Linz, will quickly start to feel a certain sense of unease. And that is, indeed, the intention. Surveillance cameras line the square, scrutinizing individual visitors. Other details also indicate that everything in the area is being carefully watched. A statue made of data storage devices stands in the square. What is its purpose? Suddenly, masked figures surge into the crowd and split it into several groups. The music shifts from well-known hits of the last few decades into deafening, meaningless noise. Two of the masked dancers climb up and over the walls, pursued by a spotlight, which suddenly directs its focus to the crowd.

Wer am 5. September 2013 an der Eröffnungsfeier der Ars Electronica auf dem Gelände der Tabakfabrik in Linz teilnimmt, wird schnell von einem unbestimmten Gefühl des Unbehagens erfasst, und das ist Absicht. Überwachungskameras säumen den Platz, die einzelne Besucher ins Visier nehmen. Auch andere Details deuten darauf hin, dass hier alles gründlich überwacht wird. Auf dem Platz steht eine Statue aus Datenträgern. Was geschieht mit ihr?
Dann beginnen maskierte Gestalten, sich in die Menge zu drängen und sie in mehrere Gruppen aufzuteilen. Die Musik, zunächst bekannte Hits aus vergangenen Jahrzehnten, wird zu einem ohrenbetäubenden Lärm. Zwei der maskierten Tänzer klettern an den Wänden hoch, wobei ein Lichtstrahl sie verfolgt, der sich dann auf einmal in die Menge richtet. Die Stimme eines

The voice of a young girl, whose face is projected large on a screen, begins to read a text. We are reminded of the 1933 Nazi book burning in the middle of Berlin, where more than 20,000 volumes were destroyed.

Those who did not go along with Nazi ideology in those days had good reason to be afraid. But shouldn't we also be afraid today, when everything we disclose on the Internet and social networks is saved, monitored, assessed, altered, deleted, and possibly used against us?

Wir sind hier is an interdisciplinary, cross-media art project in five acts, which deals with on- and offline media. The live performance in Linz is the dramaturgical climax to a three-month-long series of lead-in and follow-up debates that place the memory and interpretation of the 1933 book burning and its consequences in the 20th century in the context of the present day and facilitates reflection on these events for today's generations, and particularly the Digital Natives.

"Ours is the first age in which many thousands of the best-trained individual minds have made it a full-time business to get inside the collective public mind. To get inside in order to manipulate, exploit, control is the object now."[1] Marshall McLuhan offered this critique in 1951 in his first major work of media theory, *The Mechanical Bride,* a collage of strung-together chapters in which he analyzed the manipulative effects of advertising.

Couldn't this statement have been written down in the 1930s as a description of the Nazi propaganda machine? And wouldn't it apply just as much to the present day, in which countless purchase decisions, such as which book to buy, involve the creation and

kleinen Mädchens, dessen Gesicht groß auf der Leinwand erscheint, beginnt einen Text vorzutragen. Wir werden an die Bücherverbrennung erinnert, der 1933 mitten in Berlin rund 20.000 Bände zum Opfer fielen. Wer sich der Nazi-Ideologie nicht fügte, hatte damals allen Grund, Angst zu haben. Aber sollten wir heute nicht auch Angst haben, wenn alles, was wir im Internet, in sozialen Netzwerken von uns preisgeben, gespeichert, überwacht, ausgewertet, verändert, ausgelöscht und gegebenenfalls gegen uns verwendet werden kann?

Wir sind hier ist ein interdisziplinäres, crossmediales Kunstprojekt in fünf Akten, das über On- und Offline-Medien erzählt wird. Die Liveperformance in Linz ist der inszenatorische Höhepunkt eines dreimonatigen, vor- und nachbereitenden Online-Diskurses, der die Erinnerung und Interpretation der Bücherverbrennung von 1933 und ihre Folgen im 20. Jahrhundert in den Kontext der Gegenwart stellt und für heutige Generationen, insbesondere die der Digital Natives, reflektierbar macht.

„Wir leben in einem Zeitalter, in dem zum ersten Mal Tausende höchstqualifizierter Individuen einen Beruf daraus gemacht haben, sich in das kollektive öffentliche Denken einzuschalten, um es zu manipulieren, auszubeuten und zu kontrollieren."[1]

So leitete Marshall McLuhan 1951 sein erstes medientheoretisches Werk *The Mechanical Bride* ein, in dessen collageartig aneinander gereihten Kapiteln er vor allem die manipulative Wirkung der Werbung analysierte.

Hätte diese Aussage nicht schon in den 1930er Jahren niedergeschrieben werden können, um die Propagandamaschine der Nationalsozialisten zu beschreiben? Und würde sie nicht auch auf die heutige Situation

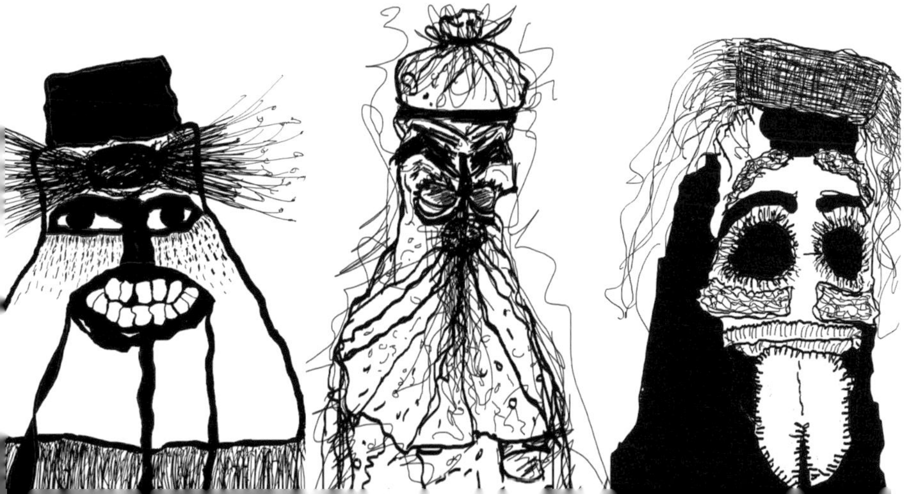

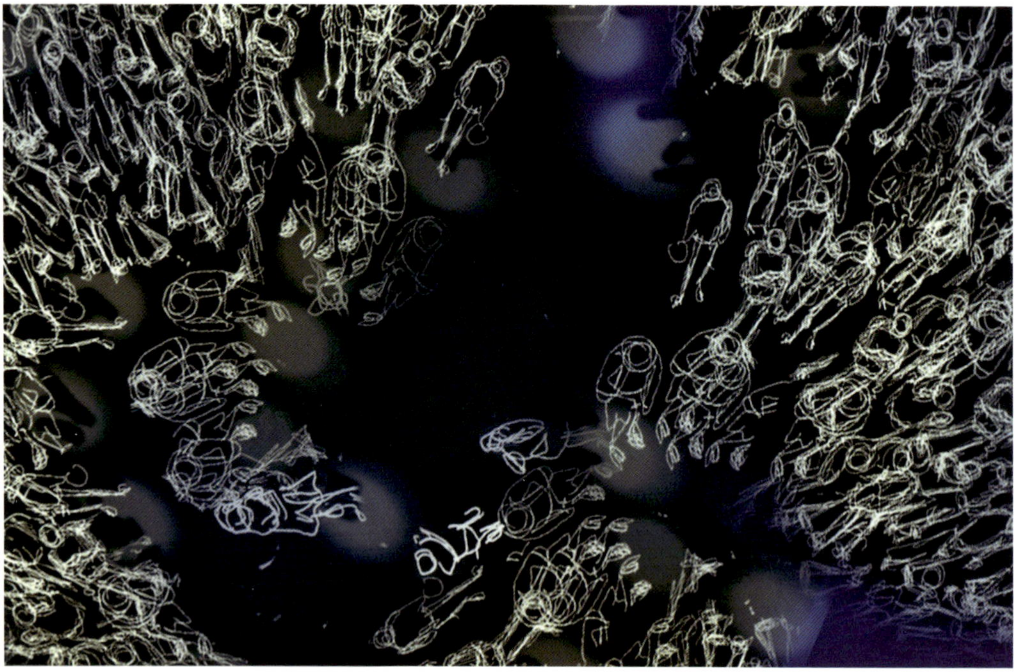

analysis of various consumer profiles? Big Brother Amazon knows exactly what we want to read next, and offers us tailor-made suggestions at the click of a mouse.

If the controlled consumers in 1950s America lived in a state that tracked Communists and did not bat an eyelid at book burnings, the controlled consumers of the 21st century live in a climate of surveillance and suspicion that prevails in the political and social day-to-day existence of the United States, many European countries and others outside Europe. The multimedia format of *Wir sind hier* turns this climate of fear into a tangible experience. But it's not just about the mere sensory and physical experience of a live-action work of art conveyed through a plethora of optical, acoustic or spoken elements. The synesthetic live performance was not designed to cloud the senses or to numb the mind, but rather to sharpen our senses and thought to all that threatens our culture, our democracy, our freedom(s), to totalitarian structures that creep unnoticed into our lives when we don't pay attention or when we are distracted by the consumer,

zutreffen, in der unzählige individuelle Kaufentscheidungen, etwa der Erwerb eines Buches, die Ermittlung differenzierter Konsumentenprofile nach sich ziehen? Big Brother Amazon weiß ganz genau, was wir auch noch lesen sollten, und ist mit entsprechenden Angeboten sofort bei der Hand.

Lebten die kontrollierten KonsumentInnen im Amerika der 1950er-Jahre in einem Staat, der Kommunisten verfolgte und auch vor Bücherverbrennungen nicht zurückschreckte, so leben sie im 21. Jahrhundert in einem Klima der Überwachung und Verdächtigung, welches das politische und gesamtgesellschaftliche Leben in den USA und vielen Ländern Europas und anderswo erfasst hat. Dieses Klima macht *Wir sind hier* durch eine crossmediale Inszenierung erfahrbar. Es geht aber nicht um das bloße sinnliche und physische Erlebnis eines mit einer Fülle an optischen, akustischen, sprachlichen und technischen Elementen arbeitenden Kunstwerks. Die synästhetische Live-Performance dient nicht dazu, die Sinne zu vernebeln und das Gehirn zu betäuben, sondern soll die Sinne und das Denken für alles schärfen, was unsere Kultur, unsere Demokratie, unsere Freiheit(en) gefährentertainment and consciousness industries.

Wir sind hier is a collective art project, carried out by the initiators of the developer team Salvatore Vanasco, Claudius Brodmann, Andy Müller-Maguhn, Cornelia Wunderlich, Arie Zinger, FM Einheit, Rica Blunck, Stephanie Geiger, Gözen Atila and Timo Maier, and in collaboration with numerous other artists, historians, philosophers, journalists, software developers and designers. The presentation on September 5 in Linz is the premiere and the climax of a continuing artistic process. A public discussion begins online two months before the live performance, on July 5, in which users are called to make contributions and take part in artistic actions on themes such as censorship, identity, cultural amputation, migration, seduction, attention control, and immersion. A selection of these will be edited and integrated in the performance in Linz.

What is the societal, political background for *Wir sind hier?* In the aftermath of the September 11, 2001 attacks—at the very latest—ostensibly democratic societies increasingly turned into "societies of control," a term coined by Gilles Deleuze around

det, was sich an totalitären Strukturen in unser Leben einschleicht, ohne dass wir es zunächst überhaupt bemerken, wenn wir nicht aufmerksam oder von der Konsum-, Entertainment- und Bewusstseinsindustrie abgelenkt sind.

Wir sind hier ist ein kollektives Kunstprojekt, an dessen Gestaltung neben dem initiatorischen Entwicklerteam Salvatore Vanasco, Claudius Brodmann, Andy Müller-Maguhn, Cornelia Wunderlich, Arie Zinger, F.M. Einheit, Rica Blunck, Stephanie Geiger, Gözen Atila und Timo Maier auch andere Künstler, Historiker, Philosophen, Journalisten, Softwareentwickler und Designer beteiligt waren und sind. Die Inszenierung am 5. September in Linz ist die Uraufführung und der Höhepunkt in einem kontinuierlichen künstlerischen Prozess. Öffentlich beginnt der Diskurs zwei Monate vor der Live-Performance am 5. Juli im Internet, wo Nutzer aufgerufen werden, sich zu Themen wie Zensur, Identität, kulturelle Amputation, Migration, Verführung, Aufmerksamkeitssteuerung, Immersion u. ä. zu äußern und an künstlerischen Aktionen teilzunehmen. Eine Auswahl der Beiträge wird redaktionell bearbeitet in die Inszenierung in Linz einfließen.

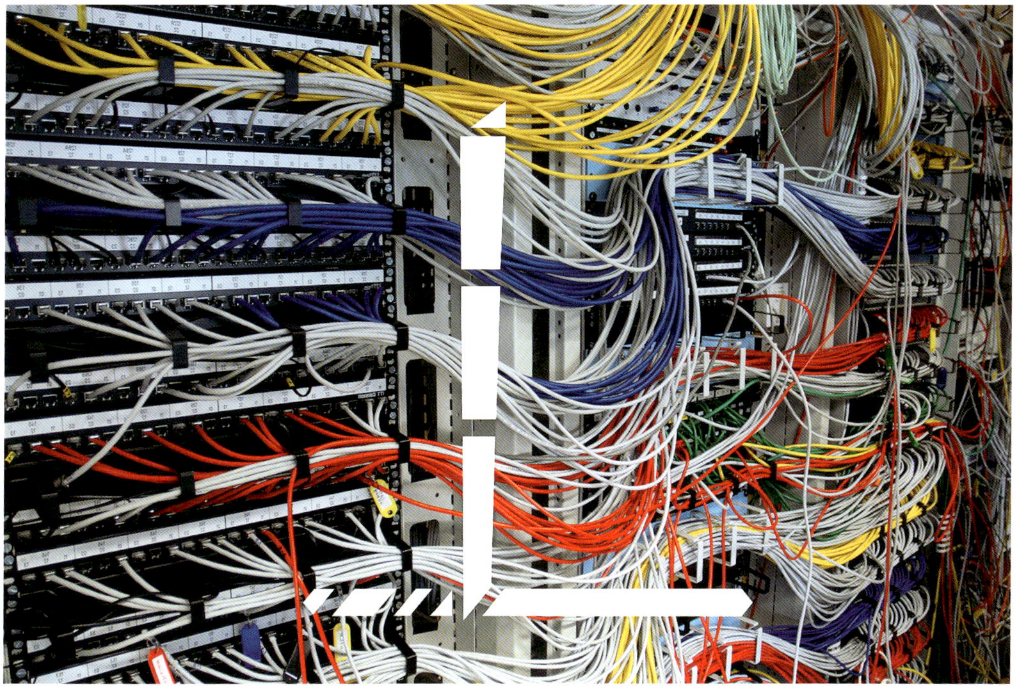

1990. We are under control continuously and to the greatest possible extent, and what eyes cannot see and ears cannot hear is determined by technological means. A slightly conspicuous head shape can become a suspicious feature for biometric identification and what we read may link us to terrorist organizations if we hit too many of the "wrong" keywords.

Ever-increasing amounts of data are being stored and even events that were once "news items" have caved to the pressure of the live-ticker news format, pressed together into one update that's barely longer than the current stock exchange listings, to be added to the world's history with as short a delay as possible. The deadline, always a known quantity, a grace period for turning in reports, is sliding closer and closer to real-time. Digital journalism was also, until recently, characterized by "finalized texts, just like in the newspaper." However, the "good old home page"[2] is also inching closer and closer to the rhythm of real-time, like a small, hungry child that can't wait for its food.

The urgency of the here-and-now knows no sustainability—a word now understood only in the environmental sense. If media reports generally fall into oblivion after a week, history also seems to fall victim to a kind of collective amnesia. Although the Third Reich still seems to be present in the media, surveys have shown that the word "Auschwitz" holds no meaning to one-fifth of Germans under the age of 30—i.e. the generation of Digital Natives. When not only historical knowledge, but also the information itself, is missing, we reach a state that not even the prescience of Walter Benjamin could have imagined. In his essay "Der Erzähler: Bemerkungen zum Werk Nikolai Lesskows" (The Storyteller: Reflections on the Works of Nikolai Lesskow, 1936/37), Walter Benjamin compares "information" with "storytelling". The tradition of storytelling is based on lived experience that is passed on through word of mouth, embodied in "farmers who have settled to till the fields" and in "trading sailors". The latter brings "tales from afar", the former "tales from the past". Both kinds of storytelling fused in the Middle Ages handicrafts trade, because "every master of the trade was a young travelling tradesman before settling in his home town or in another town."[3]

Was ist der gesellschaftliche, politische Hintergrund für *Wir sind hier?* Spätestens in der Folge der Anschläge vom 11. September 2001 verwandelten sich vermeintlich demokratische Gesellschaften zunehmend in die „Kontrollgesellschaften", als welche Gilles Deleuze sie schon um 1990 beschrieb. Es wird ständig und so viel wie möglich kontrolliert, und was Augen nicht sehen und Ohren nicht hören, wird auf technischem Wege ermittelt. Eine leicht auffällige Kopfform kann durch die Erfassung biometrischer Daten zum verdächtigen Merkmal werden und das, was wir lesen, aufgrund der Erfassung von Reizwörtern eine Nähe zu terroristischen Vereinigungen unterstellen.

Immer mehr Daten werden erfasst, und auch das, was früher einmal eine „Nachricht" war, wird unter dem Druck des Live-Tickers, der dem Weltgeschehen möglichst ohne Zeitverzug hinterherlaufen soll, auf eine Meldung zusammengepresst, die kaum länger ist als die jeweils aktuellen Börsennotierungen. Die „Deadline", die immerhin eine Galgenfrist bis zur Abgabe von Texten setzt, rückt immer mehr mit der Echtzeit zusammen. „Abgeschlossene Texte wie in der Zeitung" haben den digitalen Journalismus bisher noch geprägt, doch die „gute alte Homepage"[2] weicht immer mehr einem Echtzeittakt, der wie ein kleines Kind keinen Verzug duldet, wenn es Nahrung braucht.

Die Dringlichkeit des Augenblicks kennt allerdings keine Nachhaltigkeit – ein Begriff, der heutzutage nur noch ökologisch verstanden wird. Wenn Medienberichte in der Regel nach einer Woche völlig in Vergessenheit geraten, scheint auch die Geschichte einer Art kollektiver Amnesie zum Opfer zu fallen. So präsent das Dritte Reich in den Medien immer noch zu sein scheint, haben Umfragen gleichwohl ergeben, dass einem Fünftel der unter Dreißigjährigen, also der Digital Natives, das Wort „Auschwitz" nichts sagt. Wenn nicht nur das historische Wissen, sondern schon die bloße Information fehlt, ist ein Zustand eingetreten, den selbst der hellsichtige Walter Benjamin nicht erahnen konnte. In seinem Essay *Der Erzähler. Bemerkungen zum Werk Nikolai Lesskows* (1936/37) stellt Benjamin der „Information" die „Erzählung" gegenüber. Die Tradition des Erzählens beruhe auf der gelebten Erfahrung, die von Mund zu Mund weitergetragen wird, verkörpert im „sesshaften Ackerbauern" und im „handeltreibenden Seemann": Dieser bringt die „Kunde aus der Ferne", jener diejenige „aus der Vergangenheit". Beide Formen des Erzählens kamen

However "experience has dropped in value"[4] and with it storytelling as a "craft-like form of communication."[5] It is increasingly being displaced by a new form of communication: by the "information" that "lays claim to swift verifiability" and therefore appears more or less comprehensible." While the client mentioned here "liked to borrow from wonders, it is of vital importance that the information is plausible."[6]

Benjamin describes direct physical experiences being replaced by information, but today information itself comes under scrutiny, as its formatting and the time pressure under which it must be delivered can hardly stand up to a closer confrontation with plausibility. Long before a large-scale societal event such as the protests in Taksim Square in Istanbul in June 2013 became the subject of various analyses and news coverage, the stock exchange reaction took place.

The economic, capitalistic evaluation of events dispenses with intellectual criticism that always comes too late and for this reason is, allowed, even if it attacks the system itself. "Journalistic criticism of capitalism"[7] is allowed to spread freely—as long as it does not penetrate the secrets of the power structures themselves, a lesson learned hard by Wikileaks informant Bradley Manning or Edward Snowden, who made public the comprehensive internet surveillance being carried out by the US secret service, NSA (public means, in this sense, that the media were allowed to report about it, rather than simply repeating the "secret" information that had been exposed).

Wir sind hier uses the cultural amputation of the Nazi book burnings that took place 80 years ago as a springboard for the current project, drawing a parallel between those events and today's situation. The seven acts explore general themes such as censorship, destruction, geographic and political reorganization, migration, seduction by the consciousness industry and surveillance mechanisms, as well as the tangled, immersive developments of game and war technologies, from the 1920s to the present day. This era was shaped by the redrawing of European national boundaries after the First World War and all the resulting repercussions, up to today's supposedly unified Europe, and the accompanying cartography of the First World's bad

in den mittelalterlichen Handwerksbetrieben zusammen, denn „jeder Meister war Wanderbursche gewesen, bevor er in seiner Heimat oder in der Fremde sich niederließ".[3]

Doch „die Erfahrung ist im Kurse gefallen"[4] und damit die Erzählung als „eine gleichsam handwerkliche Form der Mitteilung".[5] Sie wird durch eine neue Form der Mitteilung zunehmend verdrängt: durch die „Information", die „den Anspruch auf prompte Nachprüfbarkeit" macht und deshalb „‚an und für sich verständlich' auftritt." Während die erzählte Kunde „gern vom Wunder borgte, ist es für die Information unerlässlich, dass sie plausibel klingt".[6]

Beschreibt Benjamin das Ersetzen unmittelbarer physischer Erfahrung durch die Information, steht heute auch die Information in Frage, da ihre Formatierung und der Zeitdruck, unter dem sie geliefert werden muss, eine nähere Auseinandersetzung mit ihrer Plausibilität gar nicht mehr zulassen. Ehe größere gesellschaftliche Ereignisse, etwa die Proteste auf dem Taksim-Platz in Istanbul im Juni 2013, zum Gegenstand differenzierter Analysen und Berichterstattungen werden können, haben die Börsenkurse schon längst reagiert.

Die ökonomische, kapitalistische Bewertung von Ereignissen verzichtet auf intellektuelle Kritik, die ihr gegenüber immer zu spät kommt und deshalb erlaubt ist, auch wenn sie das System selbst angreift. „Feuilletonistische Kapitalismus-Kritik"[7] darf grenzenlos geübt werden, sofern sie nicht in die Geheimnisse der Machtstrukturen selbst eindringt, wie der Wikileaks-Informant Bradley Manning oder Edward Snowden, der die umfassende Internet-Überwachung des US-Geheimdienstes NSA öffentlich machte (öffentlich heißt, die Medien dürfen darüber berichten, nur nicht die aufgedeckten „geheimen" Informationen weitergeben).

Wir sind hier zieht aus der heutigen Situation den Bogen zurück zu der Bücherverbrennung durch die Nazis vor achtzig Jahren und nimmt diese kulturelle Amputation zum Ausgangspunkt des Projekts. Die fünf Akte behandeln Rahmenthemen wie Zensur, Vernichtung, kartografische und staatliche Neuordnung, Migration, Verführungen durch die Bewusstseinsindustrie und Überwachungsmechanismen sowie die verschränkten und immersiven Entwicklungen von Spiele- und Kriegstechnologien – die Zeit von den 1920er-Jahren bis heute. Eine Zeit geprägt von

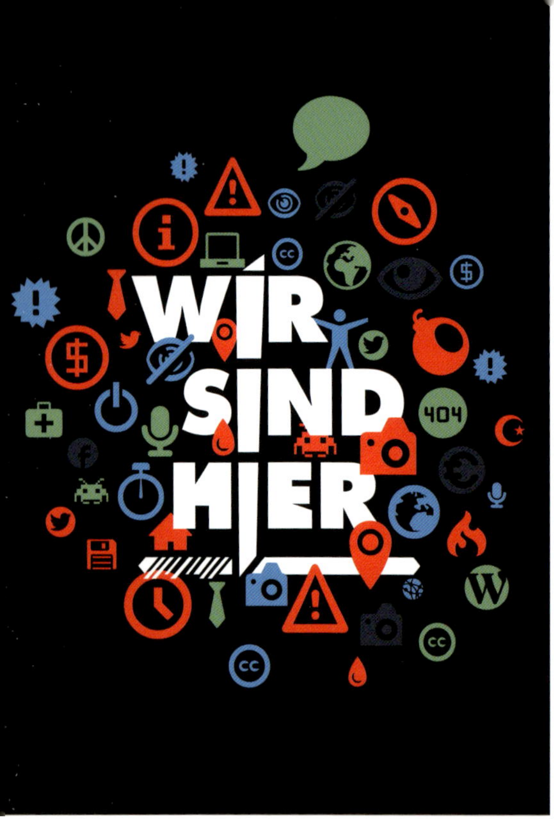

conscience about the Third World. The elaborate staging, which also offers diverse opportunities for visitor interaction, will make the situation we are in today visually, acoustically and physically perceptible. The complexity of the performance draws the audience away from the sensory barrage of passive experiences and guides them back towards real-world experiences.

Wir sind hier utilizes the full spectrum of currently available media technology to reach a goal which Russian author Viktor Shklovsky formulated nearly 100 years ago:

"In order to restore the perception of life for us, to make things palpable or the stone stony, there is the thing which we call art. The purpose of art is to allow us to experience the object, an experience that is vision and not only recognition. Art makes use of two strategies in this context: the estrangement of objects and the complication of form in order to impede perception and prolong it. For in respect to art, the perceptual process is an aim in itself and must be prolonged. Art is a means to experience the becoming of an object, which has already become is irrelevant to art."[8]

der nationalen Neuaufteilung Europas nach dem Ersten Weltkrieg mit all ihren wirkmächtigen negativen Konsequenzen bis hin zum vermeintlich einheitlichen Europa und der damit einhergehenden Kartografie des schlechten Gewissens der Ersten gegenüber der Dritten Welt. Die komplexe Inszenierung, die zudem vor Ort Möglichkeiten der Interaktion durch die Besucher erlaubt, soll visuell, akustisch und physisch erfahrbar machen, in welcher Situation wir heute sind. Ihre sich der direkten Sinneserfahrung entziehende Komplexität wird gleichsam durch den synästhetisch-digital-technologisch-involvierenden Inszenierungsansatz in die „gelebte Erfahrung" zurückgeholt.

Wir sind hier verfolgt unter vielfältigem Einsatz der heute zur Verfügung stehenden Medientechnologie ein Ziel, das der russische Schriftsteller Viktor Sklovskij vor fast hundert Jahren so formulierte:

„Um für uns die Wahrnehmung des Lebens wiederherzustellen, die Dinge fühlbar, den Stein steinig zu machen, gibt es das, was wir Kunst nennen. Das Ziel der Kunst ist, uns ein Empfinden für das Ding zu geben, ein Empfinden, das Sehen und nicht nur Wiedererkennen ist. Dabei benutzt die Kunst zwei Kunstgriffe: die Verfremdung der Dinge und die Kompliziertheit der Form, um die Wahrnehmung zu erschweren und ihre Dauer zu verlängern. Denn in der Kunst ist der Wahrnehmungsprozess ein Ziel in sich und muss verlängert werden. Die Kunst ist ein Mittel, das Werden eines Dings zu erleben, das schon Gewordene ist für die Kunst unwichtig."[8]

Auch wenn sich viele Kunstwerke der letzten hundert Jahre auf Sklovskijs Programm beziehen lassen, steht ihre „Form", auch bei Filmen oder anderen in der Zeit ablaufenden Kunstformen, in der Regel als etwas Abgeschlossenes vor uns, an dem wir uns wahrnehmend und denkend abarbeiten können, auf dessen Gestalt wir aber selbst keinen Einfluss haben. Dies gilt auch für die meisten Kunstwerke, die sich mit dem Thema Bücherverbrennung auseinandersetzen.

Bücherverbrennungen in der Geschichte

Die mutwillige Vernichtung von Büchern und anderen Kulturgütern zieht sich wie ein roter Faden durch die Geschichte. Der heute am meisten diskutierte und erinnerte Fall fand am 10. Mai 1933 statt, als Mitglieder des Nationalsozialistischen Studentenbundes und sogar viele Professoren über 20.000 Bücher aus der

Even though many works of art in the past hundred years have made reference to Shklovsky's words, their "form"—even in films or other art forms that play out over time—is generally "complete" in some way. We can perceive and think about this complete something, but have no influence on its form. The same is true for most of the works of art that deal with the book-burning theme.

Book Burnings in History

The willful destruction of books and other cultural symbols is a recurring theme throughout history. The most well-known and widely discussed incident took place on May 10, 1933, when members of the National Socialist German Students' League, as well as many professors, brought out over 20,000 books from the Humboldt University library, selected because they did not conform to the ethos of the Nazi regime. With musical accompaniment from SA and SS bands, the books were burned at what was then known as Kaiser-Franz-Josef-Platz, known today as Bebelplatz. But this was not an isolated event. In the third century B.C., the Chinese emperor Qin Shihuangdi burned the writings of all philosophical schools operating outside of the government's school of thought. In the third century AD, the Roman emperor Diocletian burned the writings of Christians in Constantinople. The Christian church itself had few qualms about destroying the works of critical or non-believer authors during the Inquisition.

In 1762, the progressive writings of Jean-Jacques Rousseau were a thorn in the side of the authorities in Paris and Geneva. His works were burned and arrest warrants issued. Religious writers and supporters of the Ancien Régime fared little better, with Robespierre, the leader of the French Revolution, ordering their destruction in 1793.

On October 18, 1817, roughly 500 members of various student groups converged at Wartburg Castle in Eisenach on the three-hundredth anniversary of Martin Luther's posting of the 95 Theses. Dozens of books were burned, described as reactionary, anti-nationalistic or un-German. The Wartburg Festival spurred Heinrich Heine's well-known quotation: "That was only the beginning. For wherever they burn books, they will also, in the end, burn human beings."

Bibliothek der Humboldt-Universität holten, die nicht der Gesinnung des NS-Regimes entsprachen. Musikalisch begleitet von SA- und SS-Kapellen wurden sie auf dem damaligen Kaiser-Franz-Josef-Platz, heute Bebelplatz, verbrannt.

Das war kein Einzelfall. Im 3. Jahrhundert v. Chr. ließ der chinesische Kaiser Qin Shihuangdi die Schriften aller anderen philosophischen Schulen außer der staatlichen verbrennen, im 3. Jahrhundert n. Chr. der römische Kaiser Diokletian in Konstantinopel die Schriften der Christen. Die christliche Kirche wiederum ging später nicht zimperlich mit den Büchern kritischer und „ungläubiger" Autoren um, deren Werke durch die katholische Inquisition vernichtet wurden.

1762 waren die aufklärerischen Schriften Jean-Jacques Rousseaus den Autoritäten in Paris und Genf ein Dorn im Auge. Es kam zu Verbrennungen und Haftbefehlen gegen den Autor. 1793 erging es religiösen und das Ancien Régime verherrlichenden Schriften auch nicht besser, als der französische Revolutionsführer Robespierre ihre Vernichtung anordnete.

Am 18. Oktober 1817 kamen etwa 500 Burschenschaftler und Mitglieder schlagender Verbindungen auf der Wartburg bei Eisenach zusammen. Es wurden Dutzende von Büchern verbrannt, die man als reaktionär, antinational oder undeutsch empfand. Dazu schrieb Heinrich Heine seinen berühmten Satz: „Das war ein Vorspiel nur, dort wo man Bücher verbrennt, verbrennt man auch am Ende Menschen." Die Abbildung einer Bücherverbrennung „zierte" das Siegel der 1873 gegründeten New York Society for the Suppression of Vice (Gesellschaft zur Bekämpfung des Lasters). Ihr Gründer, der Puritaner Anthony Comstock, soll die Verbrennung von fünfzehn Tonnen Büchern, die Zerstörung von 150 Tonnen Bleidruckplatten und von fast vier Millionen Bildern verantwortet haben.

Am 25. August 1914 brannten deutsche Truppen als Vergeltungsmaßnahme für Angriffe belgischer Partisanen die Universitätsbibliothek in Löwen nieder, wodurch auch viele mittelalterliche Handschriften zerstört wurden. In den Jahren des Russischen Bürgerkriegs (1918–1922) und in der so genannten bolschewistischen Kulturrevolution Ende der 1920er Jahre wurden Bibliotheken geplündert sowie Bücher verbrannt oder auf andere Weise vernichtet. Die Nationalsozialisten ließen im Zuge von „Eingliederungen" ins Reich auch 1938 in Mexiko und Österreich und 1941 im Elsass Bücher verbrennen.

The illustration of a book burning adorned the official seal of the New York Society for the Suppression of Vice. Its founder, the Puritan Anthony Comstock, was reputed to have destroyed more than fifteen tons of books, 150 tons of lead plates used in letterpresses, and nearly four million pictures.
On August 25, 1914, in retaliation for the attacks of Belgian guerrillas, German troops burned down the university library in Leuven, destroying with it many hand-written medieval texts. In the course of the Russian Civil War (1918-1922) and in the so-called Bolshevik Cultural Revolution in the late 1920s, libraries were looted and books burned or destroyed in other ways. In the course of their "incorporation" into the Third Reich, the Nazis also burned books in Mexico and Austria in 1938 and in Alsace in 1941.
American Senator Joseph McCarthy's hatred of Communists led him to confiscate and burn works of literature in 1953, while "anti-Communist" books and other media have been repeatedly destroyed in

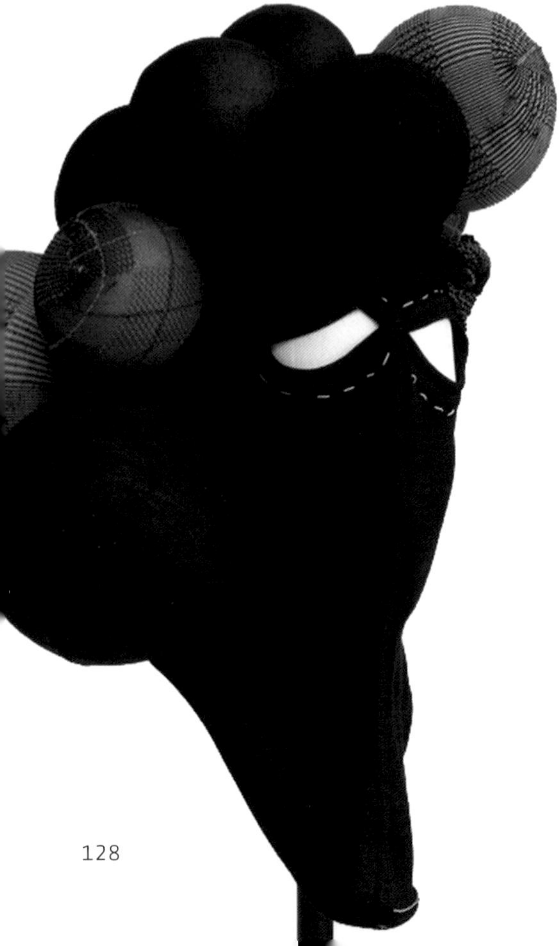

Die Kommunistenhatz des amerikanischen Senators Joseph McCarthy führte 1953 zur Beschlagnahmung und teilweise zur Verbrennung von Literatur, während in China seit der Machtübernahme der Kommunistischen Partei immer wieder öffentlich „anti-kommunistische" Bücher und Medien vernichtet werden.
Der 1988 erschienene Roman *Die satanischen Verse* von Salman Rushdie wurde von Muslimen wegen Gotteslästerung verbrannt. Unwiederbringliche historische Manuskripte wurden 1992 von den serbischen Truppen in Sarajevo, 1998 von den Taliban in Kabul zerstört. Im Juli 2010 kündigte der Prediger Terry Jones an, am Jahrestag der Terroranschläge am 11. September 2001 in Gainesville (Florida) 200 Exemplare des Koran verbrennen zu wollen, sagte die Aktion nach internationalen Protesten jedoch kurzfristig ab. Im Februar 2012 verbrannten fünf US-Soldaten in Afghanistan mehrere Koran-Exemplare, die von Gefangenen im Militärgefängnis Bagram als geheimes Kommunikationsmittel verwendet worden waren. Sie waren wohl versehentlich im Müll gelandet, wo Arbeiter in der Mülldeponie des Gefängnisses ihre Verbrennung bemerkten. Bei darauffolgenden Protesten in Afghanistan kamen rund 40 Menschen ums Leben. Barack Obama entschuldigte sich bei der afghanischen Bevölkerung für das Vorgehen der Soldaten.
In Deutschland regt sich sofort Protest, sobald nur die geringste Vergleichbarkeit mit den Bücherverbrennungen der Nazis entsteht, auch wenn sich eine Aktion gegen die Verbreitung reaktionären Gedankenguts richtet. Mit diesem Vergleich wurde der tschechische Künstler Martin Zet sogleich konfrontiert, als er im Rahmen der Berliner Biennale 2012 dazu aufforderte, Exemplare des populistischen Buches *Deutschland schafft sich ab* von Thilo Sarrazin an verschiedenen Sammelstellen abzugeben und damit aus dem Verkehr zu ziehen. Das Projekt war wenig erfolgreich, es kamen nicht viele Bücher zusammen. Man könnte es auch als schwachen künstlerischen Abklatsch dessen sehen, was der Verfassungsschutz der BRD 1956 mit der deutschen Auflage von Eustace Mullins *Secrets of the Federal Reserve* machte: Sie wurde wegen des in dem Buch enthaltenen antisemitischen Gedankenguts komplett beschlagnahmt und verbrannt.
Die Vernichtung einzelner Exemplare gedruckter Bücher ist ein symbolischer Akt, der in der Regel auch als ein solcher verstanden werden soll. Sie verhindert nicht die Verbreitung des Restes der Auflage, ebenso

China since the Communist Party came to power. Salman Rushdie's 1988 novel *The Satanic Verses* was burned by Muslims under accusations of blasphemy. Irreplaceable historical manuscripts were destroyed by Serbian troops in Sarajevo in 1992 and by the Taliban in Kabul in 1998. In July 2010, Terry Jones, an American priest from Gainesville, Florida, announced plans to burn 200 copies of the Quran on the anniversary of the September 11 attacks. After a slew of international protests, he cancelled the event shortly before it was scheduled. In February 2012, five American soldiers burned several copies of the Quran on the grounds that the books had been used for secret communication among inmates at Bagram military prison. The Qurans accidentally landed in the compound's trash, where garbage workers saw them burning. The ensuing protests in Afghanistan resulted in the loss of about 40 lives. Barack Obama offered an apology to the Afghan people for the soldiers' actions.
In Germany, the slightest hint of a comparison to the Nazi book burnings will stir up protest immediately—even if it is sparked by a campaign against the spread of reactionary ideas. The Czech artist Martin Zet was confronted with this comparison at the Berlin Biennale in 2012, when he invited people to hand in copies of Thilo Sarrazin's populist and provocative book about the cultural integration of immigrants in Germany, *Deutschland schafft sich ab* (Germany is doing away with itself) at various collection points, thereby removing it from circulation. The project met with little success; very few books were collected. It could also be seen as a weak artistic imitation of what the Federal Republic of Germany's actions for the Protection of the Constitution did with the German edition of Eustace Mullins' *Secrets of the Federal Reserve* in 1956–it was confiscated and burned due to the anti-Semitic ideas it contained.
The destruction of individual copies of printed books is a symbolic act and should generally be understood as such. Such exemplary book burning does not prevent the circulation of the edition of book, or its digital reproduction. It is, however, a different story when original manuscripts are destroyed, something which has happened often when libraries have been destroyed in the recent past.

wenig seine digitale Vervielfältigung. Anders verhält es sich mit der Vernichtung originaler Manuskripte, die bei vielen Bibliothekszerstörungen gerade in jüngerer Zeit erfolgte.

Bücherverbrennung und Vernichtung von Kulturgut als Thema der Kunst

Die totalitäre Vision, dass konsequent alle im Umlauf befindlichen Bücher vernichtet werden, findet sich in der – auch durch ihre Verfilmung durch François Truffaut – wohl am berühmtesten gewordenen literarische Darstellung des Themas Bücherverbrennung. Ray Bradburys 1953 erschienener Zukunftsroman *Fahrenheit 451* (die Hitze, bei der Bücherpapier Feuer fängt) beschreibt eine Gesellschaft, in der Feuerwehrleute, die normalerweise Brände löschen sollen, jedes einzelne Buch, das sie finden, ins Feuer werfen.
Die „Wilden", auf denen die Tanzchoreografie von *Wir sind hier* basiert, könnten Nachfahren dieser Feuerwehrleute sein. Es sind ambivalente Figuren – sie

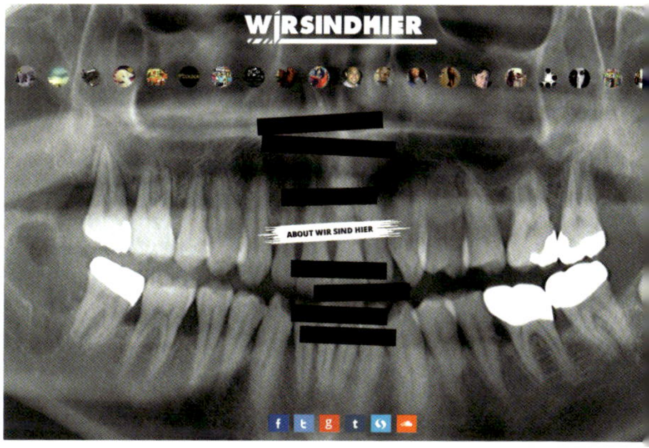

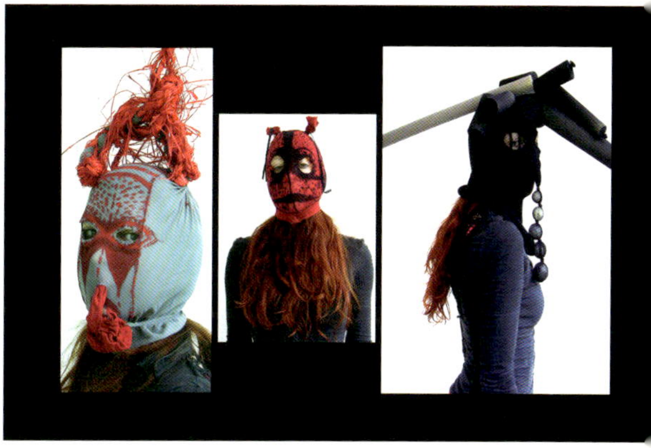

Burning Books and Destroying Cultural Heritage as a Theme in Art

The totalitarian vision of the total destruction of all books in circulation can be found in what is probably the best-known literary portrayal of book burning, Ray Bradbury's 1953 science-fiction novel *Fahrenheit 451* (the temperature at which book pages burn), as well as in the film version directed by François Truffaut. A society is depicted in which the firemen, normally responsible for putting out fires, burn every book they encounter.

The "wild men" on whom the dance choreography of *Wir sind hier* is based could be seen as descendants of these firemen. They are ambivalent characters symbolizing the eviction squads who, at the end of a war, catastrophe or reign of terror, come in to restore a sense of 'normality', and manifest themselves again in elaborately organized and controlled institutions. But does a new broom always do a better job of sweeping? Don't they always sweep aside whatever doesn't suit them? What is normality and doesn't the ordering and manipulative game of such forces just start all over again? In whose interest is and what are the consequences of the cleaning up, classifying, planning, manipulating? And are those people for whom a new order is being built in any position, in their awful situation, to think about cultural tradition, cultural new beginning, and cultural freedom when they are struggling to simply survive? Control and manipulation in the process of nation (re)building are also forms of physically nonviolent but, in their intellectual scope, aggressive restriction and amputation.

The violent silencing of cultural tradition is depicted in Bradbury's dystopia. In the visual arts, the book-burning theme is most often explored through monuments and memorials that depict silence through stark sculptural forms, or empty rooms and spaces.

On the exact site of the book burning in 1933, there can now be found the Monument to the Memory of the Book Burning, created in 1995 by Israeli artist Micha Ullman. A five-cubic-meter underground space has been carved out on Bebelplatz. On the completely whitewashed walls, shelves are installed with enough space for 20,000 books. The empty room is not accessible, but it is covered with a glass plate that allows visitors to clearly see the room.

stehen metaphorisch für die Räumungskommandos, die nach einem Krieg, einer Katastrophe oder einer Terrorherrschaft den „Normalzustand" wiederherzustellen versuchen und sich wieder in durchorganisierten und gelenkten Institutionen manifestieren. Aber kehren neue Besen immer besser? Fegen nicht auch sie beiseite, was ihnen nicht in den Kram passt? Was ist der Normalzustand und beginnt das ordnende und lenkende Spiel solcher Kräfte nicht wieder von vorne? In wessen Interesse und mit welchen Konsequenzen wird aufgeräumt, eingeteilt, entworfen, gelenkt? Und haben diejenigen, für die eine Ordnung wieder neu erbaut wird, in ihrer schrecklichen Situation überhaupt „den Kopf frei", sich über kulturelle Tradierung, kulturellen Neubeginn und kulturelle Freiheit Gedanken zu machen, wenn es um das nackte Überleben geht? Steuerung und Lenkung im Prozess des Nation(re)building sind auch Formen einer zwar gewaltlosen, aber in ihrer intellektuellen Tragweite doch gewaltsamen Beschränkung und Amputation.

Dass kulturelle Überlieferung gewaltsam zum Verstummen gebracht wird, ist bei Bradbury in Form einer negativen Utopie dargestellt. In der bildenden Kunst wird das Thema Bücherverbrennung vor allem durch Mahn- oder Denkmäler zum Ausdruck gebracht, die das Verstummen durch starre skulpturale Formen sowie Leerräume und -stellen ausdrücken.

Direkt am Ort des Geschehens 1933 in Berlin befindet sich das 1995 eingeweihte Denkmal zur Erinnerung an die Bücherverbrennung des israelischen Künstlers Micha Ullman. Ein 5 × 5 × 5 Meter großer unterirdischer Raum ist in den Bebelplatz eingelassen. An den Wänden des vollständig weiß getünchten Raumes befinden sich leere Regale für 20.000 Bände. Der leere Raum ist nicht zugänglich, aber durch eine Glasplatte abgedeckt, die den Blick in den Raum ermöglicht.

Seit 2000 steht auf dem Wiener Judenplatz das Holocaust-Denkmal der britischen Bildhauerin Rachel Whiteread. Der geschlossene, würfelförmige Block hat die Konturen einer Bibliothek.

Eine direkte Assoziation an verbrannte Bücher könnte die Bleibibliothek von Anselm Kiefer in der Sammlung Marx im Hamburger Bahnhof in Berlin wecken. Die große Bodenskulptur bezieht sich aber auch mit ihrem Titel auf die 1988 in der BRD durchgeführte „Volkszählung", ihre Größe soll die die Bürger entmündigende und zu abgezählten Erbsen erniedrigende Staatsmacht symbolisieren.

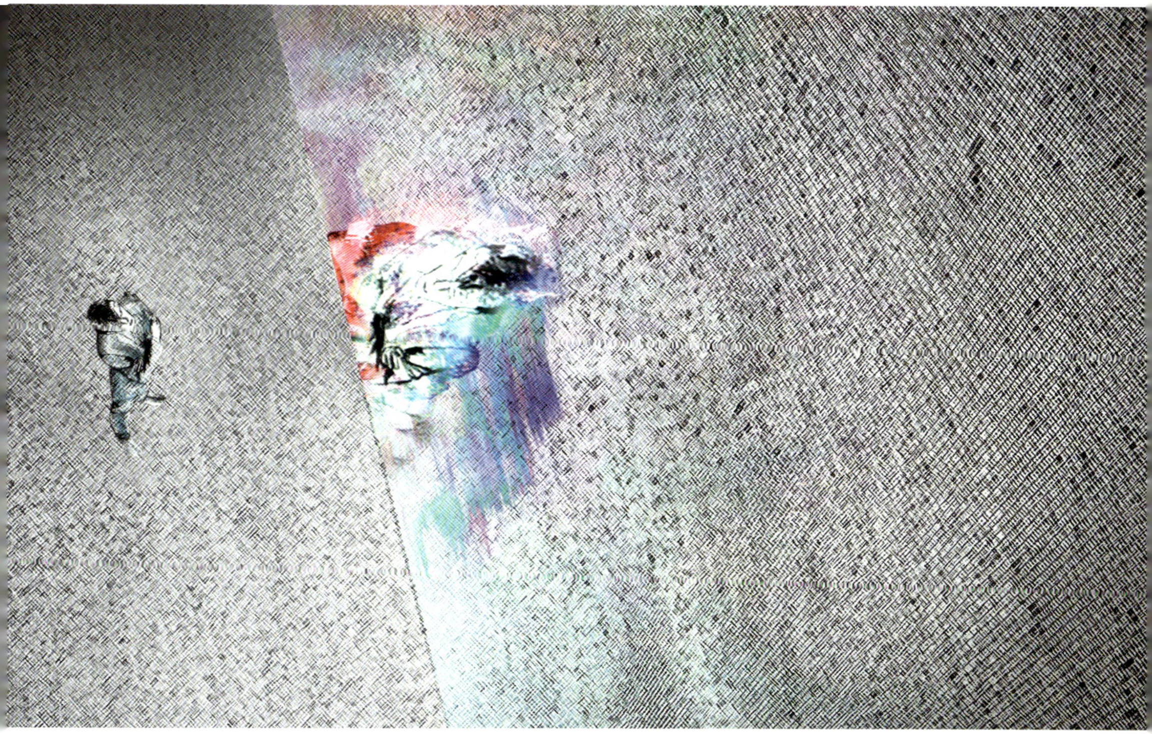

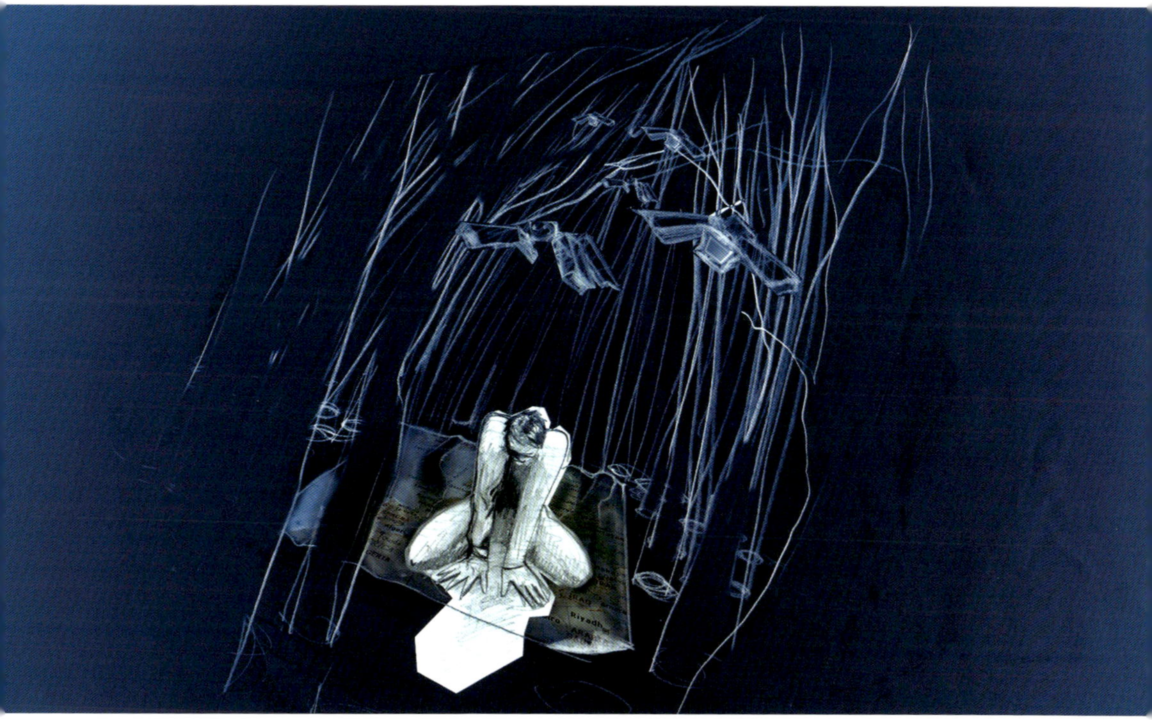

Since 2000, Vienna's Judenplatz (Jews' Square) has been the home of a Holocaust memorial constructed by the British sculptor Rachel Whiteread. The sealed, cubic block is in the shape of a library. Anselm Kiefer's lead library in the Marx Collection at Berlin's Hamburger Bahnhof (a museum complex) stirs up direct associations to burned books. The large sculpture's title also refers to the 1988 Federal Republic of Germany's population census–its size symbolizes the state's crippling of the population, reducing them to figures to be counted like peas.
At the documenta exhibition in Kassel, the Museum Fridericianum displayed an installation by Michael Rakowicz, an American artist with Iraqi-Jewish roots. He commissioned 33 Afghan and Italian sculptors to create books out of stone, to stand as imitations of precious manuscripts from the noble library which were totally burned or seriously damaged in the Fridericianum. The exhibition also made reference to the Buddha statues that were destroyed by the Taliban in 2001.
The sculptural, memorial and gravestone-like petrification is the symbolic expression for the "killing" of culture, which enforces silence. Like the remains of destroyed buildings they bear witness to the past and call to mind Diderot's words in 1767: "The ideas ruins evoke in me are grand. Everything comes to nothing, everything perishes, everything passes, only the world remains, only time endures."

Media Device Sculptures Instead of Towers of Books

Wir sind hier takes a completely different route. It is not a work of art that lends itself to meditation, but rather a process that can be influenced through the actions of individuals. It could also be described as a sculpture, but one that is accessible and always changing.
If a seemingly static sculpture is created during the two-month process leading up to the live performance, it will be based on digital communication processes. The whole process is open and depends on the collaboration of the users. They decide by vote which parts will be used, which form the sculpture will have and what will happen to the sculpture after the festival. It is a journey of discovery into the unknown depths of creative collective processes–

Auf der documenta 2012 in Kassel war im Museum Fridericianum eine Installation des US-amerikanischen Künstlers irakisch-jüdischer Abstammung Michael Rakowicz zu sehen. Von afghanischen und italienischen Bildhauern ließ er 33 Bücher aus Stein meißeln als Nachahmungen wertvoller Handschriften, die im damals die fürstliche Bibliothek beherbergenden Fridericianum gänzlich verbrannt oder schwer beschädigt wurden. Der Künstler stellte damit auch einen Bezug zu den 2001 von den Taliban zerstörten Buddha-Statuen her.
Die skulpturale, denkmalhafte und an Grabsteine erinnernde Versteinerung ist symbolischer Ausdruck für die „Tötung" von Kultur, die zum Verstummen bringt. Wie Reste zerstörter Gebäude zeugen sie von der Vergangenheit und gemahnen an Diderots Worte von 1767: „Ruinen erwecken in mir erhabene Ideen. Alles wird zunichte, alles verfällt, alles vergeht. Nur die Welt bleibt bestehen, nur die Zeit dauert fort."

Keine Büchertürme, sondern Datenträgerskulpturen

Wir sind hier geht einen anderen Weg. Es ist kein Werk, das zur Meditation auffordert, sondern ein Prozess, der durch eigene Aktion beeinflusst werden kann. Vielleicht ist es auch als Skulptur beschreibbar, dann allerdings als eine begehbare und sich ständig verändernde. Wenn im Laufe des zweimonatigen, die Live-Performance vorbereitenden Online-Diskurses eine statisch erscheinende Skulptur entsteht, basiert sie auf digitalen Kommunikationsprozessen. So können Internetnutzer die Herstellung einer neuen Art von Skulptur als nutzergeneriertes Kunstwerk unterstützen, das auf dem Festivalgelände der Ars Electronica entsteht. Der gesamte Prozess ist offen und baut auf die Einmischung der Nutzer. Sie bestimmen per Voting, welche Teile verarbeitet werden, welche Form die Skulptur haben wird und was nach dem Festival mit ihr geschieht. Es ist eine Entdeckungsreise in die unbekannten Tiefen gestalterischer Kollektivprozesse, auf die die Künstler von Anfang bis Ende zusammen mit den Nutzern gehen – der Prozess ist auch das Ergebnis. Ob am Ende ein Obelisk aus Festplatten im Internet versteigert oder eine Freiheitsstatue aus Büchern verbrannt wird, die Entscheidung liegt ganz bei den Netizen.
Wir sind hier betrifft nicht nur diejenigen, die tatsächlich in Linz vor Ort sind. Dort gibt es die Akteure auf

a journey that the artists embark on with the users from beginning to end. The process is the result. Whether an obelisk made of hard drives is auctioned on the Internet at the end, or a Statue of Liberty made of books is burned, the netizens will decide.

Wir sind hier does not just affect those who are present at the performance in Linz. The participants onstage are essentially the same as the ones who are watching from the plaza, who in turn are the same as the users who influence the piece by interacting with it online. Stages of the historical process–war, destruction, rebuilding, the incursion of media on everyday life–will all be passed in scenic review through the choreography of dancing bodies. *Wir sind hier* also poses the question of what constitutes cultural memory nowadays.

The piece creates an experience space that is shaped not only by the creative energy of the choreographed dancers, but also by the diffuse atmosphere of surveillance and menace. This ambivalence is characterized by the presence of the masked figures onstage, the so-called 'Perchten' in Bavarian and Austrian folk tradition. Are they lighthearted jesters? Are they the leaders of eviction squads, sent to clean up the scene after a war or a similar catastrophe? Or are they Bradbury's book-burning firemen in *Fahrenheit 451?*

Surveillance and Control in Art

Michael Klier's film *Der Riese* (The Giant), a movie that consisted almost entirely of footage collected through surveillance cameras in major German cities, appeared as early as 1984. But all things considered regarding the surveillance theme, *Wir sind hier* is more in the tradition of works in which the observer himself becomes involved as a protagonist in ambivalent observation situations. This is also explored in space installations and experimental designs developed by Bruce Nauman, Dan Graham and others around 1970. The visitor walks into a room or along a wall and is recorded. He can see a rear view of himself, or a view of himself with temporal delay at a different place in the installation. Nauman is interested in the video medium "as electronic mirror and surveillance device."[9]

In the set-up of seemingly simple environments, complex relationships between seeing and not

der Bühne, diejenigen, die sich auf dem Platz befinden, und diejenigen, die sich über das Internet beteiligen und das Geschehen beeinflussen. Stationen des historischen Prozesses, Krieg, Zerstörung, Wiederaufbau, die zunehmende Mediatisierung des Lebens, passieren szenisch Revue, werden in eine Choreografie tanzender Körper übersetzt. *Wir sind hier* stellt auch die Frage, wie das kulturelle Gedächtnis sich heute konstituiert. Es entsteht ein Erfahrungsraum, der von der darstellerischen Energie der Choreografie, aber auch von einer diffusen Atmosphäre der Überwachung und Bedrohung geprägt ist. Für diese Ambivalenz stehen auf der Bühne die maskierten Gestalten, die einem bayerisch-österreichischen Volksbrauch entsprechend „Wilden" heißen. Sind sie lustige Narrenfiguren? Sind sie das „Aufräumkommando", das nach dem Krieg oder einer anderen Katstrophe den „Normalzustand" wieder herstellt? Oder die Feuerwehrleute, die in *Fahrenheit 451* die Bücher verbrennen?

Überwachung und Kontrolle in der Kunst

Schon 1984 machte Michael Klier mit *Der Riese* (1984) einen Film, der fast ausschließlich aus Bildern besteht, die von Überwachungsanlagen in deutschen Großstädten aufgezeichnet wurden. Insgesamt lässt sich *Wir sind hier* unter dem Aspekt der Überwachungsthematik aber eher in die Tradition von Werken stellen, in denen die Betrachter selbst als Akteure in ambivalente Beobachtungssituationen verwickelt werden. Dies geschieht in den Rauminstallationen und „Versuchsanordnungen", die unter anderem Bruce Nauman und Dan Graham um 1970 entwickelt haben. Man läuft in einen Raum hinein oder an einer Wand entlang, wird aufgezeichnet, sieht sich selbst von hinten oder mit zeitlicher Verzögerung an einer anderen Stelle der Installation. Nauman interessiert das Medium Video „als elektronischer Spiegel und Überwachungsanlage".[9]

In ihrem Aufbau einfach erscheinender Environments entfalten sich komplexe Beziehungen zwischen Sehen/Nicht-sehen und Beobachtet-werden/Nicht-sichtbar-sein. Graham nutzt bis heute einseitig spiegelndes Glas, das er erstmals 1975 in der Installation *Two Viewing Rooms* einsetzte. Zwei direkt nebeneinander liegende Raumboxen sind durch das Glas getrennt. Der eine Raum ist dunkel, der andere hell. In der hellen Box sehen die eintretenden Besucher auf einem vor dem Spiegel platzierten Videomonitor in seeing, observer and observed unfold. Graham still uses today one-way mirrors, which he first used in his installation *Two Viewing Rooms* in 1975. Two adjacent rooms are separated by glass. One room is dark, the other illuminated. Visitors in the illuminated room can see their reflections in real-time on a monitor placed in front of the mirror. Visitors in the dark room can observe visitors in the other room, who do not realize this—until they notice that the camera showing their real-time reflections can only be behind the mirror.

In theoretical writings, Graham also occupies himself with the social and political functions of surveillance systems.[10] Quite a large number of artists carried on in Nauman's and Graham's footsteps in various ways. The most important theoretical source of inspiration on the subject of surveillance and the relationship between power and viewpoint was undoubtedly Michel Foucault. In *Discipline and Punish: The Birth of the Prison* in 1975, Foucault analyzed Jeremy Bentham's Panopticon prison concept, put forward in the early 19th century. The guards, stationed in the middle of a tower, can watch prisoners in a ring around them, but the prisoners cannot see the guards.

The camera-supervised indoor and outdoor spaces in the city, the streets, shopping malls and parking garages, bank branches, train stations and airports are not prison-like closed environments. Foucault compared these closed environments to societies of discipline, which predominated from the early 19th century past the end of the Second World War. They were characterized by closed-door institutions like prisons, hospitals, factories, schools, and families, which both regulate normal social life as well as temporarily or permanently excluding people from them, for example during a prison sentence. But even someone who never sets foot in a prison gets trapped in numerous closed environments throughout their life: in the form of school, university, long-term work, and so on.

The closed environments have not disappeared, but the societies of discipline have increasingly transformed into societies of control—a process that Gilles Deleuze describes in his development on Foucault's theory.

In societies of control, closed environments eventually resolve themselves into architectural bound-

Echtzeit ihr eigenes Bild. Im dunklen Raum können andere Besucher die Besucher im hellen Raum beobachten, die davon nichts merken – erst dann, wenn sie realisieren, dass die sie aufzeichnende Kamera sich hinter dem Spiegel befinden muss.

Auch in theoretischen Texten hat sich Graham mit der sozialen und politischen Funktion von Überwachungssystemen befasst.[10] Etliche Künstler führten das Nauman-Graham-Paradigma differenzierend weiter. Die wichtigste theoretische Inspirationsquelle des Überwachungsthemas, des Verhältnisses von Macht- und Blickbeziehungen, waren die Schriften Michel Foucaults. In *Überwachen und Strafen* analysierte Foucault 1975 das panoptische Gefängniskonzept Jeremy Benthams aus dem frühen 19. Jahrhundert. Die Wärter konnten vom Mittelpunkt der Rundanlage aus die Gefangenen in den umliegenden Zellen überwachen, waren aber selbst für diese unsichtbar.

Die kameraüberwachten städtischen Außen- und Innenräume, die Straßen, Kauf- und Parkhäuser, Bankfilialen, Bahnhöfe oder Flughäfen sind jedoch keine Einschließungsmilieus, wie es ein Gefängnis darstellt. Foucault hat die Einschließungsmilieus als kennzeichnend für die Disziplinargesellschaften analysiert, die vom frühen 19. Jahrhundert bis nach dem Zweiten Weltkrieg vorherrschten. Sie waren geprägt von festen Institutionen wie Gefängnis, Krankenhaus, Fabrik, Schule, Familie, die sowohl das normale soziale Leben regeln als auch die zeitweiligen oder grundsätzlichen Ausschlüsse aus diesem, etwa durch eine Gefängnisstrafe. Aber auch wer nicht ins Gefängnis kommt, durchläuft im Leben mehrere Einschließungsmilieus: Schule, Universität, langfristiger Arbeitsplatz usw.

Die Einschließungsmilieus sind zwar nicht verschwunden, aber die Disziplinargesellschaften haben sich zunehmend zu Kontrollgesellschaften gewandelt – ein Prozess, den Gilles Deleuze in Weiterführung von Foucaults Machttheorie zusammenfassend beschrieben hat. In der Kontrollgesellschaft lösen sich die einschließenden Milieus als architektonische Begrenzungen auf. Statt Menschen in örtlich begrenzten Milieus Regeln zu unterwerfen und zu disziplinieren, findet Kontrolle jederzeit und überall statt, ohne dass es zu physisch direkt spürbaren Zugriffen auf den – eingesperrten – Körper kommt. Man weiß nie, wo man wirklich steht. Das Gebot lautet, sich ständig weiterzuentwickeln, neu zu lernen, den Arbeitsplatz zu wechseln – wie es der amerikanische Soziologe

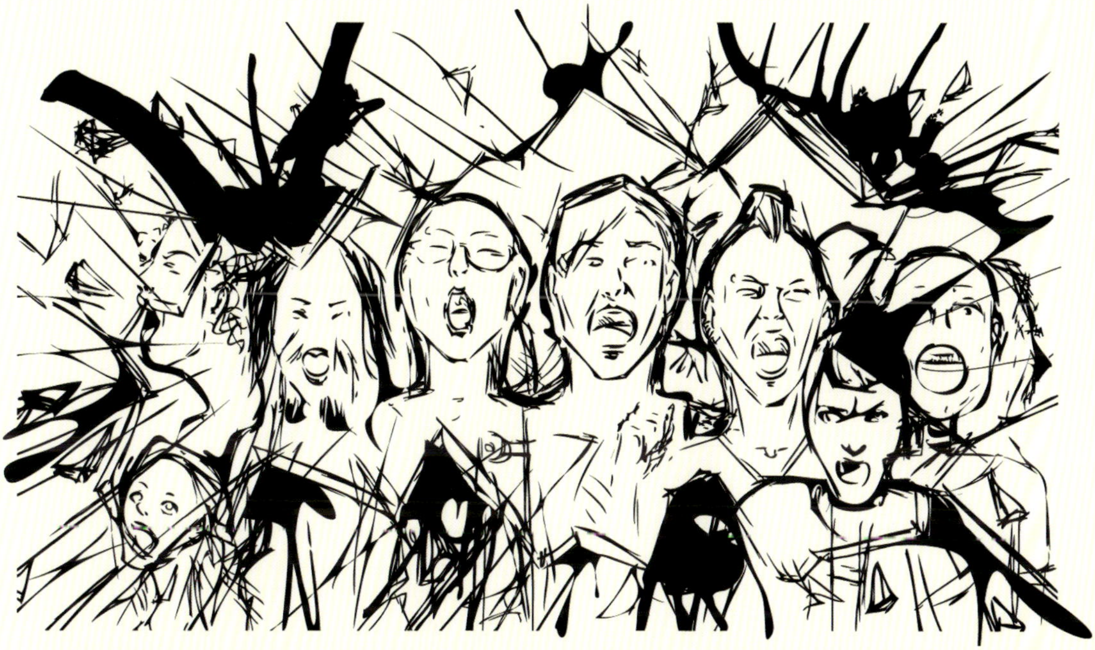

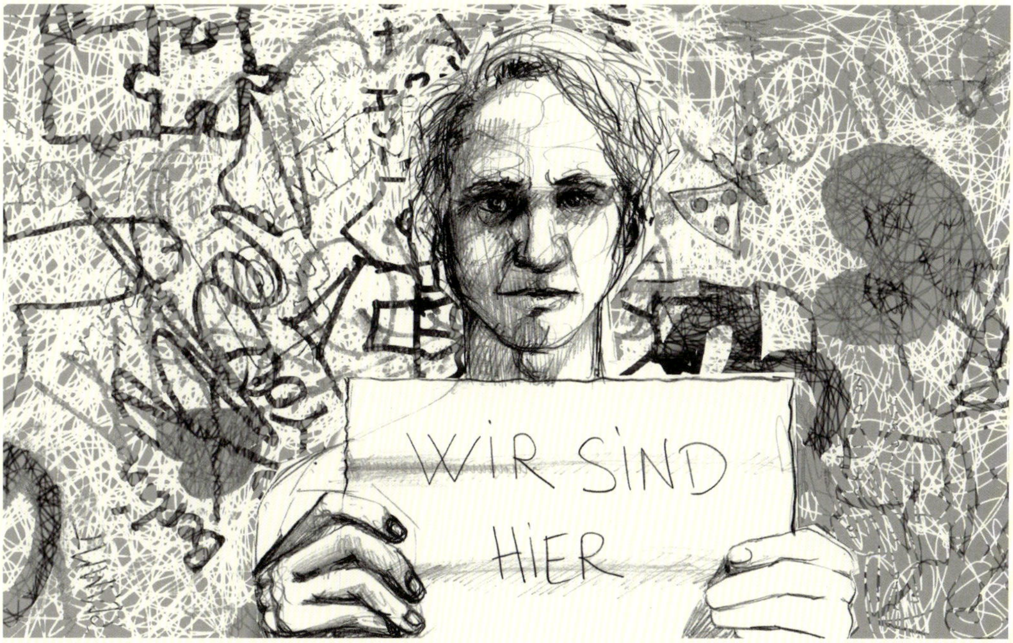
WIR SIND
HIER

aries. Rather than throwing people into physically separated areas and disciplining them, control happens everywhere at all times without showing any effect on the–imprisoned–bodies of those it affects. No one knows where he or she stands. The command rings out to develop further, learn new things, change jobs–as the American sociologist Richard Sennett described it, to be a "flexible" person. Such a person does not work in factories with fixed hierarchies, but rather in business ventures; they do not have owners, but rotating directors; these people can lose their jobs because the shareholders speculated and suffered financial ruin.
In his 1990 work, *Postscript on the Societies of Control,*[11] Gilles Deleuze sees the electronic shackle that replaces conventional imprisonment as a basic metaphor for societies of control. The convict does not have to serve time in prison, but cannot really move around freely as his location can always be monitored.

Freedom from the Shackle

Every traceable mobile phone is also its own type of electronic shackle, and every action you take on the Internet can be traced. Tell me which pages you visit and what you buy, and I will tell you who you are, what you are allowed to do and what you should do. Books are no longer being burned, but if demand is too low, they are no longer distributed or even published. It's often enough if they are just not mentioned, so that no one hears about them unless they accidentally come across them while surfing online. But there are also opportunities to become an author, such as by becoming involved with the *Wir sind hier* blog, where contributions to the given themes are edited and become part of an online publication. The voices of the users will be heard in the truest sense of the word when they read or sing Brecht's poem *Gegen Verführung* (Against Seduction) on a video or audio recording. The different voices will be mastered into a user-generated cho(i)r, to be played at the end of the performance in Linz.
Wir sind hier aims to encourage young people not to sink into a sea of historical oblivion, to extract themselves from the tick-tock of the live ticker, and to recognize how their thoughts are being far more subtly manipulated, exploited and controlled than

Richard Sennett genannt hat: ein „flexibler" Mensch zu sein. Dieser arbeitet nicht in Fabriken mit festen Hierarchien, sondern in Unternehmen, hat es nicht mit Besitzern, sondern mit wechselnden Geschäftsführern zu tun und kann seinen Arbeitsplatz verlieren, weil die Aktionäre sich verspekuliert haben.
In seinem 1990 verfassten *Postskriptum über die Kontrollgesellschaften*[11] sieht Gilles Deleuze die elektronische Fußfessel, die eine herkömmliche Haftstrafe ersetzt, als grundlegende Metapher für die Kontrollgesellschaft. Der Verurteilte muss nicht im Gefängnis verweilen, kann sich aber auch nicht wirklich frei bewegen, weil sein Aufenthaltsort immer überprüfbar bleibt.

Befreiung aus der Fußfessel

Jedes ortbare Handy ist auch eine Art elektronische Fußfessel, und auch jede Aktion im Internet ist gegebenenfalls verfolgbar. Sag mir, welche Seiten du aufrufst, was du kaufst, und ich sage dir, wer du bist, was du darfst und was du tun sollst. Bücher werden nicht mehr verbrannt, aber bei zu geringer Nachfrage nicht mehr vertrieben oder gar nicht erst veröffentlicht. Oft reicht es aber auch, dass einfach nicht über sie berichtet wird, sodass keiner sie kennt, der nicht zufällig irgendwo im Netz einen Hinweis auf sie findet. Aber es gibt heute auch andere Möglichkeiten, zum Autor zu werden, so die Beteiligung am *Wir sind hier*-Blog, wo die zu den angegebenen Themen eintreffenden Beiträge redaktionell bearbeitet und Bestandteil einer Online-Veröffentlichung werden. Die Stimmen der User werden auch im wahrsten Sinne des Wortes „gehört", wenn sie auf kurzen Webcam-Videos Bertolt Brechts Gedicht *Gegen Verführung* lesen oder singen. Die verschiedenen Stimmen werden zu einem user-generierten Cho(i)r verarbeitet, der am Ende der Aufführung in Linz gespielt wird.
Wir sind hier soll dazu beitragen, dass junge Menschen nicht in einem Meer des historischen Vergessens versinken, sich aus dem Zeittakt des Live-Tickers herausbewegen und erkennen, wie ihr Denken im fortgeschrittenen Zeitalter digitaler Netzwerke noch weit subtiler manipuliert, ausgebeutet und kontrolliert wird, als es Marshall McLuhan vor 52 Jahren am Beispiel gedruckter Werbeanzeigen vorführen konnte. Dann können sie auch in Freiheit handeln und positiv und emphatisch sagen: *Wir sind hier.*
Text: Ludwig Seyfarth

Marshall McLuhan pointed out in his analysis of printed ads fifty-two years ago. This way, they will be able to act freely, while proclaiming positively and empathetically: *We are here.*

Translated from the German by Francesca Kühlers
Edited by Catherine M. Lewis

1 Marshall McLuhan, *The Mechanical Bride: Folklore of Industrial Man.* Amsterdam 1996, p. 7.

2 Kilian Trotier, "Süchtig nach dem Augenblick", *Die Zeit,* 6 June 2013, p. 48.

3 Walter Benjamin, *Gesammelte Schriften,* vol. II, 2, Frankfurt a. M. 1977, all quotes p. 440.

4 Ibid., p. 439.

5 Ibid., p. 447.

6 Ibid., p. 444.

7 Markus Metz, Georg Seeßlen, *Kapitalismus als Spektakel,* Frankfurt a. M. 2012, p. 8.

8 Viktor Sklovskij, *Theorie der Prosa,* ed. Gisela Drohla, Frankfurt a. M. 1984, S. 13.

9 Barbara Engelbach in: *Bruce Nauman: Versuchsanordnungen. Werke 1965–1994,* Kat. Hamburger Kunsthalle 1998, p. 37.

10 See: Dan Graham, "Video in Relation to Architecture", in: D. Hall and J. Fifer, eds. *Illuminating Video,* NY: Aperture, 1990.

11 In: Gilles Deleuze, *Unterhandlungen* 1972–1990, Frankfurt/M. 1993, p. 254–262.

1 Marshall McLuhan, *Die mechanische Braut. Volkskultur des industriellen Menschen,* Amsterdam 1996, S. 7.

2 Kilian Trotier, „Süchtig nach dem Augenblick", *Die Zeit,* 6. Juni 2013, S. 48.

3 Walter Benjamin, *Gesammelte Schriften,* Bd. II, 2, Frankfurt a. M. 1977, alle Zitate S. 440.

4 Ebd., S. 439.

5 Ebd., S. 447.

6 Ebd., S. 444.

7 Markus Metz, Georg Seeßlen, *Kapitalismus als Spektakel,* Frankfurt a. M. 2012, S. 8.

8 Viktor Sklovskij, *Theorie der Prosa,* hg. von Gisela Drohla, Frankfurt a. M. 1984, S. 13.

9 Barbara Engelbach in: *Bruce Nauman: Versuchsanordnungen. Werke 1965–1994,* Kat. Hamburger Kunsthalle 1998, S. 37.

10 Siehe „Video in Beziehung zur Architektur" und Grahams Texte zu einzelnen Überwachungsinstallationen in: Dan Graham, *Ausgewählte Schriften,* hg. von Ulrich Wilmes, Stuttgart 1994

11 In: Gilles Deleuze, *Unterhandlungen 1972–1990,* Frankfurt/M. 1993, S. 254–262.

http://www.wir-sind-hier.org

Participating artists

Daniel Aigenbauer
Jovica Aleksis
Gözen Atila
Ulé Barcelos
Dominik Berg
Florian Berger
Matti Casper Blunck
Rica Blunck
Yoko Gretel Blunck
Nora Bolz
Claudius Brodmann
Chris Bruckmayr
Matthias David
Elisa de Paolis
Maria Grazia Depalmas
Daniela Dibelius
David Dorell
Carnay Dörtyol
FM Einheit
Stephanie Geiger
Horst Hörtner
Marcus Jäger
Andreas Jalsovec
Craig Johnson
Hüseyin Kartal
Angelika Katzinger
Nazli Kilerci
Johannes Kirschner
Angela Kecinski
Francesca Kühlers
Traute Kühlers
Jan Lachenmayer
Anna Livsic
Lisa Ludwig
Sybille Luhmann
Andy Müller-Maguhn
Timo Maier
Jules Marshall
Michael Mayr
Stefanie Melzer
Jürgen Mertens
Martin Mörth
Steffen Neubauer
Kien Nguyen
Bilgehan Öziş
Benjamin Olsen
Michael Platz
Laszlo Puskas
Rafa Quinonero
Lukas Sterly
Salvatore Vanasco
Christian Walter
Tyll Wibben
Philipp Wiesner
Rolf Wolkenstein
Cornelia Wunderlich
Laura Zidda
Arie Zinger

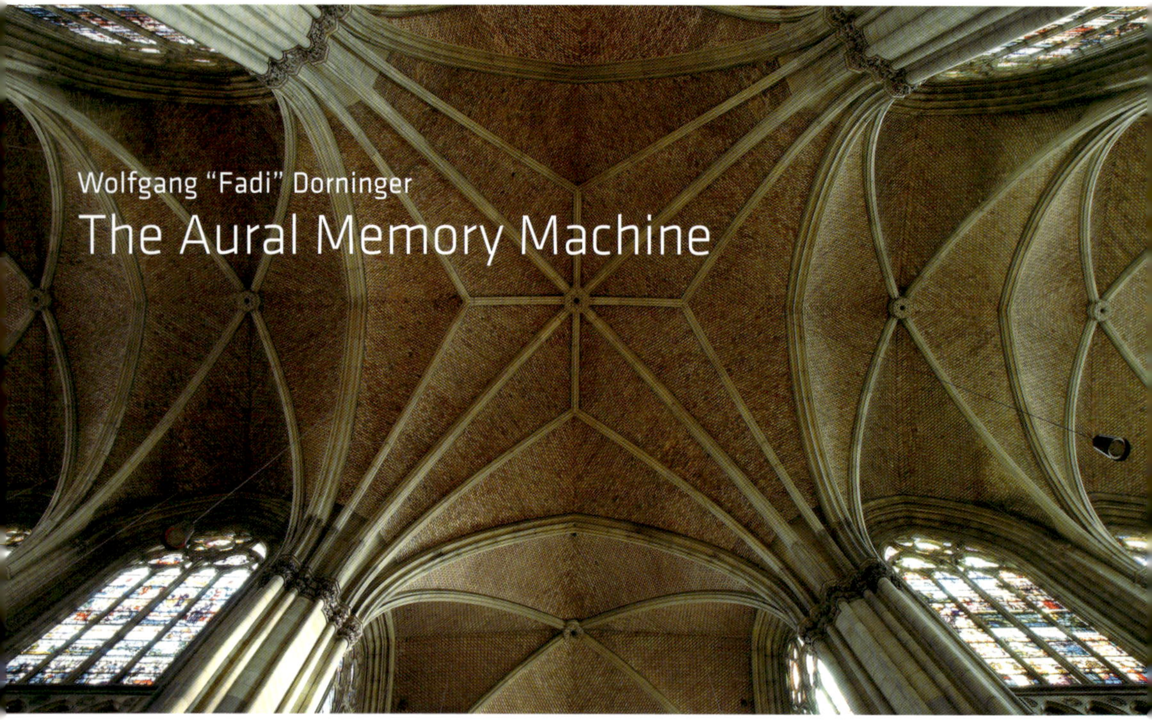

Wolfgang "Fadi" Dorninger

The Aural Memory Machine

Aural Memory Machine (AMM) is an six-channel sound installation played by visitors present in Linz's St. Mary's Cathedral. No musical training or technical skills are required of audience members; all they have to do is use a midi-keyboard to input texts that, in real time, trigger field recordings having to do with the 2013 Ars Electronica Festival theme. In this way, audience members inputting texts at six terminals can discursively get involved in the theme and simultaneously create a spatial sound installation. This is followed by a nightly highlight: a concert by Wolfgang Dorninger and friends right on site in St. Mary's Cathedral.

The text2field-recordings plug-in and the midi keyboard comprise the central control unit of *AMM.* The letters entered are displayed on a screen in real time. The same goes for the sound. Field-recordings are unique "snapshots" of an acoustic reality. In contrast to phonography, the declared aim of which is to put together an authentic collection of ambient sounds, *AMM* creates a new reality via hybridization. It's impossible to reproduce the state of the acoustic moment in St. Mary's Cathedral, which is characterized by chaotic transformations and the

Aural-Memory-Machine (AMM) ist eine Sechs-Kanal-Soundinstallation, die vom Publikum im Linzer Mariendom bespielt wird. Das Publikum braucht keine musikalischen oder technischen Vorkenntnisse, sondern gibt lediglich Text mittels Midi-Keyboard ein. Der Text triggert in Echtzeit Field-Recordings (Umweltaufnahmen) aus abgegrenzten Themenkreisen. Das Publikum kann so auf sechs Terminals gleichzeitig diskursiv am Festivalthema teilhaben und eine Raum-Klang-Soundinstallation gestalten. Abschließender Höhepunkt ist ein nächtliches Konzert von Wolfgang Dorninger mit Partnern im Linzer Mariendom.

Das Plugin „text2field-recordings" ist mit dem Midi-Keyboard die Steuerzentrale von *AMM.* Die eingegeben Buchstaben werden in Echtzeit auf einem Bildschirm ausgegeben, gleiches gilt auch für den Klang. Field-Recordings sind einzigartige Momentaufnahmen einer akustischen Wirklichkeit. Anders als in der Phonographie, wo das authentische Sammeln von Umweltklängen erklärtes Ziel ist, entsteht bei *AMM* durch das Hybride eine neue Wirklichkeit. Der Zustand des akustischen Moments im Linzer Mariendom ist nicht reproduzierbar, er ist geprägt von chaotischen

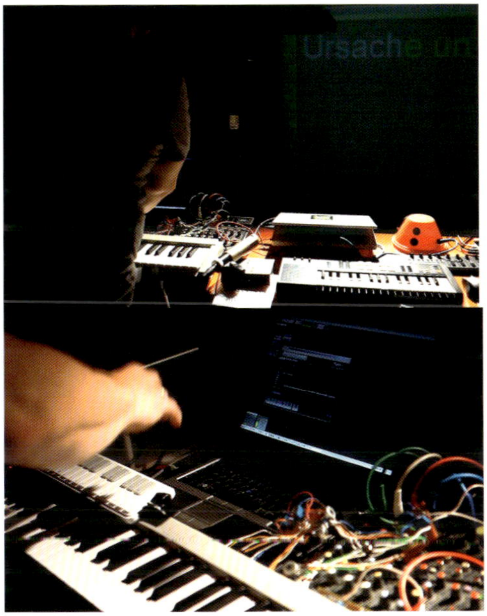

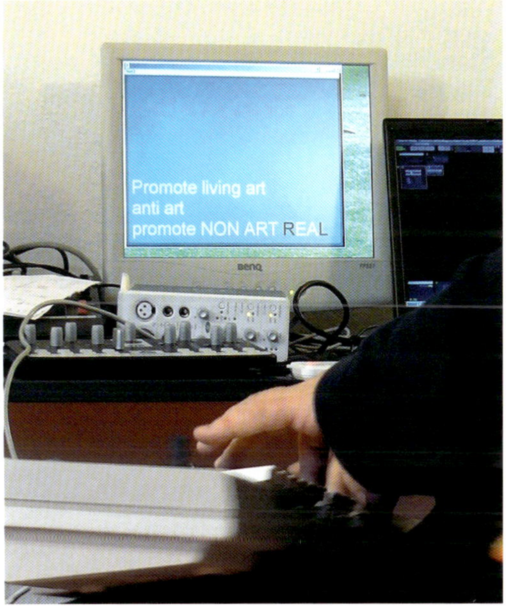

suspension of time. Phonography is the attempt to counteract the amnesia of sound, whereas this very state is the declared aim of *AMM.* Acoustic turbulence and construed relations ranging from absolute zero to utter chaos illustrate how abstract code or language can trigger complex sequences of any sort, control them or make them uncontrollable. Each individual user at one of the terminals in the cathedral must constantly face the question of whether he/she wants to produce text/code, or participate in the design of a momentary acoustic environment on site, or both. Complex questions of our time and issues related to the festival theme are made visible by this process.
The artists performing in the subsequent concert will be using the same tools, but they'll be playing selected preset texts from the Ars Electronica Catalog.

http://dorninger.servus.at

The text2field-recordings plug-in was co-financed by the Austrian Federal Ministry for Education, the Arts and Culture, Linz Kultur and the Province of Upper Austria's Department of Cultural Affairs. Programmer: Thomas Gangl, Host: Usine

Transformationen und der Aufhebung von Zeit. Versucht die Phonographie einer Amnäsie des Klangs entgegen zu wirken, so ist bei *AMM* gerade dieser Zustand erklärtes Ziel. Akustische Turbulenzen und konstruierte Relationen, ausgehend vom Nullpunkt bis ins Chaotische, verdeutlichen dabei, wie abstrakter Code oder Sprache komplexe Abläufe jeder Art in Gang setzten, steuern oder auch unkontrollierbar machen können. Jede/r einzelne/r MitspielerIn an einem der acht Terminals im Mariendom muss sich laufend die Frage stellen, ob sie/er Text/Code produzieren oder an der Gestaltung eines momentanen akustischen Environments im Dom teilhaben will oder beides. Bei diesem Prozess werden komplexe Fragestellungen unserer Zeit und des Festivalthemas sichtbar.
Beim abschließenden Konzert benutzen die Künstler dieselben Tools, spielen aber vorgegebene, ausgewählte Texte aus dem Katalog der Ars Electronica.

http://dorninger.servus.at

Das Plugin „text2field-recordings" wurde von bm:uuk, Linz Kultur und Kulturabteilung Land OÖ mitfinanziert. Programmierer: Thomas Gangl, Host: Usine

Huang Yi & KUKA

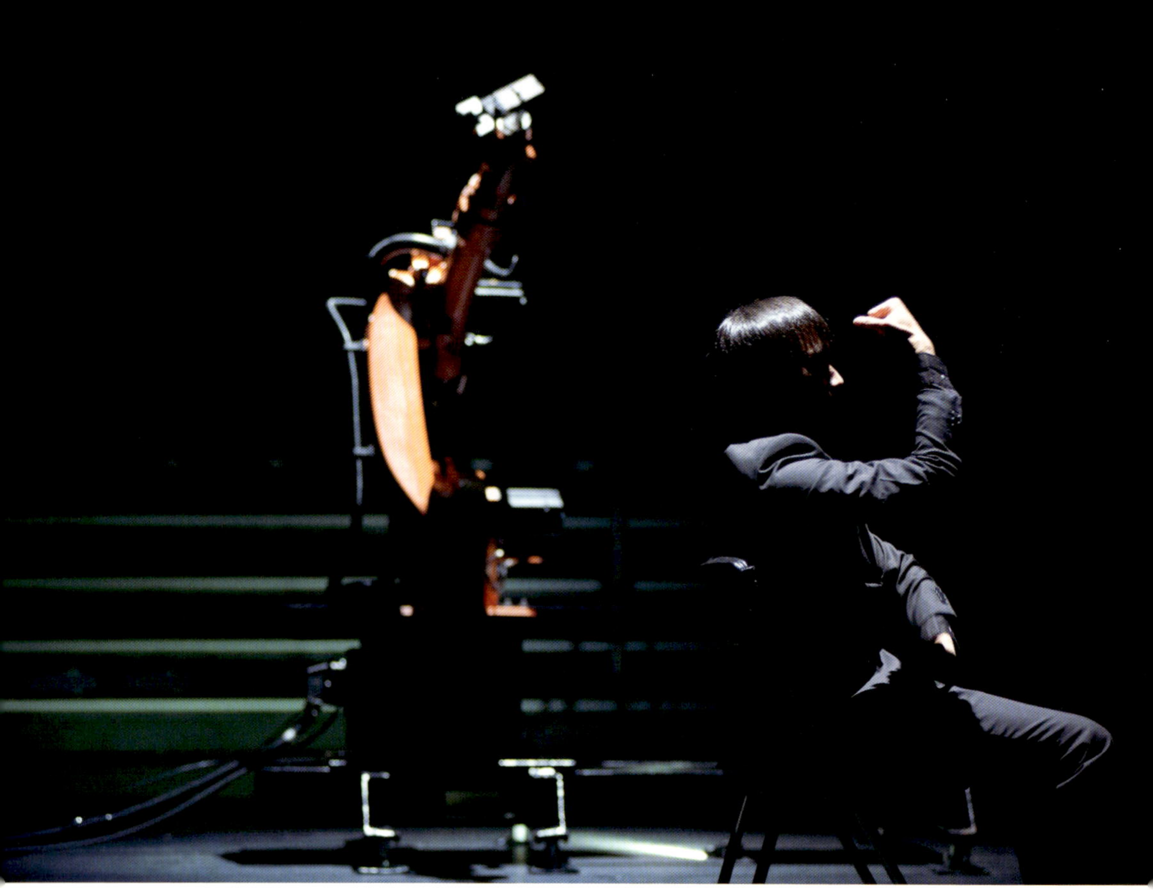

While children in the West imagined having an android as a friend, or, before that, an R2-D2 or a C-3PO, Huang Yi envisioned a best friend in the form of the blue Japanese manga robot cat, Doraemon. *Huang Yi & KUKA** represents the fulfillment of a lifelong interest in the partnership between humans and robots. Huang Yi, a dancer and choreographer, has created dance works that fuse technology and machinery with rich imagery, including a computerized violin he invented himself in *Symphony Project I Violin* (2010).
Huang Yi is a Taiwanese choreographer, dancer, experimenter and an inventor. His multiple tal-

* KUKA is a worldwide German producer of industrial robots

Während Kinder im Westen sich gerne vorstellten, einen Androiden – oder davor einen R2-D2 oder einen C-3PO – als Freund zu haben, träumte Huang Yi immer davon, die blaue japanische Manga-Roboterkatze Doraemon zum besten Freund zu haben. Mit dem Projekt *Huang Yi & KUKA** hat sich der Tänzer und Choreograf Huang Yi seinen lebenslangen Traum von einer Partnerschaft zwischen Mensch und Roboter erfüllt. Er hat Tanzstücke entwickelt, bei denen sich Technologie und Maschinen mit einer ausdrucksstarken Bilderwelt verbinden, etwa die Produktion *Symphony Project I Violin* (2010), für die er eine computergesteuerte Geige erfand.

* KUKA is ein weltweit operierender deutscher Hersteller von Industrierobotern

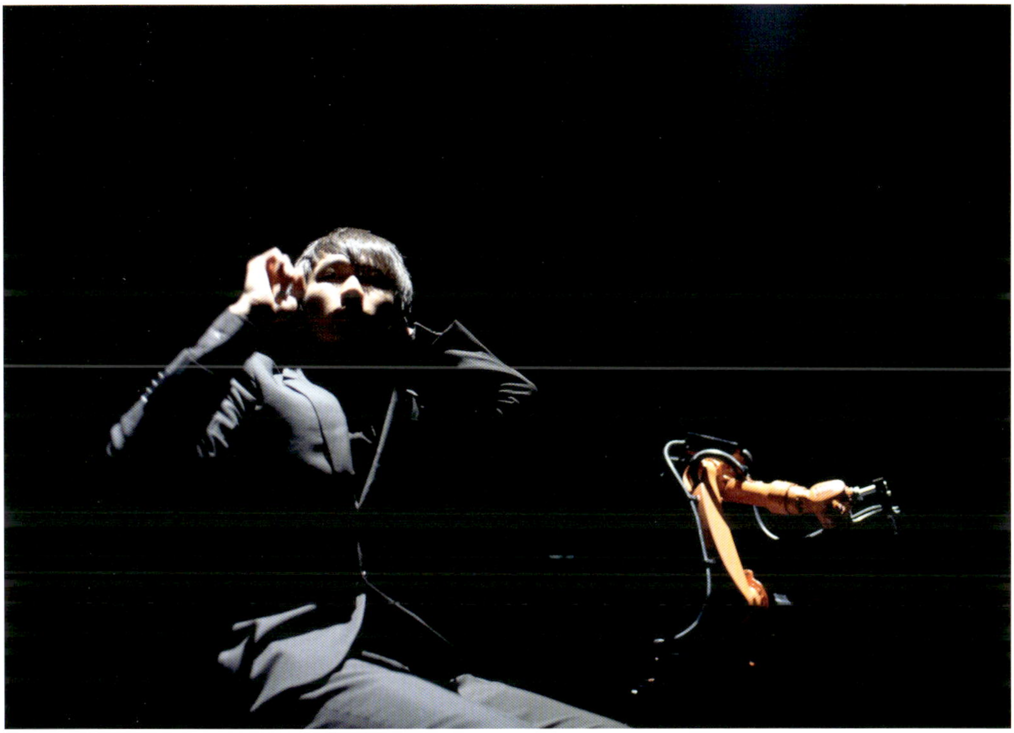

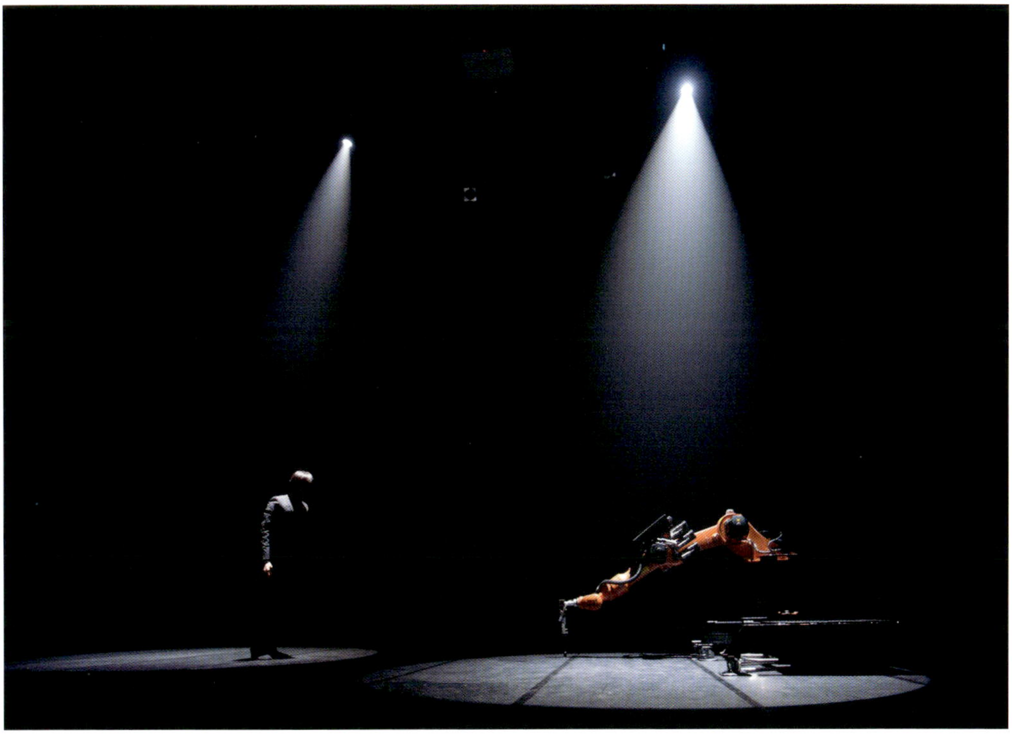

Summer Yen

ents in the fields of photography, videography and mechanics can be seen in his choreography that goes far beyond any standard performing art production. He is adept at incorporating multi-layered images and delicate body movement.
Huang Yi has won the Taipei Digital Art Performance Award twice and is known for his performance experiments, his speed and his precision in dance. His pure movement choreographies evoked the praise of the *New York Times*, which referred to him as "a spinning machine of a dance with near-continual motion." Huang creates works as if data was flowing through his limbs and mind, and he is the programmer of the body. While the world was looking at robots as tools, Huang Yi looked at himself and realized that he was a tool for dance. He reflected on how to visualize humanity, drawing upon new concepts and new technologies. The KUKA Company didn't just "lend a hand", it literally "lent an arm" to help Huang Yi realize his creative vision, making it possible for Huang to embark on a dance journey with the robotic arm, *KUKA*.

"Dancing face to face with a KUKA robot is like looking at my face in a mirror. I make KUKA mimic my movements, and I learn from him, I make myself dance like a machine."

Huang Yi's vision of a human–robot dance partnership has captivated audiences, which feel the chemistry between two living beings during their poetic dance duet and look at KUKA in a new light following a performance.

Co-commissioned by Quanta Arts Foundation
Choreographer / Robot programming: Huang Yi; Music: Arvo Pärt / Bach; Performers: Huang Yi, KUKA the robot; Lighting Designer: Huang Yi; Lighting technology / synchronized system: Ou Yen-ku; Robot Director: Inwen Lin (Taiwan KUKA Corporation); Robot Appliance Director: Yang Li-yuan.

Supported by Digital Art Center, Taipei. Sponsored by Welding Equipment & Factory Automation System and Kao Wen-hung.

Special Thanks to KUKA Roboter CEE GmbH, Taiwan KUKA Corporation, Liao Chih-hsin and Sobright Lighting Company.

Huang Yi ist ein taiwanesischer Choreograf, Tänzer, Experimentator und Erfinder. Seine vielen Talente in den Bereichen Fotografie, Videografie und Mechanik fließen auch in seine Choreografien ein, die weit über gewohnte Darbietungen der Performancekunst hinausgehen. Er ist Meister darin, mit graziösen Bewegungen vielschichtige Bilder zu verbinden und zum Ausdruck zu bringen.
Huang Yi gewann zweimal den Taipei Digital Art Performance Award und ist insbesondere für seine Performance-Experimente sowie seinen temporeichen und präzisen Tanzstil bekannt. Für seine reinen Bewegungschoreografien wurde er von der *New York Times* als „Spinnmaschine des Tanzes in nahezu permanenter Bewegung" gewürdigt. Huang Yis Performances erwecken den Eindruck, als ob Daten durch seine Glieder und seine Gedanken strömten und er ein Programmierer des Körpers wäre. Während alle Welt Roboter als Werkzeuge betrachtete, konzentrierte sich Huang Yi auf sich selbst und erkannte, dass er ein Werkzeug des Tanzes war. So begann er sich zu überlegen, wie man Menschlichkeit mithilfe neuer Konzepte und Technologien darstellen könnte. Die taiwanesische KUKA-Niederlassung hat Huang Yi bei der Umsetzung seiner kreativen Visionen nicht nur „eine helfende Hand", sondern gleich „einen ganzen Arm" gereicht, um ihm seine Tournee mit dem Roboterarm „KUKA" zu ermöglichen.

„Von Angesicht zu Angesicht mit einem KUKA-Roboter zu tanzen, das ist, wie sich selbst im Spiegel zu betrachten. Ich bringe KUKA dazu, meine Bewegungen nachzuahmen, lerne aber auch von ihm, lerne wie eine Maschine zu tanzen."

Huang Yis Vision einer Tanzbeziehung zwischen Mensch und Roboter hat das Publikum fasziniert und dazu gebracht, das poetische Duett als harmonische Verbindung zwischen zwei Lebewesen zu empfinden und KUKA nach der Performance mit anderen Augen zu betrachteten.

Aus dem Englischen von Martina Bauer

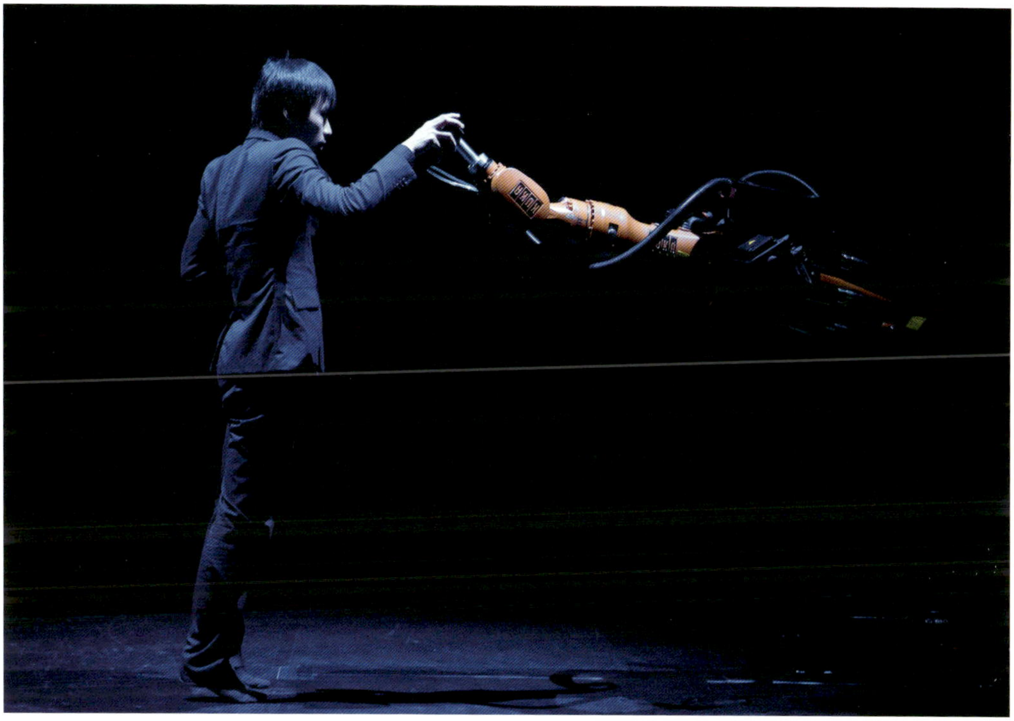

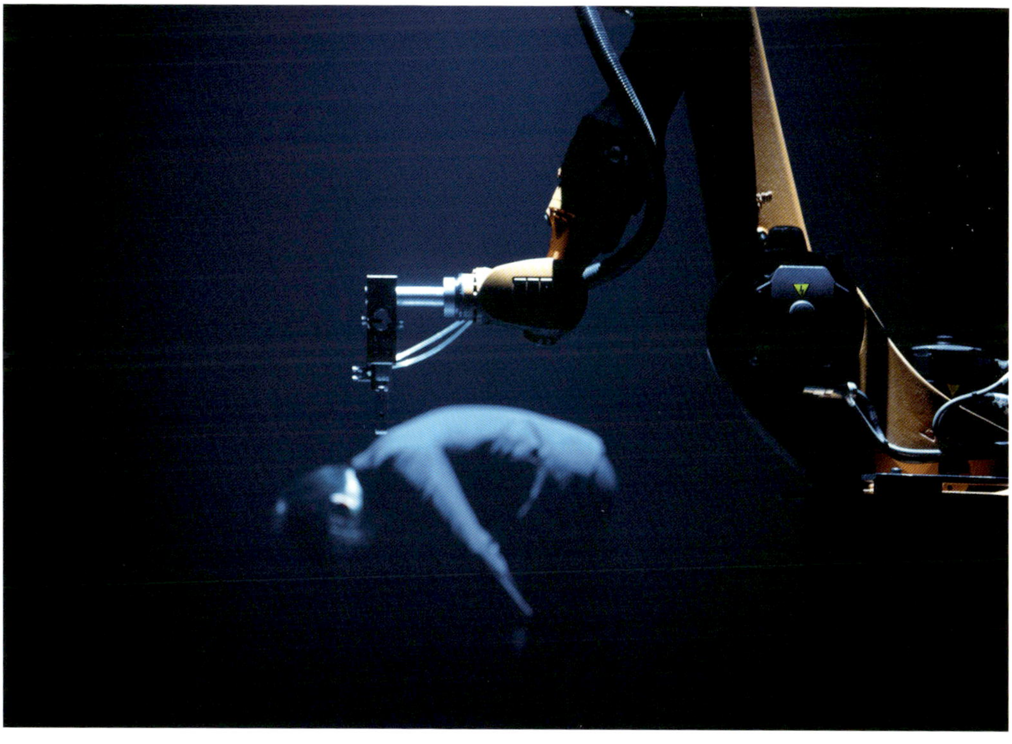

Summer Yen

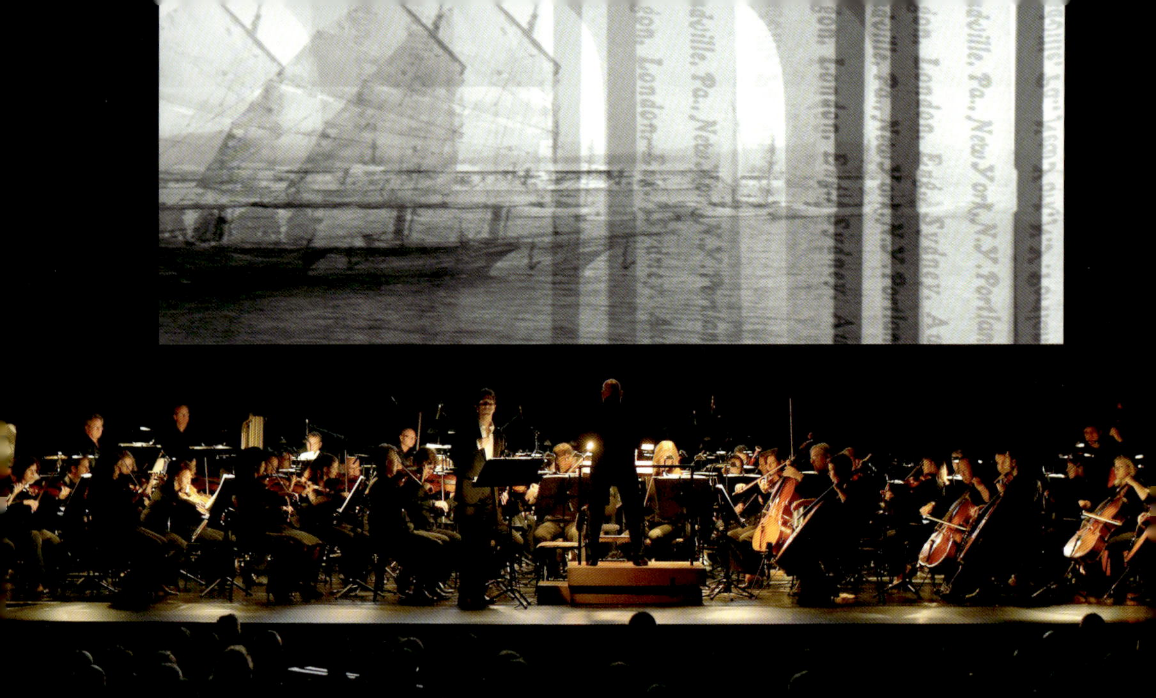

Welcome Transients

Die Große Konzertnacht

A system is said to be in a transient state when a process variable has been changed and the system has not yet reached steady-state

The Big Concert Night has been one of the absolute highlights of every Ars Electronica Festival since 2002. The outcome of close collaboration with the Brucknerhaus and the Bruckner Orchester under Chief Conductor Dennis Russell Davies is a one-of-a-kind format whose defining characteristic—aside from its epic length, of course—is staging rewarding encounters involving music of the 20th and 21st centuries, acoustic instruments and digital media, instrumentalists and laptop-keyboarders. The diversified program ranges from music composed in ink on paper to autogenerative sound sculptures. To consummate these extraordinary experiences, artists are invited each year to create live visualizations of the musical works.

Seit 2002 ist die große Konzertnacht bei jedem Ars-Electronica-Festival ein unumstrittener Höhepunkt. Aus der engen Kooperation mit dem Brucknerhaus und dem von Dennis Russell Davies geleiteten Brucknerorchester entstand ein einzigartiges Format, das sich nicht nur durch seine epische Länge, sondern vor allem durch die Begegnungen zwischen der Musik des 20. und 21. Jahrhunderts, akustischen Instrumenten und digitalen Medien, zwischen InstrumentalistInnen und LaptopistInnen auszeichnet. Von auf Papier komponierter Musik bis zu autogenerativen Sound Sculptures reicht die Bandbreite des Programms. Und als Besonderheit werden jedes Jahr KünstlerInnen eingeladen, die Musikstücke live zu visualisieren.

Transient: lasting only for a short time, momentary variation of a signal
Transients: travelers passing through, itinerant workers, people on the road, on the run, on the go ...

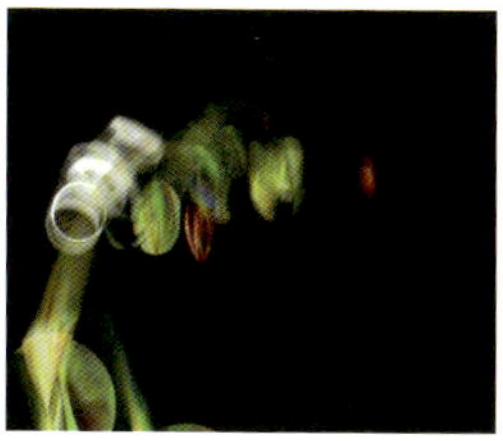 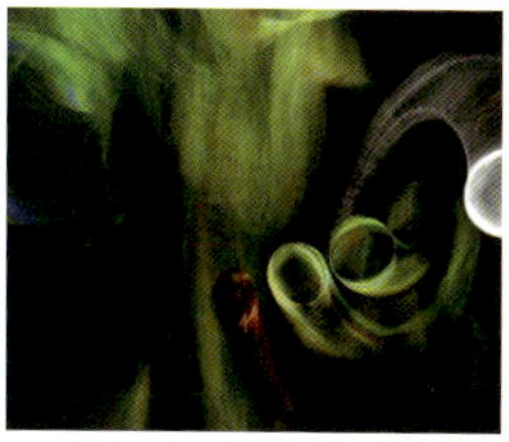 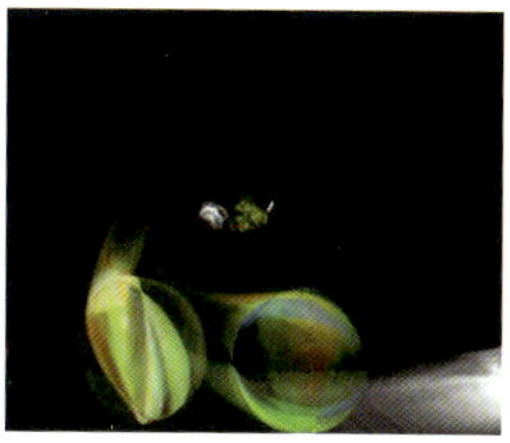 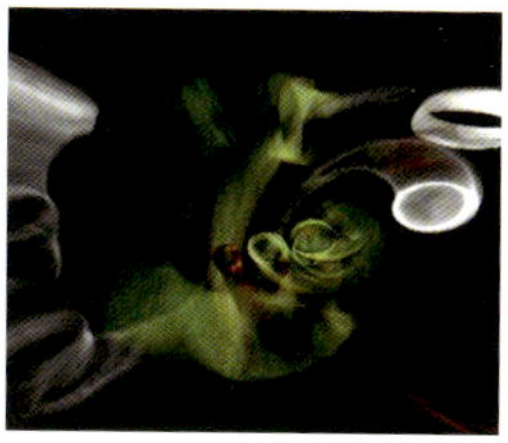

Program

Acoustic Time Travel
Bill Fontana
Created under the auspices of the Prix Ars Electronica Collide@CERN Artist in Residence Program

By the Reflecting Pool
Commissioned composition by Leah Muir
World premiere, performed by David Friedman and Bruckner Orchester Linz / Dennis Russell Davies

10th Symphony
Philip Glass
Performed by Bruckner Orchester Linz / Dennis Russell Davies

Requies
Luciano Berio
Performed by Bruckner Orchester Linz / Dennis Russell Davies

Ye Shanghai
Roberto Paci Dalò

cut.repeat
re-lay (Tobias Ehrhardt) & 19 hertz (Emanuel Jauk)

Radiologic
Carl Stone & Gil Kuno

Your-Cosmos
Daito Manabe & Satoru Higa

The visualizations of the orchestral pieces are by:
Berlin – Arístides García and more

Music animations during transitional phases by:
MFRedman Collective

TOTAL RECALL: Performance Intermezzo
The Sound of the Earth
Yuri Suzuki
Device Playing: Cassette Recorder (II)
Keith Lam and Michelle Ngai

And a retro TV impression to get things moving ...
Welcome Transients
Ernie Kovacs

Welcome Transients is the latest step in the successful collaboration of the Bruckner Orchester Linz under Dennis Russell Davies, Brucknerhaus Linz and Ars Electronica. Their aim is to test innovative ways of combining music and new visual forms of expression. Curators: Dennis Russell Davies, Heribert Schröder, Gerfried Stocker, Hans Joachim Frey

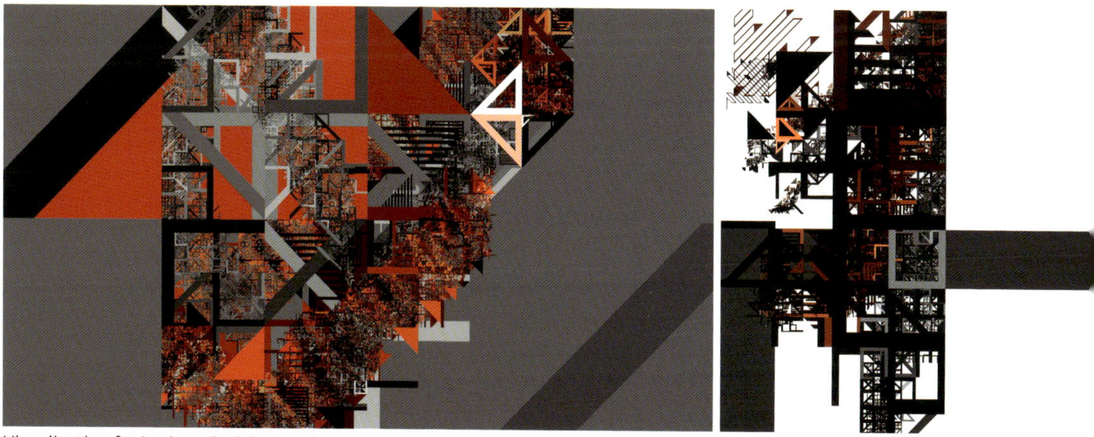

Visualization for Luciano Berio's *Requies* by Arístides García

Roberto Paci Dalò

Ye Shanghai 夜上海

"Roberto Paci Dalò's film *Ye Shanghai* (2012) is a hauntingly vivid work"
Barbara Casavecchia, Frieze Magazine

Ye Shanghai is a music-visual performance by Roberto Paci Dalò, commissioned by Massimo Torrigiani for SH Contemporary 2012 and produced by Davide Quadrio and Francesca Girelli (Arthub Asia).
The project deals with several aspects of pre-1949 Shanghainese life. At the core of this work is the story of the Shanghai Ghetto, formally known as the "Restricted Sector for Stateless Refugees". The Ghetto was an area of approximately one square mile, located in the Hongkou District of Japanese-occupied Shanghai. It housed about 23,000 Jewish refugees, relocated by the Japanese-issued Proclamation Concerning Restriction of Residence and Business of Stateless Refugees, who fled from German-occupied Europe before and during World War II. The International Settlement was occupied by the Japanese on 8 December 1941 and remained occupied until Japan's surrender in 1945.
The work is based on visual and audio materials from the years 1933–1949. This database, composed of historical media, has been converted into a contemporary art work based on live video projections and music.
The iconic material used as a point of departure for this work is *Nights of Shanghai*–a song interpreted by Zhou Xuan (1918–1957). This hit from 1937 represents the aural and sonic environment of the piece. Sampling, decomposing and recomposing create the texture that embraces the entire performance. Out of the enriched texture of this song, components made of live instrumental sounds gradually emerge, samples from archive materials (voices in English, Yiddish, Chinese) recreate soundscapes from the past, accompanied by electronics sounds. The images' database relies entirely on materials from the BFI British Film Institute's archives and consists of 35mm films shot in Shanghai by English travellers during the 30s and 40s.

Ye Shanghai ist eine Musik- und Videoperformance von Roberto Paci Dalò, die von Massimo Torrigiani für das Festival SH Contemporary 2012 in Auftrag gegeben und von Davide Quadrio und Francesca Girelli (Arthub Asia) produziert wurde.
Das Projekt beleuchtet mehrere Aspekte des Lebens in Shanghai vor 1949. Die Geschichte des Shanghaier Ghettos, formell als „Ausgewiesener Bezirk für staatenlose Flüchtlinge" bezeichnet, steht im Zentrum dieser Arbeit. Das im Bezirk Hongkou des japanisch besetzten Shanghai gelegene Ghetto umfasste rund 2,5 Quadratkilometer und war Aufenthaltsort für ca. 23.000 jüdische Flüchtlinge, die vor und während des Zweiten Weltkriegs aus dem von Deutschland besetzten Europa geflohen waren und aufgrund der japanischen Proklamation zur Einschränkung von Ansässigkeits- und Arbeitsrechten für staatenlose Flüchtlinge hierher umgesiedelt wurden. Der Internationale Bezirk wurde am 8. Dezember 1941 von den Japanern besetzt und blieb es bis zu deren Kapitulation im Jahr 1945.
Ausgangspunkt für das Werk sind Film- und Tonaufnahmen aus den Jahren 1933–1949. Die aus historischen Dokumenten gespeiste Datenbank wurde in ein zeitgenössisches Kunstwerk mit Live-Videoprojektionen und -Musik umgewandelt.
Der von Zhou Xuan (1918–1957) interpretierte Hit *Nights of Shanghai* von 1937 ist der Startpunkt dieser Arbeit und bildet den tonalen und klanglichen Hintergrund des Stücks. Sampling, Dekomposition und Rekomposition schaffen die Textur, die das gesamte Werk durchzieht, aus der sich live gespielte Instrumentalklänge langsam herausheben, während von elektronischen Sounds begleitete Archivaufnahmen (Englisch, Jiddisch und Chinesisch sprechende Stimmen) eine Klanglandschaft der Vergangenheit erstehen lassen. Die Bilddatenbank bedient sich ausschließlich des Materials aus den Archiven des British Film Institute (BFI) und enthält 35-mm-Filme, die von englischen Reisenden in den 30er und 40er Jahren gemacht wurden.
Aus dem Englischen von Michael Kaufmann

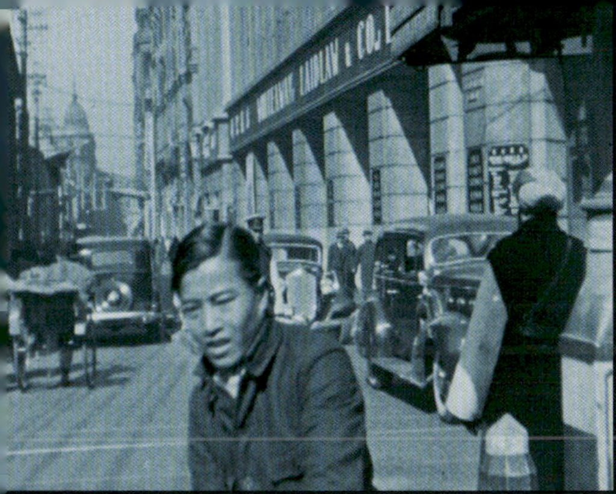

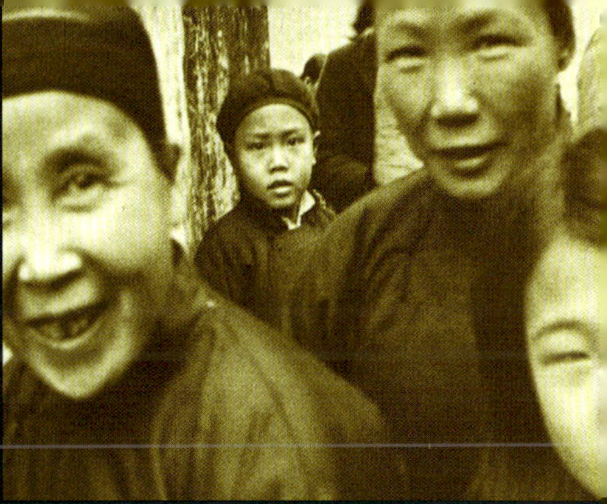

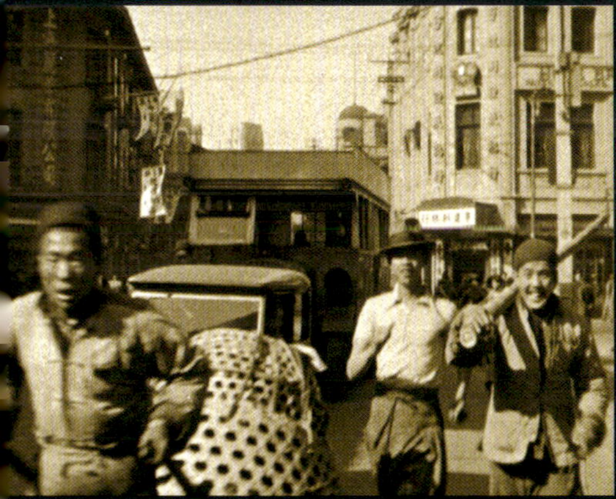

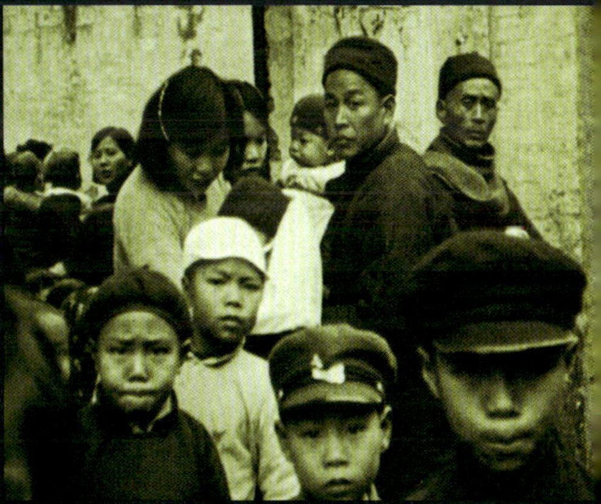

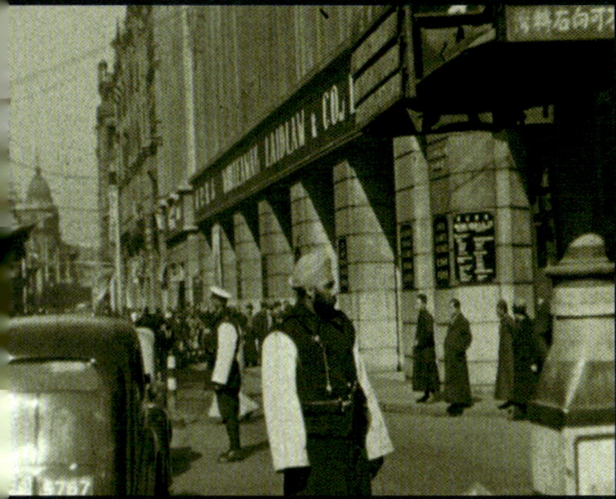

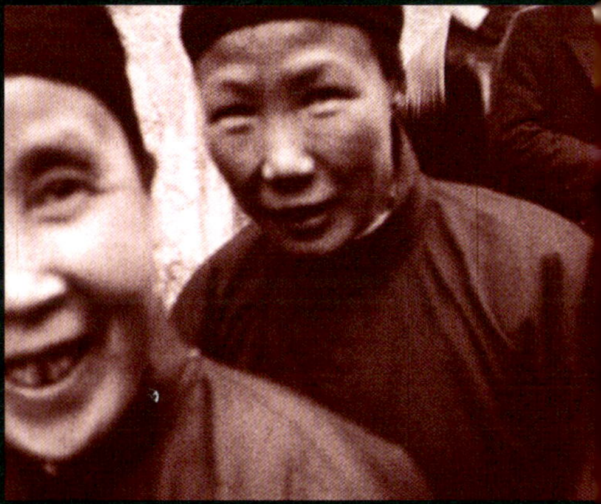

Music, film, bass clarinet, sampler & live electronics: Roberto Paci Dalò ; Farmhouse–audio post-production: Andrea Felli; film editor: Davide Capuleti; producers: Davide Quadrio, Francesca Girelli
A co-production by Arthub Asia, SH Contemporary, Giardini Pensili, NOTCH Festival, Messagerie.
In association with BFI British Film Institute. In collabora- [illegible] University of Shanghai, Home Movie–Archivio Nazionale del Film di Famiglia Bologna, La camera ottica Gorizia.
Ye Shanghai has been originally conceived in collaboration with Yu Xiaolu, Yu Xueou, Qin Mei, Sun Mengxuan (Shanghai Institute of Fine Arts, Fudan University).

Giardini Pensili is supported by the Rimini Municipality, the Province of Rimini, the Region Emilia Romagna.

voestalpine Klangwolke 2013
Bruckner lebt!

After more than three decades, the voestalpine Klangwolke is approaching Linz's musical core: Anton Bruckner, the composer who has moved people, timelessly, all over the world, with the loftiest of all feelings—music! "That such a simple man was the one chosen to give us the gift of this divine music" ... "Tony from Ansfelden" ... "this lonely giant" ... "a country bumpkin" ... "half genius, half fool"—the spectacle commences with comments by his contemporaries, underscored by powerful passages from the *8th Symphony*. With exclamation points formed by laser beams and pyrotechnic effects. The opinions about the Master could hardly have been more wide-ranging. And there's hardly another composer who led a life so charged with tension, a life with all the summits and nadirs between Heaven and Hell. And throughout it, unlucky at love—with Ida, with Rosa, with Karoline, with Aurelia, with Josefine. Actually, material for a Hollywood movie: from the drama with the *3rd Symphony*—when, at the world premiere in Vienna, both the audience and the orchestra first laughed at him and then left—to the sensation of the 8th, from the *Melancholy in my Secluded Chamber* to his triumph in London's Crystal Palace, where the brilliant organ virtuoso brought 70,000 fans to a state of rapture. They carried him off on their shoulders—Bruckner, the pop star.

Nach über drei Jahrzehnten nähert sich die *voestalpine Klangwolke* ihrem musischen Mittelpunkt: Anton Bruckner, der weltweit und zeitlos die Menschen bewegt – mit dem höchsten aller Gefühle: Musik! „Dass so ein einfacher Mensch dazu auserwählt war, uns diese göttliche Musik zu schenken" ... „der Tonerl von Ansfelden" ... „dieser Einsam-Große" ... „ein Bauerntölpel" ... „halb Genie, halb Trottel" – mit Zitaten seiner Zeitgenossen beginnt das Spektakel, untermalt von kraftvollen Takten aus der *8. Symphonie*. Mit Ausrufezeichen aus Laserstrahlen und Pyro-Effekten. Die Meinungen über den Meister könnten unterschiedlicher nicht sein. Und kaum ein anderer Komponist hat eine so spannungsgeladene Lebensgeschichte, mit allen Höhen und Tiefen, zwischen Himmel und Hölle – und immer unglücklich verliebt, in die Ida, die Rosa, die Karoline, die Aurelia, die Josefine. Eigentlich ein Hollywoodstoff: vom Drama mit der *Dritten* – als er bei der Uraufführung in Wien vom Publikum und Orchester zuerst verlacht und dann verlassen wird – bis zur Sensation seiner *Achten*. Von der *Melancholie in meinem Kämmerlein* bis zum Triumph im Londoner Kristallpalast, wo er als brillanter Orgelvirtuose 70.000 „Fans" zu Begeisterungsstürmen hinreißt und auf Schultern getragen wird. Bruckner, der Popstar.
So wie heute Parov Stelar, genialer und global erfolgreicher Musikexport aus Linz zwischen Pop, Swing, Soul und Jazz – und dreifacher Amadeus-Preisträger

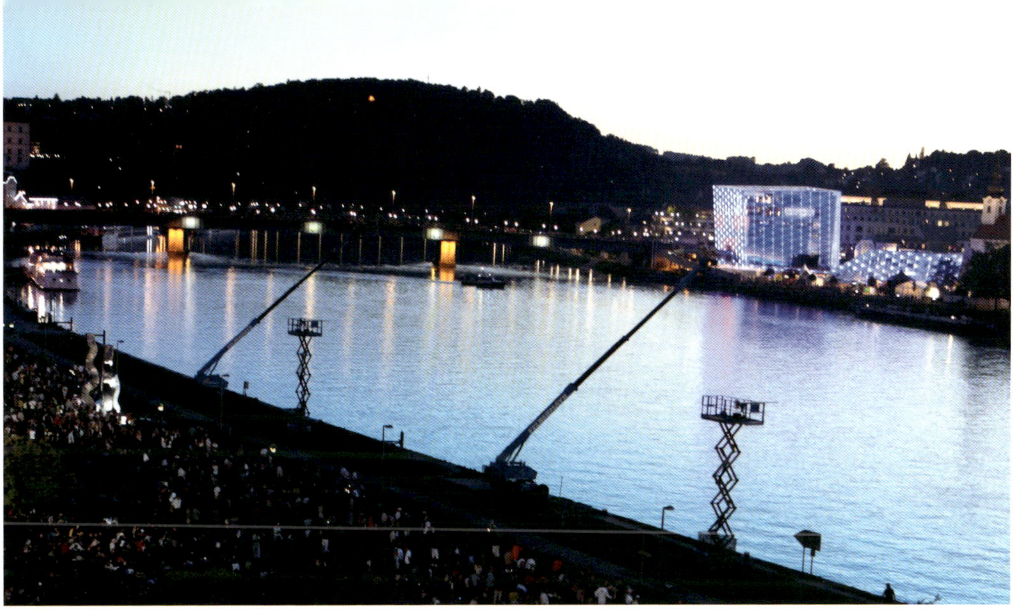

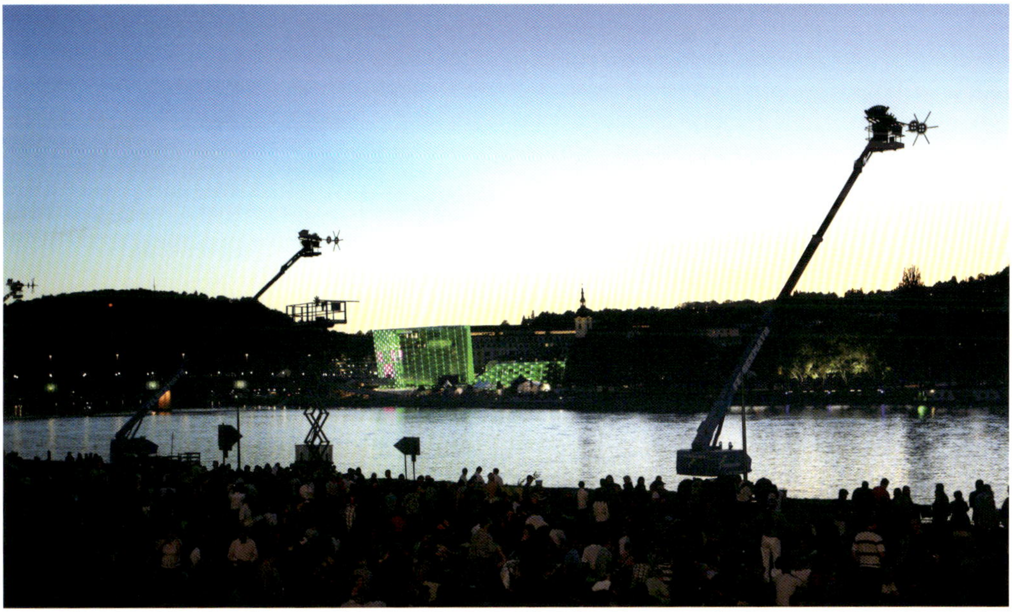

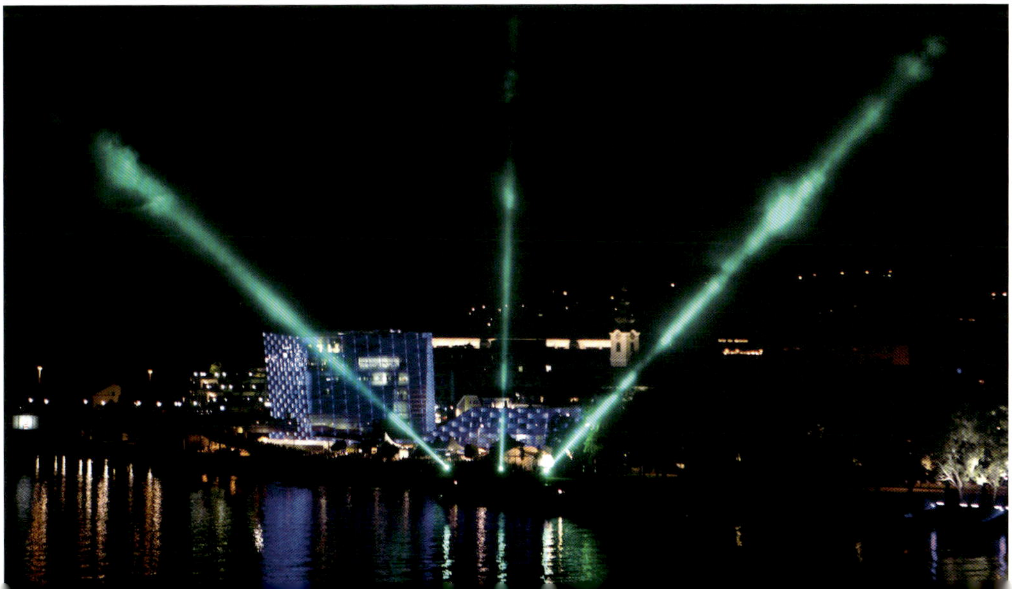

AEC, rubra, Kolb

Just like today's Parov Stelar, Linz's brilliant, globally successful musical export, a phenomenon at the nexus of Pop, Swing, Soul and Jazz, and a three-time Amadeus prizewinner in 2013. Marcus Füreder, the band's artistic front man, is a "Bruckner for our times." He too struggled for years before achieving recognition, and feels himself to be a kindred spirit.
The 2013 *voestalpine Klangwolke* will be a duet, duel and dialog between the past and the present. Parov Stelar will fuse and contrast Bruckner's supreme moments: Anton reloaded, his greatest hits meet modern times. Bruckner's symphonies will provide the soundtrack for the facts and circumstances of his life, with sequences from the finale of the *8th*, the scherzo from the 9th, and of course the adagio from his *7th*. And "divine" moments like the Kyrie from his *Great Mass in F minor* and *Dies Irae* interpreted by the St. Florian Boys Choir. "For the first time in 2013, the voestalpine Klangwolke isn't being conceived by a single artist. Instead, it will bring several very gifted individuals together on stage," explained LIVA Artistic Director Hans-Joachim Frey. "Oliver Spiecker, one of the most celebrated authors and event designers in German-speaking Europe, developed the concept and the script. We're thrilled to be working together with internationally successful choreographer Marc Bogaerts. The Ars Electronica Futurelab is supporting the big audience interaction element with a *voestalpine Klangwolke* music app. And Christoph Winterbacher will be the executive producer in charge of making it all happen. The *voestalpine Klangwolke* will thus be a joint effort by the crème de la crème."
Making a very special premiere is the *voestalpine Klangwolke* music app: "All men shall be Bruckner!" During the time leading up to the Cloud of Sound, audience members can download their free app specially programmed with the notes B-Es-Es-B, the beginning of Bruckner's famous *4th*. It turns any smartphone into a musical instrument, and the Klangwolke audience into the world's largest orchestra.

2013. Marcus Füreder, der künstlerische Kopf von Parov Stelar, ist ein „Bruckner unserer Zeit", musste auch lange Jahre um seine Anerkennung kämpfen, fühlt sich mit ihm seelenverwandt.
Die *voestalpine Klangwolke 2013* wird zum Duett, Duell und Dialog zwischen Vergangenheit und Gegenwart: Parov Stelar fusioniert und kontrastiert mit Bruckners Höhepunkten: *Anton reloaded* – seine „größten Hits" treffen die Neuzeit. Bruckners Symphonien werden zum „Soundtrack" seiner Lebenssituationen: mit Sequenzen aus dem Finale der *Achten,* aus dem Scherzo der *Neunten* und natürlich dem Adagio seiner *Siebten.* Und „heilige" Momente wie das Kyrie seiner *Großen Messe* in f-moll oder *Dies Irae,* interpretiert von den St. Florianer Sängerknaben.
„Die voestalpine Klangwolke 2013 liegt erstmals nicht in der Hand eines einzigen Künstlers, sondern bringt viele Könner auf einer Bühne zusammen", erklärt der künstlerische Leiter der LIVA, Hans-Joachim Frey. „Oliver Spiecker als einer der renommiertesten Autoren und Ereignisgestalter im deutschsprachigen Raum hat Konzept und Drehbuch entwickelt, mit Marc Bogaerts wurde ein international erfolgreicher Choreograph gewonnen, das Ars Electronica Futurelab unterstützt die große Publikumsaktion mit der *voestalpine Klangwolke*-MusicApp, und Christoph Winterbacher hält als ausführender Produzent alle Fäden zusammen. Die *voestalpine Klangwolke* wird so zur Komposition der Besten."
Eine ganz besondere Premiere ist die *voestalpine Klangwolke*-MusicApp: „Alle Menschen werden Bruckner!" Jeder Besucher kann sich schon vorab und kostenlos die speziell programmierte App mit den Tönen B-Es-Es-B herunterladen – den Beginn von Bruckners berühmter *Vierter.* Jedes Smartphone wird zum Instrument, und das Publikum zum größten Orchester der Welt.
Und wer ist Anton Bruckner? Der „Wunderbar"ste von allen: Harald Serafin, Kammersänger, Charakterkopf und ein Unikat wie Bruckner selbst. Er gibt

And who's playing Anton Bruckner? An entertainer who is himself positively wunderbar: Harald Serafin, classical vocalist, character actor, and, like Bruckner himself, one of a kind. He'll provide the profile to Linz's world-class star. And, indeed, the silhouettes could be those of brothers! Serafin will bring the genius to life with original quotes and reenactments of scenes from his life.
The Sound fetches Bruckner from his Cloud. The rehearsals have kissed him awake. But isn't he immortal anyway? *Bruckner Lives!* is the biggest story you could possibly stage before the backdrop of the Brucknerhaus.

dem Weltstar aus Linz sein Profil – und in der Tat: Die Silhouetten könnten Brüder sein! Serafin lässt das Genie lebendig werden, in Original-Zitaten und Lebens-Szenen.
Der Klang holt Bruckner von seiner Wolke, die Proben haben ihn wach geküsst. Aber ist er nicht sowieso unsterblich? *Bruckner lebt!* ist die größtmögliche Geschichte, die man auf der Bühne vor dem Brucknerhaus erzählen kann.
Text: Oliver Spiecker

Mobile App voestalpine Klangwolke 2013

"All men shall be Bruckner!" These immortal words are the motto of the iOS and Android app that the Ars Electronica Futurelab and Ars Electronica Solutions jointly developed for the 2013 *voestalpine Klangwolke*. "Bruckner Lives!" and he lives not only in the staging of this year's spectacle but also in audience members' smartphones and tablets.
Bruckner's *4th Symphony* is part of the show. It begins with long, drawn out tones played by the horn section. At precisely this moment, spectators will form the world's largest smartphone orchestra. Under the conductor's direction, all present will play the opening together—two buttons, two notes—and produce a resounding collaborative sound experience.
During the time leading up to the Klangwolke, users can also learn a few things about the great man himself. Bruckner's diary is the second part of the app. It offers insights into the facts & circumstances of the origins of Upper Austria's most brilliant son and his compositions that continue to enthrall music lovers everywhere.

Mobile App voestalpine Klangwolke 2013

„Alle Menschen werden Bruckner", so lautet das Motto für die iOS- und Android-App, die gemeinsam vom Ars Electronica Futurelab und Ars Electronica Solutions für die voestalpine Klangwolke 2013 entwickelt wurde. „Bruckner lebt!" – und er lebt nicht nur in der Inszenierung, sondern auch in den Smartphones und Tablets der Besucherinnen und Besucher.
Bruckners *4. Sinfonie* ist Teil der Show, sie beginnt mit getragenen Tönen, die von Hörnern gespielt werden, und in diesem Moment wird das Publikum zum größten Smartphone-Orchester der Welt. Unter Anleitung des Dirigenten spielen alle zusammen die Eröffnung der Sinfonie, zwei Tasten, zwei Töne, um einen einzigartigen Gesamtklang zu erzeugen.
Vor und nach der Klangwolke kann man zudem einiges über das Leben Bruckners erfahren, denn „Bruckners Tagebuch" ist der zweite Teil der App, der Einblick gibt in das Umfeld, in dem die bis heute faszinierenden Kompositionen des bedeutendsten Sohnes Oberösterreichs entstanden sind.
Text: Michael Knoll

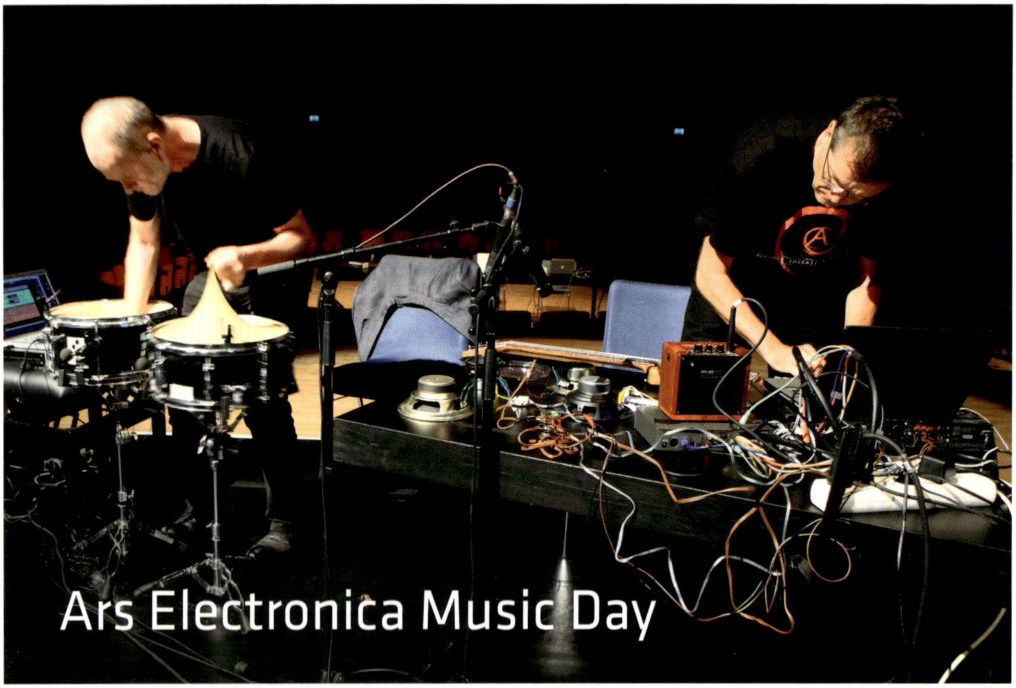

Ars Electronica Music Day

Electronic music was present at the birth of Ars Electronica. Hubert Bognermayr, Austrian composer/musician and visionary synthesizer enthusiast, was one of this festival's founders. Right from its inception, the Prix Ars Electronica too gave a high-profile position to computer music. To this day, Digital Musics & Sound Art is the category that receives the most entries.

So, it is appropriate indeed to dedicate a major themed showcase at the 2013 festival to this field of such tremendous importance to media art—one that encompasses soundart, radio art, sound sculptures and sound installations. The Brucknerhaus' concert halls and the Donaupark's alfresco ambience will serve as settings for tonal events and acoustic phenomena, listening sessions, performances, interventions and talks.

Electronic All-Request Concert

The Listening Post gets the music started in the AM. Their motto: Your wish is our command! This all-request show serves up a potpourri from among the 340 Prix Ars Electronica entries in the Archive.

An der Geburtswiege der Ars Electronica steht die elektronische Musik: Hubert Bognermayr, visionärer Synthesizerfan, österreichischer Komponist und Musiker, war einer der Gründer dieses Festivals. Auch der Prix Ars Electronica räumte von Anfang an der Computermusik breiten Raum ein. Bis heute ist die Kategorie Digital Musics & Sound Art jene mit den höchsten Einreichquoten.

Grund genug, diesem für die Medienkunst so wichtigen Feld der Musik, der Sound Art, der Radiokunst, den Klangskulpturen und Klanginstallationen einen eigenen Programmschwerpunkt zu widmen. Die Konzertsäle des Brucknerhauses und der Donaupark werden zu Klang- und Aktionsräumen, für Listening Sessions, Performances, Interventionen und Talks.

Elektronisches Wunschkonzert

Bereits am Vormittag eröffnet *Listening Post.* Unter dem Motto „Sie wünschen, wir spielen" serviert dieses Wunschkonzert ein Potpourri aus den über 340 Prix-Ars- Electronica-Einreichungen im Archiv.

Prix Forum V – Digital Musics & Sound Art

Kicking off this live performance are 2013 prizewinners in Digital Musics & Sound Art, the Prix Ars Electronica category that attracts by far the most entries. Artists Nicolas Bernier, Chris Carlson and [SjQ++] will present their works and discuss current trends and developments with Prix juror Electric Indigo.
Next up is Werner Jauk, a prominent musical theoretician and practitioner in Graz, who will deliver a special lecture entitled "Music and Media Arts" on the mediatizing of music and sound.

***TOTAL RECALL:* Special Performances**

The full-spectrum account of acoustic life on *Ars Electronica Music Day* includes several objects of a musical nature that are part of the *TOTAL RECALL* Exhibition. Yuri Suzuki, Keith Lam and Michelle Ngai will personally present their works and play installations including *The Sound of the Earth, Device Playing: Cassette Recorder (II), Toki Ori Ori Nasu–Falling Records and Quotidian Record.*

Prix Forum V – Digital Musics & Sound Art

In Sachen Live-Performances machen die diesjährigen Preisträger des Prix Ars Electronica in der Kategorie Digital Musics & Sound Art den Beginn. Das ist immer noch jene Kategorie, in die mit Abstand die meisten Einreichungen fallen. Zu hören sind Nicolas Bernier, Chris Carlson und [SjQ++], die ihre Arbeiten präsentieren und gemeinsam mit Jurymitglied Electric Indigo aktuelle Trends und Entwicklungen diskutieren.
Danach gibt der profilierte Grazer Musiktheoretiker und -praktiker Werner Jauk unter dem Titel *Music and Media Arts* eine Special Lecture zur Mediatisierung von Musik und Klang.

***TOTAL RECALL:* Special Perfomances**

Auch in der *TOTAL RECALL* Exhibition mit etlichen Exponaten musikalischer Natur regt sich am *Ars Electronica Music Day* akustisches Leben: KünstlerInnen wie Yuri Suzuki, Keith Lam and Michelle Ngai und stellen Ihre Arbeiten persönlich vor und bespielen Installationen wie *The Sound of the Earth, Device Playing: Cassette Recorder (II), Toki Ori Ori Nasu – Falling Records und Quotidian Record.*

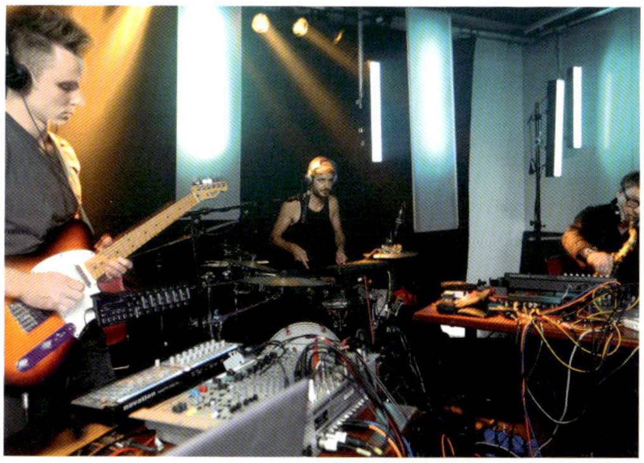

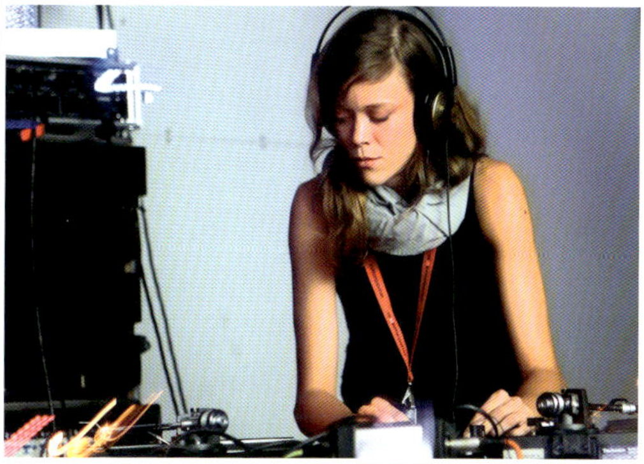

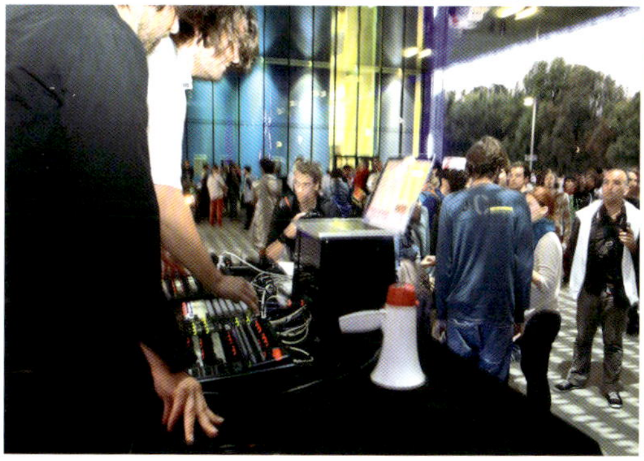

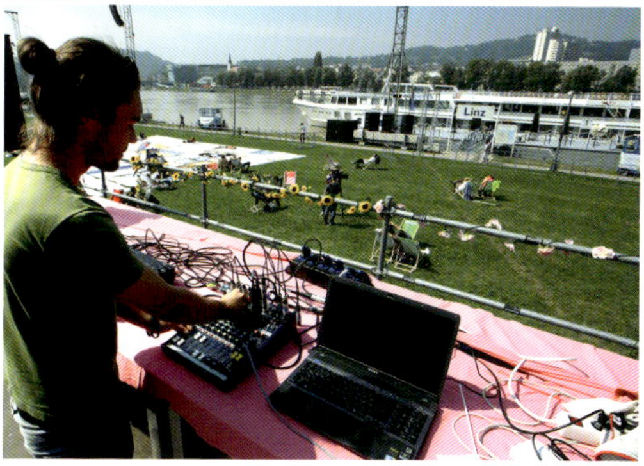

AEC, rubra

Sound is the Memory of Space
Now hear this: the Klangwolke's high-performance sound system is being placed in the service of sound art and its fine tonal and musical fabrics. *Sound is the Memory of Space* is a sonic memory sculpture that the German-Austrian label MF.Redman will acoustically erect in Donaupark. The construction components include sound & music collages containing material from international historical sound archives.

Listen and Play
The superb acoustics of the Main Hall will provide a very special setting for presentations, performances and demos by Fadi Dorninger, Daito Manabe & Satoru Higa and Roberto Paci Dalò. They'll deliver audible impressions of their work with music and sound.

Digital Musics in Concert
Taking the stage for the evening program of Digital Musics in Concert are Prix prizewinners Nicolas Bernier, Chris Carlson and [SjQ++].

Das (Welt)Raumgedächtnis
Die leistungsstarke Soundanlage der Klangwolke stellt sich an diesem Tag ganz in den Dienst der Sound Art mit ihren feinen Geräusch- und Musikgeweben. *Sound is the Memory of Space* heißt die „sonic memory sculpture", die das deutsch-österreichische Label MF.Redman akustisch im Donaupark errichtet. Klang- und Musikcollagen mit Material aus internationalen historischen Tonarchiven sind der dafür verarbeitete Baustoff.

Hören und Spielen
Bei „Listen and Play" wird die feine Konzertraumakustik des Großen Saals des Brucknerhauses zum speziellen Rahmen für Präsentationen, Performances und Demos von Künstlern wie Fadi Dorninger, Daito Manabe & Satoru Higa und Roberto Paci Dalò. Sie geben damit Höreindrücke ihrer Arbeit mit Musik und Klang.

Digital Musics in Concert
Am Abend gehört die Bühne nochmals den Prix-Preisträgern Nicolas Bernier, Chris Carlson und [SjQ++], die das Programm von *Digital Musics in Concert* bestreiten.

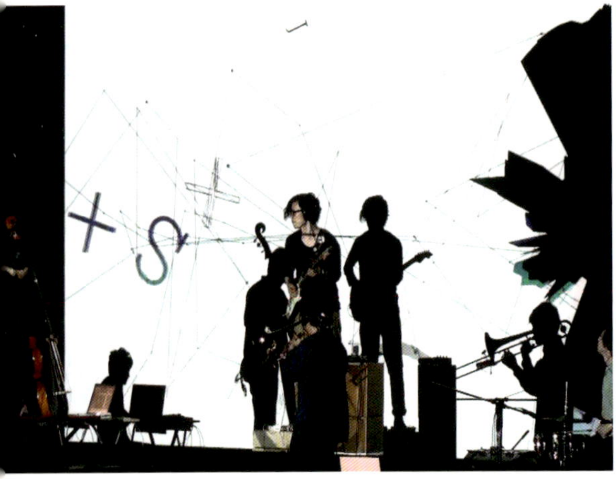
[SjQ++]

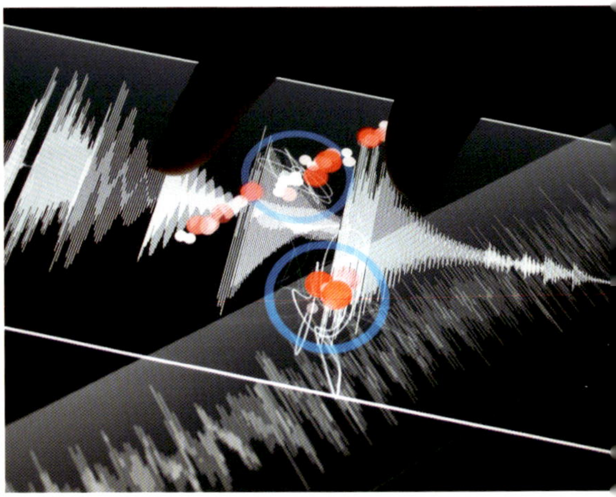
Borderlands Granular, Chris Carlson

Werner Jauk

Pop: music + media / art

Music and media art coexist in a basal interrelationship. Music is a phenomenon of the mediatization of tonal communication and thus the paradigm of a theory of media arts, of the exploration of strategies of corporeal survival in an environment "disembodied" due to mediatized interaction.
Sound is an artifact of movement; excitement is a physiological movement. Music can be considered the formalization of hearing. Anthropological theories classify music as cultivation of tonal expressivity and expressive behavior. Cultivation is associated with modern conceptions of progress. Formulated in more neutral terms, music is a product of the mediatization of the communicative quality of sound. The training of "mediators" introduces a certain degree of remoteness from the immediacy of corporeality. Mediatization also permits the assumption of differential stages of mediatization in a cultural form. Pop as well as media art will exist as interplays of immediate physicality and, simultaneously, highly mediatized "disembodiments." In more neutral terms, music is a form that goes together with the mediatization of the communicative quality of sound, with its increasing distance from the immediacy of physical and physiological "corporeality."
Gesture uses tonality and behavior indexically as reference to its origin and pictorially as iconic sign. Arbitrary signs break the connection to corporeality, and ultimately detach digital code from materiality. The formation of the work as virtuality is connected with the emergence of codes, the notation. Bodily movement depicts the conception of sound and correlates with the tonal expression of emotion. From the outset, polyphonic singing was regulated by means of such "indicative signals"; neumes are the analog representation of this movement, their

This text dispenses with formal scholarly citations and references. The use of terms clearly refers to the corresponding authorship. Detailed and comprehensive argumentation is to be found (in German) in Jauk, Werner, *pop / musik + medien / kunst. Der musikalisierte Alltag der digital culture*, epOs, Osnabrück 2009

Musik und Medienkunst stehen in einem basalen Bezug zueinander: Musik ist ein Phänomen der Mediatisierung der klanglichen Kommunikation und damit Paradigma einer Theorie der Medienkünste, der Exploration von Überlebensstrategien des Körpers in einer durch mediatisierte Interaktion „entkörperlichten" Umwelt.
Klang ist ein Artefakt von Bewegung, Erregung ist eine physiologische Bewegung. Musik gilt als Formalisierung des Hörens, anthropologische Theorien werten Musik als Kultivierung des Ausdruckslautes und -verhaltens. Kultivierung ist mit modernem Fortschrittsdenken assoziiert; neutraler formuliert, ist Musik ein Produkt der Mediatisierung der kommunikativen Qualität von Klang. Mit der Ausbildung von „Vermittlern" tritt eine Entfernung von der Unmittelbarkeit der Körperlichkeit ein. Mediatisierung erlaubt auch die Annahme unterschiedlicher Stufen der Mediatisierung in einer kulturellen Form: Pop wie Medienkunst werden als Zusammenspiel unmittelbarer Körperlichkeit und zugleich hoch mediatisierter „Entkörperlichung" existieren. Neutraler ist Musik eine Form, die mit der Mediatisierung der kommunikativen Qualität von Klang einhergeht, mit ihrer Entfernung von der Unmittelbarkeit physikalischer und physiologischer „Körperlichkeit".
Die Geste nutzt Klanglichkeit und Verhalten indexikalisch als Verweis auf den Ursprung und abbildhaft als ikonisches Zeichen. Willkürliche Zeichen lösen von der Körperlichkeit, der digitale Code schließlich von der Materialität.
Die Ausbildung des Werkes als Virtualität ist mit der Entstehung von Codes, der Notation, verbunden. Die Körperbewegung bildet die Vorstellung von Klang ab und korreliert mit dem Emotionslaut. Mehrstimmiges Singen wurde zu Beginn durch solche „hinweisenden Winke" geregelt; Neumen sind die analoge

Im Text wird auf den wissenschaftlichen Beleg, die Zitation, verzichtet; die Verwendung der Begriffe verweist klar auf die entsprechende Autorenschaft; die ausführliche Argumentation findet sich in: Jauk, Werner, *pop / musik + medien / kunst. Der musikalisierte Alltag der digital culture*, epOs, Osnabrück 2009 projection on paper, and for the first time store the sound and its full contours to memory. Their arrangement in a grid in *time & frequency* and the use of codes at the nodes (standardized by means of tempering and time measurements) of the grid system led to modern notation. Experiences from visually controlled body-environment interaction (BEI) are inscribed as a visual phenomenon onto this system of graphical codes used to save sounds to memory. It is the transfer of these "conceptual metaphors," the conceptions of physical plasticity, volume and density of sound with the concept of gravitation and their application to the representation of the pitch and length of the sound, whereby the conception of pitch is totally decoupled from the physical manifestation of the sound.

Notation, as an encoded means of mediation between the conception of sound and its physical realization, makes possible—as "objectification of the we"—arrangement of communicating voices, design as a result of communication. Notation as a system of saving information to memory is connected to the idea of the work, the final fixation of a piece of music and the overcoming of transience, both that of the act of communication as well as that of the sound, which resists the audible depiction in the moment, in the here-and-now.

High cultivation as liberation from the emotional remains of the sound's origin was achieved by music theory. Following the aesthetic of expression and imitation, disengagement from it is the assumption of the equal probability of all tone pitches; codes for sounds are now arranged deliberately (formalized in algorithms). This design of the macrostructure in time is carried on in the microstructure of the sound and the internal sound movement. Serial design is transferred into the electronically tension-controlled sound structure in *time & frequency* just as it is into the digitally computed sound stream.

Storing the sound to memory, processing it as well as its targeted generation will change the aesthetic understanding of music as arrangement of codes into understanding of the modulation of sounds. This will set in motion the "retrogression" to playing music, overcoming of visual codes, and, thus, of visual thinking in the com-position of sounds. Once, music was regarded as "referential thinking"

Abbildung dieser Bewegung, ihre Projektion auf Papier, und speichern erstmals den Klang in seiner Kontur. Ihre Rasterung in *time & frequency* und die Nutzung von Codes an den (durch Temperierung und Zeitmaße normierten) Schnittpunkten des Gridsystems führten zur modernen Notation. Diesem den Klang speichernden grafischen Codesystem sind (als visuelles Phänomen) Erfahrungen aus der sehend kontrollierten Körper-Umwelt-Interaktion (K-U-I) eingeschrieben. Es sind dies „konzeptuelle Metaphern", die Vorstellungen von physischer Plastizität, Volumen und Dichte von Klängen mit dem Konzept der Gravitation auf die Darstellung der Höhe und Länge des Klanges übertragen, wobei die Vorstellung der Höhe von der physikalischen Erscheinung des Klanges völlig entkoppelt ist.

Notation, als codierte Vermittlung zwischen der Vorstellung von Klang und seiner physikalischen Realisierung, ermöglichte als „Objektivation des Wir" das Setzen von kommunizierenden Stimmen, das Gestalten aus Kommunikation. Notation als Speichersystem ist mit der Idee des Werkes verbunden, der endgültigen Fixierung eines Musikstückes und der Überwindung von Flüchtigkeit, jener des Kommunikationsaktes ebenso wie jener des Klanges, der sich der hörenden Ab-bild-ung im Moment, im Augenblick, entzieht.

Hoch-Kultivierung als Befreiung vom emotionalen Rest der Herkunft des Klanges leistete die Musiktheorie. Nach der Ausdrucks- und Nachahmungs-Ästhetik ist die Lösung davon die Annahme der Gleichwahrscheinlichkeit aller Tonhöhen; Codes für Klänge werden nun willentlich (formalisiert in Algorithmen) gesetzt. Diese Gestaltung der Makrostruktur in der Zeit wird in jener der Mikrostruktur des Klanges und der internen Klangbewegung weitergeführt. Serielle Gestaltung wird auf die elektronisch in *time & frequency* spannungsgeregelte Klangstruktur wie den digital errechneten Soundstream übertragen.

Die Speicherung des Klanges, seine Verarbeitung, aber auch seine gezielte Generierung werden das ästhetische Verständnis von Musik als Setzen von Codes zum Verständnis der Modulation von Klängen verändern – damit werden die „Rückentwicklung" zum Musizieren, die Überwindung der visuellen Codes und damit des visuellen Denkens im Kom-ponere von Klängen eingeleitet. Einst wurde Musik als „beziehendes Denken" in Codes für Klänge gesehen, wo wir doch Klänge nach „Spannung und Lösung" erleben.

Obwohl aus der Ästhetik hochkultureller Musik stam-

in codes for sounds, whereby we nevertheless experience sounds as "tension and resolution."
Although it originated in the aesthetic of high-cultural music, this "functional" aesthetic in conjunction with the capacity to save sound to memory has just brought forth a change in Pop. The European avant-garde of electronic sound composed whole series of these; thus, the primary intention of *musique concrète* was the decomposition of the concrete. The American avant-garde made the tape recorder, the mediating memory machine, the centerpiece of musical activity and, in accordance with the trial & error method, exploited the possibilities and artifacts of mechanical manipulation of stored sounds. Tape recorded loops like tonal manipulation via phase shift become the aesthetic basis of *minimal music.*
Oriented directly on physical sound work, Pop in the "other avant-garde" made use of the availability of sound technology. Consumer technologies like overdubbing with the double cassette recorder and the mixing in of a voice by means of a built-in microphone go into the "production" of Hip-Hop. Sound processing technologies of *musique concrète* are becoming standards in the dominant sound work of Pop, whereby sound samples are not abstracted but rather used functionally as exciting elements. In doing so, technology always serves as "amplification" of the corporeality of the sound. Even if it seems "disembodied" due to its digital origins, its processing is fundamentally physical.
In contradistinction to analog sound, digital sound is freed from physical conditions. It is deliberately available in *time & frequency & space;* its deliberate calculation makes space a musical parameter. On one hand, space is decoupled from the performance location; on the other hand, precisely this is focused as emotional situation. Pop and *field recording* will be avant-garde here.
Often held in low esteem, only the "greater ease" of dealing with the sound in *digital musics* has a socio-aesthetic implication: the general accessibility of sound design. This so-called media-morphosis reverses the possibilities of the political use of music. The distinction exists only in the juxtaposition to that which is a special case.
As something freed from materiality, digital code is a *common digit;* codes are no longer converted

mend, hat diese „funktionale" Ästhetik gerade im Pop im Zusammenhang mit der Klangspeicherung eine Änderung hervorgebracht. Die europäische Avantgarde der elektronischen Klänge komponierte diese reihenmäßig, die *musique concrète* hatte primär die Dekomposition des Konkreten vor Ohren. Amerikanische Avantgarde setzte mit dem Tonband die vermittelnde Speichermaschine ins Zentrum musikalischen Tuns und nutzte nach dem *trial & error*-System die Möglichkeiten und Artefakte der maschinellen Manipulation von gespeichertem Klang; Loops aus Tonbandschleifen wie die Klangmanipulation durch Phasenverschiebung werden zur ästhetischen Basis der *minimal music.*
Direkt an körperlicher Klangarbeit orientiert, bediente sich Pop in der „anderen Avantgarde" der Verfügbarkeit der Klangtechnologie. Consumer-Technologien wie das Overdubbing mit dem Doppelcassetten-Recorder und das Zumischen einer Voice durch ein eingebautes Mikrophon gehen in die „Produktion" von Hip-Hop ein; klangverarbeitende Technologien der *musique concrète* werden zu Standards in der dominanten Sound-Arbeit von Pop – dabei werden Soundsamples nicht abstrahiert, sondern funktional als erregende genutzt. Technologie dient dabei stets als „Verstärkung" der Körperlichkeit des Klanges – selbst wenn er ob seiner digitalen Genese als „entkörperlicht" erscheint, ist seine Verarbeitung basal körperlich.
Anders als der analoge ist der digitale Klang von physikalischen Bedingungen gelöst, er ist willentlich verfügbar in *time & frequency & space;* seine willentliche Errechnung macht Raum zum musikalischen Parameter: Einerseits wird Raum vom Aufführungsort entkoppelt, andererseits wird gerade dieser als emotionale Situation fokussiert; Pop wie *field recording* werden hier Avantgarden sein.
Oftmals gering geschätzt, hat allein die „leichtere" Handhabung des Klanges in *digital musics* eine sozioästhetische Implikation: den allgemeinen Zugang zur Klanggestaltung. Durch diese Mediamorphose wird die Möglichkeit des politischen Gebrauchs von Musik umgekehrt: Distinktion besteht nun in der Gegenhaltung zum Besonderen.
Als von Materialität befreit ist der digitale Code ein *common digit;* Codes werden nicht mehr zur Vermittlung in verschiedene Stimuli konvertiert, sondern zur Erregung – multimediale Kunst wird zur multisensorischen, die Idee einer Ästhetik des digitalen Gesamt-

into various stimuli for the purpose of mediation but rather for excitement. Multimedia art becomes multi-sensory. The idea of an aesthetic of a digital *Gesamtdatenwerk* becomes the practice of full corporeal arousal.

The physical processing of generated/stored sounds is the act of overcoming the visual as the medium of the (thus rational) formation of the sound. At the same time, this is the preliminary form of the intuitive design that accompanies digitization, since immaterial codes permit design beyond the realm of the material and its *embodiments*. Deliberate design of visual codes takes place as the result of the experience of the seeing BEI and remains within the boundaries of materiality and thus of a mechanistic conception, which are formalized in algorithmic rules of arrangement. The act of overcoming this "natural" basis of the will as a conception of "shocks and thrusts" is the transgression of the mechanistic. As an alternative, there's hedonic formation—that is, according to that corporeality that is unique to the origin of music. Digital culture is necessarily a hedonic culture.

A hedonic culture approaches the status of popular culture (Volkskultur). Beyond the realm of distinguishing knowledge about the structuring of codes in rules of composition (constituting social strata), hedonic design is a basal human design that utilizes phylogenetic intentional/emotional "knowledge" about the significance of movement about us for the body. This is so because sound is a product of movement/stimulation; it informs in this way and functions as a signal and thus as a trigger of actions relevant to an individual's survival. Making music is playing with the arousal value of sound. Pop music will use the direct physical formation of technoid sound and make it popular. Hedonic design makes digital culture into a musicalized, into a pop-musicalized culture.

The availability of corresponding technologies makes direct physical formation of what are, at the same time, generated disembodied sounds popular in an additional sense. Technical availability is associated with feasibility, social availability with desirability, and psychological availability with intuitive handling of the "instruments." Instrumentation of expressive behavior becomes the para-

datenwerkes wird zur Praxis der gesamtkörperlichen Erregung.

Die körperliche Verarbeitung des gespeicherten / generierten Klanges ist die Überwindung des Visuellen als Medium der (damit rationalen) Formung von Klang – zugleich ist dies die Vorform des intuitiven Gestaltens, das mit der Digitalisierung einhergeht. Denn immaterielle Codes erlauben Gestaltung abseits des Materiellen und seiner *embodiments* – willentliche Gestaltung visueller Codes geschieht aus der Erfahrung der sehenden K-U-I und bleibt innerhalb der Grenzen der Materialität und damit mechanistischer Vorstellung, die in algorithmischen Regeln der Reihung formalisiert sind. Die Überwindung dieser „natürlichen" Basis des Willens als Vorstellung von „Schocks und Schüben" ist die Transgression des Mechanistischen. Alternativ wird hedonisch geformt, also nach jener Körperlichkeit, die dem Ursprung der Musik eigen ist. Digitale Kultur ist notwendigerweise eine hedonische Kultur.

Eine hedonische Kultur nähert sich einer Volkskultur. Abseits distinguierenden Wissens über die Strukturierung von Codes in (soziale Stände konstituierenden) Kompositionsregeln, ist die hedonische Gestaltung eine basal menschliche, die phylogenetisches intentionales / emotionales „Wissen" um die Bedeutung von Bewegung rund um uns für den Körper nutzt, denn: Klang ist ein Produkt von Bewegung / Erregung; er informiert über diese und wirkt signalhaft als Trigger für überlebensrelevantes Handeln. Musizieren ist das Spiel mit dem Erregungswert von Sound – Pop-Musik wird die direkte körperliche Formung von technoidem Sound nutzen und populär machen. Hedonische Gestaltung macht die digitale Kultur zu einer musikalisierten, zu einer pop-musikalisierten.

Die Verfügbarkeit entsprechender Technologien macht unmittelbar körperliche Formung von zugleich entkörperlicht generierten Klängen in einem weiteren Sinne populär. Technische Verfügbarkeit ist mit Machbarkeit, soziale Verfügbarkeit mit Erwünschtheit; psychologische Verfügbarkeit mit intuitivem Handling der „Instrumente" verbunden. Instrumentarisierung expressiven Verhaltens wird zum Paradigma des Interface als emotionale kommunikative Situation. Die instrumentelle Bewegung des reaktiven *touch* weicht der emotionalen Interaktion als Teil kollektiver und kollektivierender Kommunikation.

digm of the interface as emotional communicative situation. The instrumental movement of the reactive *touch* gives way to emotional interaction as part of collective and collectivizing communication.
There have been two technological developments that disrupt the dominant visually controlled body-environment interaction and transgress the mechanistic system of thinking connected with it: dynamization and encoding/digitization.
Dynamization of the environment leads, beyond "high-speed stagnation," to reversal of interaction: It's not the body that approaches the environment; rather, the environment moves in the direction of a body that has become mechanically "useless." This is the situation of phylogenetically older hearing.
Digitization resists an environment of mechanical interaction that can be grasped as analogous to the body. Hedonic regulation of the BEI is that alternative that, on the whole, regulates behavior attributable to curiosity and thus aesthetic behavior too. The body's interaction with the immateriality of a digital virtuality is necessarily a hedonic one.
Music as formalization of hearing is a dynamic form, the transience of which was overcome at an early stage by means of codes. Its arrangement takes place in hedonic fashion according to perceived "tension-resolution."
Thus, hedonically generated interaction in digital culture is ultimately musical interaction. Above all, the hedonically collective/collectivizing genesis of and reception accorded to Pop sound—a phenomenon that engenders both a political and an emotional climate—is, in this context, the avant-garde paradigm of physical life in virtuality.
Media art, like science, has an epistemological interest: generating insights about *extended perception* and the survival of the body in an environment as well as the perceptions of it that are changing as a result of media interaction with it. Music, the formalization of the medium perception as tonally controlled BEI, provides a model for this. This is so because music as a dynamic art form comprised of codes has always hedonically lived out the new facts and circumstances of the environment that only later became evident to graphic art—as formalization of analog statistical representation—by means of dynamization and encoding.

Nun sind es zwei technologische Entwicklungen, die die dominant sehend kontrollierte K-U-Interaktion irritieren und das damit verbundene mechanistische Denksystem überschreiten: Dynamisierung und Codierung / Digitalisierung.
Dynamisierung der Umwelt führt über den „rasenden Stillstand" hinaus zur Umkehrung der Interaktion: Nicht der Körper bewegt sich auf die Umwelt zu, diese bewegt sich auf einen mechanisch „unnütz" geworden Körper zu – das ist die Situation des phylogenetisch älteren Hörens.
Digitalisierung entzieht eine analog dem Körper fassbare Umwelt der mechanischen Interaktion – hedonische Regelung der K-U-I ist jene Alternative, die insgesamt das Neugierverhalten und damit auch das ästhetische Verhalten reguliert – die Interaktion des Körpers mit der Immateralität einer digitalen Virtualität ist notwendigerweise eine hedonische.
Musik als Formalisierung des Hörens ist eine dynamische Form, ihre Flüchtigkeit wurde früh durch Codes überwunden – ihre Zusammenstellung erfolgt hedonisch nach empfundener „Spannung-Lösung".
Damit ist die hedonisch generierende Interaktion in der digitalen Kultur letztlich eine musikalische. Vor allem die hedonisch kollektiv(ierend)e Genese wie Rezeption des – ein politisches als emotionales Klima schaffenden – Pop-Sound ist dabei avantgardistisches Paradigma des körperlichen Lebens in der Virtualität.
Die Medienkunst hat wie die Wissenschaft ein epistemologisches Interesse: Erkenntnis zu schaffen über *extended perception* und das Überleben des Körpers in einer sich durch mediale Interaktion mit ihr verändernden Umwelt und ihrer Vorstellung – Musik, die Formalisierung des Mediums „Wahrnehmung" als klanglich kontrollierte K-U-I, bietet dafür ein Modell. Denn jene neuen Bedingungen der Umwelt, die der bildenden Kunst als Formalisierung der analogen statischen Abbildung erst durch Dynamisierung und Codierung augenfällig wurden, hat Musik als dynamische Kunst aus Codes stets hedonisch gelebt.

Station Rose

Digital Quarter Century << ShelTeR >>

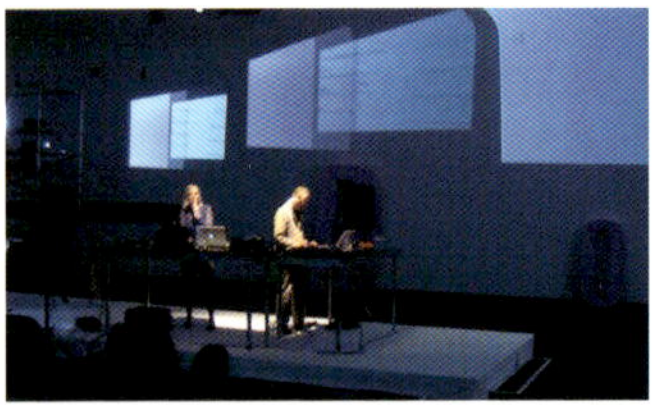

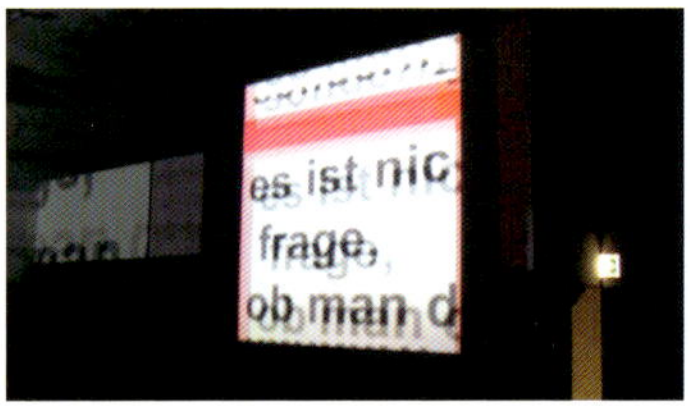

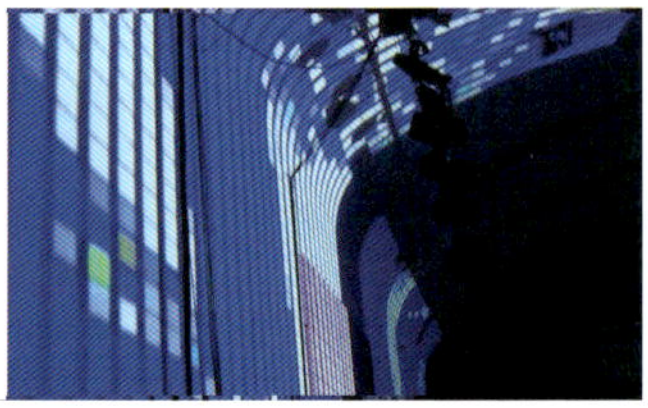

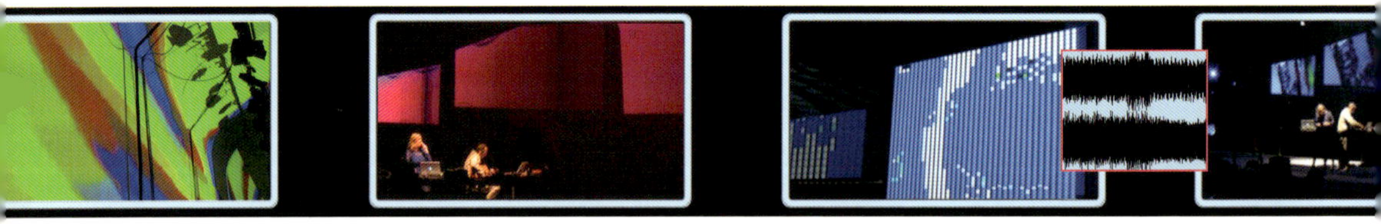

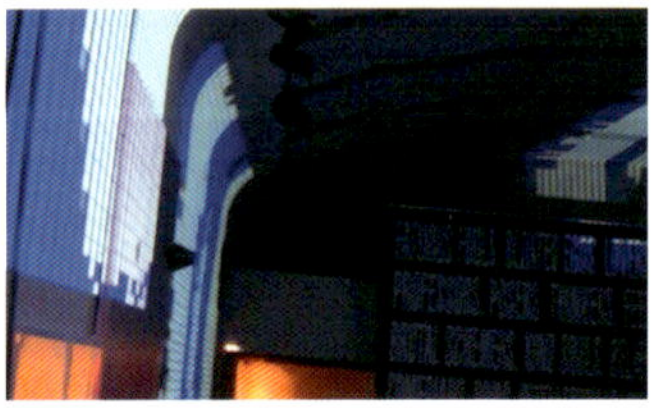

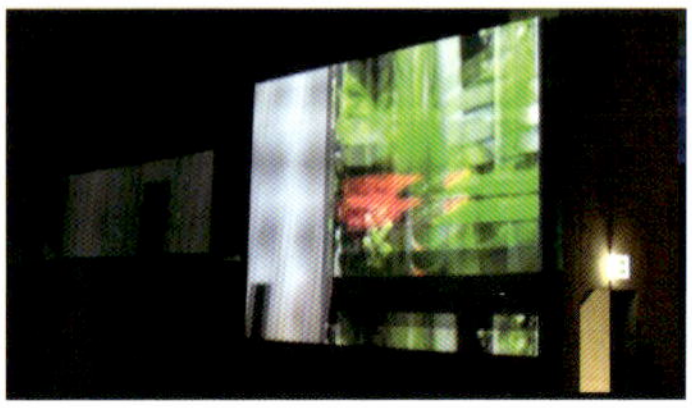

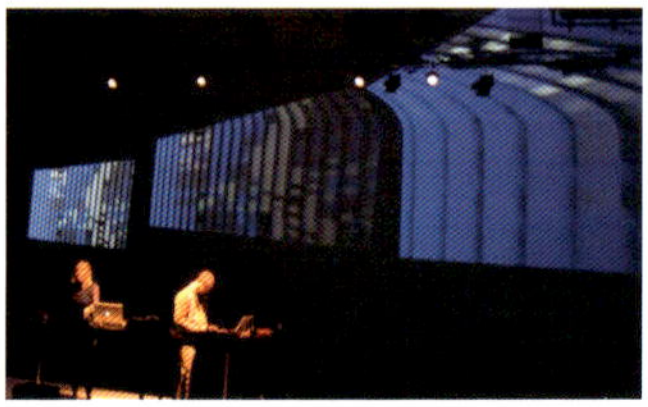

2013 is a very special year. STATION ROSE has reached the Digital Quarter Century (DQC) mark. Counting the decades is obsolete; now, the century unit is what counts. *DQC* is a current project designed to conserve cultural heritage as viewed from the perspective of artists, the pioneers of digital culture; first-hand reportage; launched in 1988 with diskettes.

:// Facts: A quarter-century ago, Elisa Rose (visual artist) & Gary Danner (musician, composer) founded Station Rose as Vienna's first address of the open digital leading edge. 1988: opening; 1989: eight months in Cairo; 1991: exile & online; 1992: Gunafa clubbing, A/V performances worldwide; beginning in 1994: digital bohème, homepage & social Web; 1999: webcasting; 2002–06: TV show on ARD; 2008: LogInCabin, books, vinyls, CD-ROMs, DVDs, CDs; since 2011: back in Vienna.

STR has now created *DQC_ShelTeR* as a playable

2013 ist ein besonderes Jahr, STATION ROSE hat das „Digital Quarter Century / DQC" erreicht. Das Zählen in Dekaden ist obsolet, nun zählt die Century-Einheit. *DQC* ist ein aktuelles Projekt, um Kulturerbe zu speichern, vom Blickwinkel der Künstler, der Pioneers of Digital Culture aus gesehen, 1st-hand Berichterstattung, 1988 mit Disketten gestartet.

:// Facts: Vor einem Viertel-Jahrhundert haben Elisa Rose (bildende Künstlerin) & Gary Danner (Musiker, Komponist) die Station Rose als erste digitale öffentliche Adresse Wiens gegründet. 1988 Opening, 1989 8 Monate in Cairo, 1991 Exil & online, 1992 Gunafa Clubbing, A/V Performances weltweit, ab 1994 Digital Bohème, Homepage & Social Web, 1999 Webcasting, 2002–2006 ARD TV-Sendung, 2008 LogInCabin, Bücher, Vinyls, CD-Roms, DVDs, CDs ... seit 2011 back in Vienna.

Mit *DQC_ShelTeR* schafft STR nun eine bespielbare Installation, eine A/V-Skulptur, ein digitales Archiv,

installation, an A/V sculpture, a digital archive, a playpen for grownups, and a way to maintain an overview of the information. Elisa Rose & Gary Danner perform live in audiovisual sessions mixed with <Nature is Cool>, station operation. *DQC* data are looped into new A/V material composed especially for the Festival. The world premiere of the *DQC_ShelTeR* performance will, in turn, be recorded. The translation of processual art into a material form has been a prime area of emphasis for years, activities STR refers to as New Media Arte Povera. This aesthetic, originally developed in Frankfurt as a response to banking sector insanity and economic crisis, retains its validity to this day. An installation and performances make it visible, audible, bring reduced sensuality, glitch art, recycling & bass into play. Sound & projection encounter wood, cloth, urban gardening and data–Contemporary Art 2013.
DQC Memory // STR Big Data: The digital quarter-century has generated an immense amount of data.
Station Rose poses questions:
Do these data belong to us? STR's watchwords: Cyberspace is Our Land
Data storage: from diskette via SCSII to Cloud & back again? What's the next step?
http://stationrose.com
Supported by: City of Linz, Linz_Kultur

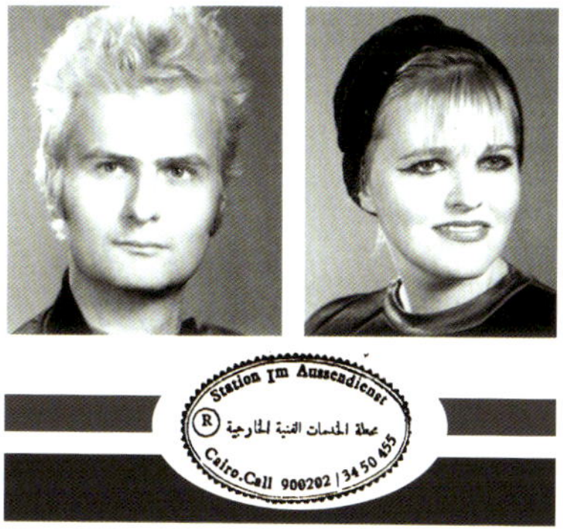

ein Spielhaus für Erwachsene, um den Überblick über die Daten nicht zu verlieren. Elisa Rose & Gary Danner performen live in audiovisuellen Sessions, vermischt mit <Nature is Cool>, Stationsbetrieb. Das „Einschleifen" von *DQC*-Daten trifft auf neue A/V-Kompositionen, für das Festival komponiert. Die Uraufführung der *DQC_ShelTeR*-Performance wird wieder recorded. Die Umsetzung der prozessualen Kunst in die Verstofflichung ist Schwerpunkt seit Jahren, von STR „New Media Arte Povera" genannt. Diese Ästhetik, noch in Frankfurt als Antwort auf Bankenwahnsinn & Wirtschaftskrise entwickelt, ist immer noch gültig. Sie wird in Installation & Performances sichtbar, hörbar, bringt reduzierte Sinnlichkeit, Glitch-Art, Recycling & Bass ins Spiel. Sound & Projektion trifft auf Holz, Stoff, Urban Gardening & Daten – Contemporary Art 2013.
DQC-Memory : // STR Big Data – das Digitale Viertel Jahrhundert hat immense Daten generiert.
Station Rose stellt Fragen:
Gehören diese Daten uns? Ein STR-Begriff ist „Cyberspace is Our Land".
Datenspeicherung – von Diskette via SCSII zu Cloud & back again ? Was ist der next step?

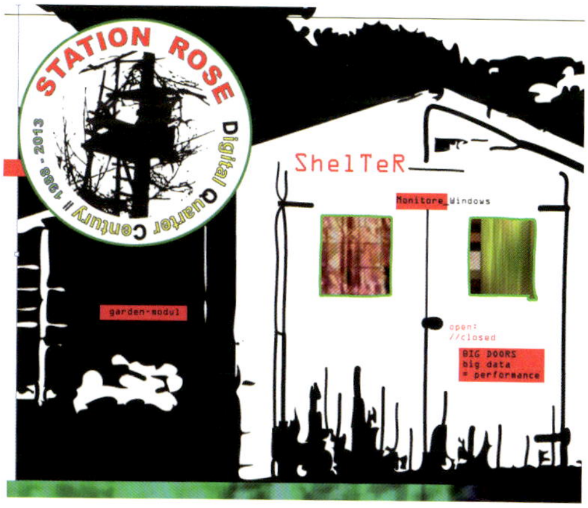

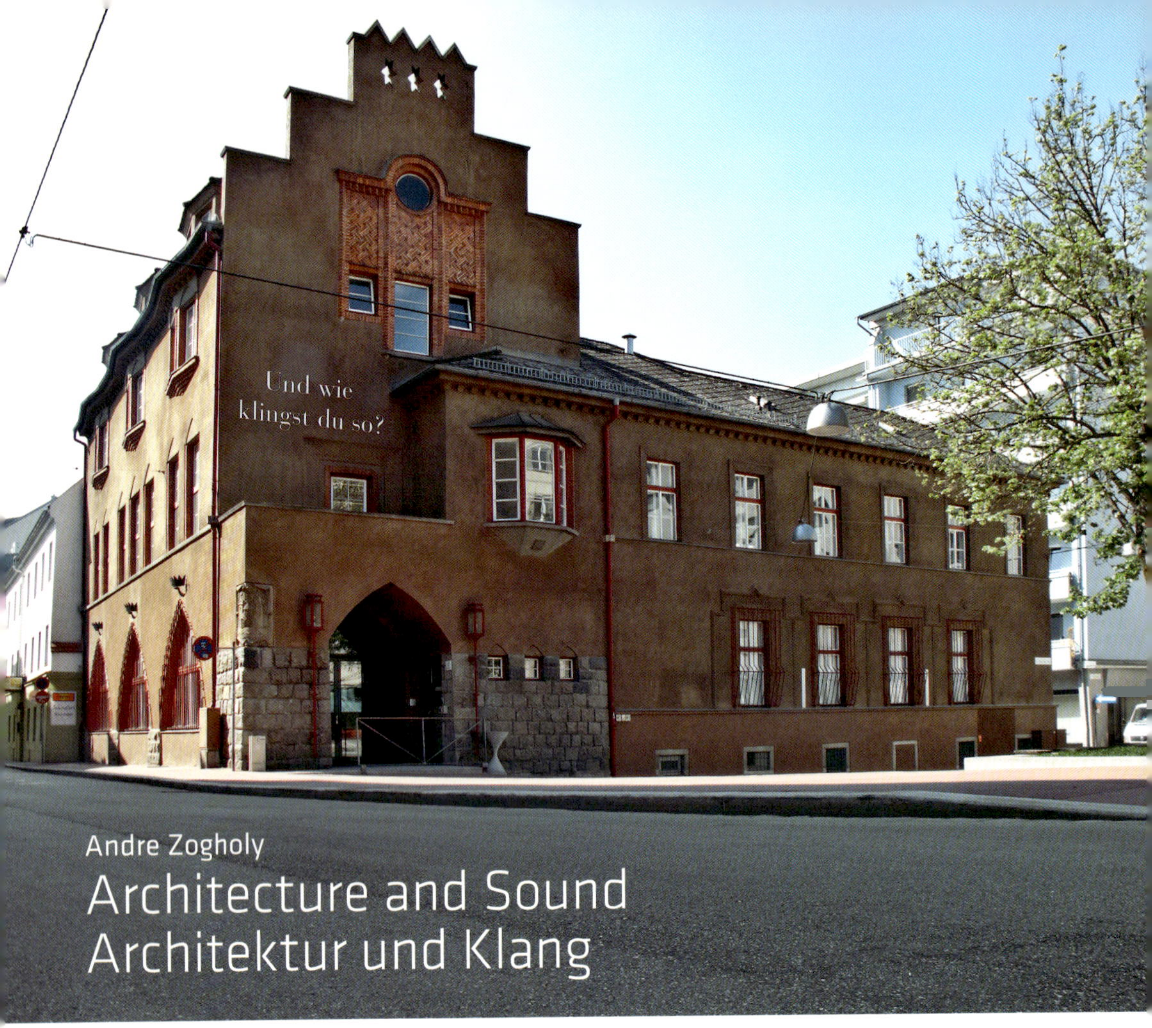

Andre Zogholy

Architecture and Sound
Architektur und Klang

The relationships between architecture and sound are highly diverse, ranging from theoretical and abstract phenomena all the way to the concrete facts and circumstances of everyday life. The history of the intellectual confrontation with this topic extends all the way back to Greek Antiquity. Most recently, it has fanned out into fields of expertise that, at first glance, hardly seem to be related to one another.

Linkages connecting architecture and sound present an interesting array of possibilities but are also fraught with discontinuities, contradictions and clashes. This is by all means a dynamic relationship that entails such heterogeneous fields as psychoacoustics, environmental acoustics, spatial acoustics and structural engineering, and touches upon questions of design and, above all, sociopo-

Die Beziehungen zwischen Architektur und Klang sind mannigfaltig und spannen einen weiten Bogen von theoretisch-abstrakten bis zu konkret im Alltagsleben fassbaren Phänomenen. Die explizite Auseinandersetzung mit dem Thema reicht weit in die griechische Antike zurück und fächert sich in der Gegenwart in Expertisen auf, die auf den ersten Blick weit auseinander zu liegen scheinen.

Verbindungen von Architektur und Klang bringen eine Vielzahl an Möglichkeiten, aber auch Widersprüche, Brüche und Konflikte mit sich. In jedem Fall handelt es sich um ein dynamisches Verhältnis, welches heterogene Felder wie etwa Psychoakustik, Umweltakustik, Raumakustik, Bautechnik, Fragen des Designs, aber auch und vor allem gesellschaftspolitische Fragestellungen betrifft, denn sowohl Architektur als auch Klang haben soziale Funktionen. Beide sind

Projects:
Wasserspiegel, Anja Barbara Aichinger, Reni Hofmüller
Mondo Mockado, Billy Roisz, Ana Threat: Enter the Voidoid
Einklinken – Ausklinken, Reinhard Gupfinger, Maurizio Nardo
Dense Room, Sun Li Lian Obwegeser, Gerald Roßbacher
Sharp Sine Square Wire Chamber Trio, Clemens Bauder, Ilpo Väisänen
Empty Spaces, Jakob Dietrich, Kai Maier-Rothe
A Balloon for Linz, Davide Tidoni
Sound Dérive, Enrique Tomás
And: Davide Tidoni, Verena Schoißengeyr, Katja Seifert, Felix Vierlinger

In addition to an extensive program of accompanying presentations, the Architecture Forum's physical premises—both indoors and outdoors—will host materializations of heterogeneous and interdisciplinary encounters with architecture and sound.

Head curator: Andre Zogholy
Assistant curator: Ewald Elmecker
Technical infrastructure: Ewald Elmecker, Hannes Franks

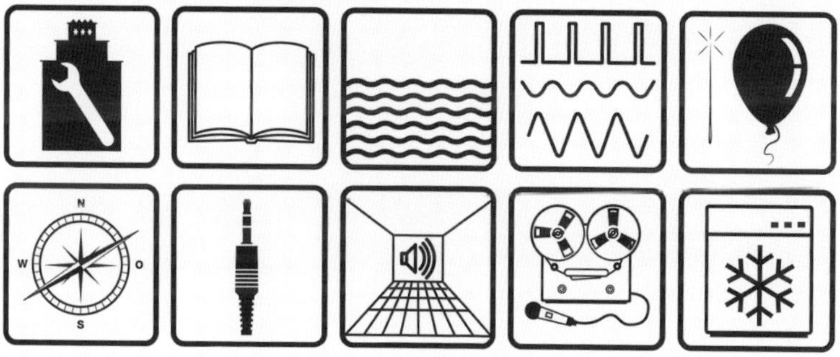

litical issues. After all, both architecture and sound have social functions. Both are embedded in the balance of power prevailing in society—reflecting it, supporting it or violating it. Acoustic space, like architectural space, is also always a setting of social interaction. As a dispositive and an element subject to the economy of power, the multifarious outcomes can manifest themselves as dystopias, utopias or heterotopias.

This much is true in any case: The relationships among architecture, space and sound, whether in the form of language, noise, music or silence, have a powerful effect on people's lives. For this reason, these relationships are interwoven with often ambivalent sociopolitical discourses.

in gesellschaftliche Machtverhältnisse eingebettet, widerspiegeln diese, unterstützen sie oder brechen mit ihnen. Der akustische wie der architektonische Raum ist immer auch Ort sozialer Interaktion. Als Dispositiv und Gegenstand der Machtökonomie können sich die Ausformungen als Dystopie, Utopie oder als Heterotopie äußern.

Fest steht in jedem Fall: Die Beziehungen von Architektur, Raum und Klang, ob nun als Sprache, Geräusch, Lärm, Musik oder Stille, prägen unser Leben wesentlich. Aus diesem Grund verschränken sich diese Verhältnisse mit oftmals ambivalenten gesellschaftspolitischen Diskursen.

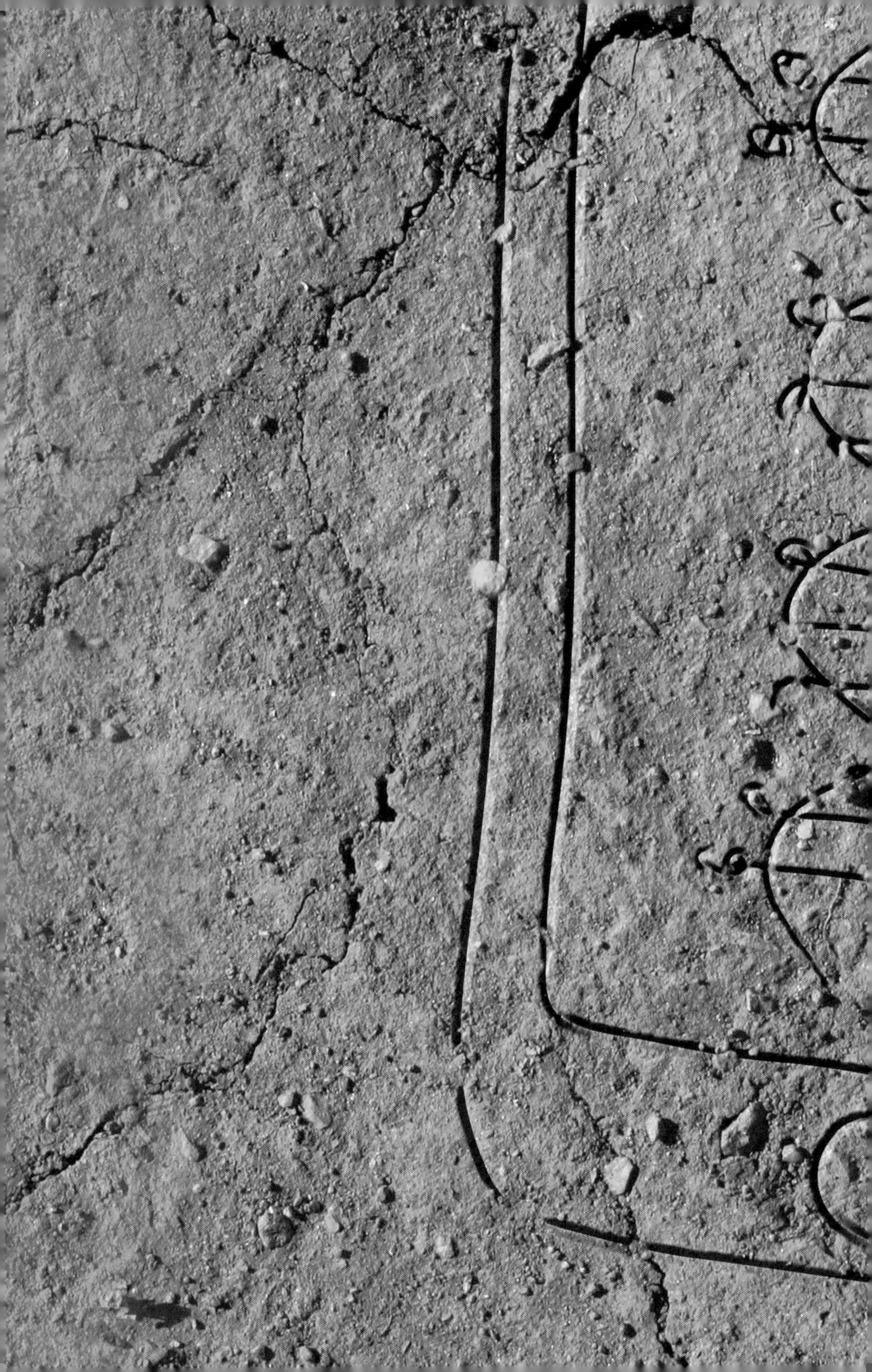

FEATURED ARTIST

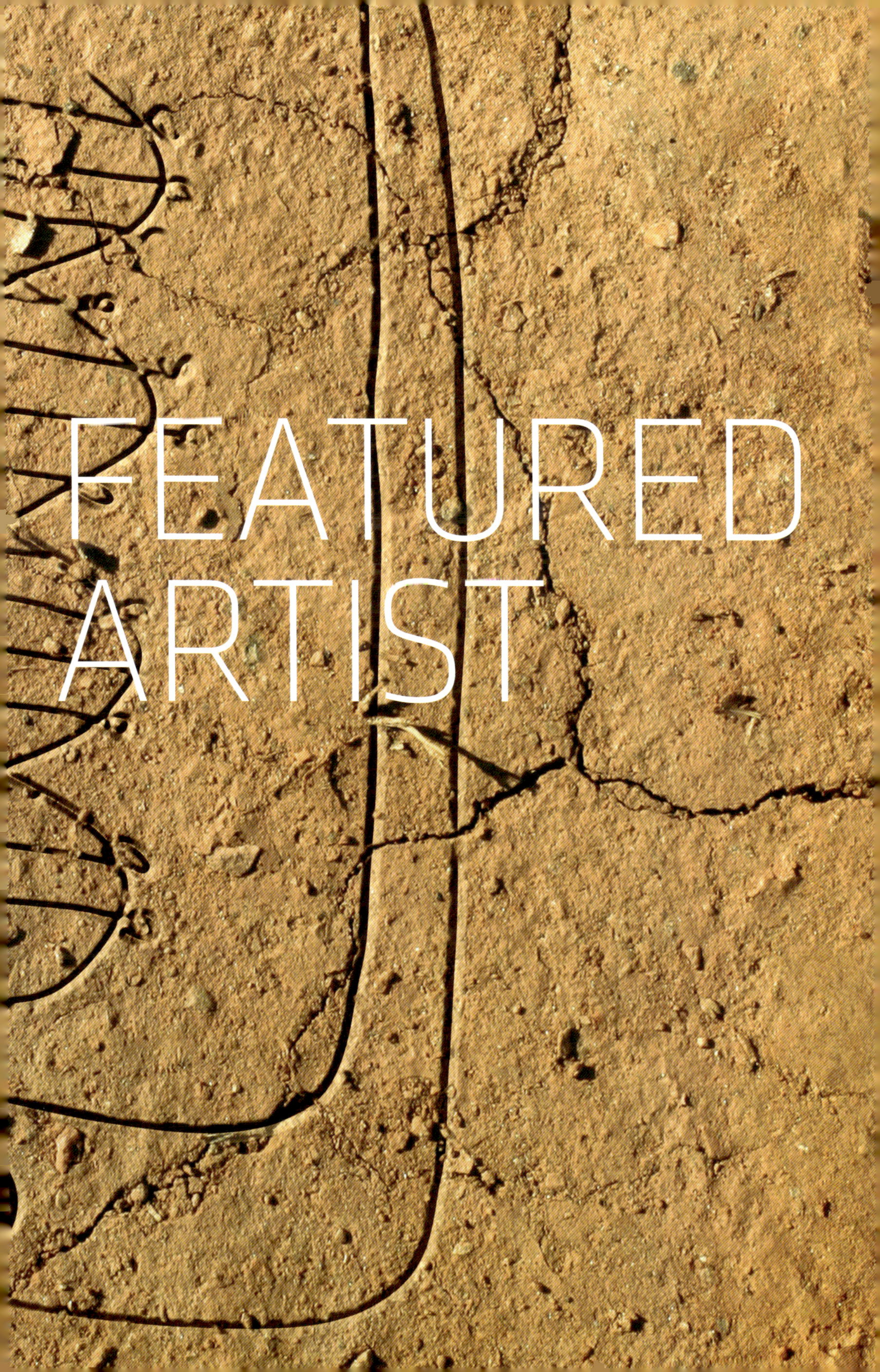

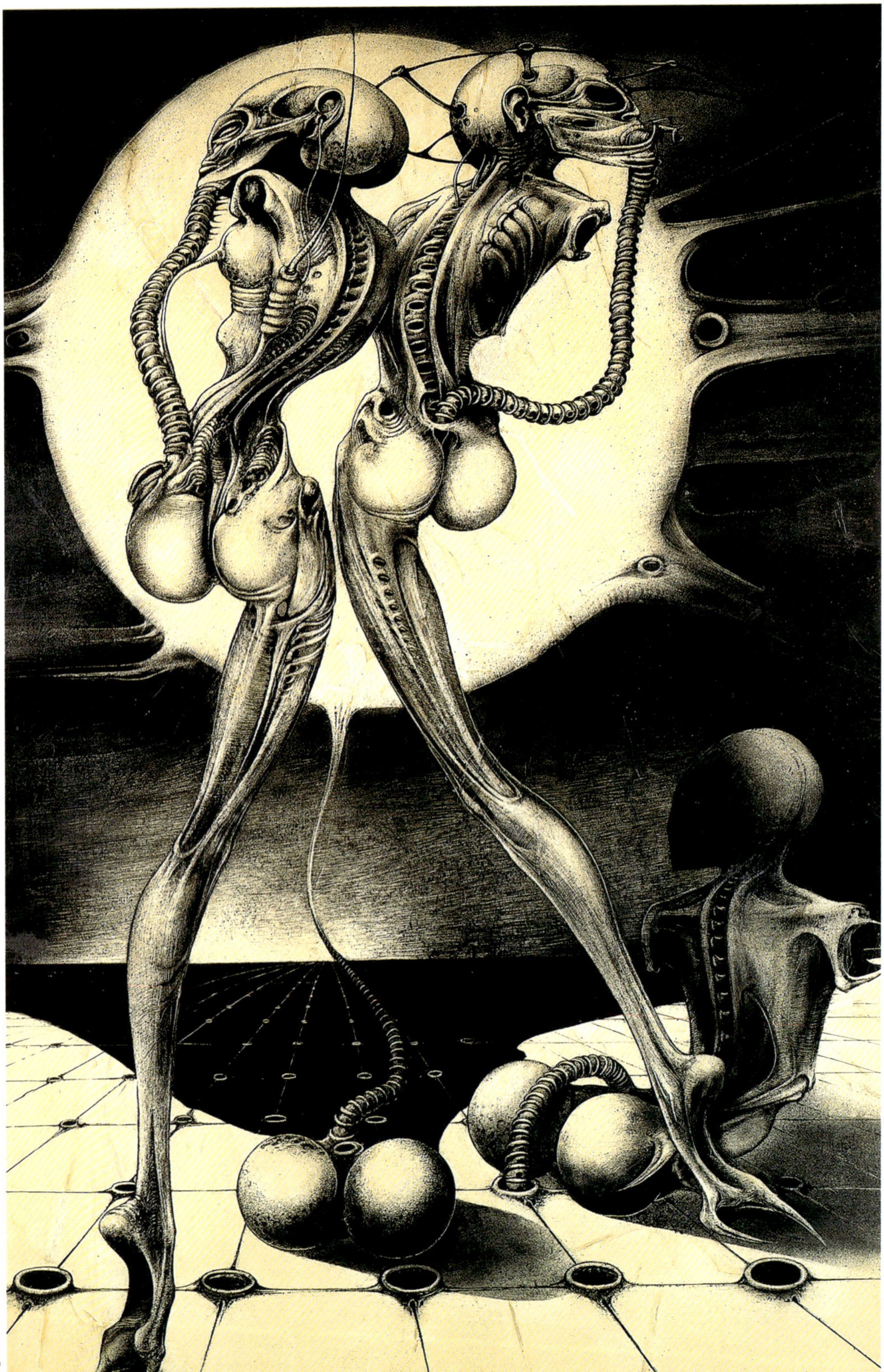

Atomkinder, 1967/68, Tusche auf Transcop-Papier, 170 x 108 cm

HR Giger

Featured Artist Ars Electronica 2013

The Art of Biomechanics

In William Gibson's 1993 novel *Virtual Light,* a tattoo parlor in the year 2005 served as the setting for this dialog.

"Lowell ... he's got a Giger.
'Giger'?
This painter. Like nineteenth-century or something. Real classical. Bio-mech."[1]

This exchange gets across the essentials about HR Giger. He's actually a 20th-century artist, born in 1940 in Chur, Switzerland, but his roots do extend back into the art history of the 19th century. He is indeed a painter, but has made the airbrush his primary tool. He's part of the 1960s avant-garde and one of the leading innovators in the fantastic art genre. His works have already attained the status of true classics, and not only among aficionados of 1990s cyberculture. He created a "biomechanical" style all his own, an astounding vision even in light of the reality of cyborgs and biotechnology.

This scene also says a lot about the reception accorded to HR Giger, whose persona is that of an art world outsider and whose work, in the wake of his blockbuster success with *Alien,* became a pop cultural phenomenon in its own right. His rediscovery in the graphic art scene has been a more recent development, one that's also associated with museums' processes of coming to terms with popular culture within the context of, on one hand, shifting concepts of what art actually is, and, on the other hand, the emergence of a broad-based cyberculture.

Die Kunst der Biomechanik

In seinem 1993 erschienenen Roman *Virtual Light* lässt William Gibson diesen Dialog in einem Tattoo-Studio des Jahres 2005 stattfinden:

Hier ist Wesentliches über den 1940 in Chur in der Schweiz geborenen HR Giger enthalten. Er ist zwar ein Künstler des 20. Jahrhunderts, aber seine Wurzeln reichen tief in die Kunstgeschichte des 19. Jahrhunderts hinein. Er ist tatsächlich Maler, hat aber den Luftpinsel (Airbrush) zu seinem zentralen Werkzeug erkoren. Er gehört der Avantgarde der 1960er-Jahre an und ist ein wesentlicher Erneuerer der Phantastischen Kunst, hat aber nicht nur aus Sicht der Cyberculture der 1990er-Jahre bereits den legitimen Status eines Klassikers. Er schuf seinen eigenen, den „biomechanischen" Stil, eine auch im Lichte von Cyborgs und Biotechnologie erstaunliche Vision.

Die Szene sagt auch viel über die Rezeption HR Gigers aus, der als Außenseiter des Systems Kunst agierte und dessen Werk seit seinem Welterfolg mit *Alien* ein Eigenleben in der Populärkultur führt. Seine Wiederentdeckung in der bildenden Kunst ist ein jüngeres Phänomen, das auch mit einer musealen Aufarbeitung von Populärkultur vor dem Hintergrund eines sich wandelnden Kunstbegriffes einerseits und dem Entstehen einer breiten Cyberculture andererseits zu tun hat.

The truth be told: the history of biomechanics begins in highly "analog" fashion; in fact, it's nothing short of artisanal. HR Giger's artistic career path was preceded by training as a designer, and engendering spaces, even entire worlds, would remain one of his passions. His art draws upon his childhood fears and obsessions, something characteristic of fantastic art as a whole. These coalesced in the early 1960s with humankind's collective fears of global atomic warfare and of being victimized by technological progress. In series such as *Atomkinder* (Atomic Children, 1967-68) and *Schachtbilder* (Shafts, 1966), HR Giger configured an aesthetic of horror. The *Schachtbilder* also contain the first of many allusions he made over the years to iconic images from art history—in this case, to the prison prints (Carceri) created by Giovanni Battista Piranesi in the mid-18th century.

The mother of all traumas is that of birth itself, the event that triggers the cycle of birth, eros and death on which HR Giger has incessantly focused. In his *Gebärmaschine* (Birth Machine, 1967), a womb depicted as the chamber of a pistol, the babies awaiting their birth are arrayed like cartridges and, as befitting HR Giger's apocalyptic visions of a perverted world, are equipped with weaponry and protective goggles. The assorted figures that inhabit HR Giger's biomechanics anticipate cyborgs, human-machine hybrids that have gone on to widespread popularity. In HR Giger's takes, these creatures exhibit predominantly female traits. Despite dystopian scenarios, it's not fear they display but rather the apathy of a collective haze—similar to the structures of the Borg civilization in the *Star Trek* cosmos.

Just as the haunting image of "Birth Machine babies" became part of a collective stock of symbols of the 1960s and '70s, the creature in *Alien* created by HR Giger was a milestone in the science fiction genre and horror filmmaking, the absolute epitome of the fears of intruders from beyond, the ultimate dread. The work entitled *Necronom IV*

Dabei beginnt die Geschichte der Biomechanik höchst „analog", ja, handwerklich. HR Gigers künstlerischer Laufbahn geht eine Ausbildung als Designer voraus, das Entwerfen von Räumen, ja, ganzen Welten wird eine seiner Leidenschaften bleiben. Seine Kunst schöpft – charakteristisch für Phantastische Kunst – aus den Ängsten und Obsessionen seiner Kindheit. Diese verbinden sich in den frühen 1960er-Jahren mit kollektiven Ängsten vor einem globalen Atomkrieg und der Übervorteilung des Menschen durch den technischen Fortschritt. In Serien wie *Atomkinder* (1967/68) und *Schachtbilder* (1966) prägt sich bei HR Giger eine Ästhetik des Grauens aus. In den *Schachtbildern* werden auch erste der über die Jahre zahlreichen Bezüge zur Kunstgeschichte deutlich, hier zu den Kerkerbildern (Carceri) des Giovanni Battista Piranesi aus der Mitte des 18. Jahrhunderts.

Am Anfang aller Traumata steht das Geburtstrauma, Teil eines HR Giger unablässig beschäftigenden Kreislaufes von Geburt, Eros und Tod. Die in der als Pistole ausgestalteten *Gebärmaschine* (1967) ihre Geburt erwartenden Babys sind – entsprechend HR Gigers apokalyptischen Visionen einer zerstörten Welt, die auf sie wartet – mit Schutzbrillen gerüstet und bewaffnet. Der Figurenreigen in HR Gigers Biomechanik nimmt den später populären Typus des „Cyborg" als Mischwesen aus Mensch und Maschine vorweg. Bei HR Giger tragen die Wesen zumeist weibliche Züge, sie zeigen trotz dystopischem Szenario keine Angst, sondern die Teilnahmslosigkeit eines kollektiven Dämmerzustandes – ähnlich den Strukturen der Borg-Zivilisation aus dem *Star Trek*-Kosmos.

So wie das Sujet der *Birth Machine Babys* Teil eines kollektiven Symbolvorrates der 1960er- und 1970er-Jahre wurde, so markierte die von HR Giger geschaffene Kreatur des Alien einen Meilenstein im Genre des Science-Fiction- und des Horrorfilms – die Verkörperung aller Ängste vor dem von Außen eindringenden, ultimativen Grauen. Das Bild *Necronom IV* (1976) veranlasste den Regisseur Ridley Scott dazu, HR Giger mit der Schaffung der Gestalt des Aliens zu betrauen. HR Giger brachte dies 1980 einen Oscar und

Li II, 1973/74, Acryl und Tusche auf Papier, auf Holz, 200 x 140 cm

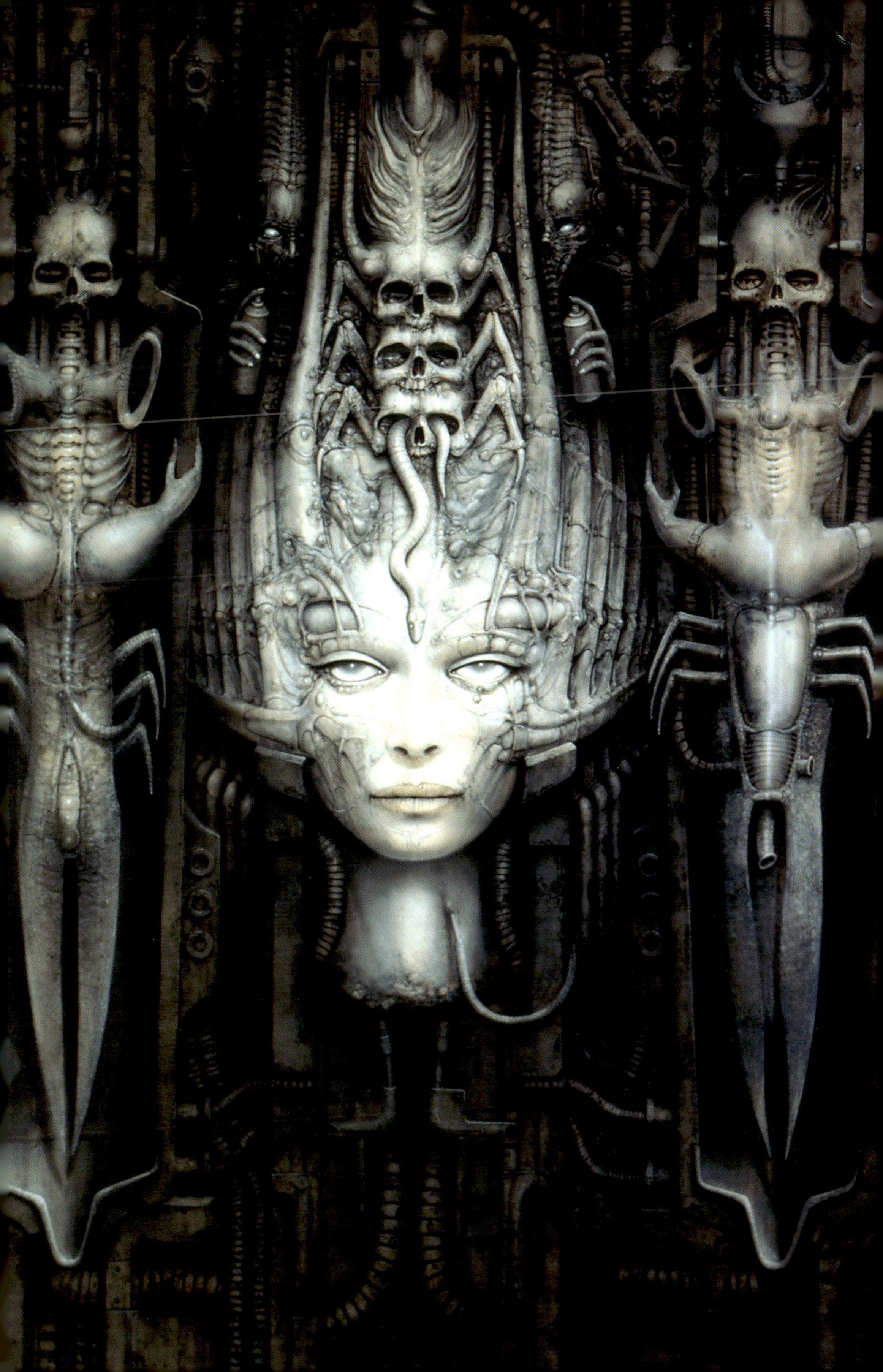

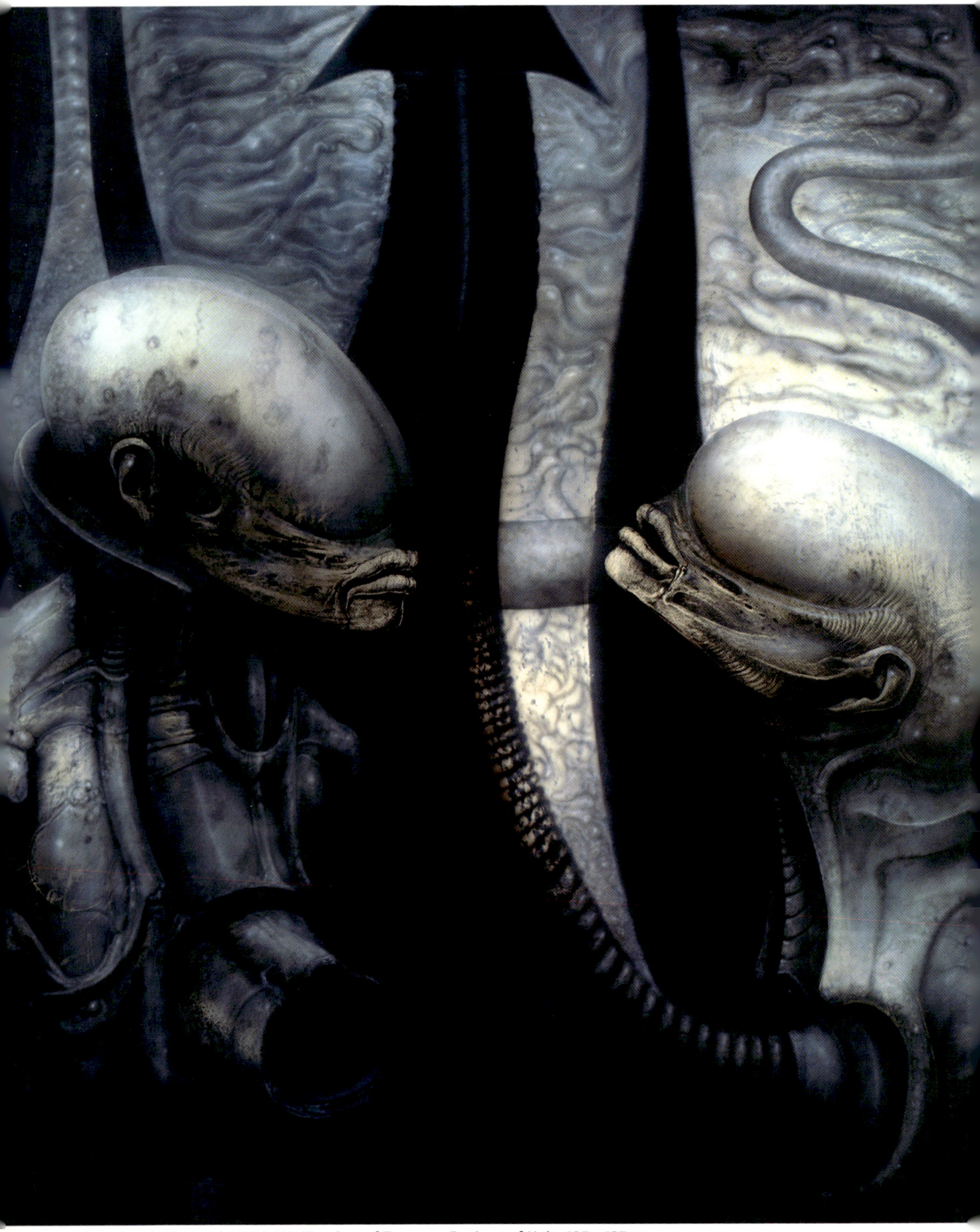

Mutanten, 2. Zustand, 1967/1975, Tusche auf Transcop-Papier, auf Holz, 105 x 127 cm

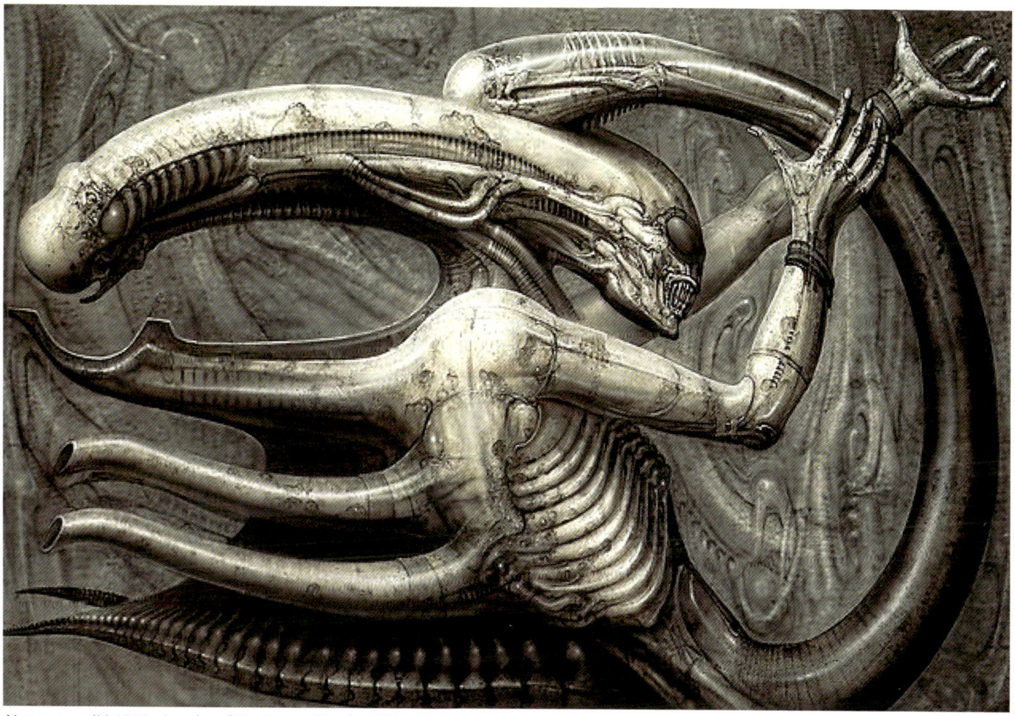

Necronom IV, 1976, Acryl auf Papier auf Holz, 100 x 150 cm

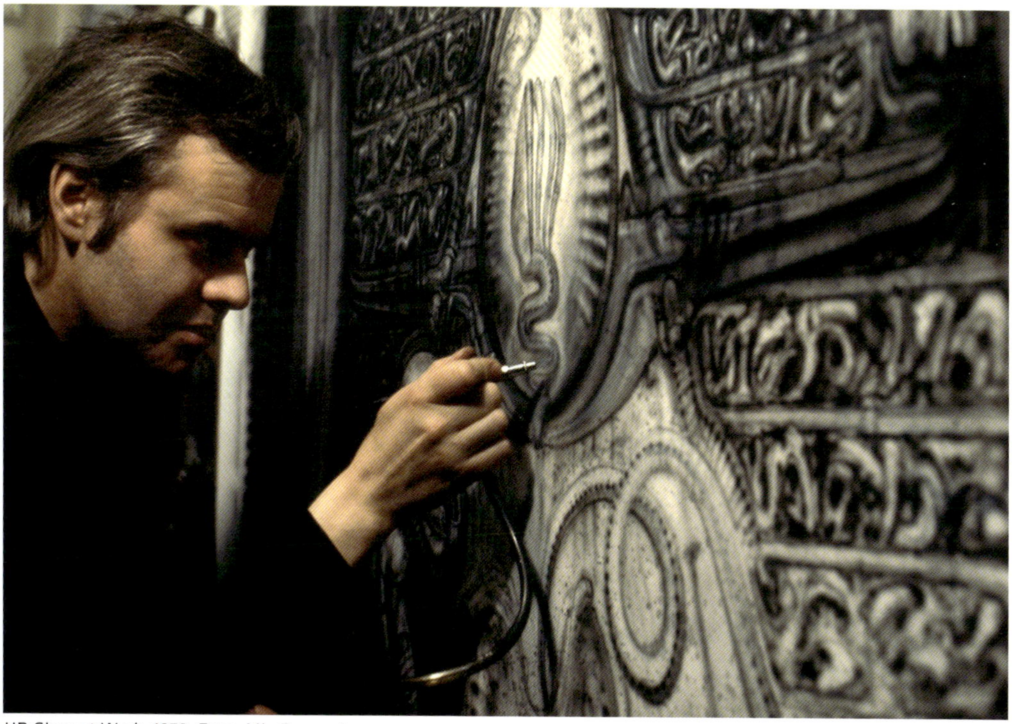

HR Giger at Work, 1978; Foto: Mia Bonzanigo

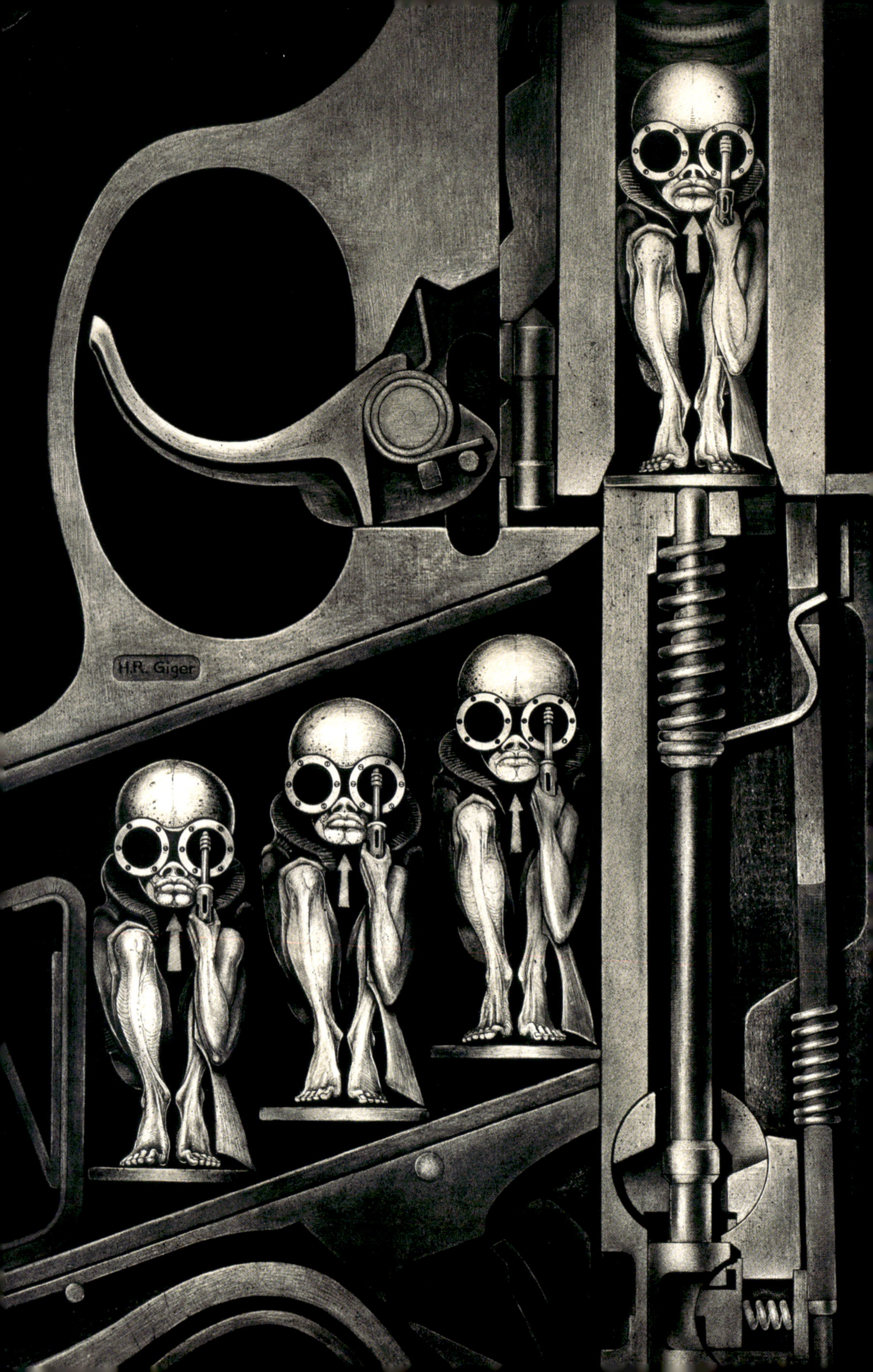
H.R. Giger

(1976) convinced director Ridley Scott to commission HR Giger to design the alien creature, which earned HR Giger an Oscar in 1980 and garnered worldwide fame for his aesthetic. Whereas the models and mockups for *Alien* were real analog objects handcrafted of wood and polyester, *Prometheus* (2012), the film Ridley Scott made more than 30 years later, took HR Giger's alien world to a whole new level. Not only had the special effects long since gone digital, the creation theme of the Prometheus myth and the flashy burst of the double helix also endowed HR Giger's visual vocabulary with new levels of meaning—a belated, monumental homage to HR Giger's artistry enunciated in the stylistic language of the cinema.

HR Giger and Ars Electronica are not only connected by a cultural "kinship"; they also share a key point on the timeline. Just as HR Giger's oeuvre is divided into periods before and after *Alien*, the history of media art and cyberculture is also marked by a watershed: the time prior to the founding of Ars Electronica, and what came next. These key events occurred in the same year: 1979.

So, the 2013 Ars Electronica Festival provides in numerous respects just the right situation for HR Giger, fantastic painter, visionary father of early cyborgs, architect of spaces populated by embodiments of our collective terror, and creator of worlds that bespeak our internal abysses in *TOTAL RECALL*—the Ars Electronica Center's Deep Space and the dark underground level at the LENTOS Museum of Art.

1 William Gibson, *Virtual Light*, Toronto, 1993, p. 241

weltweite Verbreitung seiner Ästhetik ein. Waren die Vorlagen und die Modelle bei *Alien* noch echte, analoge Handarbeit aus Holz und Polyester, so brachte Ridley Scott mehr als 30 Jahre später mit seinem Film *Prometheus – Dunkle Zeichen* (2012) die Alien-Welt des HR Giger auf eine neue Ebene: Nicht nur die Special Effects waren längst digital geworden, auch die Bildsprache HR Gigers erhielt über das Schöpfungsthema des Prometheus-Mythos und das aufblitzende Bild der Doppelhelix neu aufgespannte Bedeutungsebenen: eine späte, monumentale Hommage an HR Gigers Kunst mit den Stilmitteln des Kinos.

HR Giger und Ars Electronica verbindet nicht nur eine kulturelle „Verwandtschaft", sie teilen sich auch ein magisches Datum: So wie im Werk von HR Giger die Zeit vor und nach *Alien* unterschieden wird, so darf in der Geschichte der Medienkunst und der Cyberculture in eine Zeit vor und nach der Gründung der Ars Electronica eingeteilt werden. Das Jahr ist in beiden Fällen dasselbe – 1979.

So ist der phantastische Maler HR Giger, der visionäre Vater früher Cyborgs, der Architekt von Räumen, bevölkert von Kreaturen unseres kollektiven Grauens und der Schöpfer von Welten unserer inneren Abgründe im *TOTAL RECALL* der Ars Electronica des Jahres 2013 in mehrfacher Weise am richtigen Ort angekommen: im Deep Space des Ars Electronica Center und im dunklen Tiefgeschoß des LENTOS Kunstmuseums.

Text: Andreas J. Hirsch

1 William Gibson, *Virtual Light*, Toronto, 1993, S. 241

Gebärmaschine, 1967, Tusche auf Transcop-Papier, 170 x 110 cm

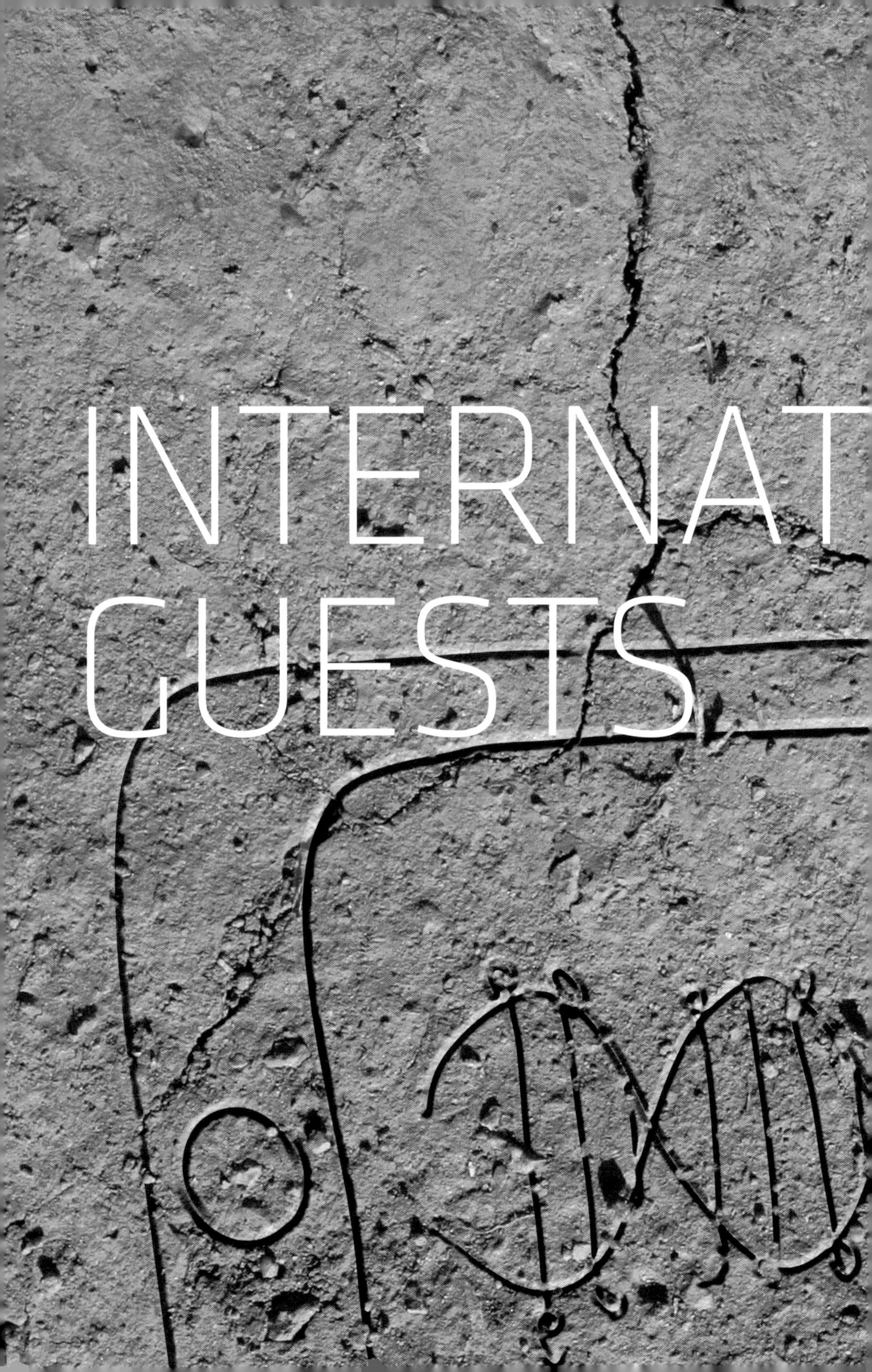
INTERNAT
GUESTS

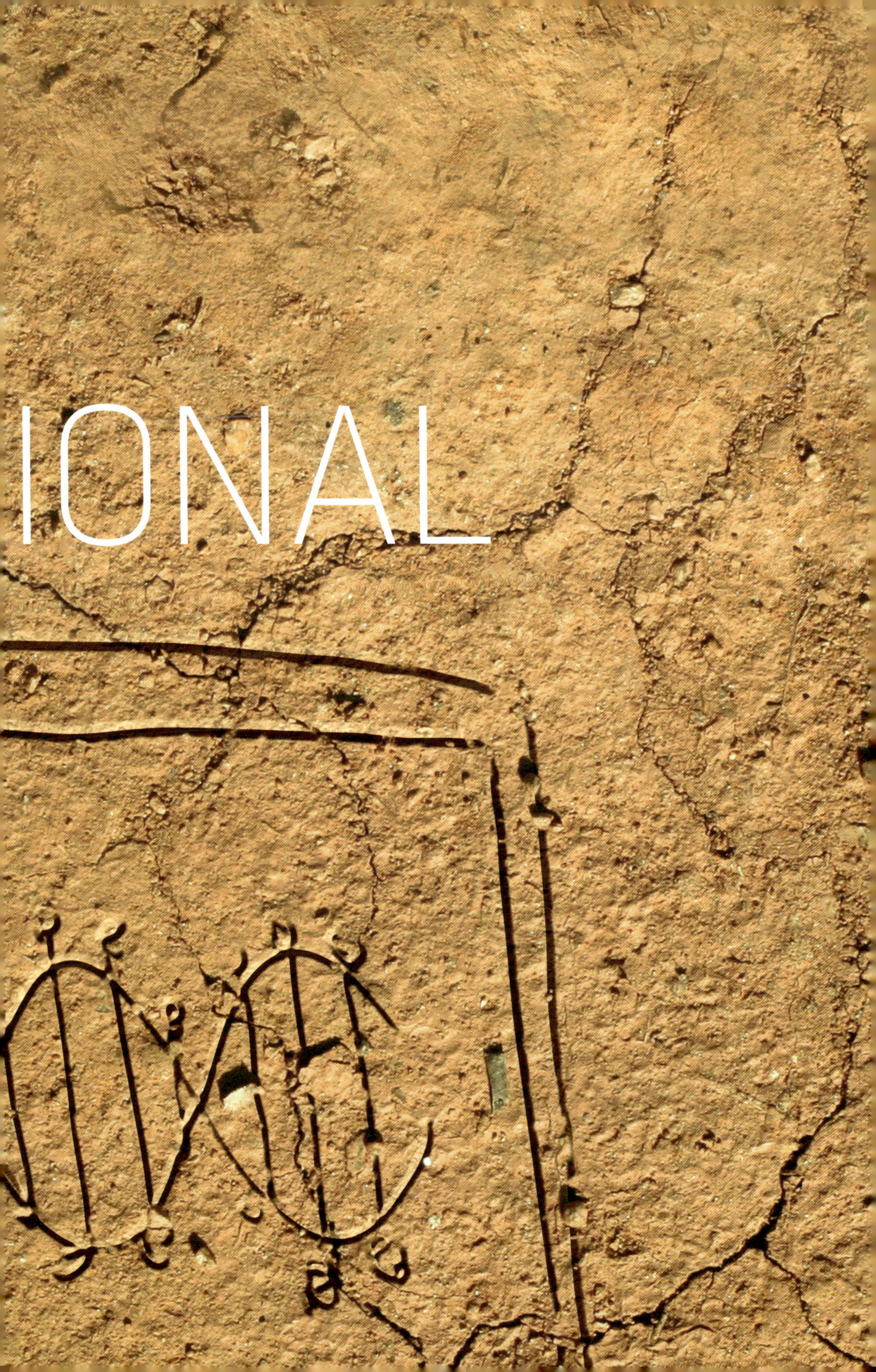
IONAL

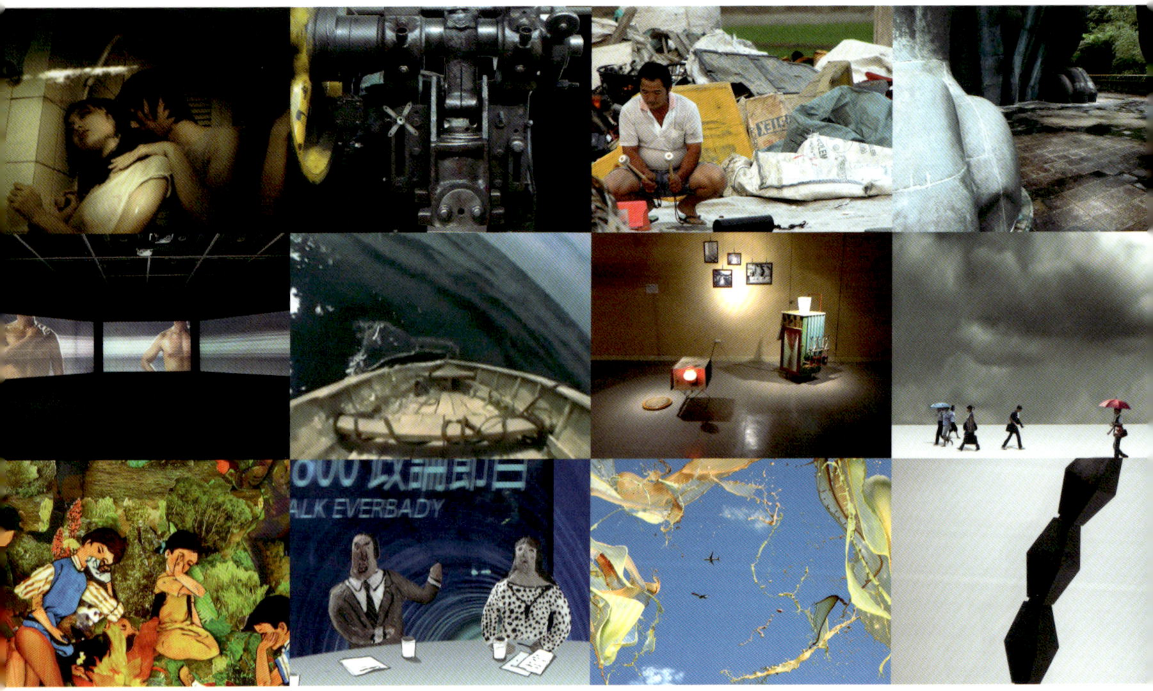

Schizophrenia Taiwan 2.0

Taiwan can be viewed as a microcosm of a world history that has led to today's globalized reality. Following successive colonization by the Portuguese, the Dutch, the Japanese, and the Chinese, this island nation has thrived on cultural exchange. In Taiwan, opposites coexist: the most advanced technology and traditional culture, the ubiquitous Chinese and 17 Austronesian tribes, democracy and corruption, a relatively small country (1/15 of the size of France) and an economic powerhouse for global high-tech industry.

Im Mikrokosmos von Taiwan spiegeln sich die historischen Entwicklungen, die zu der globalisierten Welt von heute führten. Nachdem diese schöne Insel lange unter der Kolonialherrschaft gleich mehrerer Nationen stand – Portugal, die Niederlande, Japan und China – gelingt es ihr heute, vom kulturellen Austausch zu profitieren. Taiwan steckt voller Gegensätze: Spitzentechnologie und traditionelle Kulturen, die Omnipräsenz der Chinesen und die Minderheit der siebzehn austronesischen Stämme, Demokratie und Korruption. Trotz begrenzter Fläche (1/15 von Frankreich) ist das Land ein Konjunkturmotor für die globale Hightechindustrie.

Taiwan is both a part of the world and apart from it. Like a satellite, Taiwan observes, orbits, and transmits messages to the rest of the world. The conflict between Taiwan's strong sense of national identity and its ambivalent national status in relation to China charges daily life with a tension best described as "Taiwan's schizophrenia". Schizophrenia is present even in the name "Taiwan": Tai 台 (platform) and wan 灣 (coastal). Taiwan is at once the center (the platform, the node) and the periphery (the coast, the entrance), the flow (technology) and inheritance (tradition), the east and the west, the inside and outside (of China).

Tackling these dynamic contradictions and dualities, *Schizophrenia Taiwan 2.0* also sketches the concept of the *Taiwan machine*, based on Heiner Müller's postmodernist drama, *Hamlet Machine* (1997) in which technology revolutionizes the world by breaking down the traditional narrative structure and placing media at the center of the economy. For Müller, machinery is omnipresent—a universal and permanent revolution. *Schizophrenia Taiwan 2.0* focuses on this digital revolution in the work of young Taiwanese new media artists, born between the eras of color television and smart phones in a country that manufactures 80% of the world's electronic goods. These artists are fully aware of the risks and of the potential of globalization and cybernetics and their works reflect the challenges facing Taiwan and the world as a whole.

http://www.schizotaiwan.net

SCHIZOPHRENIA TAIWAN 2.0

Curated by I-Wei Li, Pierre Bongiovanni, Ching-Wen Chang, Chien-Hung Huang

Produced by Ministry of Culture of the Republic of China 中華民國文化部, The Association of the Visual Arts in Taiwan (AVAT), SideBySide Studio e.V., La Maison Laurentine

Taiwan – Teil der Welt und gleichzeitig isoliert – beobachtet und umkreist den Globus wie ein Satellit und sendet Botschaften an den Rest der Welt aus. Der Konflikt zwischen dem stark ausgeprägten nationalen Identitätsgefühl und dem ungeklärten rechtlichen Status im Verhältnis zu China ist allgegenwärtig und prägt den Alltag. Diese Gespaltenheit lässt sich am besten als „Taiwans Schizophrenie" beschreiben. Die Schizophrenie Taiwans kommt schon im Namen zum Ausdruck: *tai* 台 (Terrasse, Plattform) und *wan* 灣 (Bucht). Taiwan ist zugleich Zentrum (Terrasse, Plattform, Knotenpunkt) und Peripherie (Bucht, Zugang), verkörpert Fortschritt (Technologie) und Erbe (Tradition), repräsentiert Osten und Westen, Innen und Außen (von China).

Schizophrenia Taiwan 2.0 thematisiert diese dynamischen Widersprüche und Dualitäten und entwirft in Anlehnung an Heiner Müllers postmodernes Theaterstück „Die Hamletmaschine" (1997) eine *Taiwanmaschine.* Müller thematisiert in seinem Werk u. a., wie Technologie die Welt revolutioniert, indem sie traditionelle narrative Strukturen aufbricht und die Medien zum zentralen Faktor der Wirtschaft macht. Maschinen sind für Müller allgegenwärtig und Ursache für eine permanente und alles erfassende Revolution. Einer solchen Revolution – der digitalen – nähern wir uns hier über die Ansätze und Arbeiten junger taiwanesischer Medienkünstler. Geboren zwischen der Ära des Farbfernsehens und des Smartphones und aus einem Land kommend, in dem 80 Prozent der elektronischen Geräte der Welt hergestellt werden, sind sie sich des Risikos und des Potenzials der Globalisierung und der Kybernetik voll und ganz bewusst. Ihre Arbeiten spiegeln die Herausforderungen wider, vor denen Taiwan und die ganze Welt heute stehen.

Aus dem Englischen von Martina Bauer

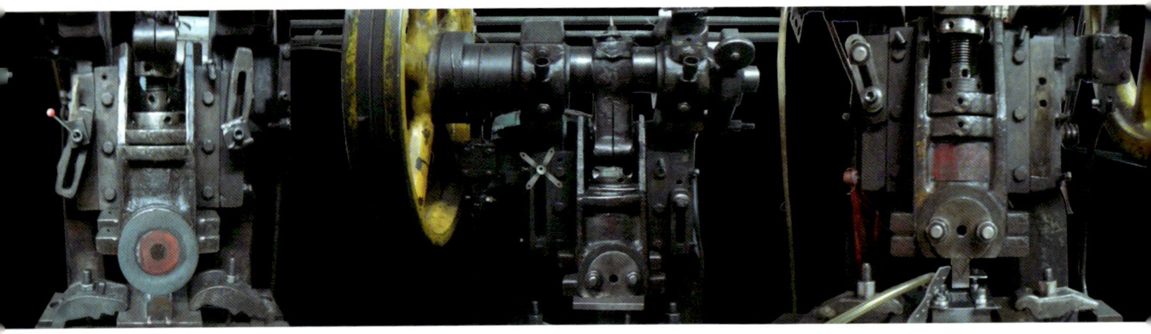

I-Chun CHEN 陳依純

Goodbye, Little Factory

Three-channel video installation, 10', 2012

Small OEM factories, with their assembly lines often based in the living rooms of Taiwanese families, are being replaced as the economy moves toward establishing global brands. But the shift from political colonization to capitalist colonization is intricately connected with the history of Taiwan and OEMs reflect not only Taiwan's economic status, but also Taiwanese society as a whole. Chen utilizes the sounds produced by the sluggish movement of these delicately rotating machineries, like the fusion of a gentle lullaby and a requiem.

Goang-Ming YUAN 袁廣鳴

Floating

Single-channel video installation

Goang-Ming Yuan's specialty is to combine technological mediums through metaphoric maneuver to investigate the human mind and consciousness. *Floating* portrays an observer adrift in a boat, moving through intrinsic and extrinsic spaces. Jumping overboard is not an option; there is no means of escape.

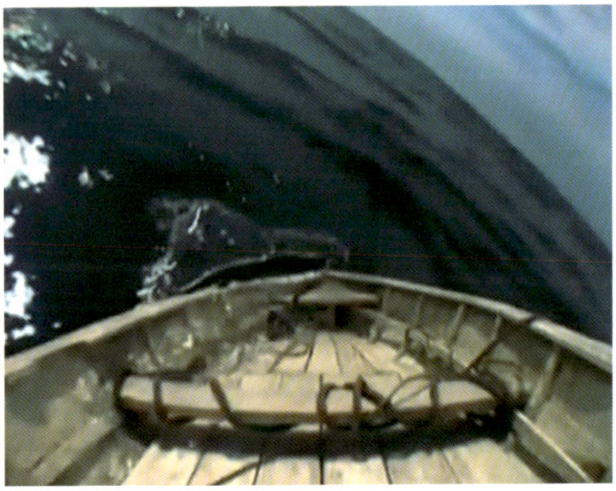

Yen-Ying HUANG 黃彥穎

Go to Africa

Single-channel video installation

Distancing himself from the glut of messages about the international art world and social issues in Taiwan, Yen-Ying Huang focuses on the theme of transformation in his work, such as the shift in identity sparked by shattered relationships that heighten sensitivity to wider networks of exchange.

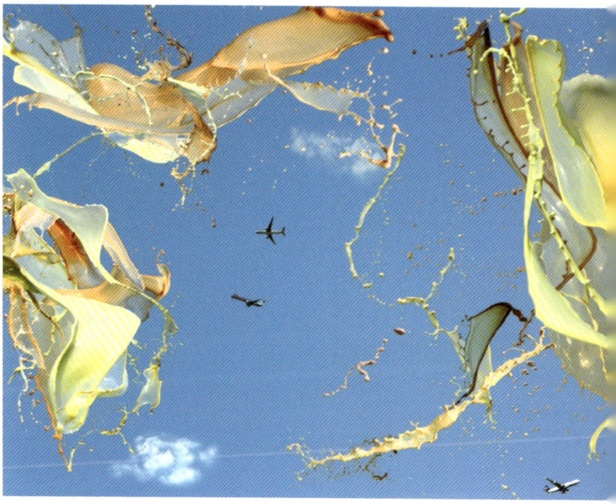

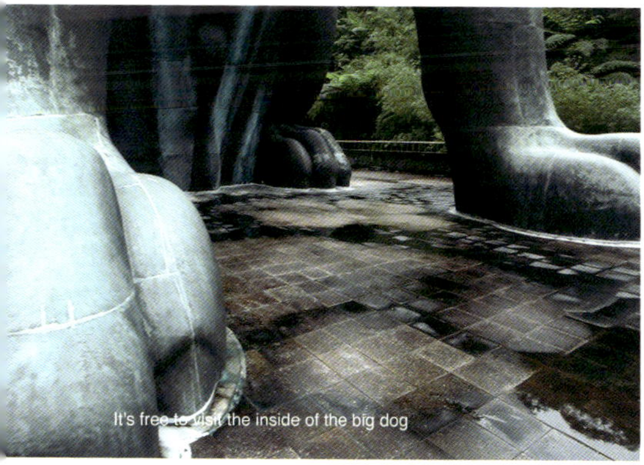

Chi-Yu WU 吳其育

The Nuclear Power Plant and the Dog

Single-channel video installation, 2011

Every nuclear power plant in Taiwan is fused with a temple of the 18th King, a dog-like Godzilla of a god. Chi-Yu Wu approaches this strange phenomenon through field investigations. The "straying gaze" of the recorder reflects the ambivalent response of the lethargic government and the anxious public in relation to Taiwan's nuclear energy policy.

Yu-Chin TSENG 曾御欽

Shivering Wall

Four-channel video installation, 2012

In his work, Yu-Chin Tseng echoes the traces that life leaves, transposing such marks onto the connections between his personal life experience and his concern for communities he belongs to. Tseng's inventiveness lies in an ambience of innocence combined with violence, while narration is carried by tagged images.

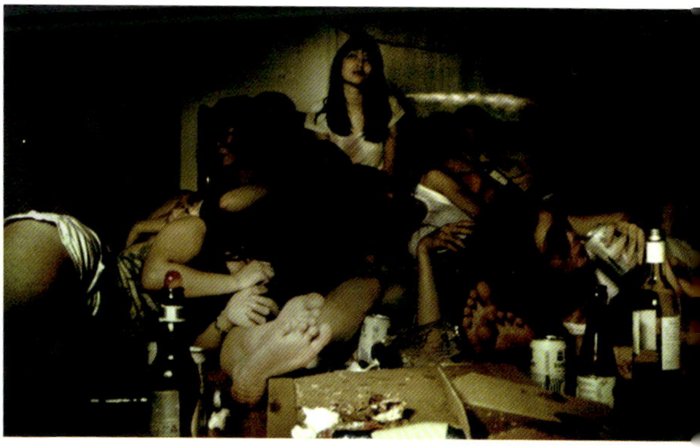

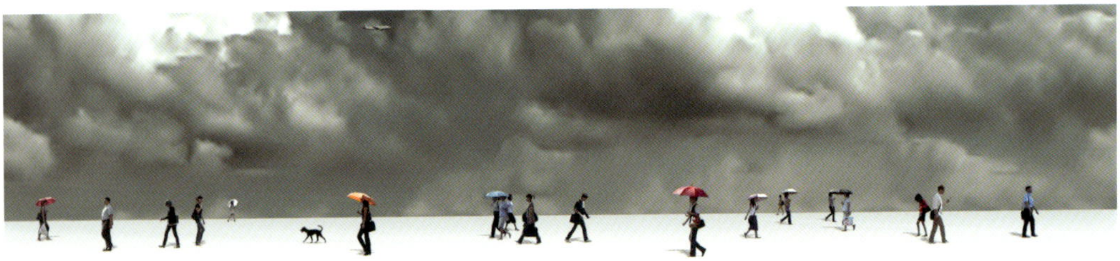

Wan-Jen CHEN 陳萬仁

The Unconscious Voyage

Three-channel video installation, 3', 2008

In the *Unconscious Voyage* there is no axis of time and space. Various pedestrians walk around endlessly, coming and going, not unlike ghosts. No one stops—there is no time to do so. Anxiety is sensed in the seemingly ordered paces. The only option is to keep on going.

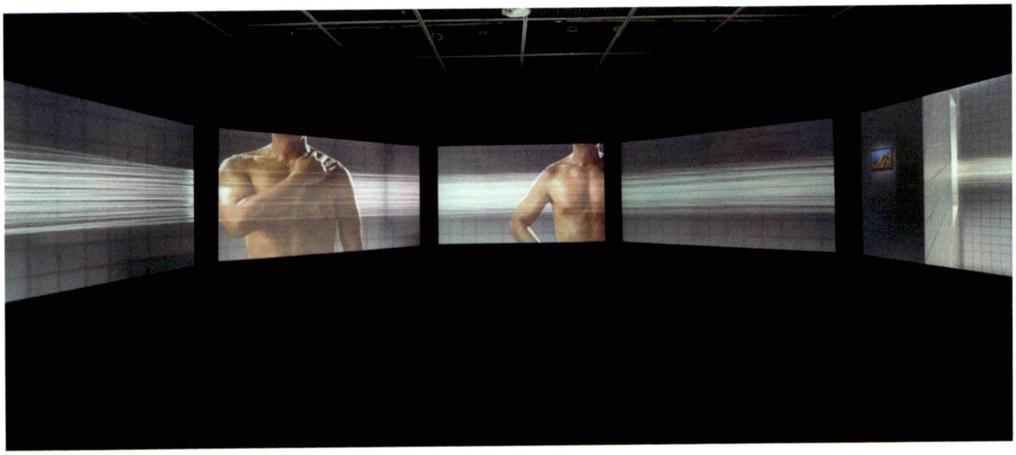

Jun-Jieh WANG 王俊傑

Project David III: David's Paradise

Single-channel video installation, 19'17", 2008

Designed as the outcome of negotiations between creation and social ethics, Wang's work is an attempt to discover the personal, intimate element in such exchanges, which reveals a poetically expressed vitality that has infiltrated cold technology.

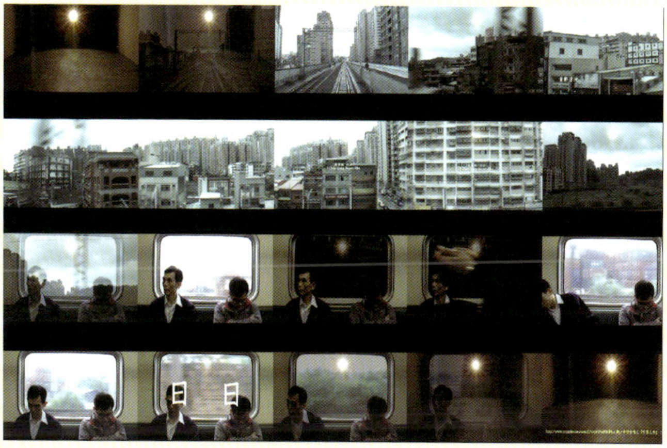

Liang-Hsuan CHEN 陳亮璇

Daily

Two-channel video installation

Turning the commonplace into eventual Images has become the compulsive disorder of news media in Taiwan. Chen focuses on the real existence of individuals outside the media. Instead of escaping to—or sheltering in—a utopia, Chen's characters act out or mimic the events taking place in a specific timeframe through ambiguous, heterogeneous images.

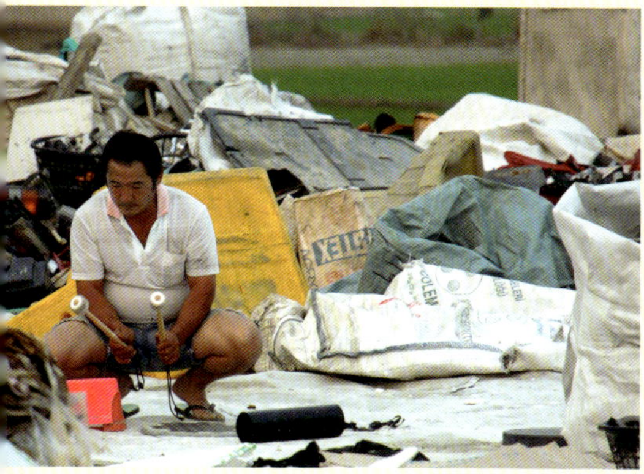

Yu-Hsien SU 蘇育賢

Plastic Man

Single-channel video installation, 09'01'', 2011

Plastic Man is the film of an authentic rock 'n' roll concert that goes far beyond conventional environmental or social documentary, questioning the paradigms and the nature of creation. The performers are Uncle Mao and his helpers, who belong to the lowest social class in Taiwan and make their living by recycling waste in the deprived areas. Uncle Mao may be humble, but he's certainly honest.

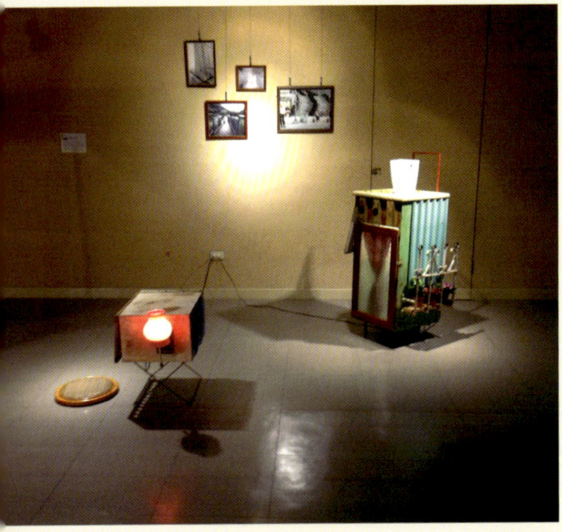

Yen-Chu LIN 林晏竹

Rambling Cases

Single-channel video installation

Rambling seems to be the state of Yen-Chu Lin's existence. Spaceships, aliens and fabricated suitcases become sophisticated symbols of nostalgia. Having landed on this planet, they are received as the real characters in Lin's cosmos. And isn't it also a compulsive disorder that, having being colonized for such a long time, we have an unquenchable wish to dwell in outer space?

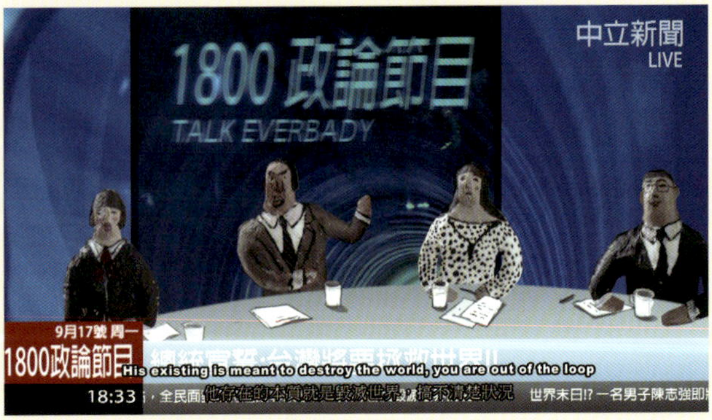

Li-Ren CHANG 張立人

"Battle City" Trailer

Single-channel video installation, 2012

Instead of resisting images of consumerism by repressing or satisfying desires, Li-Ren Chang makes use of commonplace materials and techniques to duplicate professional marketing images. While paranoid and compulsive, the process of duplication also takes new pleasure in transforming recycling into an alternative form of compulsory consumption.

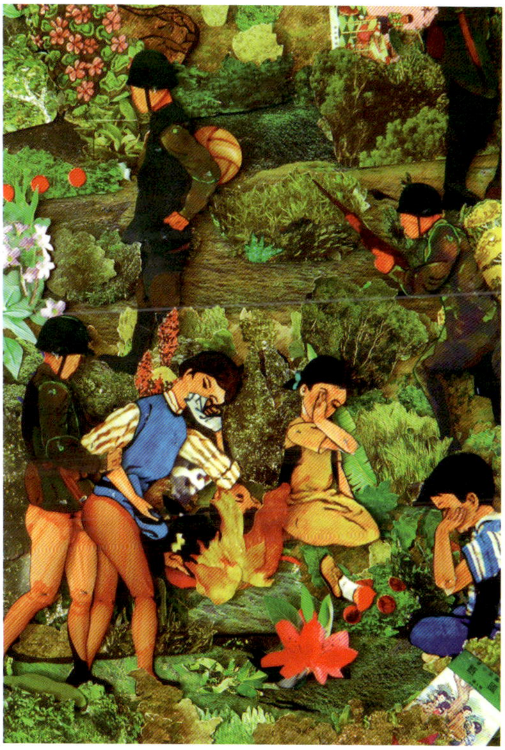

Pei-Shih TU 杜珮詩

The Adventures in Mountain Yu No.5—From Michel Foucault to Our Glorious Future

Single-channel video installation, 2011

Every colonizing regime has tried to reshape Taiwan and to create the "ideal" population by imposing their own ideologies on people's bodies and minds. Tu's critique of Taiwan's "lost history" during the national identity fabrication of national and political propaganda is visible through his flatly colorful images of Taiwan.

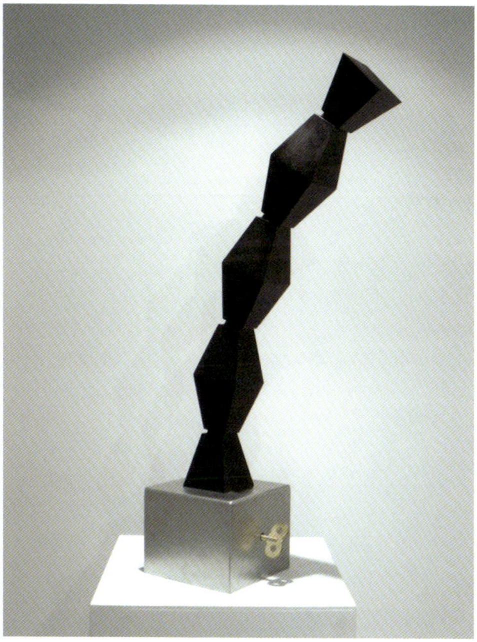

Chao-Tsai CHIU 邱昭財

The Counterattack of Fatigue

When powerful political figures or architectural masterpieces bow down, they renounce their sense of greatness. How Taiwan can stand up on the world stage if it is not recognized as an independent nation would be seen as its population's biggest concern. Chiu employs black humor to reveal how Taiwanese society is exhausted by this all-consuming fear in various scenarios.

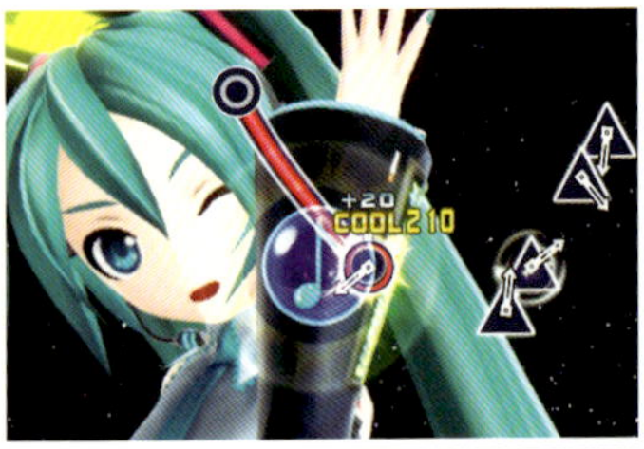

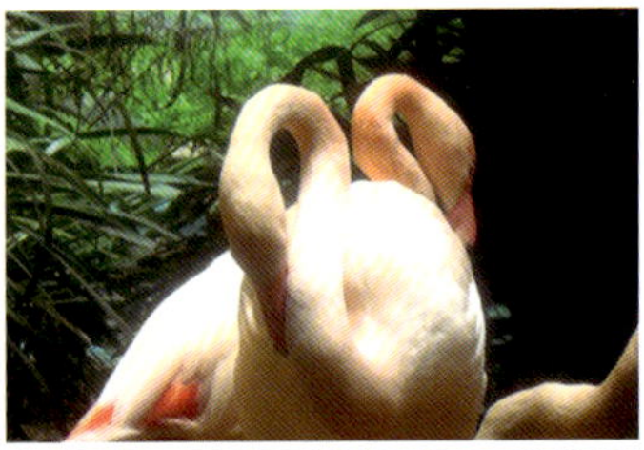

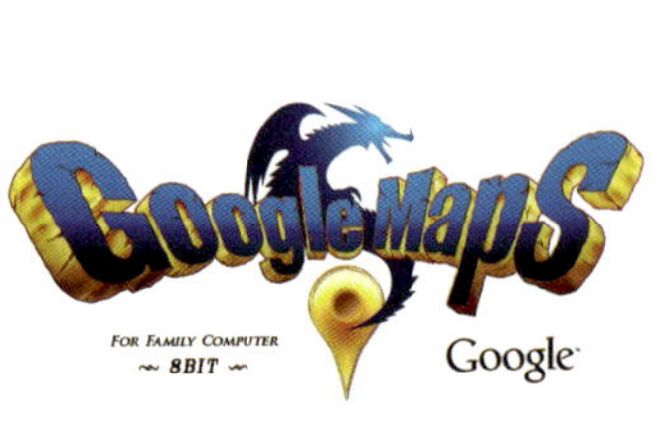

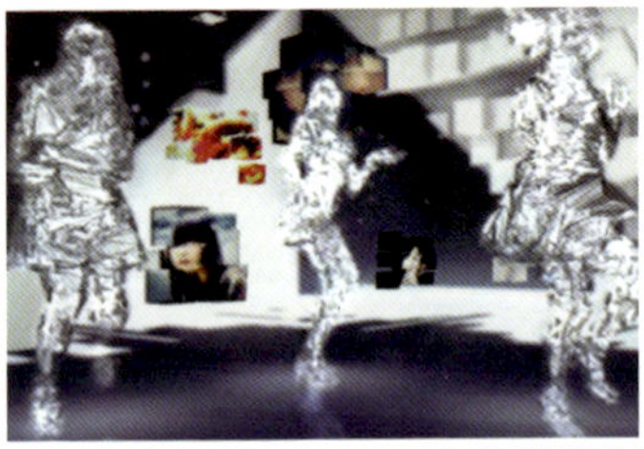

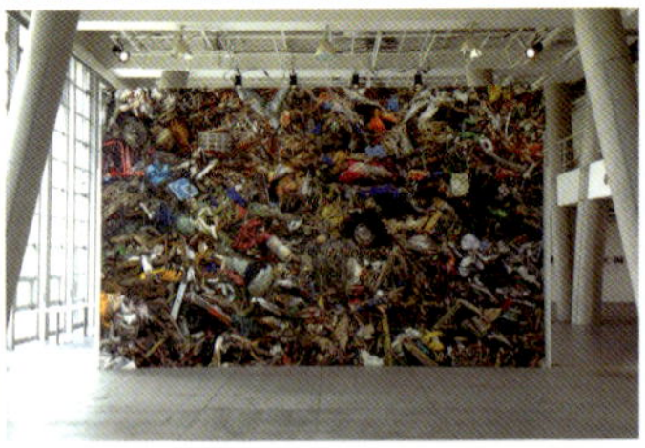

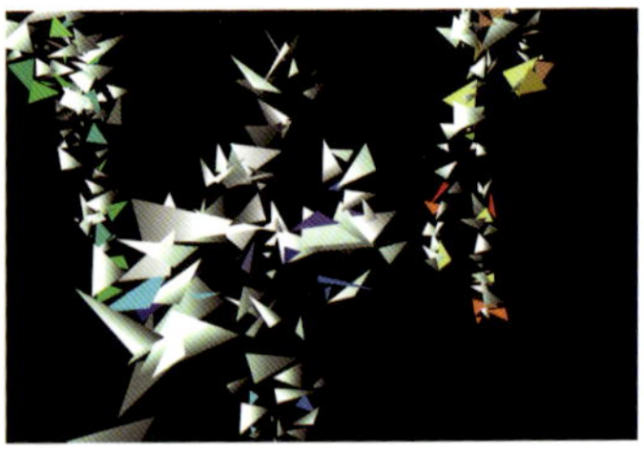

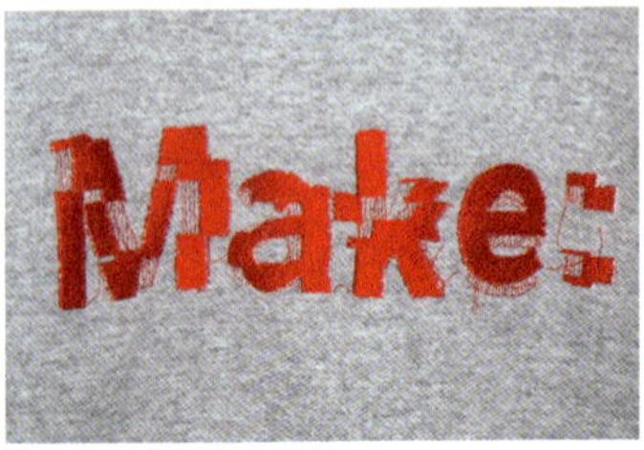

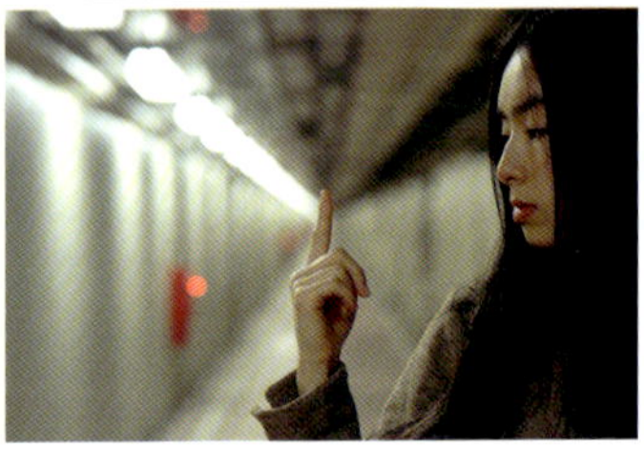

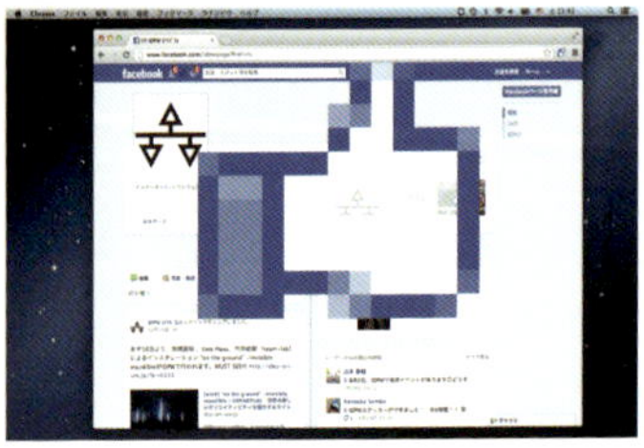

Japan Media Arts Festival

A New Platform for New Memories

The Japan Media Arts Festival honors outstanding works from a wide range of media, from animation and comics to media art and games. There are four categories of awards: Art, Entertainment, Animation and Manga.

Das Japan Media Arts Festival zeichnet herausragende künstlerische Leistungen in einem breiten Spektrum an Genres aus, von Animation und Comics bis zu Medienkunst und Spielen. Die Preise werden in vier Kategorien vergeben: Kunst, Unterhaltung, Animation und Manga.

Since the first festival was held in 1997, it has also functioned as a platform that celebrates the winners of awards and outstanding creative works of art. The 16th Festival received a record number of 3,503 entries from 72 countries and regions around the world, an indication of its already firmly established status as an international annual festival and of how it continues to grow.
A selection of award-winning works from the 16th Japan Media Arts Festival reveals how both the unique and the universal aspects of the themes "memory" and "evolution of memory" are addressed in Japanese media arts.
Japanese dolls are part of Japan's culture and tradition, and they are accorded an expressive talent that surpasses that of humans, as seen in the rich and varied creations of the *vocaloid* singing voice synthesizers, such as the virtual diva Hatsune Miku, and other data sources, such as the motion capture choreography of the techno-pop group *Perfume.* Technically accomplished platforms attract, store, and facilitate the sharing of a vast amount of works from around the globe, giving us a very modern form of memory. The Great East Japan Earthquake of March 11th, 2011 was an unprecedented catastrophe for Japan. Exceptional works created in the wake of this disaster present memory in a multi-layered manner.

http://j-mediaarts.jp/

JAPAN MEDIA ARTS FESTIVAL

Planning Director: Nae Morita
Producer/event planner to communicate cutting-edge science via the planetarium and exhibition visuals.
Advisor: Tomoe Moriyama, Curator, Museum of Contemporary Art Tokyo

Seit seiner Gründung im Jahr 1997 fungiert das Festival auch als Plattform, die den preisgekrönten KünstlerInnen und künstlerisch herausragenden Werken Sichtbarkeit verleiht. Mit 3.503 Einreichungen aus 72 Ländern und Regionen dieser Welt erzielte die 16. Auflage des Festivals einen neuen Rekord, was für seine Stellung im internationalen Kulturbetrieb spricht und von seinem steten Wachstum zeugt. Eine Auswahl preisgekrönter Werke des 16. Japan Media Arts Festival zeigt, wie die japanische Medienkunst mit den besonderen und allgemeinen Aspekten des Themas „Erinnerung" und „Evolution der Erinnerung" umgeht. Puppen sind ein fester Bestandteil der Kultur und Tradition Japans, und man spricht ihnen oft die Fähigkeit zu, ausdrucksstärker zu sein als Menschen. Die vielfältigen reizvollen Kreationen auf Basis des Software-Synthesizers *Vocaloid,* wie etwa die virtuelle Sängerin Miku Hatsune, oder die Choreografien auf Basis der Motion-Capture-Daten der Techno-Pop-Gruppe *Perfume* sind beredtes Zeugnis davon. Technisch ausgefeilte Plattformen ziehen eine enorme Vielzahl von Arbeiten von überall her an, speichern sie und ermöglichen deren Weitergabe und schaffen damit eine sehr moderne Form des Erinnerns. Das verheerende Erdbeben in Ostjapan vom 11. März 2011 war eine in diesem Ausmaß nicht gekannte Katastrophe für das Land. Die in der Folge entstandenen außergewöhnlichen Werke repräsentieren eine eigene vielschichtige Form der Erinnerung.

Aus dem Englischen von Michael Kaufmann

SOL CHORD (Shinjiro MAEDA / Rina OKAZAWA)

BETWEEN YESTERDAY & TOMORROW

Art Division Excellence Award
Web-based work

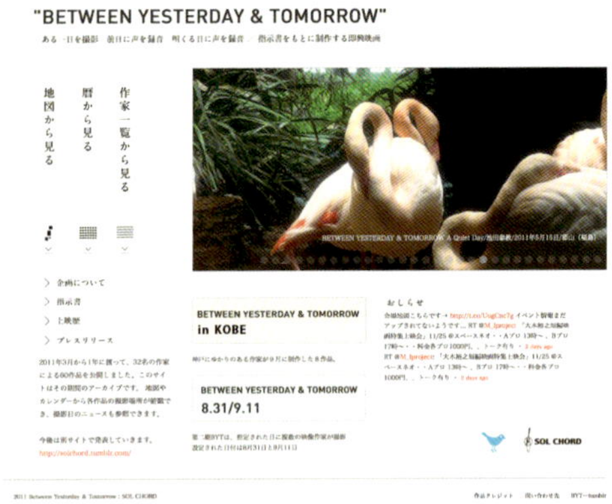

The web-based movie project *BETWEEN YESTERDAY & TOMORROW* was launched two weeks after the Great East Japan Earthquake on March 11, 2011. Based on a set of instructions provided by Shinjiro MAEDA, each filmmaker produced a five-minute film that was released on the Internet as soon as it was completed. In the first year (until March 2012), 32 artists participated in the project, producing a total of 60 works. On the website, information on the filming date and location of each work was collected in an archive, along with a sampling of the news that occurred on that day. An omnibus movie, made up of selections from each of the works, was also produced and screened at various film festivals.
http://solchord.jp/byt/

Instruction Sheet excerpt
BETWEEN YESTERDAY & TOMORROW
Instruction sheet / Shinjiro Maeda
Updated ver.04 (2011.04.08)

- Record your video and audio by the following process
  Day 1: Record audio explaining what you will shoot tomorrow, where and why you are filming it
  Day 2: Start filming
  Day 3: Record audio talking about the day before
- Edit your video shot in Day 2, and add audio from Day 1 to Day 2
- You can use audio from the video but do not add new sounds other than what's been recorded
- The length of a film should be 5 minutes including opening credits (5 seconds) and ending credits (10 seconds)
- The audio recordings of Day 1 and Day 3 should be less than 4'45 in all, including white noise

Filmmaker holds the copyright

Details: http://*solchord.jp/byt/en/instruction-sheet.html*

Yuki SANO

A few

Art Division Jury Selection
Graphic art

This life-size scale work depicts the mountains of rubble produced by the Great East Japan Earthquake in 2011. The artist has attempted to convey the reality of the rubble in both image and substance by layering oil paint atop a photograph. The work's size, an element that cannot be experienced through other media such as video or text, further imparts a sense of reality. (Size: 450 cm H x 720 cm W)

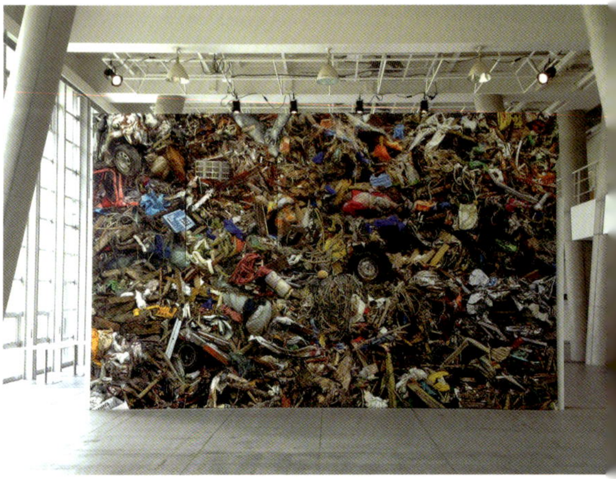

SANO Yuki

Daito MANABE / MIKIKO / Yasutaka NAKATA / Satoshi HORII / Hiroyasu KIMURA

Perfume “Global Site Project”

Entertainment Division Grand Prize

Website, Source code, Performance, Choreography, Music

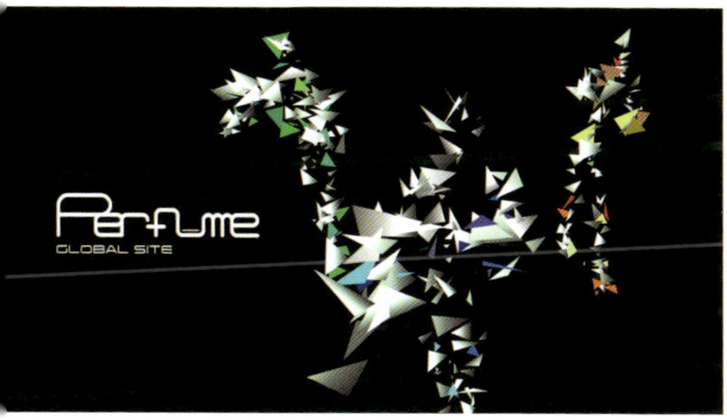

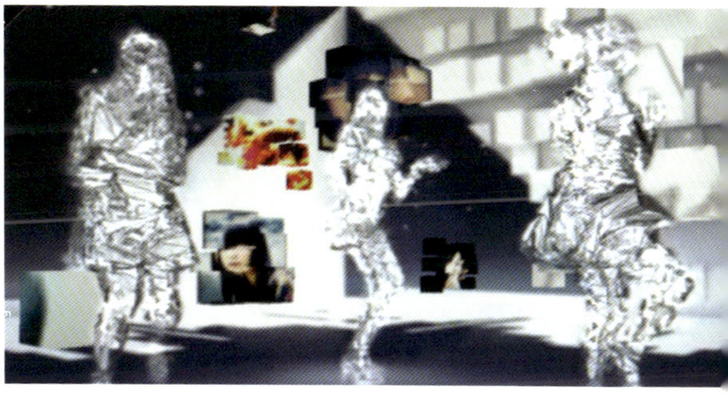

System Software: C++, Java, AS3, Max
http://www.perfume-global.com/perfume-dev.github.com
© Rhizomatiks co.,ltd. + AMUSE Inc. + UNIVERSAL MUSIC LLC

This project commemorates the global debut of the techno-pop group Perfume. Based on the concept of fans and creators together launching the group into the world, this massive project involved the planning and production of a teaser site, an open-source project, and live performances by the members of Perfume. Following the site launch, the open-source project provided free distribution of original music and choreographic motion capture data from the official website. Secondary creation by programmers was enabled by providing sample codes and extended features for the use of data via the social coding service GitHub. This gave birth to over 500 richly varied projects in countries around the world. On Perfume's global tour, works developed through this project were introduced and they performed compositions and choreography distributed through the site.

Team Project DIVA

Hatsune Miku -Project DIVA- f

Entertainment Division Jury Selection

Game

This is the latest rhythm game in the *Project DIVA* series, which features the virtual diva Hatsune Miku and has shipped over 1 million copies since 2011. Based on the concept of “playing like you're singing,” the exhilarating game comes with over 30 songs and over 80 costumes made by creators on the Internet, as well as Augmented Reality (AR) mode and other new features that make full use of the PlayStation®Vita platform.

(Game platform: PlayStation®Vita)

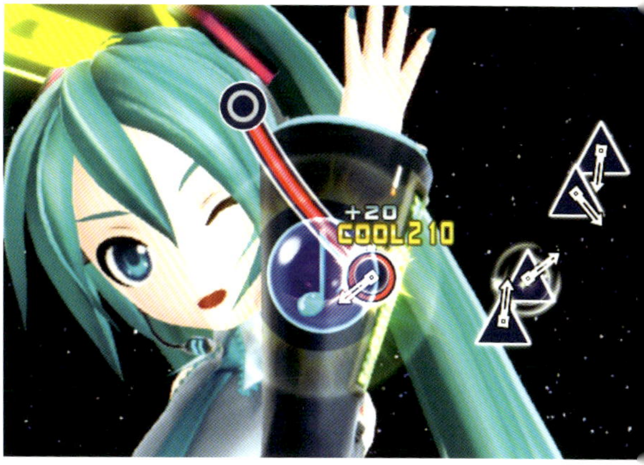

© SEGA / © Crypton Future Media, Inc.
http://www.crypton.net

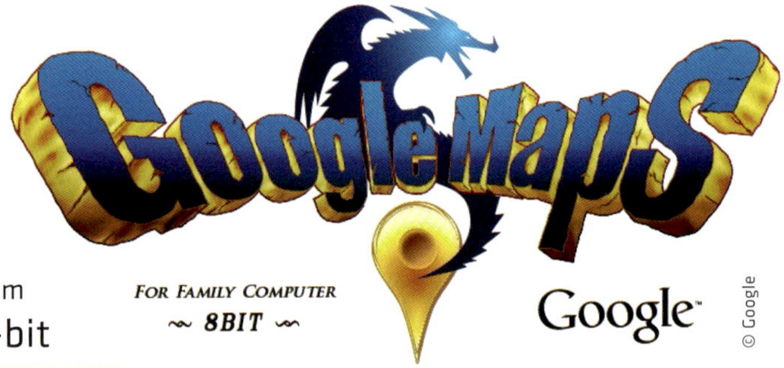

© Google

Google Maps 8-bit team

Google Maps 8-bit

Entertainment Division Jury Selection
Web, Video work

This adventure-themed entertainment product transforms Google Maps into a world reminiscent of the Dragon Quest games of childhood. When it was released on April Fools' Day, 2012, users worldwide accessed it via the Google Maps menu, and shared map coordinates and promotion clips via social media.

http://www.youtube.com/watch?v=rznYifPHxDg
Google Maps 8-bit team (Japan)

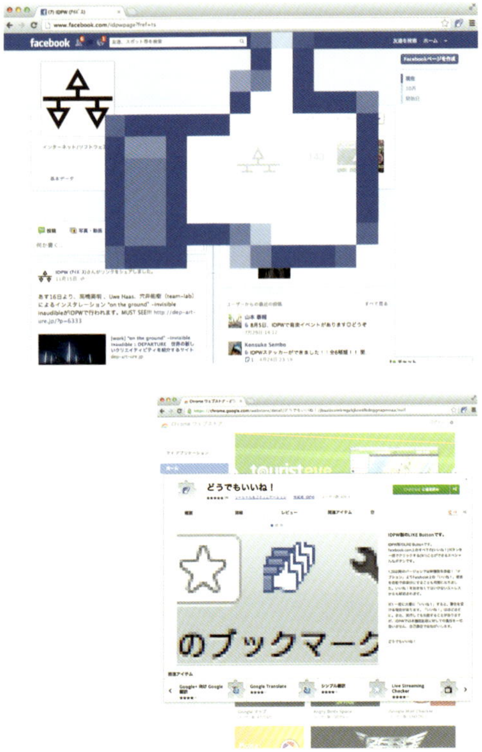

IDPW

IDPW

Whatever Button

Entertainment Division New Face Award
Website

The *Whatever Button* is an extended feature for the Google Chrome web browser that can be added to Facebook, the world's largest social networking service. The Facebook "Like" button, which carries the ultimate in low-res information (clicking it allows you to share your approval of content appearing on Facebook), has overrun the Internet at astonishing speed. By installing this free online feature, you can "Like" everything—the good, the bad, the things you think you ought to like. With one click you can automatically click every "Like" button that appears on the screen.

Software: Google Chrome extended feature
http://idpw.org/porto/w/000001/

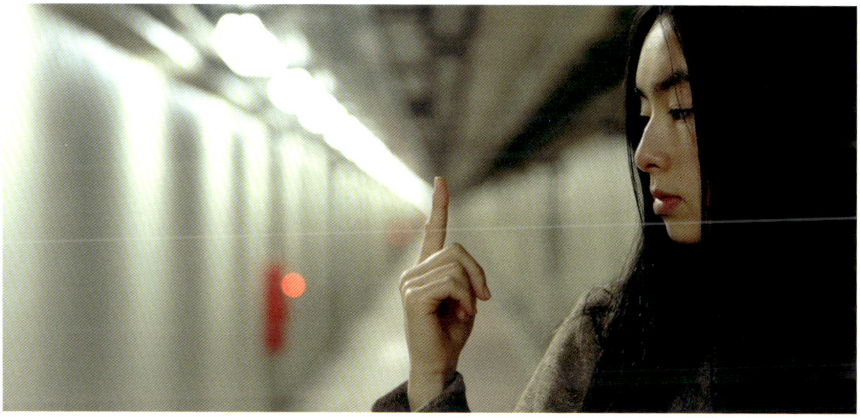

rrrrrrrroll

rrrrrrrroll

Entertainment Division Jury Selection
Web

The *rrrrrrrroll* project produces animated GIF images in which some part of the photo endlessly rotates, usually a young woman, or some object near her, against various backdrops—the sea, the mountains, the city. The creators regularly upload these images to the mixed-media blog service tumblr.

http://rrrrrrrroll.tumblr.com/

Nukeme

Glitch Embroidery

Entertainment Division Jury Selection
Digital fabrication

Using rewritten binary code embroidery data (.pes) from a computerized sewing machine, the work causes glitches in the needle's movement. The word "glitch" refers to "damage to data or machinery, or the condition of data that is damaged but still useable." This work was created by intentionally damaging data, then outputting the results of the damage.

http://nukeme.nu/
Cooperation: Make: Japan (O'Reilly Japan)

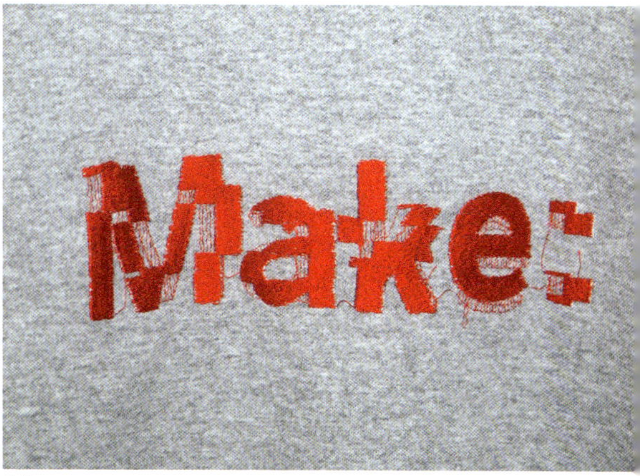

Nukeme

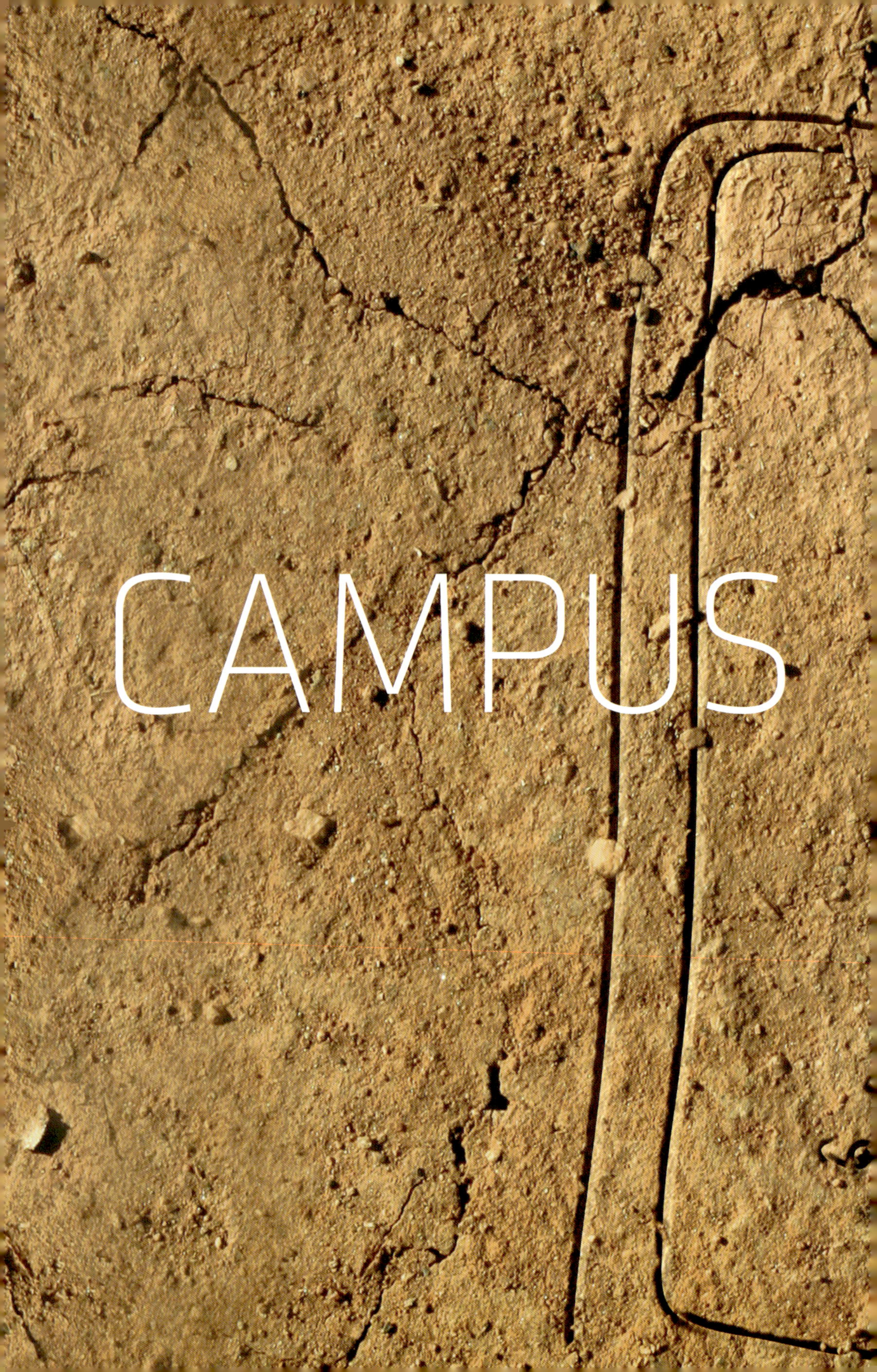
CAMPUS

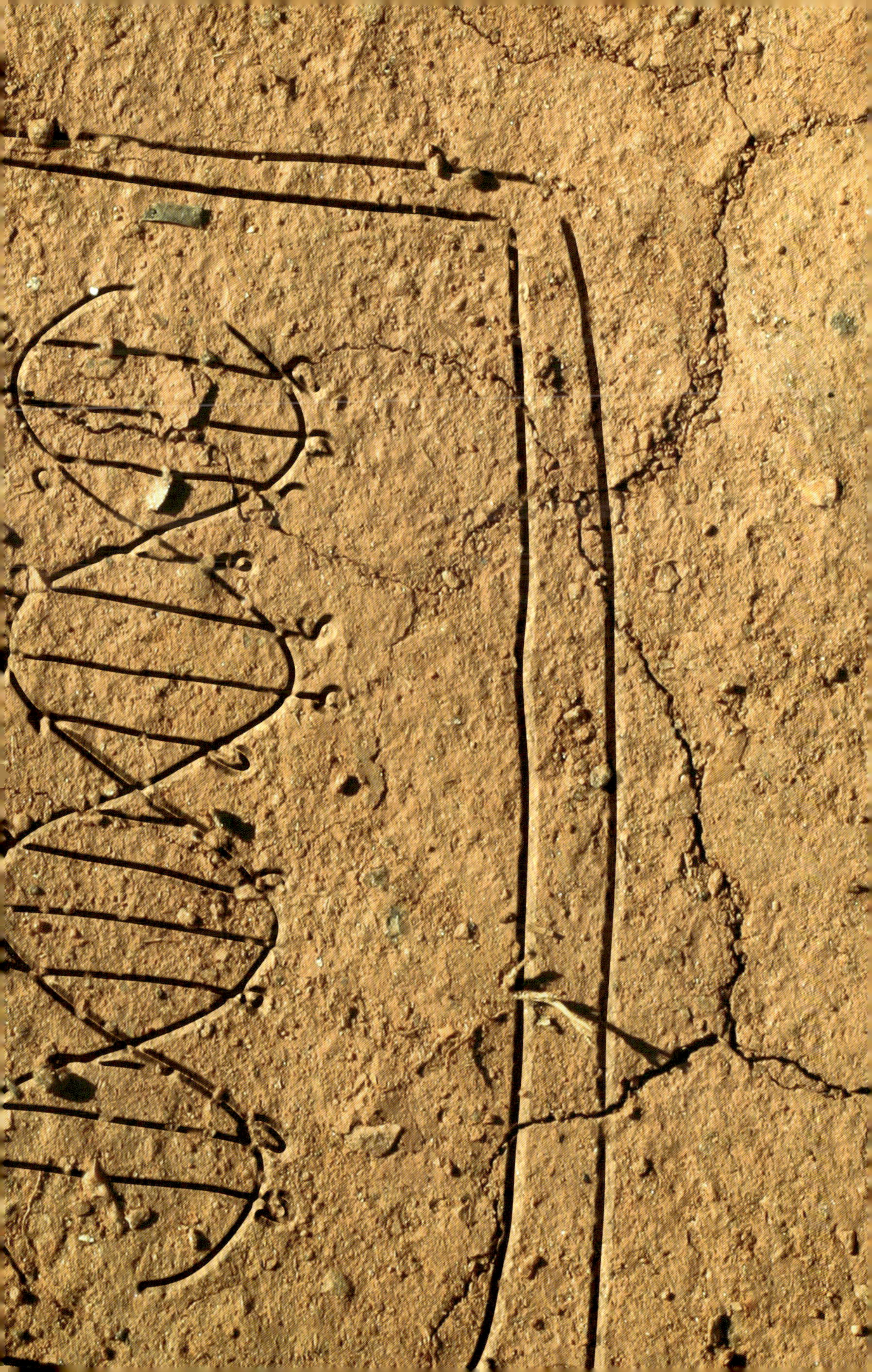

Ars Campus Israel

Collaborations continue to play a major role in creation, production, participation and manifestation of New Media Art and Technology. Ars Campus this year generates the ground for a rare opportunity for collaboration between ten leading academic Institutions in Israel. Fueled by creativity, trans-disciplinary acts and surrounded by real existential dilemmas, students and faculty artists bring forth a plethora of New Media artifacts, visions and conceptual project systems, that reflect a multiplicity of attitudes and perspectives, demonstrating a specific yet complex area of expression. The comprehensive process of reviewing the various artworks during the past months, accompanied by the Ars Campus IL Team, facilitated the encounter of diverse and sometimes polar approaches to education and to the manifestation of arts and technology in Israel. Intricate relationships exist between Art, Technology, Culture, Computation, Interaction, Performance Arts, Science, Architecture, Sound and Design adjoining in a very palpable way, reflecting the complexity of human interactions. Dependent on the departments of each school, their geographic location, their political views and the ideological identity of the students, the result is a kaleidoscopic view of new media education in a complex multi-cultural state. Through the works exhibited, the open workshops and the experimental performances, this exhibition portrays different paradigms of the educational process. There are those influenced by socio-cultural contexts, others carrying artistic expressions layered by technology interventions, those that speak through global or local involvements, and others still privileging design or material research or technological innovations. Yet all of them are reacting, questioning, criticizing and sometimes disregarding the dynamic reality of a multicultural state.

Text: Lila Chitayat

Kooperationen spielen in der Entwicklung, Produktion und Manifestation neuer Medienkunst und -technologie nach wie vor eine wesentliche Rolle.
In diesem Jahr bietet sich im Rahmen des Ars Campus die seltene Gelegenheit einer Zusammenarbeit der zehn führenden akademischen Einrichtungen Israels. Beflügelt von Kreativität und motiviert zu transdisziplinärem Handeln haben die Studierende und KünstlerInnen dieser Institutionen – trotz ihrer existenziellen Probleme in einem schwierigen Umfeld – eine Fülle von Werken, visionären Ideen sowie konzeptionellen Projekten aus dem Bereich Neue Medien präsentiert, die auf eine Vielzahl unterschiedlicher Haltungen und Perspektiven verweisen und eine sehr spezifische und äußerst komplexe Ausdrucksform ausloten. Die in den letzten Monaten mit Unterstützung des Ars Campus IL Teams erfolgte eingehende Prüfung und Bewertung der verschiedenen Kunstwerke verwies auf die unterschiedlichen und mitunter auch gegensätzlichen Ansätze in der Ausbildung und Manifestation von Kunst und Technologie in Israel.
Die komplexen Beziehungen zwischen Kunst, Technologie, Kultur, Informatik, Interaktion, Performance, Wissenschaft, Architektur, Sound und Design stehen wie immer im Zentrum der Auseinandersetzung und der Beiträge, die sich sehr konkret der Vielschichtigkeit menschlicher Interaktionen annähern. Das Ergebnis ist – je nach Abteilung des jeweiligen Instituts, dessen geografischer Lage, dem politischen Engagement und der Persönlichkeit der Studenten – sehr unterschiedlich und gibt in seiner Vielfalt einen kaleidoskopischen Einblick in die Ausbildung im Bereich Neue Medien in einem in mehrfacher Hinsicht komplexen kulturellen Kontext. Durch die präsentierten Arbeiten, die offenen Workshops und die experimentellen Performances werden unterschiedliche Paradigmen des Bildungsprozesses aufgezeigt: Einflüsse soziokultureller Zusammenhänge, künstlerische Ausdrucksformen, die sich durch vielschichtige technologische Interventionen oder globales oder lokales Engagement auszeichnen oder nach wie vor Design- oder Materialforschung oder technologische Innovationen in den Vordergrund stellen. Gemeinsam ist ihnen jedoch, dass sie auf die Realität eines multikulturellen Staates reagieren, diese hinterfragen, kritisieren oder auch bewusst ignorieren.

Aus dem Englischen von Martina Bauer

Ars Campus IL Team:

Lila Chitayat, Project Initiator and Creative Director
Yael Eylat Van-Essen, Curator
Oren Zuckerman, Strategic and Creative Advisor
Sayfan G. Borghini, Assistant Curator and Scientific Advisor
Eyal Vexler, Artistic Producer

The projects are selected from the following academic institutions:

Bezalel Academy of Arts and Design, Jerusalem
Hamidrasha Art School at Beit Berl College
H.I.T – Holon Institute of Technology
Kibbutzim College of Art & Education, Tel-Aviv
Shenkar College of Engineering and Design, Ramat Gan
Media Innovation Lab (miLAB) at IDC Herzliya
Musrara School, Jerusalem
Neri Bloomfield School of Design and Education, Haifa
Hadassah Academic College, Jerusalem
College of Management – Academic Studies (COMAS)

IL(L) Machine

We are now living in an era where new digital technologies based on automated procedures and agents are de facto mediating between us and the world, and thus cannot be perceived just as signifiers of a future horizon, but rather mark a new phenomenological phase in human existence. Many of these technologies have matured and have practical implementations which are used as part of our daily lives, and they arouse greater concern about the ways these technologies influence our emotional states and take part in constructing our identities, both as individuals and as part of the community. *IL(L) Machine* suggests and examines these new relations between automated procedures performed by machines in direct relation to real life. The works presented tackle machine automation either as entities that have physical manifestation in the world, or through actions originating in algorithms that manipulate data in virtual spaces through time, in effect reconstructing the reality we encounter. The exhibition focuses on two main perspectives in relation to automation mechanisms and hence to the ways they are emotionally and ideologically approached. The first approach derives from the realization of the power of computer algorithms in data analysis that can be considered analogous to the act of mapping. Following Deleuze and Guattari's distinction between mapping and tracing, it can be claimed that the new computational technologies enable "uncovering realities previously unseen or unimagined", and therefore unfold potential grounds.[1] Those potential grounds can reveal phenomena related to psychological, social and political issues in a way that sheds new light on historical as well as current

Wir leben in einer Zeit, in der neue digitale Technologien, die auf automatisierten Abläufen und Agenten basieren, de facto Mittler zwischen uns und der Welt sind. Sie sind daher nicht nur als Zeichen zu sehen, die den Horizont der Zukunft abstecken, sondern markieren den Beginn einer neuen phänomenologischen Phase der menschlichen Existenz. Viele dieser Technologien sind mittlerweile ausgereift und ihre praktischen Anwendungen Teil unseres Alltags, weshalb zunehmend Unbehagen bezüglich ihres Einflusses auf unsere emotionale Verfassung und die Konstruktion unserer Identitäten – als Individuen, aber auch als Teil der Gemeinschaft – aufkommt. *IL(L) Machine* thematisiert und analysiert diese neuen Beziehungen zwischen den automatisierten Abläufen der Maschinen und setzt sie in direkten Bezug zum realen Leben. Die präsentierten Arbeiten verhandeln die Automatisierung entweder in Form von Entitäten, die sich physisch in der Welt manifestieren, oder als auf Algorithmen basierende Aktionen, die Daten in virtuellen Räumen und Zeitabläufen manipulieren und die Wirklichkeit, die wir erfahren, tatsächlich neu konstruieren. Schwerpunkt der Ausstellung sind zwei wesentliche Perspektiven auf die Automationsmechanismen und die Prozesse, wie man sich ihnen emotional und ideologisch annähert. Der erste Ansatz steht in Kontext mit der Realisierung der Macht von Computeralgorithmen in der Datenanalyse, die analog zur Kartierung betrachtet werden kann. An Deleuzes und Guattaris Unterscheidung zwischen „Karte" und „Kopie" anknüpfend, lässt sich sagen, dass die neuen rechnergestützten Technologien es ermöglichen, „bisher ungesehene und nicht vorstellbare Realitäten zu entdecken", und daher potenzielle Territorien[1] eröffnen. Durch diese potenziellen Territorien können Erkennt-reality, making it possible to decipher our world in new ways. The second approach is related to the concept of "transcoding" used by Lev Manovich, which claims that computerizations of culture involve the projection of the machine's unique ontology, epistemology, and pragmatics onto the cultural space.[2] Thus, machines are not simply the tools we use, they also reconstruct our cultural reality. As such, they can be the stimulators of the constitution of new power relations and structures of control in new emerging spatial and temporal dimensions. This is related to generative mechanisms as well as to representational ones.[3] The *IL(L) Machine* exhibition shows a new generation of artists emerging from art academies and research institutions, bringing forth a critical examination of the relations to technology as the manifestation of a new era. In a country characterized by a very active and innovative high-tech industry with a charged historic identity and profound political conflicts, this critical approach leads to different perspectives regarding the influence of new technology on our society. This exhibition reflects the living and present conflict of Israeli art, which pivots around the urge to relate to complex local issues on the one hand, and on the other hand aspires to take its place within the ongoing global discourse.

Text: Yael Eylat Van-Essen

1 Corner, James. "The Agency of Mapping: Speculation, Critique and Invention". In Denis Cosgrove, ed., *Mappings* (London: Reaktion Books, 1999). 213.

2 Manovich, Lev. *The Language of New Media*. Cambridge, Mass.: The MIT P, 2001. 64-65.

3 See Bruno Latour's analysis of the automated mechanism of renaissance perspective in which he claims that the relations between objects and their representational tools, are not limited to the representation of reality, but can also serve as a means of controlling reality.
Latour, Bruno. "Visualization and Cognition: Thinking with Eyes and Hands" in *Knowledge and Society: Studies in the Sociology of Culture Past and Present*. Vol. 6, 1986, 1–40.

nisse über psychologische, gesellschaftliche und politische Phänomene gewonnen werden, die sowohl auf die historische als auch auf die gegenwärtige Wirklichkeit neues Licht werfen und ermöglichen, unsere Welt neu zu dechiffrieren.

Der zweite Ansatz bezieht sich auf den von Lev Manovich verwendeten Begriff „Transcoding", der besagt, dass die Computerisierung der Kultur die Projektion der spezifischen Ontologie, Epistemologie und Pragmatiken der Maschine auf den kulturellen Raum impliziert.[2] Maschinen sind demnach nicht einfach nur Hilfsmittel, sondern konstruieren auch unsere kulturelle Realität. Insofern können sie die Herausbildung von neuen Machtverhältnissen und Kontrollstrukturen in neu entstehenden räumlichen und zeitlichen Dimensionen provozieren. Dies bezieht sich ebenso auf generative wie auf repräsentative Mechanismen.[3]

Die Ausstellung *IL(L) Machine* präsentiert eine neue Generation von Künstlern, die aus Kunstakademien und Forschungseinrichtungen kommen und die Beziehungen zur Technologie, die als Manifestation einer neuen Epoche verstanden werden, einer kritischen Prüfung unterziehen. In einem Land, das durch sehr aktive und innovative Hightech-Industrie, eine historisch belastete Identität und gravierende politische Konflikte geprägt ist, bringt diese kritische Auseinandersetzung mit dem Einfluss neuer Technologien auf unsere Gesellschaft unterschiedliche Perspektiven hervor. Diese Ausstellung spiegelt den aktuellen Konflikt israelischer Kunst, der daher rührt, dass einerseits die Notwendigkeit besteht, die komplexen lokalen Themen aufzugreifen, und andererseits das Bestreben vorherrscht, eine Rolle im aktuellen globalen Diskus zu spielen.

Aus dem Englischen von Martina Bauer

1 Corner, James: „The Agency of Mapping: Speculation, Critique and Invention", in Denis Cosgrove (Hg.), *Mappings*, Reaktion Books, London, 1999 [S. 213]

2 Manovich, Lev: *The Language of New Media*, The MIT P, Cambridge, Mass., 2001. [S. 64–65]

3 Siehe Bruno Latours Analysen des in der Renaissance entwickelten Verfahrens der Zentralperspektive, in denen er davon ausgeht, dass sich die Beziehungen zwischen Objekten und den Instrumenten ihrer Darstellung nicht auf die Repräsentation der Realität beschränken, sondern auch zur Kontrolle der Realität dienen können.
Latour, Bruno: „Visualization and Cognition: Thinking with Eyes and Hands", in *Knowledge and Society: Studies in the Sociology of Culture Past and Present*, Band 6, 1986. [S. 1–40]

Projects

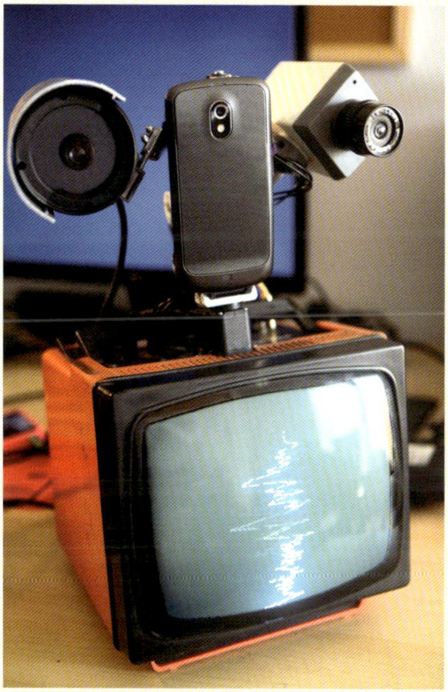

Maayan Sheleff, Eran Hadas, Gal Eshel

frankie

Kibbutzim College of Art & Education, Tel-Aviv

frankie is a documentary robot that interviews people, attempting to "learn" what it means to be human. It responds to certain emotions both with language and "eye/camera" movements, creating computer-generated, emotion-inspired videos. The video documentation is available online, forming an archive of the robot's research.

frankie is a form of "automatic" documentation that allegedly excludes the artist as an author, questioning notions of representation and participation. A well-exposed surveillance camera, it brings to the surface issues of agency, control and privacy, questioning how they affect us in a world in which every second is documented and mediated. It reflects upon our relationships with the machines that dominate our lives, and the manner in which we perform and present ourselves in the digital age.

Guy Hoffman, Roberto Aimi

Travis—Robotic Speaker Dock and Listening Companion

Media Innovation Lab (miLAB) at IDC

Travis is a robotic speaker dock and music listening companion. This robot doesn't just play your music, it experiences it with the human listener, blurring the line between hi-fi and robotic companionship.

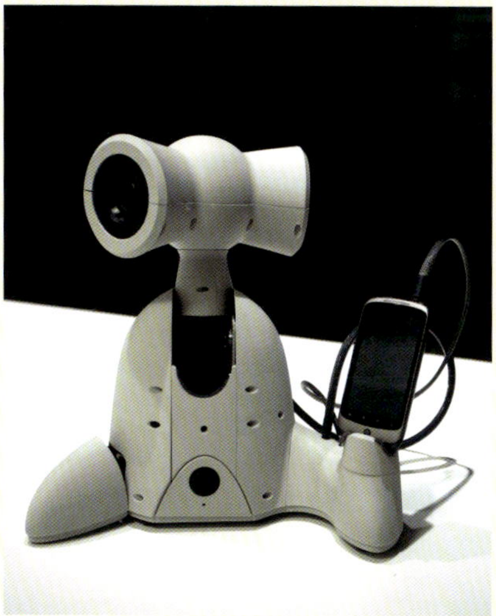

Although it does not have a shape that resembles a human creature, it feels more human than many other robots that are designed according to anthropocentric principles. As opposed to the etymological origin of the term "robot", which is connected to the Latin word "labor" and suggests the tendency to relate to the robot in terms of the robot serving the human and making his missions more efficient, *Travis,* using sophisticated voice recognition and artificial intelligence applications, focuses on the collaborative potential and offers a new perspective on man-machine relations.

Developed in collaboration with the Georgia Tech Center for Music Technology.

Alisa Goikhman

LangWidgets–Navigation System for Semantic Fields

H.I.T - Holon Institute of Technology

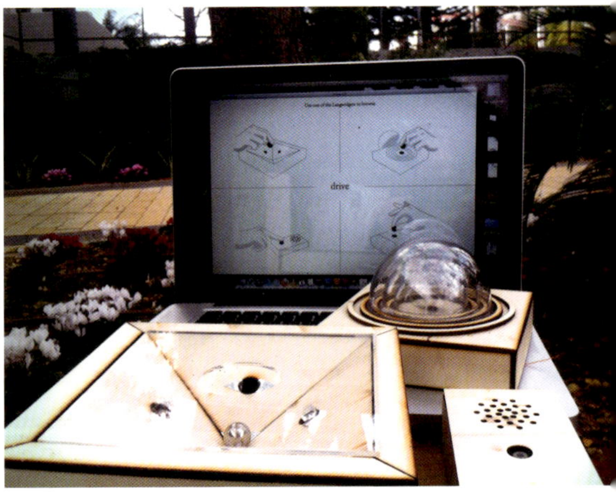

LangWidgets composes a set of designed physical widgets and interactive graphical representations to allow us to wander through foreign semantic fields, as if they were a geographical surface.
The suggested interface examines how acquired conventions of navigation can be implemented as a translation instrument by browsing through the conceptual relations between words. The goal is to find a visual and technological solution that will allow the user to experience and internalize the structure of new vocabulary through their senses rather than memorizing it. The research aims at inducing synesthesia between our verbal cognition and our orientation skills, to provide a path for sensory understanding of foreign language and culture.

Ilan Green

Sound Map 2013

Musrara School

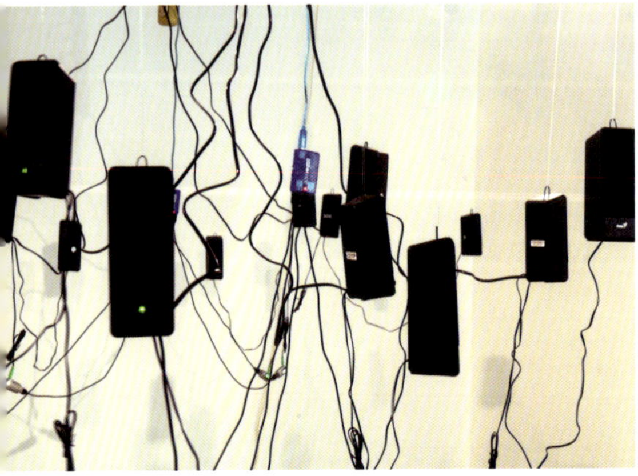

Sound Map 2013 consists of digitations of the acoustic surroundings of the old city of Jaffa, a city with a multifaceted history of political conflicts and cultural tensions, and therefore a symbolic space through which identities are defined. The environmental sound of a square kilometer is scaled down into the acoustic space, maintaining the proportions of the area sampled, similar to how geographical maps are represented in different scales. The sound of the Old City is extracted and condensed, enabling the visitor to experience the city at a (an ear) glance. Recordings took place around the clock, thus, in the reconstructed soundscape, day and night are blended in an intangible picture of this complex city.

Shaul Tzemach

Reason and Outcome

Kibbutzim College of Art & Education

This work is a study of time, movement, relations, interactions and influence, randomness and feedback. It exposes an inextricable tangle of objects moving simultaneously, reacting to the beholder in a mechanical yet interconnected fashion—each part both influences and is influenced by all others. The flexibility of the stripes and belts, the tension of the springs, cable lengths, the wheel rotation rate, fluctuations in weight, the engine power, the ability to meet resistance and the beholder's movement, while trying to understand what they are looking at, are all parameters contributing to the measure of chaos of the overall motion. The system fluctuates between states of stress and slackness, between static and erratic moments, between predictable and unexpected reactions in a mechanical metaphor of the dynamics of living systems.

Oren Zuckerman, Oran Peretz, Orad Weisberg, Ricardo Tarrasch

Ruzo

Media Innovation Lab (miLAB) at IDC

Ruzo is a crowd-sensing platform that allows urban explorers to both collect and analyze data together, in an effort to detect meaningful patterns of relations between everyday phenomena. The aim of the platform is to enable its participants through interactive data visualization to intuitively explore statistic-based relationships in the data collected by the community. *Ruzo* users join different data collection campaigns according to what they find meaningful in their daily routines and their ways of life. The resulting process of collective computation holds the potential for revealing unexpected ties between phenomena we usually perceive as being disconnected, and calls attention to new perceptions of our living environment.

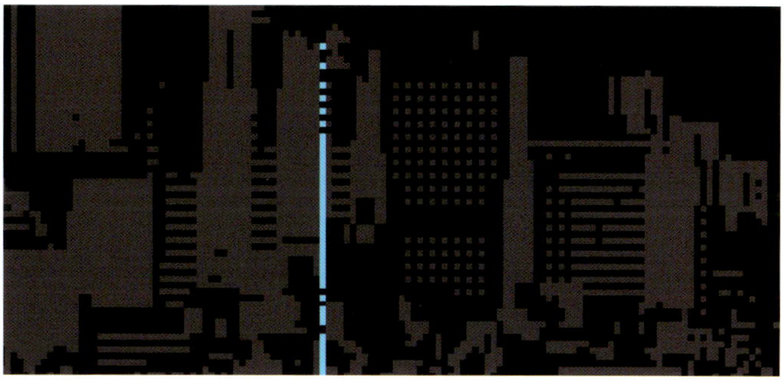

Inbal Hershtig

C.T.SOUND TLV-LINZ

Hamidrasha Art School

C.T.SOUND TLV-LINZ is a digital homage to the analogical musical box. Instead of converting notes into material and form in order to produce sound, an image is converted into MIDI language, and then played by sound-producing software. In this way, an image becomes a calculated grid of pixels, and, in turn, each one of the pixels affects both the musical notes produced and their duration. In this installation the panoramic view of the cities of Linz and Tel-Aviv are displayed and "played" as their images are scanned through time. By exposing the power of translation enabled by new technologies, the work reflects upon the interpretative aspect included in the automated act, while exploring a new kinesthetic order and a new way of "feeling" a space.

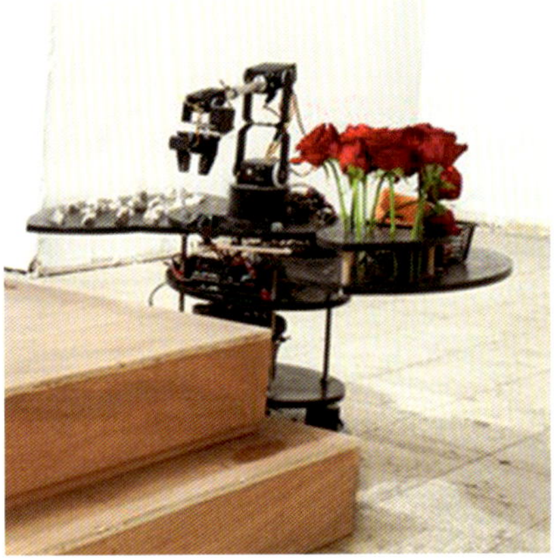

Itamar Shimshoni

Stony 1.0

Bezalel Academy of Arts and Design

Stony 1.0 is a robot that operates inside a gallery hall. The robot moves around a real life-sized double headstone. During the day it wanders around, placing a stone on the headstone—a Jewish mourning custom that signifies the visitor's intention to return, symbolically cleaning the headstone and placing a red rose on the headstone.

The name *Stony 1.0* corresponds with the term "Web 2.0" which refers to the second generation of online interactive content services. Sites are no longer static (as in first generation webs, where surfers are passive); they now let surfers create, upload and share contents in a myriad of social networks. One might say that *Stony 1.0* passively mirrors the relationship between technology and death, without creating a dichotomy between them; while at the same time, actively providing a base for this relationship so that we can participate in real-time mourning rituals.

Robotics: Zvika Marckfeld
Text: Mati Shmuelof

Adi Fleisher Peled, Yael Cohen

Mercury Retrograde

Shenkar College of Engineering and Design

Astrology has been embedded in the belief systems of different cultures around the world since antiquity. Beliefs in the effects of star constellations upon natural forces and upon human activities go so far as to influence the ways decisions are taken. A well-known astrological claim is that when Mercury is in retrograde, it affects people on earth, causing communication friction and difficulties. *Mercury Retrograde* exploits the ability to access meta-data based on individuals' internet activities in order to examine the validity of this belief. The analysis is based on twitter messages and compares the frequency of words reflecting communication problems between people and the ensuing emotional expressions of these problems.

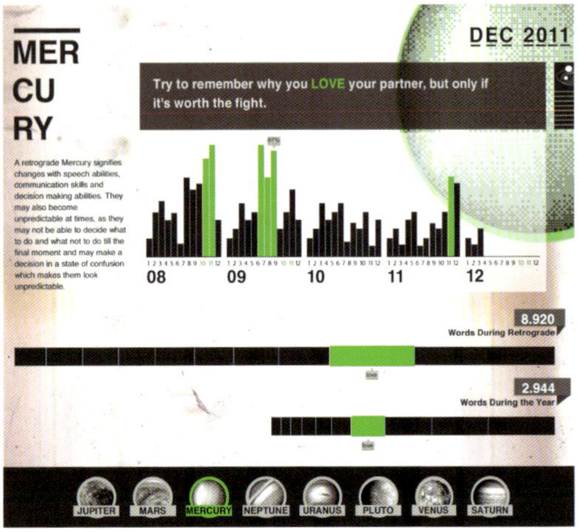

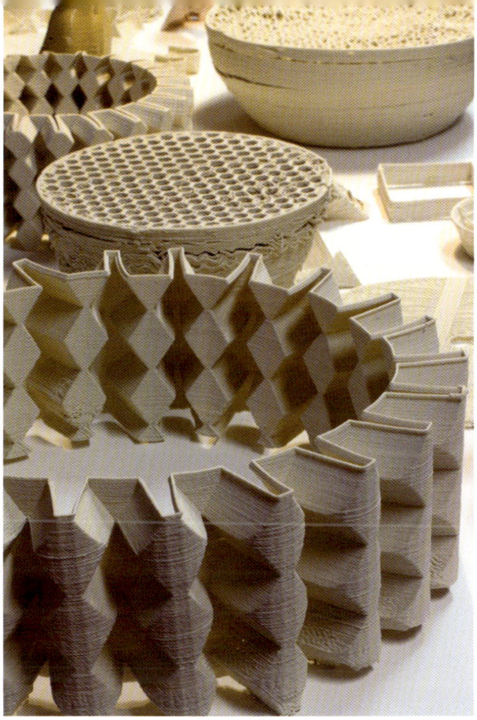

Eran Galor

Poetic Machine 3D Ceramic Printing

H.I.T – Holon Institute of Technology

The works shown in the exhibition are ceramic objects printed by a three-dimensional printer developed by Galor as the final project of his Design studies. The materials that are used for printing range from simple clay, local clay, Chinese porcelain, ceramic materials with advanced properties, and a mixture that includes organic and biodegradable materials. The objects exhibited reflect upon the evolving tension between the traditional world of pottery-making and modern technological innovation, where new sophisticated methods of manufacturing offer renewed unique and original interpretations.

Yonathan Abramson, Michael Fink

Fontify

Bezalel Academy of Arts and Design

Fontify utilizes machine-learning methodology and a database containing millions of text samples to find the most suitable font for the content of a given text in real time. *Fontify* takes a transient text message and typographically transforms it into a monumental sign. It offers its users a "double exposure" experience, the dissonance of simultaneously seeing their text as a private message and as a public object that is open to manipulation by the automatic act that interprets its emotional and cultural content. The *Fontify* online platform offers a new mapping for the intersection of cultural phenomena that were previously not related.

Gadi Ickowicz, Tal Kammer, Lihi Erel, Maya Friedman, Maya Shoham

SoundScape

Media Innovation Lab (miLAB) at IDC Herzliya

SoundScape is a guessing game of collecting and tagging sound clips. In the game, players challenge each other to guess sounds that they record in their environment. As a "game with a purpose", the casual interactions initiated by this game are utilized to build a large-scale database of text-tagged sounds. The result is a database of content- and location-tagged sound clips, which is visualized as a searchable point-cloud map. This has the potential to work on an open API to allow further research into the sound database, which can be used for computer science research, automatic soundtrack generation, the mapping of city noise and multiple other applications.

Dor Zlekha Levy

Ayooni

Hamidrasha School of Art

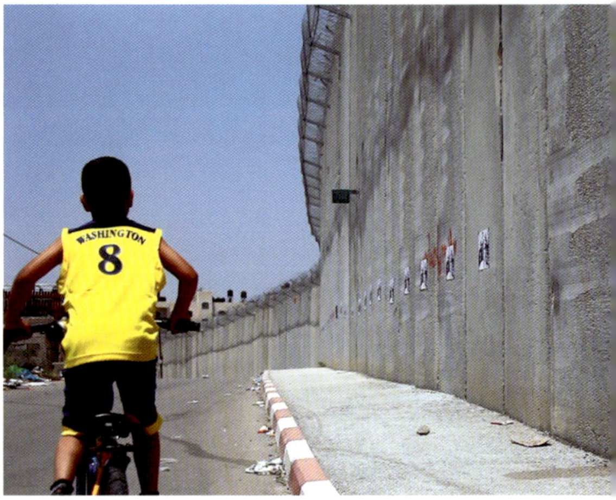

Ayooni invites viewers to journey along the politically disputed separation wall marking the border between Israel and the Palestinian occupied territories. A camera rolls by the fence, moving horizontally, tracing strips of posters hung on the wall near East Jerusalem. The posters display words of love in three languages, alongside images from old Arabic movies. The editing relates to the separation wall as a reel of 35mm film, comparing movement along the wall to that of a movie projector feed wheel. Accelerating the movement works the wall like a zoetrope device and animates the posters. The work emphasizes the conflict surrounding the wall construction, using controlling, surveillance and segregating technologies embodied by the concrete wall, as a platform not only for the emotional messages they carry, but for the display of vision technologies that make the deceitful nature of vision visible.

Daphna Levin

Visualizing Collaboration & Conflict

HIT- Holon Institute of Technology

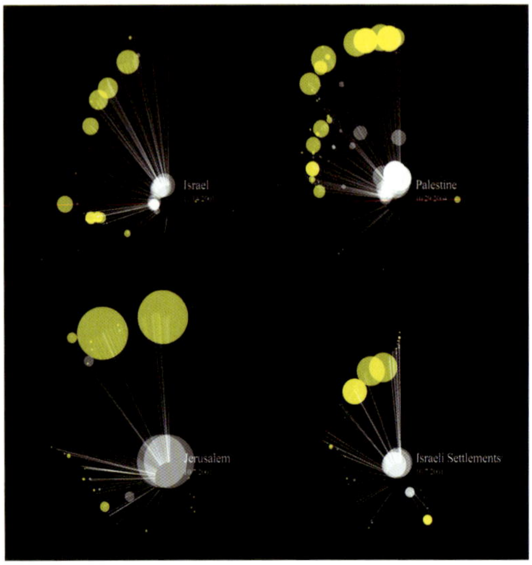

From "Paper Clip" to "Palestine", each article within Wikipedia is the outcome of a collaborative process of interactions, feedbacks, discussions, disputes, edit-wars and vandalism. By visualizing the process of collaboration within heavily disputed topics, we can research how conflict is handled in an indirect and open environment. This affords us new perspectives on dispute management and conflict resolution, especially relating to complex conflicts where attempts at resolution have so far faltered or failed altogether. This project presents what can be considered in Foucaultian terms as a tool for exposing the genealogy of discourse in a way that structurally reveals the relations between knowledge and power, and their connection to mechanisms of identity structuring.

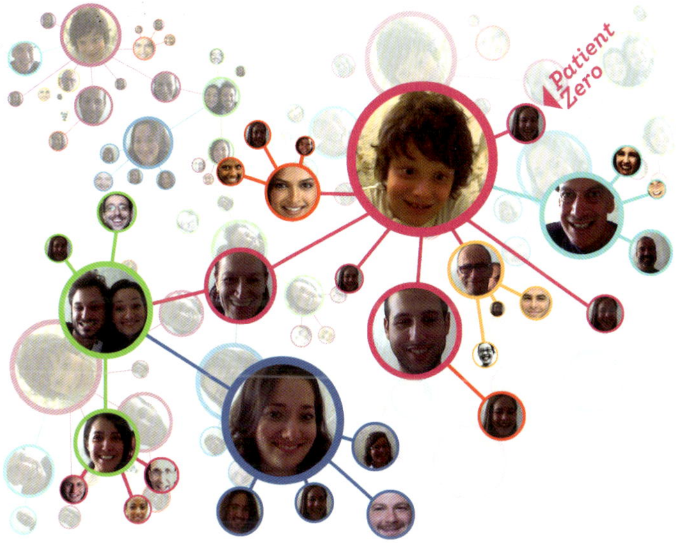

Yuri Klebanov, Roi Ronn, Yonatan Ben Yaakov

Smiletection

Bezalel Academy of Art and Design

Smilefection is a showcase of the infectious nature of smiling. The user is presented with a slideshow of smiling faces. The moment the user is "infected" by one of the smiles appearing on the screen and smiles themself, a webcam snaps a photo and their smiling face becomes a part of the slideshow. Simple data analysis can then show the expansion of the "Smiles Epidemic", and rate our users by the contagiousness of their smile. In this way, face detection and computer vision analysis done by machine, stimulate emotional reactions by viewers. The atomization of vision in this respect creates a feedback loop with the "real world", activated by our reaction to what we see.

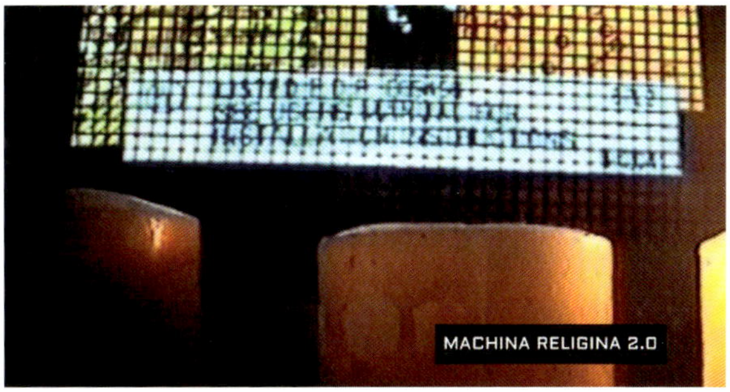

Amnon Dekel

Machina Religina 2.0

Shenkar College of Engineering and Design

Machina Religina 2.0 is a critique of the modern compulsion to see computers and technology as replacements for inner spiritual needs, knowledge and religion. A Portable prayer box, including a confessional chamber, candles, matches and volume knob, serves as the focal point. Interaction with the piece is driven by measuring light levels in the box (via the number, location and timing of candles lit), by the audio volume and by the use of stochastic algorithms that merge the data. A search algorithm and parser that take into account the light levels and the motion of kneeling participants make the selection of the presented video and audio.

Analog Illustration: Merav Salomon

Michal Rinott, Eran Galor, Shachar Geiger, Luka Or

Cubes

HIT- Holon Institute of Technology

Cubes is an interactive installation composed of 20 transparent cubes that explore the poetics of interaction and the beauty of electronics. It is a celebration of action and reaction—the "substance" of interaction and its potential for simplicity, surprise, engagement and pleasure. *Cubes* abstracts the interactive object into the simplest of forms: a cube. Keeping the form unitary allows us to explore behavior and its intricacies: a collection of 20 objects of very similar form and very different personality. The collection of *Cubes* creates a vocabulary of input types—knocking, blowing, shaking, adjusting, turning, selecting, moving closer and farther away, making light and obstructing it.

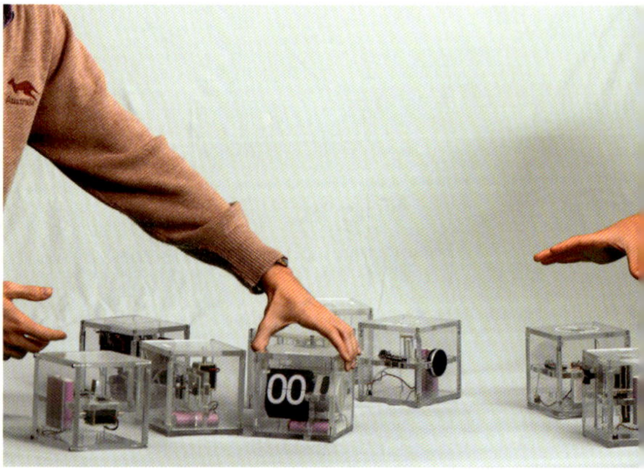

Yonatan Ben Simhon, Alessandra Villaamil, Ioni Gkliati

Futile Type

Hamidrasha School of Art

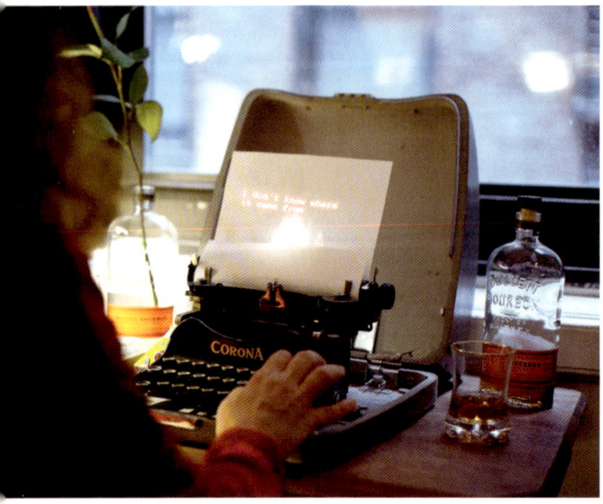

Futile Type, an interactive video installation, borrows the often-used metaphor of the typewriter to represent the deteriorating autonomy of the author and his changing relations with the reader. The user is confronted with an old dusty typewriter on a table, preloaded with a sheet of white paper on which a person smoking a cigarette is projected. When the user presses the keys of the typewriter, the hands of the projected man react and place blotches of ink on his face. Lines of verse start to appear above his head. The text is pre-written and the user cannot write back. The actual typing only influences the pace of the content flow. With every keystroke another blotch of ink covers the face of the person on the screen until he cannot breathe. The physicality of the writing machine contrasts with the virtual corporality of the breathless reader, and signifies the changing status of writing following the digital revolution.

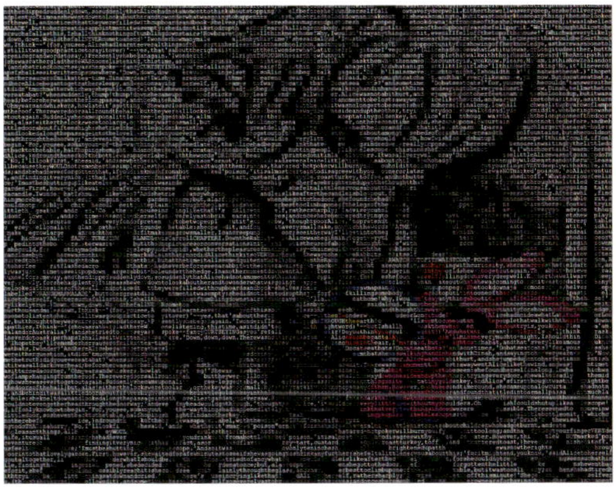

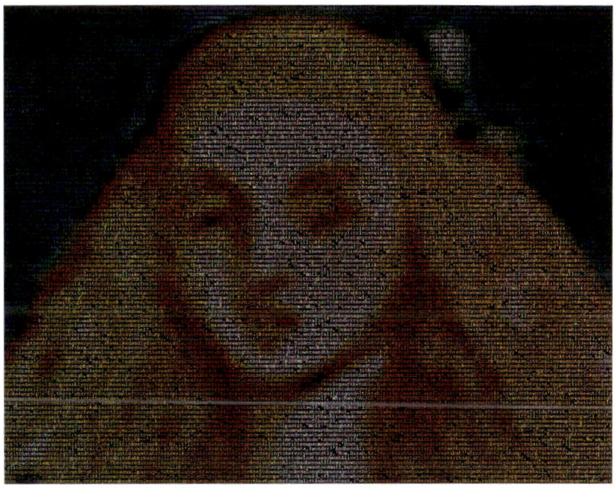

Batt-Girl

|)Own t[-]3 a§cii ho13 / 2013 /

Kibbutzim College of Art & Education

Down The ASCII Hole is an interactive net adaptation of *Alice's Adventures in Wonderland*, wandering between links of scrambled text and animated ascii-art fields. These impressions are based on the illustrations from the original book, alongside impressions of products and ads from the net.
The story is re-translated and re-born in scrambled English and coded into Leet language (see title). In order to read the texts or to view the whole image, the human body must move as a cursor: wandering, scrolling, clicking, zooming (in/out), mimicking actions that resemble everyday web surfing, asking to break from the real into the virtual. Textuality becomes hyper-textuality—The WWW as Wonderland, Alice—as a clueless-geek girl, the navigation as a poetic user experience.

Or Wolff

Olympia

Neri Bloomfield School of Design and Education

Leni Riefenstahl, a film director in the service of the Third Reich, is known for her cold, clear aesthetic work, as well as for its manipulative powers. Her well known film *Olympia*, which documents the 1936 Berlin Olympics, is the subject of this research project, presenting an analysis of the movement, composition, camera angles as well as other components of the cinematic language she used. Using computational graphic tools, the study aims to reveal the semiotic characteristics of her films in order to understand how they reflect the ideology that the film aspired to support.

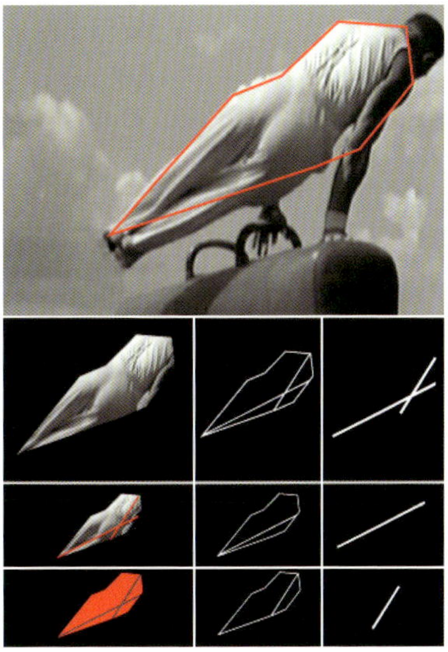

Noam Attias

OSSIS

Hadassah Academic College

This project explores a theoretical scenario in which emerging synthetic biology technologies are applied to the field of industrial design. *Ossis* is a series of objects made of artificially-grown bone tissue designed to analyze sampled DNA of organisms from the environment in order to create a new point of observation and visibility for biodiversity. The technology of identification is based on the bone's own DNA, and allows the sampling of biological information from the environment, decoding the DNA composition of organisms, and then displaying the information processed through a digital interface.

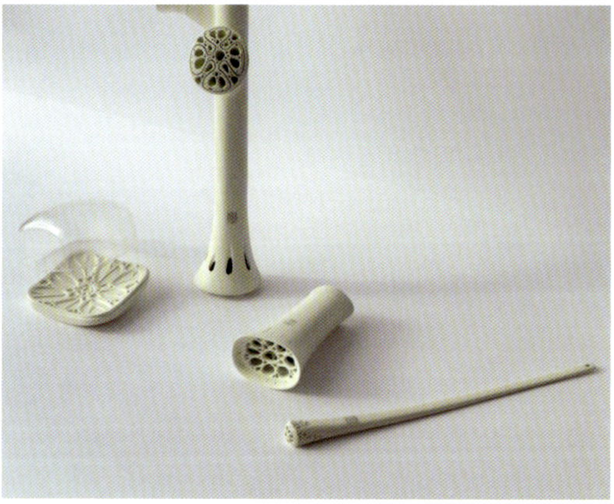

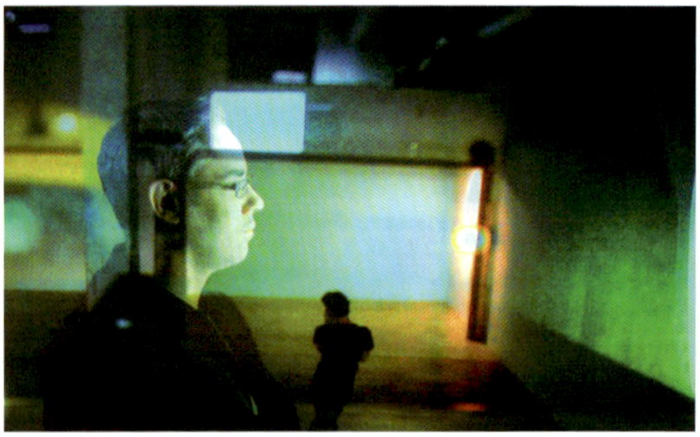

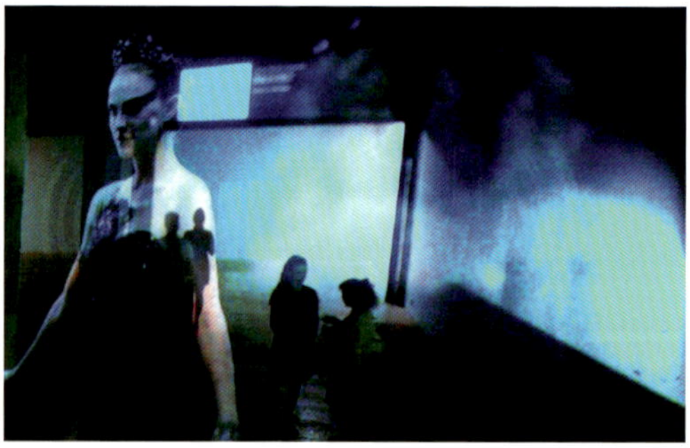

Ron Erlih

mediums

Bezalel Academy of Art and Design

mediums follows the Western tradition of accumulating information and the incessant urge for analysis and interpretation. This installation blurs the gap between the virtual and the real by merging information taken from both the exhibition space as well as from the Worldwide Web, applying algorithmic procedures in order to present a synchronic view of the world in real time.

Images captured by the Google image search engine, videos from YouTube, and facial expression analyses are used as contemporary oracles. The human body, in this work, becomes a subject of the new spatiality of our time, in which the body can be present in different places simultaneously, and be part of a borderless fluid random space of emotions and memories bounded by its hybrid existence.

Eitan Bartal

Jude

H.I.T.–Holon Institute of Technology

Jude, an inflatable PVC sculpture, creates a jarring conflict between the word "Jude", with its heavily charged historical connotations, and the light, frivolous display of the four letters that comprise the sculpture. A re-make of American artist Robert Indiana's iconic Pop Art image *LOVE,* it consists of the distorted letters *JU* over the letters *DE,* black lettering and a bright yellow background that evoke memories of the yellow Star of David, inscribed with the word *Jude,* that has become a symbol of Nazi persecution. The observer is caught between the initial playful appearance flowing from the sculpture, and darker, more complex feelings. The observer is forced to take part in the work–only if their heartbeat indicates that they have been moved by the sculpture does the statue inflate. Can the creation construct a new image for *JUDE?*

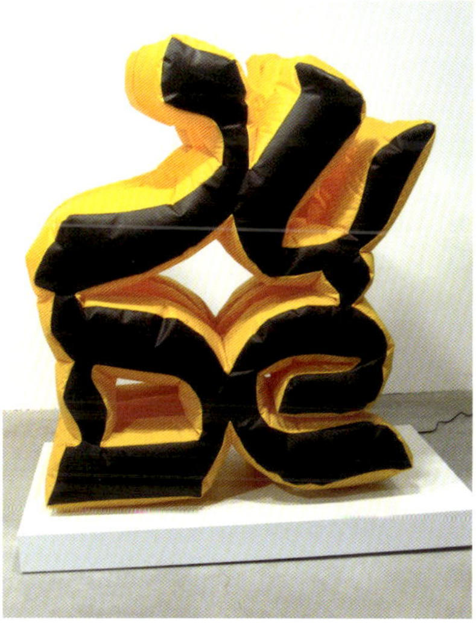

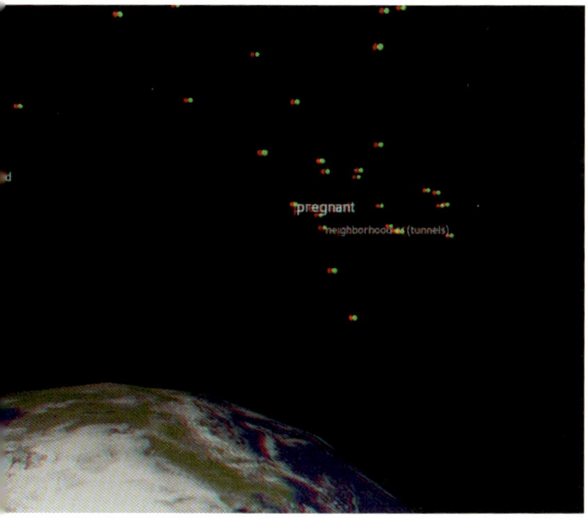

Roi Ronn

Musical Galaxy

Bezalel Academy of Arts and Design

The *musical galaxy* uses data visualization in order to translate personal music collections into three-dimensional projections in space. The resulting virtual image is a naturally navigable playlist. Audience members are encouraged to scan their personal music collections, which are then analyzed, song by song, based on their rhythm, style, the performing artist and other attributes. A tailored algorithm plots the songs into a three-dimensional space according to the analyzed attributes in a way that groups similar songs, and separates dissimilar songs. Upon completion of the process, a 3D projection of the resulting mapping is displayed, representing each song as a star in space so that the playlist owners can navigate through their own personal musical galaxy.

Inbal Pinto, Matan Zohar

Auditory Maze

Bezalel Academy of Arts and Design

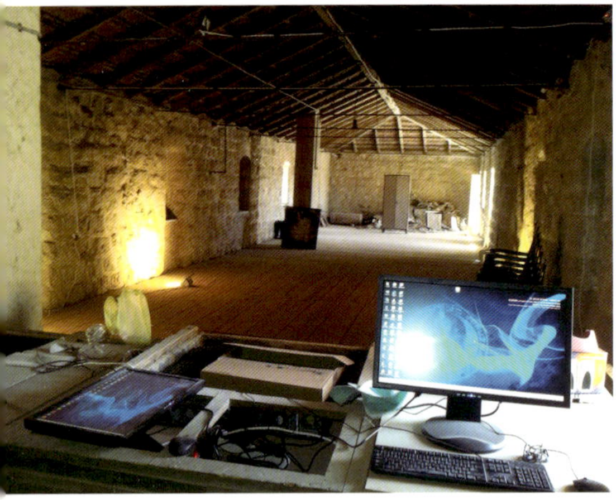

Digital technologies have extensively changed our perceptions of space, mostly due to the integration of virtual spaces in our everyday lives. Yet in actual spaces our spatial perception relies mainly on our rich visual system. We see rooms, hallways and obstacles and use them as visual signals in order to understand how the space around us is constructed and to derive the feeling it projects. Sometimes we also rely on our tactile experience, our hands on the walls of a dark corridor or a pain in our toe when it hits the corner of a room. All of these make us update our virtual mental maps.
Auditory Maze explores whether an empty space can generate this mental map of walls, corridors and corners not by the interpretation of visual inputs, but by auditory feedbacks that acoustically describe the borders and limitations of the surrounding space. By doing so, automated behavioral patterns and modes of perception are disrupted and reformulated.

Alexandra Man, David Malik, Doron Barsky, Yael Laventer, Tamar Garfunkel

Street Simon

Media Innovation Lab (miLAB) at IDC Herzliya

Street Simon is an urban game encouraging playful interactions among pedestrians. It is a large-scale sidewalk version of the classic 1980s game *Simon*, designed to be played by multiple collaborating players. The game remains faithful to both the game play and the synthesized sound effects of the original game. The motivation for this project is rooted in the realization that our idle time is increasingly taken up by using our mobile phone, disconnecting us from our surroundings. The game experience is designed to turn these short periods of idleness not only into opportunities for physical and cognitive activity, but also for a chance to look up, smile and connect with people around us.

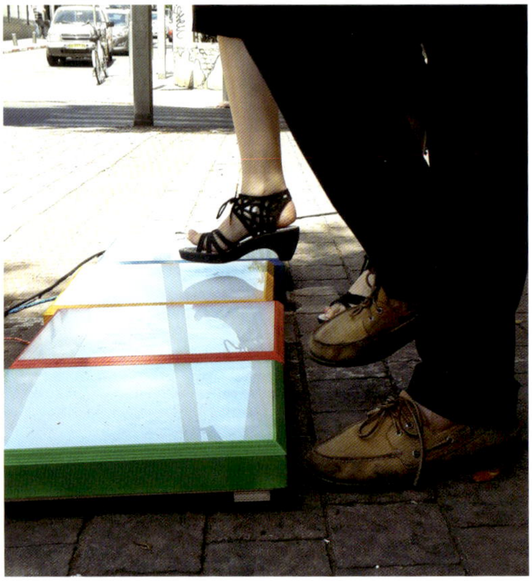

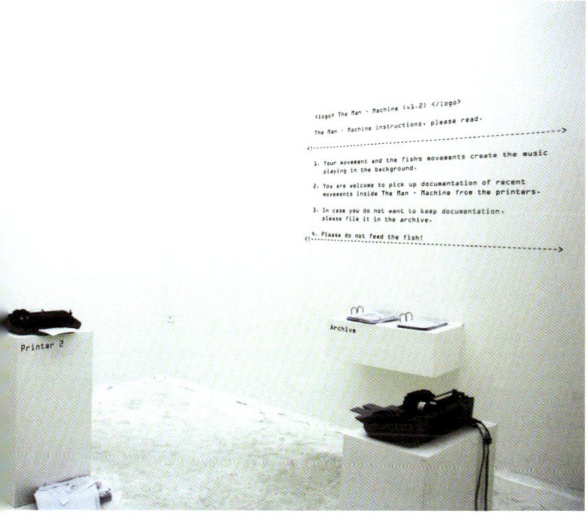

Harel Schreiber

Space Sequencer

Bezalel Academy of Arts and Design

Space Sequencer is an installation consisting of printers and a fish. The space "performs" in direct relation to the movements of the people visiting it, who are being monitored by security cameras. A program translates the movement of people in the space, mixed with the movements of a fish, into a musical sequence, which is played in real-time. The tone and level of the sound is determined by the location of the visitors in space. The sound is then translated into data: every few minutes, a printer placed in the space prints out a music sheet documenting the sound of the last minutes. The visitors can then take the score in which they took part, or file it in an archive that the artist will later use for a live performance, detached from the performative mechanism of the space. In this white poetic space, man and machine, nature and artificiality, poetry and automated writing, control and autonomy, are all vibrating actors in an emergent "mise-en-scène" of previously non-existing relations.

Moti Brecher

Songs for the drawer

Kibbutzim College of Art & Education

This interactive video and sculpture shows a projection of a man reading a poem inside a drawer. All is well, until the man's pushing of the walls makes the drawer itself start to shake and the whole work is overwhelmed by what feels like a destabilizing earthquake. The work is composed of a ready-made table drawer to which a mechanical engine is connected. A video is projected on the object and interaction takes place between the movement of the drawer, and the movements of the man who is projected inside the drawer. When the video begins to shake with the movements of the drawer, the performer starts to stumble and roll on the floor.
The work expresses the existential contradiction we are living in, particularly significant with regard to the political situation in Israel: On the one hand, our technological and intellectual capabilities lead us to believe that we are in control of our lives, but on the other hand we are aware of the essential fragile, unstable and transient nature of our existence.

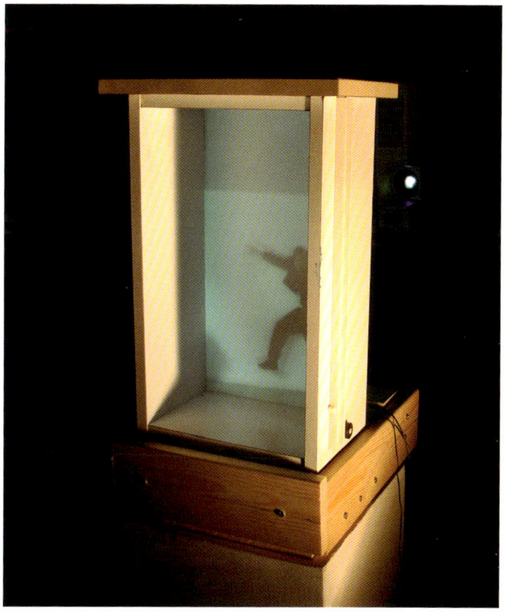

Dina Kornveits

Grandmother's Asleep

Bezalel Academy of Arts and Design

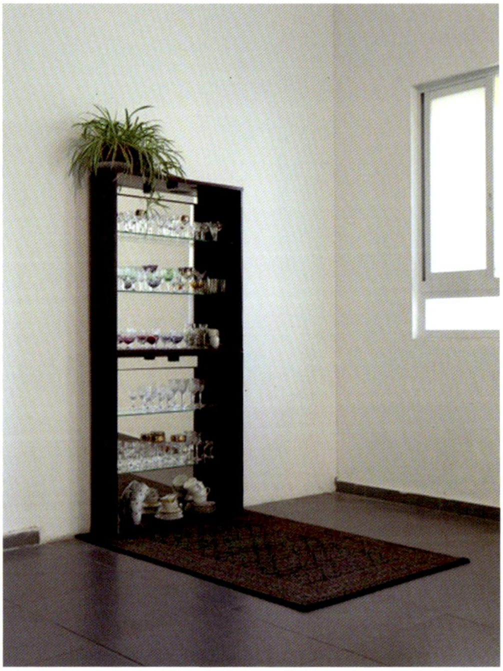

Grandmother's Asleep originates from a childhood memory in which the noise from teenagers' cars with their subwoofer sound systems in the new neighborhood used to shake the precious china cabinet that belonged to the artist's grandmother. The sound used in this project comes from bass subwoofers hidden in the cabinet, which shake the carefully displayed crystal glass and china. The china cabinet, from a time in the past, is supposed to stand still in a confined space without being exposed to unexpected and uncontrollable forces, but in this work it acquires a second nature. The previously self-contained culture indoors (the china cabinet) is confronted and fused with elements of the outdoor environment.

Ori Levin

Tears Dry on Their Own

Bezalel Academy of Arts and Design

Tears Dry On Their Own is an installation of sound and animated tissue paper. The tissue paper, which signifies something personal and private is the vehicle of a mechanical choreography. The tissue paper trembles and moves around the floor, accompanied by sound taken from the "chick flicks", Hollywood melodramas from the 1940s and 1950s. These films, also known as "weepies", originated during World War II when men were drafted and the Hollywood industry realized it had to appeal to a new, largely female target audience. The music and the sound of sobbing heroines are taken from moments of dramatic climax. Like the professional weeper or the laugh track in television shows, the tissue paper outsources emotions as it trembles and dances around the floor. Cinema has been a pioneer in "artificially" generating emotions, and the automation of new technologies is following the same empowering tracks.

Doron Segal, Jenny Bahar, Shahar Yaacoby, Itay Kurgan

Organibanitzorani

HIT–Holon Institute of Technology

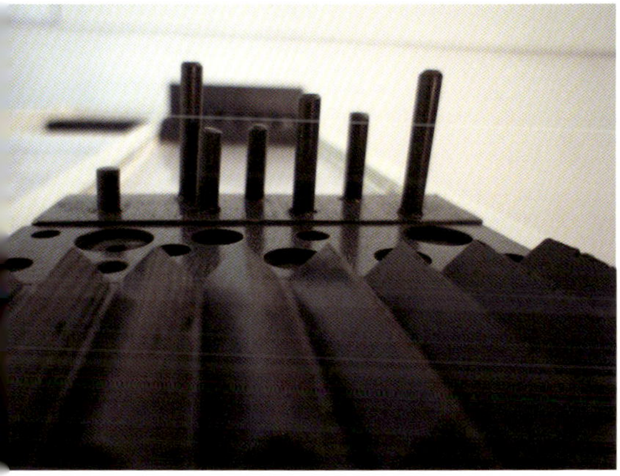

Organibanitzorani is an interaction that combines two familiar worlds, composing them into one: the physical world where every object has its own shape, weight and feel, and the world of sound, tangible yet lacking the immediacy of shapes. The interaction includes a rail on which the objects with different shapes are set. When arranging these objects on the rail, moving them back and forth creates consistent strips of sounds unique to each mix of objects. Because of the different shape, weight, and texture, connections are created between the object and the sound it produces. The system is based on RFID tags and a compatible sensor.

Liliana Farber

Mediocre

Hamidrasha School of Art

With data visualization, a logical follow-on of Big Data, a vast amount of information beyond the scope of human perception is clearly and effectively communicated through visual representation. Everything is compared now–things become transparent, even predictable. Within this mapping culture, questions of politics arise: Who is represented and how? Who is omitted? Which perspective is used? *Mediocre* appears to be a work of visualization. However, it aims in the opposite direction. The obstruction of Cognition is revealed by the work, which embodies the subjective perception of ambiguity and otherness experienced in this flooded data society. The titles chosen for the images–all relating to the history of Israel–were researched using the Google image search engine, and comment on how the information giants influence the way we construct our identities.

Lila Chitayat, Alon Chitayat, Shalom Amira

The House of the Un-happy

HIT- Holon Institute of Technology,
Bezalel Academy of Art and Design

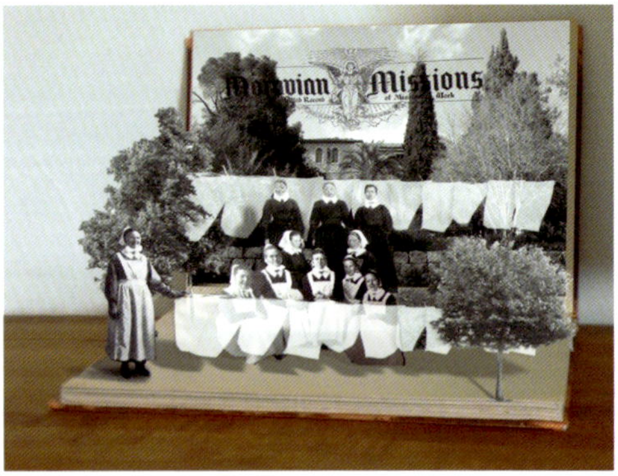

The House of the Un-happy presents fragmented memories of the old Hansen Hospital located in Jerusalem. Established in 1887 as the "Jesus Hilfe Asyl", it functioned as an open institute for leper patients till 2002, formulating a stable, transparent barrier with the neighboring society. A series of illustrated pop-up books show archived photos and texts taken from the day-to-day life as theatrical stage set scenes. With a double exposure experience using AR technology, we awaken the stories and memories of the place. Referring to the idea of heterotopic space, the hospital was based on social mechanisms of exclusion and isolation that were directed towards the leprous. This work offers, through the mediation of technology, a new emotional sphere being exposed through an intimate and personal contemplation.

Itamar Gilon, Noam Gefen, Omri Sass, Ran Snir, Sharon Heller

StreetBeat

Media Innovation Lab (miLAB) at IDC Herzliya

StreetBeat offers cultural mapping of different locations in an urban environment through patterns in the way people listen to music on their personal phones. It collects, maps and visualizes the music listened to on city streets. The *StreetBeat* mobile app senses what music is played on the phone and registers it anonymously with the server, tagging its location. Switching to the map view, users can explore new music, played by others who were there before.

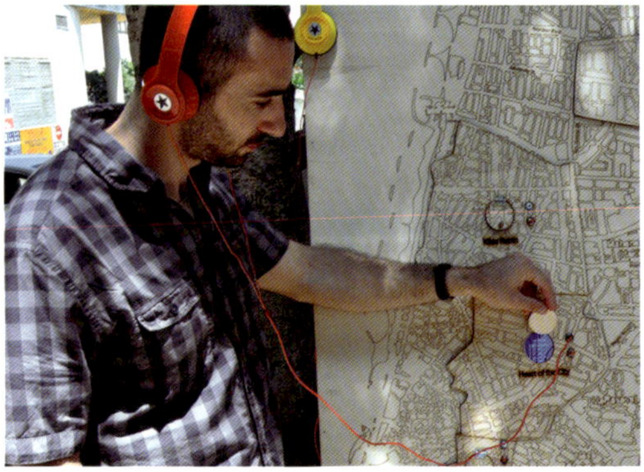

Performances

Eran Hadas, Batt-Girl, Dganit Elyakim

May b Att&ing (May be Attending) Turing Dames

Kibbutzim College of Art & Education, Tel-Aviv

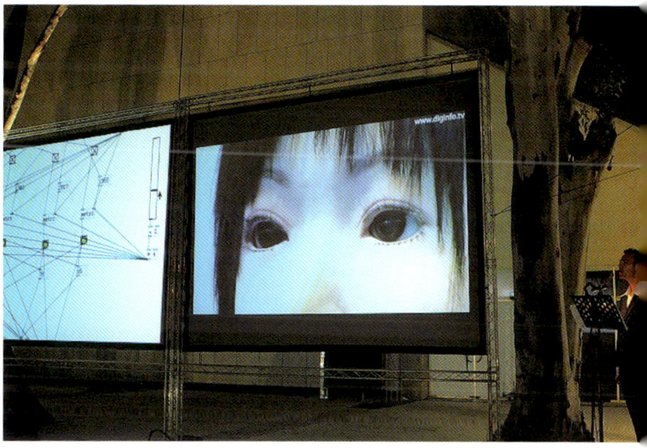

An interactive web-based opera—a virtual journey that traces fears stemming from the influence of technology, inspired by Brecht's educational plays *He Said Yes* and *He Said No*. The work incorporates materials drawn from virtual environments, such as prophetic texts dealing with the future of mankind on the web, images and animations. The opera is performed as a live show that is accompanied by music composed in real time by a computer. In the course of the plot, the audience is asked to decide between total devotion to technology or renunciation of it.

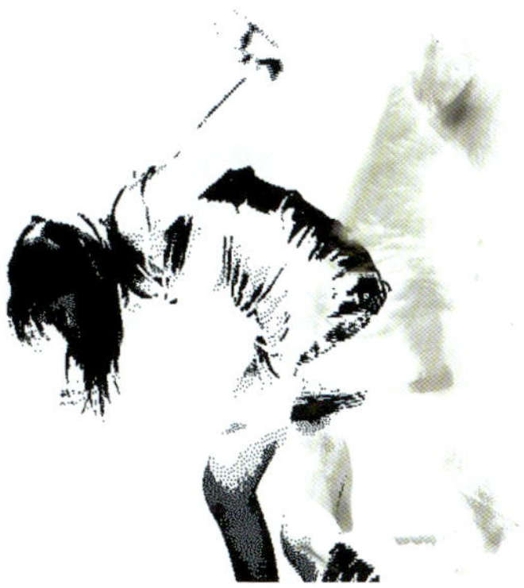

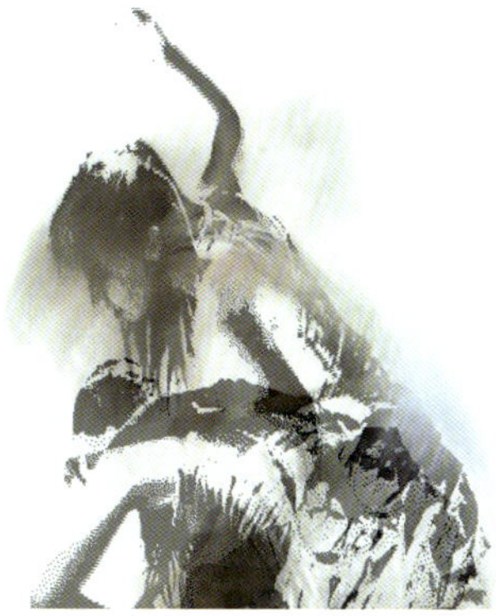

Racheli Dantess and Shimrit Paltin

DropArt Interactive

Kibbutzim College of Art & Education, Tel-Aviv

DropArt is an interactive performance that blurs the boundaries between dance and technology. The dancer's movements are composed in real time into a virtual image that is manipulated through time filters and is projected to move on stage together with the dancer. The resulting effect undermines the perception of both time and of the correspondence among the dancer's motion and the expected physical response of the passive environment. The mediation brings something else to life, a sort of *élan vital* of "things" and shadows, a new ghost in the machine. The crescendo of movements generates a dynamic space of temporal transience and of cyclical interactions between the dancer and her own randomly recomposed sequences, between the present and a chaotic arrow of time (entropy), between a machine and the subtle glitches in the audience perceptions.

Workshops

Shaul Tzemach

Video Mapping and 3D integration Workshop

Kibbutzim College of Art & Education, Tel-Aviv

The workshop introduces generative techniques and ways to integrate three-dimensional installations for real-time video mapping. The sessions on the Ars Campus will aim to build an actual video installation for a chosen architectural building in Linz. We will be using vvvv–free software with a powerful community of users, together with a variety of methods to manipulate objects in three-dimensional environments and interactive tools.

Two 4-hour sessions

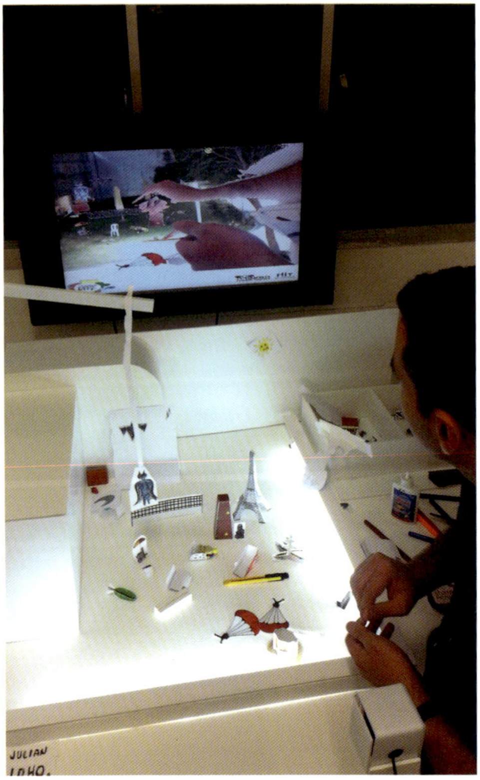

Racheli Inbal Cohen, Julian Ruiz, Nitsan Hoorgin

Design your campus

HIT–Holon Institute of Technology

Design your campus is a station that allows students, lecturers and all campus daily visitors to express their concrete wishes as to how their campus should look. The user encounters a white, half open "box", a collection of miniature objects and some papers, scissors and markers for creating customized miniature objects. When an object is placed in the "box", a screen shows the area intended for redesign in real-life, augmented with the objects. The ease of use of this seemingly playful workshop, where the augmentation imagines possible remakes of a space for us, opens the discussion to all interested users, adults and children, professionals and non-professionals. Who should be designing the habitats we use?

Ilan Green

Circuit Bending & Hardware Hacking

Musrara School

Circuit Bending & Hardware Hacking plays the antithesis of computer use. Instead of working in front of the screen with the accuracy dictated by the machine, one learns how to take apart the messy backstage of electronic toys, to rewire circuits in order to expand their capabilities, and transform what was a simple toy into a creative and original musical instrument. Step by step, the workshop explores how these toys are built and how to find their unexpected sounds, hidden where the manufacturer would have never thought. The workshop does not require any previous knowledge, just a few basic tools and a few old electronic toys.

Workshop duration 3–4 hours.

Eran Weissenstern

A hands-on workshop for building hands-off experiences PrimeSense 101

Bezalel Academy of Arts and Design

The *PrimeSense*[1] workshop on the ARS campus aims to teach participants to build their own new hands-off gaming experiences.

The four-hour workshop will include playing with some awesome *PrimeSense* demonstrations, a hands-on introduction session, a hacking competition and the presentation of the results. Basic coding experience is required for participation.

Workshop Master—Eran Weissenstern *(PrimeSense* veteran developer)

1 *PrimeSense* is the leading company in 3D sensing technology (powering the original Xbox 360 Kinect).

Yair Reshef

I'm a brave robot [brvrbt]

Shenkar College of Engineering and Design

During the workshop participants will build primitive bots that possess synthetic emotions. These animated "life-likes" help realize a thought experiment put forth by Valentino Braitenberg on the subject of synthetic psychology and cybernetics. The workshop begins with physical exercises using sensory deprivation to simulate the limiting world that bots perceive/react to. Our bots do not use binary logic, keeping circuitry analog in the B.E.A.M robotic spirit—a base responsive/exploratory nervous system.

Workshop duration 3–4 hours + open table.

Use at your own risk

Interface Cultures at Ars Electronica 2013

University of Art and Design Linz (Kunstuniversität Linz)

Use at your own risk is an allusion to a commonly used disclaimer text, warning the potential user of a certain software or hardware circuit that its makers cannot made responsible for any possible use or misuse of their inventions. When developing prototypes, the authors usually have to evaluate the potential risk or threat that their device or installation poses to the visitors within a public exhibition, which may lead to limitations of its overall use that eventually constrain the full potential of all interaction possibilities. Nevertheless the risk factor is an entire part of the making and design of novel interfaces and devices that are in direct contact with the visitors, which cannot just be ignored. This warning title reminds the spectators that experimental artworks are no exception to that rule.

Faculty: Christa Sommerer, Laurent Mignonneau, Martin Kaltenbrunner, Michaela Ortner, Marlene Hochrieser, Georg Russegger

Use at your own risk lehnt sich an die übliche Formulierung von Haftungsausschlüssen an, die potenzielle Anwender einer Software oder eines Geräts darüber belehrt, dass der Hersteller in keinem Fall für etwaige Schäden haftbar gemacht werden kann. Die Entwickler von Prototypen müssen das Risiko oder die Gefahr abschätzen, die ihre Erfindung oder Installation für Besucher einer öffentlichen Ausstellung birgt, was unter Umständen die Gesamtnutzung einschränken und letztendlich dazu führen kann, dass das volle Potenzial der Interaktionsmöglichkeiten nicht ausgeschöpft werden darf. Dennoch ist die Risikoabschätzung ein nicht zu ignorierender Bestandteil bei der Entwicklung und Herstellung von neuartigen, für den direkten Kontakt mit Besuchern gedachten Interfaces und Geräten. Dieser Warnhinweis soll den Betrachter daran erinnern, dass auch experimentelle Kunstwerke keine Ausnahme von dieser Regel darstellen.

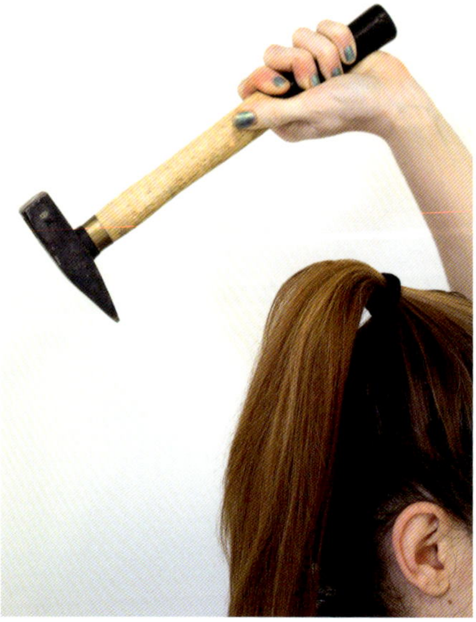

Isidora Ficovic

Think Pink

This interactive video installation uses the qualitative research method of taking interviews in the streets of Linz. The public was asked the question "Which tool would you use to destroy a desktop?" The most common answer was "the hammer".
The public decided the hammer should become the non-verbal communication tool. By hitting with the hammer the visitor of the exhibition triggers videos that are showing the interviews. Embedded sensors randomly open different videos, but only one is the key to the *Think Pink* when the monitor color changes to pink.

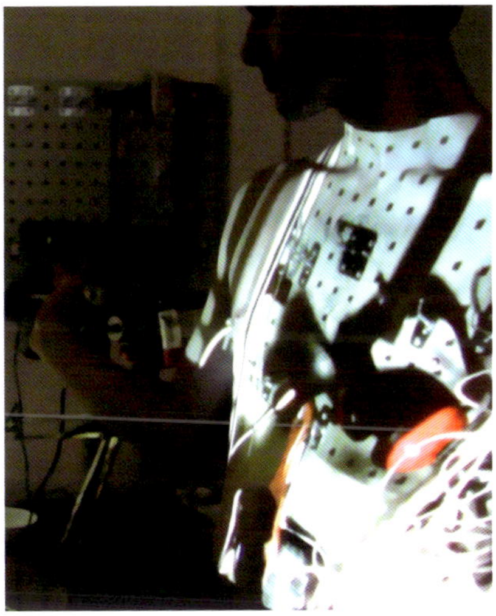

Mihaela Kavdanska

4th Skin

The *4th Skin* project visualizes what we see, touch or reflect. It is the "skin" created by our whole body & mind experience and our relations with the world around. This interactive audio-visual piece has a strong performative and site-specific component. The relations between the performer and the surroundings result in the form of ephemeral multimedia garment. The video content is created live according to the performers' explorations with mobile filming devices: their presence in a given space, bodies, movements, actions, textures, these all become part of the dynamic garment. By acting in one way or another, the performer changes the garment's content. The captured video footage is projected on the performer's body using custom-developed video tracking & video mapping solution. The *4th Skin* is a comment on the subjects of ephemerality, transience and impermanence. It reflects the sense-based exchange between oneself and the world around.

Programming by Cristian Iordache; Sound by Sorin Paun aka Randomform;
Performers: Dolma Jover Agullo & Luis Gonzaga Hoyos. A project co-produced by KOTKI visuals

Ivan Petkov

A Day In A Life

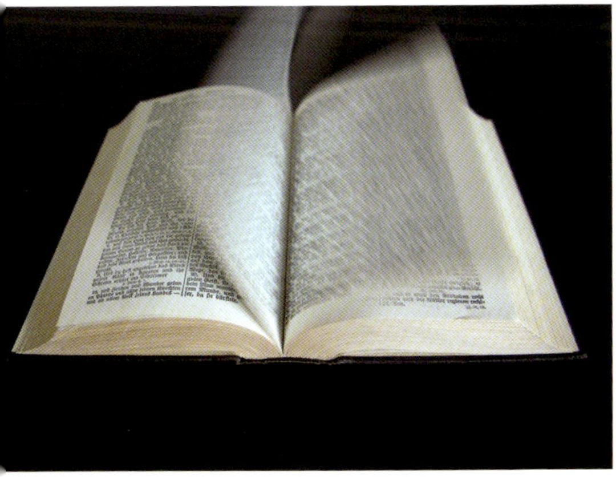

"Suffering makes you live time in detail, moment after moment." E.M. Cioran, *The New Gods*. Starting at sunrise, the pages of an empty book are turned by an airflow. At midday, the amount of the pages that have been turned roughly equals the ones that are still left. At sunset, the end of the book is reached. An unexpected usage of a book takes place in this installation. It is blank, but can still be read. In an intuitive way, without the torturous precision of the signs and by the invisible power of the wind. It reveals the time passed since the morning and the time left till dusk. It is reminiscent of a bygone era in which the active life was restricted to the daytime hours.

Veronika Krenn, Vesela Mihaylova

Acidable

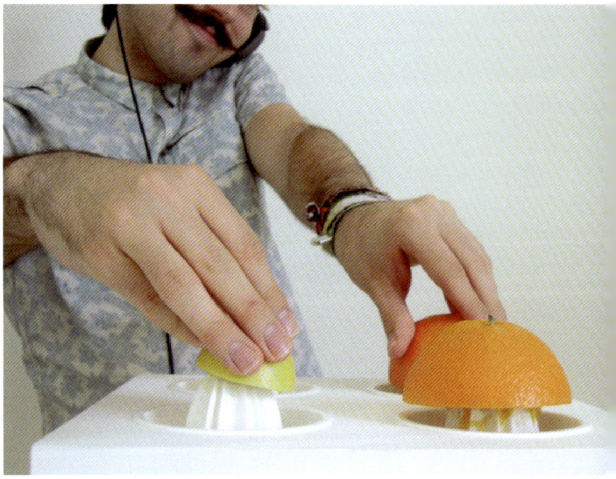

The *Acidable* is an interactive turntable and orange squeezer at the same time. Based on the familiar movement of manually squeezing a piece of citrus fruit, the interaction with the *Acidable* reaches a new level of playful experience. Depending on the pH value of the freshly pressed citrus juice, the machine creates a rhythm, and the music is modified by the motion of squeezing the fruit.
This work is an interactive experiment to bring back food production into our daily life. The visitor is invited to try out the new playful device and enjoy the freshly pressed orange juice.

Alessio Chierico

Arnulf Rainer for digital performers, concert version

Arnulf Rainer for digital performers is a reenactment from the composition *Arnulf Rainer* by Peter Kubelka, which creates its visual aesthetic from the essence of the cinematic image: light and its variations. Like digital systems, it comprises solely a binary alternation of light and no light. The storyboard is a composition that appears like a digital sequence. *Arnulf Rainer for digital performers* is based on a software that analyzes a remade composition of Peter Kubelka in real time, in order to extract the status (black or white) for each frame. Afterwards the main computer, metaphorically seen as the director, sends the status to a device ensemble meant as players, in order to perform the composition. Their interpretation becomes the real performance, which underlines the visual property of each performer. *Arnulf Rainer for digital performers* is a concert played by visual media that propose a contemporary aesthetic of the original score.

Oliver Kellow

Digital HourGlass

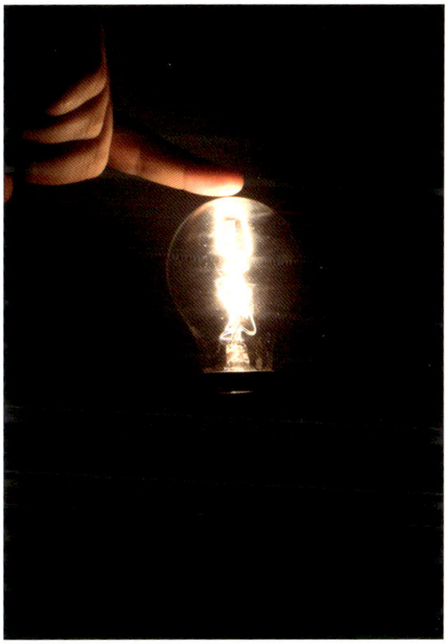

The *Digital HourGlass* is an abstracted hourglass form set in granite and extending an antenna towards the sky. Like sands running to the lower bulb, the *Digital HourGlass* will change states when the upper bulb expires. The viewer may touch the frame of the hourglass, changing the power configuration and increasing the stress on the bulb. Symbolically, it represents the consciously marked passage of time and energy, providing no reference point to gauge the amount of time or energy remaining or previously spent. The only known value is that as a physical and familiar device it must degrade and expire, the moment of transition is pure serendipity, unpredictable to both the author and the viewer. This consciousness of time, energy and decay is accentuated by the physicality of the high-consumption, antiquated Edison bulbs used. It is a simple reminder that although time and energy is always flowing, we have the opportunity and the capability to use it or alter its path.

whoun (a.k.a. Juan Cedenilla)

240313:Bit-Poems

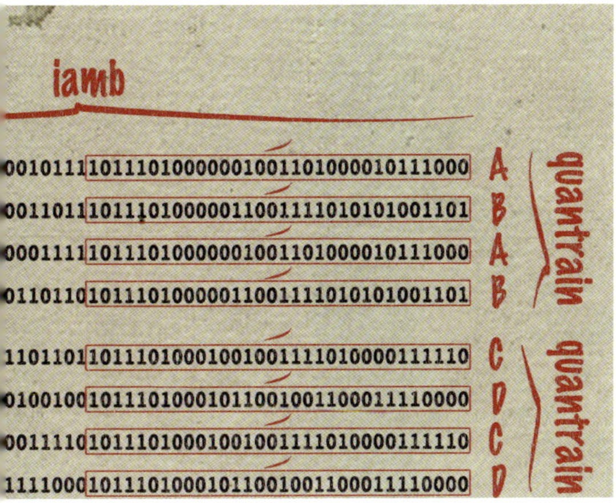

240313:Bit-Poems is a collection of several poems and a possible visualization of each of them. These bit-poems are created by rules of poetry applied to bits. The contemporary world demands a different way of perceiving the digital aesthetic. For this reason, this project aims to transfer a concept of the non-digital world to the digital world and observe the result. The starting point is something created by humans: poetry. One of the main goals of poetry is to communicate. The poetry form follows a series of rules and conditions. Communication, rules and conditions are the settings of a protocol in the digital world. Visualizing this protocol can create a better non-digital understanding of it. This allows us to explore and discover the result of the translation of such a concept.

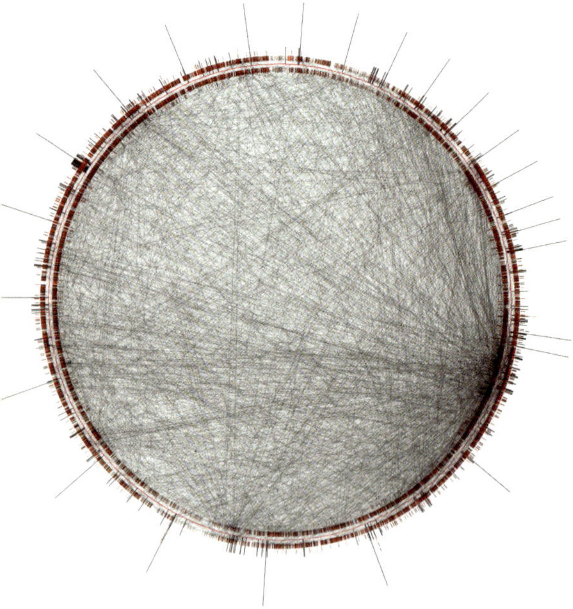

David Gann

Memories of the Future

The genome is the basic level of memory and contains the building plan for us as human beings. As we have begun to understand our genetic code and are more and more able to change it, it is time to think about and discuss the potential impact on future generations. In this work multiple users can explore an interactive audio-visual map of the human genome on a touchscreen. About 28,000 genes are positioned on a ring that represents the genome. The brightness stands for the expression level (how much gene product is produced) of a gene and the lines indicate the interaction between those. The genes are sonic grains on a long audio sample that contains many aspects of our culture and civilization. The user can associate his/her own audible memories with the sonification and gets a better spatial and relational understanding of the visualization. The user-interactions are recorded and the resulting data and musical compositions are published.

Science-Interactive.com, SymbioticCube.com

Jaak Kaevats

Street-Scape

Street-Scape is a contextual visualization of an urban environment. The walking direction of people in the street is plotted in one direction on the 5-minute timeline to make their relative distances between each other more apparent. The visualizations are rendered in a way that produces people walking 5km/h (average walking speed) with original proportions, everyone moving faster becomes thinner and everyone slower is mapped respectively wider. *Street-Scape* renders the captured people anonymous while revealing their demographic qualities such as their approximate age and gender. Thus, presenting the relative amount of children, grown-ups, older people, bikers, etc. in a particular location during the visualized time.

http://kaevats.org/street-scape

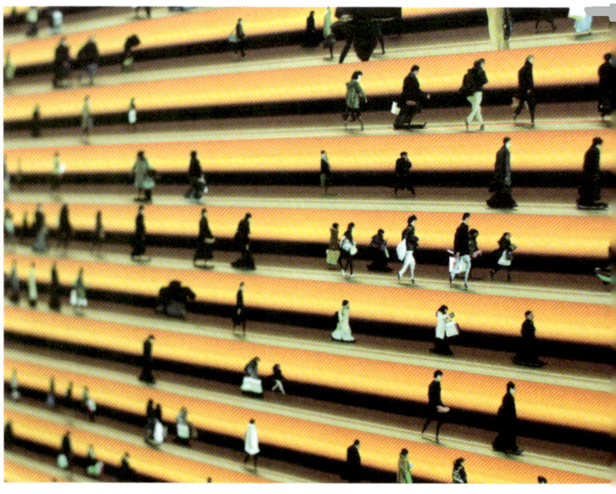

Marie Polakova, Veselina Dashinova, Jan Spurny

Micro Pets

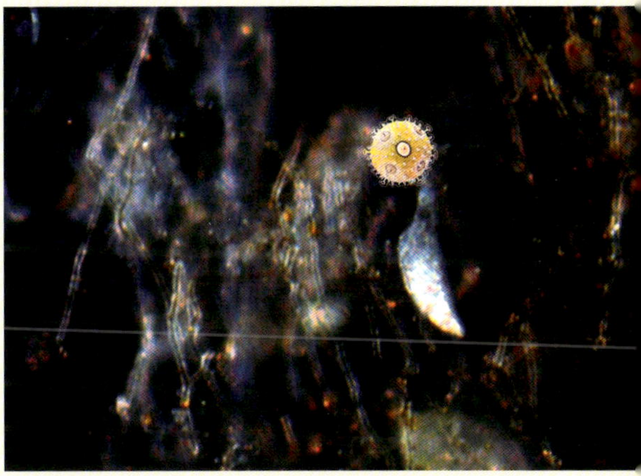

Have you ever thought that microscopic organisms could be something more then a scientific specimen or feared disease? Something you could care for and even grow to love? The *Micro Pets* project looks into the unthinkable, considering microbes of infinitesimal size as endearing and captivating creatures—as playful companions with personality and charm. The artists have addressed the difficult task of observing and understanding the natural behaviors of water microorganisms. Building on their practical and conceptual research, their aim is to design suitable nano toys for such creatures, together with "Micro Pet Lifestyle Accessories." The toys and accessories will be specially suited to the particular behavior and needs of each microorganism group. So far one can see a design of a toy and a digital simulation of the interaction between the *Micro Pets* and their toys. The next aim of the artists is to develop the design further and subsequently produce the toys.

Created at Interface Cultures Lab with support from the Ars Electronica Bio Lab.

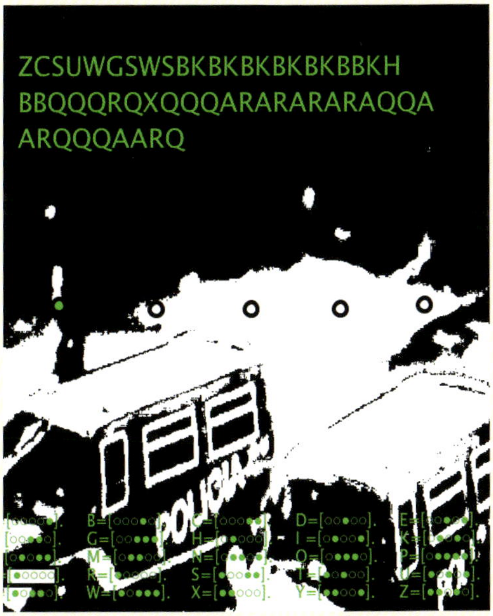

Cesar Escudero Andaluz

Random Readings

This media archeology project is based on the reinterpretation of an optical telecommunication device from 1787. It develops new interfaces (physical and graphic) by embedding current platforms such as webcams, telemonitoring systems, streaming channels or closed-circuit surveillance. The recognition system for video tracking detects the threshold color changes in five different points located on the image surface. The information collected in these five points is decoded to an alphabetic system. Finally the letters are printed on the surface of the screen together with the previous values obtained. The final result is shown as an interactive installation that combines situations in public spaces with social control factors.

http://escuderoandaluz.com

Chiara Esposito

The dream of flying

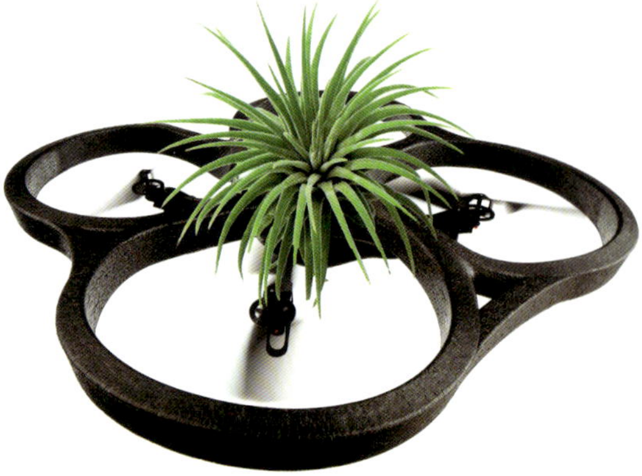

Sometimes a plant dreams of flying.
Usually we associate a plant with the ground and immobility. Movement is a feature of animals. Movements in plants are usually imperceptible and associated with growth or following the sun. Plants that are capable of rapid movements look like strange chimeras. Speed is not a feature of plants. But some plants indeed have an affinity with the air and the flight: some have no roots and get their nutrients from the air, others use the wind to let their seeds move quicker, or need the action of insects or birds to reproduce. Dandelions let their seeds fly gently, other plants spit them out like rockets. Every plant reacts to the environment in a different way. In the artwork *The dream of flying*, an interface enables a plant to control a body extension: a small flying device. The interface measures the electrical activity of the plant and uses the gathered data to control the flight. The plant works here as an actor and a sensor, creating an open system in which visitors and the environment are actively participating to influence the pattern of the flying device.

Alberto Boem

Sculpton

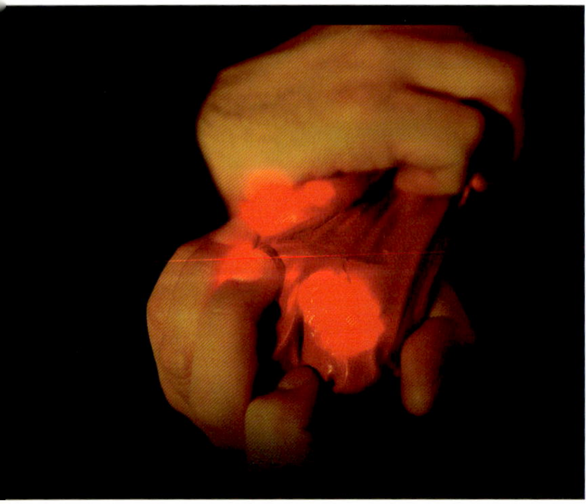

Sculpton is a malleable sonic object that uses the metaphor of sound sculpting for connecting physical information in digital audio. By manipulating the object the user can literally sculpt the sound through a real-time sound synthesis that reverberates the object structure. *Sculpton* is an attempt to develop a new kind of digital musical instruments that combines multidimensional control, tangible and malleable characteristics with organic handling. This quality has an intimate relation with the sound production: the user shapes the sound by molding the object. Beyond the idea of control, *Sculpton* represents a sonic object that promotes physical effort and engagement with musical and non-musical characteristics. *Sculpton* is an interface for musicians and performers strongly based on the idea of exploration and improvisation, a tool for composing electronic music on stage.

Nina Mengin

Suppenbrunzer

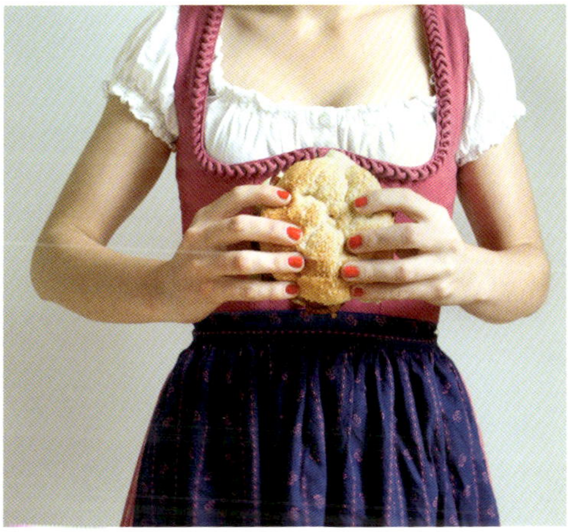

The communicative and ritual aspects of eating undergo continuous changes. Fast food and convenience food have radically changed our eating behavior. One of the consequences is that individual snacks replace ritual meals within a family. Even if we eat high quality foods, we still lack the time for a proper meal. The installation quotes a traditional Austrian dining table, but it is squeezed in between walls and can only be used by one person at a time. Snacks are available next to it, and they have to be placed on the table to activate the *Suppenbrunzer* and start the interaction. The whole procedure only takes a few seconds, in this way the *Suppenbrunzer* adapts to the prevalent food culture.

Davide Bevilacqua

Zuerst kommt das Fressen, dann kommt die Moral

Vegetarians, optimized production, low-calories drinks, bio-fast-naturally colored dishes. We are surrounded by different foods, symbols of cultures and fashions. Food has always played a central role in social gatherings, as a cultural sign and a collective ritual. Each event has indeed its own type of refreshment: wedding breakfasts, buffets, brunches. This buffet provides the suitable refreshments for the Interface Cultures' exhibition at the Ars Electronica Festival. The audience will enjoy a buffet made of experimental dishes and drinks. There will be original and collected recipes, some of them are close to the molecular kitchen, others to the DIY community. The selection follows a research led by curiosity, lust for experimenting with food, discovering how ingredients react with each other and trying out new tastes and forms for usual dishes.

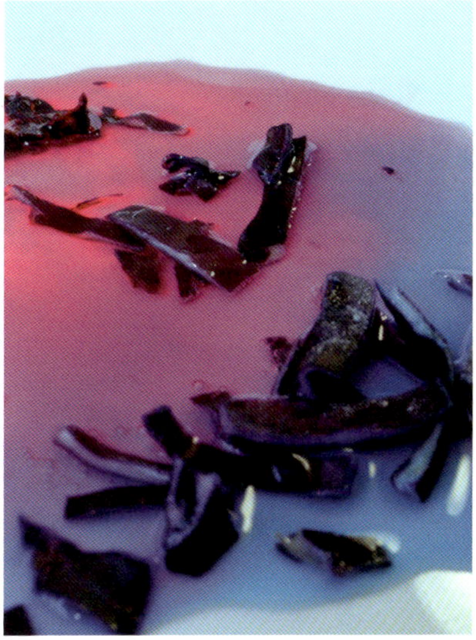

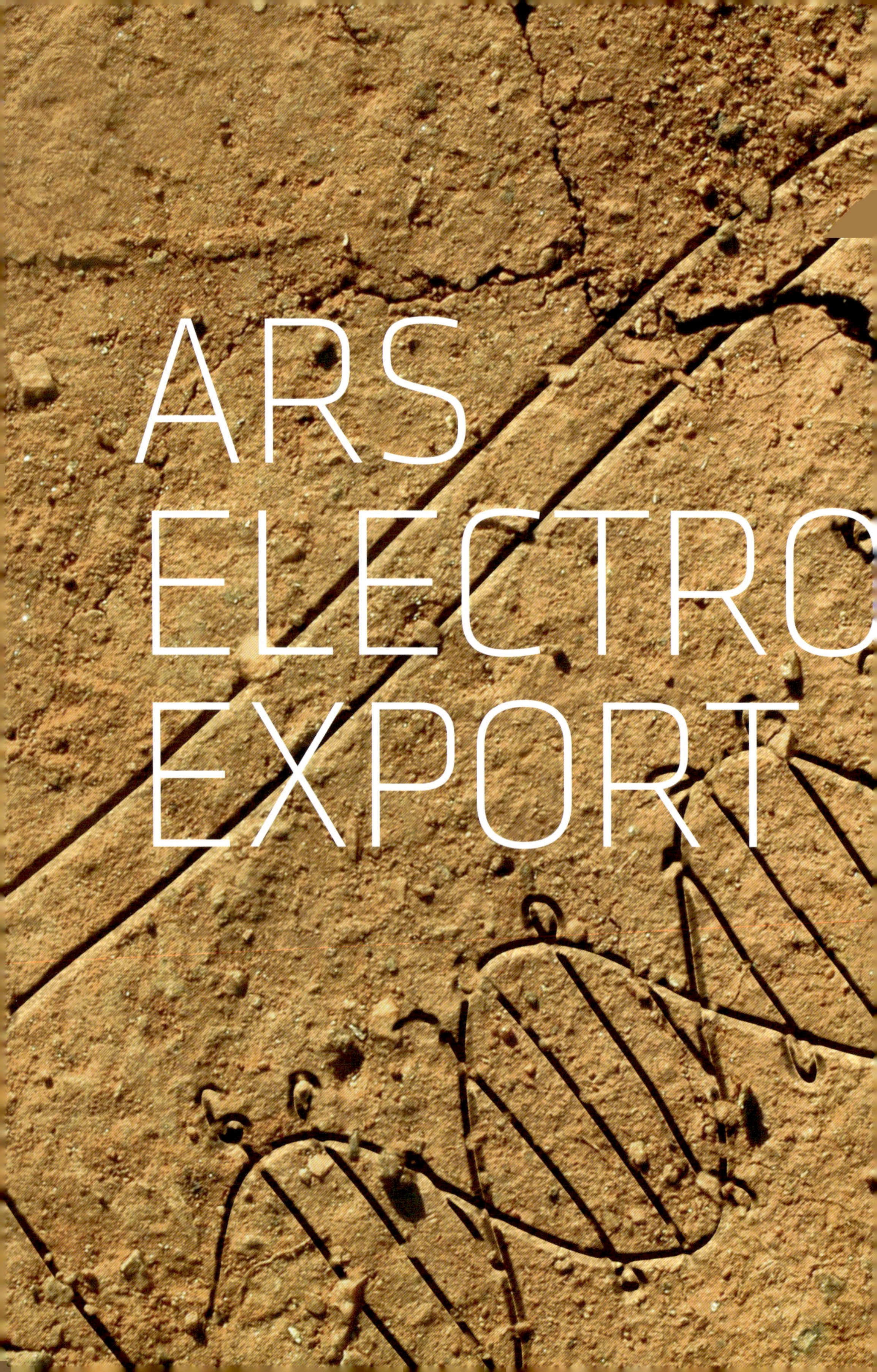
ARS
ELECTRO
EXPORT

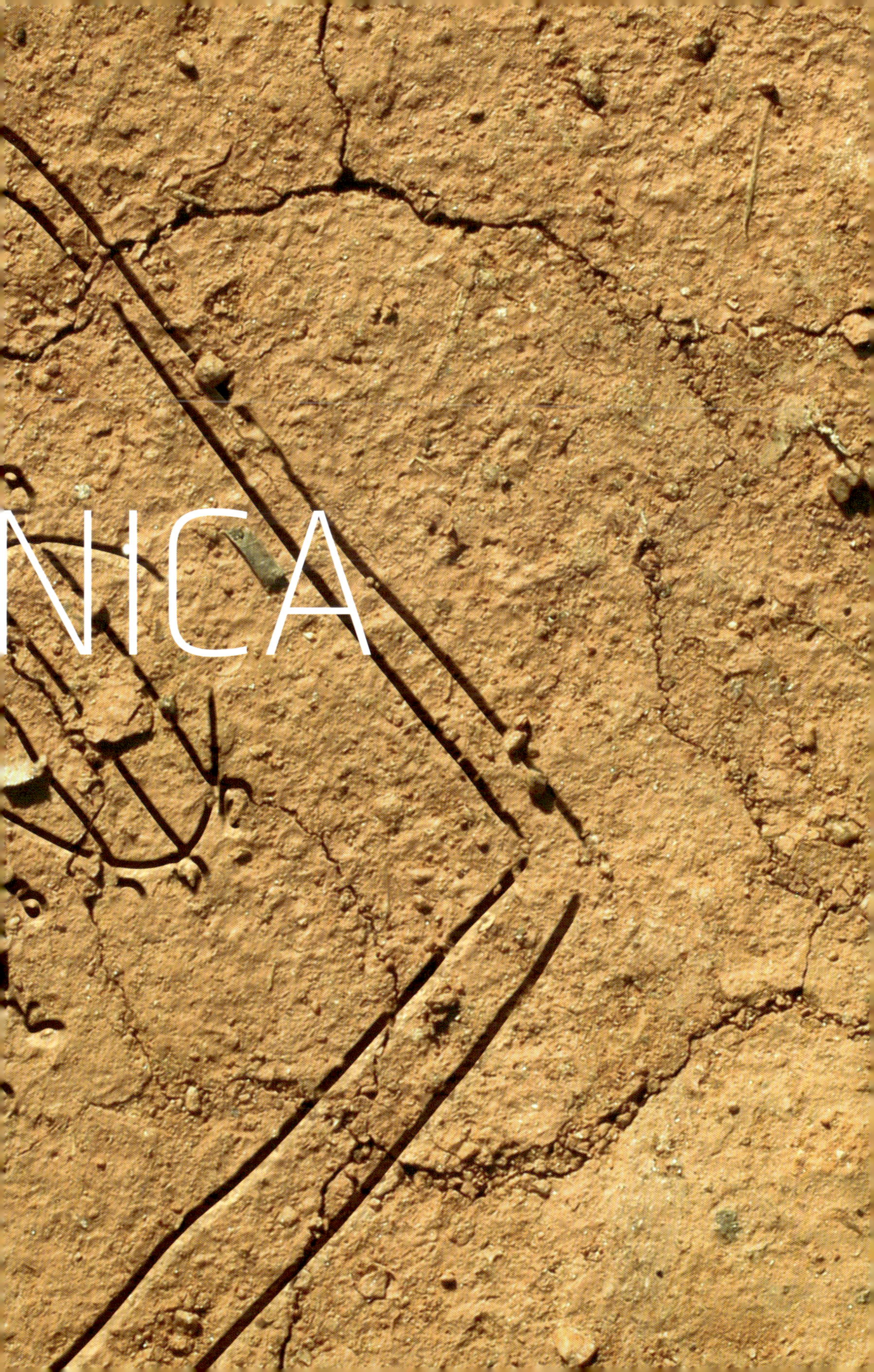
NICA

Ars Electronica Export
External Exhibitions 2012/2013

Since 2004 in response to strong international demand, Ars Electronica has developed numerous exhibitions jointly with partner institutions all over the world. Each and every exhibition was customized for the particular venue and staged in collaboration with the host institution.
Among the latest international exhibition projects are:

Seit dem Jahr 2004 hat Ars Electronica aufgrund der hohen internationalen Nachfrage gemeinsam mit internationalen Partnern zahlreiche Ausstellungen entwickelt. Jede einzelne dieser Ausstellungen wurde speziell für den Ort und gemeinsam mit den gastgebenden Institutionen zusammengestellt.
Zu den jüngsten internationalen Ausstellungsprojekten zählen:

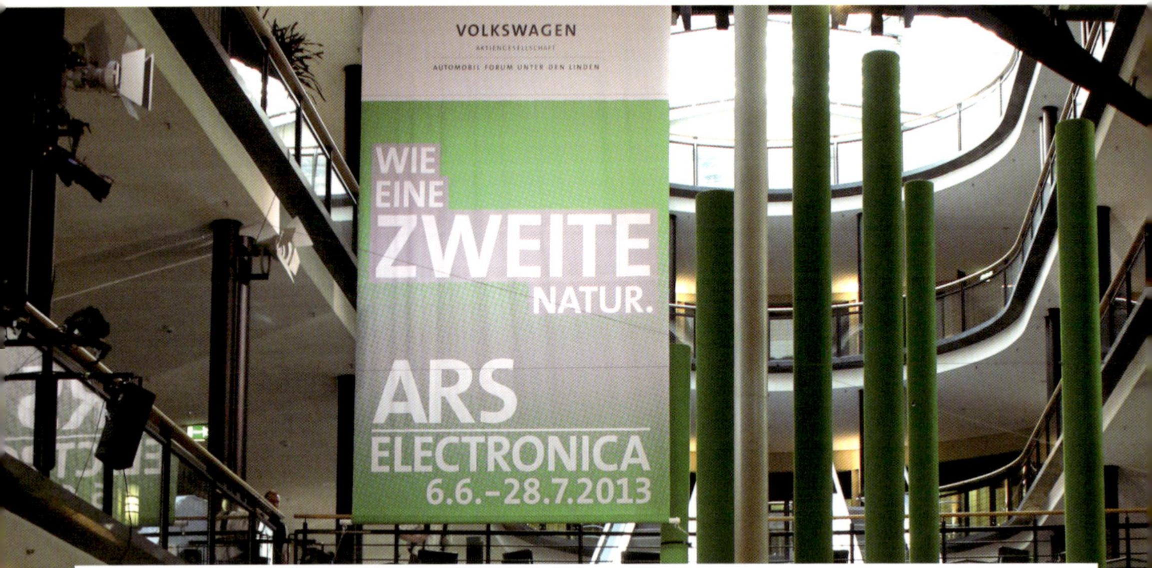

Ars Electronica – Wie eine zweite Natur

Automobil Forum Unter den Linden der Volkswagen AG
Berlin, 06.06.–28.07.2013

This fourth exhibition staged jointly by Volkswagen Automobil Forum Unter den Linden and Ars Electronica Linz scrutinizes the determinative elements in this process' past, present and future—those factors that enable us to become cognizant of what is natural and artificial in everyday life, to experience those two and differentiate between them. Artistic works, perspectives and positions selected from the media art network of the Prix Ars Electronica, the world's most prestigious and highest endowed prize honoring excellence in media art, underscore the tremendous relevance

Im Rahmen des vierten gemeinsamen Ausstellungsprojekts von Volkswagen Automobil Forum Unter den Linden und Ars Electronica Linz dreht sich alles um die Frage, was historisch, gegenwärtig und zukünftig jene bestimmenden Faktoren waren, sind und sein werden, die Natürliches und Künstliches im alltäglichen Leben erkennbar, erlebbar und unterscheidbar machen. Künstlerische Arbeiten, Perspektiven und Positionen aus dem Medienkunstnetzwerk des Prix Ars Electronica unterstreichen dabei einerseits die Relevanz dieser Fragestellung und beleuchten andererseits deren alltäglichen Auswirkungen.

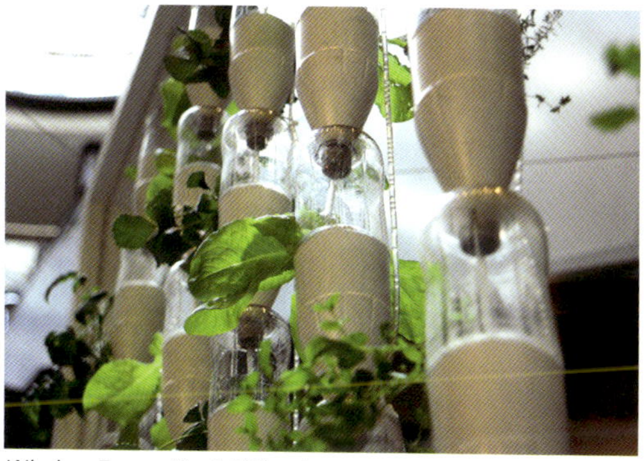

Window Farms, Daniel Warnke

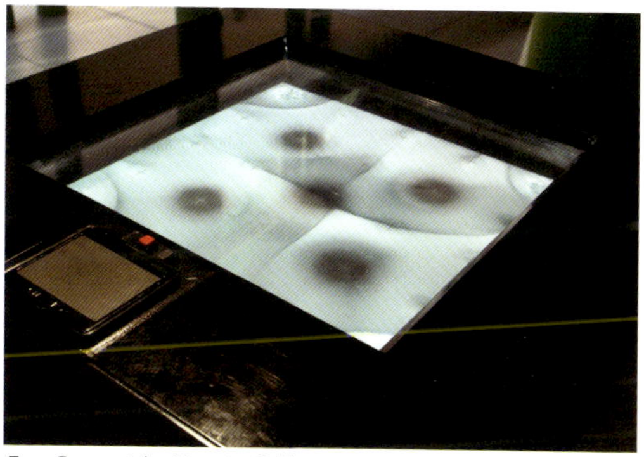

Ene-Geometrix, Masato Sekine

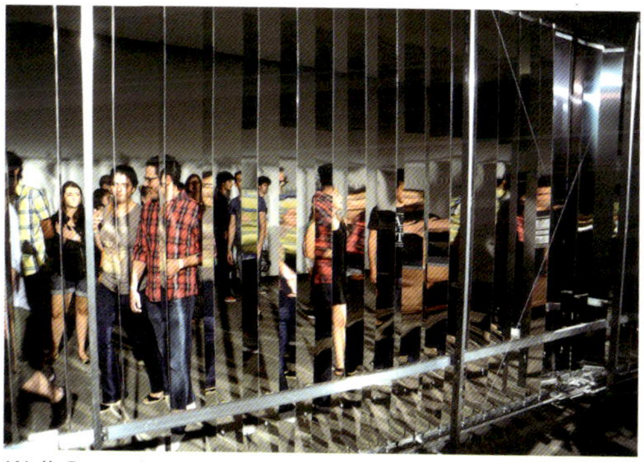

Wall, Cantoni/Crescenti

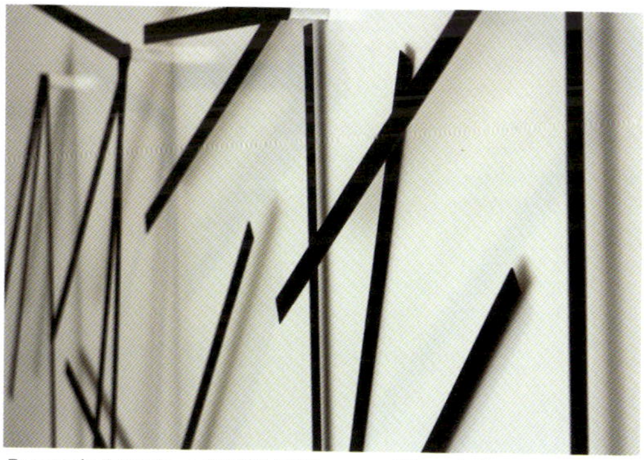

Dynamic Structure 291117, Willem van Weeghel

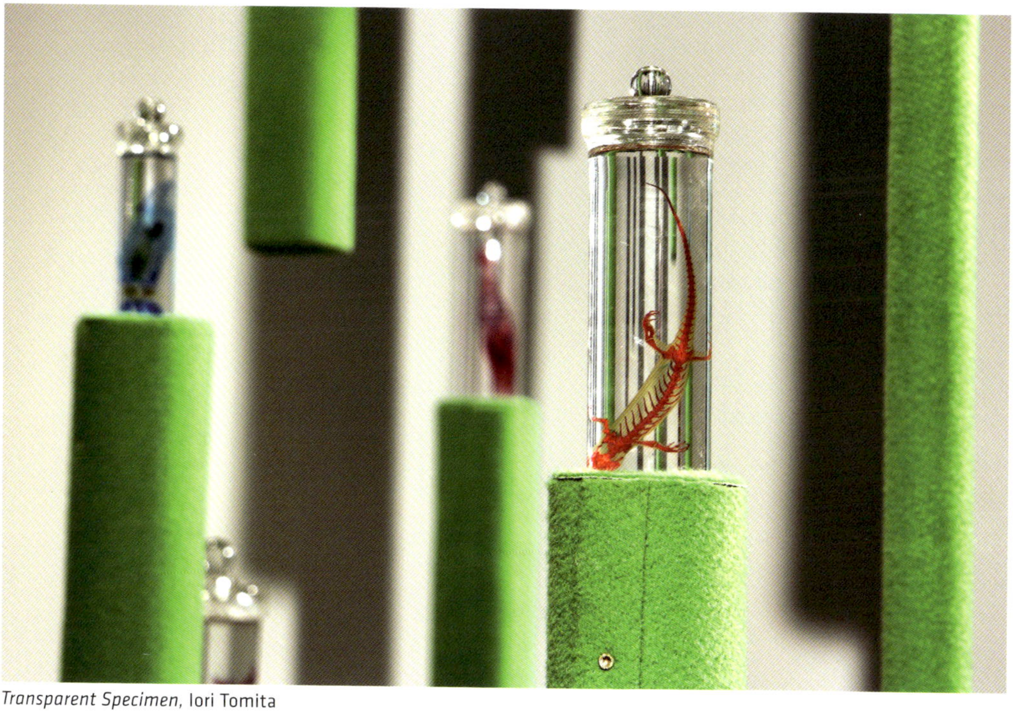

Transparent Specimen, Iori Tomita

of investigating this issue and likewise shed light on its multifarious effects on everyday life.
Each of 15 works of art uniquely manifests various approaches and associations. This show illustrates the wide array of roles artists assume, of themes their concepts and configurations encompass, of unconventional ways they choose to relate their narratives. What also becomes evident over the course of this encounter is a new type of artist, one characterized by a high level of substantive competence—which is to say artistic, scientific and sociopolitical capacities—and, with respect to art's role, one who keeps the big picture in mind.
Like a Second Nature is an exhibition produced by Ars Electronica in two site-specific variants running at Volkswagen's Automobil Forum Unter den Linden venue in Berlin and at the Ars Electronica Center in Linz.

Insgesamt fünfzehn künstlerische Arbeiten bieten unterschiedliche Zugänge und Assoziationen an. Die Schau zeigt, in welche Rollen KünstlerInnen schlüpfen, um welche Themen ihre Gedanken und Arbeiten kreisen und auf welch unkonventionelle Weise sie ihre Geschichten oftmals erzählen. Sichtbar wird dabei auch ein neuer Typ von KünstlerIn, der von sehr hoher inhaltlicher – genauer: künstlerischer, wissenschaftlicher, gesellschaftspolitischer – Kompetenz geprägt ist und der stets die Rolle der Kunst insgesamt im Auge hat.
Ars Electronica hat mit *Wie eine zweite Natur* eine Ausstellung entwickelt, die in ortspezifisch modifizierten Varianten im Automobil Forum Unter den Linden der Volkswagen AG in Berlin und im Ars Electronica Center in Linz zu sehen ist.

Earth Core-Laboratory and Elf-Scan (2003–2004), Agnes Meyer-Brandis
Dynamic Structure 291117 (2007 – 2010), Willem van Weeghel
Blinking Leaves (2003), Yasuhiro Suzuki
Plant (2010), Akira Nakayasu
The Limitations of Logic and the Absence of absolute Certainty (2008), Alistair McClymont
Wall (2012), Cantoni/Crescenti
Phantasm (2006), Takahiro Matsuo
Ene-Geometrix (2007), Masato Sekine
Prototype for a New Biomachine (2012), Ivan Henriques
Oribotics (2010), Matthew Gardiner
Window Farms (2012), Daniel Warnke
Transparent Specimen (2012), Iori Tomita
Meter Crawler (2008 – 2013), Keiko Takahashi
Tele-Present Wind (2010), David Bowen
Ars Wild Card, a project by Ars Electronica (Hideaki Ogawa, Emiko Ogawa, Manuela Naveau)

This exhibition was produced jointly by Ars Electronica and Volkswagen Aktiengesellschaft
Automobil Forum Unter den Linden, Konzernforum Berlin; director: Cornelia Schneider.
Curators: Martin Honzik, Gerfried Stocker / Ars Electronica Linz
Ars Electronica Production Crew: head of production: Michael Lettner; technical management: Karl Julian Schmidinger; project management: Stephanie Fuchs; communication: Veronika Liebl, Manuela Naveau
Ars Electronica Production Team Berlin: Memetics GmbH – Michael Badics, Berlin representative of Ars Electronica Linz GmbH
Assembly Crew: Gregor Göttfert, Simon Kopfberger, Johannes Ramsl, Raffael Wallner
Architecture: Anytime Architekten – Jürgen Haller, Christoph Weidinger, *http://any@any-time.net*

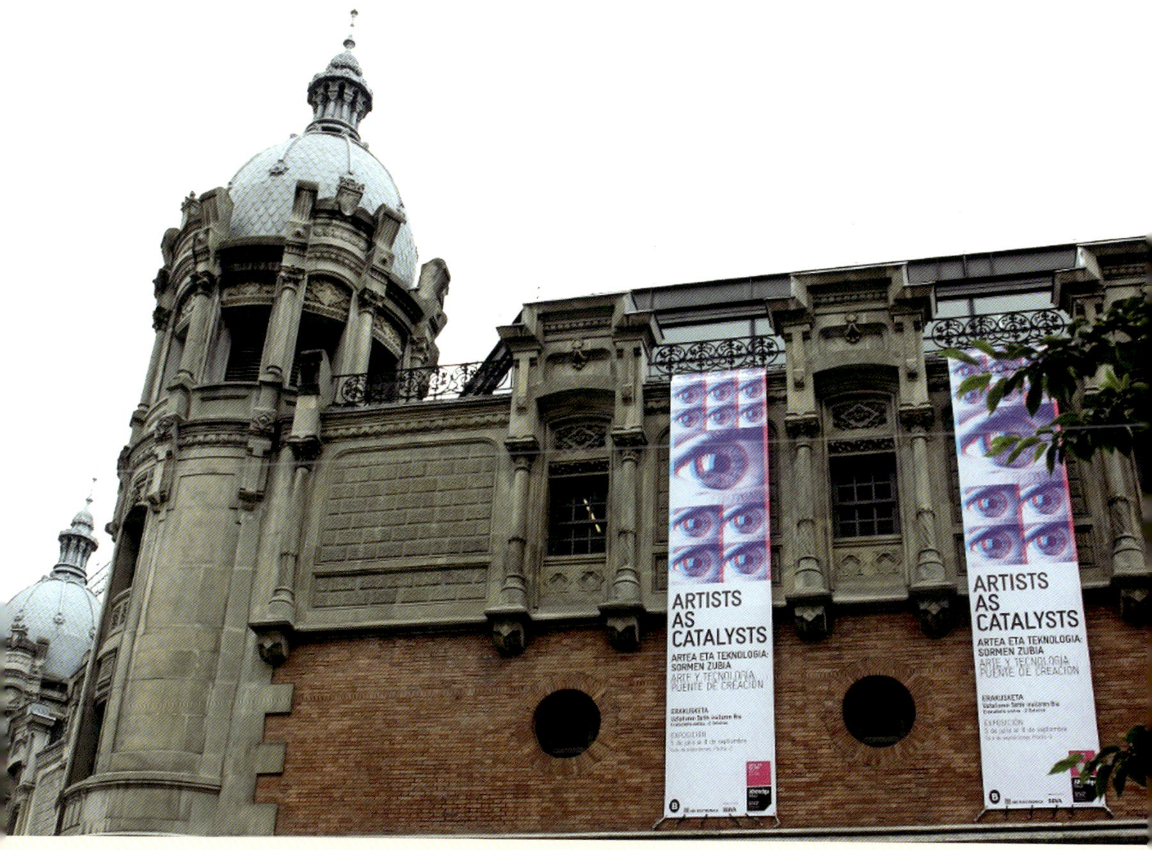

Artists as Catalysts

Alhóndiga Bilbao
Bilbao, 04.07. – 08.09.2013

"All artists are alike. They dream of doing something that's more social, more collaborative, and more real than art." (Dan Graham)

This insight inspired *Artists as Catalysts* and shaped the development of this exhibition at Alhóndiga Bilbao. In collaboration with Lourdes Fernández, director of the cultural institution that just underwent a Philippe Starck makeover, Ars Electronica has assembled a showcase of projects that endeavor to transcend conventional boundaries in an effort to inspire those who behold them.
The exhibition is subdivided into three themes:

- Environment and Sustainable Future
- Control and Manipulation of our Mediatized World
- Find Your Voice and Express Yourself

Thus, issues of pressing current relevance and matters that will also be of central importance to the future of our planet and our society.
The works on display here challenge our perceptions, affront and surprise us, call into question concepts

Dieser Satz war die Inspiration für die Ausstellung *Artists as Catalysts* in der Alhóndiga Bilbao.
Gemeinsam mit Lourdes Fernández, der Leiterin der eben erst von Philippe Starck renovierten Kulturinstitution, hat Ars-Electronica-Projekte zu einer Ausstellung zusammengestellt, die über konventionelle Grenzen hinausreichen und das Publikum in erster Linie inspirieren sollen.
Die Ausstellung kreist um drei zentrale Themen, die die Gegenwart und Zukunft unseres Planeten und unserer Gesellschaft bestimmen:

- Environment and Sustainable Future
- Control and Manipulation of our Mediatized World
- Find Your Voice and Express Yourself

Die gezeigten Werke fordern unsere Wahrnehmung heraus, stoßen uns vor den Kopf, hinterfragen Begriffe wie Privatsphäre und Öffentlichkeit, Überwachung und Kontrolle, erfassen natürliche und künstliche

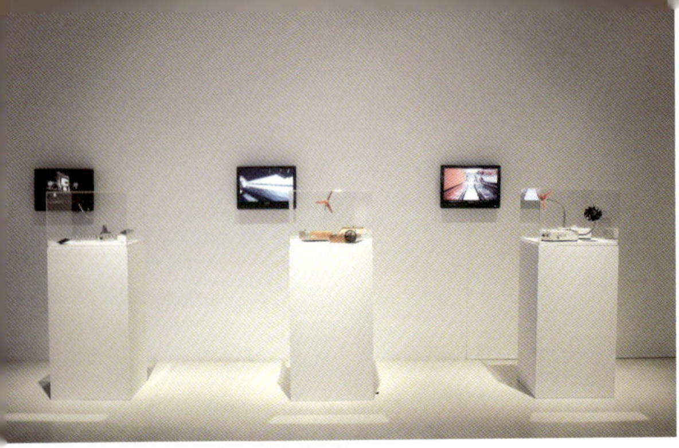
Energy Parasites, Eric Paulos

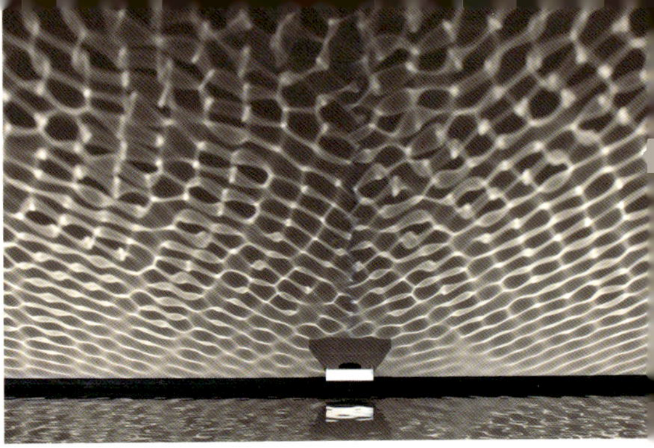
Earth, Finnbogi Pétursson

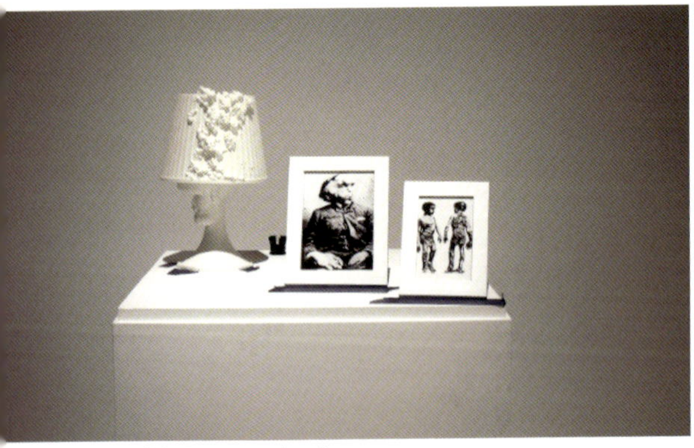
Merrick, Daan van den Berg

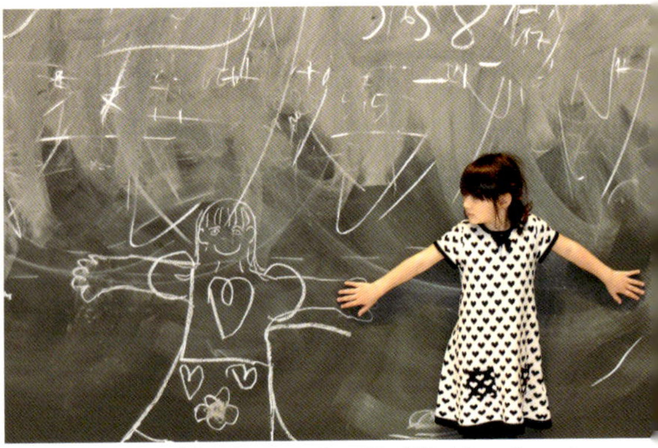
Think silent, act with noise, Josu Recalde, Mikel Arce Sagarduy, Enrike Hurtado Mendieta (ES)/EHU Zarata Lab, Bilbao

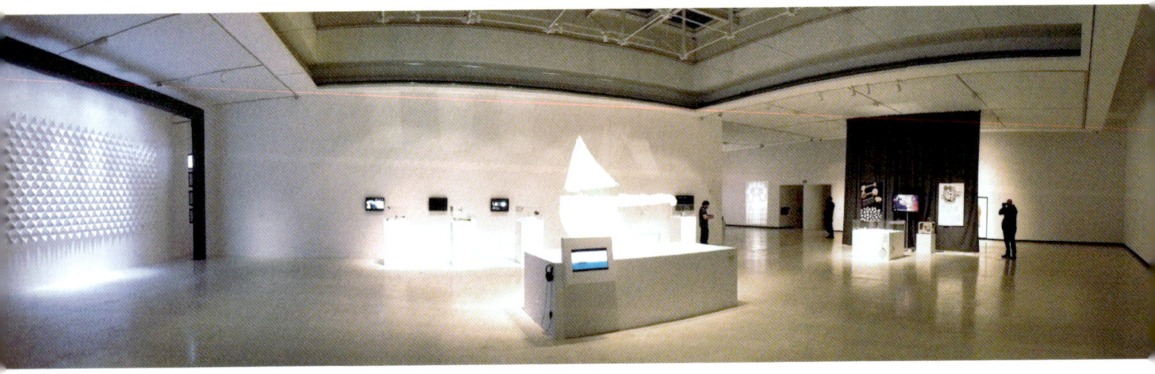
Exhibition view

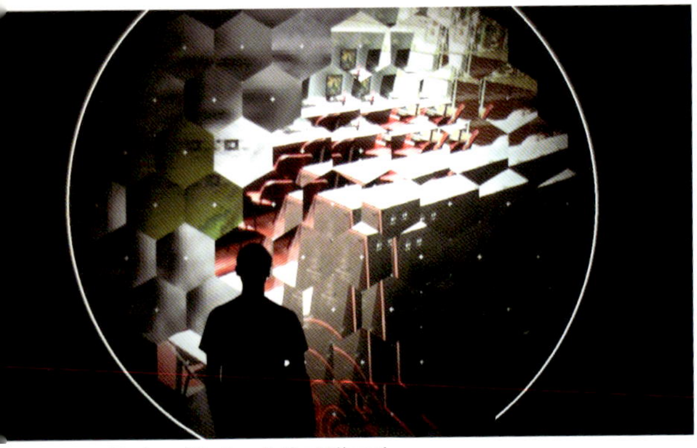
Desire of Codes, Seiko Mikami

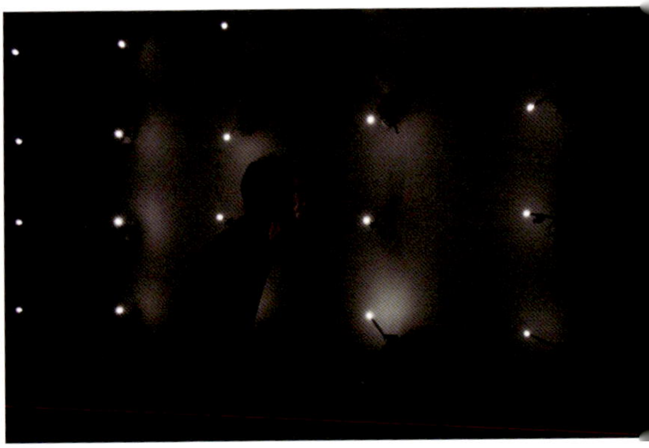
Desire of Codes, Seiko Mikami

like the private and public spheres, surveillance and control, subsume natural and artificial processes, and configure them into artistic processes in which installation visitors are expressly called upon to participate. The artists and their works function as catalysts that aim to trigger discourses, bring out new ways of considering things, open channels, and launch innovative upgrades and enhancements. Audience members are invited to engage in this confrontation, to actively scrutinize these issues, to seek answers as well as new questions. The exhibition and the works of art that comprise it constitute a start, the first step. "Express yourself" isn't just the theme of this exhibition; it's to be taken literally as a call to action.

On display are twelve works by internationally acclaimed artists. In one of the installations, the artists themselves have their say. Thus, the discourse isn't conducted anonymously; every encounter, every idea has a face.

The point of this exhibition is to showcase the highly diverse modes in which artists function as catalysts and the reactions they trigger thereby. Artists are these enzymes, the intellectual proteins of our time. They distill essential themes and reveal processes that challenge our perceptions in new and interesting ways.

Prozesse und verarbeiten sie in künstlerische Prozesse. Die BesucherInnen der Ausstellung sind explizit eingeladen, sich zu engagieren und einzubringen. Die KünstlerInnen und ihre Werke wirken als Katalysatoren, die Diskurse entfachen, Denkanstöße liefern, Türen öffnen, Veränderungen und Weiterentwicklungen anregen wollen. Die BesucherInnen sind eingeladen, diese Konfrontation anzunehmen und Antworten, aber auch neue Fragen zu suchen. Die Ausstellung und die einzelnen Werke sind ein Anfang, der erste Schritt. „Express yourself" ist nicht nur das Thema der Ausstellung, sondern durchaus auch als Aufforderung zu verstehen.

Präsentiert werden insgesamt zwölf Arbeiten von international renommierten KünstlerInnen, die auch selbst in einer Installation zu Wort kommen. Der Diskurs wird also nicht anonym geführt, sondern jede Auseinandersetzung, jede Idee hat ein Gesicht.

Die Ausstellung zeigt, auf welch unterschiedliche Art und Weise KünstlerInnen als Katalysatoren wirken und welche Prozesse und Reaktionen sie auslösen können. In gewissem Sinn sind sie „die Enzyme, die intellektuellen Proteine unserer Zeit", sie destillieren wichtige Themen und zeigen Prozesse, die unsere Wahrnehmung immer wieder aufs Neue hinterfragen.

Protei, Cesar Harada (FR/JP)
Merrick, Daan van den Berg (NL)
Newstweek, Danja Vasiliev (RU), Julian Oliver (NZ)
Energy Parasites, Eric Paulos (US)
Earth, Finnbogi Pétursson (IS)
Think silent, act with noise, Josu Recalde, Mikel Arce Sagarduy, Enrike Hurtado Mendieta (ES) / EHU Zarata Lab, Bilbao
Faceless, Manu Luksch (AT)
Light is time, folds are space, Matthew Gardiner (AU)
Street Ghosts, Paolo Cirio (IT)
Face to Facebook, Paolo Cirio, Alessandro Ludovico (IT)
Desire of Codes, Seiko Mikami (JP)
The Free Universal Construction Kit, Golan Levin (US)

This exhibition was produced jointly by Ars Electronica and Alhóndiga Bilbao; director: Lourdes Fernández
Curators: Gerfried Stocker, Manuela Naveau, Martin Honzik

Ars Electronica Production Crew: Production management / controlling: Veronika Liebl; technical supervision: Karl Schmidinger; exhibition design: Gerald Priewasser; production management: Kathrin Obernhumer; webcommunication: Michael Knoll; technicians: Simon Kopfberger, Peter Luger

Fragments Broaching the Imagination

Donumenta Regensburg, Germany
28.09. – 04.11.2012, Ostdeutsche Galerie Regensburg, Germany

This is Ars Electronica's second guest appearance at the Donumenta in Regensburg. The 2006 show dealt with "Bytes & Bodies," whereby the body as decisive medium of interaction and communication was the content of this encounter. This year's exhibition takes a poetic approach to the investigation of artistic practices that work with fragments of our digital culture. The Grafiksaal of the Ostdeutsche Galerie in Regensburg is being reconfigured to serve as the venue.
www.donumenta.de

Bereits zum zweiten Mal ist Ars Electronica zu Gast bei der Donumenta in Regensburg: War bei der damaligen Schau im Jahr 2006 die Auseinandersetzung mit „Bytes & Bodies" und dem Körper als maßgebliches Interaktions- und Kommunikationsmedium der Inhalt der Auseinandersetzung, so versucht diese Ausstellung heuer auf poetische Art und Weise künstlerische Praktiken zu untersuchen, die mit Fragmenten aus unserer digitalen Kultur arbeiten. Als Ausstellungsort wird der Grafiksaal der Ostdeutschen Galerie in Regensburg umgebaut.

Possible Futures

São Paulo
01.10. – 05.10.2012, Auditorium of the University of São Paulo, FAU-USP Faculty for Architecture and Urbanism, Brasil

Since September 2012 the *Prix Ars Electronica Archive* is online. One month later Ars Electronica presented at the University of São Paulo not only the rich amount of documentations offered online, more over Ars Electronica discussed at this conference the status quo and the possible future of archives based on selected examples of scientists, artists and historians. The symposium took place in collaboration with the University of São Paulo, in particular with Giselle Beiguelman/Faculty for Architecture and Urbanism FAU-USP and Ana Magalhaes / Museum of Contemporary Art MAC-USP.

Made possible through the support of BMEIA and the engagement of Mr. Ehrlich, Austrian embassy in Brasilia.

Seit September 2012 ist das *Prix Ars Electronica Archiv* online; auf dieser Konferenz in São Paulo präsentierte Ars Electronica nicht nur dessen Umfang, seine Inhalte und Möglichkeiten, sondern diskutierte gemeinsam mit WissenschaftlerInnen, KünstlerInnen und HistorikerInnen den Status Quo und die mögliche Zukunft von Archiven anhand ausgewählter Beispiele. Ars Electronica hat dieses Projekt gemeinsam mit der Universität São Paulo, im Speziellen mit Giselle Beiguelman, Fakultät für Architektur und Urbanismus FAU-USP und Ana Magalhaes, Museum für Zeitgenössische Kunst MAC-USP, initiiert.

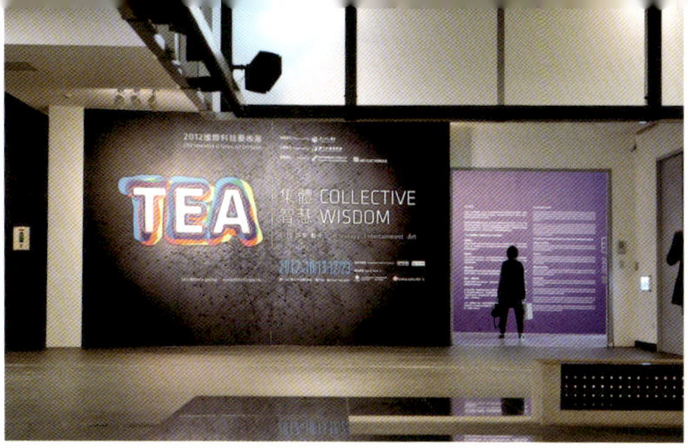

TEA Collective Wisdom

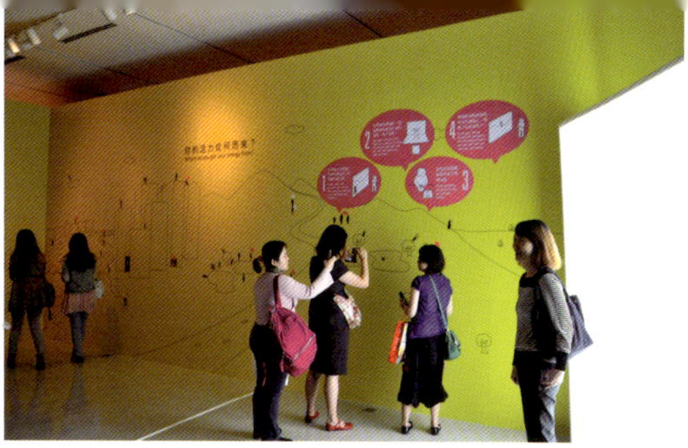

Shadowgram, Ars Electronica Futurelab

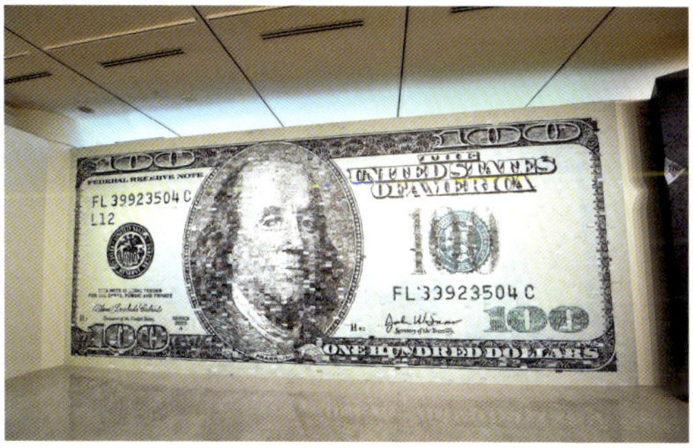

Ten Thousand Cents, Aaron Koblin

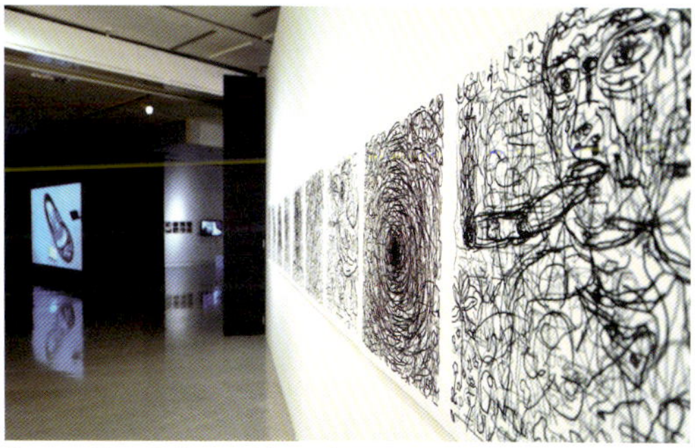

Swarm Sketch, Peter Edmunds

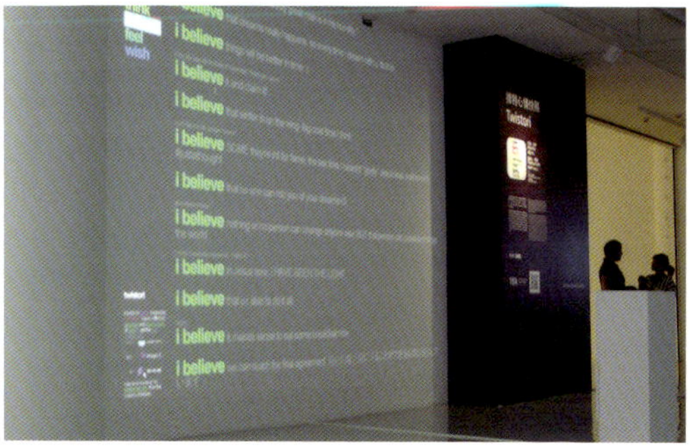

Twistori, Amy Hoy, Thomas Fuchs

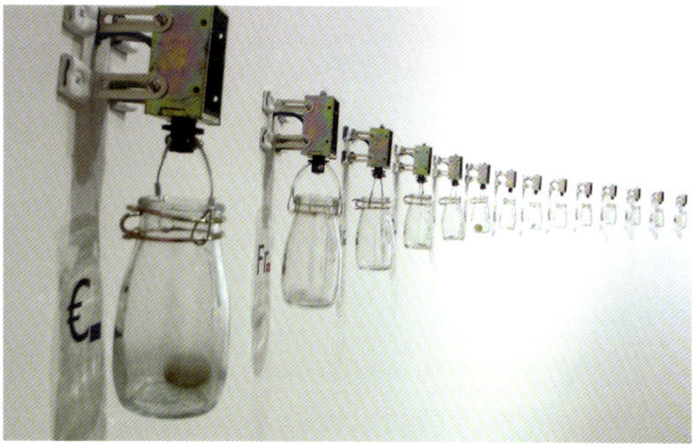

Purels/Rate Beat, Chi Tzu-Heng, Cho Li-Hang, Lee Chi-Ying, Lin Ting-Ta

TEA Collective Wisdom

Taiwan

13.10.– 23.12.2012, National Taiwan Museum of Fine Arts Taichung, Taiwan

Ars Electronica continues to make a name for itself worldwide, this time with another major exhibition at the National Taiwan Museum of Fine Arts in Taichung. "Collective Wisdom" consists of 17 selected works created from the advent of the internet in the 1990s to the present day, all of which are the outcome of some form of collective effort in which the audience plays an active role. An ancillary symposium will provide a historical overview of the development of crowdart, offer a close-up look at contemporary works in this genre, and discuss current trends.

Collective Wisdom kicks off the NTMOFA's new series of exhibitions entitled TEA (Technology + Entertainment + Art).

Zum wiederholten Male ist Ars Electronica mit einer Ausstellung im National Taiwan Museum of Fine Arts in Taichung zu Gast. Diesmal wurden 17 Arbeiten zum Thema „Collective Wisdom" zusammengestellt, die seit der Entwicklung des Internet in den 1990er Jahren und bis heute in kollektiver Art und Weise mit Publikum entstanden sind. Im Rahmen eines Symposiums wird weiters ein geschichtlicher Überblick über die Entwicklung von Crowdart gegeben, zeitgenössische Arbeiten von Künstler/innen zu diesem Thema vorgestellt und aktuelle Tendenzen diskutiert.

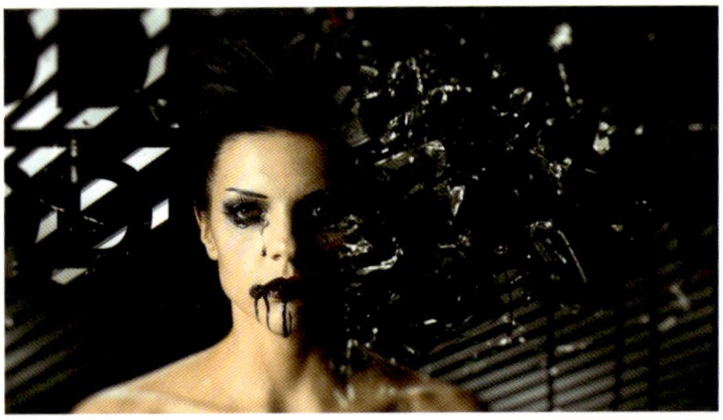
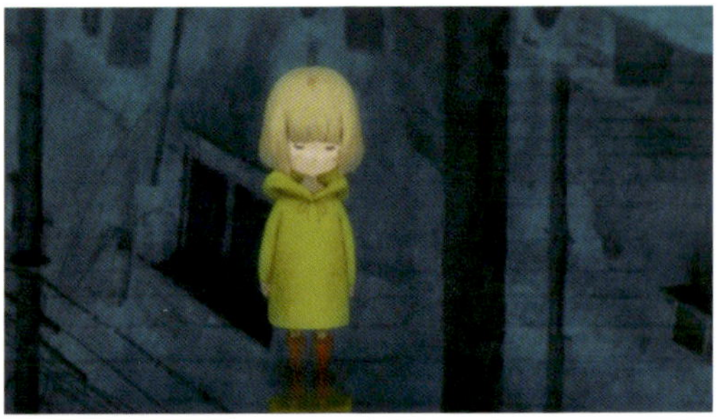
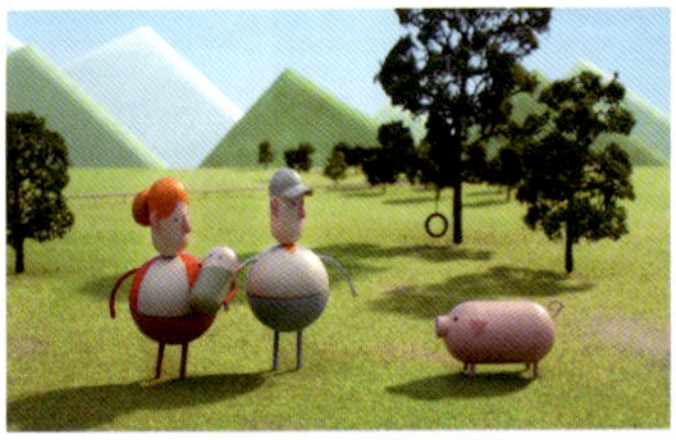
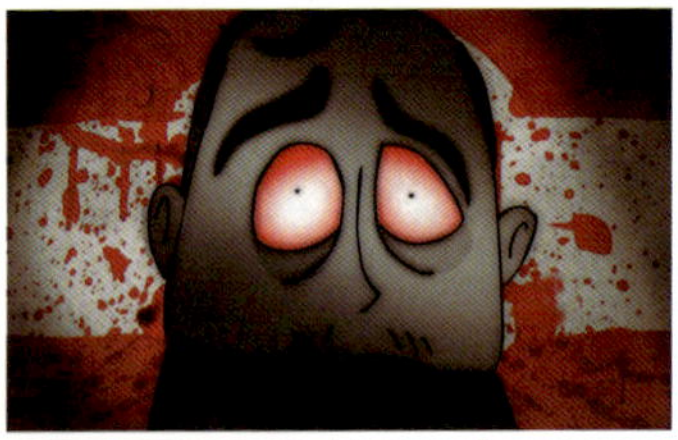
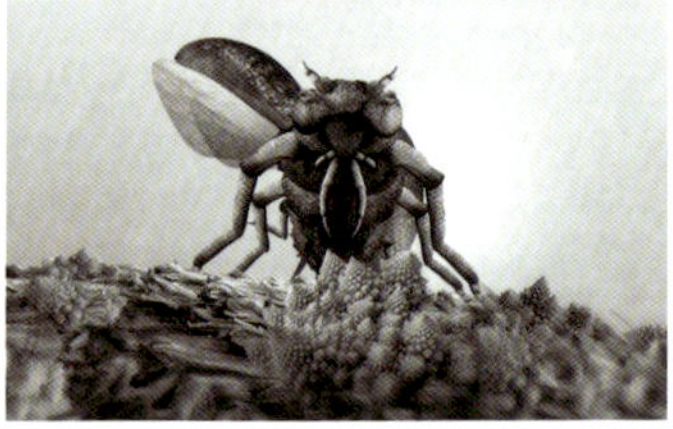
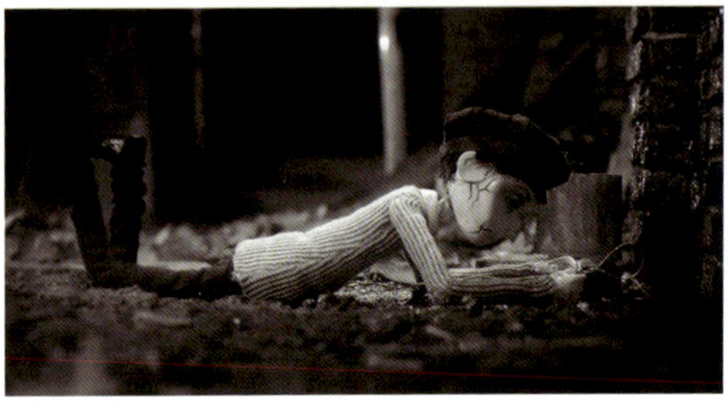
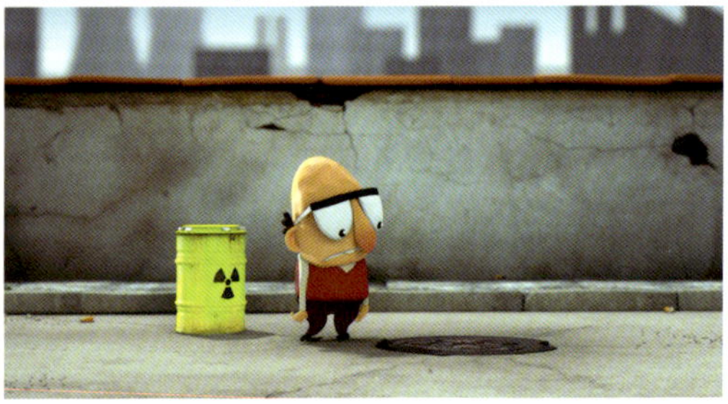

Ars Electronica Animation Festival – On Tour

The *Ars Electronica Animation Festival* screens a selection of outstanding films submitted to the Prix Ars Electronica 2012. Aproximately 100 excerpts provide an overview of what filmmakers around the world have been up to lately. Ars Electronica Linz is working together with the Austrian Foreign Ministry for the second time now to make the *Ars Electronica Animation Festival* available on Blu-ray. The films in the Festival lineup are being provided free of charge for a year to approximately 20 Austrian Cultural Forums and 100 Austrian Embassies worldwide. Educational institutions, film festivals and a wide array of cultural organizations can, in turn, obtain access to the Blu-ray free of charge at the respective Austrian facility in their country.

Das Programm des *Ars Electronica Animation Festival* ist eine Selektion der besten beim Prix Ars Electronica 2012 eingereichten Arbeiten in der Kategorie Computer Animation / VFX / Film und gibt mit rund 100 Filmausschnitten einen Überblick über internationale Positionen und Sichtweisen. Bereits zum zweiten Mal bietet Ars Electronica Linz in Zusammenarbeit mit dem BMEIA (Österreichisches Bundesministerium für Europäische und Internationale Angelegenheiten) das *Ars Electronica Animation Festival* auf Blu Ray an. Rund 20 österreichische Kulturforen sowie 100 österreichische Botschaften weltweit bekamen das *Animation Festival* gratis für ein Jahr zur Verfügung gestellt. Bildungseinrichtungen, Filmfestivals sowie diverse andere kulturelle Organisationen können ihrerseits ebenfalls gratis die Blu Ray von den entsprechenden Stellen in ihrem Land anfordern.

The *Ars Electronica Animation Festival 2012* has been presented in
An folgenden Orten wurde das *Ars Electronica Animation Festival 2012* gezeigt:

04.10.2012	Czech Republic, *AniFest Prag,* Galerie u Prstenu, Prag
October 2012	Serbia, *Center for the Promotion of Science,* Belgrad
08.10.–28.10.2012	Australia, Queensland University of Technology, *QUT Creative Industries Precinct* Parer Place Screen, Queensland
26.10.2012	Italy, *Austrian Cultural Institute,* Rome
07.11.2012	Poland, *Open City* Workshop and Conference, Katowice
07.11.–10.11.2012	Russia, *Proo-Contra of Media Culture,* Krasnoyarsk
08.11.–11.11. 2012	Spain, *Espacio ENTER* a project of ART TECH MEDIA, Tenerife
30.11.–01.12.2012	Sweden, *NMM Sweden* (New Media Meeting Sweden), Norrköping
07.12.–25.12.2012	Taiwan, *Asia University,* Taichung Government Hall, Taichung
14.02.2013	Japan, *Cinem@rt in Roppongi,* Tokyo
28.02.2013	United Kingdom, *Austrian Cultural Forum,* London
06.03.2013	Israel, *Tel Aviv International Animation Festival,* Tel Aviv
06.03.–07.03.2013	Iran, *Mohsen Gallery,* Teheran
08.03.–11.03.2013	Turkey, *CerModern,* Ankara
15.03.–14.04.2013	China, *chi K11 Art Space Shanghai,* Shanghai
28.03.–31.03.2013	Switzerland, *Electron 10 Festival,* Geneva
02.04.2013, 19:00	Slovenia, *MoTA- Museum for Transitory Art, Sonica Festival*, Ljubljana
08.04.2013, 18:00	Israel, *Holon Cinematheque,* Holon
11.04.–11.05.2013	Ukraine, *Austrian Film Weeks* in Kiev, Odessa, Lviv, Czernowitz
16.04.–21.04.2013	Mexico,*Cinema Planeta – Festival Internacional de Cine y Medio Ambiente de México,* Cuernavaca Morelos
26.04.2013	Poland, *halo!gen,* Gliwice
11.05.2013	Poland, Kronika Centre for Contemporary Arts, Bytom
07.05.–11.05.2013	Kosovo, *European Film Week,* Pristina
21.05.2013	Poland, *Non-Governmental Organizations Centre,* Gliwice

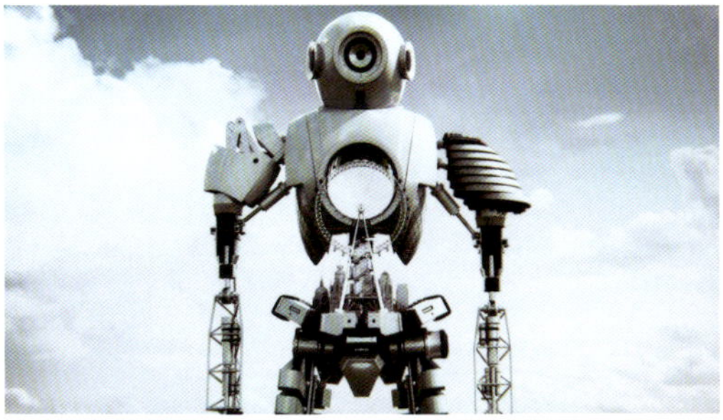
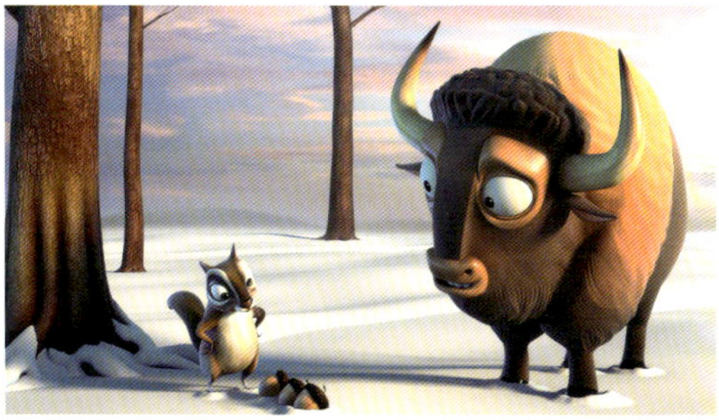
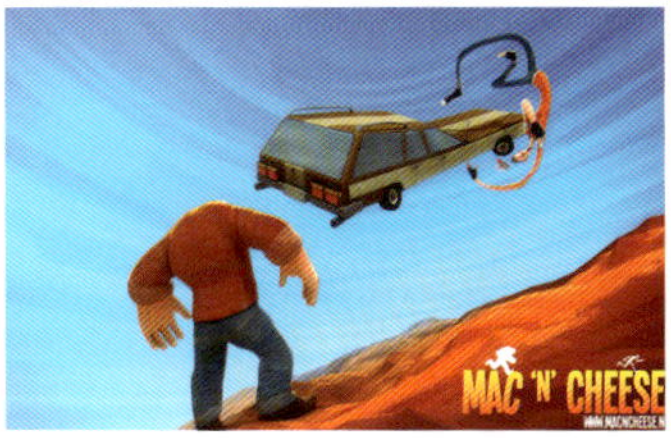

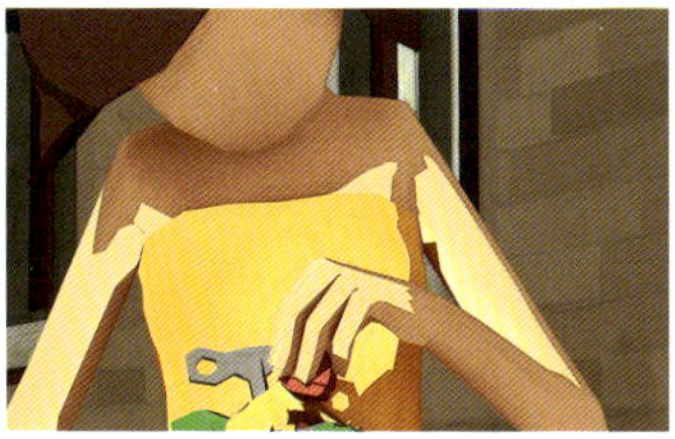
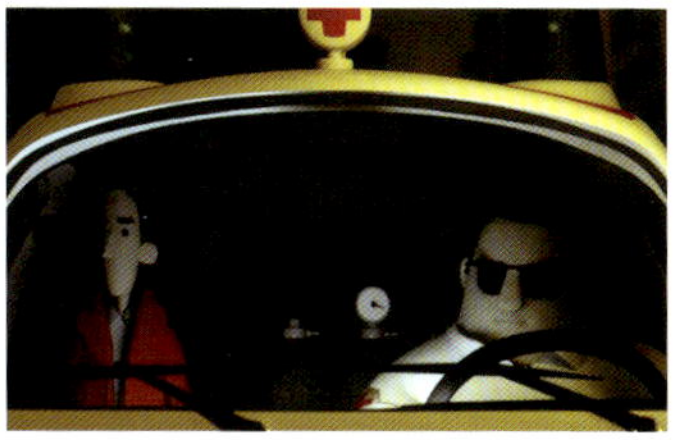

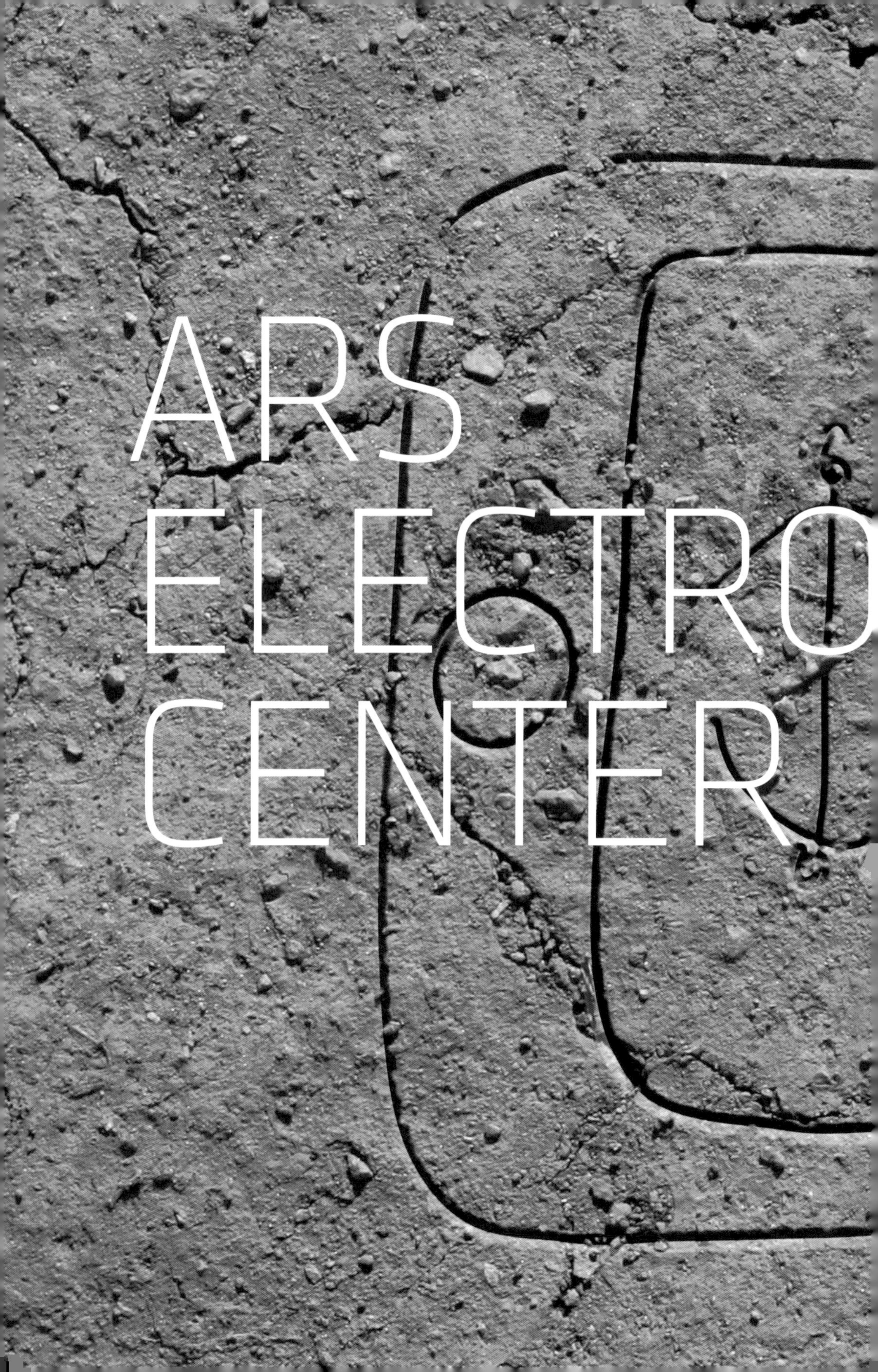

ARS ELECTRO CENTER

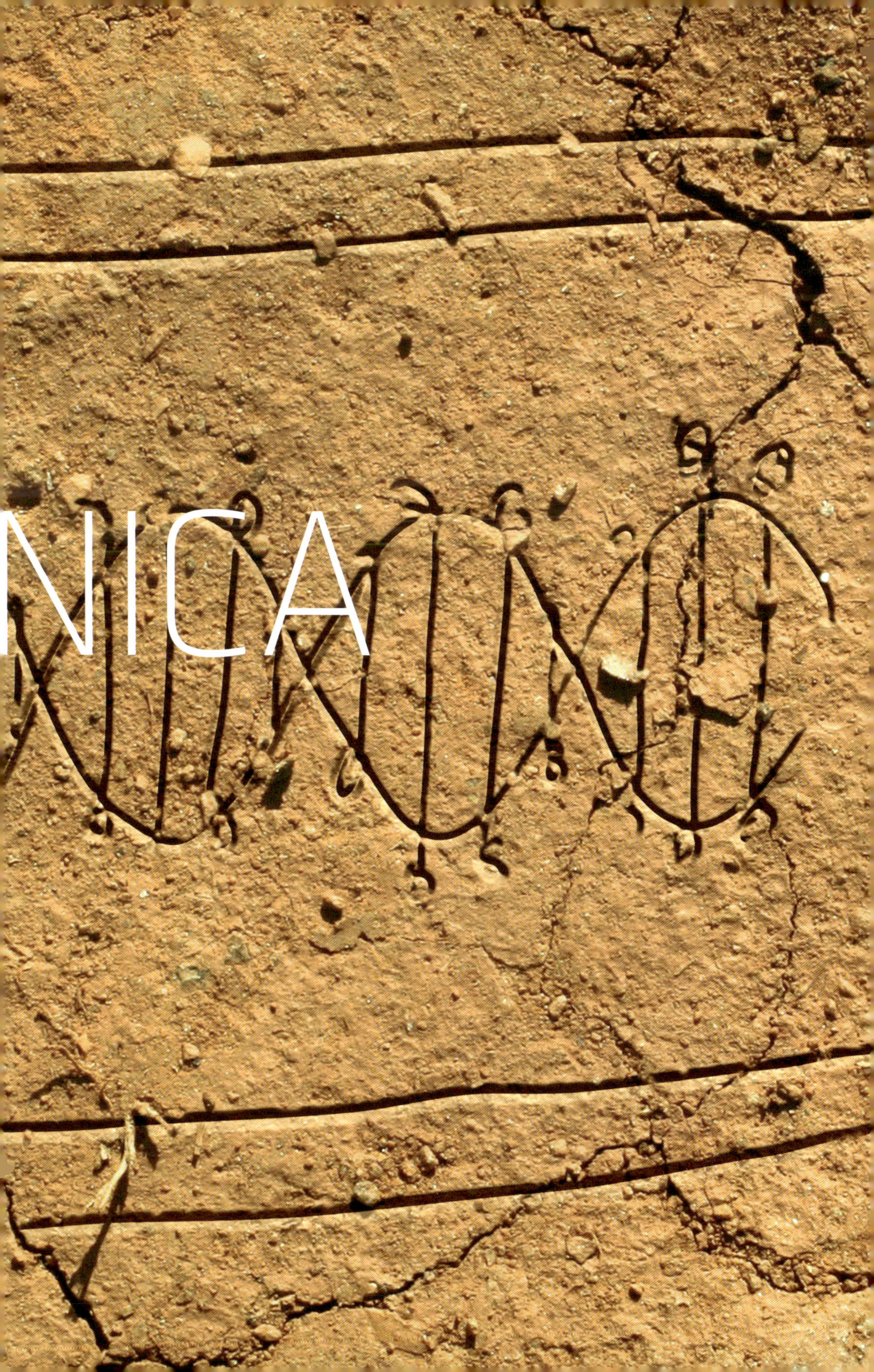
NICA

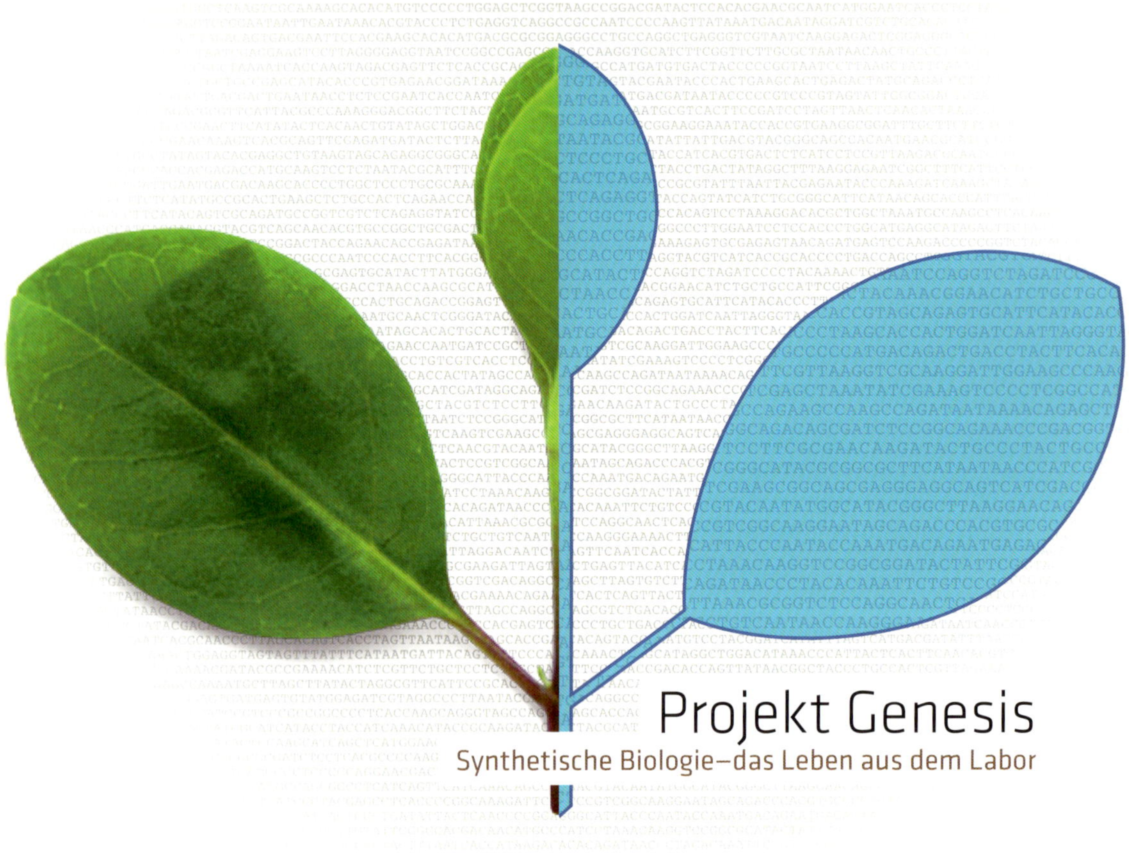

Projekt Genesis

Synthetische Biologie—das Leben aus dem Labor

Matthew Gardiner

Yours Synthetically

As a tool for shaping the future, speculation is versatile and precise—a kind of Swiss-army knife for artists and designers. It also has the habit of slipping back to the future as incidents, both real and conceptual. Case in point: Vilém Flusser paints us a colourful post synthetic biology scene in the Ars Electronica 99 Life Science catalogue (itself a reprint of a 1988 Art Forum article). He asks, "Why is it that dogs aren't yet blue with red spots, and that horses don't yet radiate phosphorescent colors over the nocturnal shadows of the land?" And follows on, being presciently speculative to ask, "Who will be the Disney of the future? He or she might, I suggest, be a molecular biologist".

By way of comeback, we need only look a little further along the Ars Electronica lineage to find Eduardo Kac—the artist as molecular biologist—and wonder if he was also reading Flusser, because he proposed something strikingly similar: *GFP-K9 (Green Flourescent Protein Canine—a glowing dog*

Die Spekulation kann ein vielseitiges und präzises Werkzeug zur Gestaltung der Zukunft sein: eine Art Schweizermesser für KünstlerInnen und DesignerInnen. Sie fällt aber mit ihren realen wie erdachten Ereignissen auch gerne in die Zukunft von gestern zurück. So entwirft etwa Vilém Flusser im Katalog der Ars Electronica 99 zum Thema *Life Science* eine farbenfrohe postsynthetische Bioszenerie. In seinem Text (selbst der Wiederabdruck eines *Art Forum*-Artikels von 1988) fragt er: „Warum eigentlich sind Hunde noch immer nicht blau mit roten Flecken? Und warum eigentlich leuchten Hasen noch immer nicht wie Irrlichter in den nächtlichen Gefilden?" Um schließlich hellsichtig zu spekulieren: „Wer ist der künftige Disney? Die Antwort: Er wird, unter anderem, Molekularbiologe sein."

Wo wir bei Comebacks sind: Nur ein wenig später in der Geschichte der Ars Electronica begegnen wir dem Künstler und Molekularbiologen Eduardo Kac und stellen uns die Frage, ob er vielleicht auch Flusser who wasn't so much *made* but rather deftly positioned as a media action to stir up the public), and *GFP Bunny* (a creature never released from the lab, but the subject of an extended custody battle). So in a world where the artist-come-Disney has been unleashed onto the world stage, though the cute glowing animals have not, we already occupy fragments of other predictions too: we've beaten Moore's law, and DNA sequencing (DNA reading) and synthesis (DNA writing) is currently running at a dramatic ten-fold increase in efficiency per year[1], becoming cheaper and cheaper per base pair.

One might think that since all the important issues in genetic artscience have been raised before, that all of the critical human issues—eugenics, trans-humanism, data security, insurance issues, ethics, transgenic art, bioart and so on—were all dealt with, artistically done-and-dusted, and died out with the "completion" of the Human Genome Project. But those issues are even more vital to readdress to the public of today. What was a once world first in 1993 is now daily business. GFP insertion is the DIYbio (Do It Yourself Biology) equivalent of the literal "hello world" in computing. Instead of Joe Davis "updating" the voyager disc for aliens and beaming a molecular DNA coded image of a vagina in *Microvenus*[2] (Joe always explains it with a serious grin) into space, we have his benefactor and collaborator George Church encoding and synthesizing a whole book (pictures and all) into DNA. A feat made simpler by co-founding a world leading synthesis company. Hello space, hello world, hello future of data, all happening today.

So if we were to reframe Flusser's question knowing what we know now—a world situated post *GFP Bunny*, post the horse/artist chimera of *May The Horse Live in Me*[3], post Stelarc's *Ear on Arm*[4], post the so-called Synthetic Genome[5] *JCVI-syn1.0* (which sounds a lot like the name of a piece of open source software, except they could have sounded cooler if they started in beta numbering) by the J. Craig Venter Institute—who would be the human with the wildly inspired vision of a earth as a new bio-technomorphed fantasia. *Who would be the designer and constructor of the new biology?*

gelesen hat, weil er etwas verblüffend Ähnliches vorschlägt: den *GFP-K9 (Green Flourescent Protein Canine* – einen leuchtenden Hund, der eigentlich nicht wirklich *geschaffen*, sondern eher geschickt in den Medien lanciert wurde, um die Öffentlichkeit aufzurütteln) und den *GFP Bunny* (ein Geschöpf, das nie das Labor verließ, aber zum Gegenstand eines langwierigen Sorgerechtstreits wurde). Nun, da der zu Disney gewandelte Künstler tatsächlich die Weltbühne betreten hat, was den niedlichen Leuchttierchen versagt blieb, haben wir es längst auch schon mit der teilweisen Verwirklichung anderer Vorhersagen zu tun: Wir haben das Moore'sche Gesetz gebrochen, und die Effizienz der DNA-Sequenzierung (das Lesen von DNA) und Synthetisierung (das Schreiben von DNA) steigt derzeit um das Zehnfache pro Jahr,[1] bei immer niedrigeren Preisen pro Basenpaar.

Angesichts des Umstands, dass alle zentralen Fragen der genetischen *Artscience* schon einmal aufgeworfen und alle kritischen Menschheitsfragen – Eugenik, Transhumanismus, Datensicherheit, Versicherungsfragen, Ethik, transgene Kunst, Biokunst usw. – längst behandelt wurden, könnte man meinen, dass sie künstlerisch erledigt, mit dem Abschluss des Humangenomprojekts an ihr Ende gekommen sind. Tatsächlich aber ist es heute umso wichtiger, diese Themen neu an die Öffentlicheit heranzutragen. Was 1993 die Welt von morgen war, ist heute Alltag. Das Einschleusen von GFP ist heute das DIY-biologische Pendant des „Hallo-Welt"-Programms in der Informatik. Statt Joe Davis' Aktualisierung der Voyager-Botschaft für Außerirdische, dem in DNA codierten Bild einer Vagina mit dem Titel *Microvenus*[2] (eine Arbeit, die Joe immer mit einem ernsten Grinsen erklärt), sehen wir heute seinen Gönner und Mitarbeiter George Church gleich ein ganzes Buch (samt Bildern) in DNA codieren – eine Leistung, die ihm auch dadurch erleichtert wurde, dass er das führende Bio-Synthese-Unternehmen der Welt mitbegründet hat. Hallo Weltraum, hallo Welt, hallo Datenzukunft, alles hier und jetzt.

Wenn wir Flussers Frage von unserem gegenwärtigen Wissenstand aus neu stellen – also einer Welt nach dem *GFP Bunny*, nach der Pferd/Künstlerin-Chimäre *May The Horse Live in Me*,[3] nach Stelarcs *Ear on Arm*,[4] nach dem am J. Craig Venter Institute erstellten sogenannten synthetischen Genom[5] *JCVI-syn1.0* (das übrigens sehr nach dem Namen eines Open-Source-Programms klingt, außer dass man versäumt hat, mit Beta-Nummerierung zu beginnen) –, wer stünde da wohl heute für die unbän-

It may well be an artist like Patricia Piccinni, whose simultaneously cute-but-frightening hyperreal silicon sculptures embody the border condition between being human and adapting to technology. *The Listener* has evolved enlarged ears that appear to feed on delicious acoustics from the media magnet of a vintage wooden speaker. The Listener's lethargic, fattened body with mutated humanesque features remind us of our suckling media saturated population. We cannot help notice the sensory wideness of the eyes that coupled with the suggestion of a smile convey a sense of inspiration, and we imagine ourselves listening. Our infatuation with technology and its flow of media, binds us, and shapes us in unknown ways.

dig kreative Vision von der Erde, die neue biotechnomorphe Fantasie? *Wer wäre Designer und Konstrukteur einer neuen Biologie?*
Es könnte durchaus eine Künstlerin wie Patricia Piccinini sein, deren zugleich liebenswerte und erschreckende hyperreale Silikonskulpturen die Schwelle zwischen Menschsein und Anpassung an die Technlogie verkörpern. *The Listener* hat vergrößerte Ohren ausgebildet, die sich vom delikaten Klang ihres Medienmagneten, einer hölzernen Vintage-Lautsprecherbox, zu ernähren scheinen. Der lethargische, verfettete Körper des Lauschenden mit den mutierten menschlichen Zügen erinnert uns an übersättigte Medienmilchferkel. Die unübersehbaren weit geöffneten sinnlichen Augen vermitteln zusammen mit dem Anflug eines Lächelns ein Gefühl der Begeistertheit, das uns selbst in die Rolle des Zuhörers versetzt. Unsere Vernarrtheit in die Technologie und ihre medialen Ströme bindet uns, prägt uns auf eine unbekannte Weise.

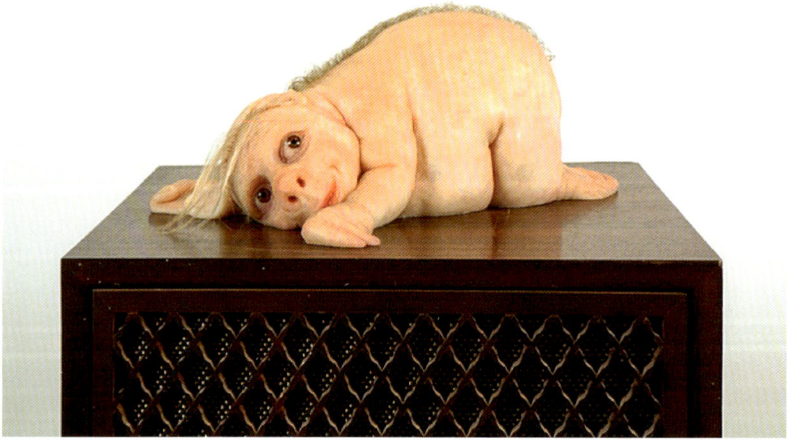

The Listener, Patricia Piccinini, 2013

The conceptual departure point for this exhibition, is the science and technology of Synthetic Biology; often defined as the design and construction of biological parts. Parts? As if we were building cars and needed to replace a bolt, fan belt or gasket? No, parts as in tiny sections of DNA code that are isolated from an organism, extracted and recombined with promoters and forcefully (perhaps using a hacked genegun like Rüdiger Trojok's) injected into natures little factories such as

Konzeptueller Ausgangspunkt für diese Ausstellung ist die Wissenschaft und Technologie der synthetischen Biologie, die oft auch als Design und Konstruktion biologischer Bauteile beschrieben wird. Bauteile? Als schraubten wir an Autos herum und müssten einen Bolzen, Keilriemen oder Dichtungsring austauschen? Nein, kurze DNA-Abschnitte werden in einem Organismus isoliert, herausgelöst und mithilfe von Promotoren rekombiniert, um sie (z. B. mit einer gehackten Genkanone wie der von Rüdiger Trojok) gewaltsam in die

the rapidly reproducing bacteria Escherichia coli (E. coli). Parts that are synthesized, printed with ever advancing technologies in longer and longer sequences. And as though it's a mating dance of rare birds, the commercial leaders in the race tout how long their sequences are.
It's a natural attraction for artists to be drawn to the frontiers of technological and social change, and Dorothy Nelkin offers an insight as to why:

"Scientific metaphors are also futuristic: they refer to the human genome as a Delphic Oracle, a trip into the future, a medical crystal ball. [...] But science has also been a source of surreal fantasies and dystopic, even apocalyptic, visions, as many artists have cast themselves as social critics."[6]

Their speculations have long since departed from communication via simple media of forms, kinetics and text; they design and construct their storylines with the functional aesthetics of natural processes as symbolic metaphors. They invent and extrapolate from science, and through their work reposition it to reframe our world view through their lenses. Works curated for *Project Genesis* carry considered critical messages for us. To confront these messages, we are challenged to engage with the thick mist of scientific mystery, to believe in the authority of peer-reviewed publications, to advance our own understanding, to get up to speed so that we too can participate in the discourse. It's a challenging exhibition for the public, because the density of information is relentless, the glossary and lexicon is highly developed and sophisticated. Each new term can be expanded into volumes of texts and experiments that warrant years of study and research. Each of these opens up new questions. It's as if there is no absolute answer, just an ever broadening set of questions. Thankfully, artists can embrace the unknown, they are comfortable in starting a project they may never finish or that may never work at all, but are they any more masochistic than the molecular biologist who spends years pipetting miniscule amounts of nature from one tube to another? The hard work of molecular biology is so repetitive and banal. We have to confront the simple fact that the artistic reinterpretation of science is much more Disney than the banality of

kleinen Fabriken der Natur wie die sich rasant vermehrenden E.Coli-Bakterien einzubauen. Teile, die synthetisiert und mit immer besser werdenden Technologien zu immer längeren Sequenzen zusammengesetzt werden (als wäre es ein Paarungstanz einer seltenen Vogelart, prahlen die Marktführer in diesem Wettrennen lauthals mit der Länge ihrer Sequenzen).
Für Künstler ist die vorderste Front technologischen und sozialen Wandels offenbar ein natürlicher Anziehungspunkt. Dorothy Nelkin lieferte eine mögliche Erklärung dafür:

„Wissenschaftliche Metaphern können auch futuristisch sein; so wird das menschliche Erbgut etwa als Orakel von Delphi, als Reise in die Zukunft, als Blick in die medizinische ‚Kristallkugel' beschrieben. [...] Doch die Wissenschaft dient auch als Quelle surrealer Fantasien und dystopischer, ja apokalyptischer Visionen, da zahlreiche Künstler nunmehr als Gesellschaftskritiker auftreten."[6]

In ihren Spekulationen haben sie die Vermittlung von Formen, Kinetik und Text mittels einfacher Medien längst überwunden; sie designen und bauen ihre Storylines heute mit der funktionalen Ästhetik natürlicher Prozesse, die sie als Metaphern einsetzen. Sie erfinden und extrapolieren aus den Wissenschaften und rekontexualisieren sie durch ihre Arbeiten, um uns die Welt aus ihrer Perspektive zu zeigen. Die für *Projekt Genesis* ausgewählten Arbeiten sind mit wohlüberlegten kritischen Botschaften gespickt. Konfrontiert mit diesen Botschaften fühlen wir uns herausgefordert, in den dichten Nebel wissenschaftlicher Mysterien einzutauchen, uns auf peer-reviewte Publikationen zu verlassen, dauernd den eigenen Horizont erweitern und uns ganz allgemein auf den neuesten Erkenntnisstand bringen, so wir an diesem Diskurs teilnehmen wollen. Es ist eine anspruchsvolle Ausstellung für das Publikum, weil die Information gnadenlos dicht, die Sprache ungeheuer komplex und das Vokabular hoch elaboriert ist. Hinter jedem neuen Begriff stehen ganze Bände an Texten und zahllose Experimente, die Jahre des Studiums und der Forschung erfordern. Und sie alle eröffnen wieder neue Fragen. Es hat den Anschein, als gäbe es keine absoluten Antworten, nur einen immer größer werdenden Fragenberg. Glücklicherweise können KünstlerInnen mit dem Unbekannten leben, haben kein Problem damit, Projekte in Angriff zu nehmen, die sie vielleicht nie vollenden werden oder die gar nicht aufgehen können. Aber natural sciences. The scientific scenarios are so fantastic that they actually beg to be made into stories, take for instance *Opimilk–Engineering transgenic cows capable of expressing Opiorphin specifically in their milk*, by Claire Dempsey et al in collaboration with Science Gallery Dublin. In the project description the authors state:

"Opiorphin is a newly researched pain-killing substance first isolated from human saliva (Wisner, Dufour et al. 2006). We wanted to use synthetic biology to produce this protein. We would envisage achieving this by inserting the gene for opiorphin into a cow, which could then produce Opiorphin specifically in its milk. The milk could then be sold in supermarkets where it would be readily available and easy to access. We hoped to highlight the need for scientific development in areas which will treat the people most in need."

Symbolically, a cow has transformed from being a domesticated mammal into a kind of synthetic factory. We build houses for cows in colder climates, we've been breeding and consuming them and their produce for generations. But only now do we begin to understand that living factories have more produce potential than nature originally evolved. We can now intervene at a new point in the biological process, rather than taking what is naturally produced in a biological system, we now synthesize a new product. A cow is a bioreactor with high output, a potential drug factory. Drinking milk or eating yoghurt could ease the hurt of chronic pain sufferers, and so what then is the issue? Is there a problem with treating an intelligent animal in this way? Then how about farming in the first place? What if we were to exchange places with the cow and our bodies became factories for new chemicals? But wait a minute, didn't the opiorphin come from a human in the first place? What actually is the difference? Nature does this job in and of itself, we're just growing the same stuff in a different place. Don't we do that in the name of medical research anyway? The task of efficiently differentiating between what is "really" natural becomes more and more obscured.

sind sie so masochistisch wie Molekularbiologen, die oft Jahre damit zubringen, kleinste Teilchen Natur von Eprouvette zu Eprouvette zu pipettieren? Ihre Arbeit ist oft extrem repetitiv und banal. Wir müssen uns mit der Tatsache abfinden, dass die künstlerische Interpretation der Wissenschaft weit disneyhafter ist als die Banalität der Naturwissenschaft selbst. Die Wissenschaft ist oft dermaßen banal, dass sie geradezu danach schreit, in Geschichten gekleidet zu werden. Geschichten wie *Opimilk – Engineering transgenic cows capable of expressing Opiorphin specifically in their milk*, die Claire Dempsey und Konsorten in Zusammenarbeit mit der Science Gallery Dublin vorgelegt haben. In der Projektbeschreibung heißt es:

„Opiorphin ist eine kürzlich entdeckte schmerzstillende Substanz, die erstmals aus menschlichem Speichel isoliert wurde (Wisner, Dufour et al. 2006). Wir wollten dieses Protein mittels synthetischer Biologie erzeugen. Wir dachten daran, dies durch Einbringung des Opiorphin-Gens in eine Kuh zu bewerkstelligen, die dann Opiorphin in ihrer Milch absondern würde. Die Milch könnte einfach im Supermarkt verkauft werden, wo sie für jedermann leicht zugänglich wäre. Wir hofften, damit die Notwendigkeit wissenschaftlicher Entwicklung in Bereichen zu zeigen, die besonders bedürftigen Menschen zugute kommen."

Hier wird die Kuh symbolisch von einem domestizierten Säugetier in eine Art Fabrik verwandelt. In den kälteren Klimazonen bauen wir Kühen Ställe, wir züchten und verzehren sie und ihre Produkte seit Generationen. Aber erst heute beginnen wir zu verstehen, dass sie als lebende Fabriken mehr Produktpotenzial besitzen, als ihnen die Natur ursprünglich mitgegeben hat. Wir können nun an einem neuen Punkt in den biologischen Prozess eingreifen. Statt davon auszugehen, was ein biologisches System auf natürlichem Weg hervorbringt, können wir nun ein neues Produkt synthetisieren. Eine Kuh ist ein leistungsstarker Bioreaktor, eine potenzielle Pharmafabrik. Milchtrinken oder Joghurtessen könnte chronische Schmerzen linden, wo liegt das Problem? Wenn ein derartiger Umgang mit einem intelligenten Tier ein Problem ist, ist dann nicht schon die Landwirtschaft ein Problem? Was wäre, wenn wir mit der Kuh tauschen und unsere Körper zu Fabriken für die Erzeugung neuer chemischer Substanzen würden?

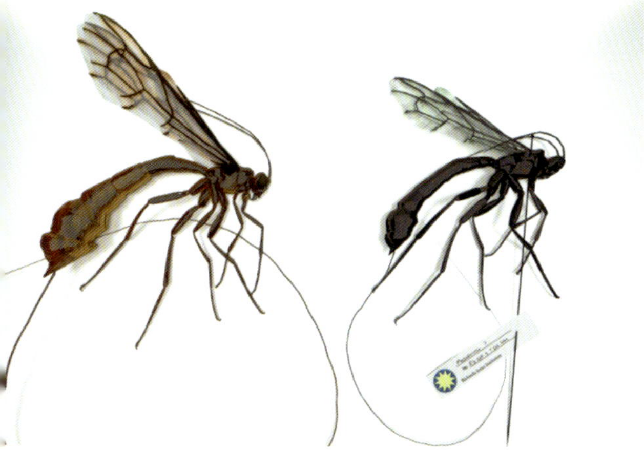

Into Your Hands They Are Delivered,
Tobias Revell, 2013

Moment mal, stammt das Opiorphin denn nicht ursprünglich vom Menschen? Wo liegt der Unterschied? Die Natur bringt das Ding doch von sich aus hervor, wir verpflanzen es lediglich an einen anderen Ort. Und tun wir das nicht im Namen des medizinischen Fortschritts? Eine effektive Unterscheidung zwischen dem „wirklich" Natürlichen und dem eigentlich Unnatürlichen wird immer schwieriger.

That there even is a natural balance is the force of contention behind Tobias Revell's *Into Your Hands They Are Delivered,* a title taken from the biblical book of Genesis. Starting with Darwin's internal struggle with the incongruency between the idea of a benevolent God, and what he was observing in the parasitic behaviour of the Ichneumon wasp, Revell proposes to re-engineer the wasp to subvert what he deems a naturalist fallacy. He contends along the lines that there never really was a nature, that nature itself is a human invention.

Tobias Revells die Genesis zitierende Arbeit *Into Your Hands They Are Delivered* („in eure Hände seien sie gegeben", Genesis 9,2:) stellt infrage, dass es überhaupt so etwas wie ein natürliches Gleichgewicht gibt. Ausgehend von Darwins Gewissenskonflikt angesichts der Unvereinbarkeit eines gütigen Gottes mit dem parasitischen Verhalten der Schlupfwespe, schlägt Revell vor, die Wespe so umzudesignen, dass sie diesen seiner Meinung nach naturalistischen Fehlschluss durchkreuzt. Er argumentiert mehr oder weniger, dass es so etwas wie eine Natur nie gegeben habe, die Natur selbst eine Erfindung des Menschen sei.

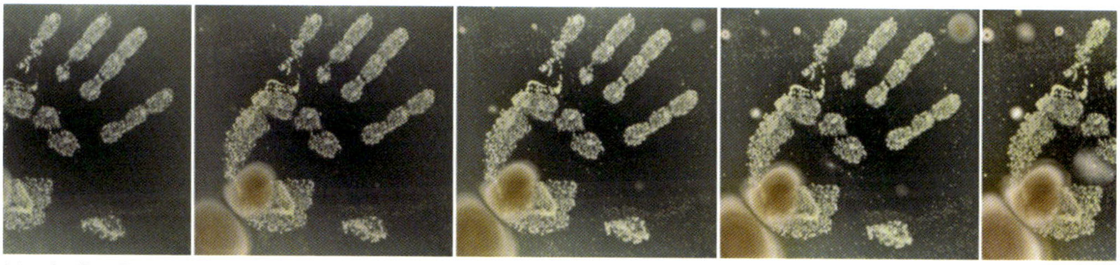

Metabodies, Sonja Bäumel, 2013

Sonja Bäumel investigates humanity's intimate relationship with nature and uses our skin as a location to ask questions. Allowing her work to go beyond genetic manipulation of a single organism, she actively cultivates, cares for, and observes bacterial imprints from humans. In *Metabodies,* she reminds us that 2-3 kg of bacteria live within each of us, and that they form a vital part of our bodies flora. Using a bio-sensor of sorts, Bäumel tries to peer into the world of bacterial commu-

Auch Sonja Bäumel untersucht und befragt die enge Verbindung des Menschen mit der Natur, wobei sie unsere Haut als Ausgangspunkt nimmt. Sie kultiviert und beobachtet bakterielle Spuren von Menschen und geht damit über die genetische Manipulation eines einzigen Organismus hinaus. Mit ihrer Arbeit *Metabodies* erinnert sie uns daran, dass in jedem von uns 2 bis 3 Kilo Bakterien leben, die einen lebenswichtigen Bestandteil unserer Körperflora bilden. Mithilfe einer Art Biosensor versucht Bäumel Einblick in die Welt bakterieller nication, of Quorum Sensing. Her subject's hands are imprinted into agar gels after activities like showering, jogging and sex. The bacteria flourish with varied colours and textures from person to person, from activity to activity. She points out that even within the immediate environment of our skin, we have diverse and populous bacterial inhabitants, all playing a vital role in our biological makeup, even down to genetic expression through a phenomenon known as epigenetics.

If we were to crossbreed Flusser's precept with the knowledge that directors like Spielberg and Tarantino began as kids with cameras (and we know from Youtube just how many of those we have today), its easy to imagine that the next genetic Disney will not be a molecular biologist, but rather a kid at home with a DIYbio kit, tinkering to build his own diesel bioreactor from instructions found on the web. David Benqué's *The New Weatherman* points towards just that, but with the added spice of Anonymous, eco-bio-activism, and a manifesto that would carve a hole in any society and environment, though reading statements like 'species galore' it is hard to find a comeback argument. If a successful (living) planet is based on variety, and evolutionary stasis equals death, then we have to avoid monocultures at all costs. Perhaps this kind of activist approach does constitute a valid third way beyond techno-progressive and environmental conservatism.

Biogenic Timestamp offers a further disruption to the technocentric world view. By creating a bacteria that displaces the metalic elements on the motherboard of a personal computer, Catts and Iwasaki disrupt the logic of computation in synthetic biology. Given time, the motherboard would be totally changed and consumed. We only need reflect on the city-like structure of the motherboard and project 10,000 years into the future, and imagine what our own urban landscape might look like. The force of biology over time is immense. Iwasaki's and Catts' *Biogenic Timestamp* offers a contemplation of time in their title, and reflect inwards with a term from computing, a timestamp, a figure denoting the number of milliseconds at which the process began. Biogenic refers to living organisms and processes. A biogenic view would be a much larger

Kommunikation, das *Quorum Sensing*, zu gewinnen. Nach Aktivitäten wie Duschen, Joggen oder Sex nimmt sie Handabdrücke von Probanden in Agar-Gel. Darin gedeihen die Bakterien je nach Person und Aktivität in unterschiedlichen Farben und Texturen. Blümel zeigt, dass es selbst im Milieu unserer Haut große und vielfältige Bakterienpopulationen gibt, die alle eine wesentliche Rolle in unserer biologischen Konstitution spielen, sogar an sogenannten epigenetischen Veränderungen beteiligt sind.

Kreuzt man Flussers Vorhersage mit dem Wissen, dass Regisseure wie Spielberg und Tarantino schon als Kinder mit Kameras zugange waren (und dank YouTube wissen wir, wie viele von der Sorte es heute gibt), ist unschwer zu erahnen, dass der nächste Disney kein Molekularbiologe, sondern ein Kind mit DIY-Biobaukasten sein wird, das gerade nach Bauanleitungen aus dem Netz einen eigenen Biodieselreaktor bastelt. David Benqués *The New Weatherman* deutet in genau diese Richtung, nur mit einem zusätzlichen Schuss Anonymous-Eco-Bio-Aktivismus und einem Manifest, das jeder Gesellschaft und Umwelt zusetzen würde, auch wenn man angesichts eines Statements wie „Arten im Überfluss" wohl kaum von einem Comeback sprechen kann. Wenn der Erfolg (das Leben) des Planeten von Artenvielfalt abhängt und Entwicklungsstillstand Tod bedeutet, dann müssen wir Monokulturen um jeden Preis vermeiden. Vielleicht ist ein solcher aktivistischer Ansatz ein legitimer dritter Weg zwischen Technoprogressismus und Öko-Konservativismus.

An einer Erschütterung der technozentrischen Weltsicht arbeitet auch *Biogenic Timestamp*. Mit der Erzeugung von Bakterien, die die Metallbestandteile eines PC-Motherboards besiedeln, unterlaufen Catts und Iwasaki die Computerlogik in der synthetischen Biologie. Mit genügend Zeit würde das Motherboard vollkommen verändert und zersetzt. Wir müssen uns nur die stadtartige Struktur des Motherboards 10.000 Jahre in die Zukunft versetzt denken und uns vorstellen, wie dann unsere urbane Landschaft aussieht. Mit der Zeit entfaltet die Biologie eine enorme Kraft. Iwasakis und Catts' *Biogenic Timestamp* verspricht eine Kontemplation über die Zeit und verwendet dazu einen Begriff aus der Computertechnik, den Zeitstempel, der den Beginn des Rechenprozesses in Millisekunden angibt. Der Begriff *biogen* verweist dagegen auf lebende Organismen und Prozesse. Eine biogene Sicht der Dinge ist mit einem viel ausgedehnteren Zeitrahmen verbunden. Die Kritik der and longer timescale. Their criticism appears to be directed towards the pace, and acceleration of synthesism in biology (progressing at ten-fold per year as noted above). We are challenged to reflect not in milliseconds, not in years, but in millenia. Life has taken aeons to evolve, tested through trial and error to refine itself, and we take a few decades and begin immediately making our own whimsical (if science can excuse me for saying that) changes. One must reflect on this purely in terms of time, and question a technology that allows us to cheat the time needed for evolution. And what happens if we consider reversing an evolution made through synthetic methods. Georg Tremmel and Shiho Fukuhara carve open a hole in genetic engineering, and state their proposition in relatively simple terms:

"The goal of the *Common Flowers / White Out* project is to develop a toolkit and the expertise that will enable non-specialists to remove previously introduced genes from genetically-modified plants. This project is inspired by the first commercially available GM flower—a blue carnation, which has been developed and commercialised by Florigene Ltd and which is currently availably worldwide."

The impact of these terms is far from simple. Hands up any scientist who can argue or define what a de-engineered organism is. Is an organism that has been engineered to add a new feature, and then had that feature removed in a clone or later decendant still engineered? Is it still a classified bio-security risk to nature? If we were to DNA sequence the de-engineered flower, and found the DNA sequence to be identical to the original unmodified flower, then what is it? Is it still transgenic, is it even possible to restore its natural state? Can it possibly carry a ghost-trace, a scar of technology, a memory of being changed? Explain to a six year old how seeds work, how the purpose of all life is to germinate and grow up and then reproduce seed for the next generation, and you'll probably get a question like "... then who planted the first seed?". A great question indeed! The question from our point of view is: who is planting and designing the new seeds? Like Flusser, we can speculate that it's not only

beiden Künstler richtet sich offenbar gegen das enorme Entwicklungstempo der synthetischen Biologie (deren Wissen, wie gesagt, jedes Jahr um den Faktor zehn wächst). Wir sind aufgerufen, nicht in Millisekunden, nicht in Jahren, sondern in Jahrtausenden zu denken. Das Leben hat Jahrmillionen gebraucht, um sich zu entwickeln, sich über Versuch und Irrtum zu verfeinern, und wir fangen schon nach ein paar Jahrzehnten an, unsere eigenen willkürlichen (die Wissenschaft möge mir den Ausdruck nachsehen) Veränderungen vorzunehmen. Man muss das nur einmal unter dem Gesichtspunkt der Zeit durchdenken, um eine Technologie infragezustellen, die es uns erlaubt, der von der Evolution benötigten Zeit ein Schnippchen zu schlagen.
Und was, wenn wir eine durch synthetische Methoden hervorgerufene Evolution rückgängig machten? Georg Tremmel und Shiho Fukuhara machen eine Lücke in der Gentechnik ausfindig und erklären ohne Umschweife, was sie vorhaben:

„Ziel des Projekts *Common Flowers / White Out* ist die Entwicklung eines Baukastens und des nötigen Know-hows, um auch Nichfachleuten das Entfernen eingeschleuster Gene aus genetisch modifizierten Pflanzen zu ermöglichen. Angeregt wurde das Projekt durch die erste kommerziell vertriebene genmodifizierte Blume – eine von Florigene Ltd entwickelte und vermarktete blaue Nelke, die weltweit erhältlich ist."

Die Bedeutung solcher Aussagen ist alles andere als einfach. Jeder Wissenschaftler vor, der sagen kann, was ein demodifizierter Organismus ist. Ist ein Organismus, dem gentechnisch ein neues Merkmal hinzugefügt und dann in einem Klon oder späteren Abkömmling wieder entfernt wurde, immer noch gentechnisch modifiziert? Stellt er immer noch ein biologisches Sicherheitsrisiko für die Natur dar? Würden wir die demodifizierte Blume sequenzieren und feststellen, dass sich ihre DNA mit der der ursprüglich unmodifizierten Blume deckt, worum handelt es sich dann? Ist sie nicht immer noch transgen, ist es überhaupt möglich, ihren natürlichen Zustand wiederherzustellen? Bleibt vielleicht eine Geisterspur zurück, eine technologische Narbe, eine Erinnerung an die Veränderung?
Versuchen Sie einem sechsjährigen Kind zu erklären, wie das mit den Samen geht, dass es der Zweck allen Lebens ist, zu keimen, heranzuwachsen und Samen für die nächste Generation zu produzieren, und Sie werden sich vermutlich die Frage einhandeln: „Aber wer

the artists hacking away at the frontier, it will be those taking nature into their own hands, they will have to speculate on the impact of their work, as scientists, as designers, as artists, and most importantly as citizens of the earth.
Matthew Gardiner, July 2013

About Project Genesis

Project Genesis evolved out of an open call titled *Yours Synthetically* at the beginning of 2013. A call supported by an EU FP7 project called *Studiolab* (see *studiolabproject.eu).* The call was designed to open dialogue between artists, designers and scientists toward an exhibition to engage the general public. *Project Genesis* presents outcomes from incubation and education projects such as *Blueprints for the Unknown* led by David Benqué at the Royal College of Art, London, *Biotricity* at RIX-C, Riga, *Organight* at Le Laboratoire, Paris, *Opimilk* at Science Gallery, Dublin, *Deep Data Prototype _1* at Medialab Prado, Madrid, *Genegun Hack* at Medical Museion, *Hybrids* at Ecole de Recherche Graphique, Brussels, and projects incubated within the Ars Electronica Futurelab: including *Metabodies, Chroma+Phy, Synthetic Memetic,* and *Common Flowers/White Out.*

Studiolab is a project funded by the European Commission. The views and opinions here expressed do not necessarily reflect those of the European Community and the Community is not liable for any use that may be made of the information contained therein.

1 George M. Church and Ed Regis, *Regenesis, How Synthetic Biology Will Reinvent Nature and Ourselves* (New York: Basic Books 2012).
2 Joe Davis and Katie Egan, "Artistic Molecules", in *Ars Electronica 2000: Next Sex.*
3 Art Orienté Objet, *May the Horse Live in me, http://archive.aec.at/#42344.*
4 Stelarc, *Ear on Arm, http://archive.aec.at/#19658.*
5 Daniel G Gibson et al, "Creation of a Bacterial Cell Controlled by a Chemically Synthesized Genome", *science,* 329 (2010), 52–56
6 Dorothy Nelkin, "The Gene as a cultural Icon. Visual Images of DNA", in: *Ars Electronica 99, LifeScience,* p 246 (first published in: *Art Journal,* spring 1996, Vol 55, No 1)

hat dann den ersten Samen gepflanzt?" Eine wirklich große Frage! Aus unserer Sicht lautet sie: Wer pflanzt und designt die neuen Samen? Wie Flusser können wir spekulieren, dass es nicht nur Künstler sein werden, die sich an den Grenzen zu schaffen machen. Es werden diejenigen sein, die die Natur selbst in die Hand nehmen, und sie werden sich Gedanken über die Folgen ihrer Arbeit machen müssen, als Wissenschaftler, Designer, Künstler, vor allem aber als Erdenbürger.
Aus dem Englischen von Wilfried Prantner

Über das Projekt Genesis

Projekt Genesis enstand aus einem Open Call mit dem Titel *Yours Synthetically,* der Anfang 2013 von dem EU-gestützten Projekt *Studiolab* (vgl. *studiolabproject.eu)* ausgeschrieben wurde. Die Ausschreibung im Siebten EU-Rahmenprogramm sollte einen Dialog zwischen Künstlern, Designern und Wissenschaftlern in Gang setzen und zu einer Ausstellung führen, die die Öffentlichkeit einbezieht. *Projekt Genesis* präsentiert die Ergebnisse von Inkubations- und Bildungsprojekten wie das von David Benqué geleitete *Blueprints for the Unknown* am Royal College of Art, London, *Biotricity* am RIX-C, Riga, *Organight* am Le Laboratoire, Paris, *Opimilk* an der Science Gallery, Dublin, *Deep Data Prototype _1* am Medialab Prado, Madrid, *Genegun Hack* am Medical Museion, Kopenhagen, *Hybrids* an der École de Recherche Graphique, Brüssel, sowie am Ars Electronica Futurelab entstandene Projekte wie *Metabodies, Chroma+Phy, Synthetic Memetic* und *Common Flowers/ White Out.*

1 George M. Church und Ed Regis, *Regenesis, How Synthetic Biology Will Reinvent Nature and Ourselves,* New York: Basic Books 2012.
2 Joe Davis / Katie Egan, „Artistic Molecules", in: *Ars Electronica 2000: Next Sex.*
3 Art Orienté Objet, *May the Horse Live in me, <http://archive.aec.at/#42344>.*
4 Stelarc, *Ear on Arm, <http://archive.aec.at/#19658>.*
5 Daniel G. Gibson et al, „Creation of a Bacterial Cell Controlled by a Chemically Synthesized Genome", in: *science,* 329 (2010), S. 52–56.
6 Dorothy Nelkin, „Das Gen als kulturelles Ikon. Die Bildsymbolik der DNA", in: *Ars Electronica 99, LifeScience,* S. 251

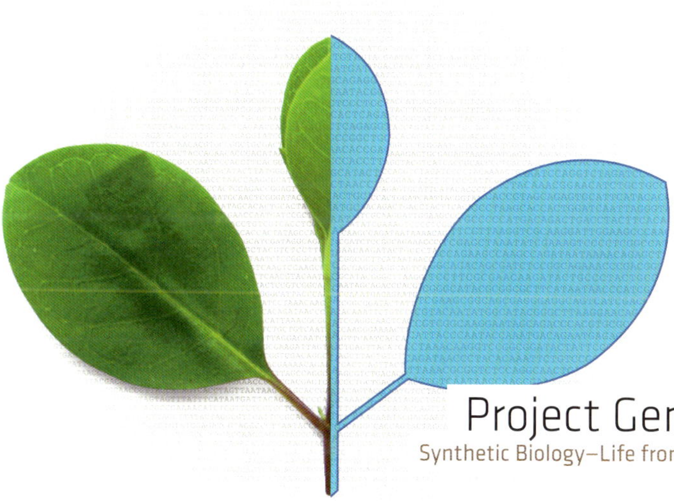

Project Genesis

Synthetic Biology—Life from the Lab

The Exhibition

Biogenic Timestamp, Hideo Iwasaki, Oron Catts (JP/AU)
Biotricity, Rasa Smit, Raitis Smite (LV)
Chroma+Phy, Theresa Schubert (DE)
Chromosome #14, Ben Fry (US)
Common Flowers/White Out, Georg Tremmel, Shiho Fukuhara (AT/JP)
Deep data prototype _1, Andy Gracie (ES)
Dynamic Genetics V Mann, Superflux (UK/DE)
Genegun Hack, Rüdiger Trojok (DK)
Hybrids, École de Recherche Graphique (BE)
Into your hands they are delivered, Tobias Revell (UK)
DIY Mobile Gen Lab, Hackteria and associated artists (CH)
Metabodies, Sonja Bäumel (AT)
Momentrium, h.o (JP)
Mousetraps 3, 14, and 18, Johanna Schmeer (UK)
Opimilk, Claire Dempsey, Aisling McCrudden, Naomi Griffin-Murtagh (IE)
Synthetic Kingdom, Daisy Ginsberg (UK)
Synthetic Memetic, Matthew Gardiner (AU/AT)
The Listener, Patricia Piccinini (AU)
The New Weathermen, David Benqué (UK)

Artistic Director: Gerfried Stocker
Curator: Matthew Gardiner
Coordinator: Christopher Lindinger
Exhibition Design: Gerald Priewasser
Project Manager: Marlene Eggenreich
Education & Culture Mediation: Andrea Fröhlich, Nicole Grüneis, Klaus Hollinetz, with support from Manuel Selg, Tamara Böhm, Andreas Leeb, Stefan Schwarzmair
Editor-in-chief: Martin Hieslmair
Graphics: My-Trinh Gardiner, Stefan Eibelwimmer
Production: Ars Electronica Center's museum infrastructure crew

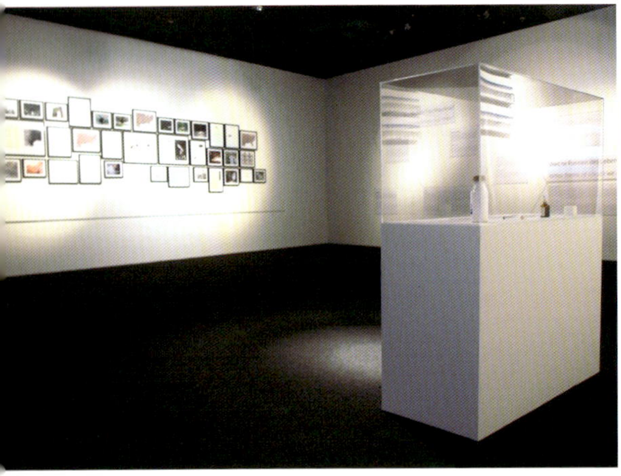

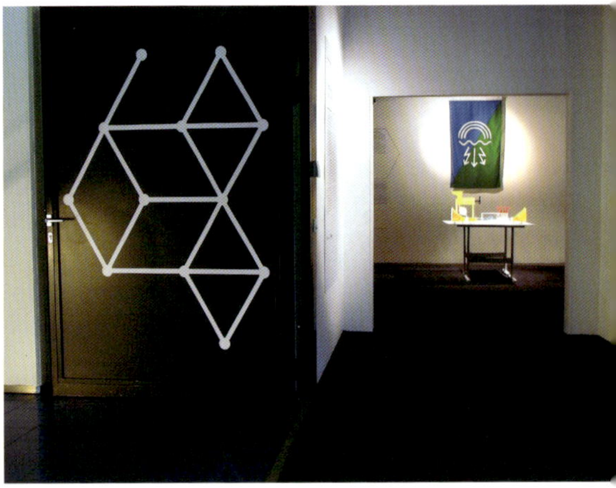

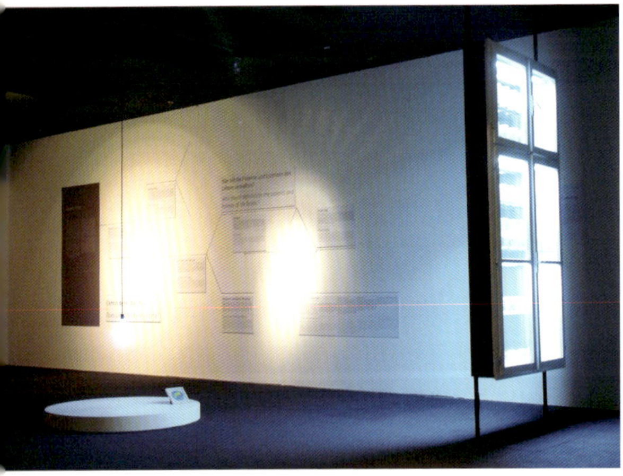

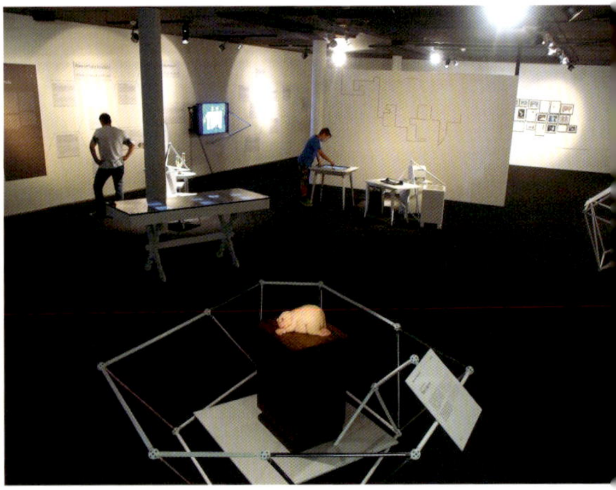

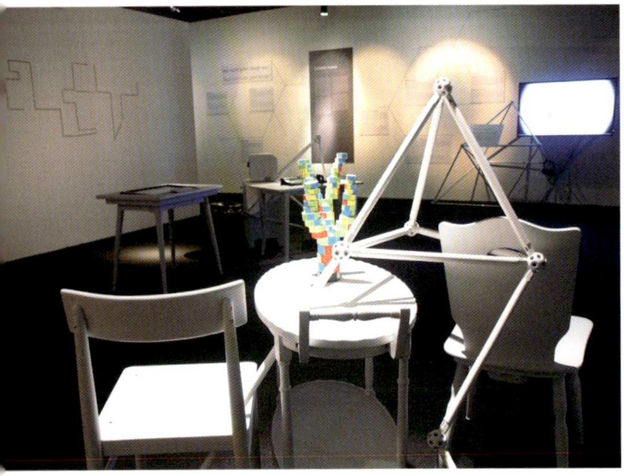

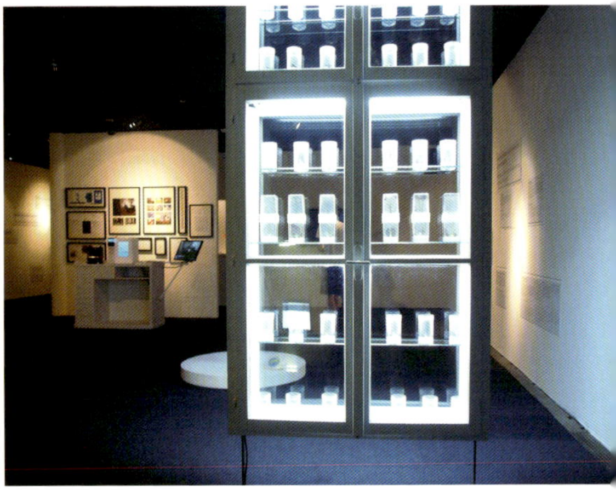

Tom Mesic

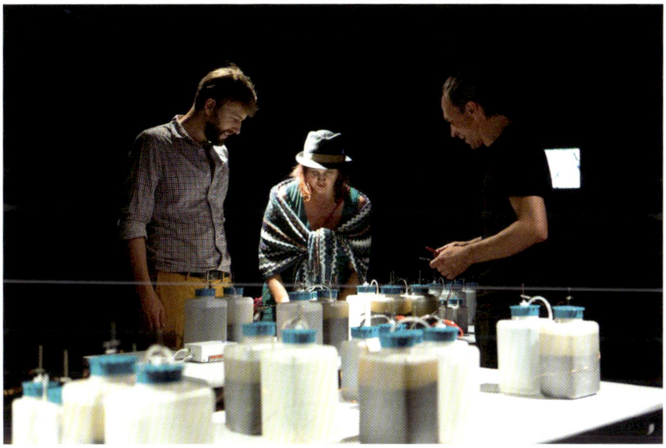

Biotricity, Rasa Smit, Raitis Smite

Tom Mesic

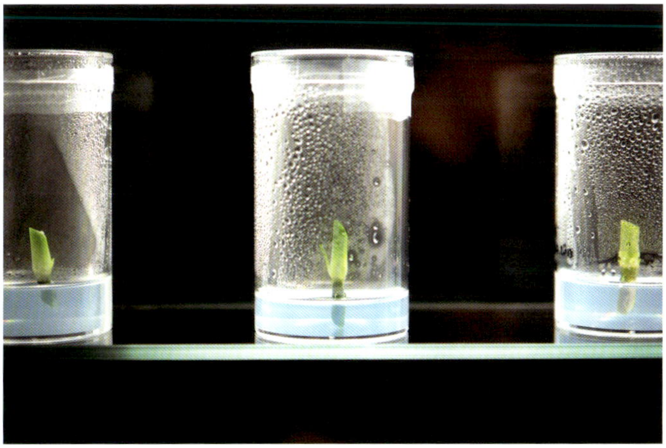

Common Flowers/White Out, Georg Tremmel, Shiho Fukuhara

AEC, Martin Hieslmair

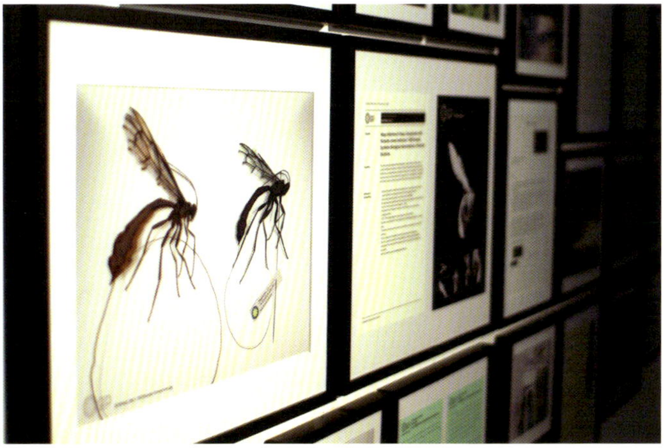

Into Your Hands Are They Delivered, Tobias Revell, Royal College of the Arts

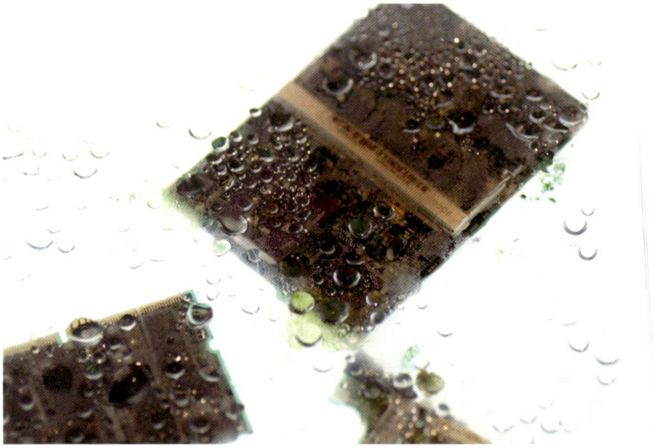

Tom Mesic

Biogenic Timestamp, Hideo Iwasaki, Oron Catts

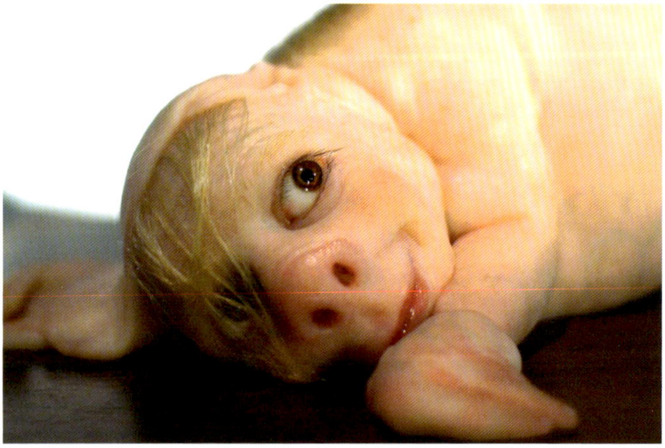

AEC, Martin Hieslmair

The Listener, Patricia Piccinini

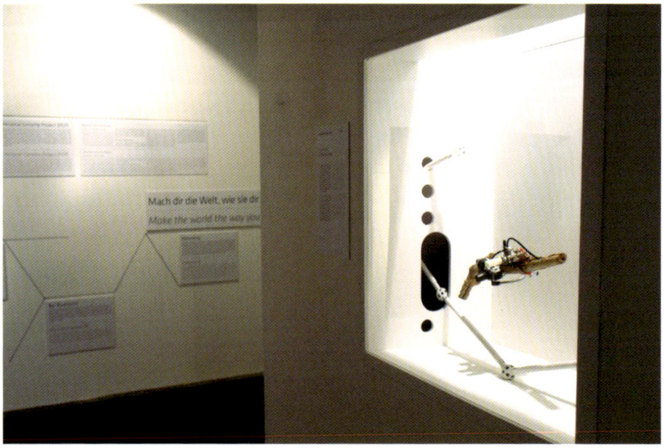

AEC, Martin Hieslmair

Gene Gun Hack, Rüdiger Trojok

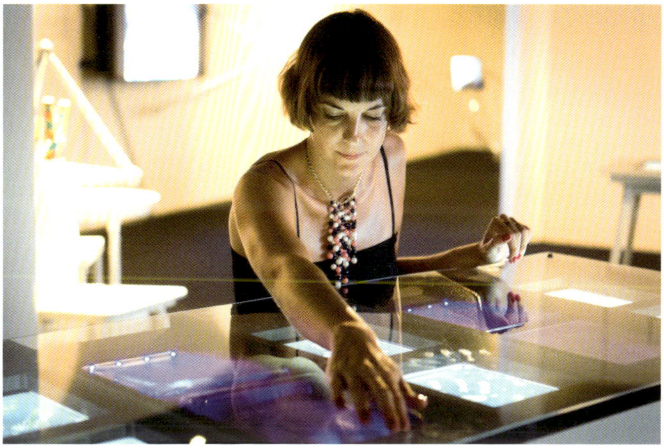

Tom Mesic

Metabodies, Sonja Bäumel

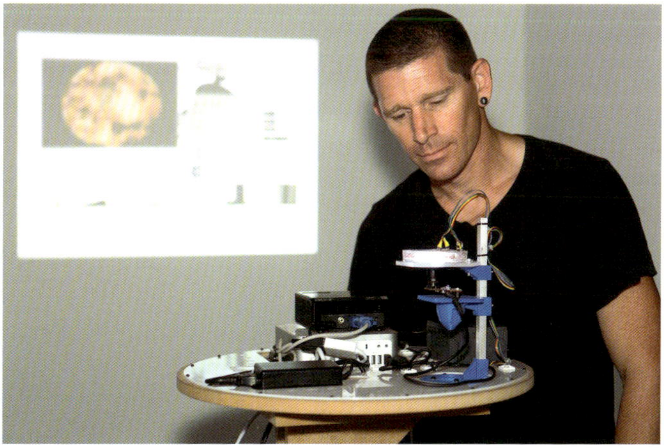

Tom Mesic

Deep data prototype _1, Andy Gracie

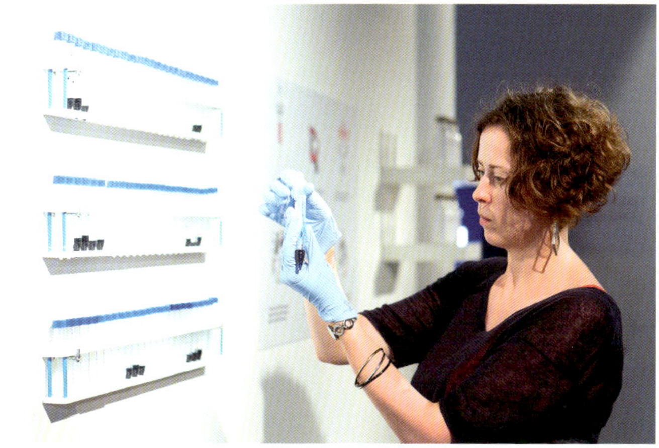

Tom Mesic

Opimilk, *Claire Dempsey*, Aisling McCrudden, Naomi Griffin-Murtagh

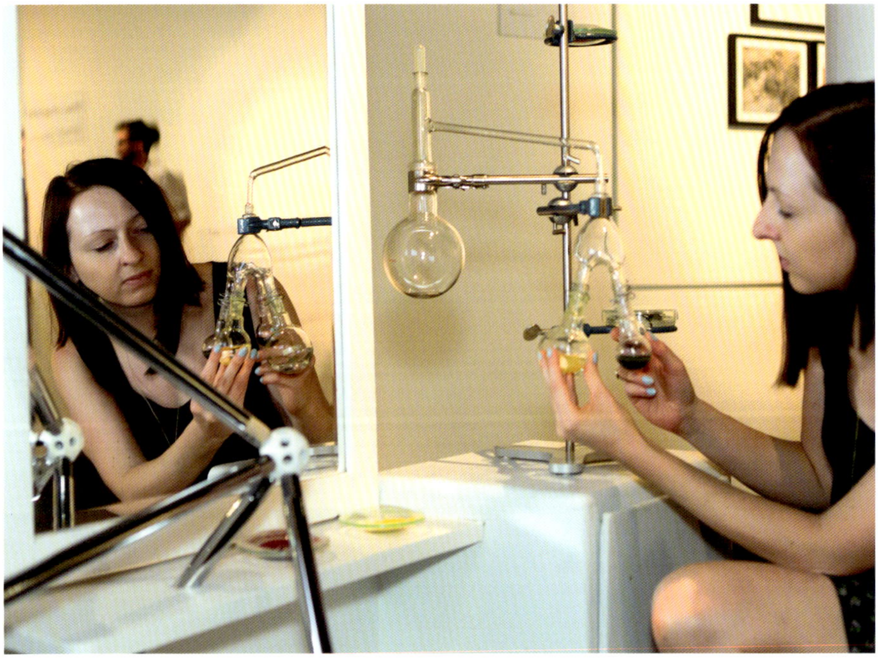

Tom Mesic

ChromaPhy+ (2013): *Theresa Schubert (AT)*

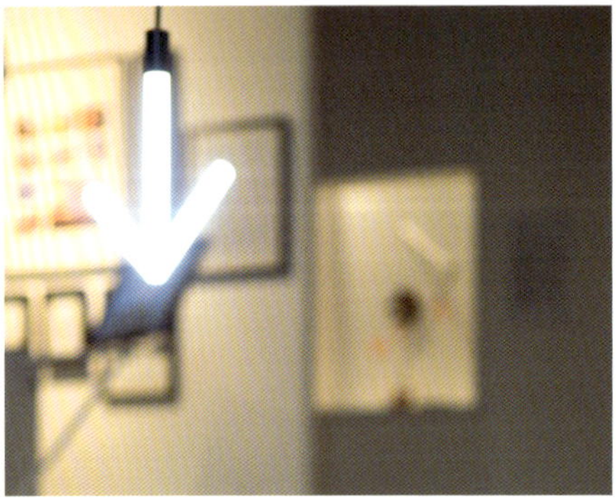

Tom Mesic

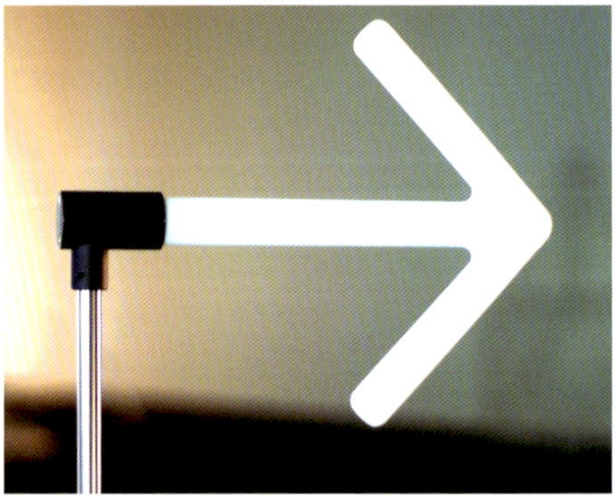

AEC, Martin Hieslmair

Momentrium, h.o

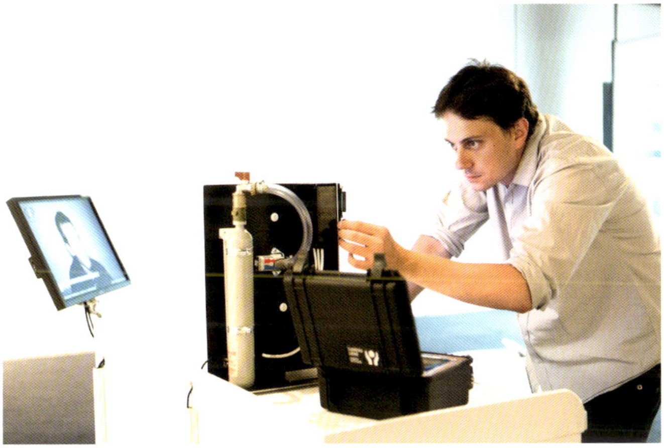

Tom Mesic

Dynamic Genetics V Mann (2013), Superflux

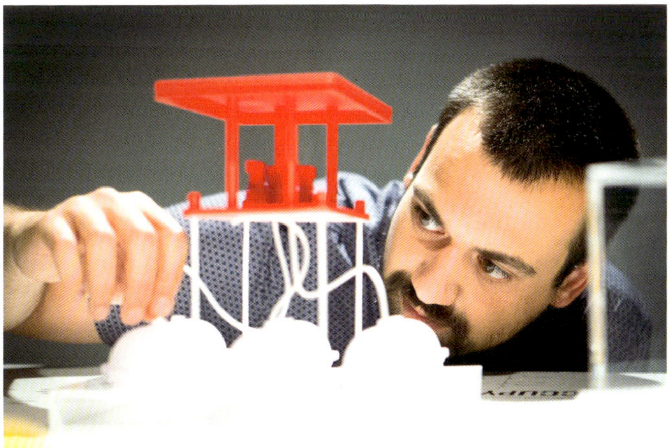

Tom Mesic

The New Weathermen, David Benqué

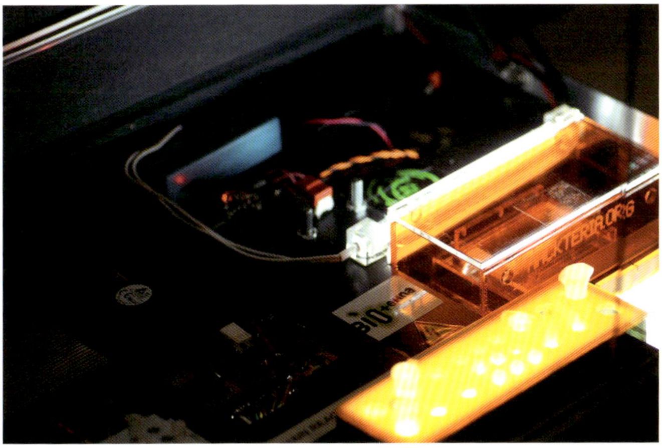

AEC,.Robertba

DIY Mobile Gen Lab, Hackteria and associated artists

Anthropocene is the term scholars now use to designate this day and age, thus describing it as the epoch in which humankind has sustainably changed the face of the Earth.
It all began with the invention of the steam engine, with the Industrial Revolution. Or perhaps much earlier—when we gave up hunting and gathering, began to cultivate fields and build settlements. But these interventions were insignificant for a very long time. It wasn't until about 1800, when our population surpassed a billion and the number of machines we had supporting us was multiplying apace, that Earth irreversibly became the Planet of the Humans. Our landscapes are formed by our hunger for raw materials; our cities and suburbs sprawl across the entire globe, their lights radiating

Anthropozän – so nennt die Wissenschaft mittlerweile unsere Zeit und beschreibt sie als Epoche, in der die Menschheit nachhaltig das Antlitz der Erde verändert. Begonnen hat es mit der Erfindung der Dampfmaschine, mit der industriellen Revolution, vielleicht schon viel früher, als wir sesshaft wurden und begannen, Felder anzulegen und Siedlungen zu errichten. Doch für sehr lange Zeit waren diese Eingriffe nicht relevant, erst seit wir ums Jahr 1800 die Milliardengrenze überschritten und immer mehr Maschinen entwickelten, die uns zur Hand gehen, ist die Erde unwiderruflich der Planet der Menschen geworden. Unsere Landschaften sind geformt von unserem Hunger nach Rohstoffen, unsere Städte und Siedlungen überziehen den gesamten Planeten und strahlen mit ihren Lichtern weit in den Weltraum hinaus. Die technischen Systeme, die out into deep space. The technical systems that we have propagated worldwide have come to be second nature to us; they've long since turned into something we take so completely for granted that we don't even notice them anymore, and we use them all too heedlessly.

Even more intensive than the networks of the Industrial Age—which were still visible and tangible—is the process of fusion that's occurred during our Digital Age. And above all since the internet became much more than technical infrastructure for data storage and dissemination, and has morphed into a social space. A setting for life itself, one that's no longer just the niche of an alternative or separate world, but rather, via the omnipresence of our stationary and mobile devices, has inseparably merged with the real spaces in which life is lived and culture engaged in by members of this society, another layer of the anthropocene that increasingly enwraps us like a natural setting of everyday life that we take as a matter of course at the very least. And even if autonomous machines remain in the realm of science fiction for the time being, we've nevertheless witnessed the emergence of a self-contained world of technical systems to which we have access only via additional systems and more devices. After all, in contrast to the natural surroundings of our everyday life, we have no sensory organs with which to perceive these new realities—we can't feel or smell the bits and bytes that surround us, and without technical aids we can't see or hear them either.

This is an ideal working environment for art meant by those who make it to be a catalyst of cultural and social transformation, and to face up to the challenge of creating passages between the real and virtual settings of life in these times. To those going about this, nature is also often a model and a source of inspiration.

Like a Second Nature is an exhibition produced by Ars Electronica in collaboration with VW Automobilforum, Berlin. The exhibition is conceived in two site-specific variants running at Volkswagen's Automobil Forum Unter den Linden venue in Berlin and at Ars Electronica Center's Robolab in Linz.

wir über den Planeten ausgebreitet haben, sind zu einer zweiten Natur für uns geworden und längst so selbstverständlich und normal, dass wir sie schon nicht mehr wahrnehmen und nur allzu achtlos nutzen. Noch viel intensiver als während des Industriezeitalters mit seinen Netzwerken, die noch sichtbar und greifbar waren, ist diese Verschmelzung im digitalen Zeitalter geworden. Vor allem seit mit dem Internet ein sozialer Raum entstanden ist, der weit über eine technische Infrastruktur für die Speicherung und Verteilung von Daten hinausgeht. Es hat sich ein Lebensraum herausgebildet, der nicht länger als Nische einer alternativen bzw. separierten Welt existiert, sondern über die Omnipräsenz der stationären und mobilen Endgeräte intrinsisch mit den realen Lebens- und Kulturräumen unserer Gesellschaft verwachsen ist – ein weiterer Layer des Anthropozän, der sich immer mehr wie eine natürliche, zumindest selbstverständliche Lebensumgebung über uns legt.

Auch wenn die Autonomie der Maschinen bis auf weiteres Science-Fiction bleibt, so ist dennoch eine Eigenwelt der technischen Systeme entstanden, in die wir nur mehr über weitere Systeme und Apparate Zugang haben, denn im Gegensatz zu unserer natürlichen Lebensumgebung haben wir für diese Realitäten keine Sinnesorgane, wir können die Bits und Bytes, die uns umgeben, nicht fühlen, nicht riechen und ohne technische Hilfsmittel auch nicht sehen und hören – ein ideales Arbeitsfeld für eine Kunst, die sich als Katalysator kultureller und gesellschaftlicher Transformation versteht und sich der Herausforderung stellt, Passagen zu schaffen, zwischen den realen und virtuellen Lebensumgebungen unserer Zeit. Die Natur ist auch dabei immer wieder Vorbild und Inspiration.

Wie eine zweite Natur ist ein Ausstellungsprojekt von Ars Electronica in Kooperation mit dem VW Automobilforum Berlin, das kontextbezogen in zwei verschiedenen Versionen realisiert wird. Zum einen im Atrium des Automobilforums in Berlin, zum andern im Robolab des Ars Electronica Center in Linz.

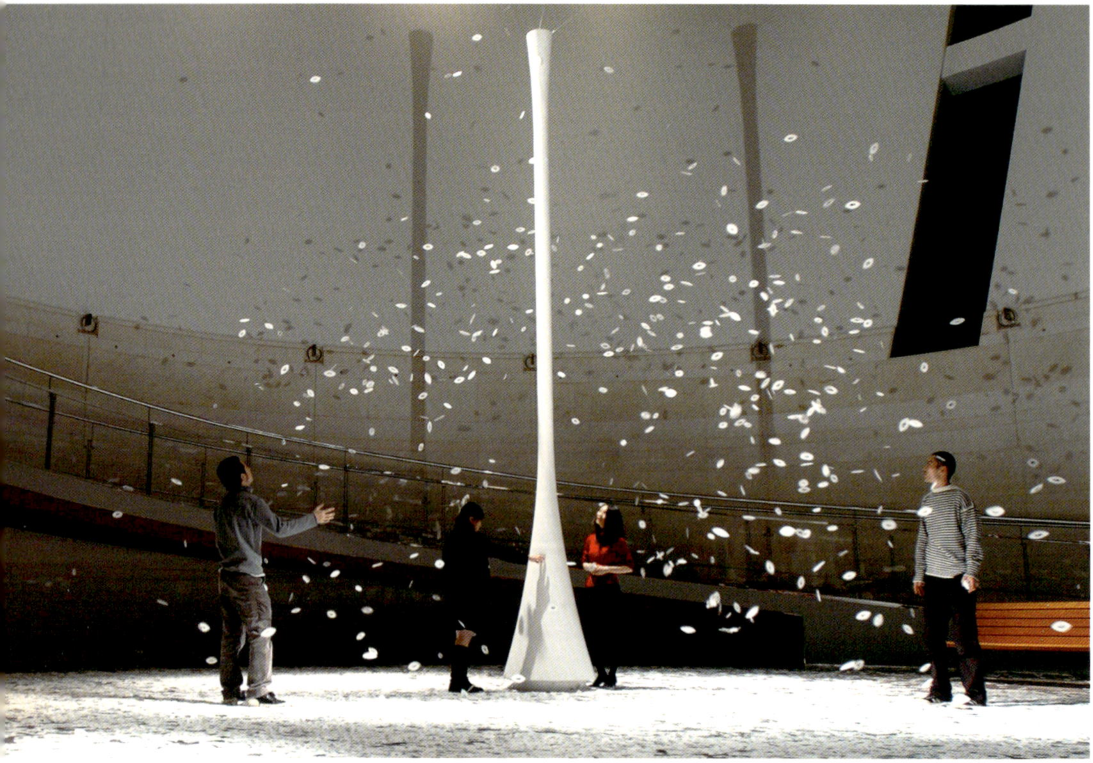

Yasuhiro Suzuki

Blinking Leaves (2003)

This sculpture is sturdily rooted in the exhibition space like a big tree trunk, but hundreds of tiny paper leaves are what makes its imposing presence truly unfold. The white leaves are blown upwards in its internal cylinder to briefly conjure up an imaginary tree with resplendent foliage in its crown. The leaves are imprinted with an open eye on one side and a closed eye on the other, which makes them seem to be winking at installation visitors during their tumbling descent to the floor. And also inviting visitors to restock the tree, since the leaves can be gathered and fed back into the sculpture to trigger another fast-forward change of seasons. Japanese artist Yasuhiro Suzuki goes more deeply into this "fluttering" and "blinking" in his 2011 book *Mabataki to Habataki.*
http://www.mabataki.com

Wie ein riesiger Baumstamm schlägt die Skulptur im Raum ihre Wurzeln, doch erst mit den Hunderten kleinen Blättern aus Papier entfaltet sie ihre ganze Pracht. Im Inneren des Zylinders werden die weißen Blätter nach oben geblasen und zaubern für wenige Sekunden einen imaginären Laubbaum in die Luft. Die mit offenen und geschlossenen Augen bedruckten Blätter wechseln bei ihrem fallenden Tanz so schnell, als ob sie den Menschen zublinzeln und sie erneut einladen würden, den Baum wieder zu „befüllen" – denn das Laub kann eingesammelt werden, um einen neuen Jahreszyklus im Schnelldurchlauf in Gang zu setzen. Dieses „Blinken" und „Flattern" greift der japanische Künstler Yasuhiro Suzuki in seinem Buch *Mabataki to Habataki* (2011) wieder auf.

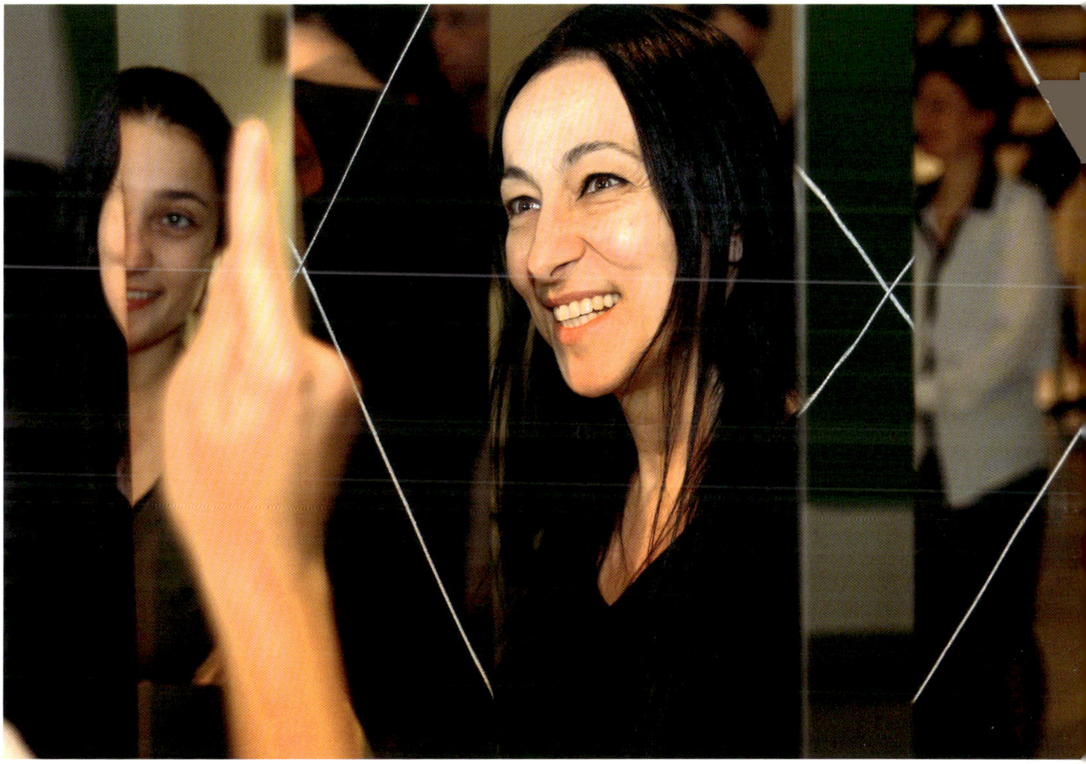

Rejane Cantoni & Leonardo Crescenti

Wall (2012)

This wall isn't the least bit inflexible; it reacts to those who confront it. *Wall* is an interactive kinetic sculpture composed of 30 vertically arrayed, mirrored-finished aluminum panels that rotate 180° in a linear sequence. The movement commences when an installation visitor moves past one end of the wall, and continues in a chain reaction like falling dominoes. One effect triggers the next. Passers-by experience a series of optical phenomena, reflections and distortions that alter the beholders' perception of reality. This interaction with installation visitors endows *Wall* with a sort of personality. The specialty of Rejane Cantoni and Leonardo Crescenti is coming up with audiovisual and haptic interfaces that make for a natural mode of exploring virtual, remote and hybrid environments.
http://www.cantoni-crescenti.com.br

Diese Wand ist nicht starr, sie reagiert auf ihr Gegenüber. 30 vertikal angeordnete Aluminiumplatten, die sich in einer linearen Abfolge jeweils um 180 Grad drehen, verwandeln *Wall* in eine kinetische, interaktive Skulptur. Der Mechanismus startet mit dem Vorübergehen an einem der Endpunkte der Installation, die Bewegung setzt sich wie bei fallenden Dominosteinen fort. Ein Effekt bedingt den nächsten. Die PassantInnen erleben eine Reihe von optischen Phänomenen, die durch Reflexionen und Verzerrungen die Wahrnehmung der Realität verändern. Durch die Interaktion mit den Menschen erhält die Wand einen Hauch von Persönlichkeit. Rejane Cantoni und Leonardo Crescenti haben sich auf audio-visuelle und haptische Interfaces spezialisiert, die das Erkunden von virtuellen, entfernten und hybriden Umgebungen auf natürlichem Weg ermöglichen

Alistair McClymont

The Limitations of Logic and the Absence of Absolute Certainty (2008)

Many people are enthralled by natural phenomena occurring on our planet. British artist Alistair McClymont constructed a model of one in order to better understand it. Thus, he literally tore a tornado out of its natural surroundings, thereby reducing the phenomenon to its essential form and then using technological aids to bring it back to life. Nevertheless, there's still that certain something—both in the original as well as the mockup—that remains essentially incomprehensible to us, something upon which we humans can exert no influence.
http://www.alistairmcclymont.com

Die Naturerscheinungen auf unserer Erde ziehen viele Menschen in ihren Bann. Der Brite Alistair McClymont hat eine davon nachgebaut, um sie noch besser verstehen zu können. So hat er einen Wirbelsturm regelrecht aus seiner natürlichen Umgebung herausgerissen, das Phänomen damit auf seine wesentlichsten Grundformen reduziert und mit technologischen Hilfsmitteln wieder zum Leben erweckt. Doch sowohl im Original als auch in der Kopie steckt ein gewisses Etwas, das für uns von Natur aus unverständlich bleibt und auf das wir Menschen keinen Einfluss nehmen können.

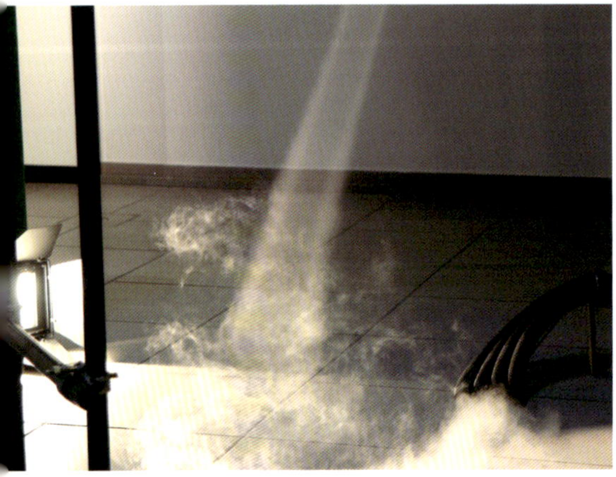

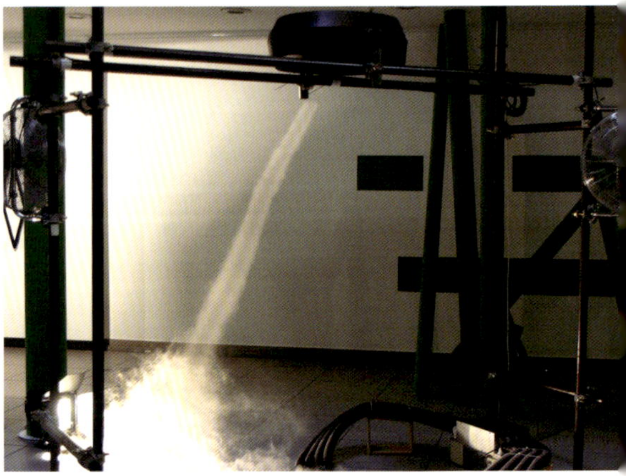

Keiko Takahashi

Meter Crawler (2008 - 2013)

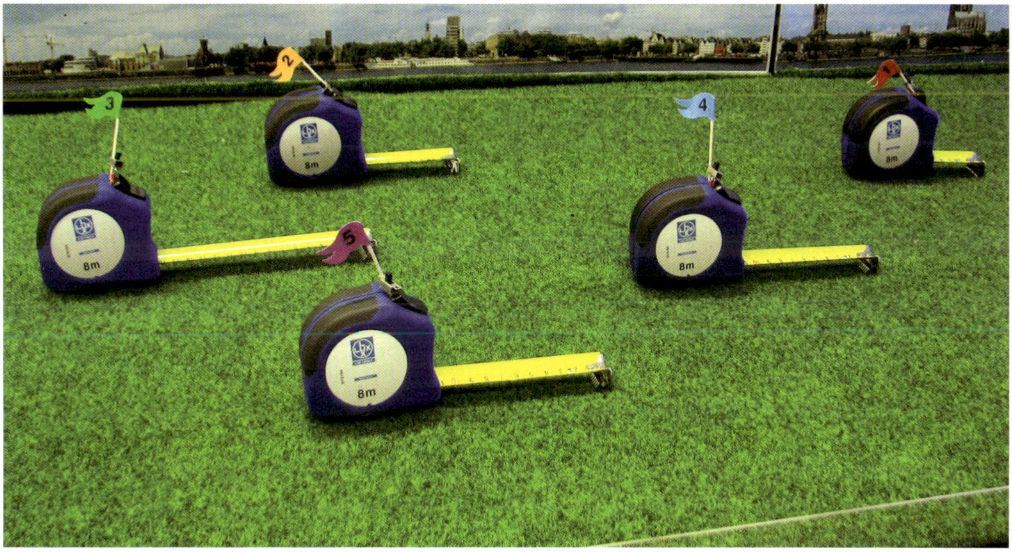

The retractable tape measure that Japanese artist Keiko Takahashi uses in this work seems no different than one any handyman has in his toolbox, but a simple technical enhancement endows this model with a life of its own. The result: an immediately recognizable resemblance to the physical appearance and leisurely locomotion of a creature with which we're all familiar. The retractable tape measure inches along like a snail. *Meter Crawler* extends its graduated band about five centimeters and digs the metal flange on the end into the ground to pull its housing forward. This case clearly illustrates how we humans, by bringing just a bit of imagination to bear, can discover similarities between nature and technology.
http://www.th.jec.ac.jp/~keiko

Äußerlich unterscheidet sich das Rollmaßband in dieser Arbeit der japanischen Künstlerin Keiko Takahashi kaum von jedem anderen. Doch mit einfachen technischen Mitteln wird dem physischen Objekt Leben eingehaucht – mit der optischen Ähnlichkeit und der nachgeahmten Bewegung stellen wir schnell einen direkten Vergleich mit einem landläufig bekannten Lebewesen her. Wie eine Schnecke kriecht das Rollmaßband über die Oberfläche: Der *Meter Crawler* streckt das Messelement etwa fünf Zentimeter aus seinem Gehäuse, krallt sich mit seinem Metallwinkel in den Boden und zieht den restlichen Körper nach. Das Beispiel zeigt ganz klar, wie wir Menschen mit einem geringen Maß an Vorstellungskraft Ähnlichkeiten zwischen Natur und Technik finden.

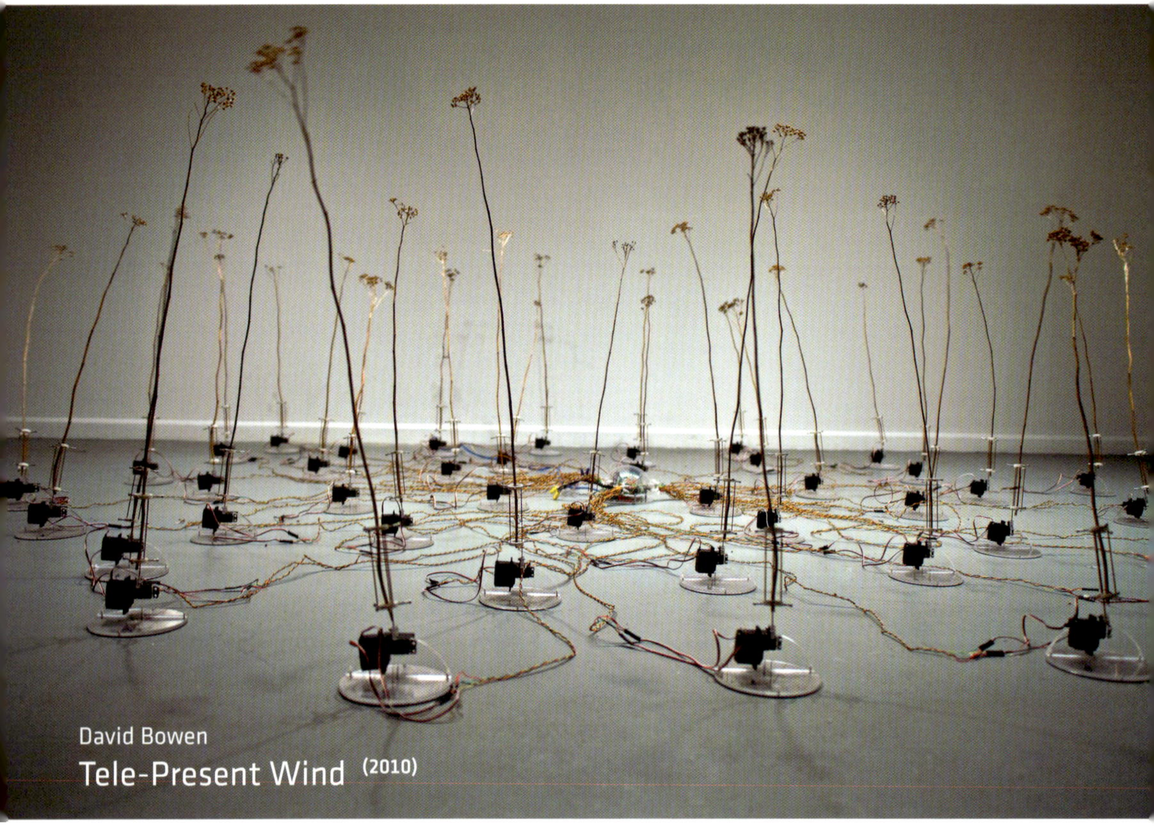

David Bowen

Tele-Present Wind (2010)

Is it possible to take the sensation of a gust of wind or slight breeze blowing outdoors and transpose it into a windowless room? How about from one spot on Earth to another? American artist David Bowen's installation does just that. An accelerometer is attached to a plant growing outdoors and records the motion of the stalk swaying in the breeze. Even the slightest puff produces data, which are transmitted into the installation space to 42 tiltable mechanical elements, each of which is mounted on the stalk of a dried plant. In real time and coordinated with wind conditions outside, the array of plants gracefully executes its synchronized dance.
http://www.dwbowen.com

Lässt sich die Empfindung einer Windböe oder eines Windhauchs im Freien in einen Raum ohne Fenster übertragen, oder gar von einem Ort der Welt zu einem anderen? Die Installation des US-amerikanischen Künstlers David Bowen macht es möglich: Ein Beschleunigungsmesser ist an einer Pflanze im Freien angebracht und nimmt die Bewegungen des im Wind schwankenden Stiels auf. Jeder kleinste Windstoß produziert Daten, die an die 42 kippbaren mechanischen Elemente im Inneren übertragen werden, an denen jeweils eine getrocknete Pflanze angebracht ist. In Echtzeit und im Gleichklang mit den äußeren Windverhältnissen setzt sich schließlich eine Gruppe von Pflanzen wieder in Bewegung.

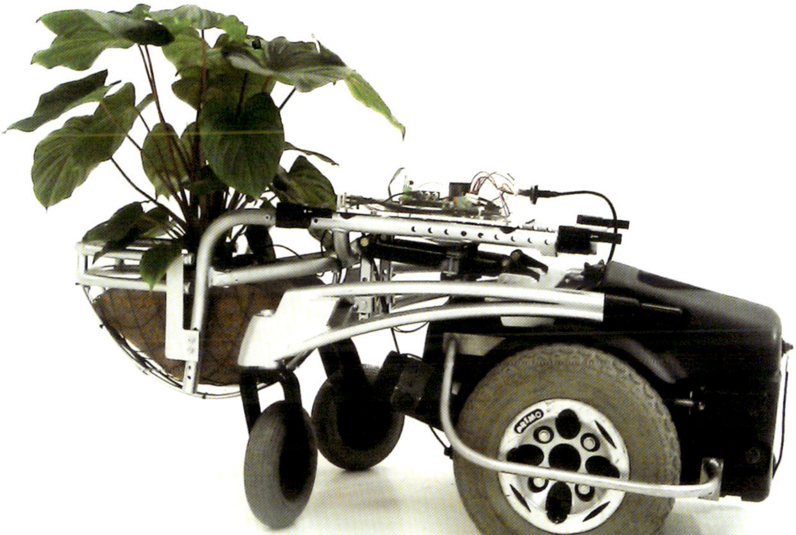

Ivan Henriques

Prototype for a New Biomachine (2012)

Now that lots of people are going high-tech, it's high time for plants to do so too. Brazilian artist Ivan Henriques' interactive BIOMACHINE explores new channels of communication among human beings, living organisms and machines. It transforms a tropical plant into a sensor. When an installation visitor touches the leaves of this Homalomena, a flowering plant of the Araceae (Arum) family, the entire plant registers this stimulus and transmits an electrical signal to an attached machine that proceeds to go into motion. The creation of this prototype will be followed up by additional research into the development of autonomous symbiotic bio-machines in which plants and mechanical devices literally merge into one unit.
http://www.ivanhenriques.com

Nicht nur Menschen sollen auf Technologien zugreifen können, sondern auch Pflanzen. Der brasilianische Künstler Ivan Henriques erforscht mit seiner interaktiven „Biomaschine" (PNBM) neue Wege der Kommunikation zwischen Menschen, lebenden Organismen und Maschinen, und verwandelt eine tropische Pflanze in einen Sensor. Wenn die Blätter der Homalomena aus der Familie der Aronstabgewächse berührt werden, nimmt die gesamte Pflanze diesen Reiz wahr und überträgt ein elektrisches Signal an eine angeschlossene Maschine, die sich daraufhin in Bewegung setzt. Dem Prototyp sollen weitere Forschungen folgen, um autonome symbiotische Biomaschinen zu entwickeln, bei der Pflanzen und Maschinen ineinander verschmelzen.

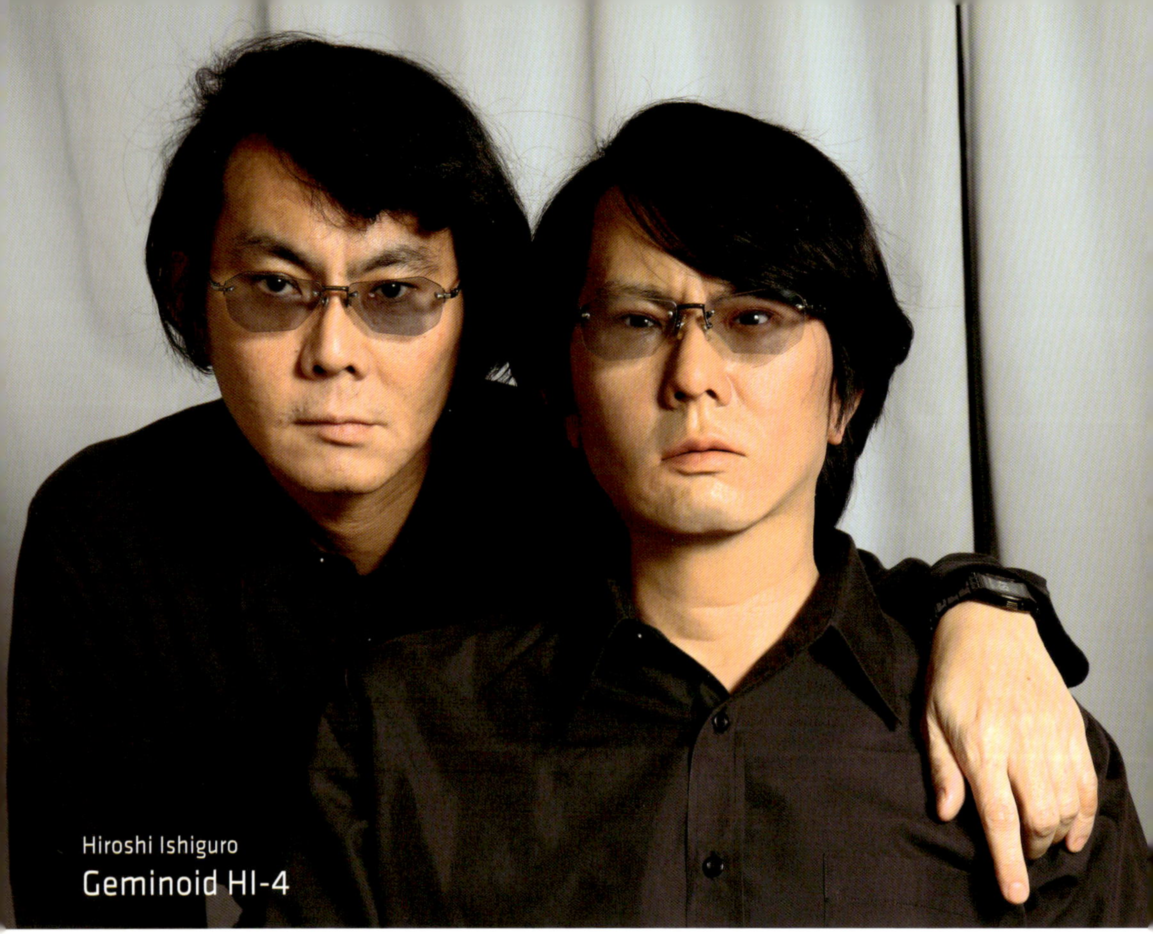

Hiroshi Ishiguro

Geminoid HI-4

In 2006, Hiroshi Ishiguro—then visiting group leader of ATR Intelligent Robotics Laboratories—created a teleoperated android replica of himself, *Geminoid HI-1.* With 46 actuators and various sensors, it was the most complicated robot in the world to date.
In 2009 Ishiguro was the featured artist at the Ars Electronica Festival, where *Geminoid HI-1* was exhibited in the main gallery of the Ars Electronica Center. The impressive exhibition made *Geminoid HI-1's* popularity spread throughout the world, and Ishiguro and Geminoid received many invitations to give talks and presentations. However, the *Geminoid HI-1* system is not suitable for transport, so Ishiguro created a more portable version, *Geminoid HI-4,* which is able to talk with visitors and has 12

Hiroshi Ishiguro schuf 2006, damals noch Gastbereichsleiter der ATR Intelligent Robotics Laboratories, *Geminoid HI 1,* einen fernbedienten Androiden als Kopie seiner Person. Mit 46 Stellmotoren und verschiedenen Sensoren ist er auch heute noch der komplexeste Roboter weltweit.
Als *Featured Artist* des Ars Electronica Festival 2009 präsentierte Ishiguro den *Geminoid HI 1* in der Main Gallery des Ars Electronica Center. Die beeindruckende Ausstellung machte *Geminoid HI 1* weltweit populär, und Ishiguro und der Geminoid erhielten zahlreiche Einladungen zu Vorträgen und Vorführungen. Doch das System hinter *Geminoid HI 1* ist für den Transport wenig geeignet, weshalb Ishiguro eine leichter zu transportierende Version, *Geminoid HI 4,* entwickelte.

actuators for facial expressions and eye and head movement. It can be split into several parts and transported as checked baggage, making it possible to hold talks at conferences all over the world. Usually, Ishiguro and *Geminoid HI-4* do not work in the same place at the same time. While one of them is giving a talk somewhere, the other may be working in Japan or some other country. In this way teleoperated androids are able to take work off our hands.

Developed by Hiroshi Ishiguro, Professor at the Department of Systems Innovation, Osaka University & Group Leader of ATR Hiroshi Ishiguro Laboratory

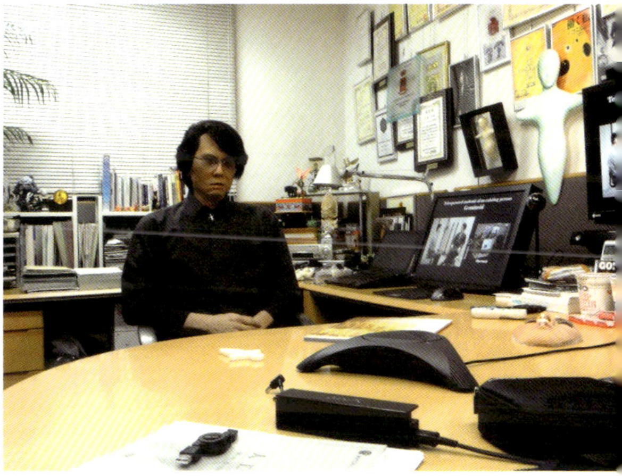

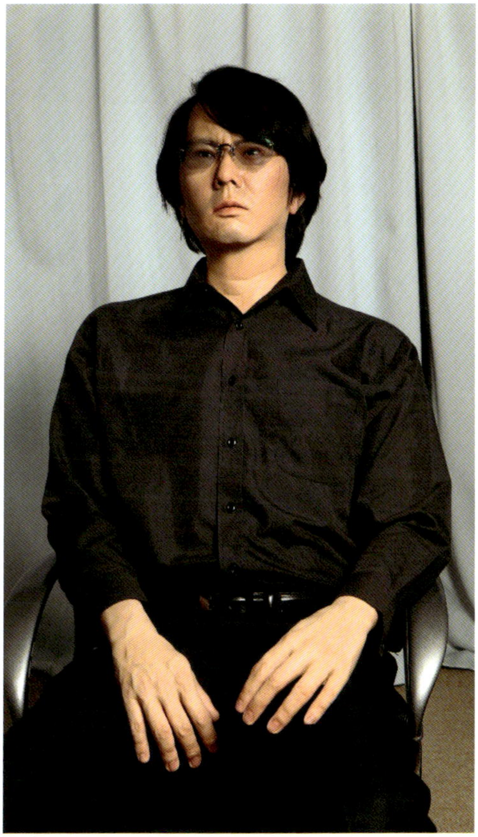

Dieser kann mit Besuchern sprechen und verfügt über zwölf Stellmotoren für Mimik, Augen- und Kopfbewegungen. Er kann in Einzelteile zerlegt und als Reisegepäck aufgegeben werden, was ihm ermöglicht, auf der ganzen Welt Vorträge zu halten. Für gewöhnlich befinden sich Ishiguro und *Geminoid HI 4* nicht zur selben Zeit am selben Ort. Während einer der beiden irgendwo einen Vortrag hält, arbeitet der andere in Japan oder einem anderen Land. Auf diese Weise sind fernbediente Androiden in der Lage, uns Arbeit abzunehmen.

Aus dem Englischen von Michael Kaufmann

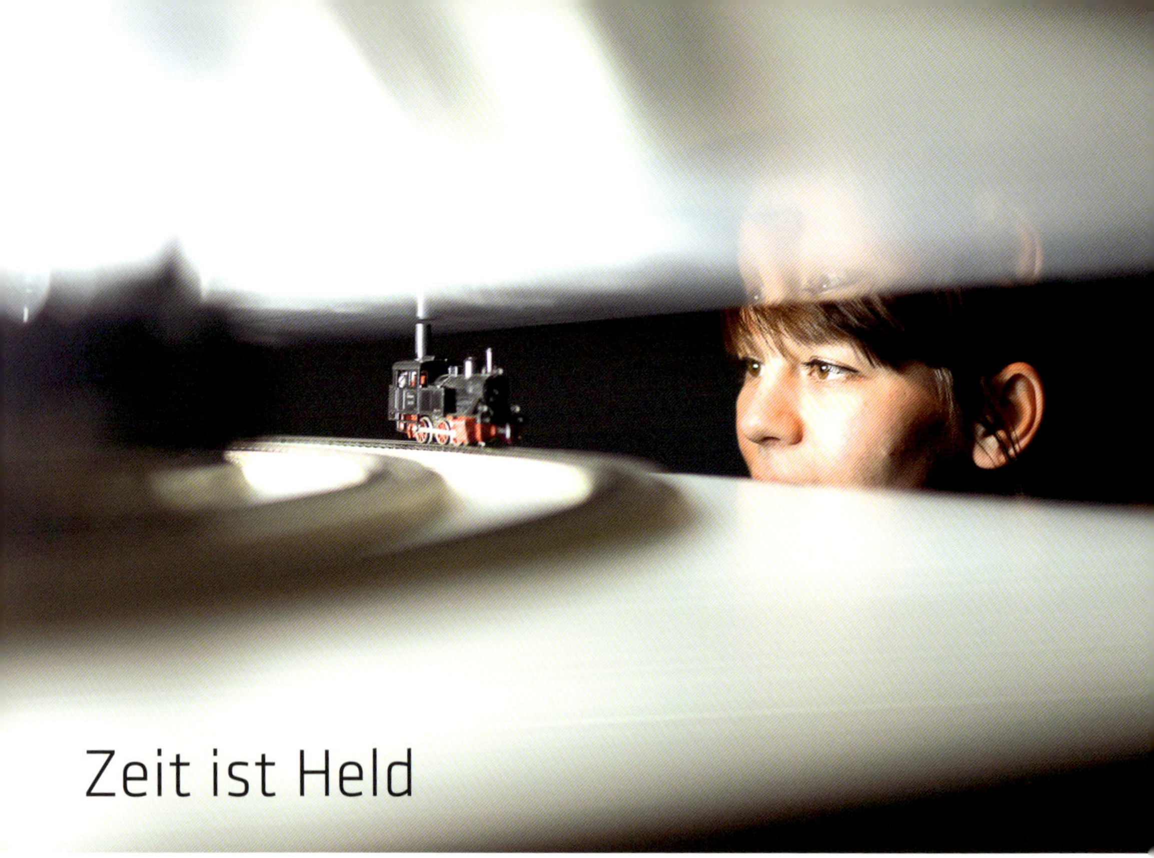

Zeit ist Held

Where does the time between birth and death go? Who controls it and how important is it for us and our fellow human beings? The relationship between one's personal pursuit of happiness and how one deals with time constitutes the substantive core of the exhibition entitled *Zeit ist Held* [literally, time is hero; actually, a play on the German expression meaning "time is money" (Geld)]. At an early stage of human existence, periodic phenomena like day and night, ebb and flow, and the change of seasons enabled people to structure their time and adjust their lives accordingly. Slowly but surely, though, our cultures and institutions erected a network of calendars and schedules, so that nowadays changes in nature scarcely impact our personal perception of time. The upshot of these structures and constraints is that we are made increasingly aware of stress in our everyday life, we are confronted by the inexorable passage of time, receive a powerful impression of life's monotony and become cognizant of constantly putting off items on our to-do list. Learning how to effectively deal with the time structures that have been imposed upon us seems to be one of the most important skills to acquire at present—after all, time is what life is all about!

Wo bleibt unsere Zeit zwischen Leben und Sterben? Wer beherrscht sie und wie wichtig ist sie für uns und unsere Mitmenschen? Das Verhältnis zwischen dem persönlichen Streben nach Glück und dem eigenen Umgang mit der Zeit bildet den inhaltlichen Kern der Ausstellung *Zeit ist Held.* Periodische Phänomene wie Tag und Nacht, Ebbe und Flut oder die Jahreszeiten ermöglichten dem Menschen früh, seine Zeit zu strukturieren und das eigene Leben daran auszurichten. Schleichend errichteten unsere Kulturen und Institutionen jedoch ein Netz aus Kalendern und Plänen, sodass Veränderungen in der Natur heute nur mehr zu einem kleinen Teil auf unsere persönliche Zeitempfindung einwirken. Diese Strukturen und Zwänge führen dazu, dass wir den alltäglichen Stress, die empfundene Unaufhaltsamkeit der Zeit, den Eindruck von Monotonie im Leben oder das ständige Aufschieben von Aufgaben immer deutlicher wahrnehmen. Den richtigen Umgang mit den uns auferlegten Zeitstrukturen zu erlernen, scheint eine der erstrebenswertesten Fähigkeiten der Gegenwart zu sein – denn Zeit ist Held.

Die Ausstellung *Zeit ist Held* wurde von Studierenden des Masterstudiengangs MultiMediaArt der

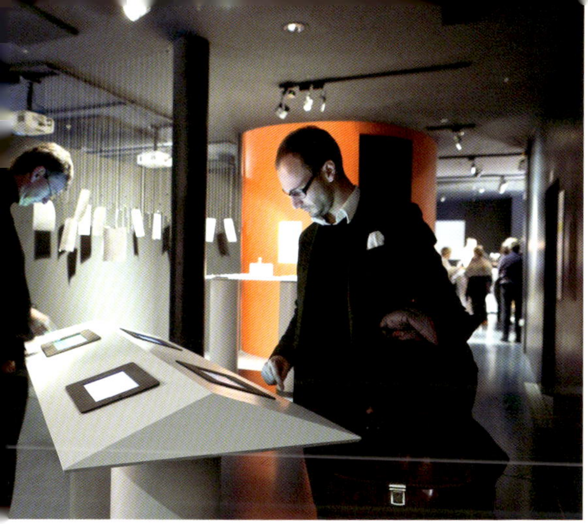

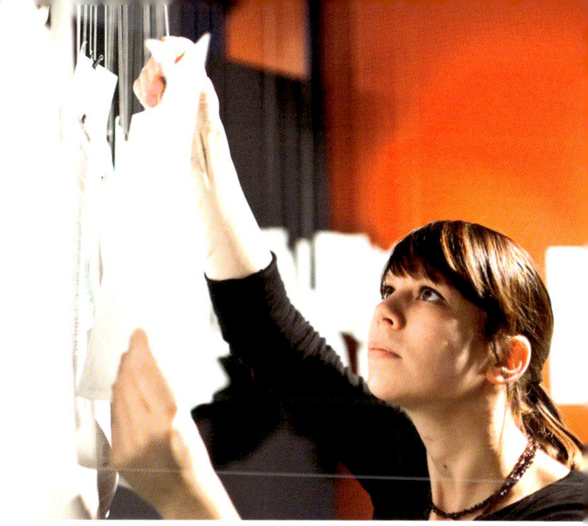

The *Zeit ist Held* exhibition was created by students in the MultiMediaArt master's program at Salzburg University of Applied Sciences. It focuses on three aspects of time. Interactive installations and visualizations showcase the time structures to which we subject ourselves, make us more cognizant of our own perception of time, and give some food for contemplation about how one budgets one's time. *The Train of Time* is a model emblematic of the synchronization of time necessitated by global networks. The fact that the world still doesn't have a homogeneous conception of time is illustrated by the *Concepts of Time* of various different cultures. Anyone who beholds the 96 webcam images in *Lamplighter* knows at a glance that day and night occur simultaneously on Earth. Detailed info-graphics show what actually takes place in a *WorldSecond*. Visitors also have the opportunity to quantify their dealings with time in order to find out whether they're suffering from *Hurry Sickness*. *Moments and Strawberries* brings in an ancient Asian point of view of time. In *Voices about Time* conversations, anecdotes and personal reflections give an account of the character of time. All of us perceive time differently, regardless of whether we're sitting in front of the computer spending *Life in the Download Progress Bar* or enjoying *The Pace of Life* at a different speed in a different country, which visitors can choose for themselves at one of several interactive stations each equipped with plenty of control knobs.

http://www.zeitistheld.at/

Zeit ist Held Team: Thomas Altmanninger, Marlene Eggenreich, Tobias Furtschegger, Friederike Krepela, Vinzenz Mayrhofer, Thomas Mühlberger / Salzburg University of Applied Sciences

FH Salzburg realisiert und richtet ihren Fokus auf drei Aspekte der Zeit: Sie führt mit interaktiven Stationen und Visualisierungen die Zeitstrukturen vor, die wir uns selbst aufbürden, sie schärft das Bewusstsein für die eigene Zeitempfindung und gibt Denkanstöße, um in Ruhe über die eigene Zeitgestaltung reflektieren zu können. So greift der *Zug der Zeit* modellhaft die durch die globale Vernetzung notwendig gewordene Synchronisation der Zeit auf. Dass die Welt noch immer keine einheitliche Auffassung von Zeit hat, darauf veweisen die *Zeitbilder* unterschiedlicher Kulturen; und wer mit dem *Laternenanzünder* 96 Webcam-Bilder auf einen Blick betrachtet, weiß genau, dass Tag und Nacht auf unserer Erde stets gleichzeitig geschehen. Detaillierte Infografiken veranschaulichen, was in einer *Weltsekunde* eigentlich geschieht. Die BesucherInnen haben außerdem die Möglichkeit, ihr eigenes Zeitverhalten zu protokollieren, um herauszufinden, ob sie zu jenen Menschen gehören, die an einer *Eilkrankheit* leiden. Nicht nur die Sichtweisen der Studierenden selbst fließen mit *Momente und Erdbeeren* in die Ausstellung ein: In *Stimmen zur Zeit* sind auch andere in Gesprächen, Geschichten und persönlichen Gedanken über die Zeit akustisch präsent. Wir alle nehmen Zeit unterschiedlich wahr, egal ob wir vor dem Computer wartend ein *Leben im Ladebalken* verbringen oder in einem anderen Land ein völlig anderes *Lebenstempo* pflegen, das sich die BesucherInnen an einer mit mehreren Reglern ausgestatteten interaktiven Station aussuchen können.

Text: Martin Hieslmair

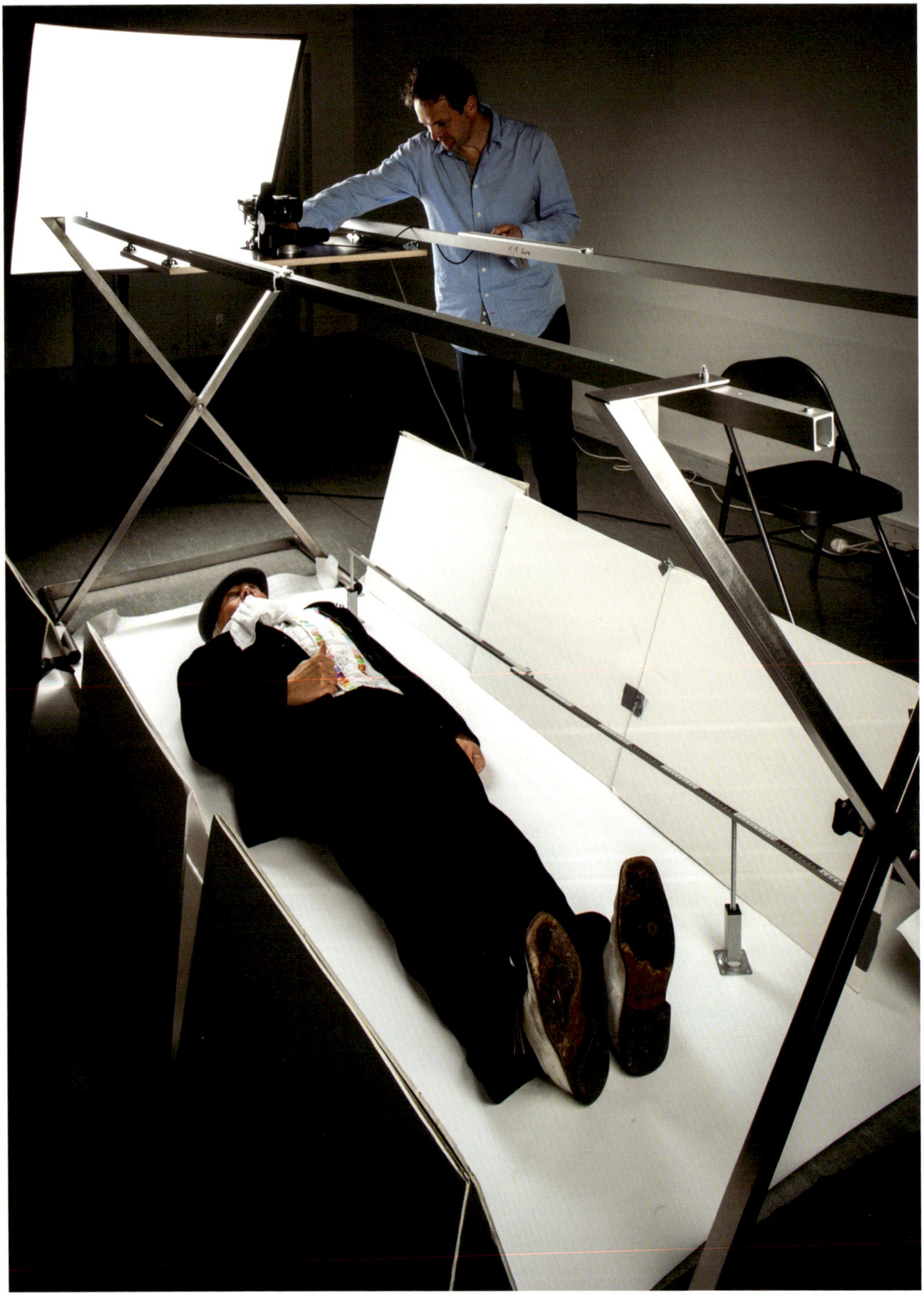

Kurt Hörbst

people_scans

Remaining stationary for minutes at a time, frozen in a pose for what seems like an eternity, one's head held in place by a support, eyes staring into an unmoving lens—all of these technical requirements of 19th-century photography have long been things of the past. And in an age in which smartphones are constantly ready to be deployed for snapshots, the duration of the exposure is now pretty much irrelevant for most cameras. Photographic portraits are taken in a matter of seconds, anyplace, at any time. The mass diffusion of profile photos in social networks underscores the unprecedented significance one's own countenance has assumed in the 21st century.

Upper Austrian photographer Kurt Hörbst's *people_scans* project and the deceleration that is its core concept provide a whole new take on modern-day portrait photography. With a high-resolution digital camera running along a specially constructed set of tracks, human subjects are systematically scanned in up to 20 individual images taken under constant lighting conditions. The individual exposures are then manually assembled with the help of an image processing program. While being photographed, the human subject is deprived of any latitude for motion. Just like in bygone days, he/she is totally exposed to the photographer for one to two minutes—though this time while lying motionless on the floor.

Minutenlanges Stillhalten, ein scheinbar ewiges Verharren in einer Pose, das mit einer Kopfstütze fixierte Starren in ein regungsloses Objektiv – all diese technischen Notwendigkeiten der Fotografie des 19. Jahrhunderts sind schon längst Geschichte. Im Zeitalter von stets für Schnappschüsse einsatzbereiten Smartphones spielt die Belichtungszeit für die meisten Kameras heute keine Rolle mehr. Fotografische Porträts entstehen in Sekundenschnelle, an jedem beliebigen Ort, zu jeder gewünschten Zeit. Die massenhafte Verbreitung von Profilfotos in sozialen Netzwerken streicht die Bedeutung des eigenen Konterfeis im 21. Jahrhundert so stark heraus wie noch nie.

Mit seinem Projekt *people_scans* und der damit verbundenen Entschleunigung der heutigen Porträtfotografie öffnet der oberösterreichische Fotograf Kurt Hörbst eine neue Perspektive: Mit einer hochauflösenden Digitalkamera und einem eigens konstruierten Schienensystem werden Menschen in bis zu 20 Einzelaufnahmen systematisch bei gleichbleibenden Lichtverhältnissen abgescannt, bevor diese Aufnahmen schließlich in einem Bildbearbeitungsprogramm manuell zusammengesetzt werden. Das Modell verliert dabei jeglichen Bewegungsspielraum und ist während dieser Aufnahmephase gezwungen, sich wie früher für ein bis zwei Minuten dem Fotografen auszusetzen – diesmal jedoch auf dem Boden liegend.

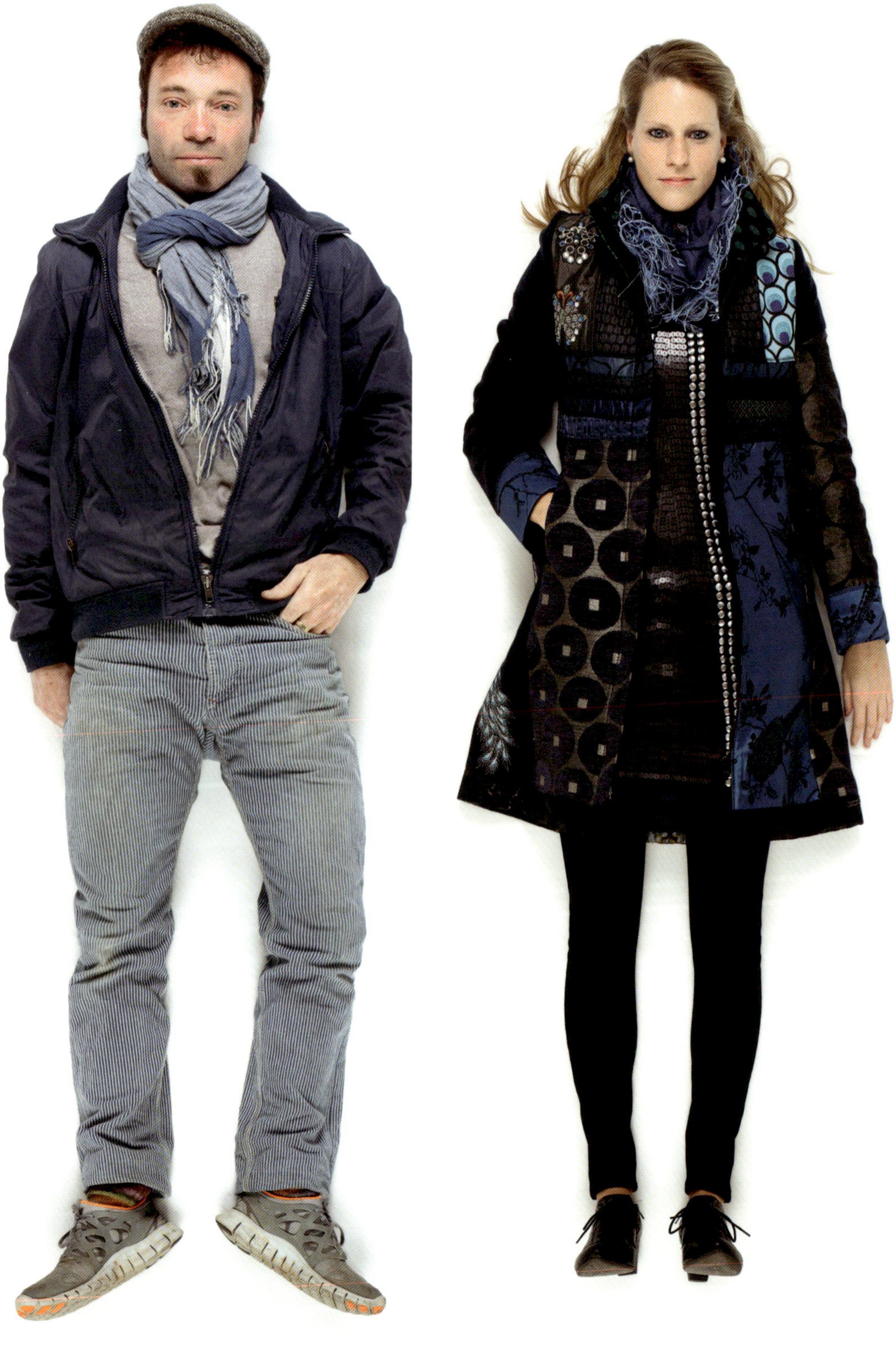

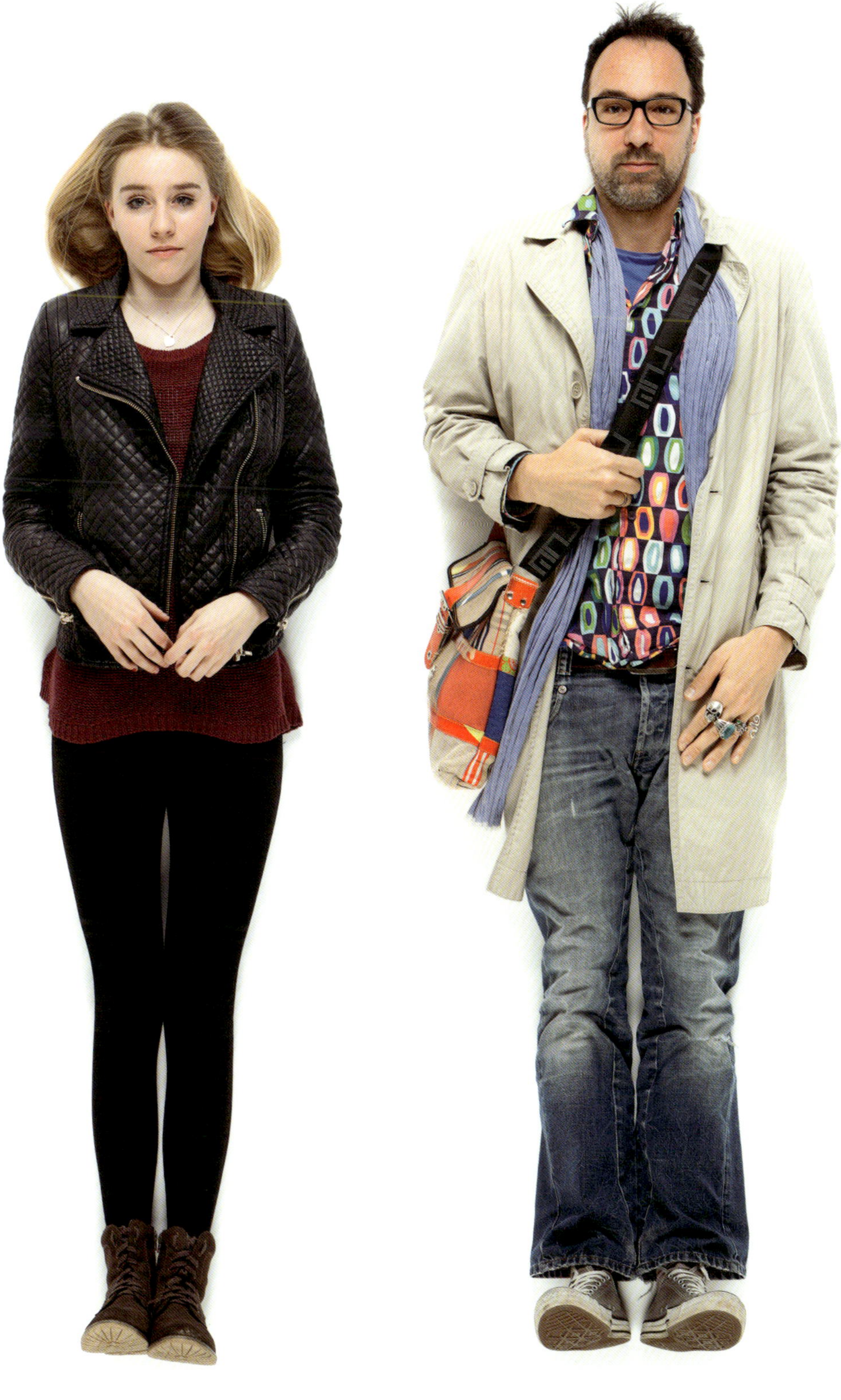

Erika Jungreithmayr, g.tec medical engineering

Faces in the MatriX
Gesichter in der MatriX

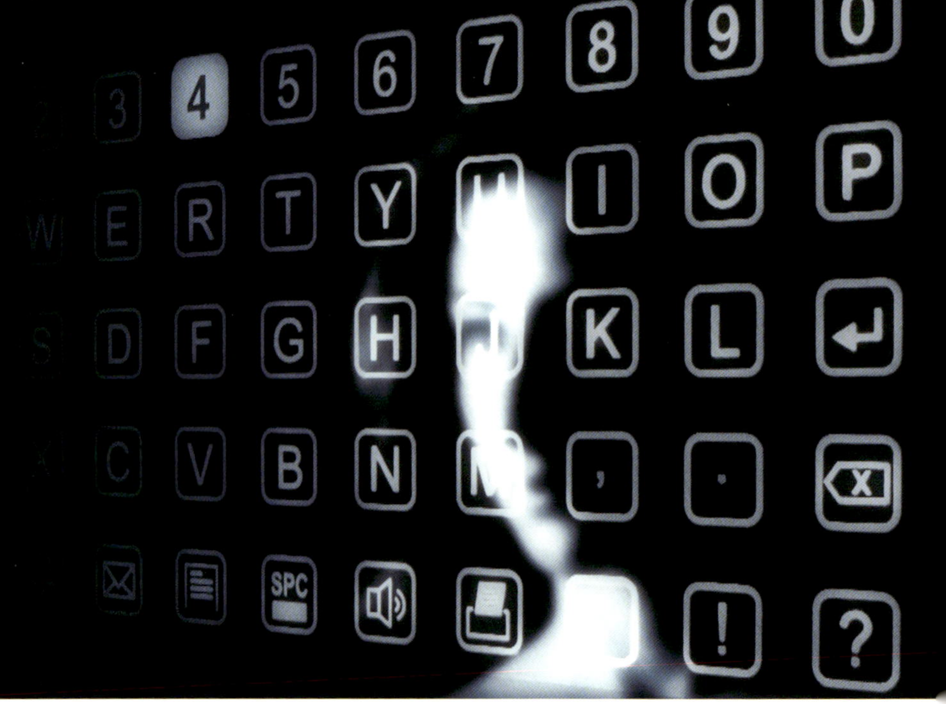

intendiX

The *Faces in the MatriX* project dispatches visitors into a digital matrix while their brain waves are measured, analyzed and visualized by a brain-computer interface (BCI). This neuroscience experiment is designed to establish whether the subject's brain reacts differently to the facial features of media personalities and celebrities than it does to unfamiliar faces.

The human brain is capable of storing all it has seen and recognizing those images when they're seen again—for instance, other people's facial features. This ultra-high-speed recognition of faces is an evolutionary achievement and serves as the basis of this research project. Put in laymen's terms, everything we see is saved to memory as a neuronal pattern in the brain. If a face, for example, is seen again, this event triggers a recognition signal

Das Projekt *Gesichter in der MatriX* entsendet BesucherInnen in eine digitale Matrix, während ihre Gehirnströme von Brain-Computer-Interfaces (BCI) gemessen, analysiert und visualisiert werden. In diesem neurowissenschaftlichen Experiment wird der Frage nachgegangen, ob unser Gehirn auf die Gesichtszüge von Medienpersönlichkeiten und Prominenten anders reagiert als auf unbekannte Gesichter.

Das menschliche Gehirn ist in der Lage, alles Gesehene zu speichern und auch wieder zu erkennen, zum Beispiel die Gesichtszüge unserer Mitmenschen. Dieses blitzschnelle Erkennen von Gesichtern ist eine evolutionäre Errungenschaft und dient als Grundlage für das Forschungsprojekt. Vereinfacht gesagt: Alles Gesehene wird als neuronales Muster im Gehirn gespeichert. Wird nun etwa ein Gesicht erneut gesehen, löst dies im Gehirn ein Wiedererkennungssignal in the brain. This neuronal signal can be measured by an electroencephalograph (EEG). At three BCI stations, visitors can directly immerse themselves into a digital world and write using only their brain waves. For this research project, they'll enter into a specially designed matrix in which they'll be confronted by countless faces. Then, measurements of the elapsed time and the strength of the neuronal recognition signals will deliver answers to the question we posed above.

The basis for the conduct of this study is intendiX, a new input interface based on EEG data. intendiX evaluates the neuronal signal flashes (P300) in the cerebral cortex. The BCI produced by Guger Technologies forwards the information directly from the brain to a computer, which then visualizes it. Visitors can experience state-of-the-art technology and try it out for themselves. They can observe their own brain waves and take part in a fascinating experiment.

An interactive research project by Erika Jungreithmayr in cooperation with g.tec medical engineering GmbH, Austria

aus. Dieses neuronale Signal ist über EEG messbar. An drei BCI-Stationen können BesucherInnen direkt in eine digitale Welt einsteigen und mittels ihrer Gehirnströme schreiben. Für das Forschungsprojekt werden sie in eine speziell designte Matrix entsandt und dort mit zahllosen Gesichtern konfrontiert – anhand der Zeitspanne und Stärke der gemessenen neuronalen Wiedererkennungssignale lässt sich unsere Ausgangsfrage beantworten.

Grundlage zur Durchführung der Studie ist das neue intendiX, eine auf EEG-Daten basierende Eingabeschnittstelle, die die neuronalen Signalfeuerwerke (P300) der Großhirnrinde berechnet. Das Brain-Computer-Interface von Guger Technologies leitet die Informationen direkt vom Gehirn an einen Computer weiter, wo sie visualisiert werden. BesucherInnen können modernste Technologie erleben und ausprobieren. Sie können ihre eigenen Gehirnströme beobachten und an einem spannenden Experiment teilnehmen.

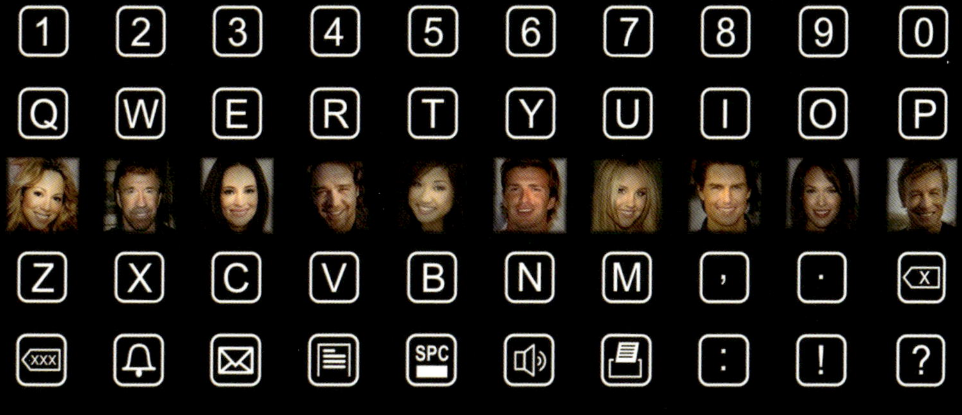

intendiX

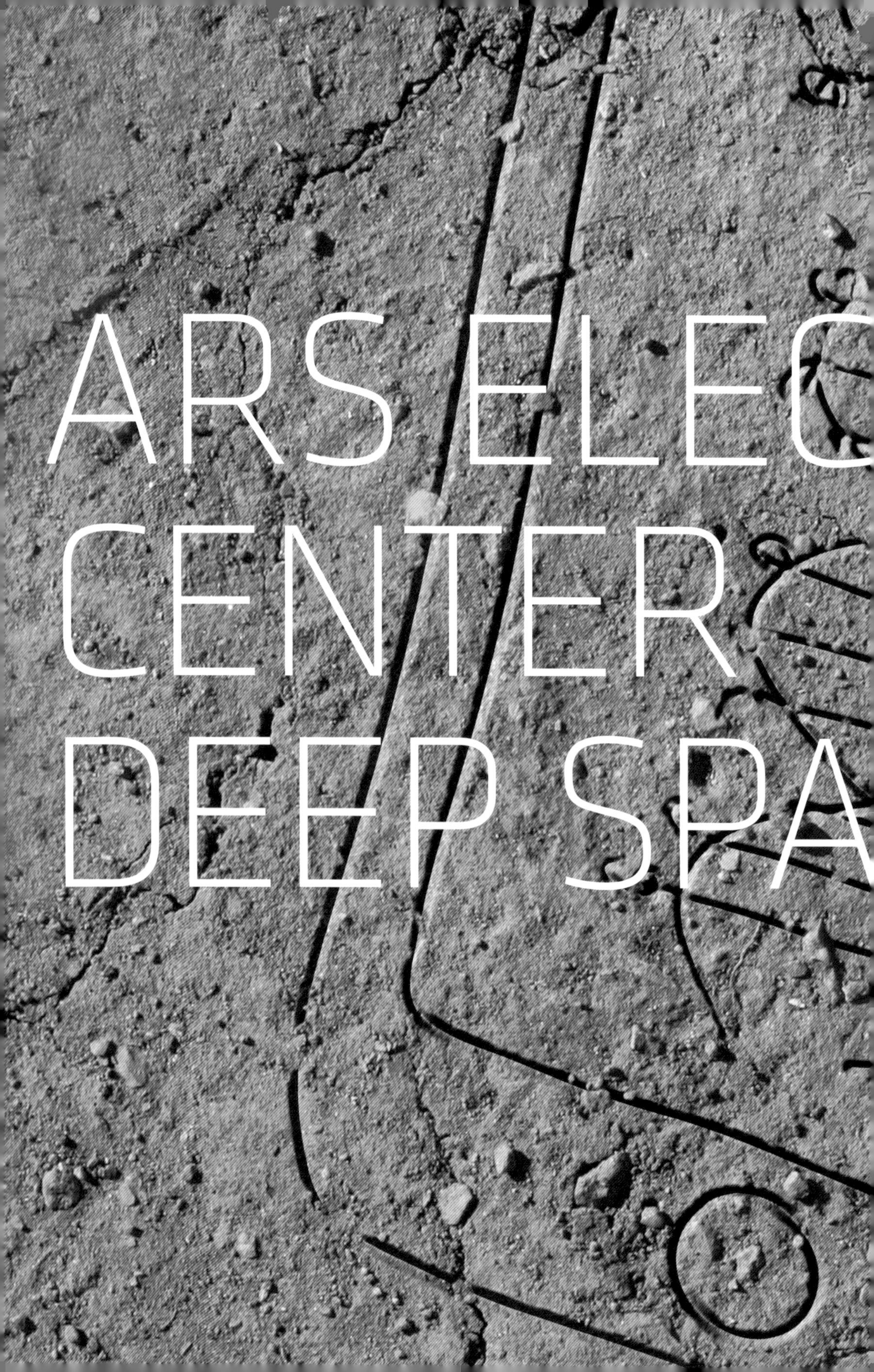
ARS ELEC
CENTER
DEEP SPA

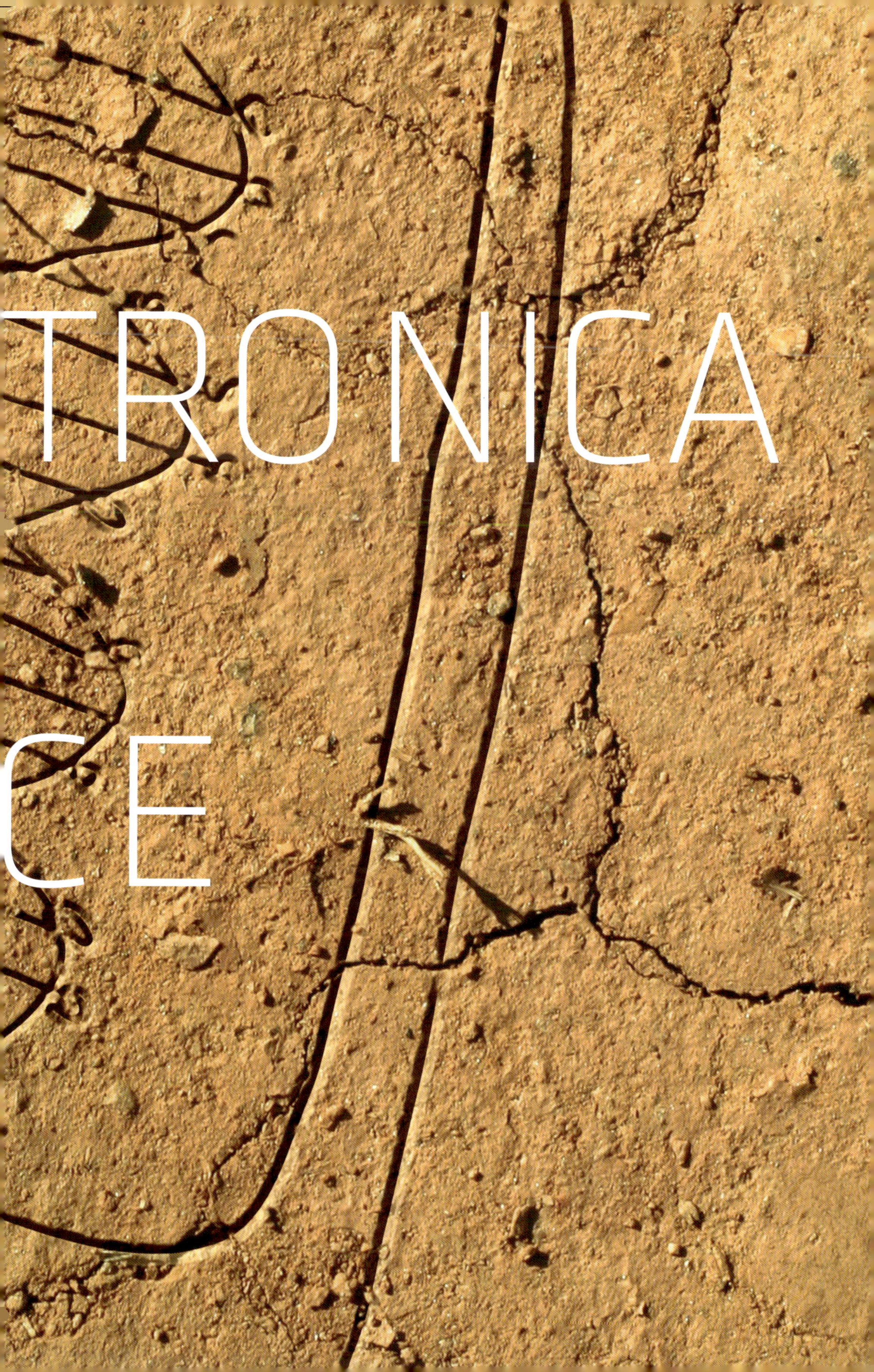
TRONICA
CE

Maki Namekawa, Dennis Russell Davies

The Memory of *Le sacre du printemps*

Piano Concert featuring Real-time Visualizations in the Ars Electronica Center Deep Space

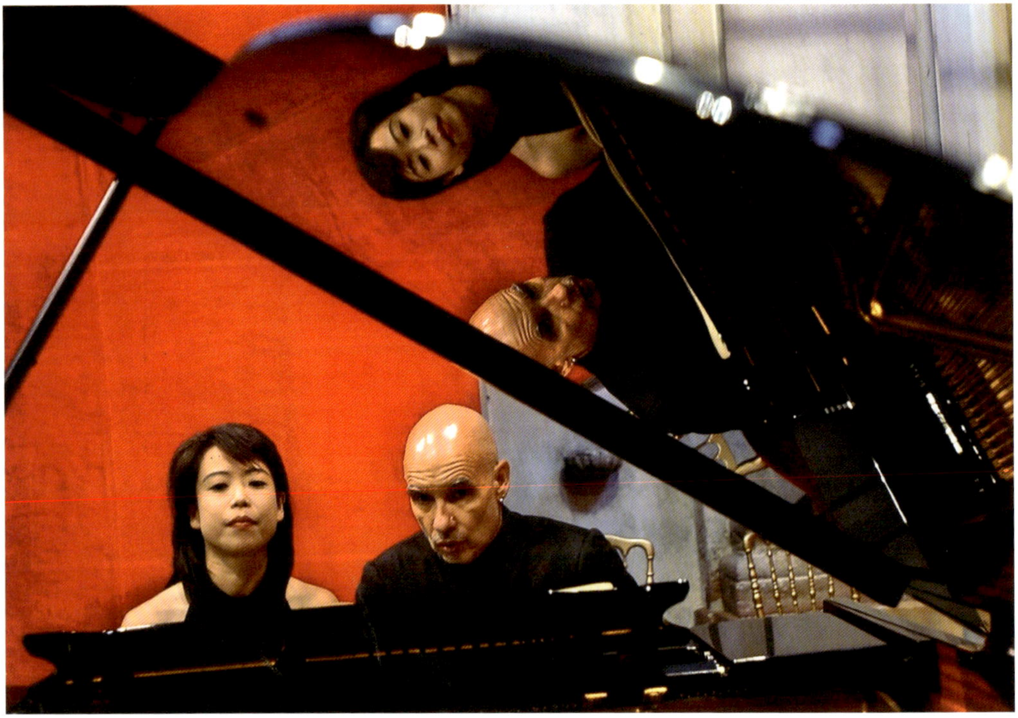

The 100th anniversary of the premiere of Stravinsky's *Le sacre du printemps* (The Rite of Spring) cannot possibly be discussed without recalling the huge scandal its debut provoked.

This piece conjures up an ancient heathen Russia that, even back then, was no more than a distant collective memory—so remote, in fact, that Stravinsky had to travel to a Center for Folk Art near Smolensk to conduct research in preparation for his "grand sacrifice." He worked on it at a time when the Industrial Revolution long since had the world in its clutches, in which men believed in the indestructibility of steel and the Titanic was sunk by

Hundert Jahre nach seiner Uraufführung kann Strawinskis *Le sacre du printemps* wohl nicht besprochen werden, ohne den großen Skandal in Erinnerung zu rufen, den seine Uraufführung provozierte.

Ein Stück, das ein altes heidnisches Russland beschwört, das auch damals für Strawinski schon nur mehr ferne kollektive Erinnerung war, die er erst in einem Zentrum für Volkskunst nahe Smolensk recherchieren musste, um daraus sein „großes Opfer" entstehen zu lassen, in einer Zeit, in der die industrielle Revolution längst die Welt in ihren Klauen hielt, in der man an die Unzerstörbarkeit von Stahl glaubte und die Titanic an einem Eisberg zerbrach, in der Henry Ford an iceberg, in which Henry Ford was manufacturing Model T cars on an assembly line and making Detroit the boomtown of the modern age, in which Marinetti was dispatching his futuristic exhibitions and manifestos throughout Europe, and the mail was already being transported by airplane.

And so, for us today, *Le sacre* is no longer a recollection of primitive heathens but rather of a time in which art was still brash and boisterous, could celebrate the joy of innovation and belief in modernity, and, by coquettishly flirting with the destruction of the old world, could get society hopped up into an utter frenzy—and all of this vigor yet unbroken by the trauma of the approaching world wars.

What makes the piano version for four hands so interesting with regard to a visualization is the much more immediate presence of the rhythmic furor inherent in this piece—raw, and not the least bit toned down by the timbre of a large orchestra, a furor that also manifests itself in the superb acrobatics of four hands and 20 fingers ceaselessly racing across the keyboard, intermingling,

mit dem T-Type Autos am Fließband produzierte und Detroit zur Boomtown der modernen Zeit machte, in der Marinetti seine futuristischen Ausstellungen und Manifeste durch ganz Europa schickte und die Post bereits mit Flugzeugen transportiert wurde.

Und so ist *Le sacre* für uns heute nicht mehr eine Erinnerung an heidnische Naturvölker, sondern an eine Zeit, in der Kunst noch ungestüm war, Freude und Glaube an das Neue und Moderne zelebrieren konnte, mit der Zerstörung der alten Welt kokettierend die Gesellschaft in helle Aufruhr versetzen konnte – noch gänzlich ungebrochen durch die Traumata der kommenden Weltkriege.

Was die Klavierfassung für vier Hände im Hinblick auf eine Visualisierung so interessant macht, ist die viel unmittelbarere Präsenz des rhythmischen Furors, der dem Stück innewohnt – roh und nicht durch die Klangfarben des großen Orchesters abgefedert, ein Furor, der sich auch in der akrobatischen Spitzenleistung der vier Hände und zwanzig Finger ausdrückt, die da unentwegt über die Tastatur rasen, sich verschränken, gefährlich nah und oft nur um Haaresbreite aneinan-

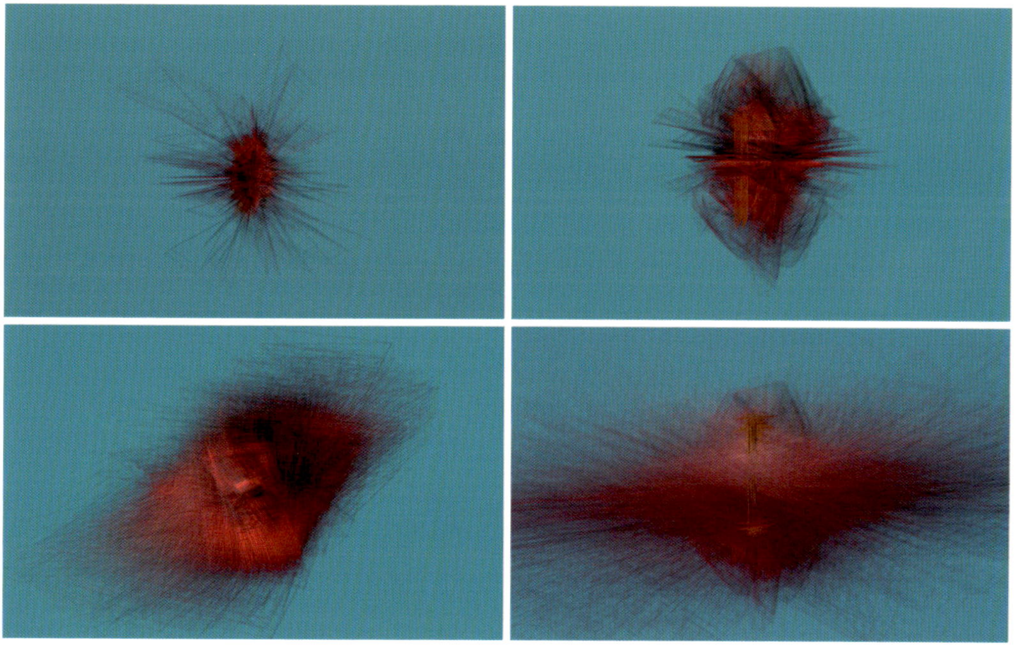

approaching one another, often dangerously close, and sometimes flying within a hairsbreadth of the two pianists' faces.

The drama of this physical spectacle is the actual unsurpassable visual attraction, above all in the intimacy that the Deep Space venue creates between the audience and the musicians. This is the compelling leitmotif of the real-time visualizations captured by Actioncams (that we're familiar with from films of performances by extreme athletes), displayed blazing across 300 m² of projection surface, and powerfully enhanced by a dialog with historical images from the U.S. Library of Congress and digital graphics right out of a Bösendorfer computerized grand piano.

der oder auch an den Gesichtern der beiden PianistInnen vorbeifliegen.

Die Dramatik dieses körperlichen Schauspiels ist die eigentlich unüberbietbare visuelle Attraktion, vor allem in der intimen Nähe, die der Deep Space zwischen Publikum und InterpretInnen herstellt. Sie ist das zwingende Leitmotiv der Echtzeit-Viualisierung, das durch aus Extremsportarten bekannten Actioncams eingefangen und auf den 300 Quadratmeter großen Projektionsflächen umspielt und überhöht wird – im Dialog mit historischem Bildmaterial aus der US Library of Congress und direkt aus einem Bösendorfer Computerflügel gesteuerten digitalen Grafiken.

Text: Gerfried Stocker

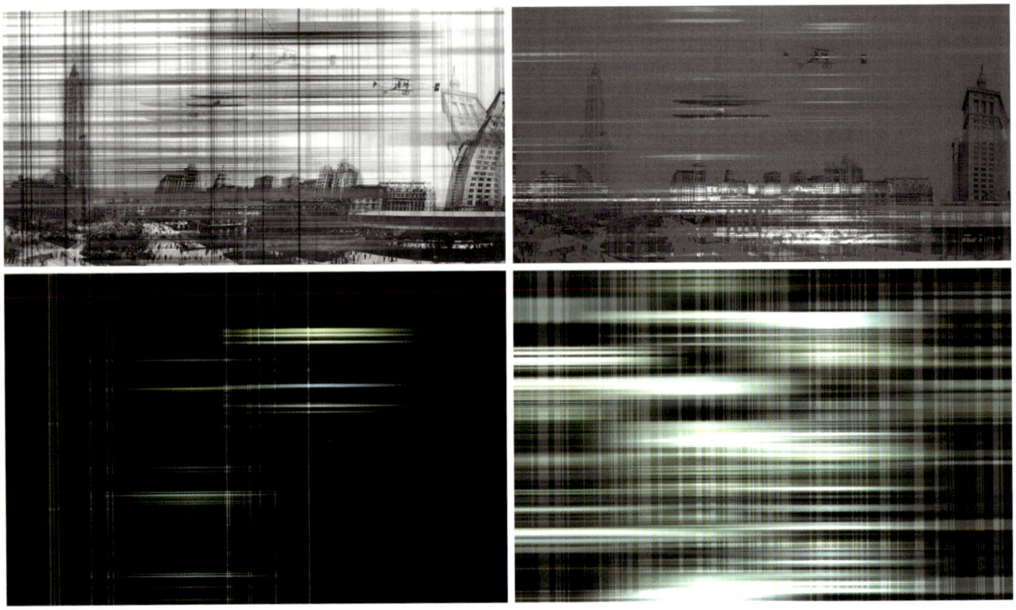

The Rite of Spring in Deep Space
Le sacre du printemps im Deep Space

It was one of the biggest scandals in music history, comparable perhaps only to the tumultuous events that accompanied the debut of Bela Bartok's ballet *The Miraculous Mandarin* at the Cologne Opera in 1926: the world premiere of Igor Stravinsky's ballet *The Rite of Spring* on May 29, 1913 at the Théâtre des Champs-Élysées in Paris. The fact that the per-

Es war einer der größten Skandale in der Musikgeschichte – vergleichbar vielleicht nur mit der unter tumultartigen Umständen stattgefundenen Premiere des Balletts *Der wunderbare Mandarin* von Bela Bartok 1926 an der Kölner Oper: die Uraufführung von Igor Strawinskys Ballett *Le sacre du printemps* am 29. Mai 1913 im Théâtre des Champs-Élysées in Paris. Nur formance was even able to proceed to completion was due solely to the unshakeable composure of the conductor. This ballet, with its unprecedented, primitive uninhibitedness and archaic gesticulations, but above all the outrageous severity of its polytonal shifts and polyrhythmic complications deeply disturbed and unnerved the audience. "People were laughing, shouting catcalls, whistling, imitating sounds made by animals," Jean Cocteau later recalled. Puccini's verdict: "...taken as a whole, it calls to mind the work of a madman." In the summer of 1913, the last peaceful summer for years to come, a ballet broke through the gateway to musical modernity with brutal rhythms and stomping chords that prefigured the horrors that World War I would abruptly rain down upon humankind.

In June 1912, a year before the world premiere of the orchestral work, Igor Stravinsky and Claude Debussy got together at the home of music critic Louis Laloy. The two composers were friends, though their approaches to the development of New Music were quite literally diametrically opposed. In Laloy's home, they first played a version of *The Rite of Spring* for four hands on the piano. Debussy found the work impressive, though he did like to refer to it as *The Massacre of Spring* after its scandal-rocked premiere.

The 31-year-old Stravinsky was devastated by the abysmal failure of *Rite*. After all, he had become accustomed to success in the wake such well-received ballets as *The Firebird* and *Petruschka* that had absolutely enthralled demanding Parisian audiences. Diaghilev, director of the Ballets Russes, had only recently said of him to his company's dancers: "Look at him. That is a man on the verge of fame." And indeed, he would later achieve fame and no small measure of it—fame even fueled by the scandal of the premiere of *Rite*.

der unerschütterlichen Ruhe des Dirigenten ist es zu verdanken, dass die Vorstellung überhaupt zu Ende geführt wurde. Das Ballett in seiner bislang unbekannten, primitiven Wildheit und seiner archaischen Gestik, aber vor allem die unerhörte Schärfe polytonaler Wendungen und polyrhythmischer Vertracktheit verstörten und verunsicherten das Publikum zutiefst: „Man lachte, höhnte, pfiff, ahmte Tierstimmen nach", erinnert sich Jean Cocteau später. Puccini urteilte: „... zusammengenommen erinnert es an das Werk eines Wahnsinnigen." Im letzten Friedenssommer 1913 riss ein Ballett das Tor zur musikalischen Moderne auf, mit brutalen Rhythmen und stampfenden Akkorden die Grauen vorausahnend, die mit dem Ersten Weltkrieg jäh über die Völker hereinbrechen sollten.

Ein Jahr vor der Uraufführung des Orchesterwerks, im Juni 1912, trafen sich Igor Strawinski und Claude Debussy im Haus des Musikkritikers Louis Laloy. Die beiden Komponisten, obwohl nun wahrlich von verschiedenen Seiten sich der Entwicklung der Neuen Musik nähernd, waren befreundet und spielten hier den *Le sacre du printemps* zum ersten Mal in einer Fassung für Klavier für vier Hände. Debussy zeigte sich von dem Werk beeindruckt, auch wenn er es nach der Skandal-Uraufführung gerne *Le massacre du printemps* nannte.

Der verheerende Misserfolg des *Le sacre* traf den 31-jährigen, erfolgsverwöhnten Strawinski hart, hatte er doch zuvor mit seinen Balletten *Feuervogel* und *Petruschka* reüssiert und das verwöhnte Pariser Publikum fasziniert. Diaghilew, der Chef der Ballets Russes, hatte ihn noch zuletzt seinen Tänzern mit „Seht ihn euch an, das ist ein Mann am Vorabend des Ruhms" vorgestellt. Und der Ruhm sollte sich später in überreichem Maße einstellen – auch befeuert vom Skandal der Uraufführung des *Le sacre du printemps*.

Text: Heribert Schröder

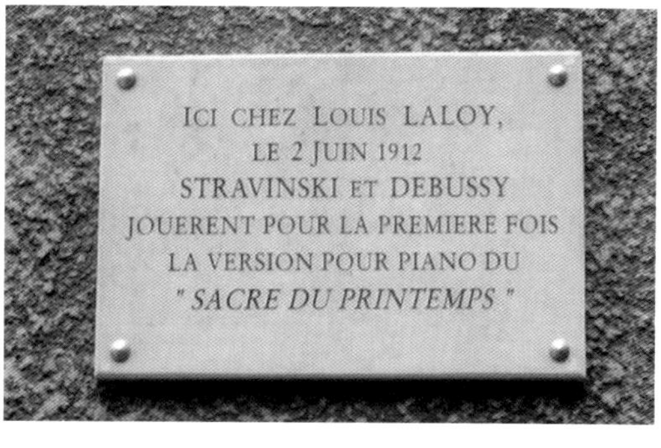

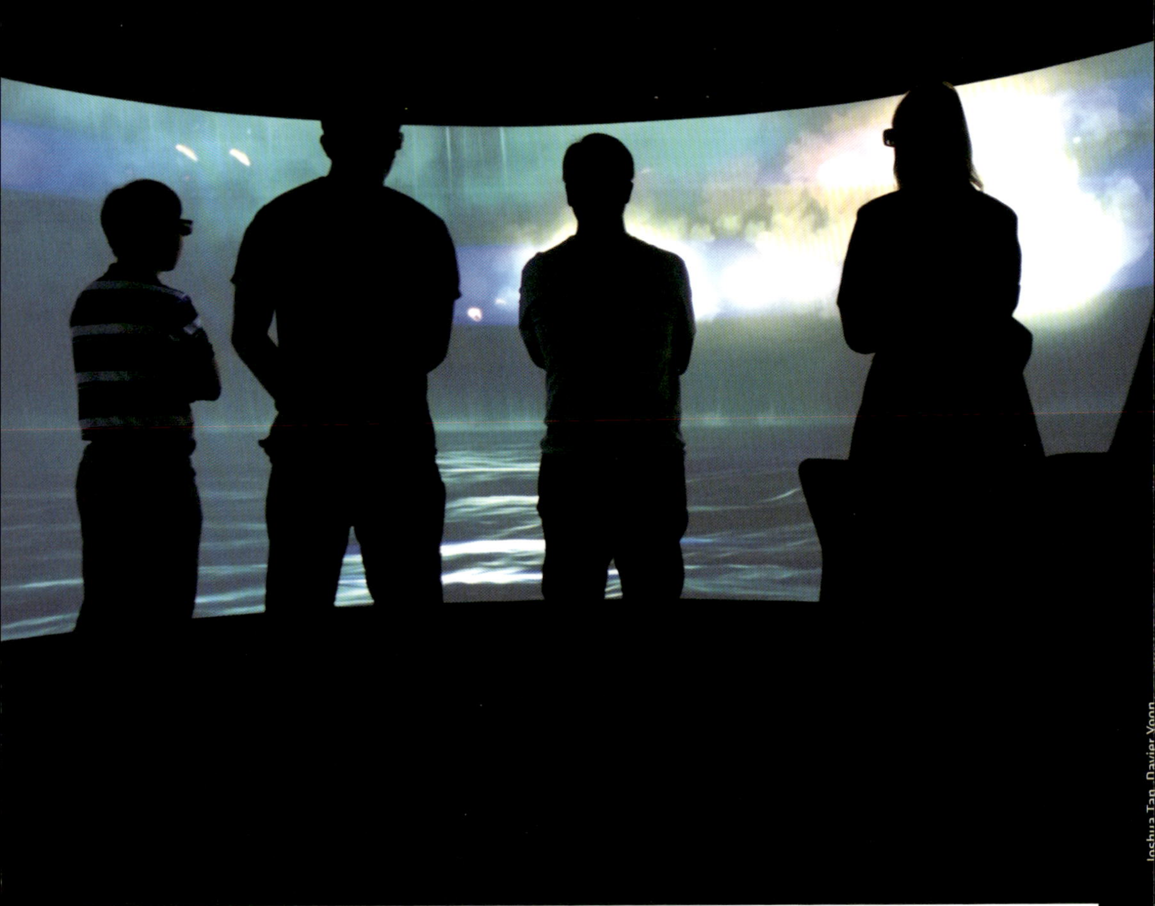

Joshua Tan, Davier Yoon

Inspired by the sacrifices made by generations preceding us and expanding upon an exploration of World War II, *Elysian Fields* fuses fantastical and historical into a surreal reconfiguration of the present.

Elysian Fields ist eine Verbeugung vor den Opfern, die unsere Vorfahren erbracht haben, und das Ergebnis einer längeren Beschäftigung mit dem Zweiten Weltkrieg. Hier verschmilzt Fantastisches und Historisches zu einer surrealen Rekonfiguration der Gegenwart.

Although my dad was a tough and hardened war veteran, he was very supportive of my decision to become a fine artist. However, at one point he was concerned as to why I blurred my images in painting, giving everything an unrecognizable appearance... "no imaginary space through which to walk with the mind's eye, no imaginary objects to desire or not to desire, no imaginary people to like or dislike". Many times he would carefully and softly critique my art, saying that he could not recognize my work or saying that he had a hard time understanding the art. He would ask for pure and simple work like a painting from the view of his window or of a cottage in the countryside.

The idea of making a war film came to me with my dad's passing like a sudden revelation. I wanted to animate a painting that would have seemingly representational clarity, but at the same time would have the freedom and bewilderment of a totally abstract story, one which we can gaze at endlessly, one we would not be able to explain either to ourselves or to others, one we could enjoy and love without necessarily knowing why.

Painting for Deep Space

Deep Space transforms the concept of painting today through technology into one of the most dynamic platforms in contemporary art. With the large-scale stereoscopic screen and an ultimate immersive canvas, Deep Space invigorates painters to create animated pictorial spaces that will draw in the viewer. The resulting unframed painting liberates image and ignites one of a kind impactful and memorable experience.

In addition to being a 3D stereoscopic screening, the film is visually articulated for the immersive 3D stereo theatre in the Institute for Media Innovation of the Nanyang Technological University in Singapore. The viewer is surrounded on all sides by long curved screens on which the film is projected, thus creating a completely different experience than seen on a cinematic frontal plane.

Obwohl mein Vater ein harter und verbissener Kriegsveteran war, hat er mich in meinem Entschluss, Künstlerin zu werden, stets unterstützt. Irgendwann aber wollte er wissen, warum ich die Bilder in meiner Malerei so verschleiere, ihnen ein Aussehen gebe, in dem nichts zu erkennen ist: „... kein imaginärer Raum, den ich im Geist durchmessen, keine imaginären Objekte, die ich begehren oder ignorieren, keine imaginären Menschen, die ich mögen oder verabscheuen könnte." Sorgsam und sanft übte er immer wieder Kritik an meiner Kunst, sagte, er könne darin nichts wiedererkennen oder es falle ihm schwer, sie zu verstehen. Er verlangte nach direkten, einfachen Arbeiten, einem Gemälde der Aussicht aus seinem Fenster oder von einem Haus auf dem Land.

Nach dem Tod meines Vaters überkam mich die Idee, einen Kriegsfilm zu machen, wie eine Offenbarung. Ich wollte ein animiertes Gemälde schaffen, das eindeutig gegenständlich war und zugleich die Freiheit und das Verstörende einer völlig abstrakten Geschichte besaß; eines, das man endlos betrachten, eines, das man weder sich selbst noch anderen erklären, eines, das man genießen und lieben kann, ohne genau zu wissen warum.

Malen für den Deep Space

Der Deep Space macht die Malerei heute mit technologischen Mitteln zu einer der dynamischsten Plattformen zeitgenössischer Kunst. Mit seiner großformatigen, stereoskopischen Projektionsfläche, einer ultimativen immersiven Leinwand, gibt der Deep Space MalerInnen die Möglichkeit, animierte Bildräume zu schaffen, die die BetrachterInnen in sich hineinziehen. Die so entstehende ungerahmte Malerei bringt eine Befreiung des Bildes mit sich und ermöglicht wirkungsvolle, einprägsame Erfahrungen.

Außer für die stereoskopische Vorführung wurde der Film auch für die Präsentation im immersiven 3D-Vorführraum am Institute for Media Innovation der Nanyang Technological University in Singapur aufbereitet. In ihm ist der Betrachtende ringsum von langen kurvenförmigen Projektionsflächen umgeben, wodurch sich ein vollkommen anderes Filmerlebnis einstellt als bei der flachen, frontal montierten Kinoleinwand.

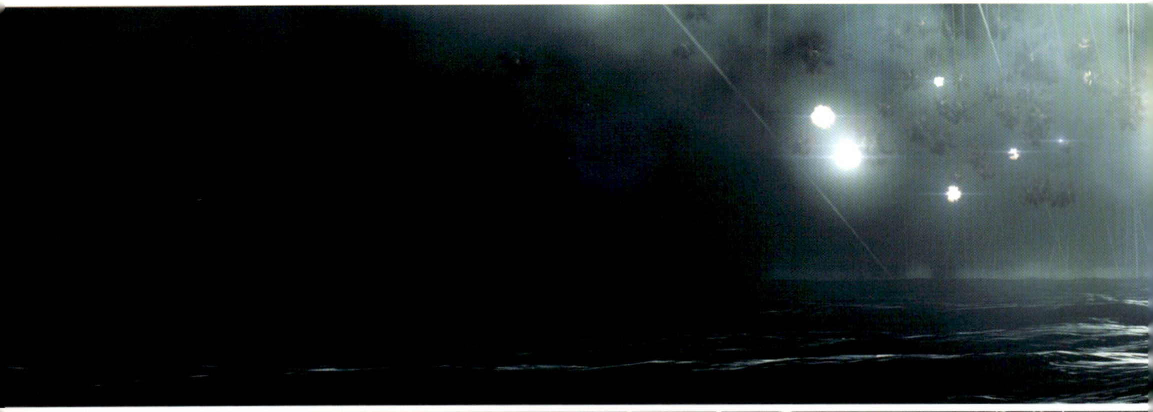

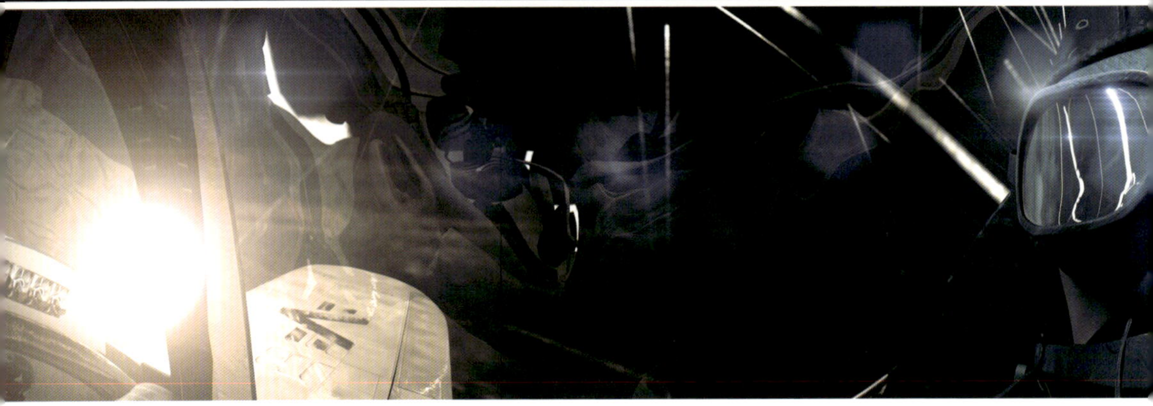

Film Synopsis

Imagined as an infinite loop, the story weaves in and out from an inevitably doomed air chase, into death, afterlife and resurrection, only to arrive at a surreal space of a parallel dimension. Conceived as the cutting of narrative out of painting and a transformation into the logic and continuity of the dream space, the concrete and explicit representation melts out into a fragile complex whole: the marvelous entangled conjunction of displaced moments in time where ephemeral experiences and verbal explanation are inadequate.

Composed of unstable fragments, the tightly woven imaginary figurative environments constantly dissolve and shift. Relentlessly pursuing each other fighter planes plunge from night to day connecting floating shores and suspended seascape horizons of the Above and the Below, signifying the realm of life and death. The time space spins an oily black

Synopsis

Angelegt als unendlicher Loop, läuft die Geschichte durch einen unausweichlich auf die Katastrophe zusteuernden Luftkampf auf Tod, Jenseits und Wiedergeburt zu, um am Ende im surrealen Raum einer Paralleldimension zu enden. Konzipiert als gemalte Erzählschnipsel und die Überführung derselben in Logik und Verlaufsform des Traums, zerfließt die konkrete, explizite Darstellung nach und nach in ein fragiles komplexes Geflecht: das wundersame Ineinandergreifen disparater Momente in der Zeit, vor dem ephemere Erlebnisse und sprachliche Erklärungen versagen.

Die dicht gefügten, aus instabilen Elementen bestehenden gegenständlichen Umgebungen zerfallen und verschieben sich permanent. Einander gnadenlos verfolgende Kampfflugzeuge stürzen aus der Nacht in den Tag, verknüpfen frei schwebende Küstenlinien und Seestück-Horizonte von Ober- und Unterwelt, das

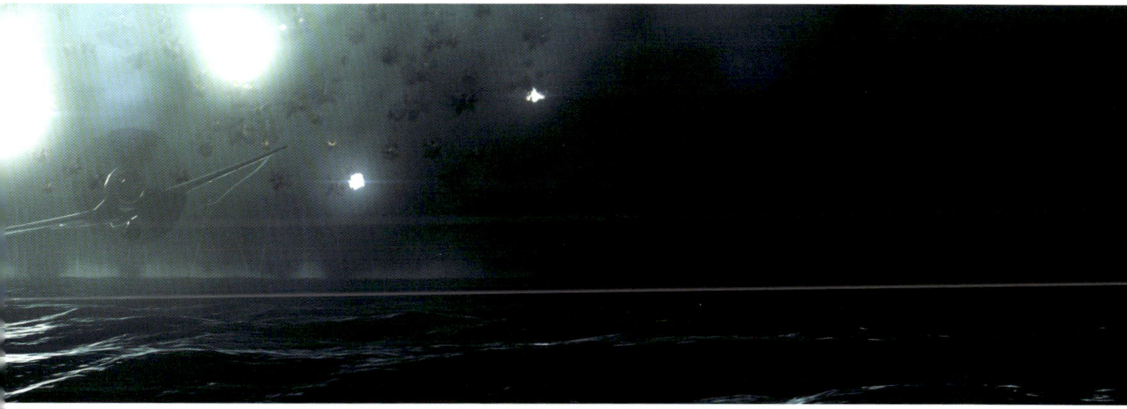

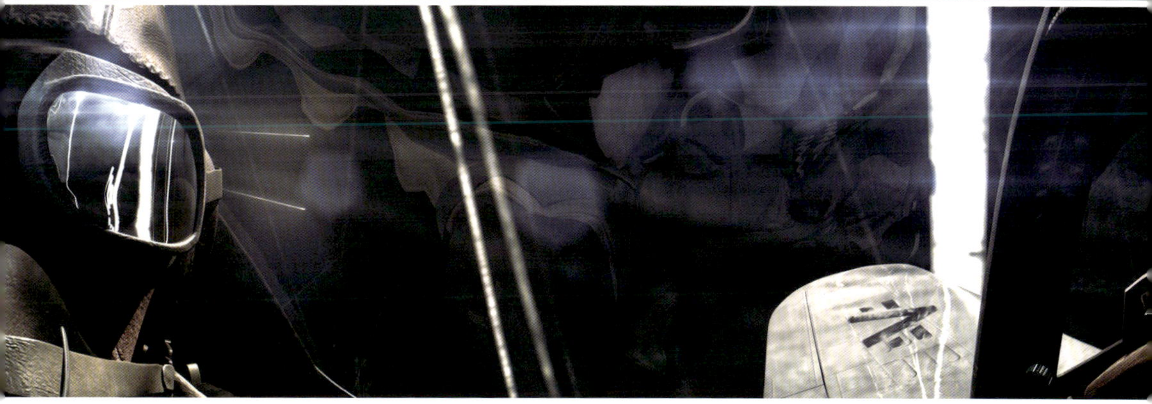

Joshua Tan, Davier Yoon

nighttime shore and a washed-out haze of early dawn into alchemical vision where *"What is the above is from the below and the below is from the above"*. Fields of poppy flowers dissolve into sleep, peace, and death. In the inferno of the afterlife the fighter is looking in and looking out from the circular gates of hell shaped as a fiery hole in the black ground, the fire in the center of the earth is a reference to our own being.

http://www.elysianfieldsfilm.com/

Elysian Fields
10:50 Stereoscopic 3D animation
Genre: War, Experimental, Surreal

Reich des Lebens und des Todes. Im Raum der Zeit wird eine ölschwarze nächtliche Küste und ein verwaschenes dunstiges Morgengrauen zu einer alchemistischen Vision verquirlt, in der das „Oben aus dem Unten und das Unten aus dem Oben hervorgeht". Blühende Mohnfelder gehen über in Schlaf, Frieden und Tod. Im Inferno des Jenseits blickt der Kämpfer in und aus dem kreisförmigen Höllentor, das in Form eines Feuerlochs vor dunklem Grund erscheint. Feuer als Zentrum der Erde, Hinweis auf unser eigenes Dasein.

Aus dem Englischen von Wilfried Prantner

This work was carried out with the generous support of the Ministry of Education Singapore
Nanyang Technological University, Institute for Media Innovation (IMI)
http://imi.ntu.edu.sg/Pages/Home.aspx
School of Art Design and Media (ADM)
http://www.adm.ntu.edu.sg/Pages/Home.aspx

Directed by Ina Conradi Chavez. Assistant Directors: Davier Yoon, Joshua Tan; Animation & Stereography: Davier Yoon, Joshua Tan; Animation Assistance: Ivan Yew; Music & Sound Design: Jeremy Goh; Title Design: Jane Chang.
ADM IT & IMI Technical Support: Thummanapalli Nagaraju, Teo Cheng Lim, Yeong Chen Hui, Koh Kian Hwa

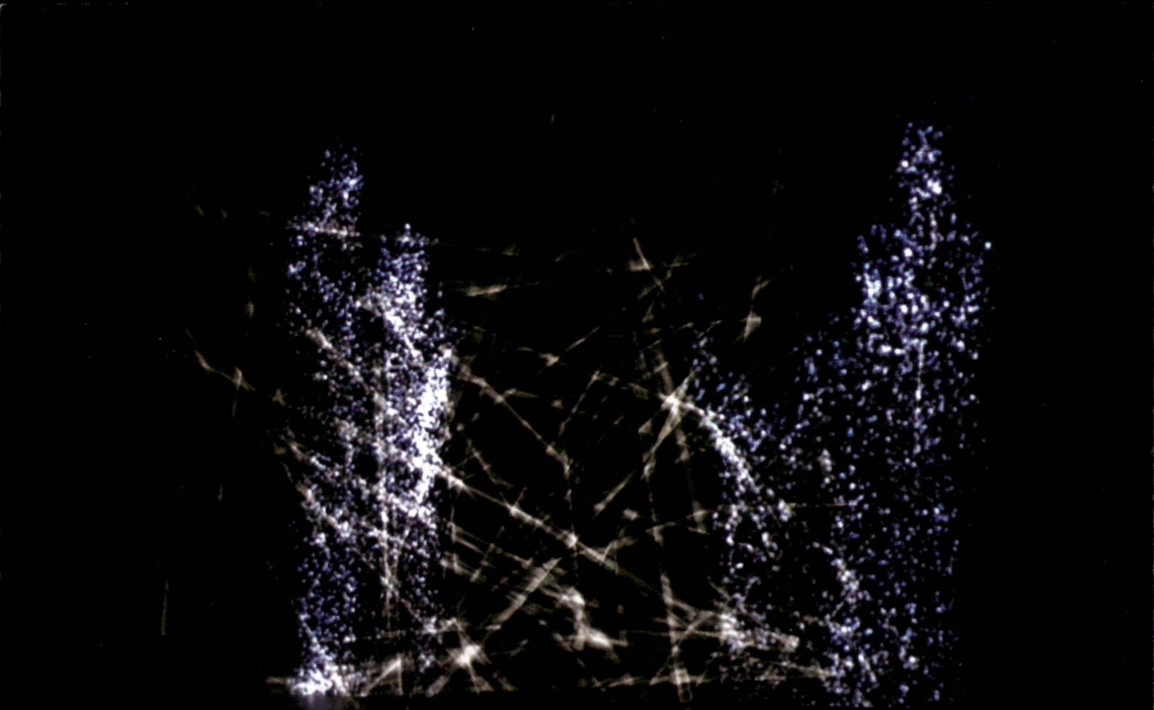

University of Applied Sciences Upper Austria

Mind Games

Our memories are not just a static collection of stored impressions, but rather the product of an active network of synapses that continually reconstruct our perception of what we experience. Two interactive installations, created by students, lecturers and friends of the Hagenberg Campus of the University of Applied Sciences Upper Austria, offer visitors to the Ars Electronica Center's Deep Space a playful approach to memory and experience.

Clockworld

The Virtual Reality installation *Clockworld* features the experience of controlling a virtual android on two levels: its material form and its internal mental constructs, the latter of which can be shaped by visitors' interactions with the installation.
Clockworld forgoes one of the classical principles of animation by giving all the control to its viewers. Thus, they become the animators and can leave their own traces in this virtual world. These traces remain in the virtual memory of the installation so that past interactions are visible for future audiences.

Unser Gedächtnis besteht nicht aus einer statischen Sammlung von gespeicherten Erinnerungen, sondern fungiert auch als ein aktives Netzwerk aus Synapsen, die unsere Vorstellung vom Erlebten kontinuierlich neu generieren. Zwei interaktive Installationen von Studierenden, Lehrenden und Freunden der Fachhochschule Oberösterreich laden Besucher ein, im Deep Space des Ars Electronica Center mit Erlebnis und Erinnerung aktiv zu spielen.

Clockworld

In der Virtual-Reality-Installation *Clockworld* können Besucher einen virtuellen Androiden auf zwei Ebenen erleben: einerseits im Zustand seiner materiellen Existenz, andererseits in dessen Gedankenwelt, die sie sogar mitgestalten können. Dabei bricht *Clockworld* ein klassisches Konzept der Animation: Der Betrachter wird selbst zum Animator und kann seine eigenen Spuren in der virtuellen Welt hinterlassen. Die Daten der Besucher bleiben im virtuellen Gedächtnis der Installation bestehen und sind für spätere Besucher auch sichtbar.

Team: Benedict Bleimschein, Martin Kienmeyer / Digital Arts, University of Applied Sciences Upper Austria

Re:collection

The devices we use to record and store data have become much more than just transitory containers of analog and digital information—over time they themselves have become part of our memories. Just looking at treasures such as phonograph records, audio cassettes and obsolete game cartridges brings back memories of the past.
The game installation *re:collection* invites the audience to rescue discarded storage devices to prevent their eventual destruction. Collecting these functional artifacts is not without its risks, however—participants need to eliminate impending dangers and defend their vulnerable source of energy.

Re:collection

Speichermedien sind nicht bloße Behälter, die Daten für eine unbestimmte Zeit aufbewahren, sondern werden auch selbst zu Teilen unseres Gedächtnisses. Ob Schallplatte, Audiokassette oder veraltetes Spielmodul, allein der Anblick von solchen Schätzen erweckt in uns Erinnerungen an frühere Zeiten.
In der Spielinstallation *re:collection* können Besucher gemeinsam obsolete Speichermedien vor ihrer Vernichtung retten. Dabei müssen die Sammler aber Gefahren aus dem Weg räumen und stets ihre Energiequelle verteidigen.

Team: Jeremiah Diephuis, Wolfgang Hochleitner, Michael Lankes / University of Applied Sciences Upper Austria
Thomas Heller, Thomas Raffatzeder, Gernot Raudner, Manuel Wieser / Radiated Pixel

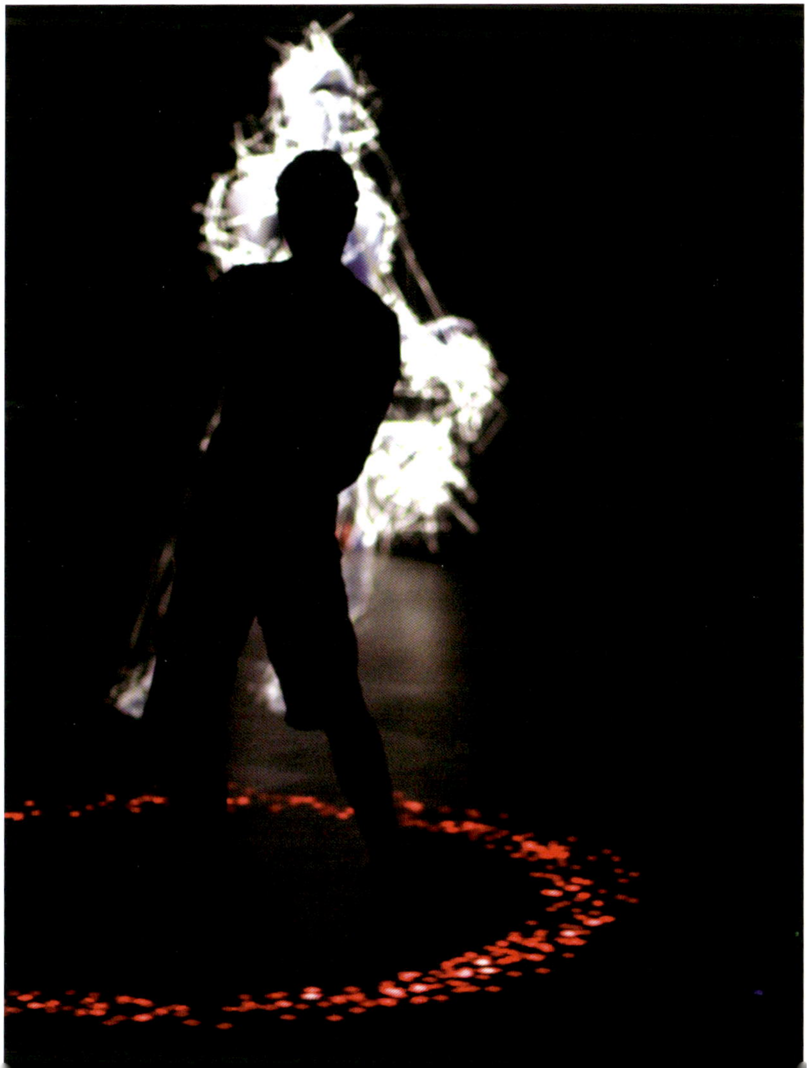

Alan Kwan

Bad Trip

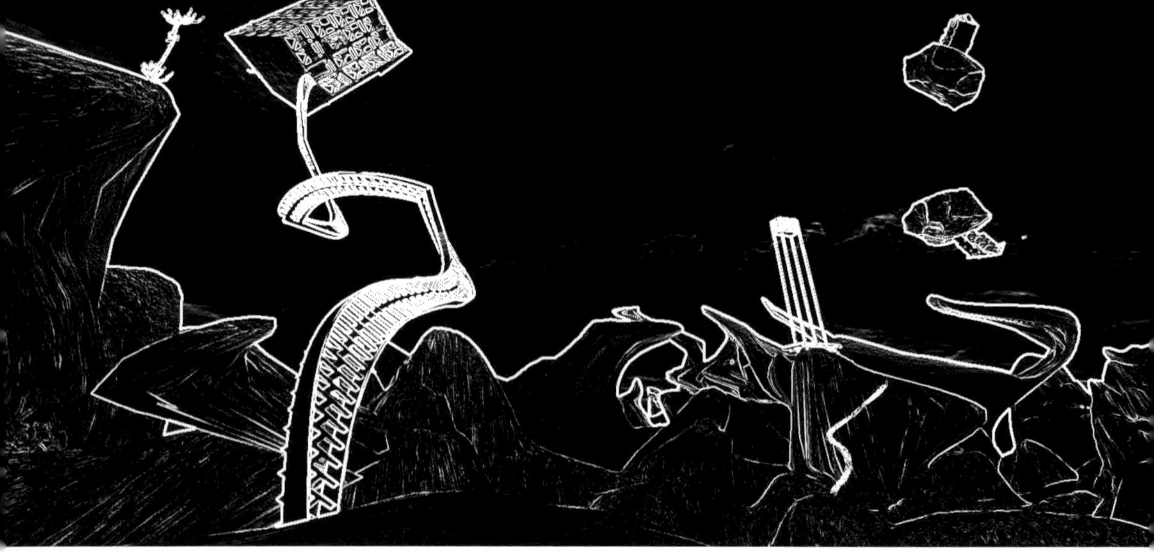

Bad Trip is an immersive virtual reality installation that enables people to navigate the creator's mind using a game controller.
Since November 2011, every moment of his life has been documented by a video camera mounted on glasses, producing an expanding database of digitalized visual memories, which are stored in a virtual world that he built and designed using custom virtual reality software. Every night, he uploaded new memories to the world and built new houses to store them in. Thus, a virtual mindscape has been created where people can navigate and experience his memories and dreams of the artist.

Creator, Visual Design, Programming: Alan Kwan; Sound Design: Zach Polis; Music: Vertigo by Robert Rich

Special Thanks: IP Yuk-yiu, Tamas Waliczky, George Huang, Kelvin Wong, School of Creative Media, City University of Hong Kong

Bad Trip ist eine immersive virtuelle Realität, in der man mithilfe eines Game-Controllers durch die Erinnerungen des Künstlers navigieren kann.
Eine auf einer Brille montierte Kamera hat seit November 2011 jeden Augenblick seines Lebens in einer immer größer werdenden Datenbank von Videoclips als digitalisierte Erinnerungen festgehalten. Diese Erinnerungen sind, mittels einer vom Künstler selbst konzipierten und entwickelten Virtual-Reality-Software, in einer virtuellen Welt abgespeichert. Jede Nacht wurden neue Erinnerungen in diese Welt hochgeladen und neue Gebäude geschaffen, um sie zu speichern. So entstand eine navigierbare virtuelle Gedankenwelt, in der man Erinnerungen und Träume des Künstlers aufsuchen und erfahren kann.
Aus dem Englischen von Michael Kaufmann

ITAF 2013

International Teletext Art Festival*

"Any sufficiently advanced technology is indistinguishable from magic." (Arthur C. Clarke)

Considering that teletext has been used by millions of people daily during its 40 years of existence, it has so far remained a relatively unexplored territory for artistic creation.

Ever since it was launched by the BBC in 1973, there have been several serious efforts to open up teletext for art, but it has never gained the status it deserves as an art form.

Now that High Definition has become established as a standard and the race towards crisp images has slowed down, a growing number of artists has returned to the basic structures of electronic art. This can be seen as the main reason for the revival of teletext in this context. Other phenomena explaining the sudden interest in teletext art, especially among young artists, is the retro factor. The minimal aesthetics and limited technical possibilities make teletext a unique medium and also an

Täglich von Millionen Menschen genutzt, und das seit über 40 Jahren – der Teletext ist der erste interaktive Informationsdienst des elektronischen Zeitalters. Und schon bald nach seiner Einführung haben auch Künstler die gestalterischen Besonderheiten dieses Mediums erkannt. Nur sechs Farben plus weiß und schwarz sind möglich, die Grafik basiert auf Pixeln, das Bildformat ist klar festgelegt. Diese minimale Ästhetik und die begrenzten technischen Möglichkeiten stellen eine interessante Herausforderung für die künstlerische Produktion dar – von Post-Punk bis Concept Art. Die Möglichkeiten, die der Teletext als künstlerisches Ausdrucksmittel bietet, sind noch lange nicht ausgeschöpft.

Der Teletext nutzt die vertikale Austastlücke bei der Fernsehübertragung, in der nur geringe Informationsbits übertragen werden können. Technisch ist der Videotext in seiner über 40-jährigen Geschichte

* in ARD Text, ORF TELETEXT and SWISS TELETEXT

quel Meyers, The journey of the sun

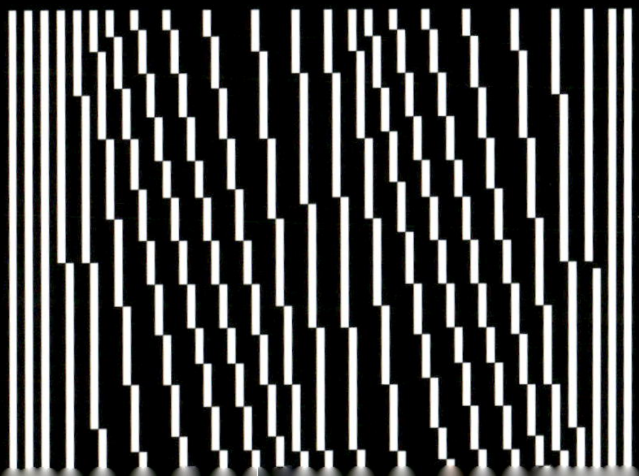

A, Black & White No 2

interesting challenge for artists: To make teletext pages a specific file format and editor are needed. A teletext page can be perceived as a grid of 24 rows and 40 columns. To change the colours of the graphics, text and background or to add a blink effect, a control character needs to be inserted. Each time a control character is placed it uses up one space in the grid, which then appears black.

The artworks can be viewed with teletext editors or made into animated images, but the true forum for teletext art is of course teletext itself. To make it possible for more artists to have their works broadcast, the Helsinki-based FixC artists Co-operative launched the international Teletext Art Festival ITAF in 2012 in collaboration with Finnish YLE Television and ARD Text. An open call attracted a fascinating diversity of engaging works ranging from minimalistic structures to post punk and conceptual art. The works were viewed by over 540,000 people on ARD Text and received extensive international media coverage.

The positive outcome has inspired the organizers to launch ITAF2013. As a new feature to the ITAF concept, a group of experts will select one of the participating artists to receive the Teletext Art Prize and the public can vote for their favourite artist. A total of 15 artists are featured in the competition, including: LIA, Ubermorgen, Manuel Knapp, Daniel Egg, Marc Lee, Raquel Meyers, Kathrin Günter, Max Capacity and Dragan Espenschied + works by FixC cooperative members out of competition.

The International Teletext Art Festival is a FixC cooperative project *http://www.fixc.fi* made in collaboration with ARD Text *http://www.ard-text.de*, ORF TELETEXT *http://teletext.orf.at* and Swiss TXT *http://www.teletext.ch.*

unverändert geblieben. Für die Erstellung von Teletext-Seiten müssen besondere Eingabeeditoren und Dateiformate verwendet werden. Eine Seite hat nur 24 Zeilen und 40 Spalten. Um die Grafik-, Text- oder Hintergrundfarbe zu ändern oder ein Blinken einzufügen, muss jeweils ein Steuerzeichen gesetzt werden. Dieses Archaische, die Reduktion auf einzelne Pixel, hat in der heutigen Welt der HD-Auflösung einen starken visuellen Reiz. Elemente der Teletext-Ästhetik finden sich an vielen Stellen – auf Hauswänden und in Graffitis, in Videos und Animationsfilmen und auf Webseiten im Internet.

Die in Helsinki beheimatete Künstlerkooperative FixC organisierte 2012 in Zusammenarbeit mit dem finnischen Fernsehen YLE und dem ARD Text in Deutschland ITAF, das erste Internationale Teletext Art Festival, um den Künstlern der elektronischen Kunstszene die Präsentation ihrer Arbeiten zu ermöglichen. 17 Künstler aus verschiedenen Ländern beteiligten sich an dem ersten Festival, das von über 540.000 Besuchern bei ARD Text gesehen wurde.

In diesem Sommer geht das Festival in die zweite Runde. An ITAF 2013 sind neben ARD Text auch ORF Teletext und der Schweizer Teletext beteiligt. Insgesamt 15 Künstler nehmen am Wettbewerb teil – darunter LIA, Ubermorgen, Manuel Knapp und Daniel Egg aus Österreich sowie Marc Lee aus der Schweiz. Erstmalig zeichnet eine Expertenjury einen der beteiligten Künstler mit dem Teletext Art Prize 2013 aus. Das Publikum erhält zudem die Möglichkeit, für sein favorisiertes Kunstwerk zu stimmen. Das Festival wird von der finnischen Künstlerkooperative FixC kuratiert.

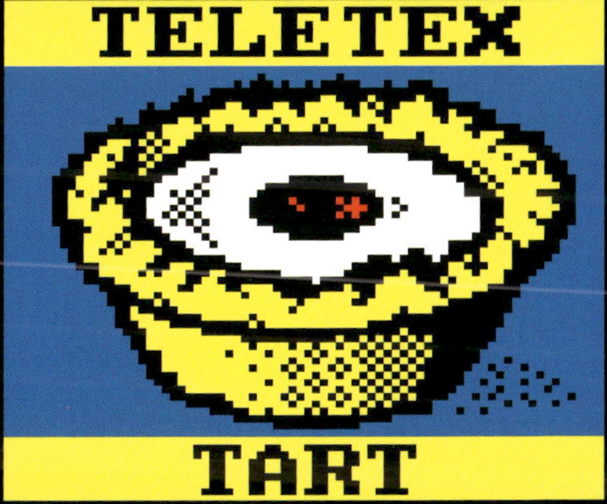

Dan Farrimond, Teletextart

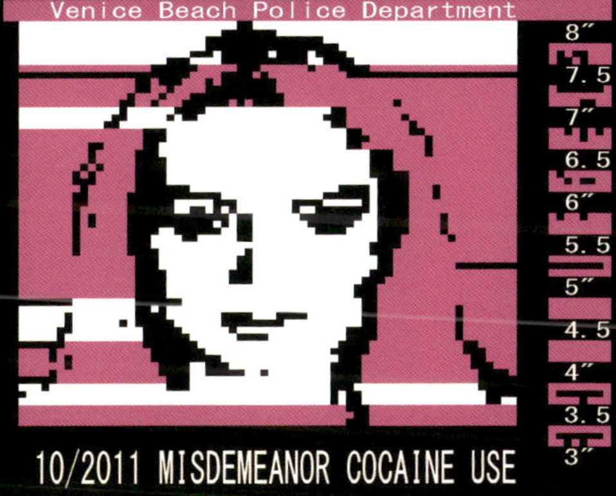

Kathrin Guenter, Lindsay Lohan's Mug Shot Cabinet

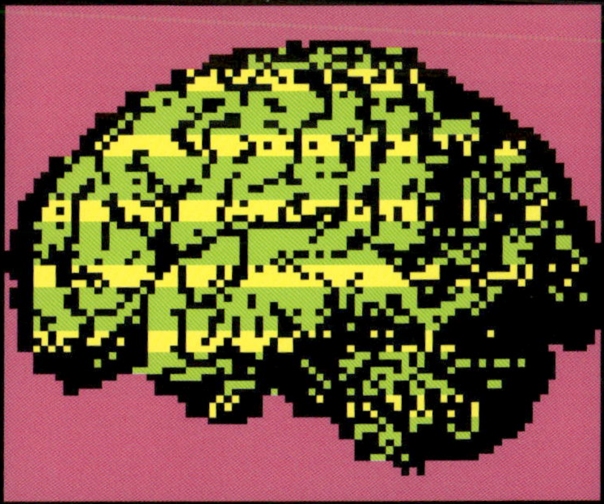

Max Capacity , Brain

Max Capacity, CITYX1

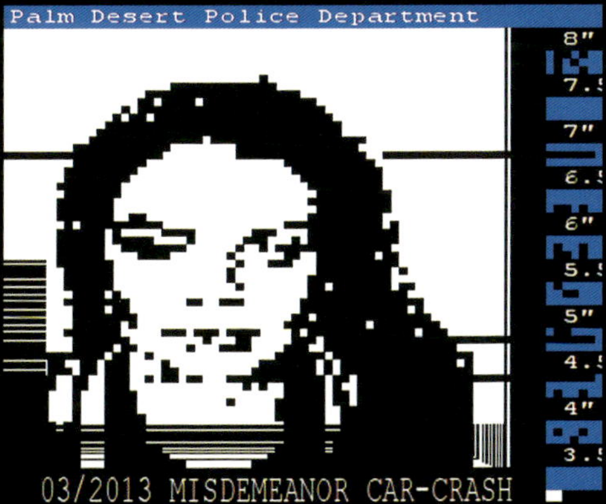

Kathrin Guenter, Lindsay Lohan's Mug Shot Cabinet

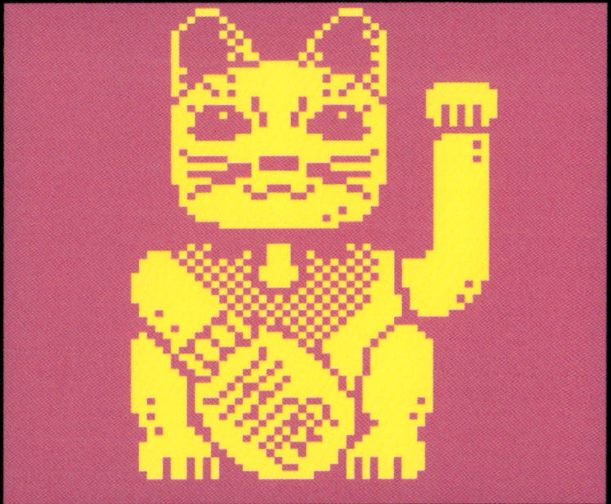

Dragan Espenschied

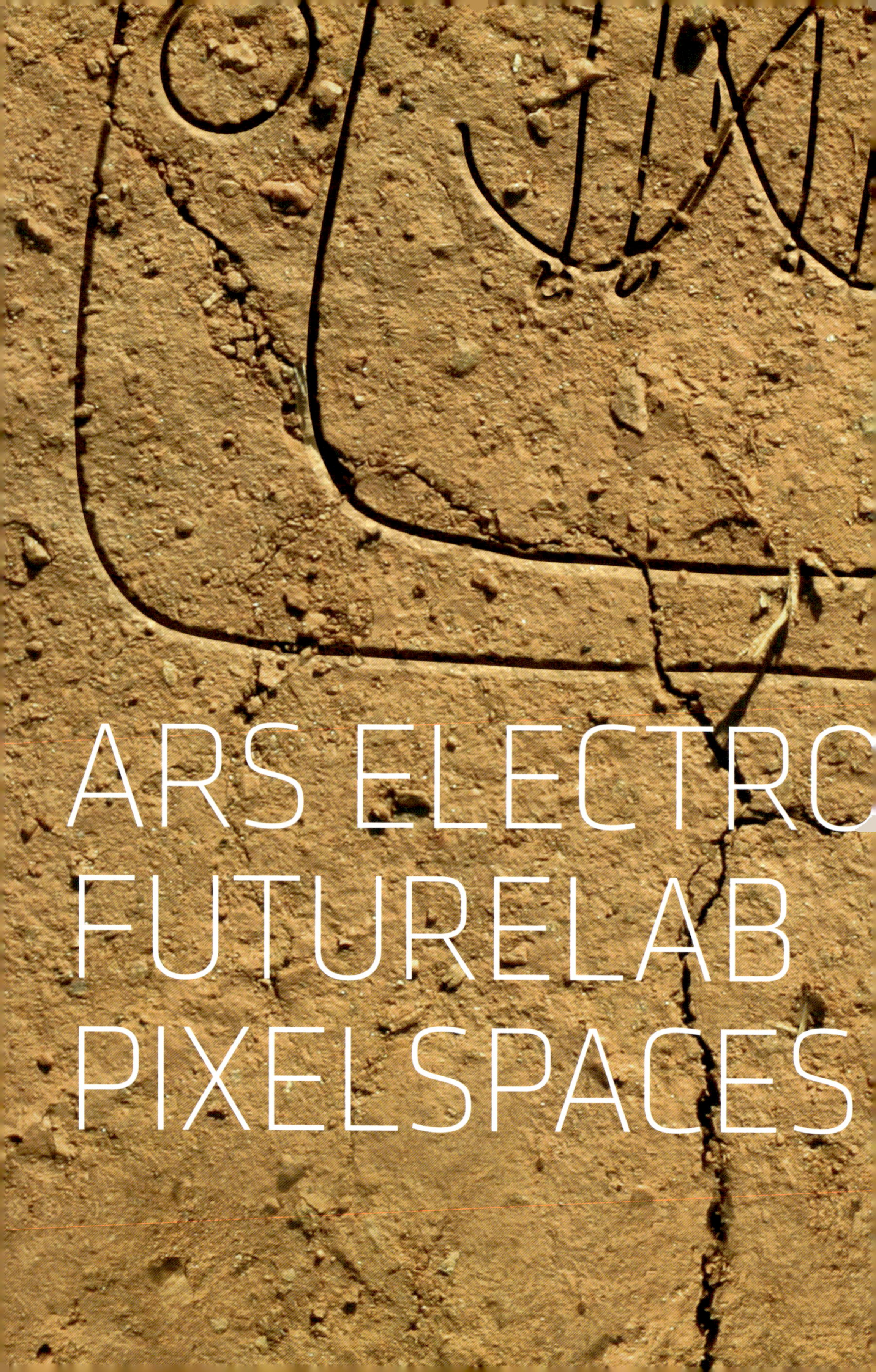
ARS ELECTRO
FUTURELAB
PIXELSPACES

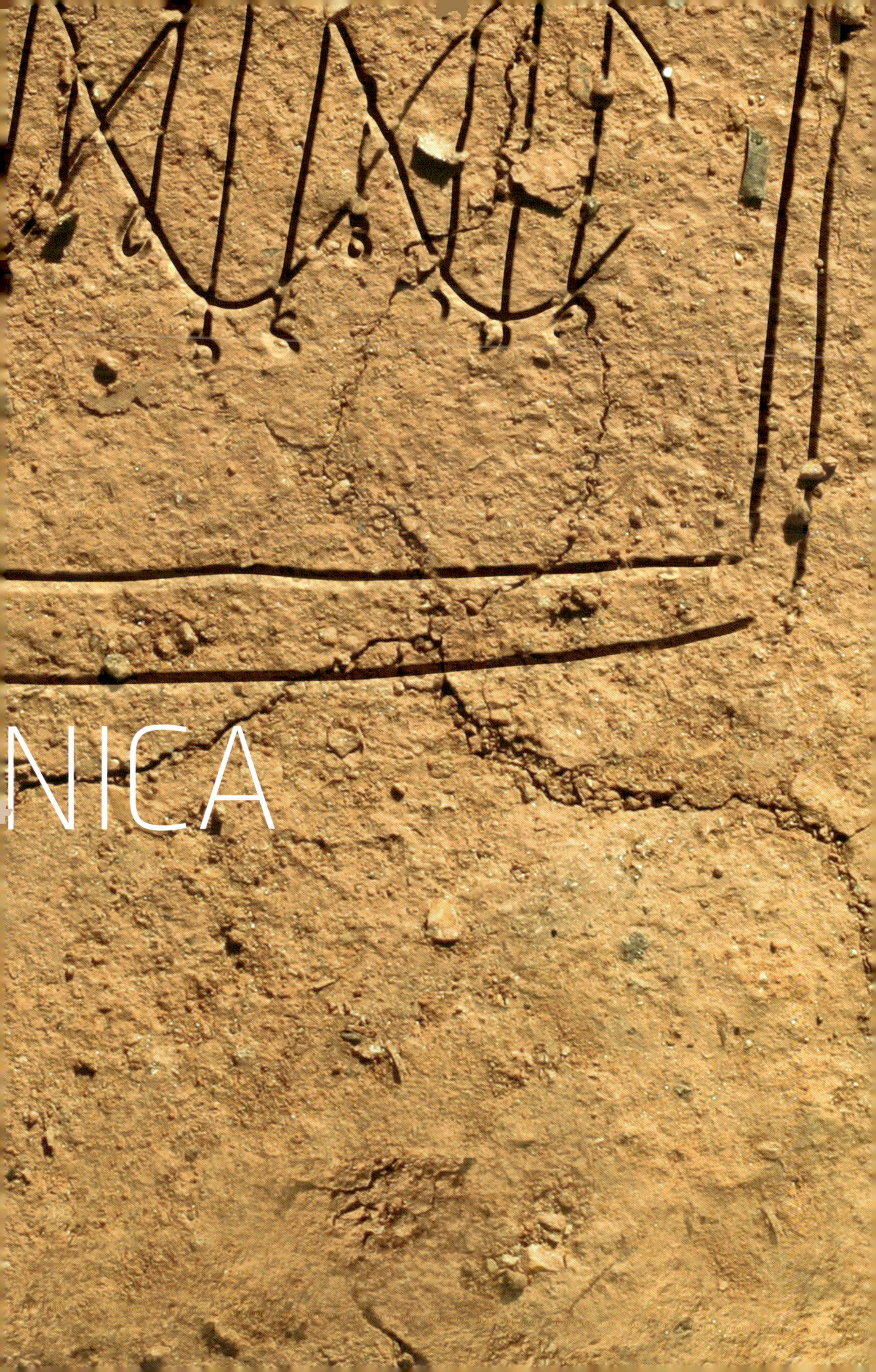
NICA

PIXELSPACES 2013

Pixelspaces is an annual conference that the Ars Electronica Futurelab has been staging since 2001. It includes a symposium and exhibition that deal with various current issues in the area of digital culture. As the conclave of a transdisciplinary community of freelance (media) artists, staffers at up-and-coming as well as established media labs and institutions, and scientists in a broad spectrum of disciplines, *Pixelspaces* is a setting for communication about and exhibition of current research approaches in the artistic-scientific and technological confrontation with socially relevant issues.
The programmatic point of departure of *Pixelspaces* was delivered by the increasingly complex interconnections among experimental fields and concrete tasks being carried out in the fields of computer gaming, architecture and virtual/augmented reality. Before this background and as part of an overall effort to address the latest currents in these fields, the conference has focused on, negotiated and even provoked new efforts to transcend boundaries between different artistic and scientific disciplines. Accordingly, non-institutionalized individual manifestations of interdisciplinarity have not only provided the themes of the annual *Pixelspaces* conferences; the trend as a whole has also occupied the focus of attention.
Two highlights of *Pixelspaces 2013* are *Inside Ars Electronica Futurelab* and *Inside Ars Electronica Solutions*, close-up looks at current projects of the Ars Electronica Futurelab and Ars Electronica's Solutions division set up in 2012. One very high priority effort is *Spaxels*, which has been substantially enhanced and upgraded over the past year. Insiders will also present a few of their international joint ventures, including those being staged in conjunction with the Ars Electronica Residency Network and the Lab Academy.

Pixelspaces ist die seit 2001 vom Ars Electronica Futurelab jährlich im Kontext des Ars Electronica Festivals realisierte Konferenzreihe, bei der im Rahmen eines Themensymposiums und einer Themenausstellung aktuelle Strömungen aufgegriffen und aus der Sicht eines Atelier/Labors diskutiert werden. Die Themenverankerung von *Pixelspaces* ist seit den Gründungstagen als eine komplexer werdende Verwebung von Computer Gaming, Architektur und Virtual/Augmented Reality zu verstehen. Das Potenzial dieses Crossovers schlägt sich nicht mehr nur im experimentellen Sektor nieder; Forschungs- und Projektergebnisse zeigen einen Grad der Professionalisierung, der dem Aufmerksamkeitsbereich kommerziell agierender Unternehmen ebenso wenig entgangen ist wie den universitären Bildungseinrichtungen, die die Kreativen der Zukunft ausbilden sollen.
Als Plattform für die Zusammenkunft einer Community aus freischaffenden Medienkünstlern, etablierten Medienlaboren und -instituten sowie Newcomern auf beiden Seiten ist *Pixelspaces* Kommunikations- und Schauraum aktueller Forschungsansätze in der künstlerisch-wissenschaftlichen und technologischen Auseinandersetzung mit gesellschaftlich relevanten Fragestellungen.
Pixelspaces 2013 gewährt mit *Inside Ars Electronica Futurelab* und *Inside Ars Electronica Solutions* Einblick in aktuelle Projekte des Ars Electronica Futurelab und der 2012 gegründeten Ars Electronica Solutions. Ein besonderer Schwerpunkt liegt dabei auf dem Projekt *Spaxel*, das seit letztem Jahr grundlegend weiterentwickelt wurde. Auch die vielfältigen Kooperationen mit internationalen Partnern, die u. a. auch im Rahmen des *Ars Electronica Residency Network* und der *Lab Academy* stattfinden, werden vorgestellt.

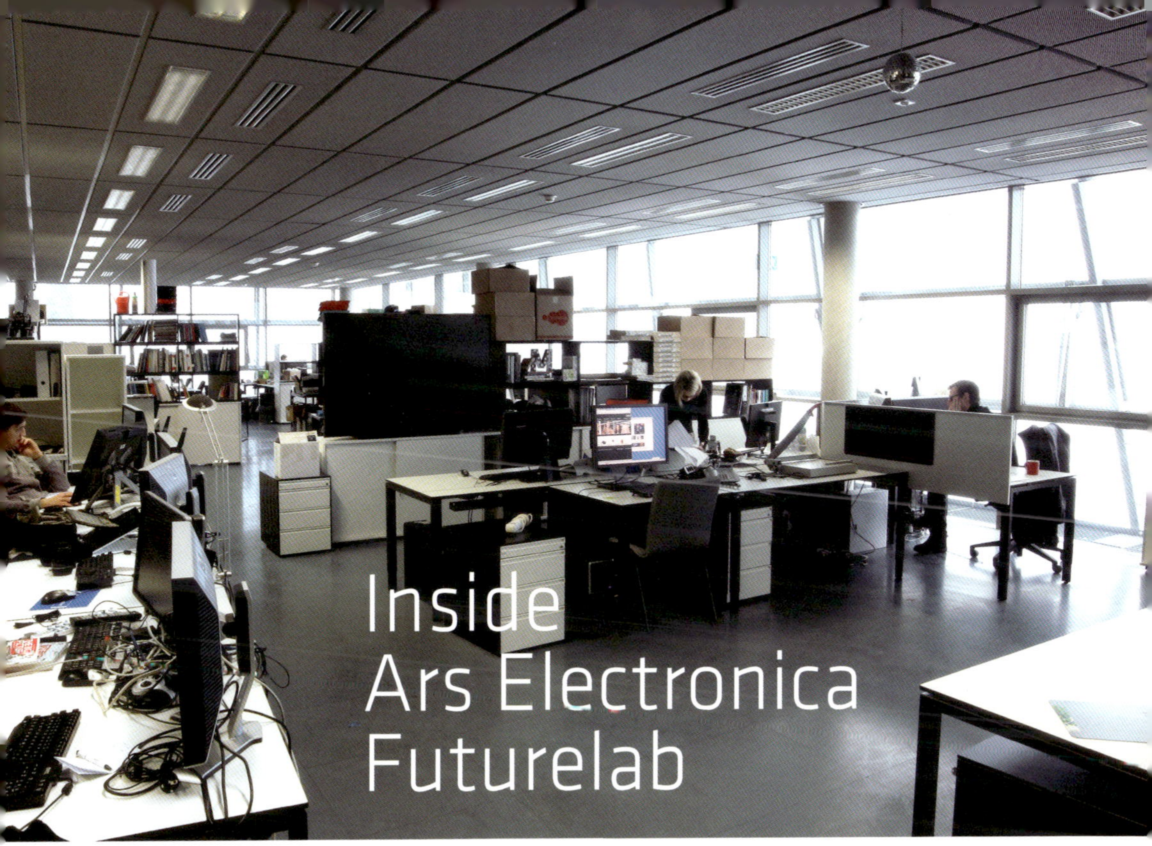

Inside Ars Electronica Futurelab

Ars Electronica Futurelab focuses on the future at the nexus of art, technology and society. The lab understands its works as sketches of possible future scenarios in art-based, experimental forms. In this way, the lab's projects use methods and strategies of applied science, the results of which reveal new knowledge and experiences of societal relevance in art and science. The team bases its work commitment upon transdisciplinary research and work that results in a variety of different disciplines at the lab. Having Artists and Researchers from all over the globe collaborating with—and taking residencies at—the Ars Electronica Futurelab, is fundamental to this Atelier/Laboratory.

Curiosity and hope evolve expertise to excellency

The range of activities of the Ars Electronica Futurelab focuses on expertise developed over the years in fields of radical innovation in art and technology such as Creative Catalysts, Functional and Information Aesthetics, Interaction Ecology, Persuasive Technologies, new forms of Virtual Reality and Robotinity.
Besides the Futurelab's research topics, with proj-

Das Ars Electronica Futurelab befasst sich mit Zukunftsfragen am Schnittpunkt von Kunst, Technologie und Gesellschaft. Es versteht seine Arbeiten als Skizzen einer möglichen Zukunft kunstgestützter experimenteller Formen. Seine Projekte setzen daher auf Methoden und Strategien angewandter Wissenschaften, deren Resultate gesellschaftlich relevante neue Erkenntnisse und Erfahrungen in Kunst und Wissenschaft liefern. Das Team setzt bei seinen Aufgaben auf eine transdisziplinäre Forschung und Arbeitsweise, weshalb im Lab in einer Vielzahl von Disziplinen sehr gute Ergebnisse erzielt werden. Ein wesentlicher Aspekt des Atelier/Labors ist es, Künstler und Forscher aus aller Welt zur Zusammenarbeit mit oder zu einer Residency am Futurelab zu gewinnen.

Neugier und Hoffnung machen aus Fachwissen Exzellenz

Das Ars Electronica Futurelab kann in seinen Aktivitäten auf ein Fachwissen zurückgreifen, das im Lauf vieler Jahre in Bereichen radikal innovativer Kunst und Technologie wie Creative Catalysts, Functional & Information Aesthetics, Interaction Ecology, Persuasive Technologies, neuer Formen von Virtual Reality oder Robotinity erworben wurde.

ects that are created both as contracted research in collaboration with industrial partners and as funded national and international research grants, the lab hosts programs for international exchange and education.

The *Ars Electronica Residency Network* conducts highly elaborated scientist- and artist-in-residence programs with national and international Partner Organizations.

The *Ars Electronica Futurelab Academy* represents the structural interface with the academic world of education. With this program for educational collaborations with international universities and an additional focus on a strongly practice-based Ph.D. program at the Ars Electronica Futurelab in collaboration with the University of Newcastle (Australia), international academic institutions create a sustainable interface with the Futurelab.

The *Inside Ars Electronica Futurelab* exhibition, part of Futurelab's curated contribution to Ars Electronica's *Pixelspaces* conference, offers a strongly practice-oriented, behind-the-scenes look at current Futurelab projects, in addition to the other *Pixelspaces* conferences and exhibitions. With hands-on demos and pre-prototype presentations this new, "beyond presentation slides" format aims to make tangible the established practice of transdisciplinarity in the lab.

Text: Horst Hörtner

Neben den Forschungsprojekten des Futurelab, die zum Teil Auftragsarbeiten in Kooperation mit Industriepartnern sind und zum Teil durch nationale und internationale Forschungssubventionen finanziert werden, bietet es auch internationale Austausch- und Bildungsprogramme an.

Das *Ars Electronica Residency Network* führt gemeinsam mit nationalen und internationalen Partnerorganisationen hoch spezialisierte Wissenschafts- und Artist-in-Residence-Programme durch.

Die *Ars Electronica Futurelab Academy* stellt das strukturelle Bindeglied zur akademischen Welt dar. Aufgrund der Zusammenarbeit mit internationalen Universitäten im Rahmen dieses Bildungsprogramms und eines stark praxisbezogenen PhD-Studiums, das das Ars Electronica Futurelab in Kooperation mit der australischen Universität Newcastle anbietet, unterhalten viele internationale akademische Institutionen einen regen Austausch mit dem Futurelab.

Die Ausstellung *Inside Ars Electronica Futurelab,* Teil des vom Futurelab kuratierten Beitrags zur *Pixelspaces*-Konferenzreihe und als Ergänzung zu deren Konferenzen und Ausstellungen gedacht, zeigt einen sehr praxisnahen Blick hinter die Kulissen laufender Futurelab-Projekte. Mit praktischen Demos und Präsentationen von Pre-Prototypen möchte dieses neue, „über Präsentationsfolien hinausgehende" Format die im Futurelab etablierte Praxis der Transdisziplinarität veranschaulichen.

Aus dem Englischen von Michael Kaufmann

Horst Hörtner

SPAXEL – embodied spaces

Technology makes possibilities
Design makes solutions
Art makes questions [...]
John Maeda

"Spaxel" is the term the Ars Electronica Futurelab invented to refer to a pixel freely positioned in real space. This concept of 3-D spatial depiction radically differs from any procedure ever used before to render 3-D images. In 2012, the spaxel opened up a new field of artistic experimentation and investigation.

Ever since the first cave paintings, human beings

Technology makes possibilities
Design makes solutions
Art makes questions [...]
John Maeda

Mit „Spaxel" bezeichnet das Ars Electronica Futurelab einen frei im realen Raum positionierten Bildpunkt. Dieses Konzept zur räumlichen 3D-Darstellung ist radikal anders als alle bisher bekannten Verfahren der 3D-Darstellung. 2012 öffnete sich damit ein neuer Raum für künstlerisch, investigative Experimente.

Seit den ersten Höhlenmalereien erstellen wir Menschen flache Abbildungen unserer Umgebung – Bild-

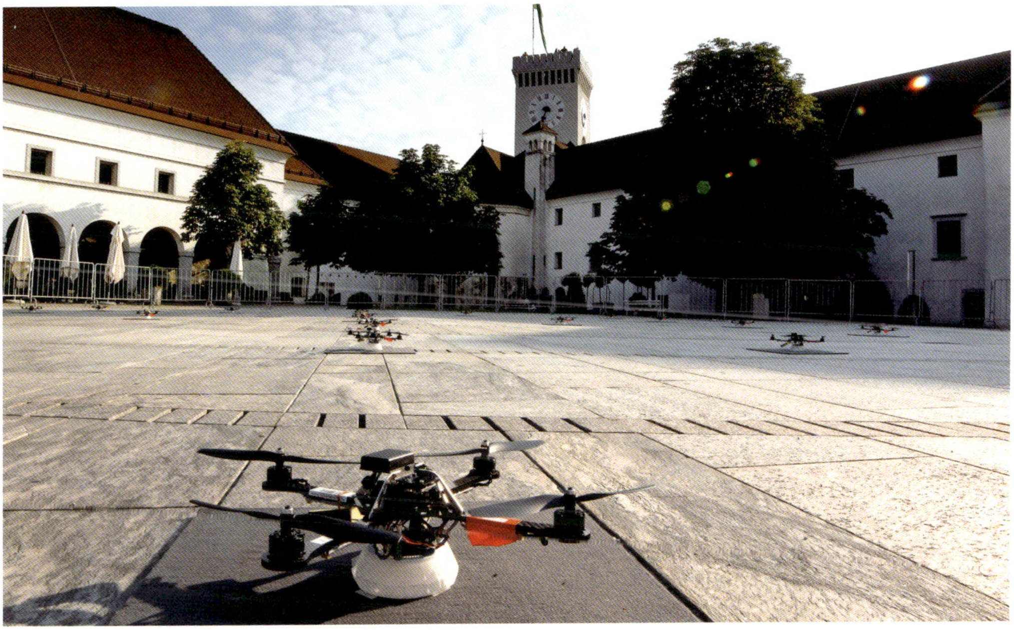

AEC

Quadcopter, Spaxel performance, Ljubljana 2013

have been creating two-dimensional representations of our surroundings—points of color on a more or less flat surface. The third dimension flowed into the design process at about the same time in the form of sculptures and reliefs. The technique of foreshortened perspective was already being employed in these early paintings; nevertheless, the development of a geometrically and thus mathematically construable central perspective wasn't consummated until the Renaissance. It's said to have been invented by Filippo Brunelleschi in 1410. About 30,000 years after the first cave paintings, human beings developed moving pictures—beginning with shadow plays, then as a reproduction of reality (*phenakistoscope*, 1830), later also as artificially generated animation (*praxinoscope*, Émile Reynaud, 1877), thereafter as depictions of our physical surroundings on film (Lumière Brothers, 1895). The computer-generated image was born considerably later in scientific laboratories (*Whirlwind*, MIT, 1945-1952). A milestone along the way was the invention of the cathode ray tube by Ferdinand Braun in 1897.

Thus, for no fewer than 115 years now, our screens or "electronic moving picture displays"—whether analog or digital—have been a fixed configuration of

punkte auf einer mehr oder weniger ebenen Fläche. Die dritte Dimension fließt etwa zur selben Zeit in Form von Skulpturen und Reliefs in die Gestaltung ein. Schon unter diesen frühen Malereien finden sich perspektivische Verkürzungen, doch die geometrische, also mathematisch konstruierbare (Zentral-)Perspektive wird erst in der Renaissance vollständig entwickelt, als ihr Entdecker gilt Filippo Brunelleschi (1410). Etwa 30.000 Jahre nach den ersten Höhlenmalereien entwickelte der Mensch das Bewegtbild – beginnend mit Schattenspielen, dann als Reproduktion der Wirklichkeit (*Lebensräder*, 1830), später auch künstlich generierte Trickaufnahmen (*Praxinoskop*, Emile Renault 1877), danach die Ab-Bildung unserer Umgebung auf Film (Brüder Lumière, 1895). Das computergenerierte Bild wurde unwesentlich später in den Labors der Wissenschaft geboren (*Whirlwind*, MIT 1945–1952); dazwischen lag die Erfindung der Kathodenstrahlröhre von Ferdinand Braun (1897).

Unsere Bildschirme oder „elektronischen Bewegtbildanzeigen" – ob analog oder digital – sind also seit 115 Jahren (!) eine starre Anordnung von Lichtpunkten, zweidimensional auf einer mehr oder weniger ebenen Fläche in Spalten und Zeilen angeordnet. Alle Möglichkeiten zur Darstellung elektronischer Bilder basieren auf einer zweidimensionalen Matrix von Lichtpunkten.

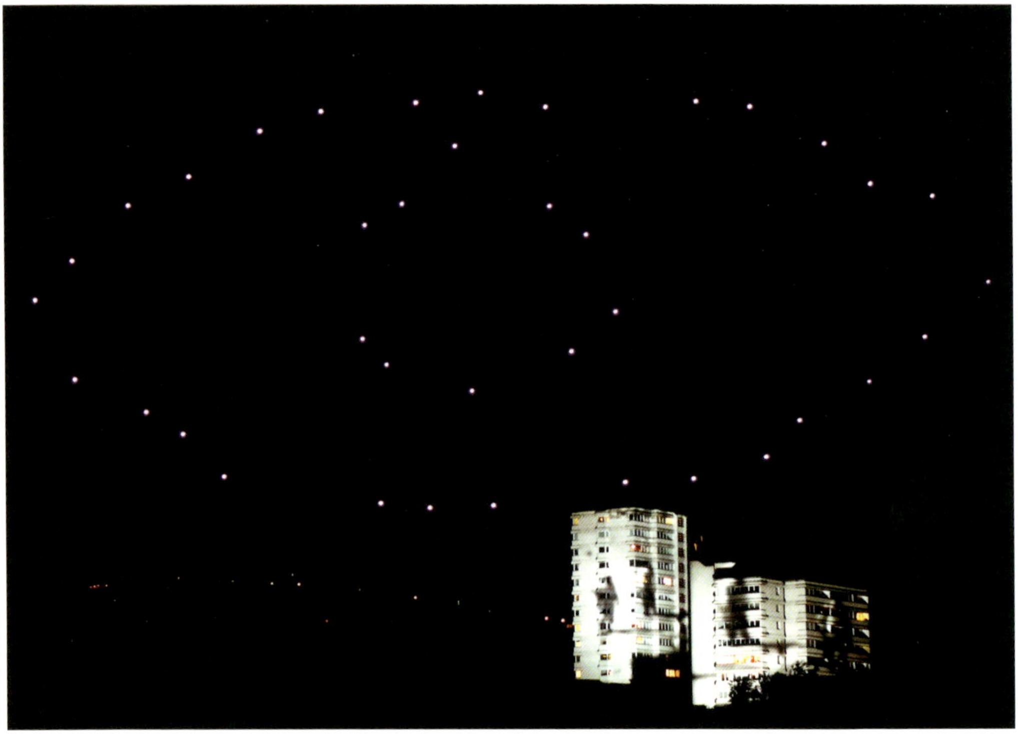

Reinhard Winkler

Quadcopter forming the shape of an eye, Linz 2012

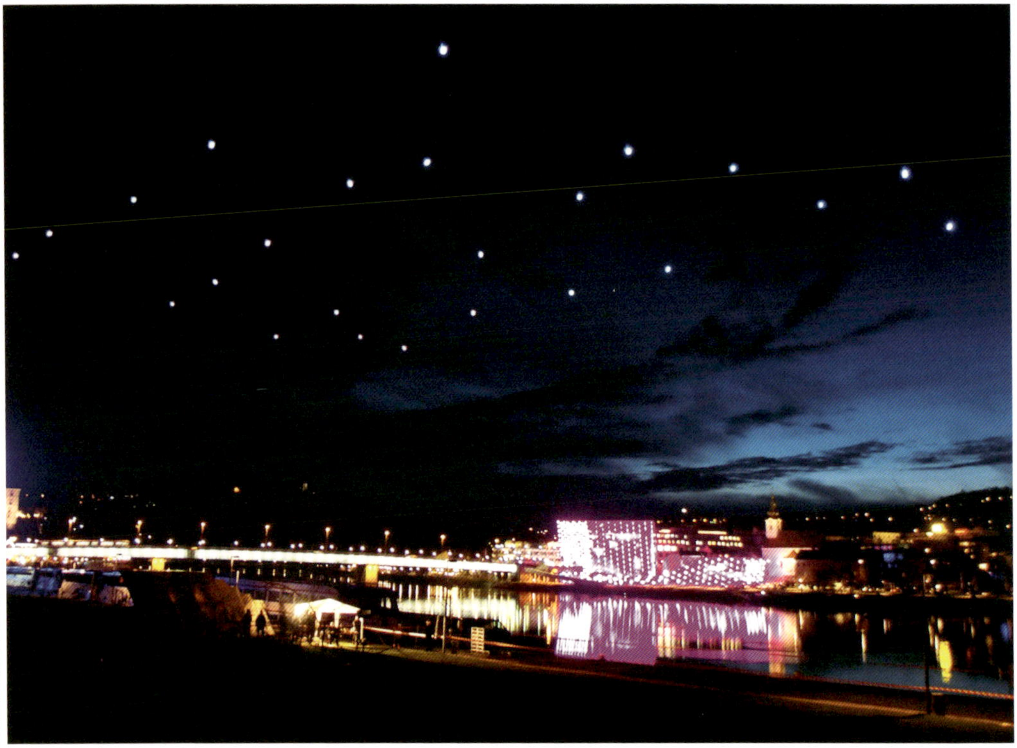

AEC, Martin Hieslmair

Spaxel performance, Linz 2013

points of light arrayed two-dimensionally on a more or less even surface in rows and columns. All the options of depicting electronic images are based on a two-dimensional matrix of pixels. And procedures for representing three-dimensional images don't change this rigid lineup of pixels either.
We have already witnessed a few approaches to expanding the two-dimensional matrix. As early as 2006, *Source*, an installation that Andrew Schoben created for the London Stock Exchange, gave pixels arranged in a stack of 2-D matrices the freedom to move about along the z-axis. The same goes for *Kinectic Sculpture*, Art+Com's 2008 work for the BMW Museum in Munich, in which a single 2-D matrix (made up of metal balls functioning as pixels) is suspended by cables and driven by a motor to overcome the third dimension. The *flyfire* concept developed in 2010 by MIT SENSEable City Lab and ARES Lab was another effort to come to terms with the third dimension; it used, at least conceptually, unmanned aerial vehicles (UAVs) to maneuver the individual pixels.
This was a brand new approach to the three-dimensional depiction of moving images in real space. Analytically speaking, the fundamental concept of the above-mentioned projects is aptly captured by the term voxel. These volumetric picture elements make up a construct that utilizes the pixels of several two-dimensional pixel matrices stacked along a third axis for visualization purposes.
But just consider how much more potential is inherent in an approach that completely negates the a priori existence of a matrix and solves the problem of visualizing the third dimension by endowing all pixels with complete freedom to move back and forth in all three dimensions, and the capability of assuming any form by correspondingly positioning the individual pixels in space. These are spaxels! In contrast to pixels and voxels, the position of each individual point to light is not influenced by the position of all the others. A rigid positional interrelationship among the pixels is a thing of the past. Regardless of the "carrier medium" used to reallocate spaxels—whether you implement this concept with UAVs as the Ars Electronica Futurelab demonstrated for the first time in 2012, or if you come up with some other technical solution like bioluminescent creatures, for example—the concept

An dieser starren Anordnung der Lichtpunkte ändern auch die Verfahren zur dreidimensionalen Bilddarstellung nichts.
Einige Ansätze zur Erweiterung der zweidimensionalen Matrix wurden jedoch bereits realisiert. Andrew Schoben hat mit seiner Arbeit *Source* bereits 2006 für die Londoner Börse eine Installation realisiert, die den Bildpunkten mehrerer übereinandergelagerter 2D-Matrizen die Freiheit gibt, in die Z-Achse zu wandern. Ähnlich verhält es sich mit der Arbeit *Kinectic Sculpture* von Art+Com (2008) für das BMW-Museum in München, in der eine einzige 2D-Matrix aus – als Bildpunkte fungierenden – Metallkugeln, an Seilen hängend und motorengetrieben die dritte Dimension überwindet. Das Konzept *flyfire* des MIT SENSEable City Lab und des ARES Lab nimmt sich 2010 ebenfalls der dritten Dimension an und nutzt, zumindest im Konzept, UAVs (Unmanned Arial Vehicle) als Träger der einzelnen Bildpunkte.
Damit wird ein neuer Weg der dreidimensionalen Darstellung von Bewegtbildern im realen Raum beschritten. Analytisch betrachtet, kann das, den zuvor erwähnten Projekten zugrundeliegende Konzept mit Voxel beschrieben werden. Ein Voxel *(Volumetric Picture Element)* ist jenes Konstrukt, das sich mit Bildpunkten mehrerer zweidimensionaler entlang einer dritten Achse gestapelter Bildpunkt-Matrizen für die Visualisierung beschäftigt.
Wie viel weiter führt das inhaltliche Potenzial eines Ansatzes, der die A-priori-Existenz einer Matrix völlig negiert und das Visualisierungsproblem der dritten Dimension dadurch löst, dass alle Bildpunkte mit allen sechs Freiheitsgraden ausgestattet werden, und jede beliebige Form durch die entsprechende Positionierung der Einzelbildpunkte im Raum darstellt? Das sind Spaxel! Anders als bei Pixel und Voxel bleibt beim Spaxel jede Position eines jeden Bildpunktes unbeeinflusst von der Position aller anderen. Es gibt kein starres Ortsverhältnis der Bildpunkte zueinander mehr.
Ob man dieses Konzept, wie vom Ars Electronica Futurelab 2012 erstmals demonstriert, mit UAVs löst oder ob man in Zukunft vielleicht über biolumineszierende Lebewesen nachdenkt – welche technische Lösung auch immer für den „Träger" eines Spaxels gefunden werden mag, das Konzept bleibt aufrecht. Das *Space Picture Element* meint weniger einen choreografierten, leuchtenden Drohnen-Schwarm als vielmehr einen Paradigmenwechsel in der dreidimen-

remains valid. The *space picture element* refers only secondarily to a choreographed, luminous swarm of drones; of prime importance is the intrinsic paradigm shift in three-dimensional depiction. This paradigm shift is made possible by dispensing with a rigid picture matrix and replacing the stereographic principle with real spatial representation of the third dimension. The virtual space becomes a real physical space without need for any additional translational aids.

The highest degree of resolution ever achieved by a spaxel display is 49 at the 2012 *voestalpine Klangwolke,* the Cloud of Sound spectacle produced during the Ars Electronica Festival. A formation of 50 spaxels has taken off for test flights not open to the public and not captured on video. This resolution (swarm density) leaves plenty of room for improvement; nevertheless, one must resist the temptation to compare the density of a spaxel swarm with the resolution of a 2-D matrix.

Spaxels afford the possibility of concentrating picture points precisely at the substantive focal point of a scene. There's a dynamic interrelationship between resolution and density. The example of a line quickly makes this clear. In a two-dimensional matrix of 49 pixels (7 x 7), a vertical line consists of a maximum of seven points, and 42 pixels just sit there doing nothing. In the case of 49 spaxels, on the other hand, the line, regardless of whether it's horizontal, vertical or oblique, is comprised of 49 points of light. In a spaxel display, all available points of light can be utilized to depict the image itself; thus, spaxel density cannot be equated with the pixel resolution of a conventional display. Nevertheless, for obvious reasons, a substantial increase in swarm density is just as desirable as boosting the speed of the vehicles (UAVs at present) used to shift the points of light. Our R&D efforts in all crucial technical areas (battery, LED, the drone itself) have top priority and we're implementing enhancements and upgrades on almost a weekly basis. Thus, achieving a larger, more maneuverable spaxel formation in the very near future is a very real prospect.

In any case, we're not all that concerned with the question of what is still feasible despite the spaxel display's physical constraints with respect to familiar forms of representation (still images, videos);

sionalen Darstellung. Dieser Paradigmenwechsel wird dadurch möglich, dass die starre Bildmatrix wegfällt und das stereografische Prinzip durch die realräumliche Darstellung der dritten Dimension ersetzt wird. Der virtuelle Raum wird zu einem realen, physischen Raum – ohne jede weitere Übersetzungshilfe.

Die höchste bis zum heutigen Tag erreichte Auflösung eines Spaxeldisplays besteht aus 49 Spaxel (Ars Electronica 2012, *voestalpine Klangwolke).* Bei nicht öffentlich zugänglichen Testflügen waren es 50 Spaxel, allerdings undokumentiert und nicht belegbar. Die Auflösung (bzw. Dichte) lässt zwar durchaus noch zu wünschen übrig, jedoch muss man der Verführung widerstehen, die Dichte eines Spaxel-Schwarms mit der Auflösung einer 2D-Matrix zu vergleichen.

Mit Spaxel besteht die Möglichkeit, Bildpunkte dort zu konzentrieren, wo das inhaltliche Hauptaugenmerk einer Szene liegt. Auflösung und Dichte stehen in einem dynamischen Verhältnis zueinander. Am Beispiel einer Linie wird das sehr schnell klar: Bei einer 2D-Matrix von 49 Pixel (7 x 7) besteht eine vertikale Linie aus maximal 7 Bildpunkten. Die restlichen 42 Pixel sind dazu da, das *Nichts* darzustellen! Bei 49 Spaxel hingegen wird die Linie durch 49 Bildpunkte dargestellt. Egal ob sie horizontal, schräg oder vertikal verläuft. Bei einem Spaxel-Display können alle zur Verfügung stehenden Bildpunkte zur Darstellung des *Inhaltes* genutzt werden. Die Spaxel-Dichte ist also nicht gleichzusetzen mit der Bildpunktauflösung eines herkömmlichen Displays. Eine substanzielle Erhöhung der Schwarmdichte ist aber aus nachvollziehbaren Gründen genauso notwendig wie die Erhöhung der Geschwindigkeit der einzelnen Bildpunkte-Träger (derzeit UAVs). In allen geforderten technischen Bereichen (vom Akku über die LEDs bis zur Drohne selbst) wird die Entwicklung mit Nachdruck vorangetrieben, und daher finden sich technische Verbesserungen nahezu im Wochenrhythmus. Eine viel versprechende Aussicht also auf agilere, größere Spaxel-Schwärme bereits in den kommenden Monaten ...

Es beschäftigt uns aber weniger die Frage, was trotz der physikalischen Beschränkungen eines Spaxel-Displays in Bezug auf bekannte Darstellungsformen (Bild, Video etc.) noch machbar bleibt, sondern viel eher die Frage, welche bislang unmöglichen Darstellungsformen durch Spaxel erst ermöglicht werden. Wir müssen beginnen, Inhalte anders zu denken und Fragen neu zu formulieren.

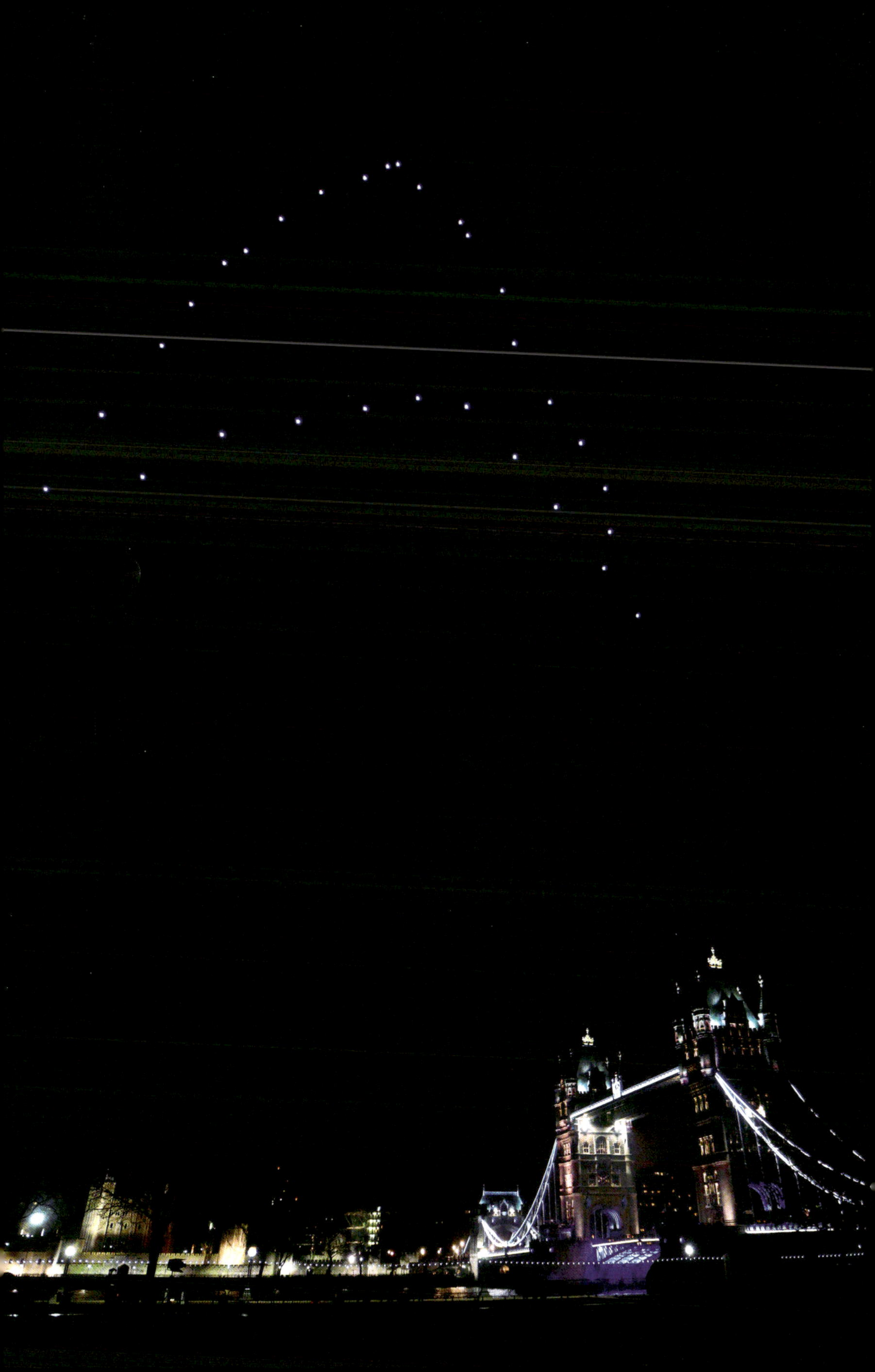

instead, we're focused on what heretofore impossible forms of portrayal are now very doable indeed thanks to the spaxel. We have to start reconceptualizing content and reformulating questions.
Regardless of the physical facts and circumstances that confront us today, we first have to explore those (design) criteria on the basis of which the optimal distribution of spaxels in space is algorithmically determined, and which already takes into consideration the shifts necessary to form subsequent content. Where exactly does the transition from "clearly determined" to "totally illegible" set in? What specific elements give rise to the tremendous enthusiasm that's positively tangible at these spaxel performances and to the rave reviews they consistently garner from audience members of all social strata and age groups?
The term "spaxel performance" refers to formation flights that take place on almost a weekly basis in Linz as well as shows staged worldwide. The Ars Electronica Futurelab was commissioned by Paramount Pictures to form the *StarTrek* fleet logo in the night sky above London. Spaxels were part of an elaborate mise-en-scène in conjunction with the *Murmuration* project staged in Bergen, Norway. In Ljubljana, Slovenia, the swarm hovered above the castle in the heart of the old city during a live performance of Tchaikovsky's *1812 Overture.* And just as this catalog is going to press, the Ars Electronica Futurelab crew is busy conducting all the measurement & test flights in the approval process mandated by Australia's Civil Aviation Safety Authority prior to the next big spaxel show on the campus of Queensland University of Technology in Brisbane on August 18, 2013.

The Spaxel Concept or "The Convergence of Realities"

One observation seems especially important. If our real physical surroundings become our projection screen—actually morph into a display—can that which is displayed on it still be called a representation or is it the case that a depiction positioned in real space is itself that which is displayed? Spaxels call for ideas and concepts of so-called real world augmentation. A computer-generated graphic depicted by means of spaxels doesn't only look like it's part of our real world (as is so with aug-

Ungeachtet der physikalischen Bedingungen, die wir heute vorfinden, sind erst jene (gestalterischen) Kriterien auszuloten, auf deren Grundlagen die optimale Verteilung der Spaxel im Raum – die bereits die Veränderung zum nachfolgenden Inhalt berücksichtigt – algorithmisch bestimmt wird. Wo genau liegt der Scheitelpunkt zwischen „eindeutig determiniert" und „absolut unleserlich"? Woraus genau speist sich die bei allen Spaxel-Performances spürbare und immer wieder rückgemeldete Begeisterung der Betrachter aller Gesellschaftsklassen und Altersstufen?
Mit „Spaxel-Performances" sind hier die nahezu wöchentlich stattfindenden Flüge in Linz ebenso gemeint wie die internationalen Auftritte. Für Paramount Pictures zeichnete das Ars Electronica Futurelab das Logo der *StarTrek*-Flotte in den Nachthimmel über London; beim Projekt *Murmuration* in Bergen waren die Spaxel Teil der Inszenierung im Bühnenraum, und in Ljubljana, Slowenien, startete der Schwarm zur Live-Aufführung von Tschaikowskis *Ouverture solennelle 1812* hoch über die Burg im Herzen der Stadt. Zeitgleich zum Redaktionsschluss des vorliegenden Katalogs absolvierte das Team des Ars Electronica Futurelab gerade die Zulassungsprüfungen der australischen Luftraumbehörde CASA in Brisbane und führte alle notwenigen Mess- und Testflüge für eine Show am Campus der Queensland University of Technology in Brisbane am 18. August 2013 durch.

Das Spaxel-Konzept oder „die Konvergenz der Realitäten"

Eine Beobachtung scheint besonders wichtig: Wenn unsere reale Umgebung zu unserer „Leinwand" – zum Display – wird, ist das Dargestellte dann noch Abbild oder wird aus einer im Realraum positionierten Darstellung nicht bereits das Dargestellte selbst? Mit Spaxel sind Ideen und Konzepte einer *real world augmentation* gefordert: Eine durch Spaxel dargestellte computergenerierte Grafik sieht nicht nur so aus, als wäre sie Teil unserer realen Welt (wie in der Augmented Reality), sie *ist* Teil unserer realen Welt. Damit sind die Spaxel auch nicht mehr den klassischen Kategorien von Virtual Reality, Augmented Reality oder Mixed Reality zuordenbar.
Ist die Darstellung einer Kaffeetasse real, wenn sie – aus Millionen Spaxels kreiert – auf dem Tisch steht? Ja, weil sie ihren Platz im Realraum einnimmt. Da die Spaxel-Tasse aber im nächsten Moment zu einem

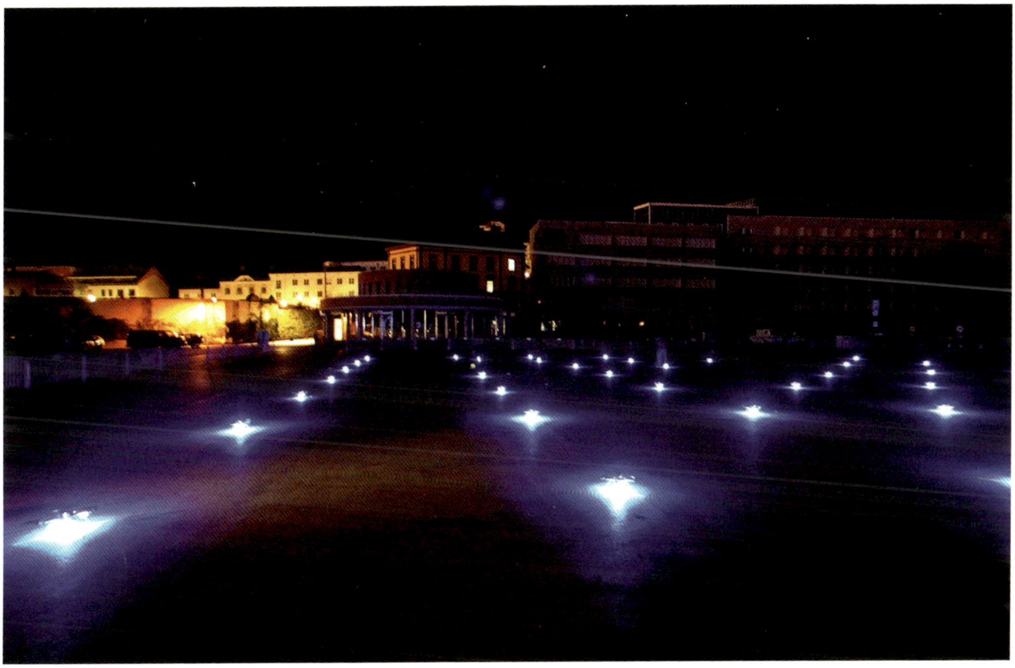
Gregor Hartl

Spaxel performance, voestalpine Klangwolke, Linz 2013

mented reality); it *is* part of our real world. Accordingly, spaxels can't be assigned to conventional categories such as virtual reality, augmented reality or mixed reality.

Is the representation of a coffee cup real if it—created out of a million spaxels—sits on a table? Yes, because it occupies its place in real space. But since the spaxel cup can suddenly turn into a bird and fly away, the term *real* doesn't do justice to it. After all, the bird's act of flying away is already inherent in the spaxel swarm—in the system—when it's still a cup. In contrast to a lump of clay that can likewise be reshaped from a cup into a bird by means of manual intervention, here it's the swarm itself (the render farm, the computer, the display) that engineers this metamorphosis. The real cup is virtually a bird. None of the options the established terminology places at our disposal completely captures the convergence of these two states, being simultaneously virtual and real, the convergence of the display with that which is displayed. The upshot of this is, necessarily, the introduction of a new term. And in light of the above elaborations, *converged reality* seems most incisive to me.

Vogel werden und wegflattern kann, greift der Begriff „real" zu kurz, denn dem Spaxelschwarm – dem System – ist das „Wegflattern als Vogel" bereits zu jenem Zeitpunkt, als es noch Tasse ist, eingeschrieben. Anders als der Tonklumpen, dessen Form durch einen manuellen Eingriff ebenfalls verändert werden kann – von der Tasse zum Vogel –, ist es hier der Schwarm (die Renderfarm, der Computer, das Display) selbst, der diese Veränderung vollzieht. Die reale Tasse ist virtuell ein Vogel. Keine der etablierten Begrifflichkeiten trägt der Konvergenz dieser beiden Zustände, gleichzeitig virtuell und real zu sein, der Konvergenz des Displays mit dem Dargestellten Rechnung. Daraus ergibt sich notwendigerweise die Einführung eines neuen Begriffs, und aus zuvor Gesagtem scheint mir *converged reality* dafür am treffendsten zu sein.

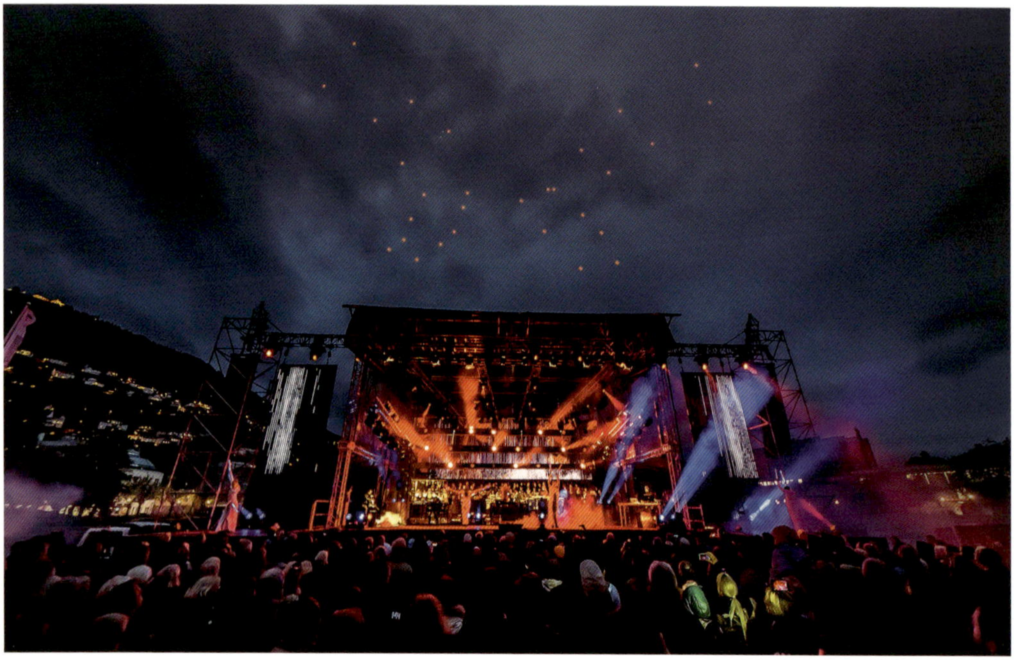

Ralph Larmann

35 quadcopters are protagonists of the opening event *Murmuration* at the Bergen Festival in Norway.

phase7 + Ars Electronica Futurelab

Murmuration

Murmuration was the Ars Electronica Futurelab's first collaborative project with phase7, the Berlin-based artists' network. For the opening of the Bergen (Norway) International Festival, they jointly staged an outdoor performance featuring 30 quadcopters, seven musicians, eight dancers, and a chorus of 150 youngsters. The Ars Electronica Futurelab's spaxel extended Phase 7's stage show into the heavens above Bergen and visualized the show's grand finale with enchanting light formations. The upshot was a multimedia light sculpture composed of high-tech and performance that reached high up into the night sky—a resounding, constantly shifting architecture that illuminated the modern individual's contradictory and instinctive swarm behavior on the artistic and metaphysical level. Following the tremendous success in Bergen, additional performances of *Murmuration* at other international venues are currently being planned. The shows in Bergen, Norway were staged in May 2013.

phase7 + Ars Electronica Futurelab

Murmuration

Murmuration heißt das erste Kooperationsprojekt des Ars Electronica Futurelab mit dem Berliner Künstlernetzwerk phase7. Anlässlich der Eröffnung der internationalen Festspiele Bergen in Norwegen wurde gemeinsam eine Outdoor-Performance mit 30 Quadcoptern, 7 Musikern, 8 Tänzern und einem 150-köpfigen Jugendchor konzipiert. Die Spaxel des Ars Electronica Futurelab erweiterten die Bühnenshow von Phase7 in den Himmel über Bergen und visualisierten das große Finale der Show mit zauberhaften Lichtformationen. Es entstand eine multimediale Lichtskulptur aus Hightech und Performance, die bis in den Nachthimmel reichte – eine klingende, sich stetig verschiebende Architektur, die das widersprüchliche und instinktive Schwarmverhalten des modernen Individuums auf künstlerischer und metaphysischer Ebene durchleuchtete. Weitere internationale Wiederaufführungen von *Murmuration* sind nach dem großen Erfolg in Bergen geplant. Die Shows in Bergen, Norwegen, fanden im Mai 2013 statt.

http://murmurationbyphase7.wordpress.com/

TOSCA + Ars Electronica Futurelab

Visualizations for TOSCA's *Odeon*

Rupert Huber and Richard Dorfmeister (aka TOSCA) premiered their new album *Odeon* at Linz's Musiktheater together with vocalists Sarah Callier Robert Gallagher, Rodney Hunter and Jay Jay Jones as well as the Wiener K&K String Quartet.

Each individual musical expression, every acoustic event and frequency delivered input for the visualization software the Ars Electronica Futurelab developed especially for *Odeon*. The output was sent in real time to five light objects and the stage backdrop, a jumbo projection screen. The visual vocabulary thus expressed the continual shifts of the performance's inherent dualities: sound and silence, light and shadow. As befitting the basic feeling *Odeon* evokes—a sense of skepticism rather associated with the Blues—the stage set was immersed in monochrome tones.

TOSCA and Ars Electronica Futurelab also produced this extraordinary show in Prague, Budapest, Graz and Bratislava.

Rupert Huber und Richard Dorfmeister (aka TOSCA) präsentierten gemeinsam mit den vier VokalistInnen Sarah Callier, Robert Gallagher, Rodney Hunter und Jay Jay Jones sowie dem Wiener K&K Streichquartett im Linzer Musiktheater ihr neues Album *Odeon*.

Jeder einzelne musikalische Vorgang, jedes Klangereignis und jede Frequenz bildeten einen Input für die Visualisierungssoftware, die das Ars Electronica Futurelab eigens für *Odeon* entwickelt hat. Fünf Lichtobjekte und eine Großprojektion im Bühnenhintergrund wurden auf diese Weise in Echtzeit bespielt. Die visuelle Sprache bringt dabei den steten Wechsel der Dualitäten Ton und Stille, Licht und Schatten zum Ausdruck. Passend zur skeptischen, mehr dem Blues zugewandten Grundhaltung von *Odeon* wird das Bühnenbild in monochrome Farbräume getaucht.

TOSCA und Ars Electronica Futurelab zeigten die Show auch bei Auftritten in Prag, Budapest, Graz und Bratislava.

Text: Johanna Mathauer

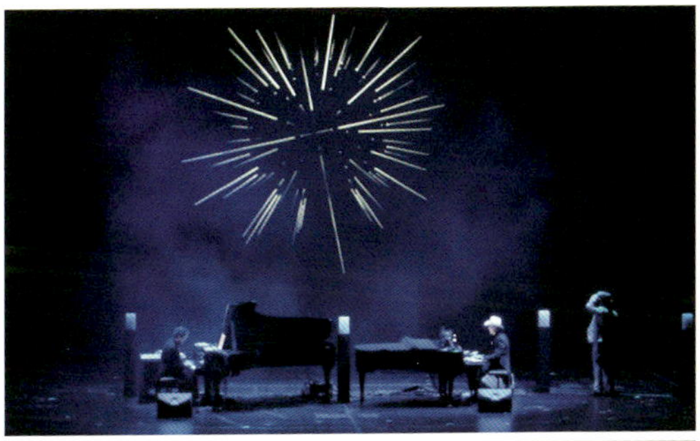

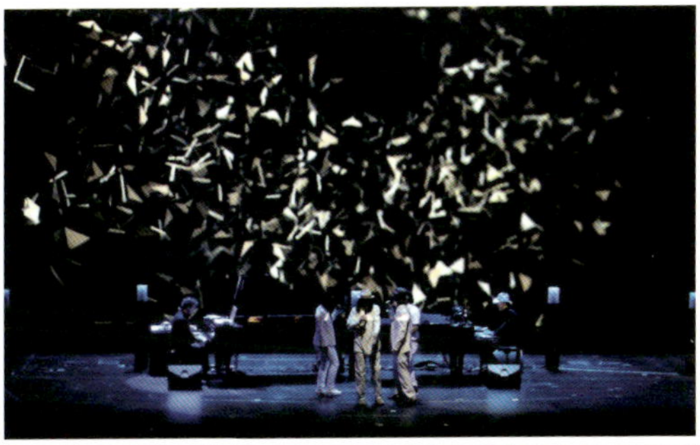

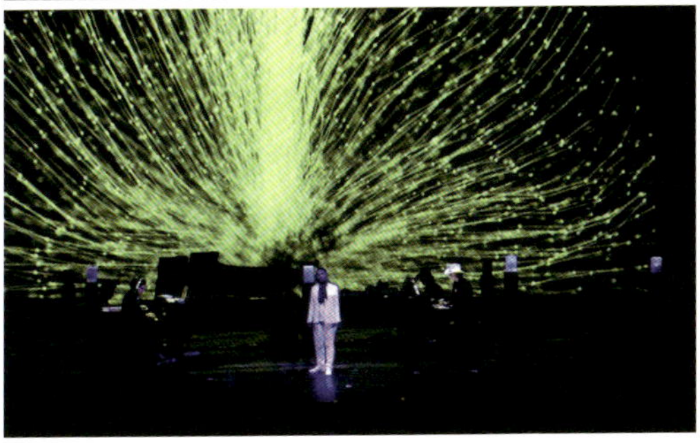

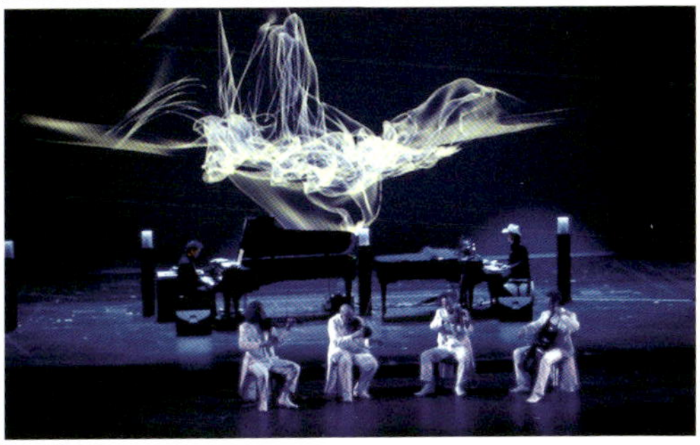

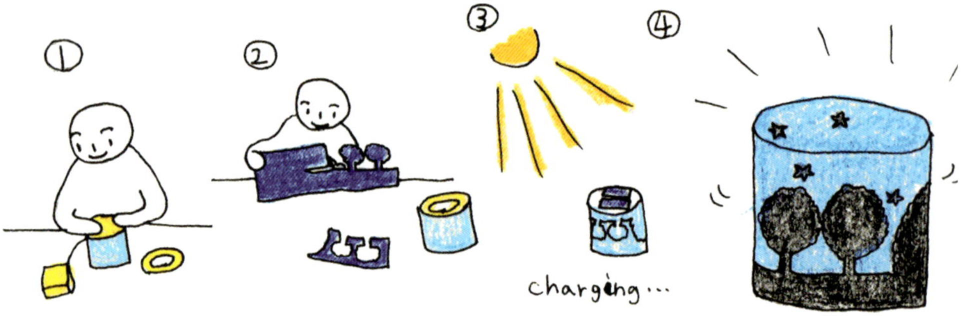

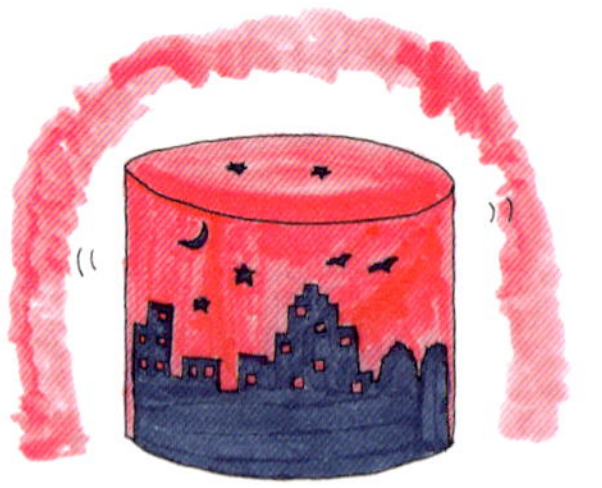

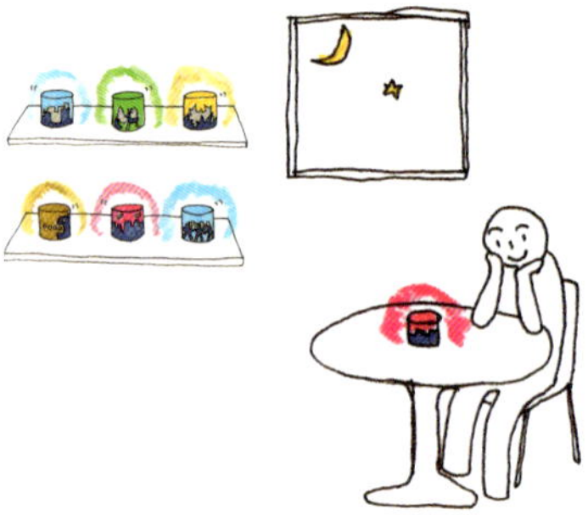

ELEKIT Japan Co., LTD + Ars Electronica Futurelab

Candlescape – Create a world in the light

The *Candlescape* is a media art construction kit developed through a collaborative research by Ars Electronica Futurelab and Elekit (EK Japan: *www.elekit.co.jp*). Elekit is a Japanese pioneering company in the edutainment electronics kits business. Firstly, participants construct the LED-candle kits. After assembly, the unit is turned upside down for charging. The charged power is used for rotating the gear unit and turning on the LED light. Secondly, the participants express an animated world. Inside of the *Candlescape*, there are two transparent rotating layers on which the participants express their memorable experience by various methods. The layers are lit up by a LED light inside the *Candlescape* and what is expressed on the layers emerges as shadows on the outer screen. Rotating the layers with the unit system allows us to see a poetic silhouette world in the wavering light. The unit is designed for intuitively setting the properties of the two layers' movements (rotating speed and direction) and the light settings (lightness and color) of the LED-candle in analog ways. The *Candlescape* is a creative environment that gives people a magical experience through animation.

This project plans to realize a commercial product based on the research result. The 2010 research col-

Candlescape besteht aus einem Medienkunst-Bausatz, der im Rahmen eines gemeinsamen Forschungsprojekts des Ars Electronica Futurelab und der Firma Elekit (EK Japan: *www.elekit.co.jp*) entstand. Elekit ist ein führendes japanisches Unternehmen, das für elektronische Bausätze im Schulungsbereich bekannt ist. Zunächst setzen die Teilnehmer die LED-Kerzen aus den Bausätzen zusammen. Das fertige Modell wird auf den Kopf gestellt, um es zu laden. Der Strom wird für den Drehantrieb und das LED-Licht genutzt. Dann gestalten die Teilnehmer eine animierte Welt. Im Inneren der *Candlescape* befinden sich zwei transparente rotierende Scheiben, auf denen die Teilnehmer ihre unvergesslichen Erlebnisse auf unterschiedliche Weise zum Ausdruck bringen können. Eine LED-Lichtquelle im Inneren des *Candlescape* beleuchtet die Scheiben, und die darauf befindlichen Darstellungen werfen ihren Schatten auf den äußeren Schirm. Durch die Rotation der Scheiben zeigt sich eine poetische Welt aus Schattenbildern. Das Design des Objekts ermöglicht eine intuitive Festlegung der Bewegungseigenschaften der beiden Scheiben (Rotationsgeschwindigkeit und -richtung) und der Lichteinstellungen der LED-Kerze (Helligkeit und Farbe). *Candlescape* ist eine Kreativumgebung, die den Benutzern mittels Animation magische Erfahrungen vermittelt.

laboration between Ars Electronica Futurelab and Elekit resulted in the commercial product "SWITCH" 2 years later, and Ars Electronica Futurelab and Elekit are currently collaborating on a long-term project, *Media art kit in our daily lives.*

Die Forschungsergebnisse dieses Projekts sollen auch in ein kommerzielles Produkt einfließen. *SWITCH,* das erste von der Forschungsgemeinschaft entwickelte Produkt, wurde zwei Jahre nach der Präsentation erfolgreich auf den Markt gebracht. Das Ars Electronica Futurelab und Elekit arbeiten derzeit gemeinsam an einem langfristigen Projekt zum Thema Medienkunst-Bausätze im Alltag.

Aus dem Englischen von Martina Bauer

Radio FRO + Ars Electronica Futurelab

openAIR – Accessibility in Radio Production

The Ars Electronica Futurelab was commissioned by Radio FRO to develop software and hardware to provide substantially more barrier-free operation of a radio station by people with disabilities.

The entire sequence of a live broadcast can be prepared in advance with very user-friendly software designed without submenus. You can arrange playlists of the songs you'd like to air, insert slots for live conversations, and determine which functions you'll need, which means that you can prepare for a lot of the operations called for during the live broadcast of a show and thereby make these production steps much less stressful than when they have to be performed while you're on the air.

The new mixing console's 10 push-buttons can carry out a wide array of commands—for instance, fade in/fade out, muting a microphone and returning it to normal pick-up, and toggling between audio sources. This enables the operator, for example, to fade in four microphones at the push of a button while simultaneously fading out the music, a procedure that would call for handling at least five controllers on a conventional mixing console.

Das Ars Electronica Futurelab hat im Auftrag von Radio FRO eine Soft- und Hardwarelösung entwickelt, die das Radiostudio speziell für Menschen mit Beeinträchtigung um ein Vielfaches zugänglicher macht.

Der gesamte Ablauf einer Live-Sendung kann vorab in der einfach und ohne Untermenüs gestalteten Software vorbereitet werden. Man legt die Playlists der Lieder an, die man abspielen möchte, platziert Slots für Live-Gespräche, legt fest, welche Funktionen man braucht, und hat so während der Live-Ausstrahlung der Sendung vieles vorbereitet, was sonst im Stress der Produktion schwierig wäre.

Die zehn Druckknöpfe am neuen Mischpult können eine Vielzahl an Befehlen ausführen, beispielsweise Einfaden, Ausfaden, Mikros scharf oder stumm schalten bzw. zwischen Audioquellen wechseln. So kann man mit einem Knopfdruck vier Mikros einfaden und gleichzeitig die Musik ausfaden lassen, ein Vorgang, der an einem normalen Mischpult das Bedienen von mindestens fünf Reglern erfordern würde.

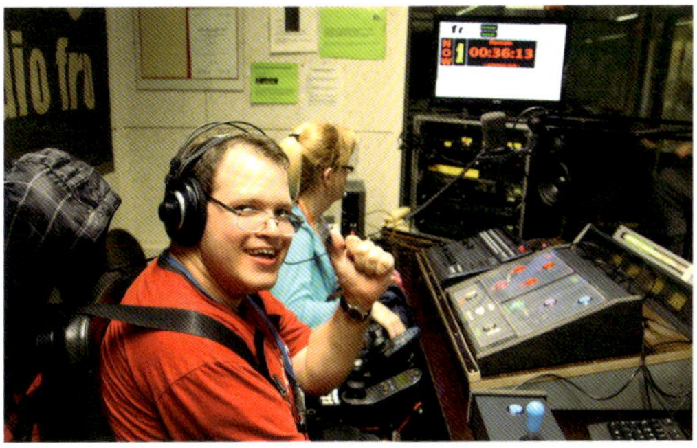

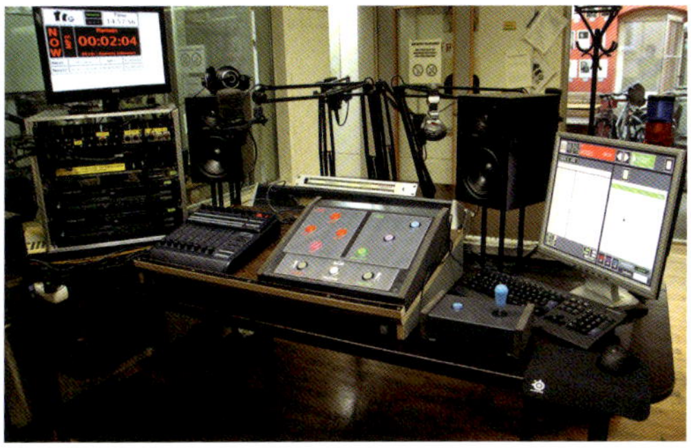

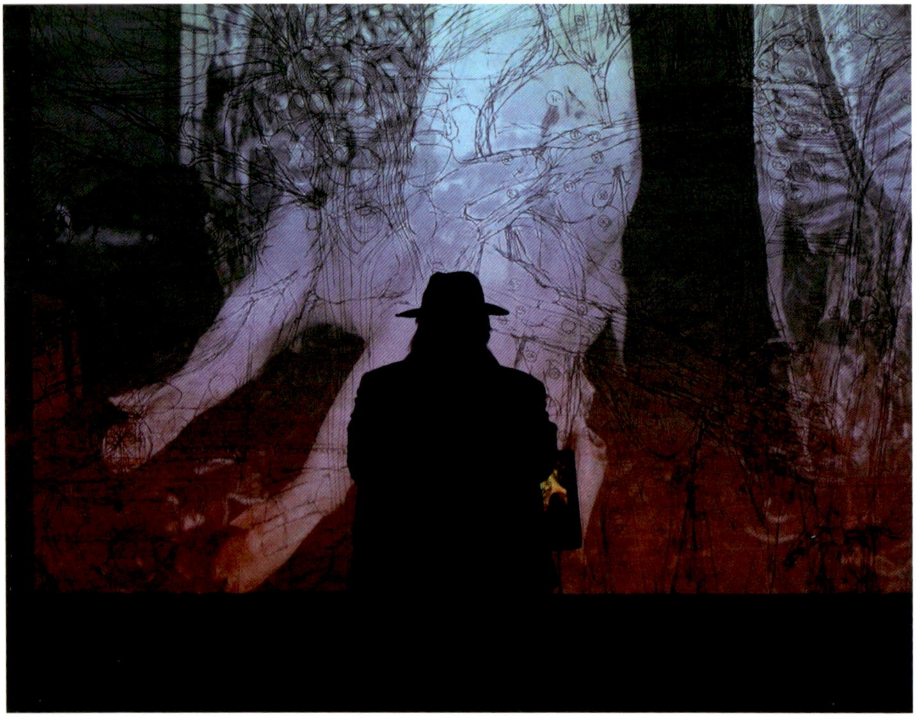

AEC, Michael Knoll

nitsch museum + Ars Electronica Futurelab

Hermann Nitsch – SINNE UND SEIN

Retrospektive, jumbo interactive projection

To mark the artist's 75th birthday, the nitsch museum staged *Hermann Nitsch–SINNE UND SEIN Retrospective,* and the Ars Electronica Futurelab designed a jumbo interactive projection screen for this exhibition. The 8x4-meter panorama display in the "Chapel" at the nitsch museum in Mistelbach, Lower Austria, opens up totally new insights into the artist's work. Users can navigate via touchscreen through gigapixel images and explore the most finely rendered details within Hermann Nitsch's world of imagery, structures inaccessible to the naked eye. The selection of works on exhibit accurately reflects the diversity of this important painter's artistic creativity. The installation is accompanied by tonal environments that were also composed by the artist. The interplay of visual, tactile and acoustic stimuli engenders a mode of experiencing Nitsch's work that is as novel as it is intense.

Anlässlich des 75. Geburtstags von Hermann Nitsch zeigte das nitsch museum die *Hermann Nitsch – SINNE UND SEIN Retrospektive.* Das Ars Electronica Futurelab gestaltete für die Ausstellung eine interaktive Großbildprojektion. Die acht mal vier Meter große Panoramaprojektion in der „Kapelle" des Mistelbacher nitsch museum eröffnet völlig neue Einblicke in das Werk des Künstlers. Via Touchscreen können die BesucherInnen durch Gigapixel-Bilder navigieren und dabei feinste Strukturen und Details in Hermann Nitschs Bildwelten erkunden, die mit bloßem Auge nicht erkennbar sind. Die Auswahl der gezeigten Werke spiegelt die Vielfalt des künstlerischen Schaffens von Hermann Nitsch wider. Unterstützt wird die Installation durch Klangwelten, die ebenfalls vom Künstler selbst stammen. Das Zusammenspiel von visuellen, taktilen und akustischen Reizen eröffnet dabei ein ebenso neuartiges wie intensives Erleben der Arbeit von Hermann Nitsch.

Text: Johanna Mathauer

Overview—In Touch with the Earth

Overview in Deep Space at the Ars Electronica Center provides stunning insights into The Blue Planet. The experience of a globe is redefined by breathtaking stereoscopic projections on a jumbo 16 x 18-meter screen featuring 8x Full HD resolution. Developed in cooperation with Japan's Miraikan—National Museum of Emerging Science and Innovation, *Overview* depicts Earth from outer space and delivers impressive images of a wide array of fascinating phenomena—migratory behavior of the arctic tern, global petroleum usage, current crises and much more. Rounding off this experience are free-as-a-bird exploratory flights to the world's most interesting destinations.

Mit *Overview* im Deep Space des Ars Electronica Center wird der Blaue Planet noch greifbarer. Das Erfahren eines Globus wird neu definiert durch atemberaubende stereoskopische Projektionen auf insgesamt 16 mal 18 Metern in achtfacher Full-HD Auflösung. In Zusammenarbeit mit dem japanischen Science Center Miraikan wird ein Blick aus dem Erd-Orbit offenbart, der eindrucksvoll das Zugverhalten der Küstenseeschwalbe, den globalen Erdölverbrauch, aktuelle Brandherde und weitere spannende Themen vermittelt. Abgerundet wird das Erlebnis durch freie Erkundungsflüge zu den interessantesten Destinationen des Planeten.

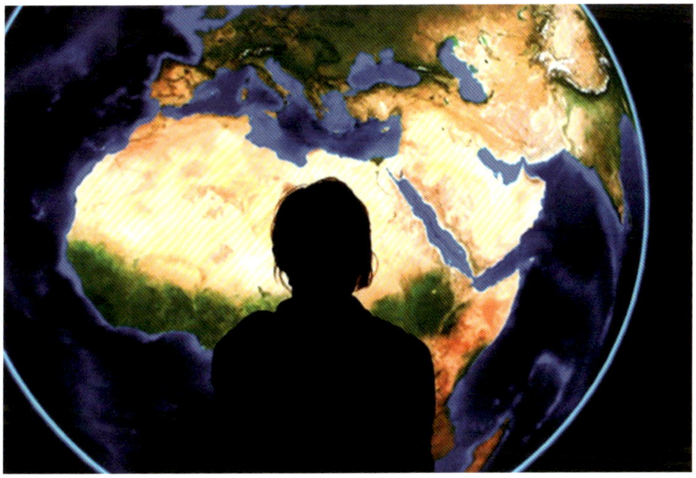

This project was produced in Deep Space by the Ars Electronica Futurelab on the basis of NASA World Wind SDK and with the use of data from the following sources (listed by topic)
Dieses Projekt wurde Im Deep Space durch das Ars Electronica Futurelab verwirklicht, basierend auf dem Nasa Worldwind SDK und unter Verwendung folgender Datenquellen (nach Themengebiet):

Seasonal Variation of Solar Radiation: JRA-25 long-term reanalysis (Japan Meteorological Agency, Central Research Institute of Electric Power Industry)
The Arctic Tern Migration: Greenland Institute of Natural Resources
Pacific Bluefin Tuna Migration: Census of Marine Life TOPP Project
The Seasons on Earth: NASA's Earth Observatory
Earth at Night: NOAA's National Geophysical Data Center
Land Cover: Global Mapping Project (International Steering Committee for Global Mapping / Geospatial Information Authority of Japan / Chiba University)
Forest map: Global Mapping Project (International Steering Committee for Global Mapping / Geospatial Information Authority of Japan / Chiba University)
Forest Fire: Wataru Takeuchi Institute of Industrial Science, the University of Tokyo
CO_2 Concentration Past and Present: Japan Meteorological Agency
Earth Surface Temperature: University of Wisconsin SSEC
Earthquakes in the World: U. S. Geological Survey
Bathymetric Charts: NASA's Earth Observatory
Tsunami 3.11: NOAA Center for Tsunami Research, NASA's Earth Observatory

Ars Electronica Residency Network

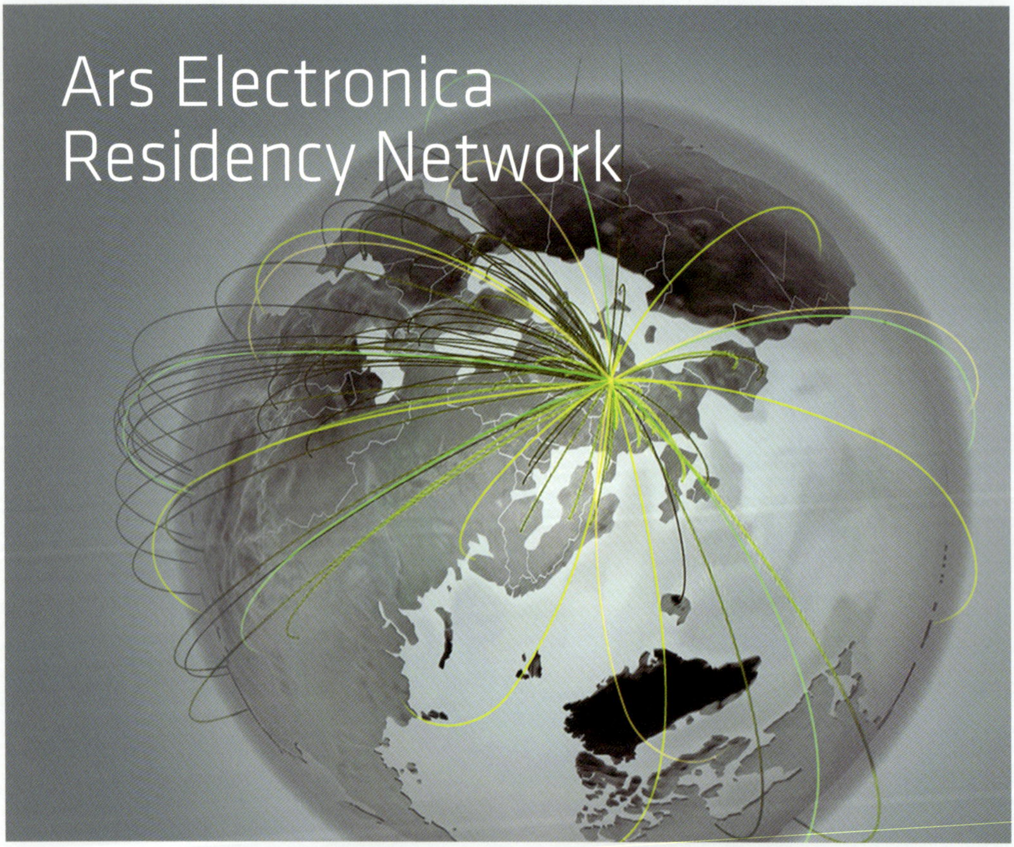

AEC

The *Ars Electronica Residency Network* (AERN) is a coalition of excellence consisting of Ars Electronica Linz and prominent partner institutions all over the world that offer extraordinary opportunities and challenges for artists and scientists. This network is open to academic institutions, museums, cultural organizations and research facilities, private firms, government agencies and NGOs. What they all have in common is their interest in conducting an artist- or researcher-in-residence program.
AERN offers many different programs that tar-

Das *Ars Electronica Residency Network* (AERN) ist ein Network of Excellence zwischen Ars Electronica Linz und namhaften Partnerinstitutionen weltweit, das außergewöhnliche Möglichkeiten und Herausforderungen für KünstlerInnen und WissenschaftlerInnen anbietet. Es ist offen für akademische Einrichtungen, Museen, Kultur- wie auch Forschungseinrichtungen der öffentlichen Hand sowie für Privatinitiativen und Wirtschaftspartner. Allen gemeinsam ist dabei das Anliegen der Durchführung eines Artist- oder Research-in-Residence-Programmes.

get a wide array of artists and scientists. Some of these residencies focus on specific issues. A few feature working conditions tailored to those who have already made a name for themselves in their chosen profession; others are especially designed to nurture the talents and potential of promising young people. Fostering interdisciplinary as well as intercultural exchange is very high on this network's agenda.
Several of the residencies emphasize creating works of art (e.g. Collide@CERN); others, such as [the next idea] voestalpine Art &Technology Grant, are suited to scientists, designers, architects, artists or engineers.
The aim is to implement optimal framework conditions for artists- and researchers-in-residence–for example, by providing access to advanced technical production infrastructure or by facilitating opportunities to encounter extraordinary individuals, issues or settings as a means of achieving the best possible outcome for the participating artists and scientists as well as the host organizations.

Mit seinen unterschiedlichen Teilprogrammen richtet sich das *Ars Electronica Residency Network* an eine große Bandbreite von KünstlerInnen und WissenschaftlerInnen. So bestechen manche der hier versammelten Residencies durch ihr verstärktes Augenmerk auf Fragestellungen und Arbeitsbedingungen für bereits am Höhepunkt ihrer Kariere befindliche KünstlerInnen und WissenschaftlerInnen; andere Residencies verstehen sich wiederum als Förderung der Potenziale von jungen Talenten. Interdisziplinärer und auch interkultureller Austausch ist ein weiteres wichtiges Anliegen dieses Netzwerks.
Sind einige der Residencies eng auf Kunstproduktion fokussiert (etwa Collide@CERN), öffnen sich andere prototypisch für Wissenschaftler genauso wie für Designer, Architekten, Künstler oder Ingenieure (etwa [the next idea] voestalpine Art &Technology Grant).
Ziel ist es, optimale Rahmenbedingungen für Artists- und Researchers-in-Residence zu schaffen, z. B. durch Zugang zu avancierten technischen Produktionsmöglichkeiten, durch ein Umfeld, in dem die Begegnung mit außergewöhnlichen Personen, Themen und/oder Öffentlichkeiten möglich ist, um so für Künstlerinnen und WissenschaftlerInnen wie auch Veranstalter die bestmöglichen Effekte zu erzielen.

voestalpine + Ars Electronica

[the next idea] voestalpine Art and Technology Grant

The objective of this grant awarded jointly by voestalpine and Ars Electronica is to foster the development of extraordinary, innovative ideas. In selecting recipients, the jury shortlists projects that transcend the boundaries of discrete disciplines and defy pigeonholing in a particular scientific field, area of business or artistic genre. The winner of a competition conducted in conjunction with the Prix Ars Electronica receives a € 7,500 cash stipend and the opportunity to spend up to three months at the Ars Electronica Futurelab, Ars Electronica's in-house R&D division, where the recipient can work with Futurelab staffers to upgrade and enhance his/her idea.
This year's subsidy is going to *Hyperform*, a project that deals with the subject of folding and 3D printing, and is taking an exciting, innovative approach to production processes. The most extraordinary

Dieses gemeinsam von voestalpine und Ars Electronica im Rahmen des Wettbewerbs Prix Ars Electronica ausgeschriebene Stipendium hat die Förderung und Weiterentwicklung von ungewöhnlichen und innovativen Ideen zum Ziel. Im Zentrum der Aufmerksamkeit stehen dabei Projekte, die über ihre jeweiligen disziplinären Grenzen hinausragen und deren Verortung in etablierten Kategorisierungen wie Wissenschaft, Wirtschaft oder Kunst nicht mehr eindeutig möglich ist. Diese im Rahmen des Prix Ars Electronica vergebene Förderung umfasst ein Stipendium in der Höhe von 7.500 Euro sowie die Möglichkeit, bis zu drei Monate im Ars Electronica Futurelab, der R&D Abteilung der Ars Electronica, zu verbringen und gemeinsam mit den ForscherInnen vor Ort das Projekt weiterzuentwickeln. Dieses Jahr wurde dem Projekt *Hyperform* das Stipendium zugesprochen, das sich mit dem Thema Faltung und 3D-Druck auseinandersetzt und völlig neue Wege thing about *Hyperform* is that the potential range of applications of printed and foldable 3D elements is almost infinite, and it can be utilized just about everywhere—in designers' ateliers and scientists' labs as well by DIY aficionados working at home. In the context of this residency, the Ars Electronica Futurelab functions as a setting in which grant recipients can take their idea to the next level and, above all, as an incubator designed to enable this technology to be made available to as many people as possible.

im Kontext innovativer Produktionsverfahren aufzeigt. Das Spezielle daran ist, dass die Bandbreite möglicher Anwendungen von gedruckten und faltbaren 3D-Elementen fast ins Unendliche reicht und überall zum Einsatz kommen kann: in DIY-Communities genauso wie bei Designern oder im Wissenschaftsbetrieb. Das Ars Electronica Futurelab funktioniert im Kontext dieser Förderung als Ort, an dem die Weiterentwicklung dieser Idee auf ein neues Level gehoben wird, und vor allem als Inkubator, der es ermöglichen soll, diese Technologie so vielen Leuten wie möglich zugänglich zu machen.

Text: Bernhard Böhm

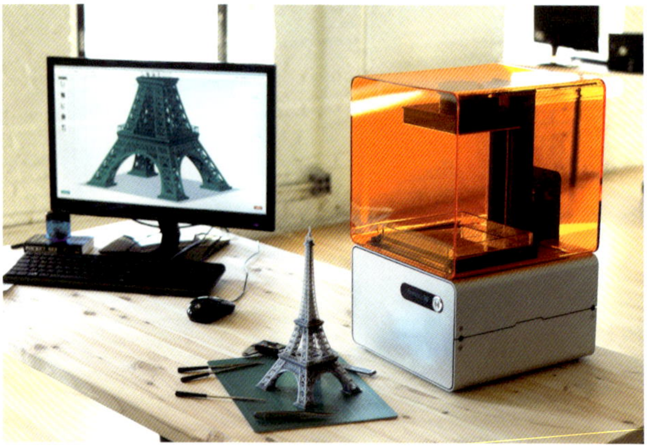

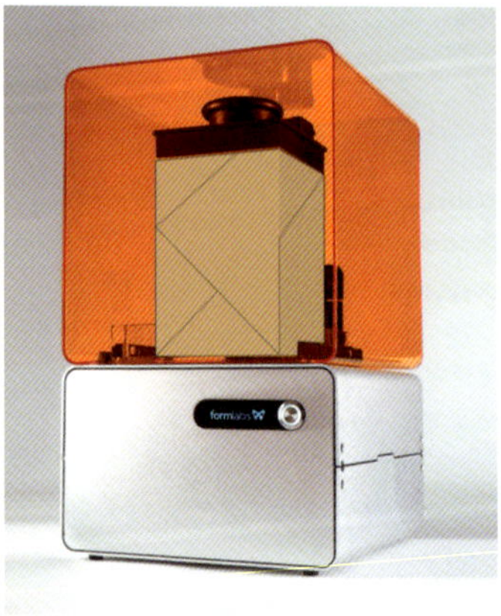

Marcelo Coelho, Skylar Tibbits, Natan Linder, Yoav Reches

Hyperform

[the next idea] voestalpine Art and Technology Grant

Desktop 3D printers are becoming increasingly accessible, but they are inherently limited by a small print volume, placing severe constraints on the type and scale of objects we can create. *Hyperform* seeks to address this problem by identifying computational and material folding strategies that will allow large scale objects to be compressed into a minimal volume. We hope that these techniques will not only help democratize and make more accessible our future means of production, but will also unleash a host of new aesthetic and design opportunities.

Text: Marcelo Coelho

3D-Desktopprinter werden zwar immer leichter zugänglich, aber sie sind grundsätzlich durch ein geringes Druckvolumen limitiert, was die Art und Größe der damit herstellbaren Objekte erheblich einschränkt. *Hyperform* versucht, diesem Problem durch die Entwicklung algorithmischer und materieller Falttechniken zu begegnen, mit denen sich große Objekte auf ein möglichst kleines Volumen komprimieren lassen. Mit diesen Techniken hoffen wir nicht nur zur Demokratisierung und Zugänglichkeit unserer künftigen Produktionsmittel beizutragen, sondern auch eine ganze Fülle neuer ästhetischer und gestalterischer Möglichkeiten zu eröffnen.

Aus dem Englischen von Wilfried Prantner

CERN + Ars Electronica

Prix Ars Electronica Collide@CERN

Since 2011, the world's largest particle physics laboratory, CERN outside Geneva and home to the Large Hadron Collider has enjoyed a cultural partnership with Ars Electronica, Linz.
Working with the transdisciplinary Futurelab team at Ars, the Prix Ars Electronica Collide@CERN Residency Award was created as part of the Collide@CERN–Creative Collisions between the Arts and Science, the artists residency programme initiated and created by CERN in 2010 following a 4-month feasibility study which I carried out.
Our partnership has led now to two successful open calls for artists from any domain working with the digital to win a fully funded two-month residency at CERN, and one month at Futurelab to develop the ideas inspired by particle physics. The first winning artist, Julius von Bismarck, created the light installation called *Versuch Unter Kreisen* which was showcased at the OK Center in Linz during the Ars Electronica Festival in 2012. This piece has now become the set for a new dance piece called *Quantum* in an unexpected creative collision with another Collide@CERN artist, the Swiss choreographer Gilles Jobin. Gilles was the recipient of the second award in the artists residency programme, Collide@CERN Geneva, and his new CERN-inspired dance piece with Julius's installation as its setting won the prestigious Hermes Foundation New Settings Award. As a result, *Quantum*, which has its

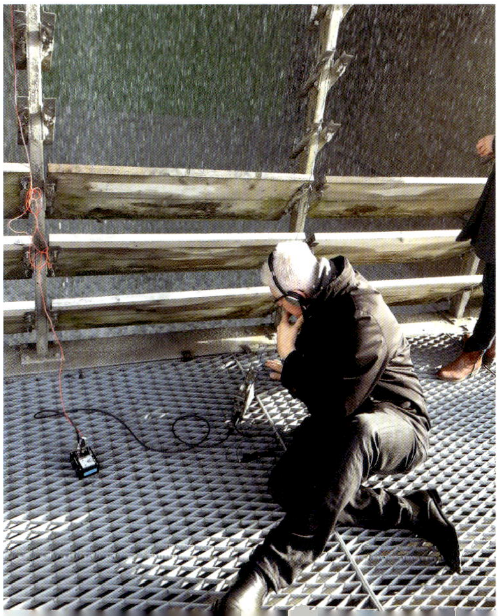

Seit 2011 ist das bei Genf ansässige CERN, das weltweit größte Forschungszentrum für Teilchenphysik und Heimstatt des Large Hadron Collider, mit der Ars Electronica durch eine kulturelle Partnerschaft verbunden.
In Zusammenarbeit mit dem transdisziplinären Futurelab-Team wurde der Prix Ars Electronica Collide@CERN Residency Award ins Leben gerufen. Er ist ein Teil des Künstlerresidenzprogramms Collide@CERN–Creative Collisions between the Arts and Science, welches am CERN 2010 aufgrund einer von mir über vier Monate erstellten Machbarkeitsstudie eingerichtet wurde.
Unsere Partnerschaft blickt mittlerweile auf zwei erfolgreiche Open Calls zurück, bei denen KünstlerInnen aus allen Bereichen des Digitalen einen voll remunerierten zweimonatigen Aufenthalt am CERN und einen einmonatigen am Futurelab gewinnen konnten, um von der Teilchenphysik inspirierte Ideen auszuarbeiten. Der erste Gewinner, Julius von Bismarck, entwickelte die Lichtinstallation *Versuch Unter Kreisen,* die beim Ars Electronica Festival 2012 im Offenen Kulturhaus OÖ gezeigt wurde. Die Arbeit ist inzwischen in einer unerwarteten kreativen Kollision mit einem anderen Collide@CERN-Künstler, dem Schweizer Choreografen Gilles Jobin, zum Bühnenbild für das Tanzstück *Quantum* geworden. Gilles war der zweite Gewinner im Künstlerresidenzprogramm Collide@CERN Geneva, und sein neues CERN-inspiriertes Tanzstück mit Julius' Installation als Bühnenbild gewann die angesehene New-Settings-Förderung der Fondation Hermès. Daher wird *Quantum,* das im September 2013 am CERN uraufgeführt wird, nun auch auf Tour nach Paris und New York gehen. Das zeigt, wie sich die Residenz für die beiden ersten Künstler im gesamten Collide@CERN-Programm ausgewirkt hat. Es wird interessant sein zu sehen, was es mit einem international renommierten Künstler wie Bill Fontana macht.
Wie aber steht es nun mit den WissenschaftlerInnen: Welchen Einfluss hatten die Künstler auf sie? Diejenigen, die mit den Künstlern in Kontakt kamen, gaben an, es habe ihre Sicht auf die Welt verändert, ihr Interesse für die Künste geweckt oder sie aus

Bill Fontana
Collide@CERN winning artist 2012

world premiere at CERN in September 2013, will now go on international tour to Paris and New York – thus showing the impact the residency experience has had on the first two artists on the whole Collide@ CERN programme. So it will be fascinating to see what impact it will have on an artist of Bill Fontana's international stature.

What of the scientists and the impact the artists have had on them? The scientists who have encountered the artists have said it has changed the way they look at the world, turned them on to the arts, or liberated them from very channeled ways of thinking, realizing that detours can be as interesting as directed thought. Many scientists at CERN have also encountered the artists in unexpected ways through the curated interventions in the laboratory, which are designed to shock, surprise and disturb the scientists in order to create new ways of looking and experiencing their daily working spaces.

For example, Julius kidnapped 30 particle physicists and took them in underground tunnels to a hidden room to drink coffee in the dark and discuss what they could "see" in their minds' eyes in the blackness. CERN inspiration partner James Wells is working long after the residency has ended with Julius on making a new art piece, and we are investigating where to show it.

In addition, the runners up to the last two year's of Prix Ars Electronica Collide@CERN are given curated 5-day-visits to the laboratory, and we are supporting them in the development of the projects which come out of their visits, including helping them find funding. So an exciting portfolio of additional transdisciplinary Prix Ars Electronica Collide@CERN work will be emerging over the coming years too, showing our work together.

CERN is immensely proud to be working with Ars Electronica on the Collide programme as our international partners, for what was envisaged initially as a 3-year programme. Part of this success of the partnership is undoubtedly to do with the fact that we share core values, beliefs and understanding of how arts, science and technology intersect and together form culture. In the 21st century, it is from their interaction that creative thinking and making across—as well as beyond—borders will happen to further innovation.

Text: Ariane Koek

eingefahrenen Denkmustern befreit, ihnen klar gemacht, dass Umwege genauso interessant sein können wie zielgerichtetes Denken. Viele WissenschaftlerInnen am CERN sind den Künstlern auch unvorbereitet in kuratierten Interventionen im Labor begegnet, die die WissenschaftlerInnen schockieren, überraschen und irritieren sollen, damit sie ihre tägliche Arbeitsumgebung neu sehen und erleben lernen.

Julius zum Beispiel schnappte sich 30 TeilchenphysikerInnen und führte sie durch unterirdische Gänge zu einem versteckten Raum, wo er mit ihnen im Dunkeln Kaffee trank und diskutierte, was sie vor ihrem inneren Auge „sehen". James Wells, sein Inspirationspartner am CERN, arbeitete mit ihm lange nach Ende der Residenz an einer neuen Arbeit weiter, und wir sind gerade auf der Suche nach einem Ort, wo wir sie zeigen können.

Zusätzlich erhalten die Zweitplazierten der letzten beiden *Prix Ars Electronica Collide@CERN Residencies* kuratierte Fünf-Tages-Aufenthalte am Zentrum, und wir unterstützen sie bei der Entwicklung von sich daraus ergebenden Projekten, bis hin zur Beschaffung von Geldmitteln. So ist zu erwarten, dass unsere Zusammenarbeit in den kommenden Jahren noch ein spannendes Portfolio weiterer transdisziplinärer Prix-Ars-Electronica-Collide@CERN-Arbeiten hervorbringt.

CERN ist immens stolz darauf, mit Ars Electronica als internationalem Partner am vorerst auf drei Jahre angelegten Collide-Programm zusammenzuarbeiten. Zum Teil ist der Erfolg der Partnerschaft sicherlich darauf zurückzuführen, dass wir die gleichen Grundwerte und Überzeugungen teilen und dasselbe Verständnis davon haben, wie Kunst, Wissenschaft und Technologie ineinandergreifen und gemeinsam eine Kultur bilden. Im 21. Jahrhundert wird kreatives, Disziplinen und Grenzen überschreitendes, innovationsförderndes Denken und Handeln aus dem Zusammenspiel zwischen diesen Bereichen hervorgehen.

Aus dem Englischen von Wilfried Prantner

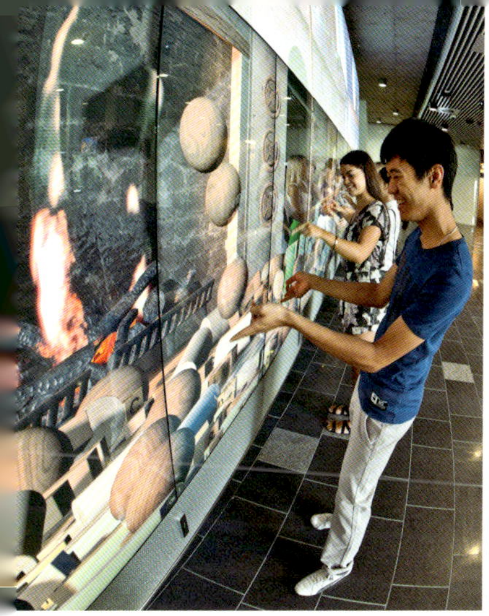

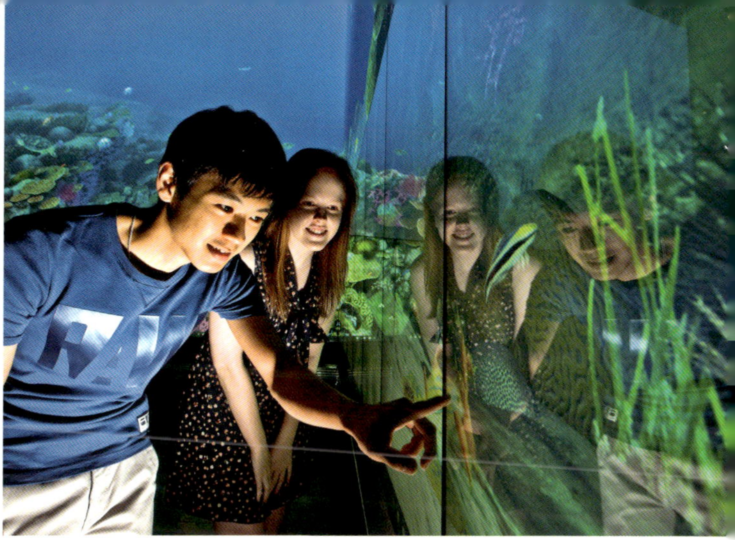

QUT Queensland University of Technology + Ars Electronica Futurelab

Inter-virtual

The Cube is one of the world's largest digital interactive learning and display spaces dedicated to providing an inspiring, explorative and participatory experience of QUT's Science, Engineering, Technology and Mathematics (STEM) research. Soaring across two storeys in QUT's new Science and Engineering Centre, *The Cube* displays projects inspired by QUT's diverse research and produces interactive projects that support public discovery and participation. The Cube is an exemplar of the possibilities that can be generated when working at the nexus of science, art and society.

As part of the development of new and innovative presentation and representation of STEM, The Cube is creating content through a number of production streams; internally, externally and through residencies. *The Cube's* residency stream is seeking inspirational digital creatives and technologists to produce innovative world-class projects inspired by the research endeavours of QUT. These creatives will produce work that will place *The Cube* at the cutting edge of public digital display and interaction environments. To support QUT in this mission, *The Cube* has teamed up with Ars Electronica, as part of the Ars Electronica Residency Network, to develop and offer an annual, invitation-based, residency opportunity.

Text: Lubi Thomas

The Cube ist einer der weltweit größten digital-interaktiven Lern- und Ausstellungsräume. Er ist dazu gedacht, eine inspirierende, explorative und partizipatorische Erfahrung von der an der Qeensland University of Technology (QUT) betriebenen Forschung in den MINT-Fächern (Mathematik, Informatik, Naturwissenschaft und Technologie) zu vermitteln. In dem sich über zwei Stockwerke des neuen Science and Engineering Center erstreckenden Raum werden von der breit gefächerten Forschungstätigkeit der Universität inspirierte Projekte vorgestellt sowie interaktive Arbeiten realisiert, die der Öffentlichkeit Einblicke in neue Entwicklungen geben und sie daran teilhaben lassen. *The Cube* ist ein Musterbeispiel für die Möglichkeiten, die sich an der Schnittstelle von Wissenschaft, Kunst und Gesellschaft auftun.

Im Zusammenhang mit der Entwicklung einer neuen und innovativen Präsentation und Repräsentation der MINT-Fächer generiert *The Cube* auch Inhalte durch eine Reihe von internen, externen und mittels Residencies erzeugten Produktionsströmen. Mit den Residenzen versucht *The Cube* inspirierende digitale Kreative und Technologen für die Produktion erstklassiger, innovativer Projekte auf Grundlage der QUT-Forschungsarbeiten zu gewinnen. Diese Arbeiten sollen *The Cube* an der vordersten Front öffentlicher digitaler Ausstellungs- und Interaktionsenvironments positionieren. Zur Unterstützung dieses Vorhabens hat sich *The Cube* mit der Ars Electronica und ihrem Residency Network zusammengetan, um eine jährliche, auf Einladung basierende Residency zu entwickeln und anzubieten.

The OHMI Trust + Ars Electronica Futurelab

The OHMI Ars Electronica Competition

At the end of the first year of this unique competition, the OHMI Ars Electronica competition entries have been exceptional. For those new to the project, the challenge is to create instruments that will enable people with physical disabilities to participate in mainstream music making. It arises from the simple recognition that traditional musical instruments require two highly dexterous hands to play. The task is exceptionally challenging. Musical instruments may look simple, but their potential to express musical subtlety and dexterity is extremely hard to reproduce "without the use of one hand and arm"—as the competition rules demand.

The 2013 entries include highly inventive mechanical adaptations as well as several built around sophisticated electronics enabling them to emulate orchestral instruments. There are two categories of award: instruments that are playable now and for concepts that are judged to have high potential for development.

Text: Stephen Hetherington

http://*www.ohmi.org.uk*

Nach Ablauf des ersten Jahrs des OHMI-Ars-Electronica-Wettbewerbs lässt sich sagen, dass sämtliche Einreichungen von außerordentlicher Qualität sind. Für all jene, die mit dem Projekt nicht vertraut sind: Die Aufgabe besteht in der Entwicklung eines Musikinstruments, das Menschen mit Beeinträchtigungen ermöglicht, am Mainstream-Musikleben teilzunehmen. Die einfache Erkenntnis dahinter ist, dass herkömmliche Musikinstrumente nur mit zwei äußerst geschickten Händen gespielt werden können. Somit stellt diese Aufgabe eine außergewöhnliche Herausforderung dar. Musikinstrumente mögen einfach aussehen, aber die Vielfalt musikalischer Nuancen und die Gewandtheit im Umgang mit dem Instrument ist „ohne den Einsatz einer Hand und eines Arms" – wie es die Wettbewerbsregeln vorschreiben – nur schwer zu erreichen.

Die Einreichungen für 2013 umfassen sowohl äußerst ausgefeilte mechanische Adaptierungen als auch auf ausgeklügelter Elektronik basierende Emulationen von Orchesterinstrumenten. Es gibt zwei Preiskategorien: eine für bereits jetzt spielbare Instrumente und eine für Konzepte mit vielversprechendem Entwicklungspotenzial.

Aus dem Englischen von Michael Kaufmann

The winners of the OHMI-Ars Electronica Competition 2013:

Playable Category:

Toggle-Key Saxophone
David Nabb (University of Nebraska)
Stelling Wind & Brass of Kearney, Nebraska (US)
http://www.youtube.com/watch?feature=player_embedded&v=XtRd2cUgGeg

Concept Category:

Eigenharp Pico with clamp
Eigenlabs, MERU (UK)
http://www.youtube.com/watch?v=f9qPf31xYnY

Magic Switch
Ruud van der Wel (NL)
http://www.youtube.com/watch?v=MW25iPS7yfc

The Virtuosic Hand Controller
Laurel Pardue (UK)
http://nime2013.kaist.ac.kr/program/papers/day1/poster1/245/245_Paper.pdf

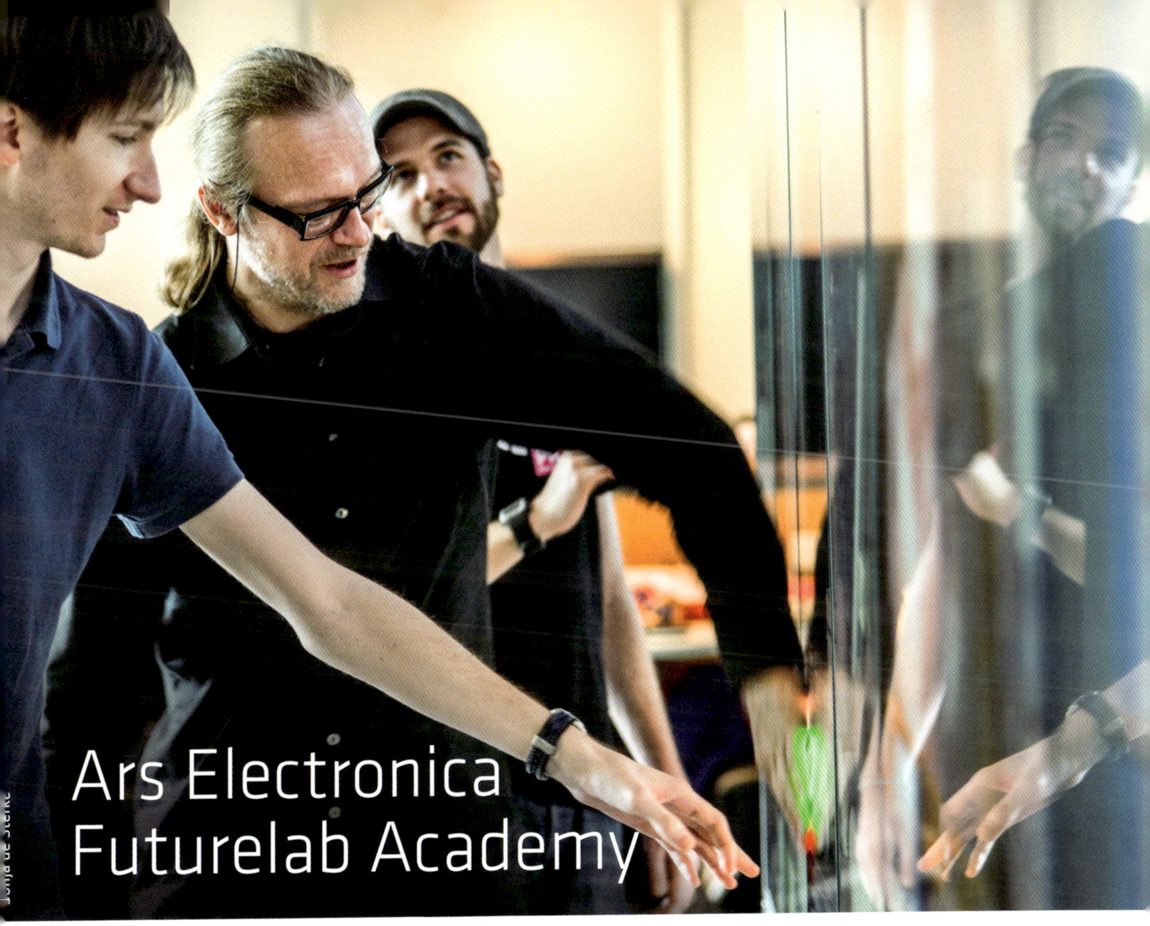

Ars Electronica Futurelab Academy

Ars Electronica Futurelab Academy was created to support students from international partner universities to realize innovative projects in the field of media art. The format's unique features contain the Ars Electronica Futurelab's expertise and the possibility to participate in the Ars Electronica Festival. Selected team members from the Ars Electronica Futurelab conduct workshops and seminars, which are open to a group of students. The topics of these lectures will be determined jointly beforehand, with the partner institutions being able to select from a variety of workshop topics. During the lectures, the students develop artistic concepts together with the lecturer/s from the Ars Electronica Futurelab, which are to be realized in the course of the semester. Finally, the students' artworks are assessed by the university professor together with the Ars Electronica Futurelab, with the aim of presenting the best works in a special exhibition at the Ars Electronica Festival.

Die *Ars Electronica Futurelab Academy* wurde gegründet, um Studenten internationaler Partneruniversitäten bei der Realisierung innovativer Medienkunstprojekte zu unterstützen. Das Format zeichnet sich insbesondere durch die transdisziplinäre Expertise des Ars Electronica Futurelab und die Möglichkeit der Teilnahme am Ars Electronica Festival aus. Teammitglieder des Ars Electronica Futurelab leiten Workshops und Seminare, an denen eine Auswahl von Studenten teilnehmen kann. Die Inhalte werden gemeinsam vorab bestimmt, wobei die Partnerinstitutionen aus einer Vielzahl von Themen wählen können. Während der Lehrveranstaltungen entwickeln die Studenten gemeinsam mit einem Dozenten des Ars Electronica Futurelab künstlerische Konzepte, die im Lauf des Semesters umgesetzt werden. Abschließend werden von einem Universitätsprofessor gemeinsam mit dem Ars Electronica Futurelab die Arbeiten der Studenten bewertet und die besten ausgewählt, die wiederum beim Ars Electronica Festival im Rahmen einer Sonderausstellung präsentiert werden.

Queensland University of Technology + Ars Electronica Futurelab

QUT

This year the featured institution is the Queensland University of Technology (QUT), with students from the faculties of Creative Industries and Science and Engineering with backgrounds in Interactive and Visual Design, Games and Interactive Entertainment, Marketing and Technology Innovation. Students have worked with the theme "Layers of the City", to find new ways of expressing, uncovering and relating to aspects of the urban environment. For presentation at the special exhibition, three works have been chosen.

Dieses Jahr wurden vom Partnerinstitut Queensland University of Technology Studierende der Fakultäten Kreativwirtschaft, Wissenschaft und Technik mit Kenntnissen in den Bereichen Interaktives und Visuelles Design, Spiele und interaktive Unterhaltung, Marketing und Innovationstechnologie eingeladen. Die Studenten haben sich mit dem Thema „Schichten der Stadt" auseinandergesetzt und versuchen, neue Wege zu finden, um Aspekte städtischer Lebensbereiche neu zu entdecken, zu interpretieren und zum Ausdruck zu bringen. Drei Arbeiten wurden für die Präsentation bei der Sonderausstellung ausgewählt.

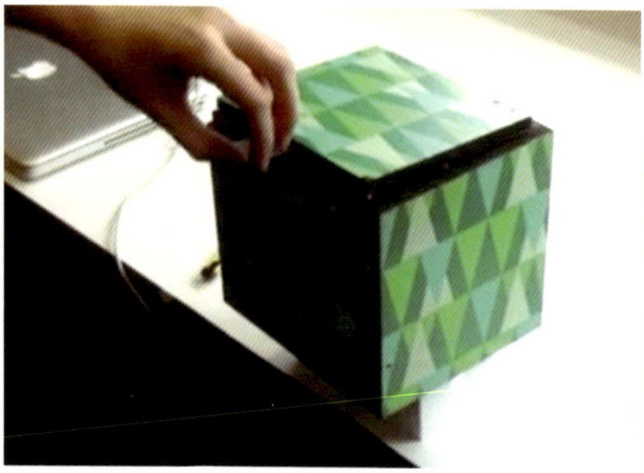

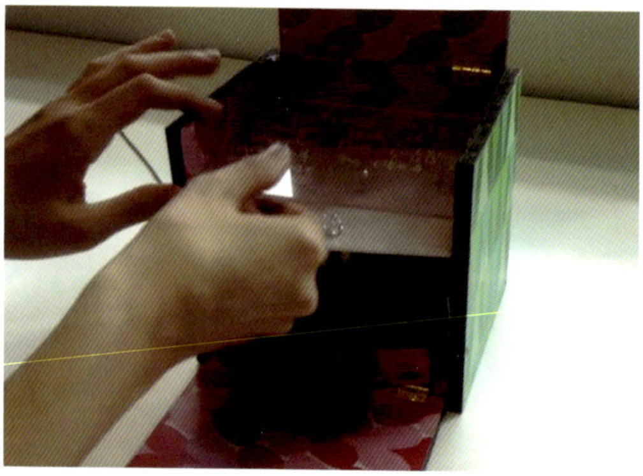

Trail of Traits (Alice Brown, Andy Bates) is a collection of discovery boxes, taking participants on a treasure hunt as a means of exploring the urban space within a given location. Visual clues and riddles form part of each box, leading participants on a trail which re-discovers the arts, history, culture and environment of the city. These boxes demand attention with colorful patterns and the chiming of bells that invite the public to become part of the adventure. The artwork has no beginning and no end point. Users come across these interactive treasure chests, which capture the attention of pedestrians, with motion sensors that trigger the chiming of bells.

Trail of Traits (Alice Brown, Andy Bates) ist eine Sammlung sogenannter *Discovery Boxes*, die die Teilnehmer zu einer Schatzsuche verführen, bei der sie den städtischen Raum in einem bestimmten Areal erforschen. In jeder Box befinden sich visuelle Hinweise und Rätsel, die die Teilnehmer auf einen Pfad führen, auf dem sie Kunst, Geschichte, Kultur und Umgebung der Stadt neu entdecken können. Mit bunten Mustern und Glöckchengeläut wecken diese Boxen das Interesse der Passanten und laden sie ein, sich auf dieses Abenteuer einzulassen. Diese Kunstaktion hat keinen Anfang und kein Ende. Durch Zufall stoßen die Passanten auf die interaktiven Schatzkisten, die mit von Bewegungssensoren ausgelöstem Glöckchengeläut auf sich aufmerksam machen.

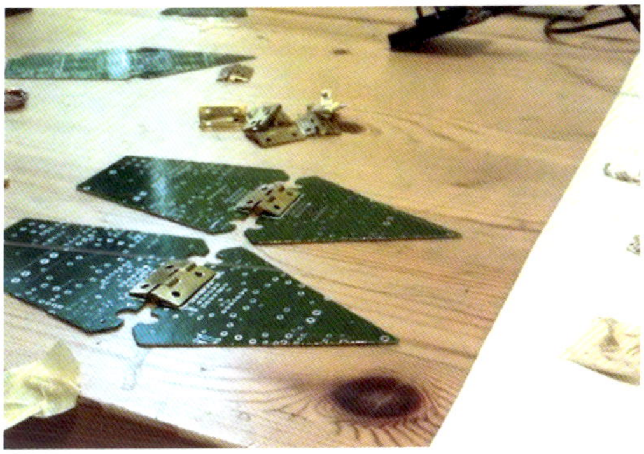

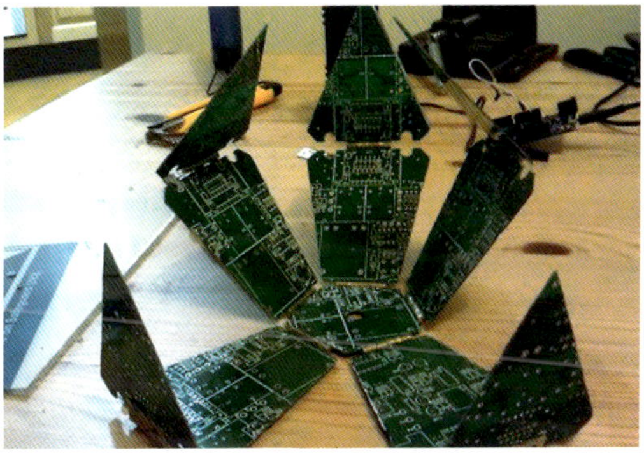

Flow[er] (Jeniffer Heng, Vidhi Shah) is an interactive flower that responds to movement. As a user comes closer to the work, it senses their presence and slowly "blossoms" by opening up. The flower is made up entirely of old circuit boards collected from a recycled items store. Old cables are used to attach the petals to a rotational motor, which makes them open and close. *Flow[er]* is inspired by the cycles and flow of energy of creation and destruction in cities as compared to the cycles in nature. Our movements and our actions have the ability to create beauty, the question is, what do you think is beautiful?

Pixel Streets (Michael Hiley, Declan Brincat, Yonghan Ji) is an interactive experience to engage a passing audience with a simple experience and encourage thinking in new ways about urban decoration. A camera detects the color of the clothing of people passing by and uses this color to light up part of the LED façade of the Ars Electronica Center. The aim is to allow people to interact with their urban environment in a new way, creating a feeling of presence and belonging in the city. The color of their clothing can influence the lights of the night and hopefully spark the users' curiosity and provide them with a unique traveling experience when they visit the city.

Flow[er] (Jeniffer Heng, Vidhi Shah) ist eine interaktive Blume, die auf Bewegung reagiert. Nähert sich ein Teilnehmer der Arbeit, spürt die Blume dessen Gegenwart und „blüht" langsam auf. Sie besteht zur Gänze aus alten Leiterplatten aus einem Recycling-Laden. Die Blütenblätter wurden mit alten Kabeln an einem Rotationsmotor befestigt, der das Öffnen und Schließen der Blütenblätter bewirkt. *Flow[er]* ist von den schöpferischen und zerstörerischen Energiezyklen und -strömen in Städten inspiriert, die jenen der Natur gegenübergestellt werden. Wir können mit unseren Bewegungen und Handlungen Schönheit erschaffen, wobei sich die Frage stellt, was als schön empfunden wird.

Pixel Streets (Michael Hiley, Declan Brincat, Yonghan Ji) ist ein interaktives Erlebnis für Passanten, die in das Projekt einbezogen und angeregt werden, neue Möglichkeiten der Stadtgestaltung zu entdecken. Eine Kamera erfasst die Farbe der Kleidung von Passanten, die auf der LED-Fassade des Ars Electronica Center wiedergegeben wird. Die Intention ist, dass die Bewohner der Stadt mit ihrem urbanen Umfeld auf eine neue Weise interagieren, um ein Gefühl der Präsenz in der Stadt und der Zugehörigkeit zu ihr zu entwickeln. Die Farbe der Kleidung beeinflusst die nächtliche Beleuchtung, weckt auf diese Weise hoffentlich die Neugier der Passanten und bereitet den Besuchern der Stadt ein unvergessliches Erlebnis.

Aus dem Englischen von Martina Bauer

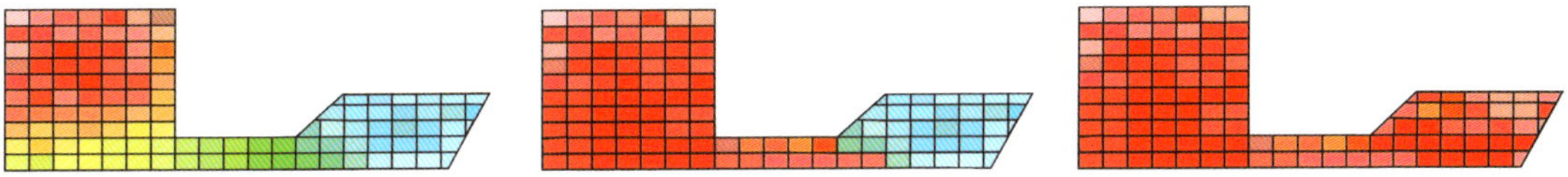

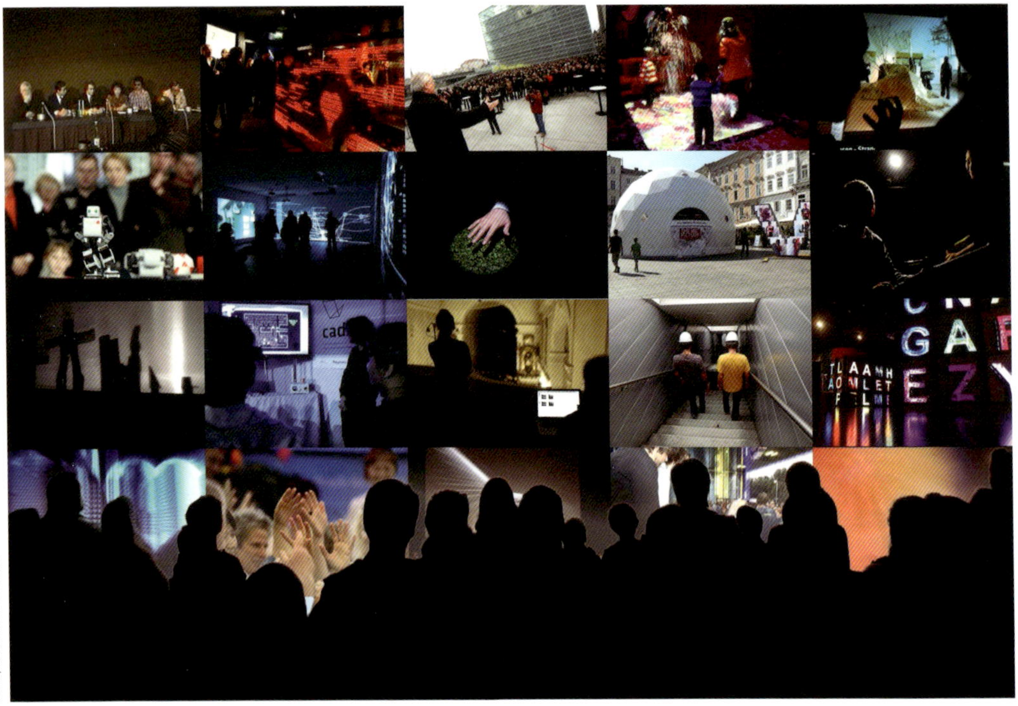

AEC, Kristefan Minski

Queensland University of Technology + Ö1 + Ars Electronica

Projekt Bienenstock (Project Bee Hive)

Another collaborative effort with Queensland University of Technology (QUT) is the "Bienenstock" [Beehive] project.
Bienenstock (Bee Hive) is an installation which is featured in ORF's Ö1 Mobile Atelier, Hauptplatz. The monument is symbolic of the activity taking place therein. The swarm goes out collecting content of the Ars Electronica Festival 2013 and then comes back to deposit into the *arcHIVE*. The many screens attached to its surface display an impression of the festival happening by sucking on the *arcHIVE*. One can interact to influence this impression or can also join the swarm and contribute to the pool of subjective experiences. *Bienenstock* is an artistic experiment to treating the actuality of the Ars Electronica Festival. It is built on the foundation of dissatisfaction toward traditional documentary approaches, a fascination with readily available subjective video apparatus and the growing online trend of immediate (quick & dirty) AV expressionism.

www.aec.at/bienenstock
Text: Kristefan Minski
In Kooperation mit IKONO TV

Eine weitere Kooperation mit QUT ist das Projekt *Bienenstock*.
Bienenstock (Bee Hive) ist eine Installation im Mobilen Ö1 Atelier am Hauptplatz. Es handelt sich um ein Monument für die darin stattfindende Aktivität. Die Leute schwärmen aus, um Inhalte des Ars Electronica Festival 2013 zu sammeln, und legen sie nach ihrer Rückkehr im *arcHIVE* ab. Die zahlreichen an seiner Außenseite angebrachten Bildschirme geben den Eindruck vom Festival wieder, der durch das Saugen am *arcHIVE* entsteht. Beeinflussbar ist dieser Eindruck, indem man miteinander interagiert oder mit ausschwärmt und zum Bestand subjektiver Erfahrungen beiträgt. *Bienenstock* ist ein künstlerisches Experiment über den Umgang mit der Aktualität des Ars Electronica Festivals. Das Projekt geht von der Unzufriedenheit mit traditionellen dokumentarischen Ansätzen aus und arbeitet mit der Begeisterung für die leichte Herstellung subjektiver Videos und den wachsenden Online-Trend eines unmittelbaren (quick & dirty) AV-Expressionismus.

Aus dem Englischen von Wilfried Prantner

University of Newcastle + Ars Electronica Futurelab

Imagination, Collaboration and Innovation

In 2012 the School of Creative Arts at the University of Newcastle (Australia) and Ars Electronica began a series of research and residency projects. Horst Hörtner was invited in April of 2012 to meet with key university staff and give presentations on interdisciplinary research. Following on from this, in December Ars Electronica and Creative Arts collaborated on an international telematic project as part of the International Space Time Concerto Competition. 2013 marks the beginning of a postgraduate research program which will involve artists from Ars Electronica wishing to convert their work into a PHD or Masters degree. In parallel to this initiative, the School of Creative Arts has established an international research program where artists/researchers can work with key researchers in Newcastle on interdisciplinary projects.

Text: Richard Vella, University of Newcastle

2012 riefen die School of Creative Arts an der University of Newcastle (Australien) und Ars Electronica eine Reihe von Forschungs- und Residenzprogrammen ins Leben. Im April 2012 wurde Horst Hörtner zu einem Treffen mit führenden Vertretern der Universität und einer Reihe von Vorträgen über interdisziplinäre Forschung eingeladen. Daraus ergab sich im Dezember zwischen der Ars Electronica und Creative Arts eine Zusammenarbeit bei einem telematischen Projekt im Rahmen der International Space Time Concerto Competition. 2013 wurde ein Postgraduierten-Forschungsprogramm aus der Taufe gehoben, bei dem KünstlerInnen der Ars Electronica ihre Arbeit in einen PhD oder ein Master-Diplom weiterführen können. Gleichzeitig hat die School of Creative Arts ein internationales Forschungsprogramm aufgelegt, bei dem Künstler-/ForscherInnen mit SpitzenforscherInnen in Newcastle an interdisziplinären Projekten arbeiten.

Aus dem Englischen von Wilfried Prantner

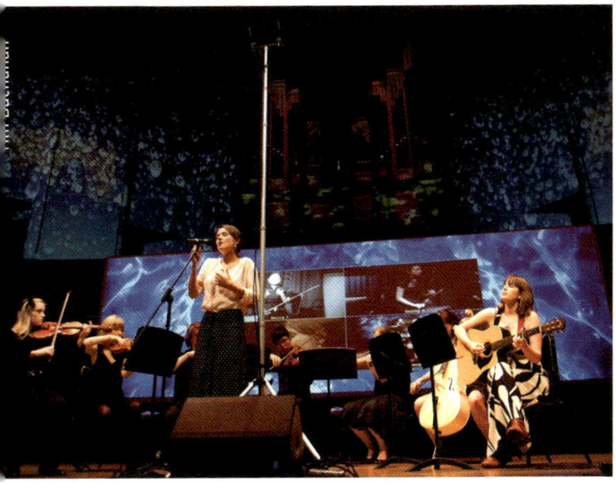

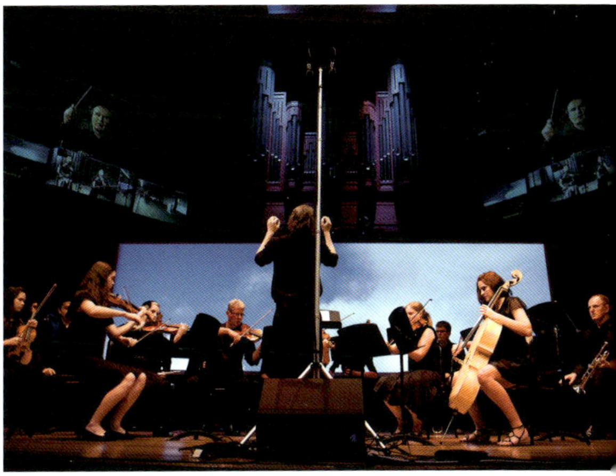

Connecting Cities: A European Network of Media Façades

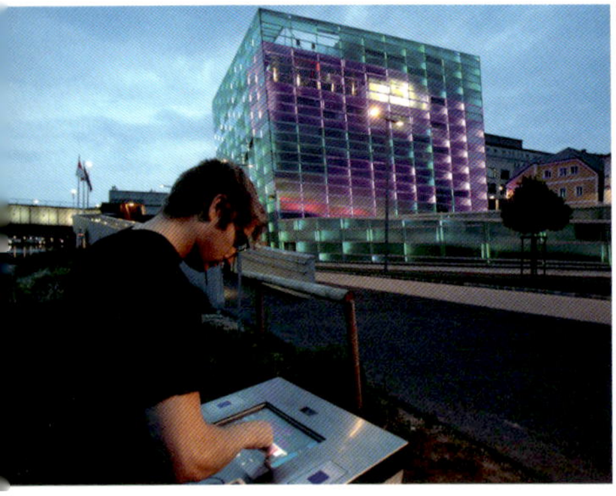

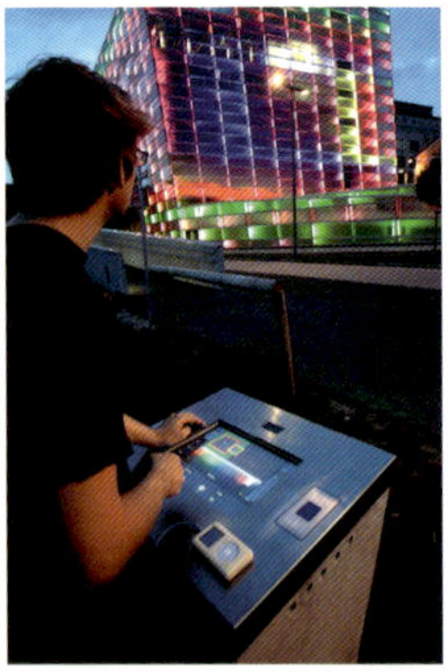

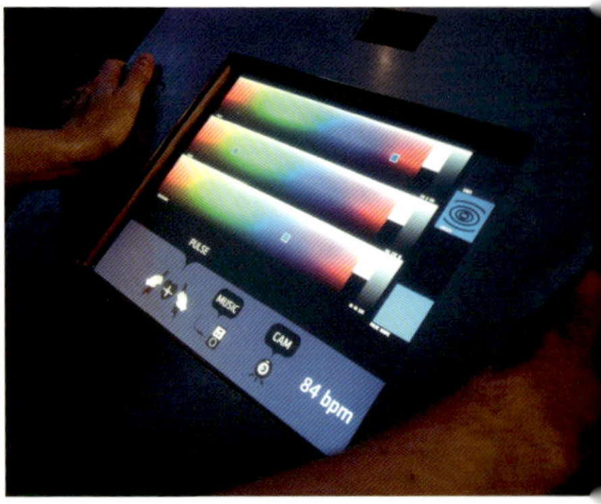

Networked City 2013: Aarhus – Berlin – Brussels – Dessau – Helsinki – Istanbul – Linz – Liverpool – Marseille – Madrid – Montréal – Riga – São Paulo – Vienna – Zagreb

"When you shine, I shine. When you smile, I smile" – this literally holds true for couples of LED façades and urban screens throughout Europe and beyond, if they are part of the *Connecting Cities* network. In the frame of this EU-funded culture project, the Ars Electronica Futurelab—together with high-class partners such as the German Public Art Lab, the Medialab-Prado in Madrid, FACT in Liverpool or the Belgian iMAL Center—interlinks media façades and large-scale screens to open up real-time interaction windows between distant cities. It's evident that the number of urban media screens is increasing worldwide. In contrast to their typically commercial usage, *Connecting Cities* will support the exchange of artistic or socially relevant contents. Imagine a networked grid of urban screens and lights in 15 cities, serving as public communication platform, reacting on each other's visuals, or even glowing synchronously. As façades interact in real-time across borders, so will the local artistic communities, activists and audiences to find out more about their European neighbors.

Through a series of *Connecting Cities* events, workshops, conferences and programs like artist and researcher residencies or mobile urban media labs, three types of city visions will be explored:

„Wenn du strahlst, strahle auch ich. Wenn du lächelst, lächle auch ich" – dieser Refrain gilt in wörtlichem Sinn für miteinander verbundene LED-Fassaden und Urban Screens – digitale Bildschirme im öffentlichen Raum –, wenn sie Teil des Netzwerks *Connecting Cities* sind, das sich über ganz Europa und darüber hinaus erstreckt. Im Rahmen dieses von der EU unterstützten Kulturprojekts vernetzt das Ars Electronica Futurelab – gemeinsam mit Partnern wie dem Public Art Lab in Berlin, dem Medialab-Prado in Madrid, FACT in Liverpool oder dem iMAL Center in Brüssel – Medienfassaden und großformatige Bildschirme, um Echtzeit-Interaktionsfenster zwischen weit entfernten Städten zu eröffnen. Es ist offensichtlich, dass die Anzahl der Urban Screens weltweit im Ansteigen begriffen ist. Im Unterschied zu deren üblicher kommerzieller Nutzung fördert *Connecting Cities* den Austausch von künstlerisch oder gesellschaftlich relevanten Inhalten. Man kann sich das Projekt als einen Verbund von vernetzten Urban Screens und LEDs in 15 Städten vorstellen, die als öffentliche Kommunikationsplattform dienen und auf die jeweiligen visuellen Elemente wechselseitig reagieren oder sogar synchron leuchten. Mit der grenzenüberschreitenden Echtzeit-Interaktion der Fassaden werden auch lokale Künstlergruppen, Aktivisten und das Publikum miteinander in Verbindung treten und so mehr über ihre europäischen Nachbarn erfahren.

- *Networked City 2013:* City-to-city communication via urban media façades
- *Participatory City 2014:* Community building through involvement of the public
- *Visible City 2015:* Invisible data streams become sensible on media façades

During the Ars Electronica Festival 2013, Linz serves as one of the *Networked City* venues. Three outstanding art projects are displayed on the Ars Electronica Center's interactive LED surface or in one of its exhibition spaces:

Über eine Reihe von Veranstaltungen, Workshops, Konferenzen und Programmen, wie Residencies für Künstler und Wissenschaftler oder mobile urbane Media-Labs, werden im Rahmen von *Connecting Cities* drei Stadtvisionen ausgelotet:

- *Networked City 2013:* Kommunikation von Stadt zu Stadt über urbane Medienfassaden
- *Participatory City 2014* Gemeinschaftsbildung durch Einbindung der Öffentlichkeit
- *Visible City 2015:* Unsichtbare Datenströme werden auf Medienfassaden wahrnehmbar.

Während des Ars Electronica Festivals 2013 ist Linz einer der Standorte des Projekts *Networked City.* Auf der interaktiven LED-Fassade des Ars Electronica Center oder in einem der Ausstellungsräume werden drei herausragende Kunstprojekte gezeigt:

h.o (Junichi Yura, Naohiro Hayaishi, Hideaki Ogawa, Emiko Ogawa and Taizo Zushi)

Connecting Monsters

The *Connecting Monsters Project* is an artistic project to create Monsters, which are activated by the words of ordinary people living in Istanbul and Linz, on symbolic media façades in these two cities. These Monsters will act like mediums, conveying the mood of each city to people in both places.

Developments in information technologies such as the Internet and social media have given us previously unimaginable access to and insight into the daily lives of individuals. Traditionally, conveying controlled information via mass media to people influenced their relationships to information and society. Nowadays it is individuals who are voicing and conveying their opinions to the world at large, with no time delay. What collective power do these individuals have?

Monsters on public screens at Beşiktaş Square in Istanbul and the Ars Electronica Center in Linz will

Das *Connecting Monsters Project* ist ein Kunstprojekt, bei dem Worte der Bewohner von Istanbul und Linz Monster auf Medienfassaden in diesen beiden Städten aktivieren können. Die Monster fungieren dabei als Medium, das den Menschen die Stimmung in der jeweils anderen Stadt vermittelt.

Entwicklungen in der Informationstechnik wie das Internet oder soziale Medien gewähren uns einen bisher unvorstellbaren Zugriff und Einblick in den Alltag des Einzelnen. Früher war die Beziehung der Menschen zu Information und Gesellschaft durch kontrolliert über die Massenmedien lancierte Meldungen geprägt. Heute kommuniziert das Individuum seine Meinung und teilt sie der Welt ohne Zeitverzögerung mit. Welche kollektive Macht üben diese Individuen aus?

Auf den Videowänden am Beşiktaş-Platz in Istanbul und am Ars Electronica Center in Linz werden Mons-

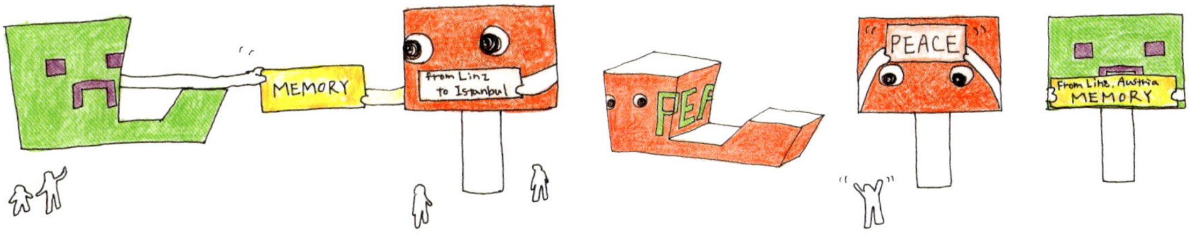

hold up placards bearing words from Twitter tweets for passersby to see. If someone reacts to a word, the Monster interacts with them. The Monster in Linz shows words tweeted in Linz on the façade, and its body assimilates the words and the AEC visitors. Both Monsters regularly visit the façade in the other city, where they communicate the real-time mood—based on the collective words tweeted in each city—to the people. People watching the Monster will probably sense the flow of power coming through the Monster from another place.

The 1651 book *Leviathan*, by Thomas Hobbes, is concerned with the structure of society and legitimate government. Monsters are created very differently in the media age today. This project aims to provoke discussions about the collective power of society, and of individuals, as visualized in the Monsters.

www.howeb.org

ter Tafeln mit Wörtern aus Twitter-Meldungen halten, um sie Passanten zu zeigen. Reagiert jemand auf ein Wort, so interagiert das Monster mit dieser Person. Auf der Fassade in Linz präsentiert das Monster in Linz verfasste Twitter-Meldungen, und sein Körper passt sich an das Wort und den Besucher des AEC an. Beide Monster statten der Fassade in der jeweils anderen Stadt regelmäßig Besuch ab und vermitteln den Menschen dort – anhand der in jeder Stadt getweeteten Wörter – die aktuelle Stimmung in der jeweils anderen Stadt. Beobachtet man das Monster länger, wird man vielleicht den Machtfluss wahrnehmen, der sich vom anderen Ort durch das Monster überträgt.

Das 1651 veröffentlichte Buch *Leviathan* von Thomas Hobbes befasst sich mit der Gesellschaftsstruktur und der rechtmäßigen Regierung. Im heutigen Medienzeitalter werden Monster grundlegend anders erschaffen. Dieses Projekt soll eine Diskussion über die in den Monstern versinnbildlichte kollektive Macht der Gesellschaft und die Macht des Einzelnen in Gang bringen.

Aus dem Englischen von Michael Kaufmann

Orkan Telhan & Mahir M. Yavuz

United Colors of Dissent

United Colors of Dissent (UcoD, http://ucod.org) is a data-driven performance designed for live public interaction. Inhabitants of a public space respond to a series of questions using their mobile phones and interact with each other in real time through a media façade. The performance intends to capture the linguistic and socio-cultural profile of different communities in urban environments by creating dynamic visualizations that map the prejudices, assumptions, and biases we may have about each other.

United Colors of Dissent (UcoD, *http://ucod.org)* ist eine datenbasierte Performance, die für eine öffentliche Live-Interaktion konzipiert wurde. Die Bewohner eines öffentlichen Raumes beantworten mithilfe ihrer Handys eine Reihe von Fragen und interagieren über eine Medienfassade in Echtzeit miteinander. Die Performance versucht, das sprachliche und soziokulturelle Profil verschiedener Gemeinschaften in einem urbanen Umfeld durch dynamische Visualisierungen zu erfassen, die die Vorurteile, Vorbehalte und Voreingenommenheiten abbilden, die wir anderen gegenüber haben.

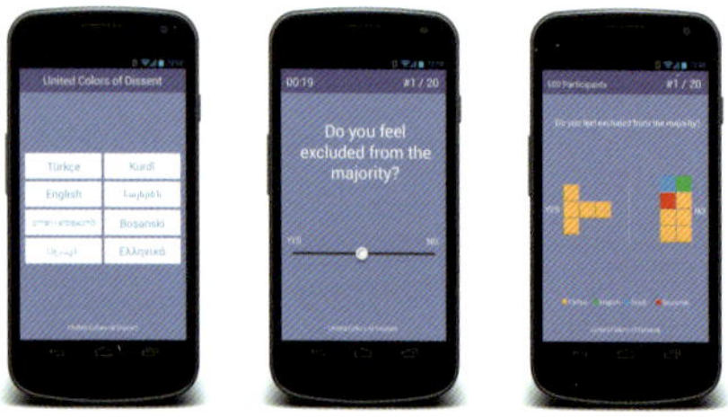

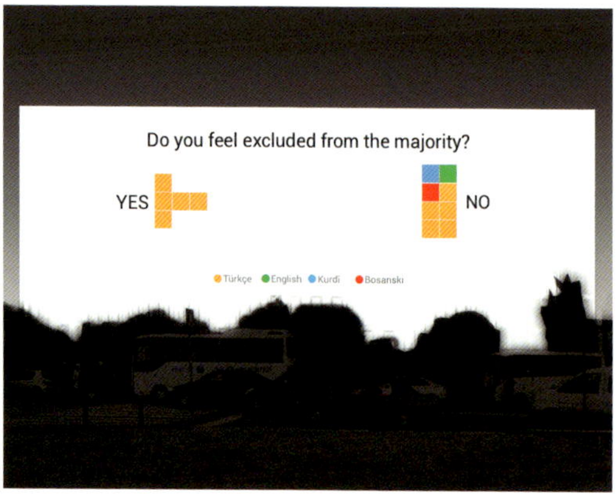

Mar Canet & Vavara Guljajeva

Binoculars to ... Binoculars from ...

Binoculars to ... Binoculars from ... is an artwork that connects a number of cities in an extraordinary way: instead of offering a view that rests in front of the binocular, a viewer is virtually carried to a different city. However, this kind of opening a real-time window to another location does not stay one-directional. While looking into the binocular, the viewer's eye gets captured and displayed on an urban screen or large-scale display at the observed place. Hence, the inhabitants of another city will see the huge-scale eye of an observer looking at them.

Text: Veronika Pauser, Martina Mara

Binoculars to ... Binoculars from ... ist ein Kunstwerk, das eine Reihe von Städten auf außergewöhnliche Weise miteinander verbindet: Ein Fernglas bietet dem Betrachter nicht die vor ihm liegende Ansicht, sondern versetzt ihn virtuell in eine andere Stadt. Das Echtzeitfenster zu dem anderen Ort öffnet sich jedoch nicht nur in eine Richtung. Während der Betrachter in das Fernglas schaut, wird sein Auge erfasst und auf einem Urban Screen, der sich auf dem beobachteten Platz befindet, großformatig abgebildet. Die Bewohner einer anderen Stadt sehen somit das überdimensionale Auge eines Beobachters.

Aus dem Englischen von Martina Bauer

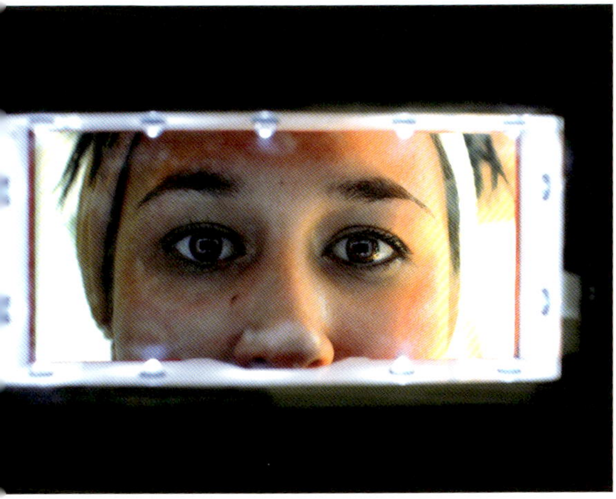

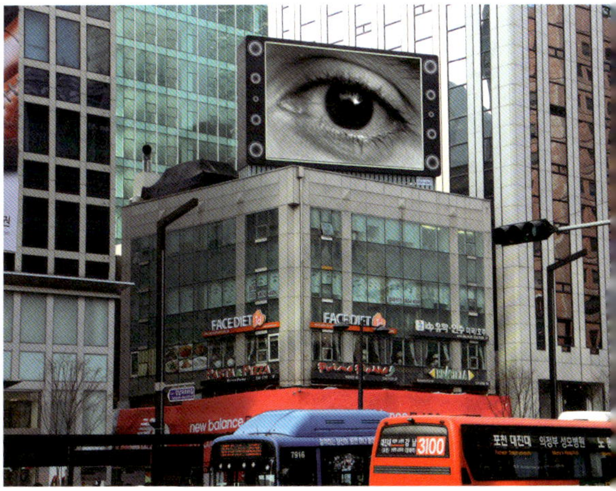

Connecting Cities Network initiated by Public Art Lab in co-organization with Ars Electronica, Media Architecture Institute, FACT, Amber Platform, Museum of Contemporary Art Zagreb, m-cult, Medialab-Prado, iMAL, Foundation Riga 2014 and Videospread, in association with Mutek Montreal, Marseille-Provence 2013, Aarhus University, Quartier des spectacles Montréal, Foundation Bauhaus Dessau, Verve Cultural São Paulo; funded by the European Commission – Programme Culture; supported by Streampark TV and ARTE Creative.

http://www.connectingcities.net

Studiolab

Studiolab is a 3-year Europe-wide initiative that merges the artist's studio with the research lab. Funded by the EC Seventh Framework Programme in 2011, Studiolab is a European network that provides a platform for creative projects that bridge divides between science, art and design.
This year's project in the course of Studiolab is called *Yours Synthetically* and is a subtle reflection on the formulaic conclusion to a letter: "Yours Sincerely". In essence, pointing to the reading and writing of biology taking place in Synthetic Biology through the self-assembling language of DNA.
http://www.studiolabproject.eu

Studiolab ist eine auf drei Jahre angelegte europaweite Initiative, die das Künstleratelier mit dem Forschungslabor verbindet. Das 2011 vom Siebten Rahmenprogramm der Europäischen Kommission finanzierte Unternehmen ist ein europäisches Netzwerk, das eine Plattform für kreative Projekte zur Verfügung stellt, die Differenzen zwischen Wissenschaft, Kunst und Design überbrücken.
Das diesjährige Projekt im Rahmen von Studiolab trägt den Titel *Yours Synthetically* und ist eine subtile Reflexion auf die geläufige Briefgrußformel: „Yours Sincerely". Er verweist im Grunde auf die biologischen Lese- und Schreibprozesse, die in der Synthetischen Biologie bei der Selbstassemblierung von DNA stattfinden.
Aus dem Englischen von Wilfried Prantner

Sphæræ
an inflatable multi-dome pavilion

As part of the Studiolab open call, *Yours Synthetically,* the ArtScience Interfaculty and Synergetica Lab present a series of multi-sensory performances and installations in the context of synthetic biology. Transpiring inside *Sphæræ,* these spherically projected artworks evoke the transformation of prebiotic conditions into the complex behavior and dimensionality of synthesized living cells.

"There is, however, a well-defined difference between the magical and the scientific imitation of life. The former copies external appearances; the latter is concerned with performance and behavior. Until the scientific era, what seemed most alive to people was what most looked like a living being. The vitality accorded to an object was a function primarily of its form". [1]

Since Walter's seminal premonitions of bio-programming (coincidentally, published the same year as the discovery of the double helical structure of DNA), the revolutionary epoch of genetic sequencing followed, and shortly thereafter synthetic biology emerged, redefining the very concept of living

Im Rahmen des Open Calls *Yours Synthetically* von Studiolab präsentieren ArtScience Interfaculty und Synergetica Lab eine Serie von multi-sensorischen Performances und Installationen zum Thema synthetische Biologie. Im Pavillon *Sphæræ* erinnern die Projektionen auf das Innere der Kugel an die Verwandlung aus dem vor-biotischen Zustand in das komplexe Verhalten und die Dimensionalität synthetisierter Lebendzellen.
William Grey Walter schreibt in seinem 1953 erschienen Buch *The Living Brain,* dass es einen klaren Unterschied zwischen der magischen und der wissenschaftlichen Nachahmung von Leben gäbe: Erstere kopiere äußerliche Erscheinungsmerkmale, während es der zweiten um Leistungsfähigkeit und Verhalten gehe. Bis zum Anbruch der wissenschaftlichen Ära erschien das am Lebendigsten, was die größte Ähnlichkeit mit einem Lebewesen aufwies. Das einem Objekt zugestandene „Leben" sei primär eine Funktion seiner Form.[1]
Auf Walters wegweisende Vorahnung der Bio-Programmierung (zufällig im selben Jahr veröffentlicht wie die Entdeckung der Doppelhelixstruktur der DNA)

matter. Empowered by the tools and insight of synthetic biologists, artists have also joined the pursuit of the origins of life and the re-writing of its code.

1 Wiliam Grey Walter, *The Living Brain*, 1953

folgte die revolutionäre Epoche der genetischen Sequenzierung, aus der kurz darauf die synthetische Biologie entstand, die das Konzept der lebenden Materie komplett neu definierte.
Ausgestattet mit den Werkzeugen und Erkenntnissen der synthetischen Biologie, suchen Künstler nun ebenfalls nach dem Ursprung des Lebens mit der Absicht, dessen Code neu zu schreiben.
Aus dem Englischen von Michael Kaufmann

1 Siehe William Grey Walter, *Das lebende Gehirn*, Köln 1961, München 1963

Projects

Hyper-Rainforest [space-shifted portable version]
Francisco López (NL/SP)
http://franciscolopez.net/

Shadow Puppet?
Dieter Vandoren, Mariska de Groot (NL)
http://mariskadegroot.com
http://dietervandoren.net

Polar
Nenad Popov (image), Erfan Abdi (sound) (NL)
http://morphogenesis.eu
http://www.erfanabdi.com

Hydro-Acoustic Study
Paul Prudence (UK)
http://www.transphormetic.com

Biosphere
Eduard Haiman, Michael Holub, Evgeny Vaschenko, Vadim Smakhtin (RU, UA)
http://mathrioshka.ru, http://v4w.enko.ffspace.info

Runaway AV
Bas van Koolwijk (NL)
http://www.basvankoolwijk.com

10000 Peacock Feathers in Foaming Acid
Evelina Domnitch, Dmitry Gelfand (NL)
http://portablepalace.com

Citadels
Matthijs Munnik (NL)
http://www.matthijsmunnik.nl

Covex
Joris Strijbos, Yanila Rius Manzanares (NL)
http://jorisstrijbos.nl, http://www.yamilarios.com

On Growth and Data
Martijn van Boven (NL)
http://www.474746.org

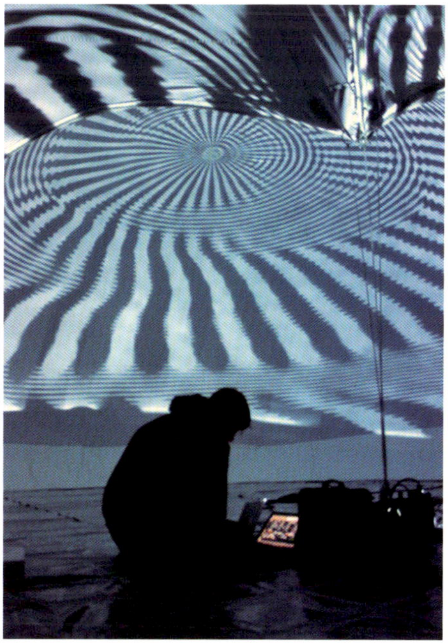

Polar, Nenad Popov (image), Erfan Abdi (sound) (NL)

#43.5
Joost Rekveld (NL)
http://www.lumen.nu/rekveld

Gut Feeling
Eric Parren (USA)
http://ericparren.net

Supported by European Commission Seventh Framework Programme (FP7), Amsterdams Fonds voor de Kunsten, Stimuleringsfonds Creatieve Industrie

Fachhochschule Salzburg + Ars Electronica Futurelab

CADET

In the Center for Advances in Digital Entertainment Technologies (CADET) research project funded by the FFG–Austrian Research Promotion Agency's Cooperation & Innovation (COIN) program, the Salzburg University of Applied Sciences and the Ars Electronica Futurelab are teaming up their technical capabilities and design skills in order to decisively strengthen Austria as a place to do business in the field of creative engineering. The aims of the CADET development initiative are to conceive and upgrade technologies and applications in the area of mixed reality entertainment. Its specific R&D objective is to enhance immersion, participation and interaction in digital entertainment and communication. The possibility of introducing a person's own body, motions and emotions into a networked virtual world will significantly change our understanding of multimedia production and entertainment.

In dem von der FFG im Rahmen des COIN-Programmes finanzierten Forschungsprojekt CADET (Center for Advances in Digital Entertainment Technologies) bündeln die Fachhochschule Salzburg und das Ars Electronica Futurelab ihre technischen und gestalterischen Kompetenzen, um damit den Bereich des „Creative Engineering" am Standort Österreich entscheidend zu stärken. Ziele des Aufbau- und Entwicklungsvorhabens CADET liegen in der Konzeption und Entwicklung von Technologien und Anwendungen im Bereich des Mixed Reality Entertainments. Die Entwicklungs- und Forschungsschwerpunkte verfolgen dabei das Ziel, Immersion, Partizipation und Interaktion in der digitalen Unterhaltung und Kommunikation zu steigern. Die Möglichkeit, den eigenen Körper, seine Bewegungen und Emotionen in eine vernetzte virtuelle Welt einzubringen, wird unser Verständnis von multimedialer Produktion und Unterhaltung maßgeblich verändern.

Text: Roland Haring

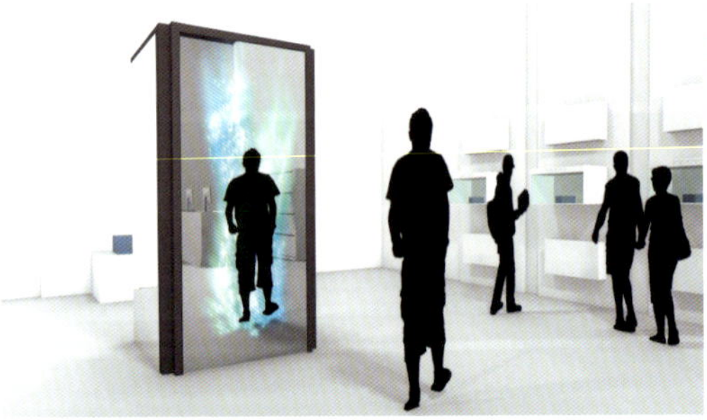

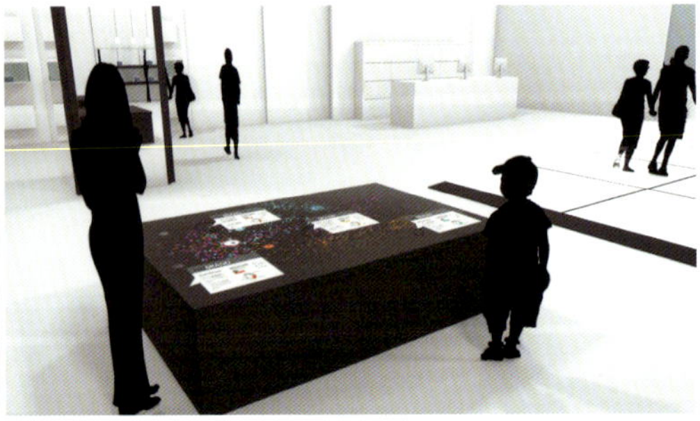

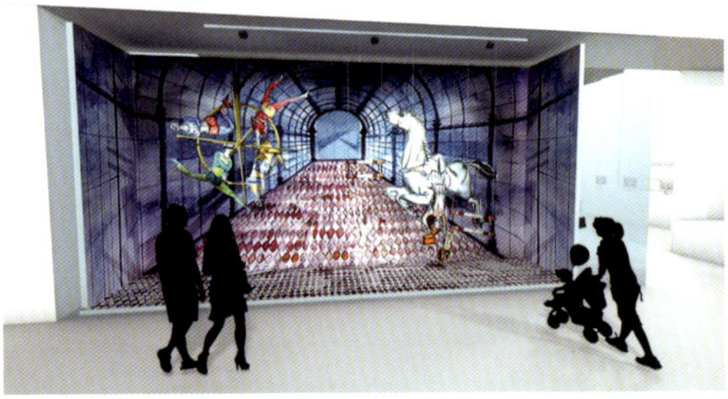

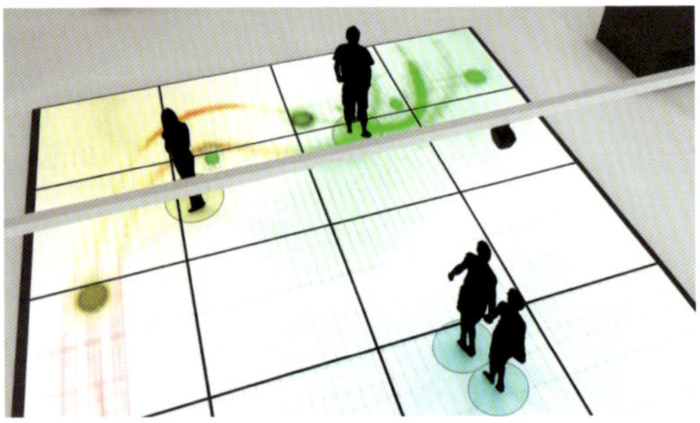

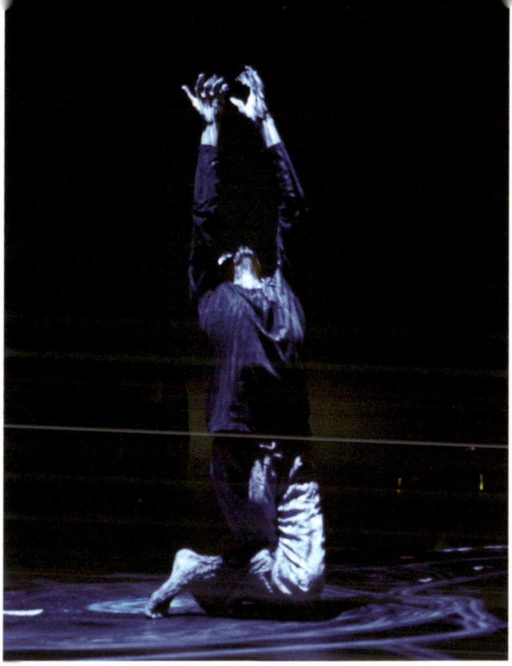

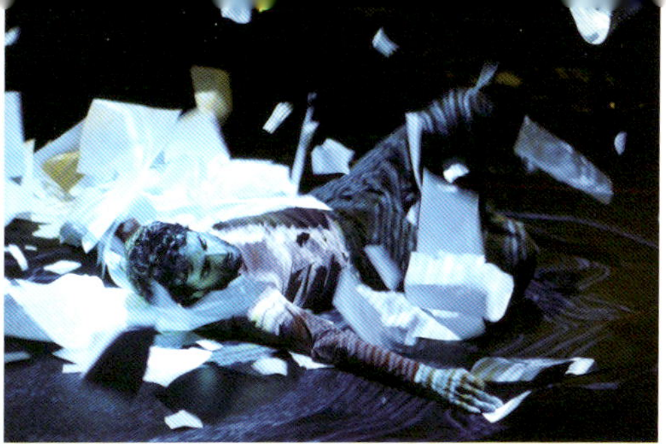

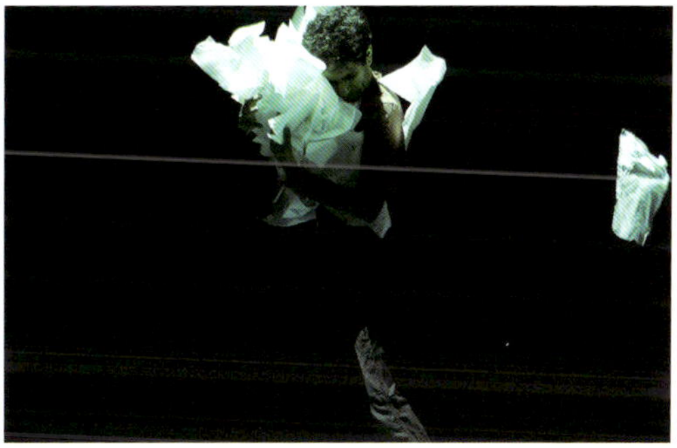

Aakash Odedra, Lewis Major + Ars Electronica Futurelab

Resonate

British dancer/choreographer Aakash Odedra and Australian choreographer Lewis Major team up with Ars Electronica Futurelab to create a dance performance blending technology such as tracking, visualisations, projections and more. Training initially in Kathak, Aakash's performance experience relates to a wide range of dance styles. He is intensely interested in collaborating with different disciplines in order to elucidate his artistic vision in dance. Aakash and Lewis approached Ars Electronica Futurelab to explore the idea of warped and exaggerated realities and the confusion that a dyslexic person feels trying to make sense of language and literature. The main focus of the following joint R&D experiments, which took place this spring in Linz, was on how the physical experience of being dyslexic can be revealed through visuals, light, sound and movement. During this year's festival the outcome of this experiment series will be presented to a public audience for the first time. In intimate work in progress sessions, the artists will dance, explain and show the upcoming work based on the storyboard and the musical score, enriched by interactive projections, wind-machine sculptured paper storms and murmurations of starling swarms.

Text: Roland Haring, Michael Knoll, Anand Bhatt

Der britische Tänzer/Choreograf Aakash Odedra und der australische Choreograf Lewis Major entwickeln gemeinsam mit dem Ars Electronica Futurelab eine Tanzperformance, die Technologien wie Tracking, Visualisierungsverfahren, Projektionen und dergleichen mehr miteinander verbindet. Ursprünglich als Kathak-Tänzer ausgebildet, bezieht sich Aakash in seiner Praxis auf eine breite Palette an Tanzstilen und arbeitet mit unterschiedlichen Disziplinen zusammen, um seine künstlerischen Visionen im Bereich Tanz zu verdeutlichen. An das Ars Electronica Futurelab wandten sich Aakash und Lewis mit dem Ziel, die Idee verzerrter oder übersteigerter Realitäten zu untersuchen und der Verwirrung nachzuspüren, die Legastheniker empfinden, wenn sie versuchen, Sprache und Literatur zu verstehen. Bei den gemeinsamen R&D-Experimenten, die dieses Frühjahr in Linz stattfanden, ging es in erster Linie um die Erforschung von Möglichkeiten, die physische Erfahrung der Legasthenie mittels Visuals, Licht, Ton und Bewegung begreifbar zu machen. Während des diesjährigen Festivals werden die Ergebnisse der Versuchsreihe erstmals öffentlich präsentiert. In intimen Work-in-Progress-Sessions werden die Künstler tanzen und das im Entstehen begriffene Stück anhand des Storyboards und der musikalischen Partitur erläutern. Dazu kommen interaktive Projektionen, von Windmaschinen erzeugte Papierstürme und Formationsflüge von Starenschwärmen.

Aus dem Englischen von Wilfried Prantner

Hakuhodo Inc. + Ars Electronica Futurelab

Innovation Catalyst

Creative questions thrown at society by artists often constitute the driving powers behind the shaping of our future lives. The craziest idea can point out the direction in which we are heading. The next step is to implement these ideas in real life. Hakuhodo Inc., a century-old ad agency in Japan which has long been looking into the "insights of *Sei-Katsu-Sha* (= consumers as living people with lives, not sample numbers of consumption)" and realizing this philosophy in diverse areas of communication design services, and Ars Electronica, the global hub of creativity, have started a completely new collaboration project to increase innovation in society through developments of new consumer products, services and communication frameworks.

Die kreativen Fragen, mit denen Künstler die Gesellschaft konfrontieren, sind die eigentliche Triebkraft für das Leben der Zukunft. Die extremsten Ideen weisen die Richtung, in die es geht. Als nächstes gilt es, diese Ideen in die Tat umzusetzen. Hakuhodo Inc., eine seit 100 Jahren bestehende japanische Werbeagentur, die seit langem auf die Einsichten des *Seikatsusha* setzt (das heißt: Konsumenten als in ihren Lebensalltag eingebundene Menschen und nicht als statistische Größen betrachtet) und diese Philosophie in vielen Bereichen des Kommunikationsdesigns umsetzt, hat sich mit Ars Electronica, der globalen Drehscheibe in Sachen Kreativität, zu einem völlig neuen Kooperationsprojekt zusammengetan, das durch die Entwicklung neuer Konsumgüter, Dienstleistungen und Kommunikationssysteme Innovation in der Gesellschaft fördern will.

Aus dem Englischen von Wilfried Prantner

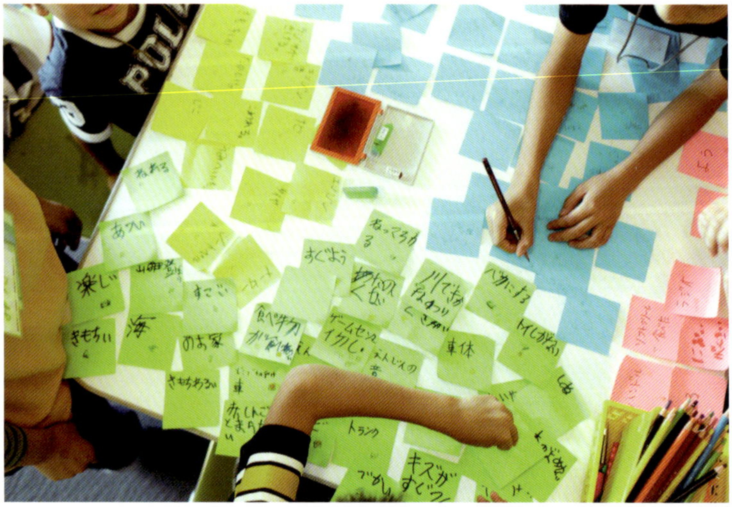

Hakuhodo Inc.

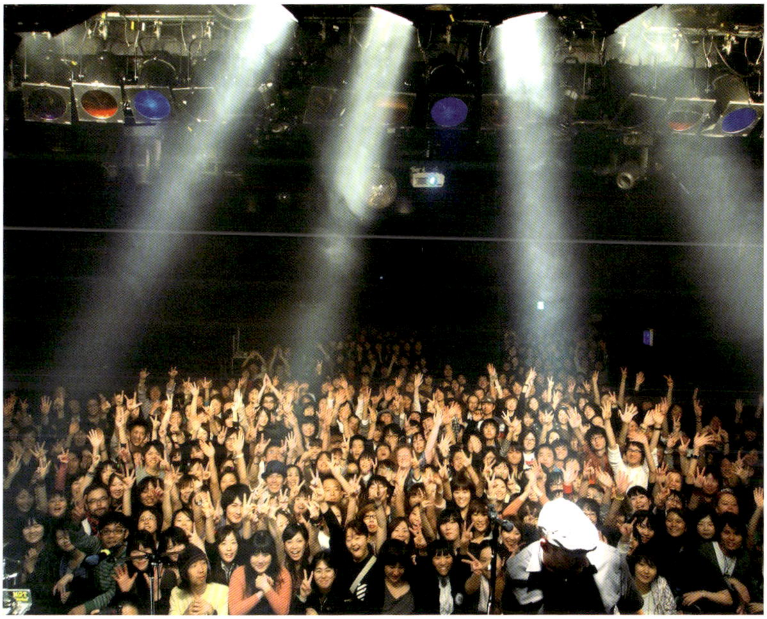

Damian J. Kulash, Jr.

OK Go + Ars Electronica Futurelab

The Future Rock Show

Pixelspaces 2013 will focus on the quest for the future of live entertainment. Musicians, artists and curators from around the world will come together to discuss the possibilities that have emerged from the explosion of interactive technologies in recent years and will assess new forms of performance and how they will grapple with the ways in which these tools are changing the dialog of performance. What will future live shows look like? How can one create new forms of audience participation that thoughtfully engage but do not interrupt the audience attention? Is the combination of different artistic disciplines required to overcome the challenging oscillation between presentation and participation? Are these radical developments solely the purview of the technological elite? Or will these changes affect us all?

In cooperation with Hakuhodo Inc.

Pixelspaces 2013 macht sich auf die Suche nach der Zukunft des Live-Entertainments. MusikerInnen, KünstlerInnen und KuratorInnen aus der ganzen Welt werden über die Möglichkeiten diskutieren, die sich aus der explosiven Entwicklung interaktiver Technologien in den letzten Jahren ergeben haben, sowie eine Einschätzung neuer performativer Formen und ihres Umgangs mit der durch diese Tools bedingten Veränderung des performativen Dialogs vornehmen.

Wie werden Live-Shows in Zukunft aussehen? Wie lassen sich neue Formen der Publikumsbeteiligung schaffen, die das Publikum klug in das Geschehen einbeziehen, ohne seine Aufmerksamkeit zu beeinträchtigen? Bedarf es einer Verbindung unterschiedlicher künstlerischer Disziplinen, um das problematische Schwanken zwischen Präsentation und Partizipation zu überwinden? Sind diese radikalen Entwicklungen lediglich eine Sache der technologischen Elite oder betrifft dieser Wandel uns alle?

Aus dem Englischen von Wilfried Prantner

Miraikan + Ars Electronica
Cultural Communication Program

The National Museum of Emerging Science and Innovation (Miraikan) is a Japanese science center that opened in 2001 in Tokyo. Miraikan's philosophy views "science and technology as part of our culture, and providing an open forum for all to ponder and discuss the future roles of science and technology". Permanent displays and exhibitions provide people with a chance to enjoy hands-on contact with science and technology, for example, a wide range of events that include workshops and talks. While exchanging opinions and ideas with Science Communicators, visitors can experience the technological progress of today, from simple day-to-day issues to the latest technologies, global environment and space exploration. At Miraikan people can get a scientific perspective on what is happening in our world today and join in discussions about the future that lies ahead of us.

Miraikan and Ars Electronica have started working on a cultural communication program to spread scientific and technical culture on a global level.

At the Ars Electronica Festival 2012, Maholo Uchida and Hajime Narukawa presented the project *Tsunagari & AuthaGraph,* which dealt with the festival theme, the "Big Picture". Maholo Uchida's presentation showed the audience a new perspective of the earth as a gigantic ecosystem, introducing the *Tsunagari Project* with the *Geo-Cosmos,* an organic light-emitting sphere display system, which is exhibited at Miraikan.

In April 2013, Ars Electronica Futurelab and Miraikan completed the development of the *Virtual-Globe* – a system to show *Geo-Cosmos* contents in Ars Electronica Center's Deep Space. This cultural communication program establishes innovative infrastructure for freely exchanging contents developed by both institutes. The Deep Space program at the Ars Electronica Center regularly includes contents from Miraikan.

Das National Museum of Emerging Science and Innovation (Miraikan) ist ein 2001 in Tokio eröffnetes Wissenschaftszentrum. Gemäß seiner Philosophie, „dass Wissenschaft und Technologie ein Teil unserer Kultur sind", und dem damit einhergehenden Ziel, „ein allen zugängliches Forum zur Betrachtung und Erörterung der künftigen Rolle von Wissenschaft und Technologie zu schaffen", zeigt das Miraikan permanente Arbeiten und Installationen, die Besuchern eine unmittelbare und spielerische Auseinandersetzung mit Wissenschaft und Technologie ermöglichen, einschließlich eines umfassenden Angebots an erfahrungsbezogenen Kursen und Vorträgen. Im Austausch von Meinungen und Ideen mit Wissenschaftsvermittlern können Besucher aktuelle technologische Entwicklungen hautnah miterleben, und zwar von einfachen Alltagsdingen bis hin zu den neuesten technischen Errungenschaften, von globalen Umweltfragen bis zur Weltraumforschung. Das Miraikan ist ein Ort, an dem man ein wissenschaftliches Verständnis vom heutigen Geschehen in der Welt gewinnen und in Diskussionen über zukünftige Entwicklungen eintreten kann.

Miraikan und Ars Electronica haben ein gemeinsames Vermittlungsprogramm zur Verbreitung wissenschaftlicher und technischer Kultur auf globaler Ebene gestartet.

Beim Ars Electronica Festival 2012 zum Thema THE BIG PICTURE präsentierten Maholo Uchida und Hajime Narukawa das *Tsunagari-* und das *AuthaGraph-*Projekt. Die Präsentation vermittelte dem Publikum anhand des im Miraikan installierten kugelförmigen Displaysystems *Geo-Cosmos* eine neue Sicht des gewaltigen Ökosystems Erde.

Im April 2013 stellte das Ars Electronica Futurelab die Entwicklung des *Virtual-Globe* fertig – eines Systems, mit dessen Hilfe Inhalte des *Geo-Cosmos* im Deep Space des Ars Electronica Center gezeigt werden können. Damit wurde eine innovative Infrastruktur zum freien Austausch von Inhalten zwischen den beiden Instituten geschaffen. Das Programm des Deep Space im Ars Electronica Center bezieht regelmäßig Inhalte vom Miraikan ein.

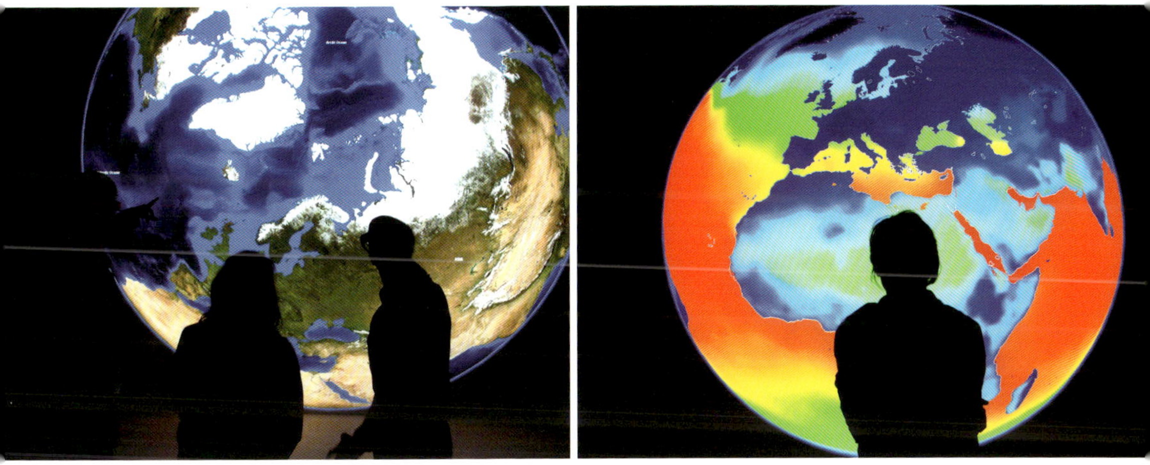

Virtual-Globe, Ars Electronica Center

Virtual-Globe in Deep Space

Virtual-Globe is a platform developed by Ars Electronica Futurelab to show contents of Miraikan's symbolic installation *Geo-Cosmos* in Deep Space at the Ars Electronica Center. The most important consideration was compatibility, so that the same contents could be shown in both systems, *Geo-Cosmos* and Deep Space. Although the same contents are shown in both infrastructures, visitors will experience different perspectives—Miraikan's "Geo-Cosmos" shows the globe in space, while the AEC's *Virtual-Globe* gives the audience a closer view of the earth with information provided by infotrainers. For both museums, this cultural platform is a powerful catalyst to get people talking about global issues.

Virtual-Globe ist ein vom Ars Electronica Futurelab entwickeltes System, mit dessen Hilfe sich Inhalte der ikonischen Miraikan-Installation *Geo-Cosmos* im Deep Space des Ars Electronica Center darstellen lassen. Priorität hatte dabei die Herstellung von Kompatibilität, um die gleichen Inhalte auf beiden Plattformen zeigen zu können. Trotz gleicher Inhalte werden die Besucher allerdings jeweils etwas anderes wahrnehmen. Zeigt der *Geo-Cosmos* im Miraikan die Erde als im Raum schwebende Kugel, so ist sie auf dem *Virtual-Globe* im Ars Electronica Center – eingebettet in Narrative von Infotrainern – aus größerer Nähe zu sehen. In beiden Museen bildet die Plattform einen wirkmächtigen Katalysator, um Diskussionen über globale Fragestellungen in Gang zu setzen.

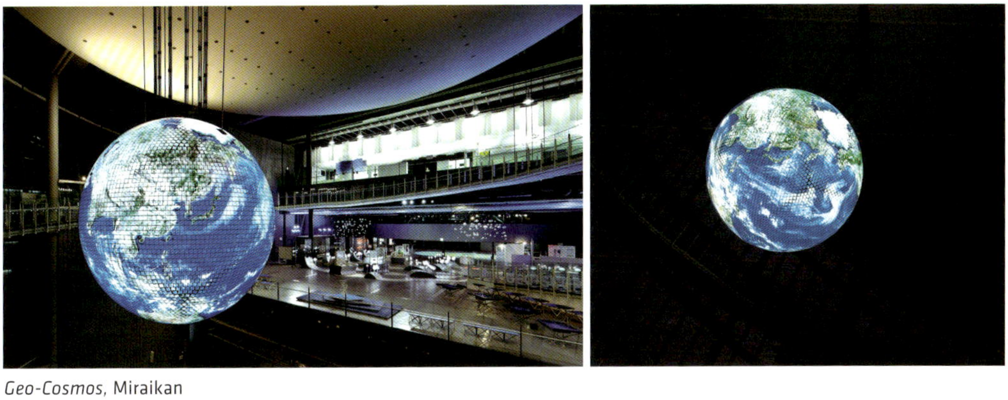

Geo-Cosmos, Miraikan

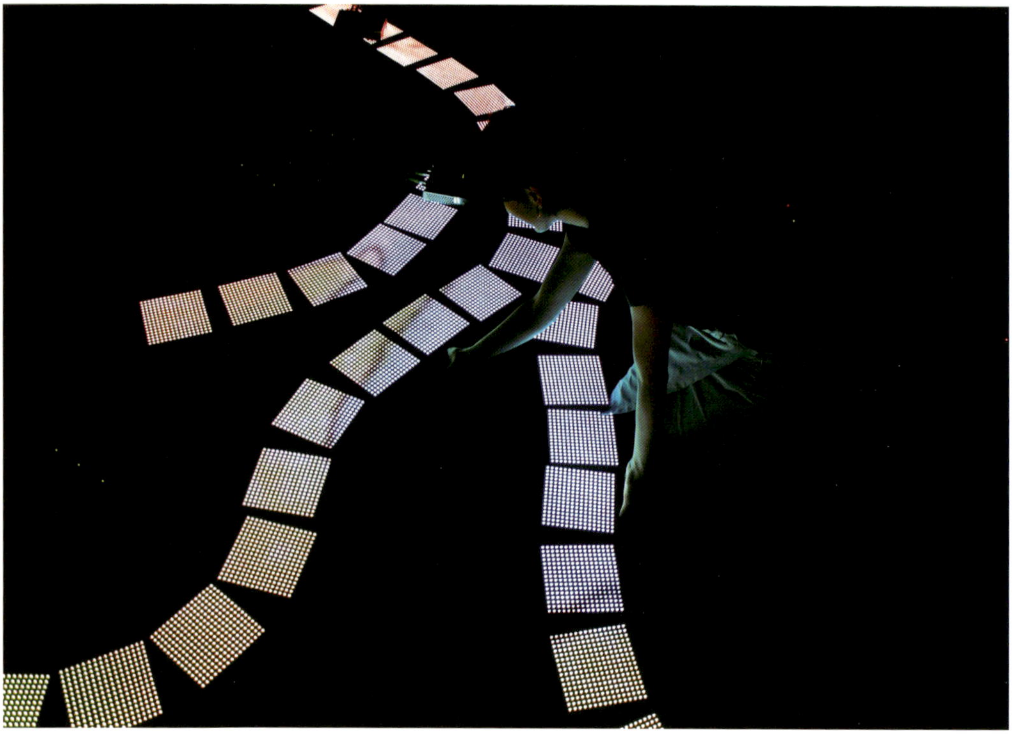

Your-Cosmos

At the Ars Electronica Festival 2013, Ars Electronica Futurelab is showing *Your-Cosmos,* a project that gives a new perspective on the world by re-using Miraikan's LED panels from the old *Geo-Cosmos.* While the old *Geo-Cosmos* gave people a perspective, taking a panoramic view of the earth by constructing LED panels as a globe, this new installation of *Your-Cosmos* gives visitors the opportunity to freely construct their own perspectives. Daito Manabe and Satoru Higa, Japanese artists, have been invited to hold a special workshop by using this unique installation. The *Geo-Cosmos* perspective will be transformed into various forms of "Cosmos" and the project will provide new insights on understanding the world in different ways. *Your-Cosmos* is a participatory workshop and installation in which participants can connect LED panels and construct their own world.

Im Rahmen des Ars Electronica Festivals 2013 präsentiert das Futurelab *Your-Cosmos,* ein Projekt, das eine neue Sicht der Welt vermittelt, indem es die LED-Panels des guten alten *Geo-Cosmos* im Miraikan einer neuen Verwendung zuführt. Wo *Geo-Cosmos* mit der kugelförmigen Anordnung der LED-Panels ein panoramatisches Bild von der Erde bietet, ermöglicht *Your-Cosmos* Besuchern, sich ihr eigenes Bild davon zu machen. Die japanischen Künstler Daito Manabe und Satoru Higa wurden eingeladen, einen speziellen Workshop mit dieser einmaligen Installation abzuhalten. Dabei wird das Bild des *Geo-Cosmos* in verschiedene „Kosmen" verwandelt, um neue und andere Möglichkeiten des Weltverständnisses zu erschließen. *Your-Cosmos* ist ein Workshop und eine Installation, bei der die Teilnehmer die LED-Panels miteinander verbinden und so ihre eigene Welt erschaffen können. Der *Geo-Cosmos* im Mirakan mit seinen zu einem

Miraikan's *Geo-Cosmos* creates a perspective as if we are viewing the earth from space, by making the LED panels into one huge globe. Technological developments in social media have led to dramatic changes in communication between people. How are the perceptions of the world changing? And how are the new perceptions changing the way to create the world?

Your-Cosmos provides visitors with a framework to create a LED panel world together by assembling LED modules like LEGO blocks. It's not just about understanding other people's viewpoints, but about experiencing and working out ways of constructing a world together.

The interactive exhibit, *Your-Cosmos,* also represents a way of thinking that is characteristic of Ars Electronica: the proposal of new forms and new worlds.

Text: Hideaki Ogawa, Emiko Ogawa

riesigen Globus angeordneten LED-Panels zeigt die Erde wie sie vom Weltall aus zu sehen ist. Die technologische Entwicklung in den sozialen Medien hat die zwischenmenschliche Kommunikation drastisch verändert. Wie verändert sich dadurch die Wahrnehmung der Welt? Und wie verändern neue Formen der Weltwahrnehmung unsere Möglichkeiten, die Welt zu gestalten?

Your-Cosmos gibt Besuchern die Möglichkeit, die LED-Module wie Legosteine zusammenzusetzen und so gemeinsam eine Welt zu erschaffen. Dabei geht es nicht nur darum, den Standpunkt anderer zu verstehen, sondern auch darum, hautnah zu erleben, was es heißt, zusammen mit anderen eine Welt zu schaffen. Insofern steht die interaktive Ausstellung *Your-Cosmos* auch für ein Denken, das kennzeichnend für Ars Electronica ist: eines, das ständig neue Formen und Welten hervorbringt.

Aus dem Englischen von Wilfried Prantner

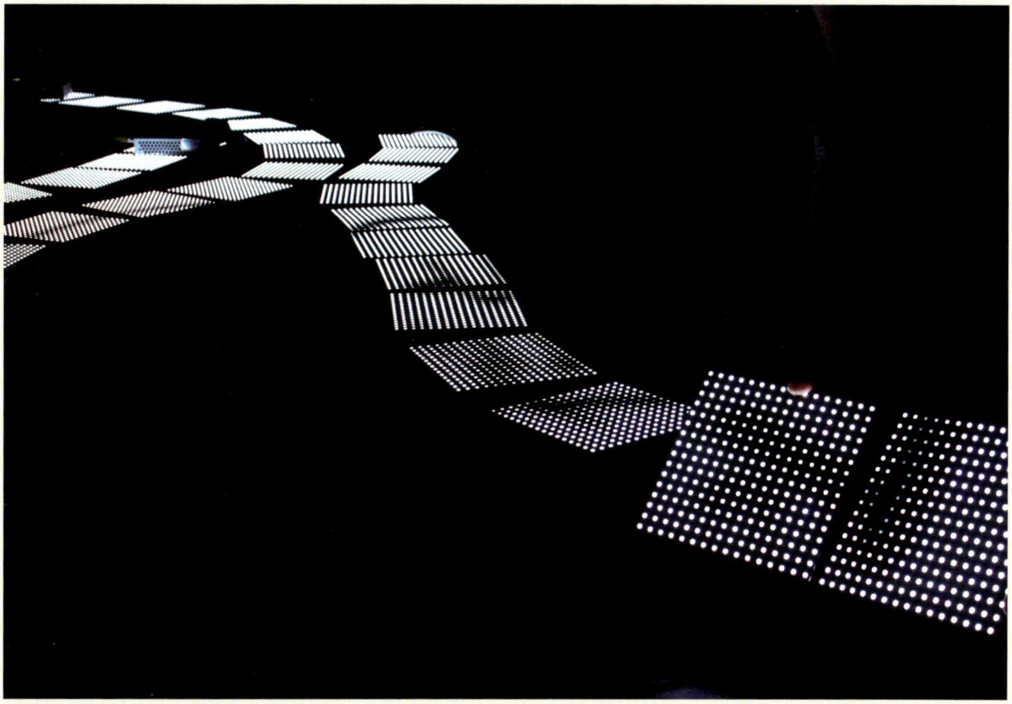

Knowledge Capital Osaka + Ars Electronica Futurelab

Ars Electronica Creative Cloud

Ars Electronica Creative Cloud is a workshop series held in the Knowledge Capital of Osaka in a brand-new creative hub for innovation through a fusion of human creativity and technology. Ten creative workshops will be conducted in this cultural program curated by Ars Electronica, starting June 2013 to May 2014, including cutting-edge talk sessions by international artists and Ars Electronica members. This event is held under the auspices of both Knowledge Capital and Kansai Telecasting Corporation.

The venue of this event is located in the center of Osaka and it is a complex facility and incubation center for advanced technology and innovation. *The Lab.* in the Knowledge capital consists of open experimental laboratories used by industries and universities and the venue functions as a unique intersection where general visitors, industries, universities and creators meet.

Each month during the *Ars Electronica Creative Cloud*, three days are filled with talks and workshops. On the first day an artist and an Ars Electronica member hold the Cloud Talk. The talks will provide in-depth insight into many interesting topics on the cutting-edge of art, technology and society.

Artists fill the second and third day with workshops. Every workshop is based on creative expression, exploration and activity, all shaped by the unique experience and vision of the respective artist. On the second day a member of Ars Electronica will present the latest projects and news, offering the community in Osaka insight into the creative processes in Linz. Through these workshops, the program aims to stimulate social discussion and action for new creativity based in the Knowledge Capital Osaka.

http://kc-i.jp/en/

Ars Electronica Creative Cloud steht für eine Workshopreihe, die in der Knowledge Capital in Osaka, einem brandneuen Innovationszentrum, das sich der Fusion von menschlicher Kreativität und Technologie widmet, abgehalten wird. Im Rahmen des von Ars Electronica kuratierten Kulturprogramms werden zwischen Juni 2013 und Mai 2014 zehn Kreativworkshops veranstaltet, die auch Gesprächsrunden mit internationalen Künstlern und Mitarbeitern von Ars Electronica umfassen. Die Reihe steht unter der Schirmherrschaft der Knowledge Capital und der Kansai Telecasting Corporation.

Der Veranstaltungsort ist ein Gebäudekomplex im Zentrum Osakas, ein Inkubationszentrum für Hightech-Entwicklungen und Innovationen. Im *The Lab.* der Knowledge Capital befinden sich offene Experimentallabore, die von Industrieunternehmen und Universitäten genutzt werden, und der gesamte Veranstaltungsort fungiert als einmaliger Treffpunkt für interessiertes Publikum, Vertreter aus Industrie und dem Universitätsbereich sowie für kreative Köpfe.

Während der *Ars Electronica Creative Cloud* finden an drei Tagen jeden Monats Gesprächsrunden und Workshops statt. Am ersten Tag führen ein Künstler und ein Vertreter von Ars Electronica den *Cloud Talk*. Diese Gesprächsrunden sollen detaillierte Einblicke in brandaktuelle Themen aus den Bereichen Kunst, Technologie und Gesellschaft bieten.

Am zweiten und dritten Tag leiten die Künstler die Workshops. Im Zentrum dieser von den Erfahrungen und Visionen des jeweiligen Künstlers geprägten Veranstaltungen stehen künstlerischer Ausdruck, Forscherdrang und aktives Handeln. Ebenfalls am zweiten Tag wird ein Vertreter von Ars Electronica die aktuellsten Projekte und Neuigkeiten vorstellen, um der Community in Osaka einen Einblick in die kreativen Prozesse in Linz zu gewähren. Ziel dieser Workshops ist es, der sozialen Diskussion und den kreativen Prozessen in der Knowledge Capital Osaka neue Impulse zu geben.

Aus dem Englischen von Michael Kaufmann

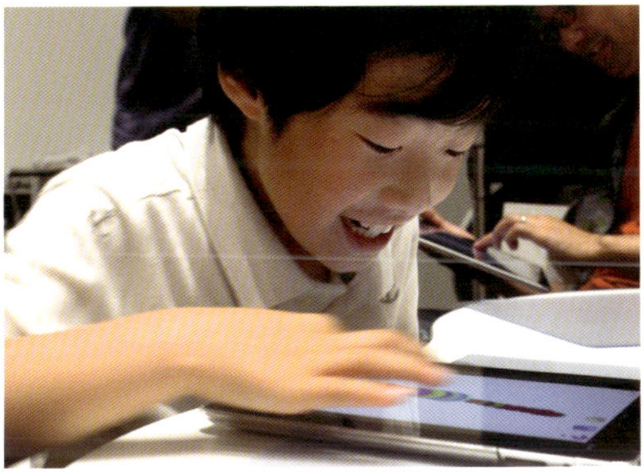

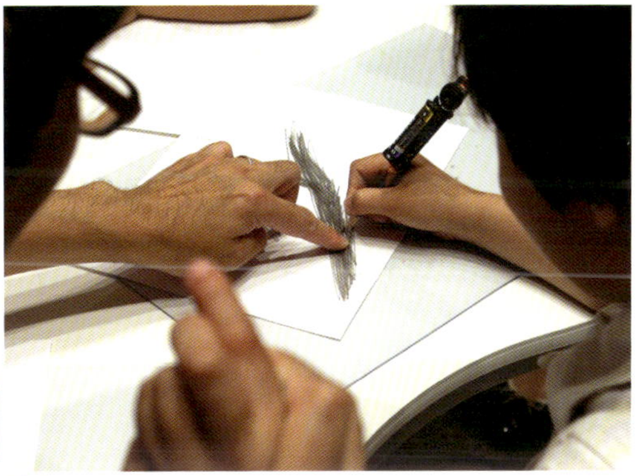

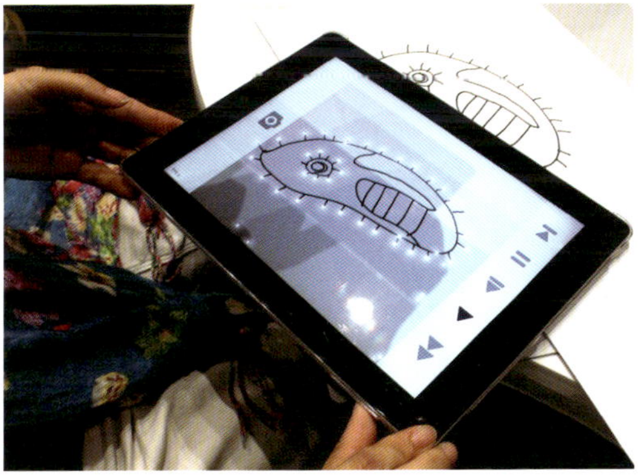

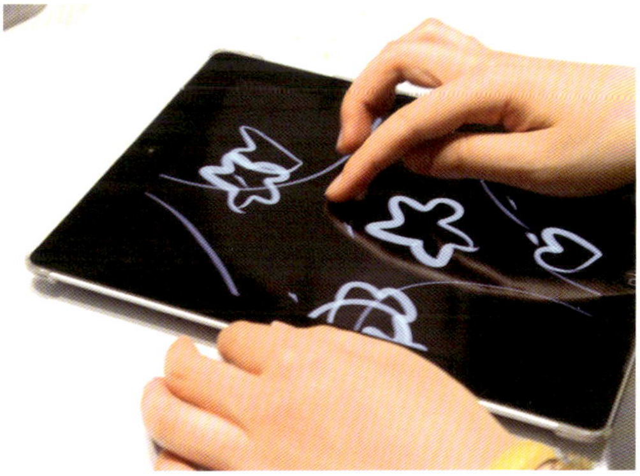

Drawing++ / Creative platform, with Zach Lieberman and Gerfried Stocker

Ars Electronica Creative Cloud 2013

June: Zach Lieberman and Gerfried Stocker, *Drawing++* / Creative platform
July: Sam Auinger and Horst Hörtner, *Thinking with your ears* / Future of lab
August: Greg Saul and Christoph Kremer, *SketchChair* / Future of education
October: Ursula Damm and Martin Honzik, *Grow your city* / Art and Society
November: Michael Doser and Gerfried Stocker, *Seeing the invisible* / Art and Science
December: Christopher Lindinger and Hideaki Ogawa, *Digital Creativity* / Art and Innovation

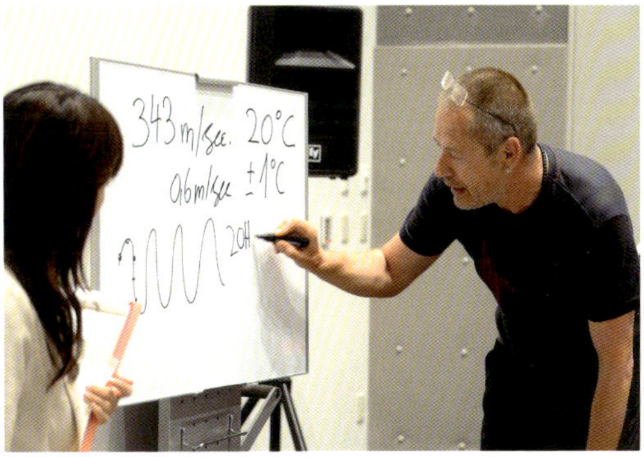

Thinking with your ears / Future of lab, with Sam Auinger and Horst Hörtner

Inside Ars Electronica Solutions

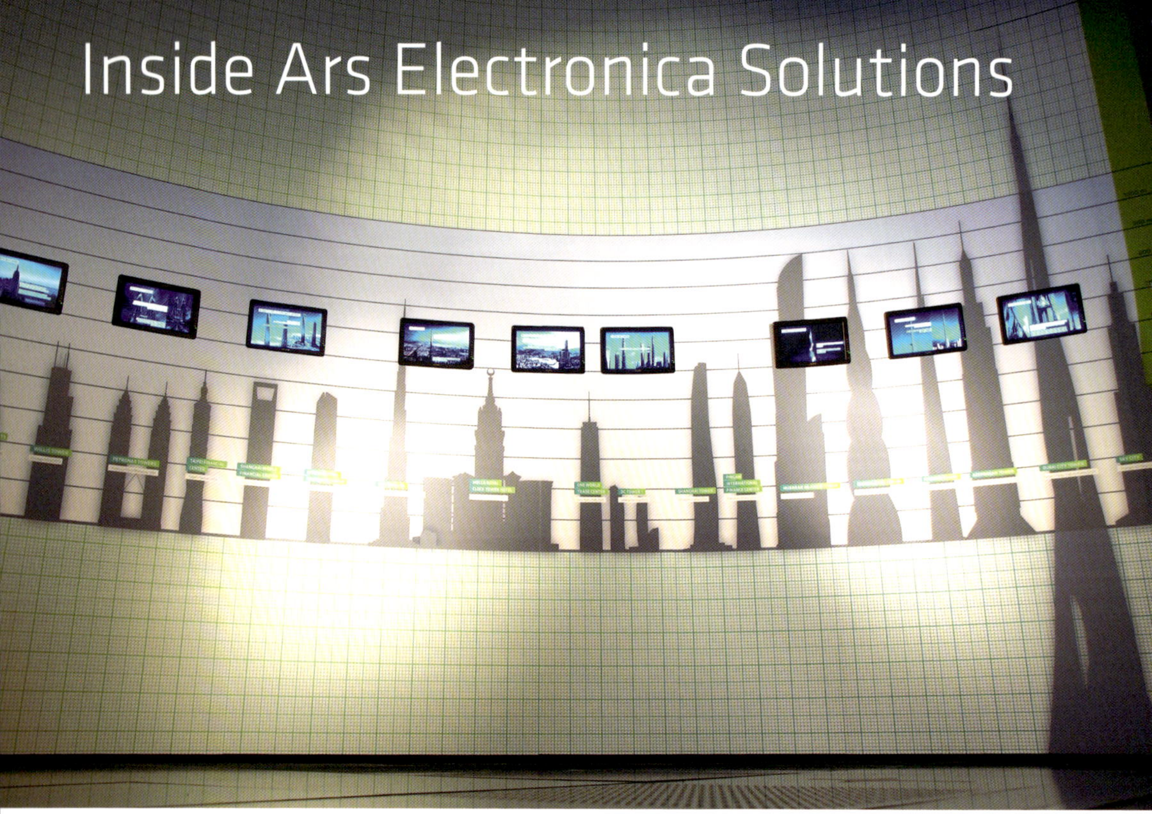

Ars Electronica's newest division, Ars Electronica Solutions, creates customized, networked solutions for interactive products and services in three areas: Event & Show Design, Brandlands & Exhibitions, and Shop Experience. The primary aim of what we do is communicating and visualizing information. Our solutions can be deployed in very diverse ways that transcend the boundaries between different business sectors.

In carrying out assignments, Ars Electronica Solutions relies on the comprehensive competence network of Ars Electronica—first and foremost, real-world R&D results achieved by the Ars Electronica Futurelab that does groundbreaking work on the leading edge of such fields as media art, design, interaction, virtual reality and real-time graphics. The mission is to take prototypes to the next level: serial production and mass marketing. In the con-

Als jüngste Ausprägung von Ars Electronica schafft Ars Electronica Solutions vernetzte Lösungen für interaktive Produkte und Dienstleistungen in den Geschäftsfeldern „Event & Show Design", „Brandlands & Exhibitions" und „Shop Experience". Diese Lösungen dienen primär der Informationsvermittlung und -visualisierung und können branchenübergreifend auf vielfältige Weise eingesetzt werden.

Bei der Realisierung von Projekten stützt sich Ars Electronica Solutions auf das umfassende Kompetenznetzwerk von Ars Electronica. So greifen wir bei der Realisierung von Projekten primär auf die Forschungs- und Projektergebnisse des Ars Electronica Futurelab zurück, das in Bereichen wie Media Art, Design, Interaktion, Virtual Reality und Echtzeitgrafik Pionierarbeit leistet. Aus Prototypen entstehen somit serienreife Produkte, womit im Kontext von Ars Electronica die Prozesskette von der Idee und Vision über

text of Ars Electronica, the process chain proceeds from idea and vision to prototype development to creation of an innovative product.
In bringing our projects to fruition, we take advantage of the latest communications trends and state-of-the-art technologies. This creative work always exemplifies Ars Electronica's media art approach, and lives up to Ars Electronica's claim to innovation excellence.

Event & Show Design
Our multifaceted portfolio in the Event & Show Design area encompasses real-time 3D, augmented reality, virtual environments & ambient design, as well as interface design for product presentations—for example, at trade shows—and the Spaxels, Ars Electronica's quadcopter swarm.

Brandlands & Exhibitions
Ars Electronica Solutions' Brandlands & Exhibitions professionals conceive and produce media-based exhibitions, interactive installations, and participative formats for a wide array of communications objectives and usage scenarios. In going about this, we design sites and experiences that provide visitors with exciting identification and participation possibilities, and that stay with them beyond the confines of the exhibition scenario.

Shop Experience
In configuring a shop experience, Ars Electronica Solutions focuses on smart deployment and integration of multimedia solutions and interactive installations that prompt customers' purchase decisions in retail settings. (Mobile) shop-/product experience and (media) art-in-store are the primary keys to successful, persuasive marketing.

http://www.aec.at/solutions

eine prototypische Entwicklung hin zum innovativen Produkt geschlossen wird.
Bei der Umsetzung der Projekte bedienen wir uns innovativer Kommunikationstrends und neuester Technologien. Dabei verfolgen wir in unserem Schaffen den medienkünstlerischen Ansatz und Innovationsanspruch von Ars Electronica.

Event & Show Design
Das vielseitige Portfolio dieses Geschäftsbereichs umfasst sowohl Real-Time-3D, Augmented Reality, Virtual Environments und Ambient Design als auch Interface Design zur Produktpräsentation – z. B. auf Messen – und den Ars-Electronica-Quadcopter-Schwarm „Spaxel".

Brandlands & Exhibitions
Ars Electronica Solutions „Brandlands & Exhibitions" konzipiert und realisiert medienbasierte Ausstellungen, interaktive Installationen und partizipative Formate für unterschiedliche Kommunikationszwecke und Einsatzszenarien. Dabei designen wir Orte und Erlebnisse, die den BesucherInnen spannende Identifikations- und Partizipationsmöglichkeiten bieten und sie auch über das Ausstellungsszenario hinaus begleiten.

Shop Experience
Mit „Shop Experience" fokussiert Ars Electronica Solutions auf die smarte Umsetzung und Integration von Multimedia-Lösungen und interaktiven Installationen zur Verkaufsförderung für den Handel. (Mobile) Shop-/ Product Experience und (Media) Art-in-Store bilden dabei die primären Säulen.

Text: Roland Reiter, Bernd Albl, Michael Badics

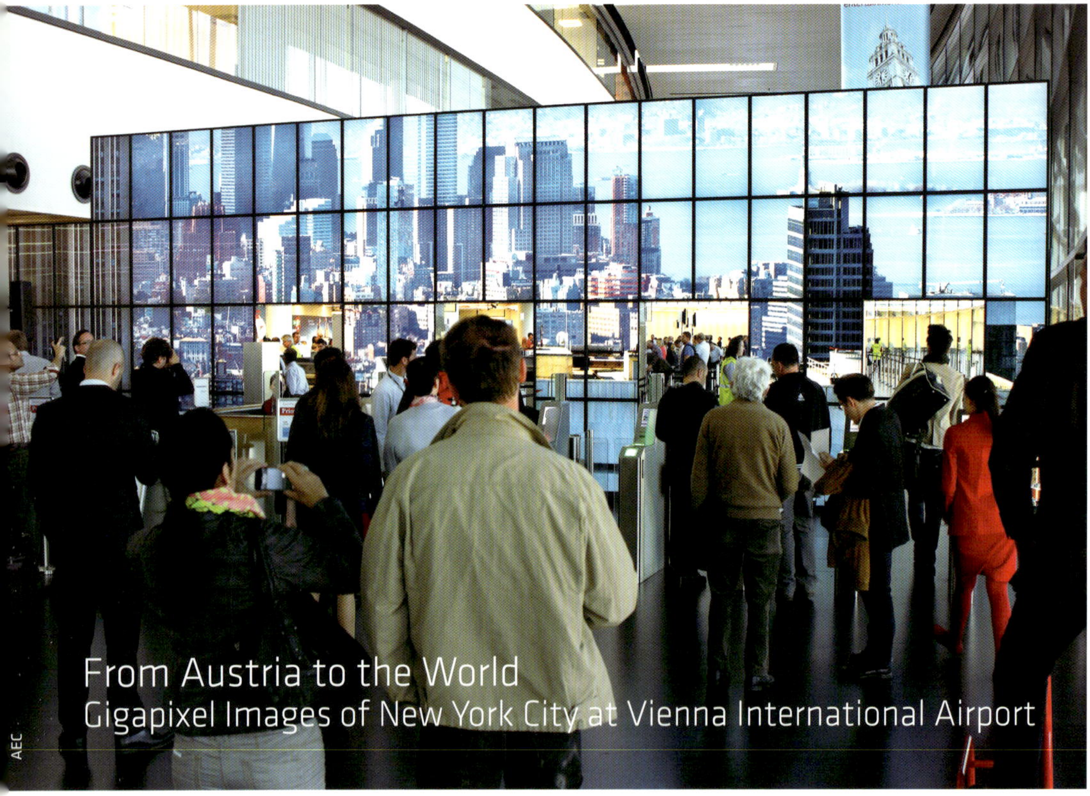

From Austria to the World
Gigapixel Images of New York City at Vienna International Airport

AEC

Five gigapixel images offer fascinating, high-definition views of New York City to passengers at Vienna International Airport (VIA). To present these extraordinary visuals to travelers in Check-In 3, the security area in VIA's newest terminal, 165 screens have been clustered into a 15-meter-wide, 9-meter-high display with a projection surface delivering a whopping 530 megapixels.

The shots of the Manhattan cityscape are the work of multiple-prizewinning Austrian photographer Lois Lammerhuber. The software that converts individual stills into an impressive pan through

Fünf Gigapixelbilder eröffnen den Passagieren am Flughafen Wien einen faszinierenden und detailreichen Blick auf New York City. Dabei fügen sich im Check-in 3, dem Securitybereich des neuen Flughafenterminals, 165 Screens zu einem gigantischen, 15 Meter breiten und 9 Meter hohen Display mit einer Anzeigefläche von mehr als 530 Megapixeln zusammen.

Die Aufnahmen der New Yorker Stadtlandschaft stammen vom vielfach ausgezeichneten österreichischen Fotografen Lois Lammerhuber, während die Software, die aus den einzelnen Bildern eine beeindruckende

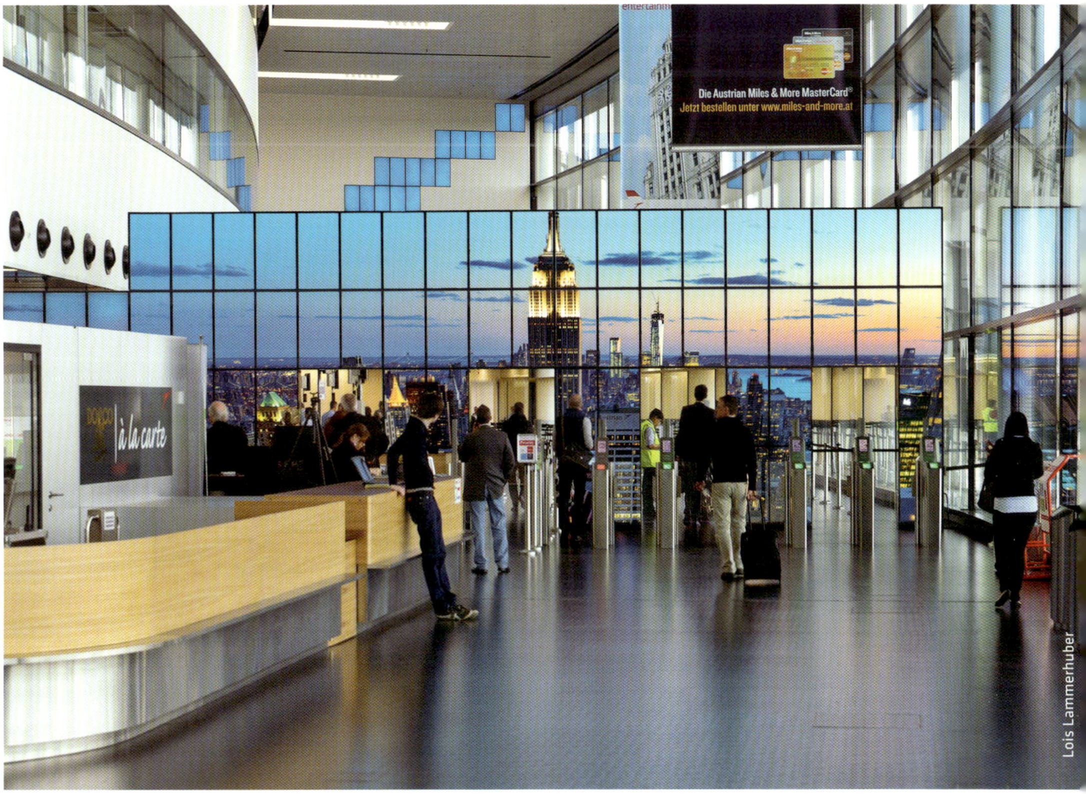

Lois Lammerhuber

the Big Apple was developed by Ars Electronica. It takes 60 servers with combined processing power of 720 gigahertz to break up the high-definition pictures into tiny fragments, distribute them to the servers, and thus achieve loss-free depiction of the gargantuan images. The result of this prototypical interplay of hardware & software components is not only an impressive sight to behold; it's also the latest outcome of a joint effort by Ars Electronica and VIA to showcase media art in public spaces.

Kamerafahrt durch Manhattan erstellt, von Ars Electronica entwickelt wurde. Sechzig Server und eine Prozessorleistung von 720 Gigahertz sind notwendig, um die hoch aufgelösten Bilder in winzig kleine Schnipsel zu zerlegen, sie auf die Server zu verteilen und dadurch eine verlustfreie Darstellung der riesigen Bilder zu erzielen. Das Resultat dieses prototypischen Zusammenspiels von Hard- und Softwarekomponenten ist nicht nur ein optisches Vergnügen, sondern auch jüngstes Beispiel für das gemeinsame Anliegen von Ars Electronica und dem Flughafen Wien, Medienkunst im öffentlichen Raum zugängig zu machen.

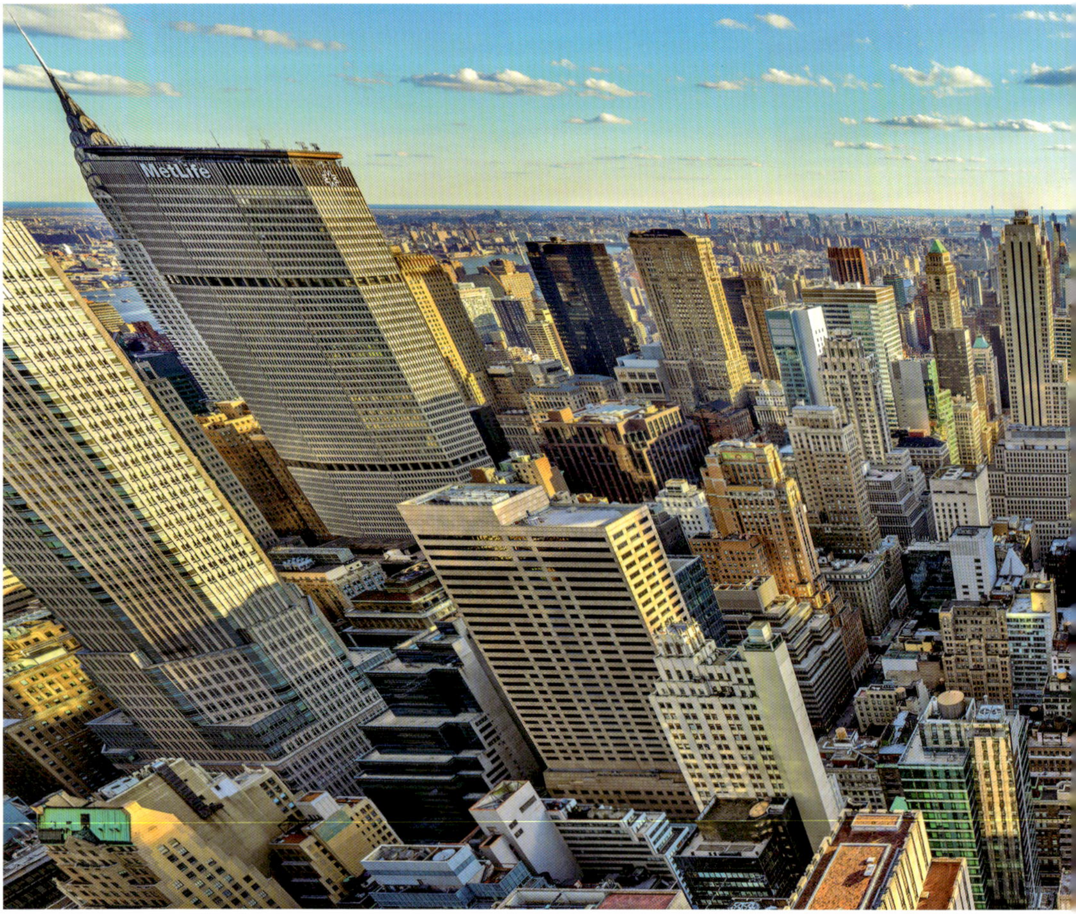

Lois Lammerhuber

Gigapixel image New York, Lois Lammerhuber

A window in the office suite of a bank on the 61st floor of Rockefeller Center seemed to me and my technical advisor, Martin Ackerl, to be the best location for this extreme photo shoot. Once the contractual arrangements to use the office were consummated, I got to work on "Heaven and Hell" by first having the pane of glass in the window removed. But then we made an extremely unpleasant discovery: warm air flowing in through the open window produced an optical shimmer that made it impossible to take crystal-clear images. Due to safety considerations and access restrictions, find-

Die beste Position für dieses Extrem-Fotoshooting schien mir und meinem Technical Advisor, Martin Ackerl, das Fenster eines Bankhauses im 61. Stockwerk des Rockefeller Center zu sein. Nachdem der Standort vertraglich vereinbart wurde, setzte ich Himmel und Hölle in Bewegung, um die Scheibe des Fensters ausbauen zu lassen. Wir mussten dann allerdings feststellen, dass die aus dem Fenster strömende warme Luft ein optisches Flirren erzeugte, das gestochen scharfe Fotos unmöglich machte. Sicherheitsbedenken und Zutrittsbeschränkungen machten eine neue Standortwahl zu einer logistisch mindestens ebenso

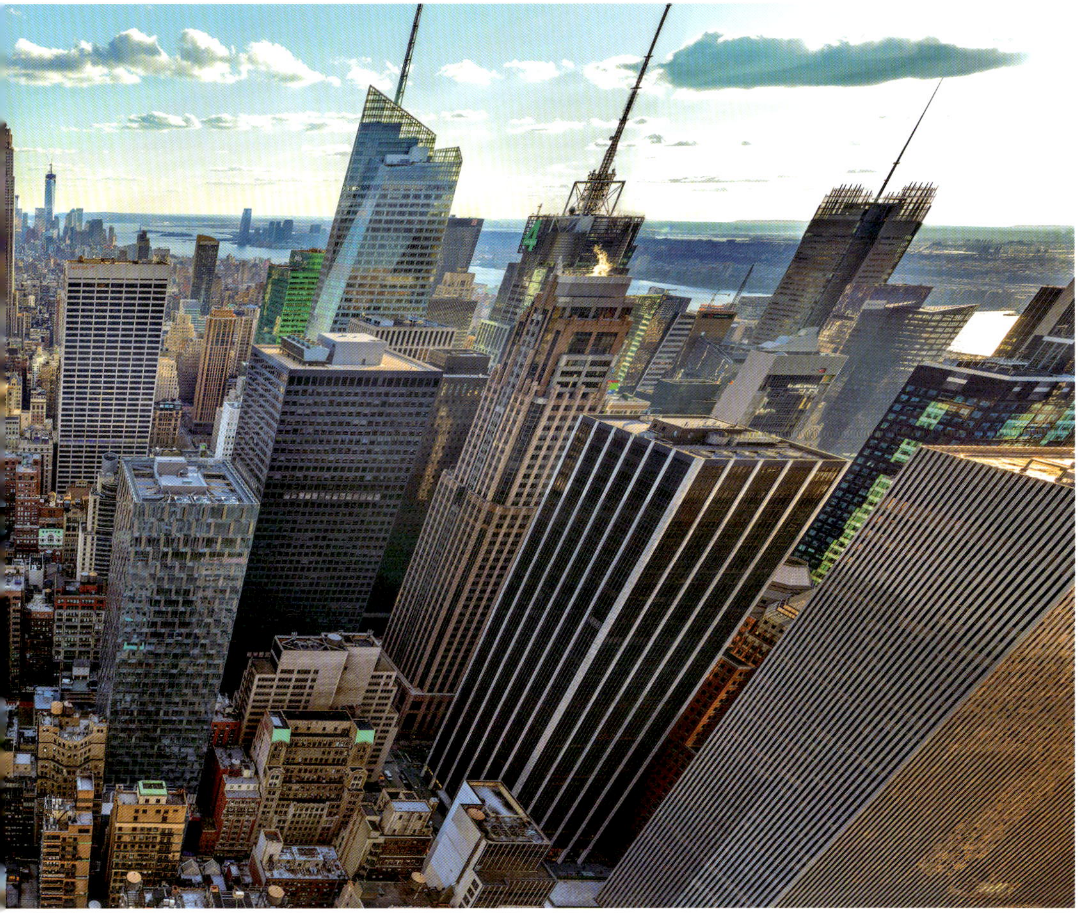

ing a new location became a logistical challenge no less daunting than the timing of the weather, the responsibility of Michael Staudinger, director of Austria's National Weather Service in Vienna. It took five months to find the perfect day! The pictures were finally taken from a wind-protected balcony on the same floor. We worked for two days, taking approximately 2,600 photographs totaling 62 gigabytes of data. Post-processing the images took a whole week, and another 22 hours of computing time was required to assemble the individual shots into gigapixel images.

großen Herausforderung wie das Wetter-Timing, das in den Händen von Michael Staudinger, dem Direktor der ZAMG in Wien, lag. Es dauerte fast fünf Monate, bis der ideale Tag gefunden war. Aufgenommen wurden die Bilder dann auf einem windgeschützten Balkon desselben Stockwerks. Zwei Tage lang arbeiteten wir an den Bildern, für die wir rund 2.600 Fotos machten, das sind 62 Gigabyte Daten. Die Nachbearbeitung der Bilder nahm eine ganze Woche, die reine Rechenzeit, um die einzelnen Bilder zu Gigapixelbildern zusammenzubauen, nochmals 22 Stunden in Anspruch.

Text: Lois Lammerhuber

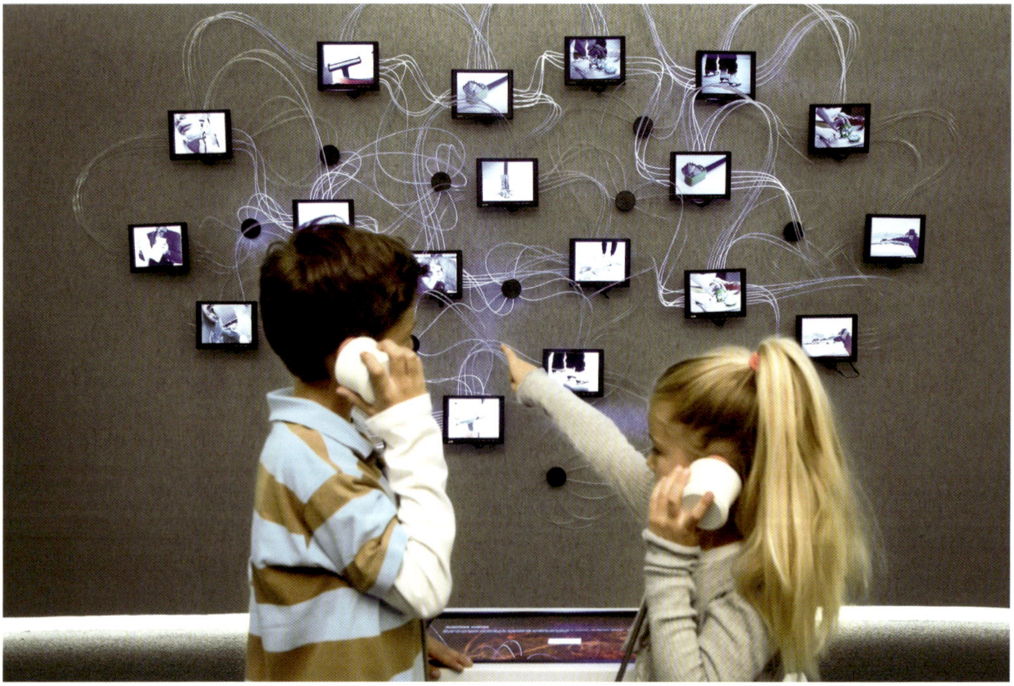

MED-EL
Audioversum

For MED-EL, a Tyrol-based manufacturer of medical electronic devices, Ars Electronica conceived and produced the *Audioversum* in Innsbruck. This interactive exhibition accommodated by a 1,000-m² space offers visitors uncommon insights on the subject of hearing. Installations developed especially for this exhibition and its customized Soundlab provide visitors with a fun, creative way to obtain new perspectives on acoustic perception. For instance, they can free virtual birds in Binaural Game, play melodies on large-scale mockups of hair cells, and create a Soundogramm, an audio communiqué featuring shadow pictures. The interactive informational level and diversified didactic approach effectively get across interesting material well worth knowing about the world of hearing.

Für die Firma MED-EL Elektromedizinische Geräte Gesellschaft m.b.H. konzipierte und realisierte Ars Electronica in Innsbruck die interaktive Ausstellung *Audioversum*, die auf über 1.000 Quadratmetern ungewöhnliche Einblicke in das Thema Hören bietet. Die eigens für diese Ausstellung entwickelten Installationen und das Soundlab eröffnen den BesucherInnen auf spielerisch-kreative Weise neue Perspektiven auf die akustische Wahrnehmung. So können die BesucherInnen etwa im „Binauralen Spiel" virtuelle Vögel befreien, auf überdimensionalen Haarzellen Melodien spielen oder ein „Soundogramm" – eine Audiobotschaft mit Silhouettenbild – erstellen. Die interaktive Informationsebene und vielfältigen didaktischen Programme vermitteln dabei Wissenswertes und Spannendes aus der Welt des Hörens.

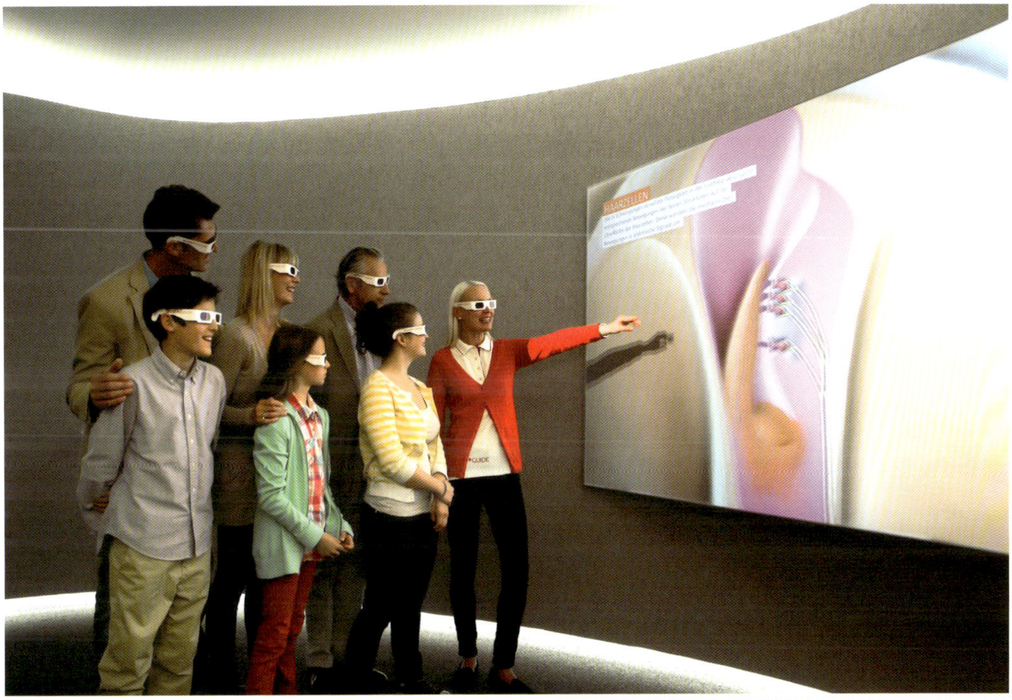

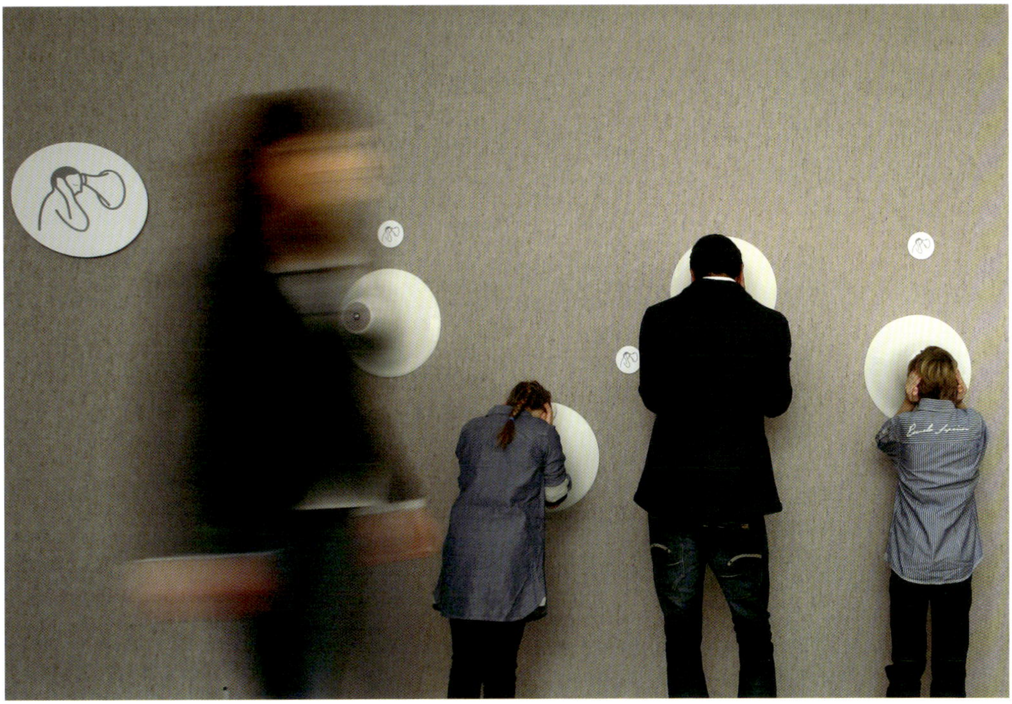

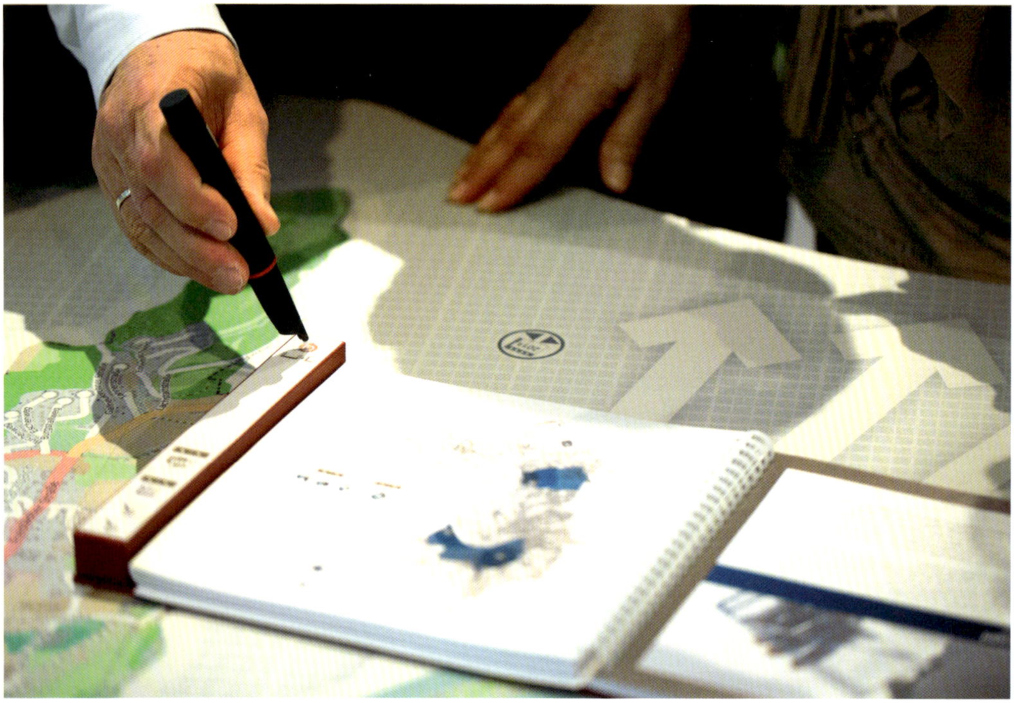

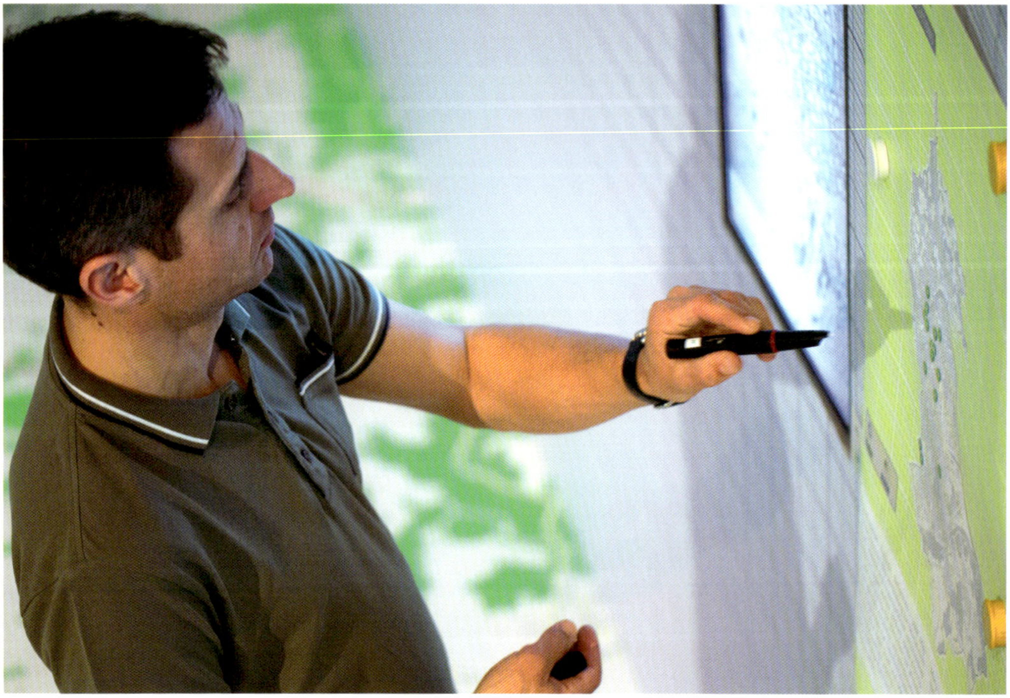

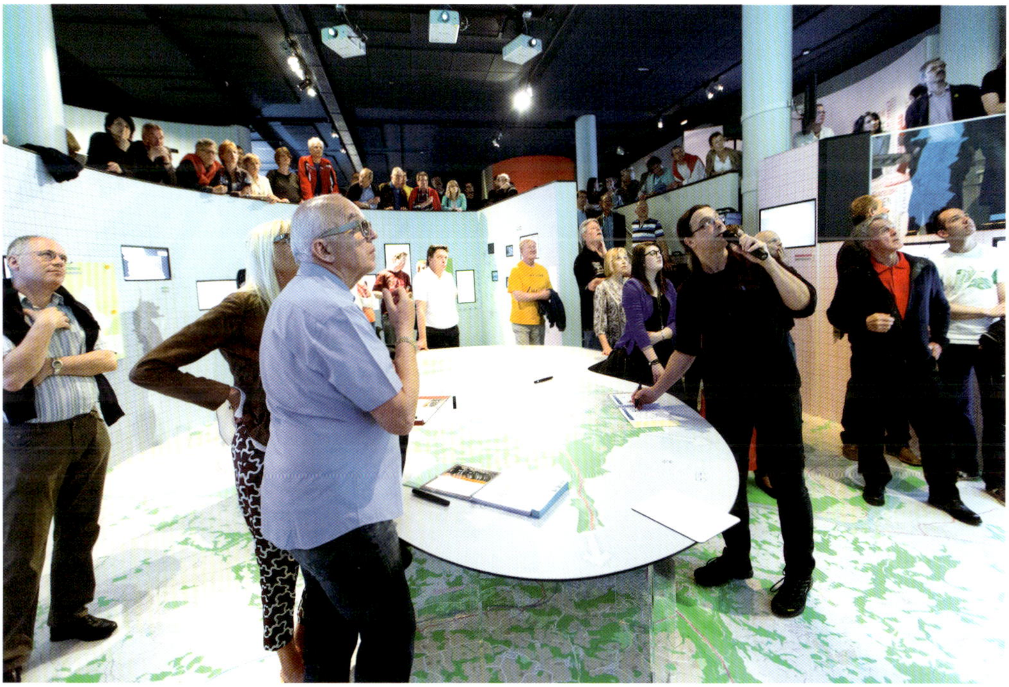

Tom Mesic

GeoPulse – Ars Electronica Center

GeoPulse enables visitors of the Ars Electronica Center to interactively explore Linz and other cities of the world via a futuristic simulation & visualization tool. A digital pen is the users' key to this "walk-through databank," where the smart stylus makes for a convenient, effective way to interact with books, maps, wall surfaces and other objects. The highly diverse information about the particular city they access thereby is displayed on screens in the installation space.

With its user-friendly mode of interaction, this unique spatial experience extends a cordial invitation to visually, intuitively deal with complex information and the implications buried within the data. This makes for a fun way to compare essential facts about local and global processes, and to consider interrelationships within these metro areas from new perspectives. Photos, videos, texts, maps, infographics, statistics and other data about a wide array of urban topics are made available.

Mit *GeoPulse* ist es den BesucherInnen des Ars Electronica Center möglich, Linz und andere Städte der Welt interaktiv über ein zukunftsweisendes Simulations- und Visualisierungswerkzeug zu erkunden. Mithilfe eines digitalen Stifts betreten die BesucherInnen diese „begehbare Datenbank" und tippen auf Buchseiten, Stadtpläne, Wandoberflächen und andere Objekte. Dadurch rufen sie eine Vielfalt an Informationen zur jeweiligen Stadt ab, die auf Screens dargestellt werden.

Mit seiner einfachen Interaktion lädt dieser einzigartige Erlebnisraum ein, verborgene und komplexe Informationen verschiedenster Städte visuell und intuitiv zu erfahren. Auf spielerische Weise kann man wissenswerte Fakten zu lokalen und globalen Prozessen vergleichen und Zusammenhänge in den Städten aus neuen Perspektiven erfahren. Bilder, Videos, Texte, Karten, Infografiken, Statistiken und andere Daten zu den unterschiedlichsten urbanen Themen stehen zur Verfügung.

Musiktheater Linz

Interactive Installations at Linz's Musiktheater

For Linz's new music theater, Ars Electronica created a series of interactive installations set up in the facility's Lobby. The *MusiktheaterFries*, *SpielTisch*, *HörBar* and *CineBox* give visitors a comprehensive glimpse of the diverse genres that make up the world of music theater, while also offering a convenient way to access information about current productions. The *MusiktheaterFries* blends the narrative tradition of historical tapestries with the immersive world of digital media: The visitor's "aura" appears on the frieze itself as a glimmering apparition and brings to life prominent protagonists from music history on the 15-meter-long fabric. Users can get more in-depth info on these subjects at the *SpielTisch*. The *HörBar* and *CineBox* provide details about current productions and musicians.

Für das neue Musiktheater Linz realisierte Ars Electronica eine Reihe von interaktiven Installationen im KlangFoyer. Mit dem *MusiktheaterFries*, dem *SpielTisch*, der *HörBar* und der *CineBox* wird den BesucherInnen ein umfassender Einblick in die Vielfalt von Genres aus der Welt des Musiktheaters ermöglicht. Zudem werden damit Informationen zu aktuellen Produktionen auf spielerische Weise zugänglich gemacht. Dabei verschmilzt auf dem *MusiktheaterFries* die Erzähltradition historischer Wandteppiche mit der immersiven Welt digitaler Medien: Die „Aura" der BesucherInnen erscheint als funkelnder Schein auf dem Fries und erweckt ProtagonistInnen aus der Musikgeschichte auf dem fünfzehn Meter langen Gewebe zum Leben. Am *SpielTisch* können die BesucherInnen weiter in diese Themenbereiche eintauchen, während *HörBar* und *CineBox* Informationen zu den aktuellen Inszenierungen und MusikerInnen vermitteln.

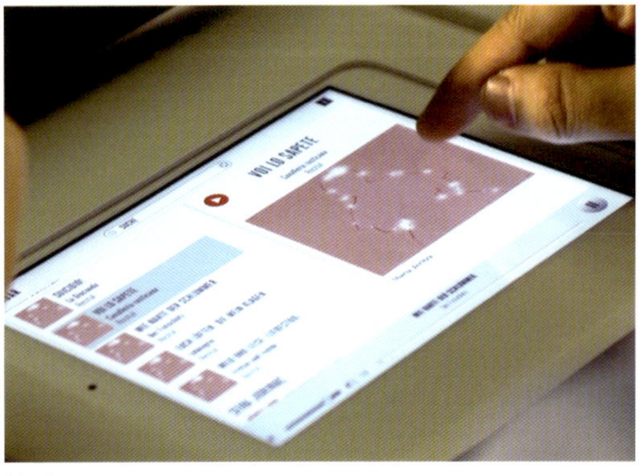

AEC, Martina Hechenberger

HörBar

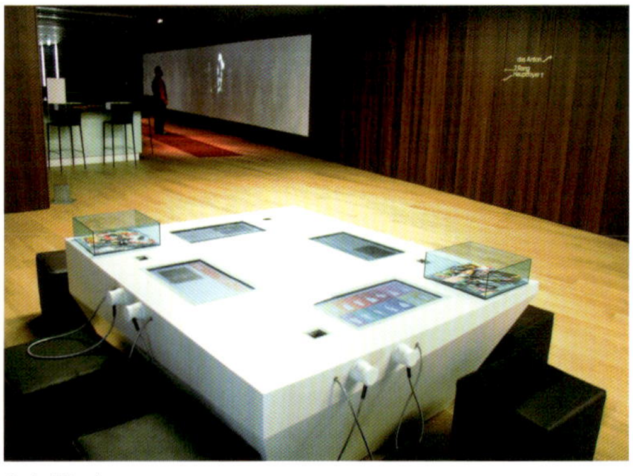

AEC, Roland Reiter

SpielTisch

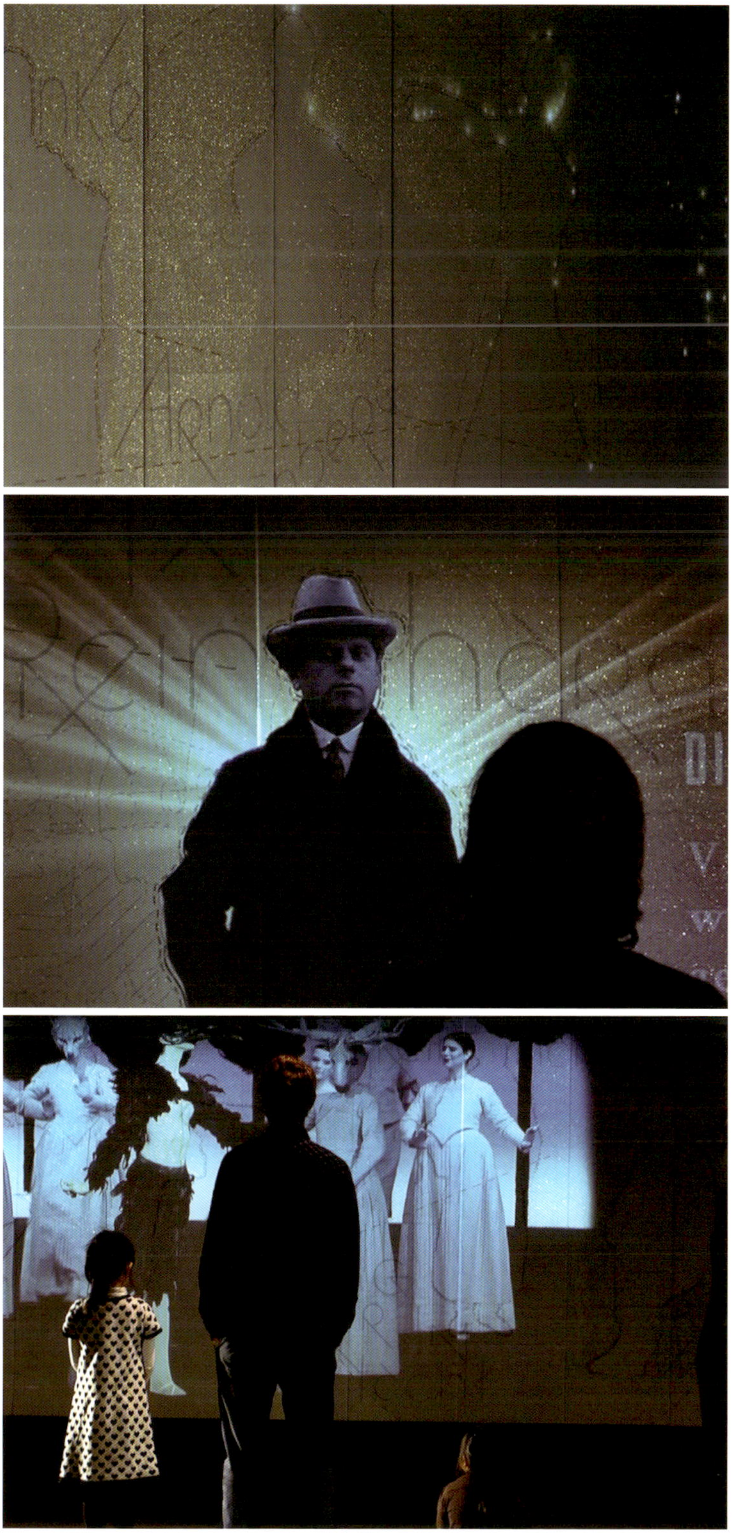

AEC, Martina Hechenberger

MusiktheaterFries

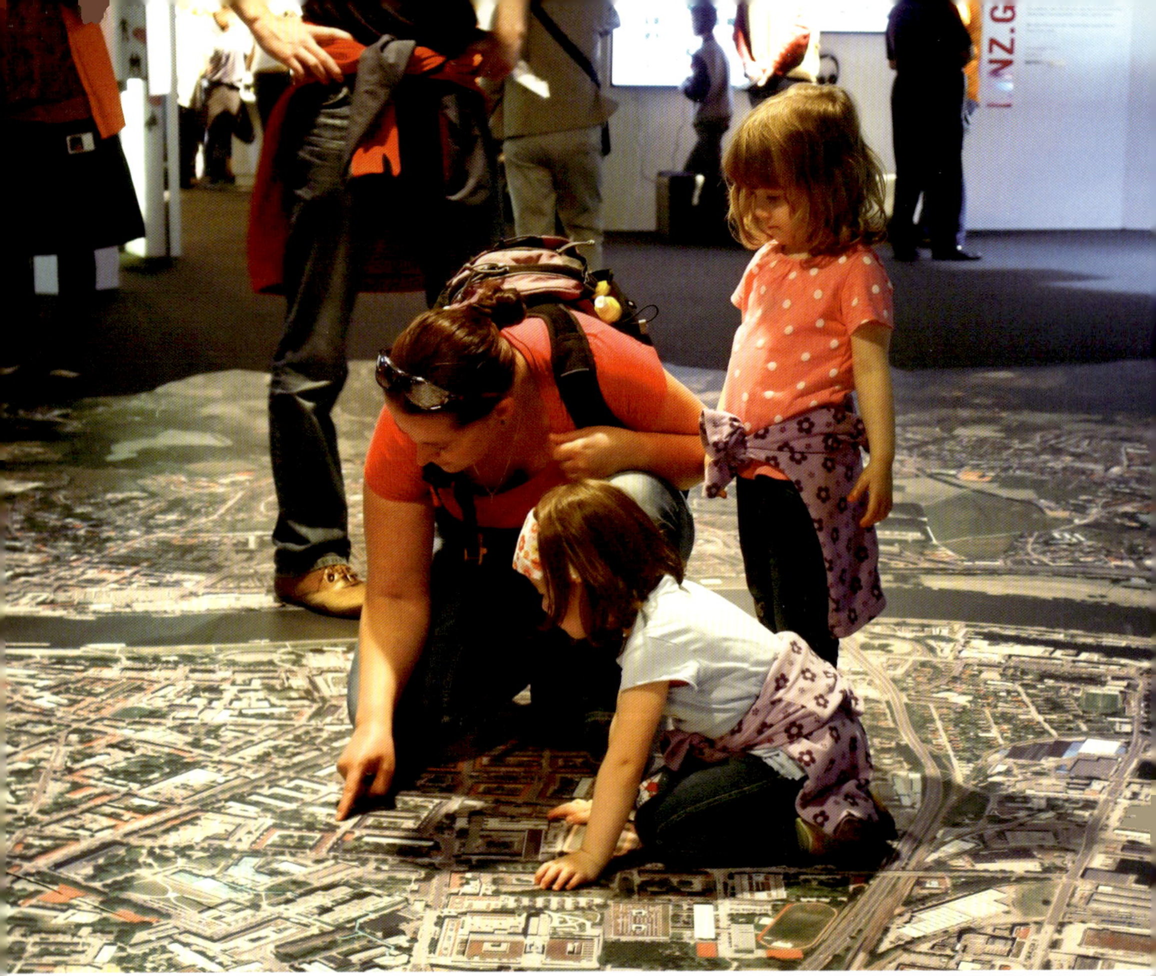

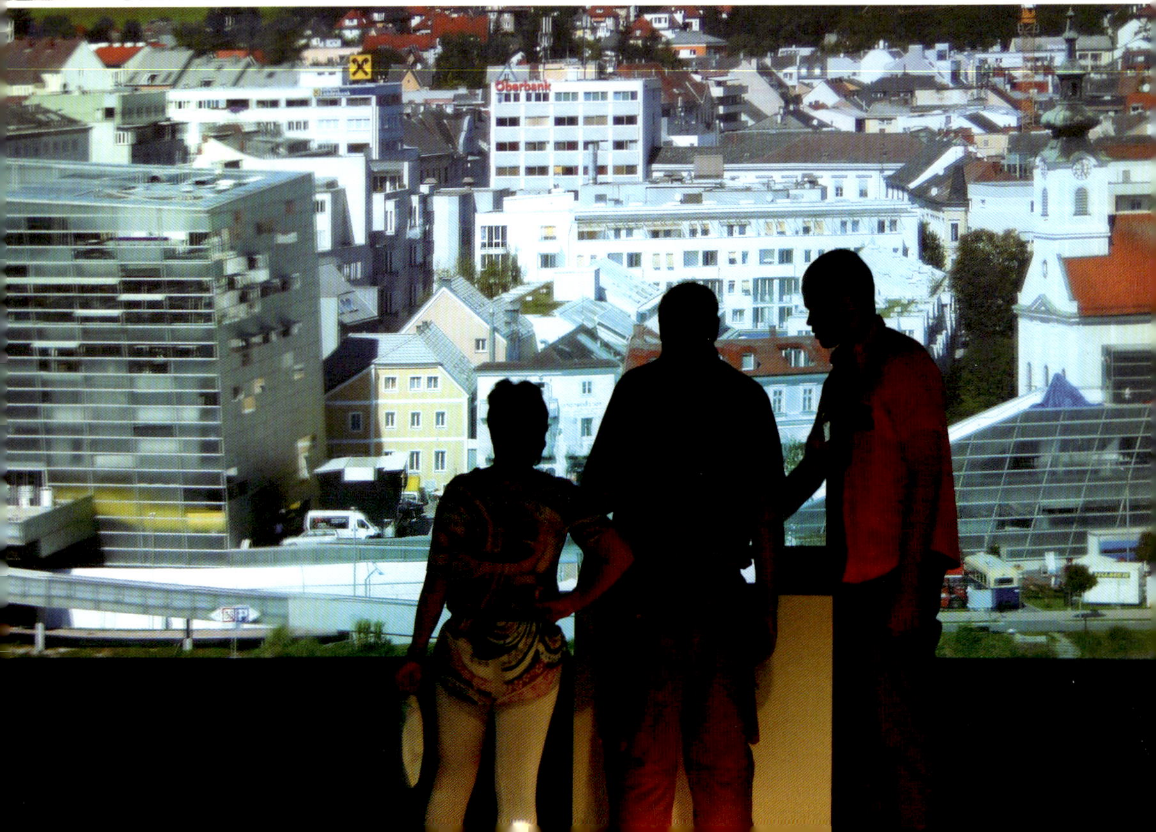
Oberbank

Stadt Linz

Linz verändert 2013

The *Linz verändert* (Linz Changes) exhibition tent set up at the fair held semiannually in Linz's Urfahr neighborhood is a project of Unternehmensgruppe Stadt Linz, the city's municipal services provider. Its 12 interactive installations present interesting and important information about Upper Austria's capital city. This project developed by Ars Electronica invites visitors to learn little-known facts about their immediate environment in a most entertaining way. At *We Are Linz* visitors combine their own photo segments—head, trunk, legs—with those of other visitors. "Views" is an interactive table that displays historical images of Linz and juxtaposes each one to its contemporary counterpart. In addition to the most popular attractions from previous *Linz verändert* shows such as Finger Marathon, SimLinz and Energy Ticket, the new installations focus on Linz as a place to enjoy music—for instance, at the brand new Musiktheater—and showcase the city's tremendous cultural diversity.

Das Ausstellungszelt *Linz verändert* auf dem Gelände des Urfahraner Jahrmarktes in Linz ist ein Projekt der Unternehmensgruppe Stadt Linz. Zwölf interaktive Stationen präsentieren hier Verblüffendes und Wissenswertes aus der und über die Landeshauptstadt. Die von Ars Electronica entwickelten Installationen laden die BesucherInnen ein, erstaunliche Fakten über ihren unmittelbaren Lebensraum auf spielerische und unterhaltende Weise zu erfahren: Bei *Wir sind Linz* lassen sich Aufnahmen von BesucherInnen kombinieren, während der interaktive Tisch *Ansichten* historische Aufnahmen aus Linz aktuellen Bildern gegenüberstellt. Zusätzlich zu beliebten Stationen aus vergangenen Jahren, wie z. B. *Finger Marathon, SimLinz* und *Energie Ticket,* fokussieren die neuen Installationen *Linz als Kulturstadt* und *Linz macht Musik* auf die Kulturstadt Linz – ein Fokus, der etwa der Eröffnung des Linzer Musiktheaters und der kulturellen Vielfalt in Linz Rechnung trägt.

AEL, Martin Hieslmair

AEC, Stephan Pointner

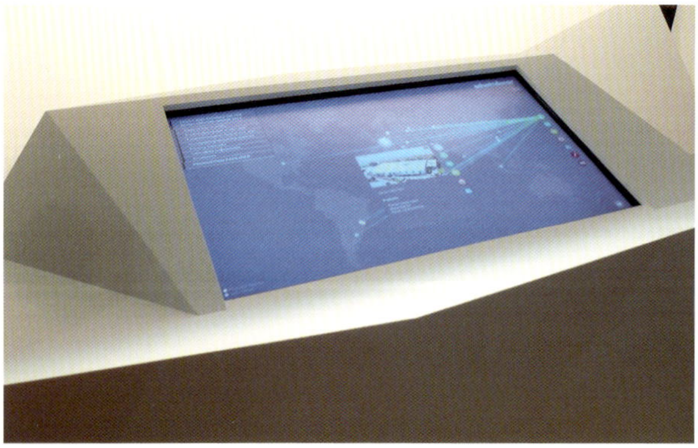

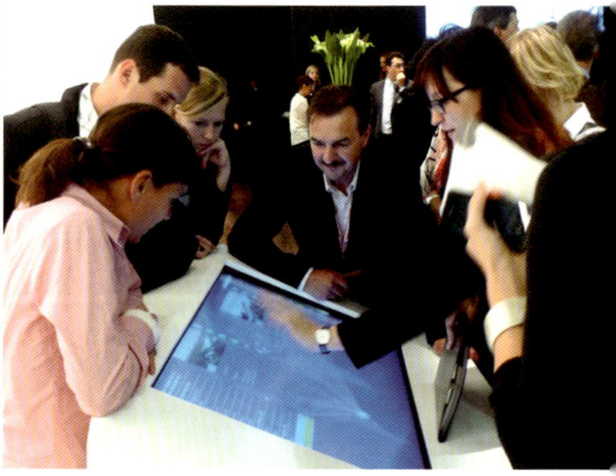

Schattdecor

Digital World by Schattdecor

Digital World by Schattdecor is an interactive presentation tool developed for that company's stand at interzum 2013 in Cologne. Visitors to the world's largest trade show for suppliers to the furniture and interior finishing industry encountered a convenient way to get acquainted with Schattdecor's products and services via multitouch technology and to locate their nearest branch office. With this presentation tool, multiple users are able to access the interactive content simultaneously.

Für die Präsentation von Schattdecor auf der interzum 2013 in Köln wurde ein interaktives Präsentationstool entwickelt, das den MessebesucherInnen die *Digital World by Schattdecor* nahe brachte. Die BesucherInnen waren auf der weltweit größten Messe der Möbelzulieferindustrie dazu eingeladen, die digitalen Kompetenzen des Unternehmens via Multitouch-Technologie zu erforschen, Standorte zu entdecken und Service- und Produktkompetenzen standortbezogen abzurufen. Das Präsentationstool ermöglichte es dabei mehreren Usern gleichzeitig, sich mit den interaktiven Inhalten auseinanderzusetzen.

Österreich Werbung
The atb experience

For Austria's national inbound tourism organization, Ars Electronica Solutions produced the *atb experience*—six terminals displaying an interactive brochure that provides users with access to statistics, photos and real-time data related to tourism in Austria's nine provinces. In the brochures, visitors can browse maps and use an Anoto pen to select towns and regions about which they'd like to view detailed tourism-related information. The requested info promptly appears on screen.
A spinoff of *GeoPulse*, the *atb experience* is the first project designed by Ars Electronica Solutions in which a folder containing wide-ranging geo-referenced content is accessed by means of a digital stylus. Among the highlights are 59 Flash animation sequences delivering the key facts about tourism in Austria—e.g. number of overnight stays, energy usage and water supply. The attractively designed brochure was also a popular give-away that, via QR code, enabled visitors to get additional information about the individual tourism-related topics on the Österreich Werbung website.

Für die *atb experience* der Österreich Werbung realisierte Ars Electronica Solutions sechs Terminals, die den BesucherInnen mithilfe einer interaktiven Broschüre Statistiken, Bilder und Real-Time-Daten zum Tourismus in den österreichischen Bundesländern zugängig machen. Die BesucherInnen wählen in der Broschüre mit einem Anoto-Stift Orte, Bundesländer oder Bezirke auf Landkarten aus, zu denen detaillierte tourismusbezogene Daten abgerufen werden können. Die Ausgabe der gewünschten Informationen erfolgt auf Screens.
Basierend auf *GeoPulse* von Ars Electronica Solutions wurde somit erstmals ein Folder entworfen, der via Digitalstift umfassende georeferenzierte Inhalte digital abrufbar macht. Dabei liefern u. a. 59 Flash-Animationen verblüffende Fakten zum Tourismus in Österreich, wie etwa zur Anzahl der Übernachtungen, zum Energieverbrauch und zur Wasserversorgung. Die ansprechend gestaltete Broschüre war auch ein beliebtes Give-Away, das es den BesucherInnen via QR-Code ermöglichte, zusätzliche Informationen zu den einzelnen Tourismus-Themen auf der Website der Österreich Werbung abzurufen.

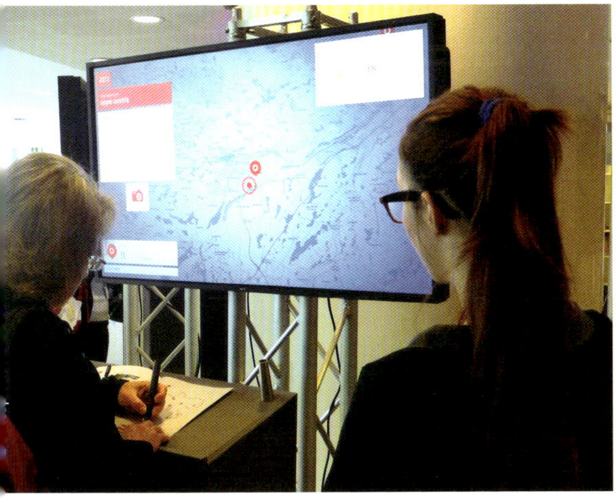

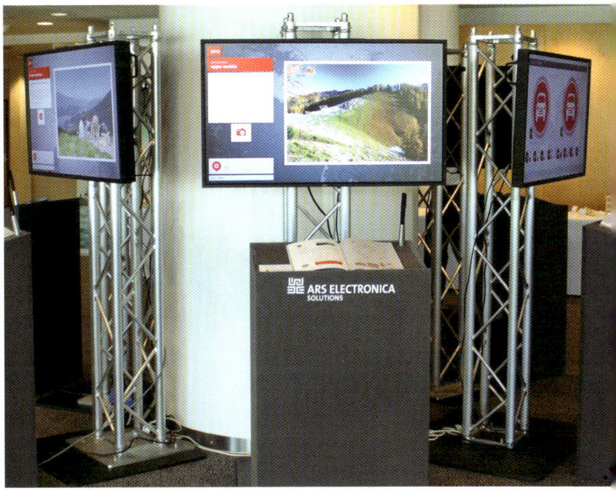

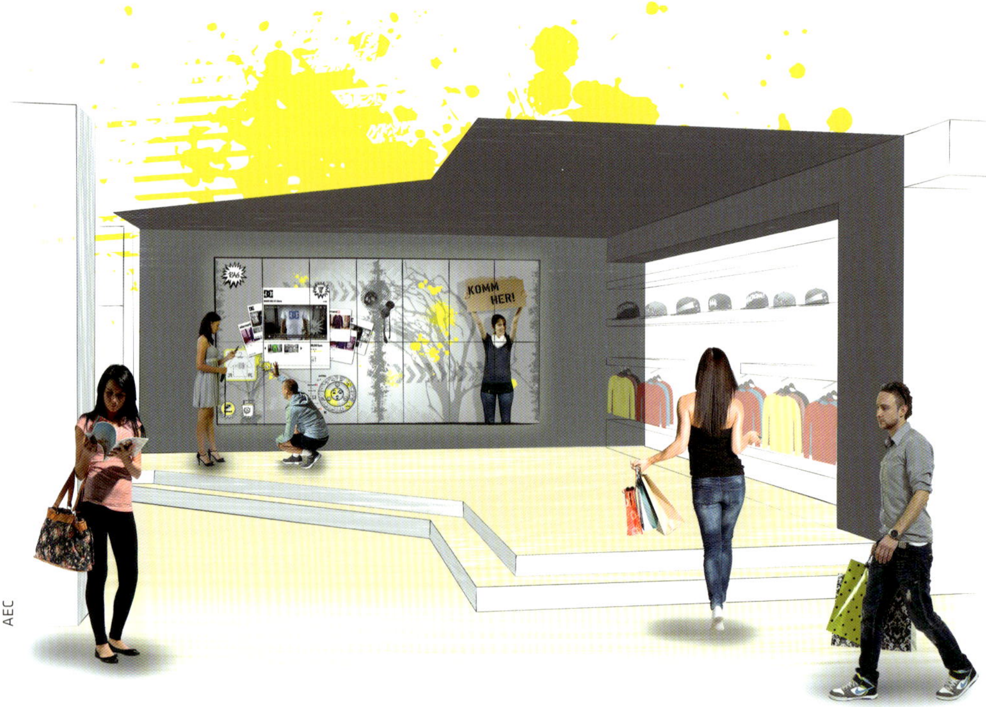

AEC

Umdasch Shopfitting, RAG

RAG Wall

Prototype of a new shop format in a world of digital retailing

In cooperation with Umdasch Shopfitting, Europe's leading shop design firm, fashion retailer RAG and Samsung, Ars Electronica Solutions developed an interactive shopping wall that lets customers browse RAG's product portfolio by interacting with the Wall via RFID code on physical objects.
As an up-to-date interface at the point of sale (POS) for in-store customers as well as online shoppers, the Wall combines the haptic product experience with the possibilities of digital product information and online features. The utilization concept encompasses multiple levels (advertising & promotion, online marketing in-store), whereby interaction is via touch and the actual merchandise. The Wall allows for presentation of RAG's entire product line at the POS. Thus, in these times of digital retailing, it creates an innovative experiential space for customers at the POS.

Gemeinsam mit Umdasch Shopfitting – Europas führendem Unternehmen im Bereich Ladenbau –, dem Fashion-Einzelhändler RAG und dem Technologieunternehmen Samsung entwickelte Ars Electronica Solutions eine interaktive Shopping Wall, die es den KundInnen ermöglicht, das Produktportfolio der Firma RAG zu erkunden, indem sie über physische Objekte via RFID-Code mit der Wand interagieren.
Als zeitgemäßes Interface am Point of Sale (POS) für Kunden des stationären Handels, aber auch für Online-Shopper verknüpft sie das haptische Produkterlebnis mit den Möglichkeiten der digitalen Produktinformation und Online-Funktionalitäten. Das Nutzungskonzept umfasst mehrere Ebenen (Werbung/Promotion, Online-Marketing im Geschäft), wobei über Touch und die echte Ware interagiert wird: Die RAG-Wall ermöglicht die Präsentation des gesamten Warensortiments am POS und schafft damit in Zeiten der digitalen Konsumwelt einen neuartigen Erlebnisraum für Kunden am POS.

Liebherr

Slide Presenter

Liebherr's compact L 506 earthmover made its public debut at bauma 2013, the world's largest trade show. With the *Slide Presenter*, visitors to their booth could access position-related information about the L 506 and via touchscreen get details in five different languages. This installation has lots of advantages: robust construction, simple to use, works outdoors and features a barrier-free design. Accessing and viewing the earthmover are made possible by the seepage pit principle and an in-ground foundation.

Liebherr stellte der breiten Öffentlichkeit mit dem Compactlader L 506 auf der bauma 2013, der weltweit größten Messe, eine Neuheit im Segment der Radlader vor.

Mit dem *Slide Presenter* können BesucherInnen durch Verschieben positionsbezogene Informationen zum Gerät und mittels Touch Detailinformationen in fünf Sprachen abrufen. Neben der robusten Bauweise, der einfachen Bedienung und der Outdoorfähigkeit zeichnet die Installation auch die barrierefreie Bauweise aus. Der Zutritt und die Sicht zum Gerät werden durch ein Sickerschacht-Prinzip und ein Fundament im Erdreich ermöglicht.

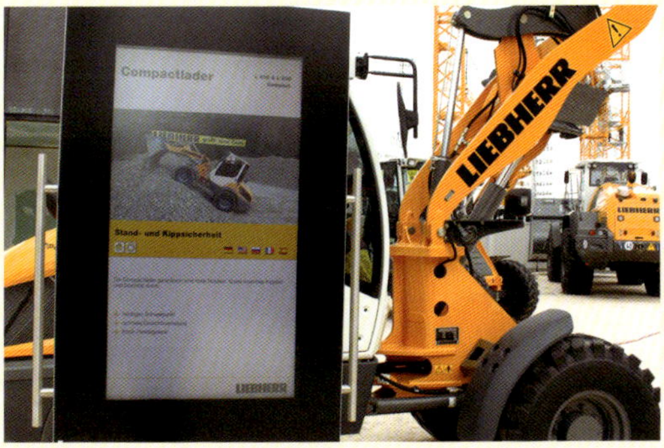

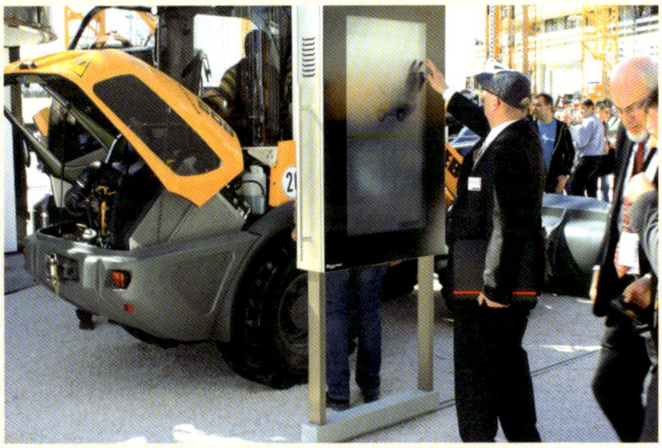

AEC, Stephan Pointner

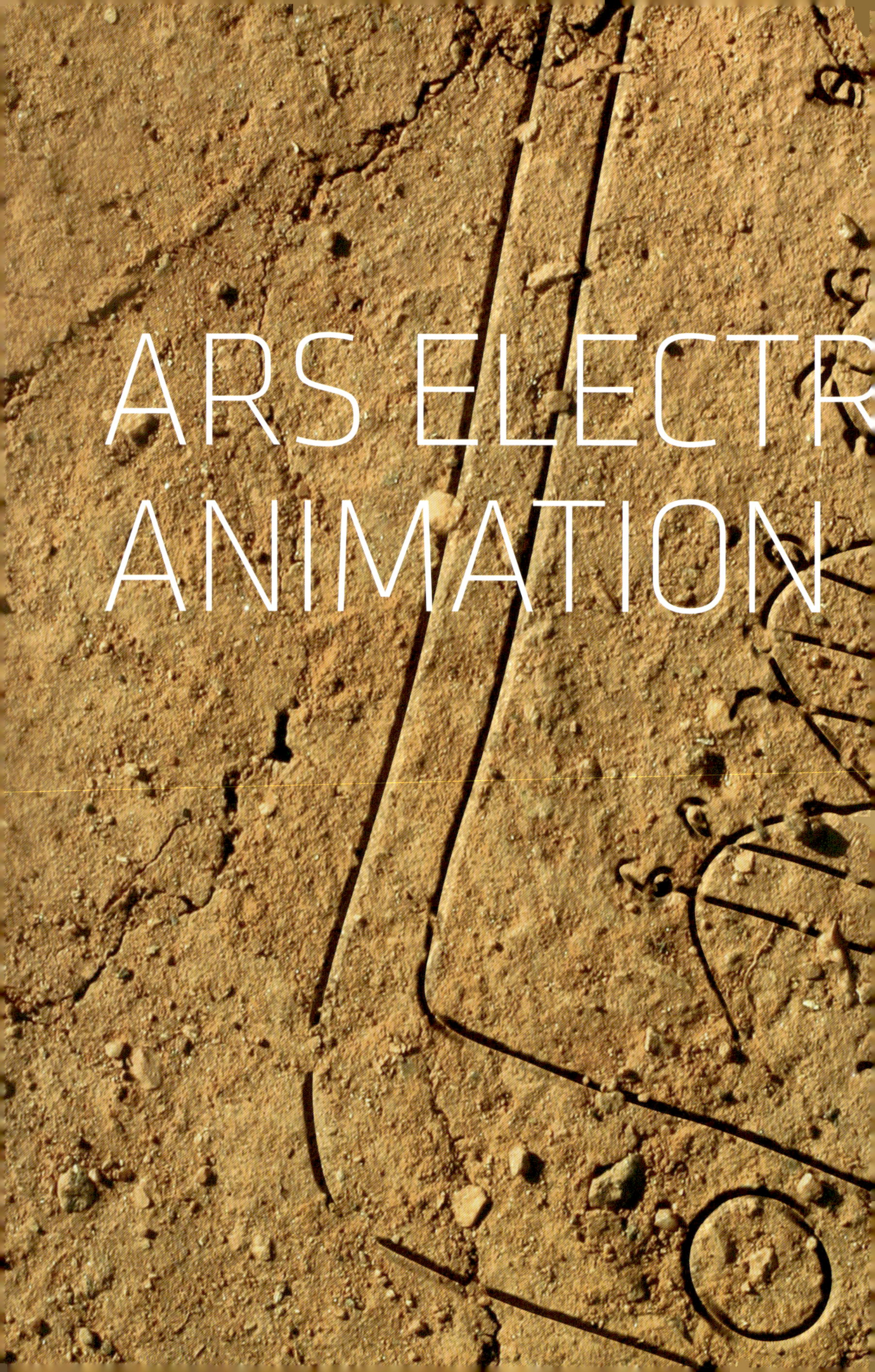
ARS ELECTR
ANIMATION

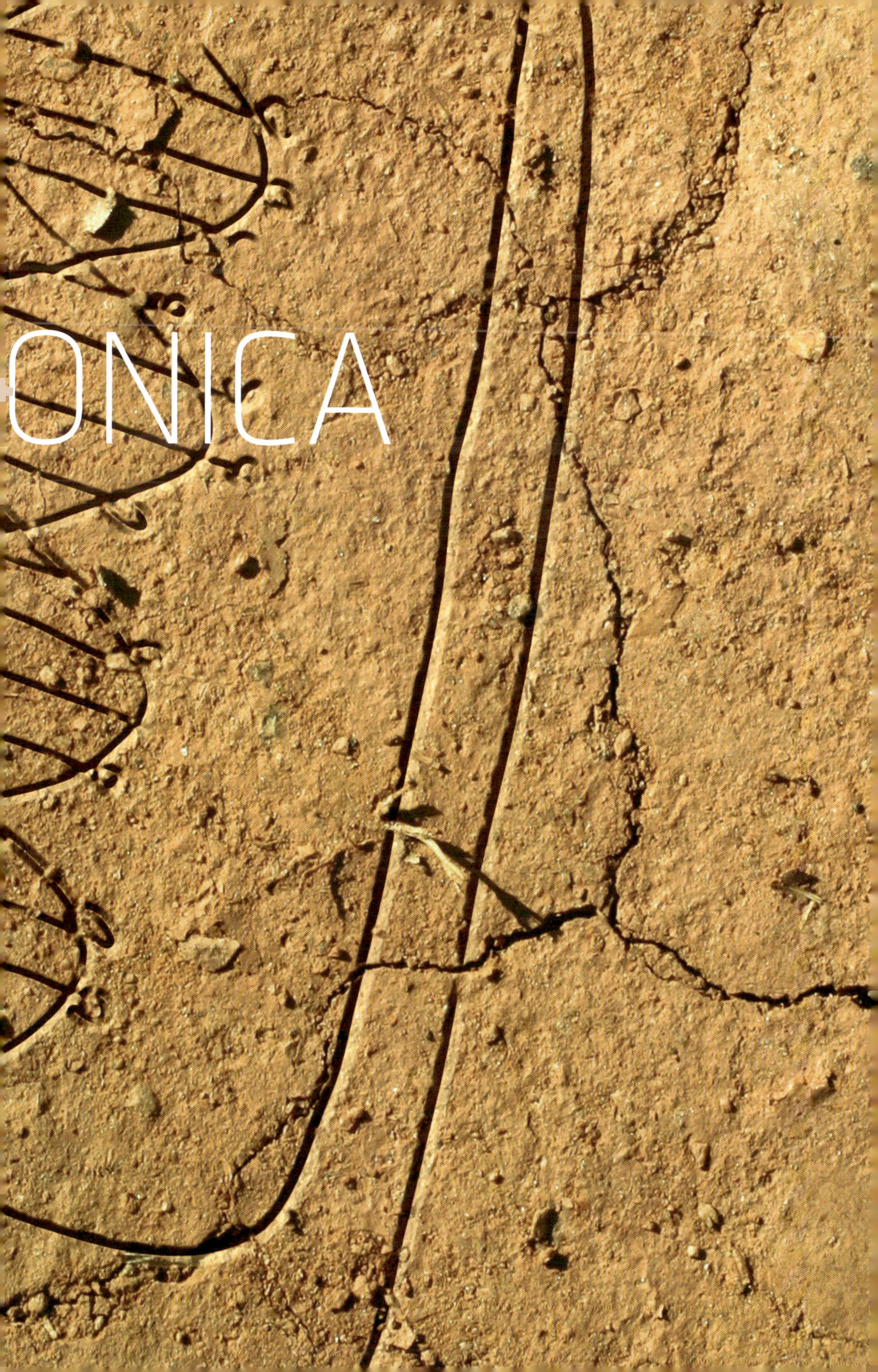
ONICA

Jürgen Hagler

Expanded Digital Animation

Mapping an Unlimited Landscape

The Prix Ars Electronica, one of the first international competitions for digital media art, has continued to document the genealogy of Digital Animation with its category "Computer Animation/Film/VFX" since the mid 1980s. This category has featured tech demos, short films produced with tools developed by their creators, artistic avant-garde animations, commercial films, visual effects works, and narrative character animations. In the early 1990s, the Computer Animation category was expanded to include Visual Effects, and in the early years of the new millennium, Film. Examining the most recent winners reveals a wide range of media forms: hybrid stop-motion animations, found-footage films, generative and interactive works, installations in an exhibition context and building façade projections.

This propensity for Computer Animation to expand and merge with other fields is unmistakable. On the one hand, there is an apparent danger for this field to develop into an interdisciplinary fringe domain. On the other, the very fact that it has continually expanded offers substantial potential for a new orientation. Is the field of Computer Animation experiencing an existential crisis? Or is the context of an unlimited field actually an essential core element?

Der Prix Ars Electronica, einer der wichtigsten Wettbewerbe für digitale Medienkunst, dokumentiert anhand der Kategorie „Computer Animation / Film / VFX" anschaulich die Genealogie der digitalen Animation: Seit Mitte der 1980er Jahre wurden Tech-Demos, Kurzfilme mit eigens entwickelten Werkzeugen, künstlerisch-avantgardistische Animationen, kommerzielle Filme, Visual-Effects-Arbeiten sowie narrative Charakteranimationen ausgezeichnet. Anfang der 1990er Jahre wurde die Kategorie „Computeranimation" durch „Visuelle Effekte" erweitert und Anfang 2000 durch den Zusatz Film „ergänzt". Ein Blick auf die letzten Preisträger zeigt eine breite Palette an Erscheinungsformen: hybride Stop-Motion-Animationen, Found-Footage-Filme, generative und interaktive Arbeiten, Installationen im Ausstellungskontext und Fassadenprojektionen.

Die Auflösung der Grenzen des Genre Computeranimation sind unverkennbar. Einerseits läuft sie damit Gefahr, sich in einem interdisziplinären Grenzgebiet zu verlaufen. Andererseits birgt diese Erweiterung Möglichkeiten für eine Neuorientierung. Steckt die Computeranimation also in einer Sinnkrise? Oder macht diese permanente Verortung in einem unlimitierten Grenzgebiet ihr eigentliches Wesen aus?

Digitale Animation durchdringt, einerseits als solche erkennbar und andererseits als Simulation

Digital Animation has become a pervasive element in our daily lives, at times visibly recognizable as a simulation and at others almost indistinguishable from real-world content. Moving images created with computer technology constitute a very diverse spectrum, particularly in hybrid forms, and are products of a highly interdisciplinary collaboration of individuals from the worlds of industry, research, art and science. In this unlimited domain, animation is ubiquitous and yet, simultaneously, undifferentiated. To even attempt to define what Digital Animation is, it becomes necessary to more closely examine this dynamic and constantly expanding field.
A symposium entitled *Expanded Digital Animation: Mapping an Unlimited Landscape* will be held as part of the Ars Electronica 2013. A collaboration between the Hagenberg Campus of the University of Applied Sciences Upper Austria, the Ars Electronica Festival and LENTOS Kunstmuseum, it aims to address the transgression of borders, hybrid forms and fringe areas within the field of Computer Animation.

Speakers: Memo Akten, Suzanne Buchan, Joreg Dissel, John Gerrard, Friedrich Kirschner, Davide Quagliola, Semiconductor, Virgil Widrich, Karin When, Benjamin Wiederkehr

unkenntlich, zusehends unseren Alltag. Dabei treten die Bewegtbilder aus dem Computer in sehr unterschiedlichen und vor allem hybriden Formen in einem breiten und interdisziplinären Feld von Kunst, Industrie bis zu Forschung und Wissenschaft auf. Aufgrund dieser „Grenzenlosigkeit" wird Animation allgegenwärtig und undefinierbar zugleich. Um die Frage „Was ist Digitale Animation?" aktuell beantworten zu können, ist ein Blick auf dieses dynamische, sich permanent ausdehnende Feld unumgänglich.
Im Rahmen der Ars Electronica 2013 findet eine Fachtagung mit dem Titel *Expanded Digital Animation: Mapping an Unlimited Landscape* statt. Die von der Fachhochschule Hagenberg und Ars Electronica in Zusammenarbeit mit dem LENTOS Kunstmuseum veranstaltete Fachtagung beschäftigt sich mit Entgrenzungen, Randgebieten und Vermischungen in der Computeranimation.

Organizers:
Jürgen Hagler, Sabine Retschitzegger, Alexander Wilhelm / University of Applied Sciences Upper Austria | Digital Media Department
http://www.fh-ooe.at/
http://www.expandedanimation.com/

Ars Electronica Animation Festival 2013

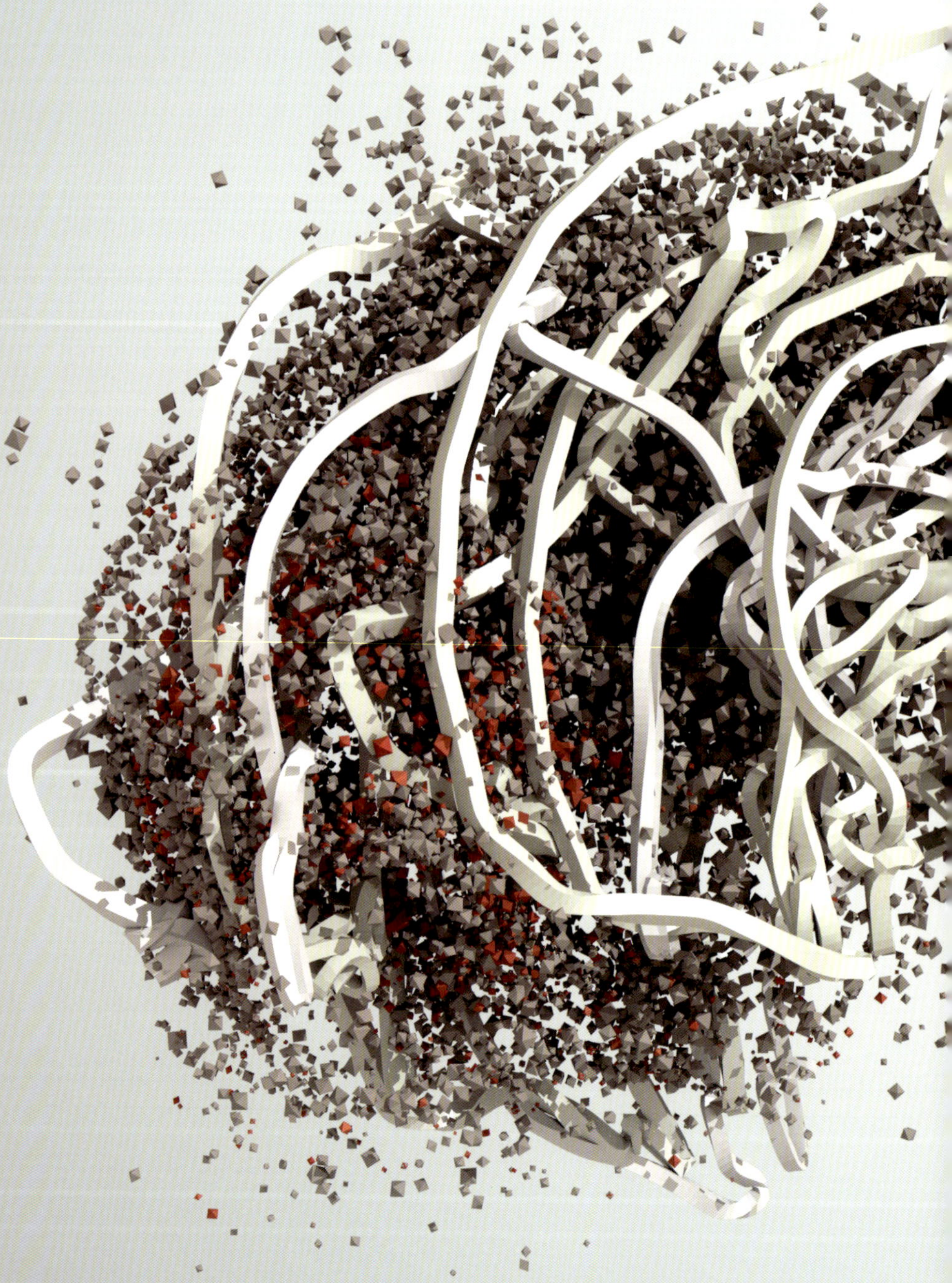

Forms, Quayola, Memo Akten

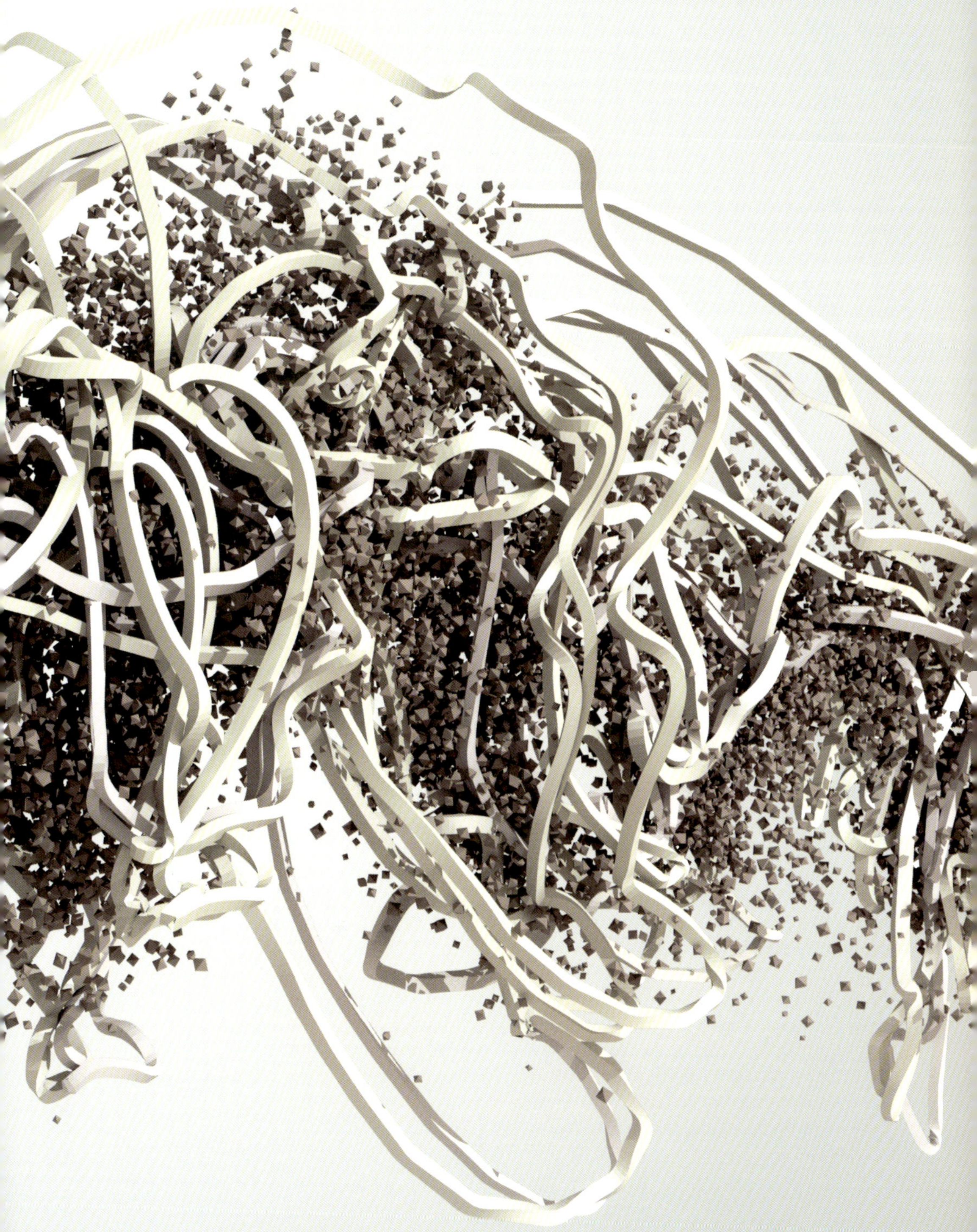

The Ars Electronica Animation Festival is a compilation selected from all entries to the 2013 Prix Ars Electronica's Computer Animation/Film/VFX category. It offers an overview of the positions and points of view of artists worldwide, and impressively documents not only the genre's explosive growth of late but also its marvelous substantive and stylistic diversity.
775 films from 73 countries were submitted for prize consideration this year. Even a quick perusal of the selected films reveals the broad spectrum of what's being produced now. Digital animation—sometimes recognizable as such, sometimes unidentifiable as a realistic simulation—increasingly pervades our everyday life. These computer-generated motion pictures appear in a diverse array of often hybrid forms in a very wide-ranging and interdisciplinary field at the nexus of art, industry, science and R&D. From high-tech VFX used in the movies and games turned out by major Hollywood studios all the way to conventional techniques like hybrid stop-motion animation, found-footage films, generative and interactive works, special effects, installations in an exhibition context and façade projections—the submissions to the 2013 Prix competition deliver a sharp, colorful picture of digital productions' successful crossings of the boundaries separating discrete fields and art forms. The substantive spectrum ranges from abstract and experimental works to traditional narrative films.
Each of these eight programs is a compact summary of current trends as evidenced by this year's entries to the Prix Ars Electronica. They're grouped on the basis of content as well as formal criteria.
There's been a striking increase in the number of computer animation works submitted to the Prix Ars Electronica's u19–CREATE YOUR WORLD category for Austrian youngsters under 19 years of age. The maturity and quality of these efforts have constantly been a source of pleasant surprise. *Young Animations* is a delightful assortment of this year's best. As an added bonus, there's *Japan Media Arts Festival Selection*, a one-hour showcase of animated films that have been honored by the Japan Media Arts Festival. The 10 programs that comprise the 2013 Ars Electronica Animation Festival provide a dense narrative full of insights into the world of motion pictures.

Das *Ars Electronica Animation Festival* ist eine Auswahl aus den Einreichungen der Kategorie Computer Animation / Film / VFX des Prix Ars Electronica 2013. Es gibt einen Überblick über internationale Positionen und Sichtweisen und zeigt eindrücklich nicht nur das expansive Anwachsen des Genres, sondern auch seine Vielfalt im Inhaltlichen wie auch im Gestalterischen.
775 Filme aus 73 Ländern waren in diesem Jahr eingereicht. Ein Blick auf die ausgewählten Filme zeigt die breite Palette an aktuellen Erscheinungsformen. Digitale Animation durchdringt, einerseits als solche erkennbar und andererseits unkenntlich als Simulation, zusehend unseren Alltag. Dabei treten die Bewegtbilder aus dem Computer in sehr unterschiedlichen und vor allem hybriden Formen in einem äußerst breiten, interdisziplinären Feld von Kunst, Industrie oder Wissenschaft und Forschung auf.
Diese reichen von hochtechnologischen VFX der Film- und Gamewelt aus den großen Hollywood-Studios bis hin zu traditionellen Techniken. Hybride Stop-Motion-Animationen, Found-Footage-Filme, generative und interaktive Arbeiten, Special Effects, Installationen im Ausstellungskontext und Fassadenprojektionen – das sind die Stichworte zu den Einreichungen 2013, die den grenzüberschreitenden Charakter in der digitalen Produktion deutlich machen. Das inhaltliche Spektrum reicht dabei von abstrakten und experimentellen bis hin zu traditionell narrativen Filmen.
Die Programmschienen fassen in kompakter Form die diesjährigen Trends in den Einreichungen zum Prix Ars Electronica 2013 nach inhaltlichen und formalen Gesichtspunkten zusammen. Eine markante Zunahme an Computeranimationen verzeichnet die Kategorie u19 – CREATE YOUR WORLD des Prix Ars Electronica. Das ist jene Kategorie, die junge Menschen in Österreich unter 19 Jahren zum Mitmachen einlädt und die mit ihren Ergebnissen immer wieder überrascht. Grund genug, ein Best-of der Animationen aus dieser Wettbewerbskategorie in *Young Animations* zu zeigen Ergänzend dazu wird in der *Japan Media Arts Festival Selection* ein einstündiges Programm preisgekrönter Animationsfilme des Japan Media Arts Festival präsentiert. Mit seinen insgesamt zehn Programmen gibt das diesjährige *Ars Electronica Animation Festival* einen kompakten Einblick in die Welt der bewegten Bilder.

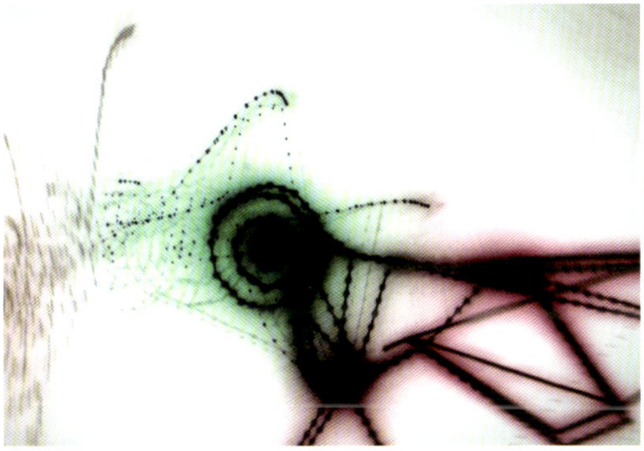

Snail Trail, Philipp Artus

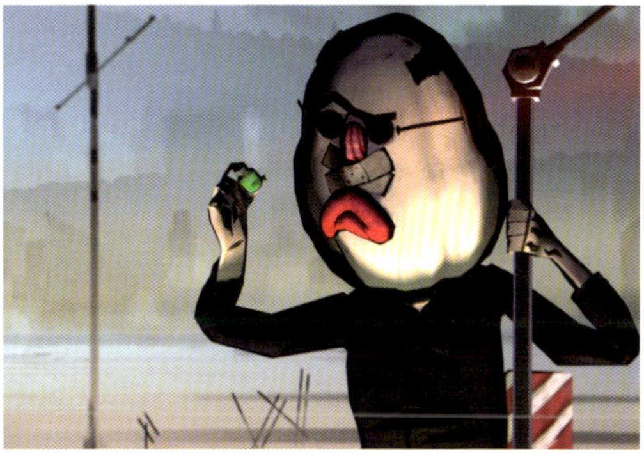

The Animation Tag Attack, The Animation Tag Attack Team

Experimental

The *Experimental* program presents innovative design forays in various forms and genres. The experimental approach can apply to any element—to the storytelling itself, for instance, to new forms of production in the blog format, to serial animation produced by several designers, or to object-space interaction & deconstruction. And we encounter these experimental forms in narrative films, abstract works, and even seemingly conventional documentaries.

Das Programm *Experimental* untersucht gestalterische Experimente in unterschiedlichen Formen und Genres. Der experimentelle Charakter betrifft Storytelling ebenso wie neue Produktionsformen im Blogformat, als Kettenanimation produziert von mehreren Gestaltern, Objekt-Raum-Interaktion und -Dekonstruktion. Diese Experimentalformen begegnen uns in narrativen genauso wie in abstrakten Filmen und im scheinbar traditionellen Dokumentationsformat.

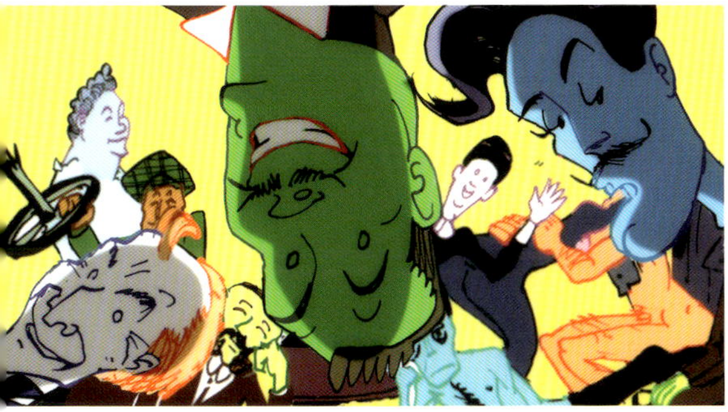

Die Telefonbuchpolka, benjamin swiczinsky

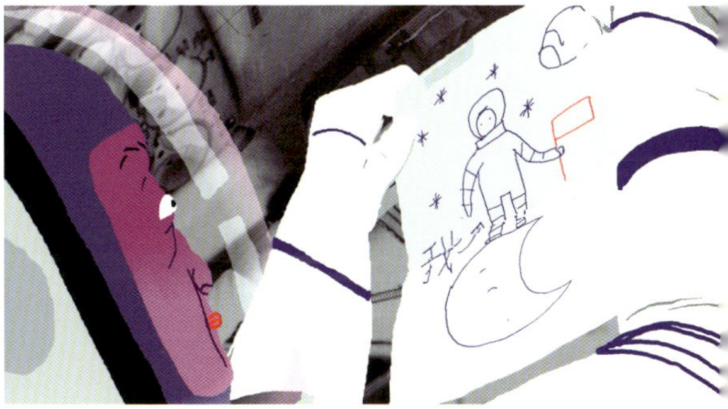

Let's Go!, Alexis Beaumont, Remi Godin

Music & Images

This program showcases the various modes of interplaying music and images. The lineup includes experimental works configuring interaction between the audio and the video, classic examples of visual music, and conventional music videos from across the cultural spectrum. They're generated with the use of technological tools ranging from high- to low-tech. To perk up the mix with some comic relief, there's funny stuff too.

Music & Images zeigt die unterschiedlichsten Spielarten im Zusammenwirken von Musik und Bild. Experimentelle Arbeiten mit Interaktion zwischen Bild und Sound sind ebenso zu sehen wie Beispiele, die sich dem klassischen Bereich der Visual Music verpflichten, oder gängige Musikvideos aus unterschiedlichen Kulturbereichen, die ganz unterschiedliche technologische Tools einsetzen, von Low-Tec bis High-Tec. Und auch das Komisch-Humoristische hat hier seinen Platz – für Abwechslung ist also gesorgt.

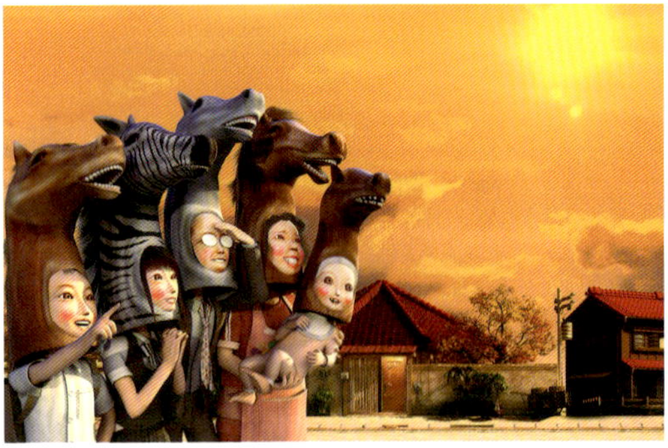

The Carousel Family, Te-Yu Liu

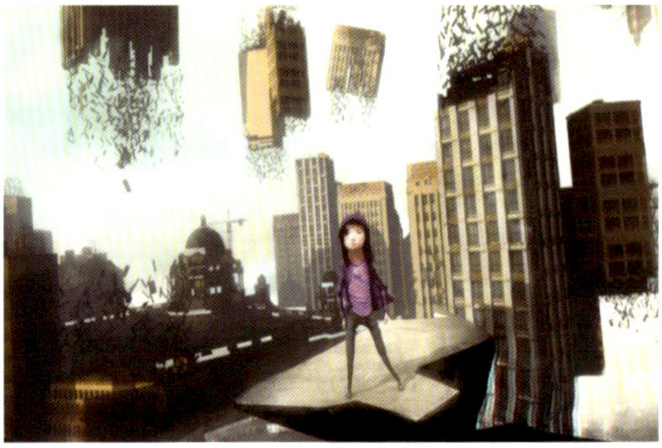

Here To Fall, Kris Kelly, Evelyn McGrath

Mental States

Remembrances of childhood and things (not) experienced, shortcomings, issues defying closure, and disturbances make up this program. All the selected films describe sensitive and highly personal mental states and give accounts of people in states of acute emergency. Early-childhood memories of experiences (had and not had), deficient parental relationships, and disorders like autism are some of the things these films deal with in this thematically very specially defined program of storytelling.

Erinnerungen an die Kindheit, Nicht-Erfahrenes, Defizite, Unbewältigtes und Störungen – um diese Themen kreist *Mental States.* Alle ausgewählten Filme beschreiben sensibel und höchst persönlich mentale Zustände und erzählen von Menschen in Ausnahmezuständen. Beispielsweise werden frühkindliche Erfahrungen/Nichterfahrungen, defizitäre Elternbeziehungen, aber auch Störungen wie Autismus bearbeitet – ein thematisch speziell definiertes Programm von Storytelling.

Narration

The short narrative film has become a mainstay in the field of computer animation and in digital filmmaking as a whole in recent years. Not-your-everyday love stories, a hilarious promenade at the French court that culminates in catastrophe, reflections that lead an unpleasantly insistent life of their own, a pushy blue crocodile as flatmate—these are a few of the films on this lineup that are all part of a master narrative: computer animation letting storytellers give free rein to their imagination!

Der narrative Kurzfilm gewinnt in der Computeranimation bzw. im Digital Filmmaking in den letzten Jahren zunehmend an Bedeutung. Nicht alltägliche Liebesgeschichten, ein urkomisches Defilée am französischen Hof, das im Desaster endet, Spiegelbilder, die ein penetrantes Eigenleben führen, ein aufdringliches blaues Krokodil als Mitbewohner, – das sind nur einige Beispiele aus einem Programm, das zeigt: Computeranimation setzt dem Geschichtenerzählen keine Grenzen – die Grenze ist immer nur die Fantasie!

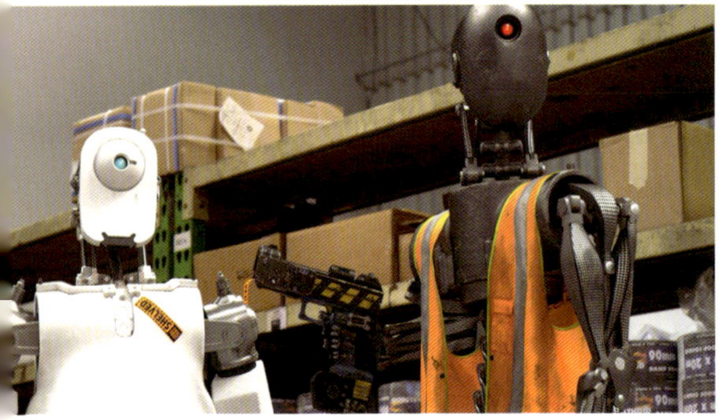

Shelved, James Cunningham

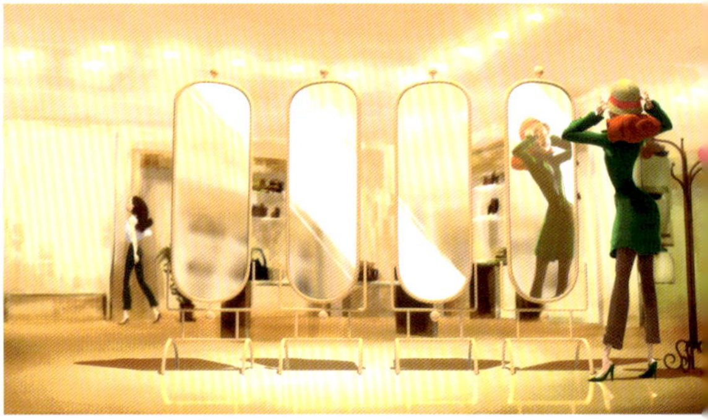

Refection, Yoshimichi Tamura / Planktoon

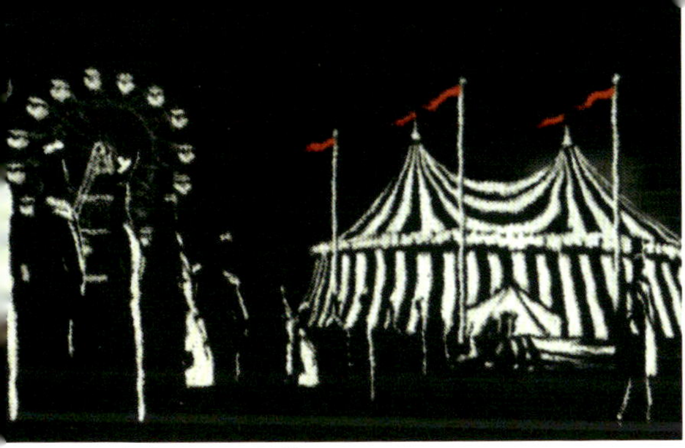

Evolution, Hamer Hall

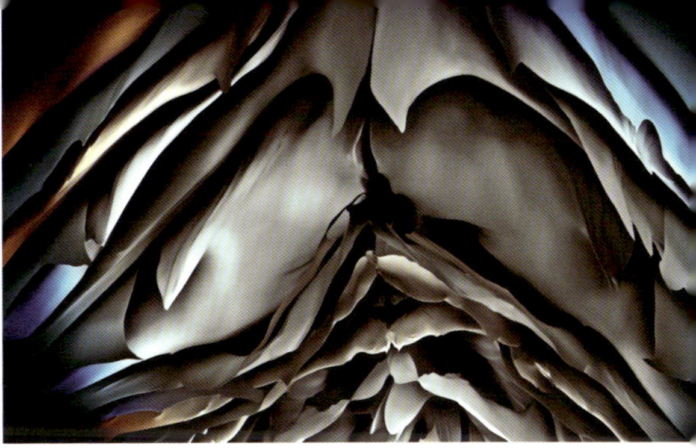

Scrape, Robert Seidl

Expanded Digital Animation

3D visualizations in interior spaces and on building façades as well as in performative settings have solidly established themselves in the field of computer animation. High-performance projection technology and software packages have made it possible to bring excellent motion pictures into the public sphere. Museum galleries and façades can serve as the showcases for these often interactive works; so can trade shows and theatrical productions. Some of the projects featured in this lineup were commissioned by museums, municipalities and corporate clients; others were developed by the artists themselves. All the works screened here have this in common: conveying digital images into a spatial context.

3D-Visualisierung in Räumen und auf Gebäuden in Städten wie auch im performativen Bereich sind seit längerer Zeit ein Thema in der Computeranimation. Leistungsstarke Projektionstechnologie und Software-Pakete bringen das bewegte Bild immer öfter in den öffentlichen Raum. Museumsräume- und -fassaden werden dafür ebenso zum (teils interaktiven) Showcase wie kommerzielle Messen und Shows. Die in diesem Programm vorgestellten Projekte sind Auftragsarbeiten von Museen, Kommunen und industriellen Partnern, aber auch individuelle Projekte von Künstlern. All die hier gezeigten Projekte haben den gemeinsamen Nenner einer Erweiterung des digitalen Bildes im räumlichen Kontext.

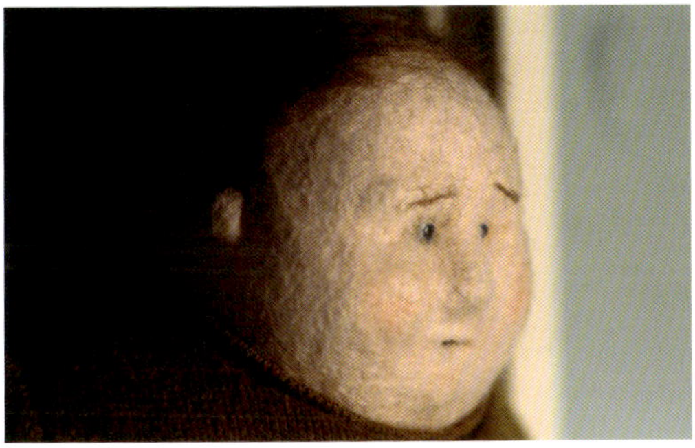

Oh Willy..., Emma De Swaef, Marc James Roels / Beast Animation

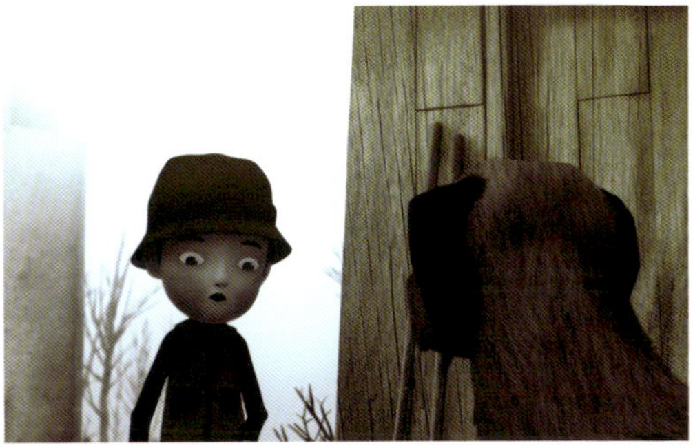

Palmipedarium, Jérémy Clapin / Papy3D Production

Memories

A diary written by a man in whose everyday life nothing ever happens; "Rien à faire" is what he inscribes, day after day. Willy seeks re-socialization from the nudist colony in which his mother lives. A little boy flees into a dream world from which he ultimately can't escape. And Bill attempts to reunite his fractured psyche. These four films serve as proxies as it were for the visualizations of worlds of feeling and remembrance, a discipline in which animation truly shines.

Ein Tagebuch schreibender Mann, in dessen Alltag nichts passiert: „Rien à faire" notiert er jeden Tag. Willy will sich aus dem Nudistencamp seiner Mutter rücksozialisieren. Ein kleiner Junge flüchtet sich in Traumwelten, denen er letztendlich nicht entkommt, und Bill versucht, seine gespaltene Psyche wieder zusammenzubringen: Vier Filme, die gewissermaßen als Vertreter für die Visualisierung von Gefühls- und Erinnerungswelten stehen, eine Paradedisziplin in der Animation.

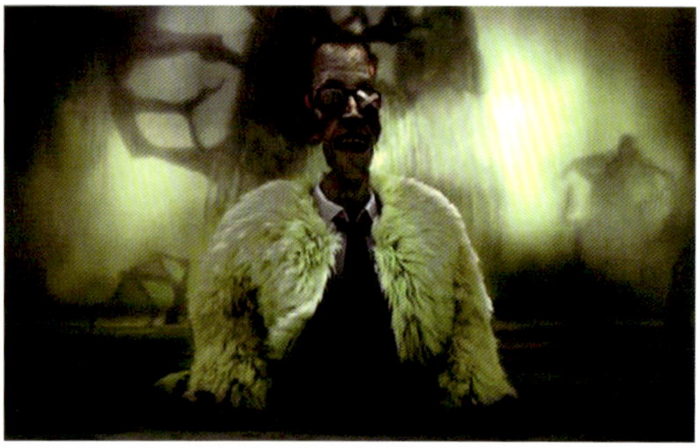

Lonely Bones, Autour de Minuit Productions & STUDIO ROSTO A.D.

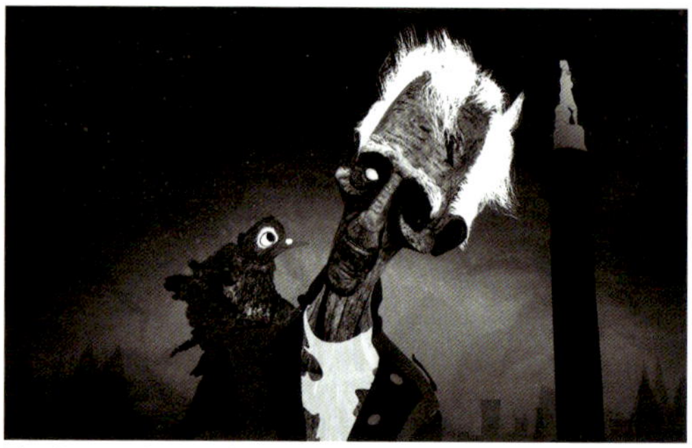

The Hungry Corpse, Gergely Wootsch

Late Nite

Sexual obsessions, violent fantasies, blood, death and persecution—this is a lineup for after dark and for viewers with strong nerves!

Sexuelle Obsessionen, Gewaltvorstellungen, Blut, Tod und Verfolgung – das ist das Programm zur späten Stunde, geeignet nur für starke Nerven!

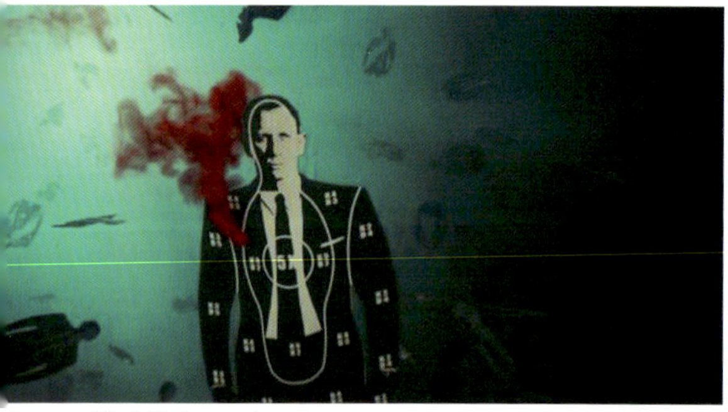

Skyfall, Framestore

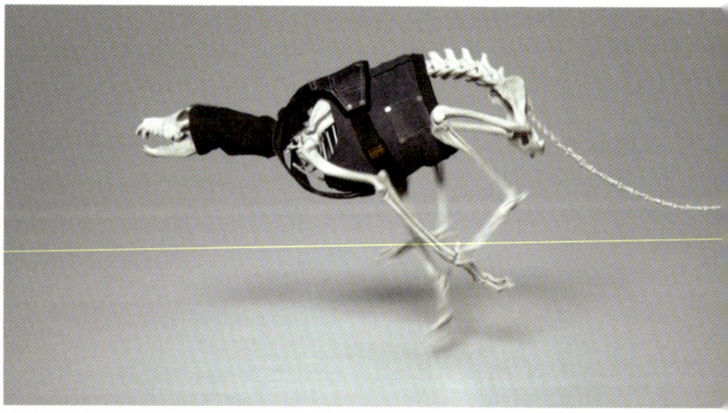

G-Star: The Art of RAW, Glassworks Amsterdam

Advertisement & VFX

Computer animation and VFX have long since become part of everyday life in advertising, the film business and the booming game industry. Up to now, all of them—commercials, VFX and games—have been solidly in the hands of major studios and on the copyright leash of film production giants. Nevertheless, a growing number of alternatives have emerged. Open source and Creative Commons are the bright spots here.

Computeranimation und VFX sind längst Alltag in der Werbung, im Filmbusiness und in der boomenden Game-Industrie. Alle – Werbung, VFX und Games – sind bislang überwiegend in der Hand großer Studios und am Copyright-Gängelband der Filmproduktionsriesen. Allerdings gibt es mittlerweile immer mehr Alternativen. Open Source und Creative Commons sind die Stichworte dazu.

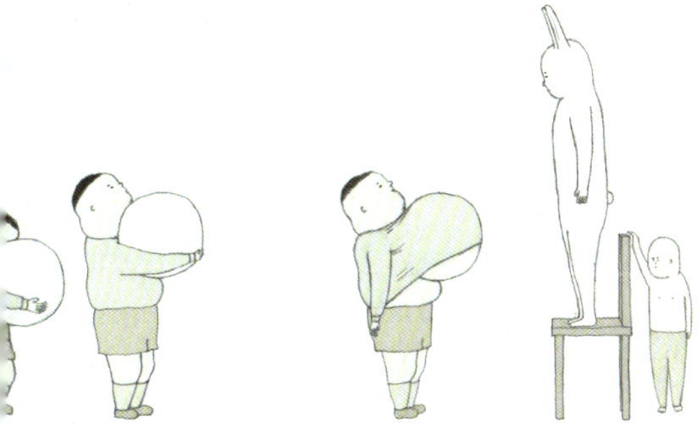

The Great Rabbit, Atsushi Wada

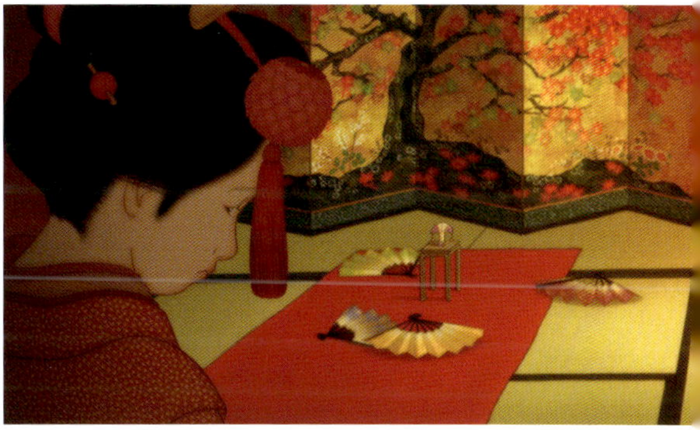

Combustible, Katsuhiro Otomo

Japan Media Arts Festival Selection

The *Japan Media Arts Festival* honours outstanding works from a wide range of media in four award categories: Art, Entertainment, Animation and Manga. It also serves as a platform that celebrates the winners of awards and outstanding creative works of art.

Das *Japan Media Arts Festival* ehrt herausragende künstlerische Leistungen in einem breiten Spektrum an Genres in den vier Kategorien: Kunst, Unterhaltung, Animation und Manga. Dabei fungiert es auch als Plattform für die Ausstellung preisgekrönter Künstler und künstlerisch wertvoller Werke.

Young Animations

Witty, off-beat, subtle, tragic and serious animated work produced by young filmmakers will be screened during the Festival Ars Electronica. Every year, gifted young filmmakers submit their movies to u19 – CREATE YOUR WORLD (Austria), bugnplay (Switzerland), MB21 (Germany) and C3<19 (Hungary). The greatest hits will be featured in young animations.

Witzige, schräge, subtile, tragische und ernste Animationen, von jungen Menschen produziert, werden im Rahmen des Ars Electronica Festival gezeigt. Jedes Jahr reichen begabte FilmemacherInnen ihre Animationen bei u19 – CREATE YOUR WORLD (Österreich), bugnplay (Schweiz), MB21 (Deutschland) und C3<19 (Ungarn) ein. Die besten davon werden in Young Animations gezeigt.

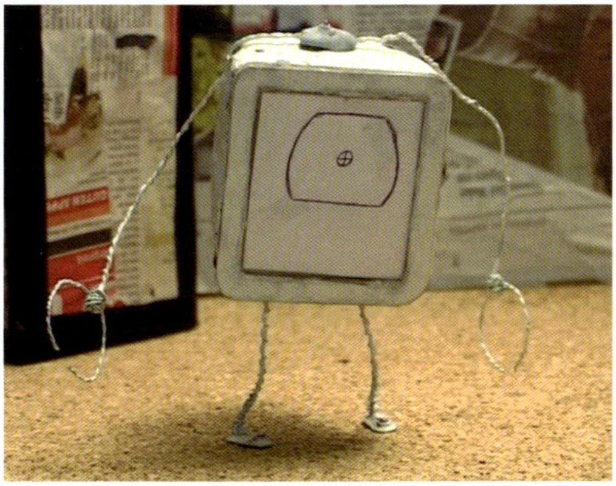

Tit for Tat, Benjamin Lewek

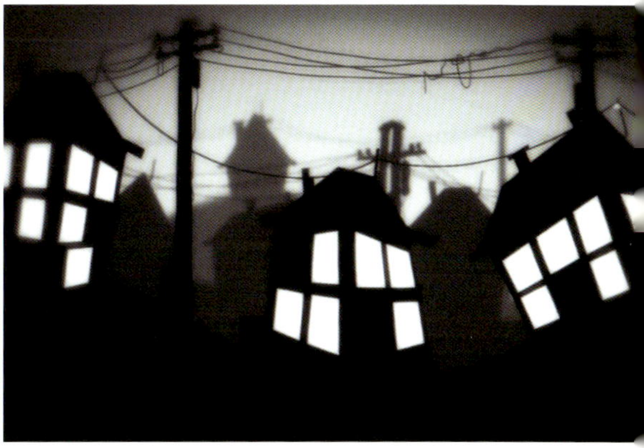

Urban, Máté Varga

Prix Ars Electronica 2013

International Competition for CyberArts

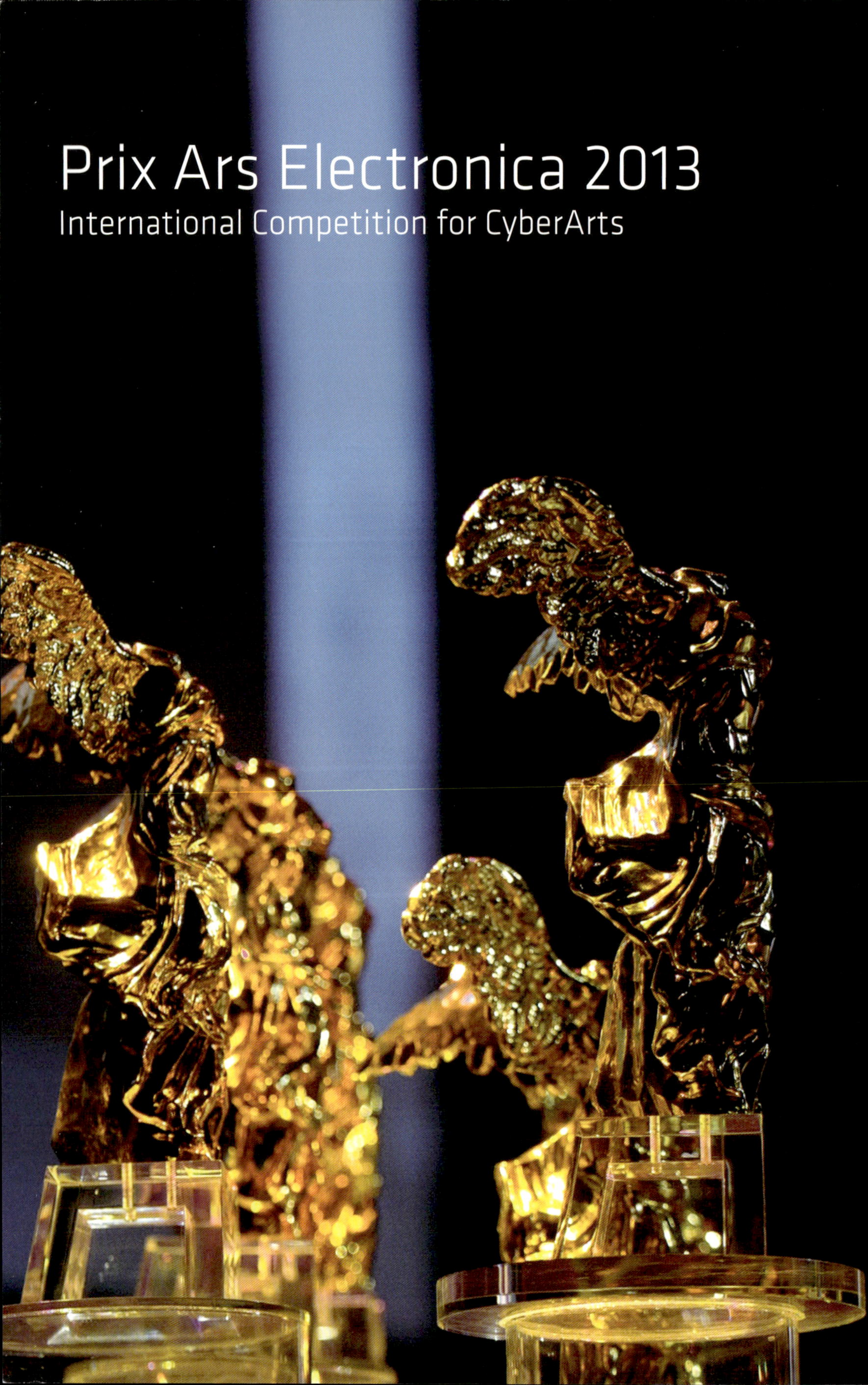

Since 1987, the Prix Ars Electronica is a seismograph for the latest innovations at the interface of art, technology and science, and thus an important barometer of trends in the digital arts. With 4,071 entries submitted from 73 countries, the Prix Ars Electronica has once again underscored its status as key bellwether in the dynamic field of cyberarts.
The 2013 Prix Ars Electronica invited submissions in the following seven categories: Computer Animation/Film/VFX, Digital Communities, Digital Musics & Sound Art, Hybrid Art, Interactive Art, [the next idea] voestalpine Art and Technology Grant and u19 – CREATE YOUR WORLD that reflect the ongoing diversification of digital media art as well as the continuing development of the Prix Ars Electronica itself. Juries made up of prominent experts from all over the world selected the winners of 6 Golden Nicas, 12 Awards of Distinction, 1 [the next idea] Grant and 72 Honorary Mentions. Honorees also received a total of 117,500 euros in prize money.
This year, a jury also selected the second recipient of the Prix Ars Electronica Collide@CERN Award, the new artist-in-residence program established by CERN and Ars Electronica.
Selected works from this year's Prix Ars Electronica will be on display in the CyberArts 2013 exhibition at the OK Offenes Kulturhaus.
You'll find the results of the 2013 Prix Ars Electronica and detailed descriptions of the prizewinning projects in:
CyberArts 2013
International Compendium of Prix Ars Electronica
H. Leopoldseder / C. Schöpf / G. Stocker (Eds.)
Hatje Cantz, Ostfildern-Ruit

Der Prix Ars Electronica ist seit 1987 Seismograph für aktuelle Innovationen an der Schnittstelle von Kunst, Technologie und Wissenschaft und damit wichtiger Trendbarometer der digitalen Künste. Mit 4.071 eingereichten Projekten aus 73 Ländern unterstreicht der Prix Ars Electronica einmal mehr seinen Stellenwert als wichtiger Indikator im dynamischen Umfeld der Cyberarts. Folgende sieben Kategorien wurden im Rahmen des Prix Ars Electronica 2013 ausgeschrieben: Computer Animation/Film/VFX, Digital Communities, Digital Musics & Sound Art, Hybrid Art, Interactive Art, [the next idea] voestalpine Art and Technology Grant und u19 – CREATE YOUR WORLD. Allesamt spiegeln die fortschreitende Diversifizierung digitaler Medienkunst, aber auch die kontinuierliche Weiterentwicklung des Prix Ars Electronica wider. Internationale und hochkarätig besetzte Fachjuries entschieden über die Vergabe von 6 Goldene Nicas, 12 Auszeichnungen 1 [the next idea] grant und 72 Anerkennungen. Es ergehen 117.500 Euro Preisgeld an die GewinnerInnen.
Darüber hinaus wurde in diesem Jahr zum zweiten Mal der Prix Ars Electronica Collide@CERN Award vergeben, das 2012 von CERN und Ars Electronica ins Leben gerufene Artist-in-Residency-Programm. Ausgewählte Arbeiten des Prix Ars Electronica werden in der Ausstellung CyberArts 2013 im OK Offenes Kulturhaus im OÖ Kulturquartier präsentiert.
Die Ergebnisse des Prix Ars Electronica und detaillierte Beschreibungen der Gewinnerprojekte finden Sie in:
CyberArts 2013
International Compendium of Prix Ars Electronica
H. Leopoldseder / C. Schöpf / G. Stocker (Eds.)
Hatje Cantz, Ostfildern-Ruit

Computer Animation / Film / VFX

Golden Nica Computer Animation / Film / VFX

Forms
Quayola (IT), Memo Akten (TR)
www.memo.tv/forms
www.quayola.com/forms

Awards of Distinction Computer Animation / Film / VFX

Duku Spacemarines
La Mécanique du Plastique (FR)
http://lamecaniqueduplastique.fr

Oh Willy...
Emma De Swaef (BE), Marc James Roels (BE) / Beast Animation
www.beastanimation.be

Honorary Mentions Computer Animation / Film / VFX

Ars Rata
Moritz Palnstorfer (AT), Christian Schulze (DE)
http://vimeo.com/christianschulze/arsrata

Ballpit
Kyle Mowat (CA)
http://vimeo.com/49178869

Björk – Mutual Core
Andrew Thomas Huang (US)
www.youtube.com/watch?feature=player_embed-ded&v=ZM80F_J-QHE

It's Such a Beautiful Day
Don Hertzfeldt (US)
www.bitterfilms.com

MeTube: August sings Carmen 'Habanera'
Daniel Moshel (DE) / Moshel Film
www.metube.at

Palmipedarium
Jérémy Clapin (FR) / Papy3D productions
www.muiye.com www.papy3d.com

Rollin' Safari
Kyra Buschor (CH), Anna Habermehl (DE), Constantin Paeplow (DE)
www.facebook.com/RollinWild

Shelter
Carl Burton (US)
http://vimeo.com/37156003

Snail Trail
Philipp Artus (DE)
www.philippartus.com

Subconscious Password
Chris Landreth (CA)

The Carousel Family
Te-Yu Liu (TW)
http://vimeo.com/61404549
http://cargocollective.com/chrisfishshop

Under an Alias
Nerdworking (TR)
http://vimeo.com/51209455

Digital Communities

Golden Nica Digital Communities

El Campo de Cebada
http://elcampodecebada.org

Awards of Distinction Digital Communities

Refugees United
http://info.refunite.org

Visualizing Palestine
www.visualizingpalestine.org

Honorary Mentions Digital Communities

African Digital Art Network
www.africandigitalart.com

Casastristes
http://casastristes.org

Indian Memory Project
www.indianmemoryproject.com

ipaidabribe.com – Crowdsourcing Against Corruption
www.ipaidabribe.com

Kyberia
http://kyberia.sk

Labmovel
www.labmovel.net

Metropolitalia
www.metropolitalia.org

NicoNicoGakkai Beta
http://niconicogakkai.jp

Numbeo – cost of living
www.numbeo.com

oiga.me, a platform for citizenship's lobby
https://oiga.me/

Seeed Studio–Open Hardware Facilitator
www.seeedstudio.com

The East Japan Earthquake Archive
http://e.nagasaki.mapping.jp

Special Mention Digital Communities
Aaron Swartz (US)

Digital Musics & Sound Art

Golden Nica Digital Musics & Sound Art

frequencies (a)
Nicolas Bernier (CA)
http://vimeo.com/48493242
www.nicolasbernier.com

Awards of Distinction Digital Musics & Sound Art

[SjQ++]
[SjQ++] (JP)
http://sjq.jp/sjqpp

Borderlands Granular
Chris Carlson (US)
www.borderlands-granular.com

Honorary Mentions Digital Musics & Sound Art

0b0000.tms
Typingmonkeys (JP)
http://typingmonkeys.jp

Albireo2.1
Mark Malmberg (US)
www.markmalmberg.com

altogether disproportionate
Michael Edwards (UK)
www.sumtone.com

Cube with Magic Ribbons
Simon Katan (UK)
www.info.simonkatan.co.uk/soundcircuit

Duali
Suguru Goto (JP)
http://suguru.goto.free.fr

Equilibrium Variant
Roberto Pugliese (IT)
www.robertopugliese.com

Gedichterbe
AGF (DE)
http://gedichterbe.poemproducer.com

and VI (inertia)
Grischa Lichtenberger (DE)
http://grischa-lichtenberger.com
www.raster-noton.net

La Biblioteca Ciega
Nicolás Varchausky (AR)
www.varchausky.com.ar

The Half
Intermedia Chef (KR)
http://vimeo.com/62248561
http://youtu.be/2vTUqpVlrLg

The Sound of the Earth
Yuri Suzuki (JP/UK)
yurisuzuki.com/works/the-sound-of-the-earth-2/

Works for Wave Field Synthesis
Robert Henke with Christoph März, Edgardo Gómez, Rafael Santiago, Volodomyr Taranovych, Silje Nes, Jan Brauer, Christian Losert, Dusan Bracic, Anna Bogner, Nicolas Probst, Michel Wähling, Jessica Ekomane, Thomas Maier (DE)
roberthenke.com

Hybrid Art

Golden Nica Hybrid Art

The Cosmopolitan Chicken Project
Koen Vanmechelen (BE)
www.koenvanmechelen.com

Awards of Distinction Hybrid Art

Five Variations of Phonic Circumstances and a Pause
Tania Candiani (MX)
www.taniacandiani.com
http://vimeo.com/63364803

Mycotecture
Phil Ross (US)
http://philross.org

Honorary Mentions Hybrid Art

Oh!m1gas: biomimetic stridulation environment
Kuai Shen (EC/DE)
http://kuaishen.tv/0hm1gas

Breathing Bike
Matt Hope (UK)
http://matthope.org

Hidden Fields
David Glowacki (US) with Phil Tew (UK), Laura Kriefman (UK), Joseph Hyde (UK), Thomas Mitchell (UK), Lisa May Thomas (UK), Emma Harrie (UK)
http://danceroom-spec.com

Hu.M.C.C. – Human Molecular Colonization Capacity
Maja Smrekar (SI)
www.mayayoghurt.net
www.majasmrekar.org

MEMORY VAPOR
Dmitry Gelfand (NL), Evelina Domnitch (NL)
http://portablepalace.com/memoryvapor.html

Microbial Schöppingen
Mick Lorusso (US)
www.micklorusso.net

Nanohana Heels – Healing Fukushima
Sputniko! (JP/UK)
www.sputniko.com

Nomadic Plants
Gilberto Esparza (MX)
www.plantasnomadas.com

N_Polytope: Behaviors in Light and Sound After Iannis Xenakis
Chris Salter (US/QC/CA) in collaboration with Sofian Audry (QC/CA), Marije Baalman (NL), Adam Basanta (QC/CA), Elio Bidinost(QC/CA), Thomas Spier (DE)
http://chrissalter.com

Pancreas
Thomas Feuerstein (AT)
http://thomasfeuerstein.net

Suspect Inversion Center
Paul Vanouse (US)
www.paulvanouse.com

The Blind Robot
Louis-Philippe Demers (CA/SG)
www.processing-plant.com

Interactive Art

Golden Nica Interactive Art

Pendulum Choir
Michel Décosterd (CH), André Décosterd (CH) / Cod.Act
http://codact.ch

Awards of Distinction Interactive Art

Rain Room
rAndom International (UK)
http://random-international.com

Voices of Aliveness
Masaki Fujihata (JP)
http://voicesofaliveness.net

Honorary Mentions Interactive Art

AHORA. A song in the Hypertemporal Surface
Hernán Kerlleñevich (AR), Mene Savasta Alsina (AR)
http://cargocollective.com/operadora/ahora

Angles Mirror
Daniel Rozin (US)
http://vimeopro.com/bitforms/rozin/video/61823984

Blaus
Playmodes (ES), MID (ES)
http://playmodes.com/web/blau
http://mediainteractivedesign.com/en/blaus

Descriptive Camera
Matt Richardson (US)
http://mattrichardson.com/Descriptive-Camera

Down with Wrestlers with Systems and Mental Nonadapters!
Dmitry & Elena Kawarga (RU)
www.kawarga.ru

Dronestagram
James Bridle (UK)
http://instagram.com/dronestagram

Exploded Views 2.0
Marnix de Nijs (NL)
www.marnixdenijs.nl

Ishin-Den-Shin
Olivier Bau (FR), Yuri Suzuki(JP), Ivan Poupyrev (RU)
www.ishin-den-shin.com

Necomimi
Neurowear (JP)
http://neurowear.com

Perfume Global Site Project
Perfume (Aa-Chan, Kashiyuka, Nocchi) (JP), Daito Manabe (JP), Mikiko (JP), Yasutaka Nakata (JP), Satoshi Horii (JP), Hiroyasu Kimura (JP)
http://perfume-dev.github.com

The Kuramoto Model (1,000 Fireflies)
David Allan Rueter (US)
http://1000fireflies.net

Voice Array
Rafael Lozano-Hemmer (MX)
www.lozano-hemmer.com

u19 – CREATE YOUR WORLD

Golden Nica u19 – CREATE YOUR WORLD

Visual:Drumset
Dominik Koller
http://drum.dominikkoller.net/

Awards of Distinction u19 – CREATE YOUR WORLD

Soilution – Erde mit Zukunft
Magdalena Irnstötter, Magdalena Giesshammer, Doris Plasser, Elisabeth Winkler, Christina Proßegger, Theresa Eichhorn, Jessica Saria, Iris Rosenstatter, Lukas Schmidbauer, Christoph Unterraßner, Anna Greier, Daniel Groder, Florian Mackinger, Peter Schnitzhofer, Martin Pfaffinger, Sandra Mackner, Christiane Bachmann, Fabian Sanin, Martina Windsperger, Christina Zieher, Johannes Schmitzberger, Simon Kletzl, Philipp Klieber, Sebastian Perschl
HLFS Ursprung
http://hlfs.ursprung.at

Destino/ facebook/ BluCar/ Nur Kreide
Isidor Dietrich
http://www.youtube.com/Realbrickanimations

Non-cash prize u14

Feldversuche
Florian Bührle

Non-cash prize u10

Lernprogramme für die Volkschule
Sasan Hoseini, Arian Hoseini
http://members.aon.at/u19lernspiele

Honorary Mentions

Schulgedächtnis – Eine interaktive Rauminstallation
Magdalena Barteder, Flora Besenbäck, Marina Burankova, Anna Döcker, Magdalena Gollner-Hollnbuchner, Anna Greifeneder, Andrea Grünstäudl, Martina Gundolf, Fabia Hahn, Luise Heininger, Johanna Hirth, Monika Huber, Thomas Kirchweger, Anja Labner, Valentin Lichtenberger, Orenda Mohan, Carina Oberleitner, Lisa Maria Palasser, Iris Piringer, Sandra Prandstätter, Jasmin Rammerstorfer, Kathrin Schinnerl, Cornelia Schraml, Laura Starsich, Lena Strasser, Bibiana Traxler, Theresa Winter, Birgit Wögerbauer, Sarah Zauner, Eva Zöchbauer, Nina Blaschke, Johanna Doblinger, Jana Katzlberger, Alina Bittner, Simone Hart
HBLA für künstlerische Gestaltung Linz

Modern Media Guide
Christoph Auer, Kristina Cvetkovska, Melanie Eder, Nicolla Ivanov, Matus Porubsky, Fabian Zechmeister, Jan Kuschel, Raffael Hagleitner
BRG Kandlgasse Wien
http://www.modernmediaguide.at/

Kompositur
Sabine Bischinger, Barbara Pfaller, Madlen Weingartner, Razila Semic, Melisa Mujcinovic, Ines Tiefenbacher, Karoline-Melpomeni-Hermine Schager
BRG Horn

Gekommen um zu bleiben: Zur falschen Zeit im falschen Land
Kübra Börekci, Chiara Fürpass, Tunahan Harmankaya, Ali Özenir, Ana Protrka, Atilla Kahraman
BRG/ORG Henriettenplatz, Wien
http://www.schuelerradio.at/sendungen/2013-02-14

Biogas für Burkina Faso
Johannes Egger, Patrick Maier, Dražen Petrović, Simon Zigala
HTL Anichstraße Innsbruck

stop war – start thinking
Michael Dunkel, Nikolaus Müller, Georg Schneider, Philipp Unger
HTL RennwegWien
https://www.facebook.com/StopWarStartThinking
http://www.youtube.com/watch?v=oaP_uIQsmLA

Dictatorship of Perfection
Simon Stix
https://www.youtube.com/watch?v=eieV_jjGvog
A Moving Picture
Elisabeth Bloder,
BRG Kepler Graz

Konstruktion eines Fortbewegungsmittels nach dem Vorbild einer Ameise
Gabriel Krög
HTL Vöcklabruck

Massageschulranzen
Lena Sophia Wagner
8 Jahre

[the next idea]
voestalpine Art and Technology Grant

[the next idea]
voestalpine Art and Technology Grant

Hyperform
Marcelo Coelho (BR), Skylar Tibbits (US), Natan Linder (IL), Yoav Reches (IL)
www.cmarcelo.com sjet.us
http://formlabs.com

Honorary Mentions [the next idea]

GravityLight
Martin Riddiford (UK), Jim Reeves (UK)
http://deciwatt.org
www.therefore.co.uk

Prix Ars Electronica Collide@CERN
Artists Residency Prize

Prix Ars Electronica Collide@CERN
Artists Residency Prize

Bill Fontana (US)
www.resoundings.org

Honorary Mention

Ale de la Puente
www.aledelapuente.com

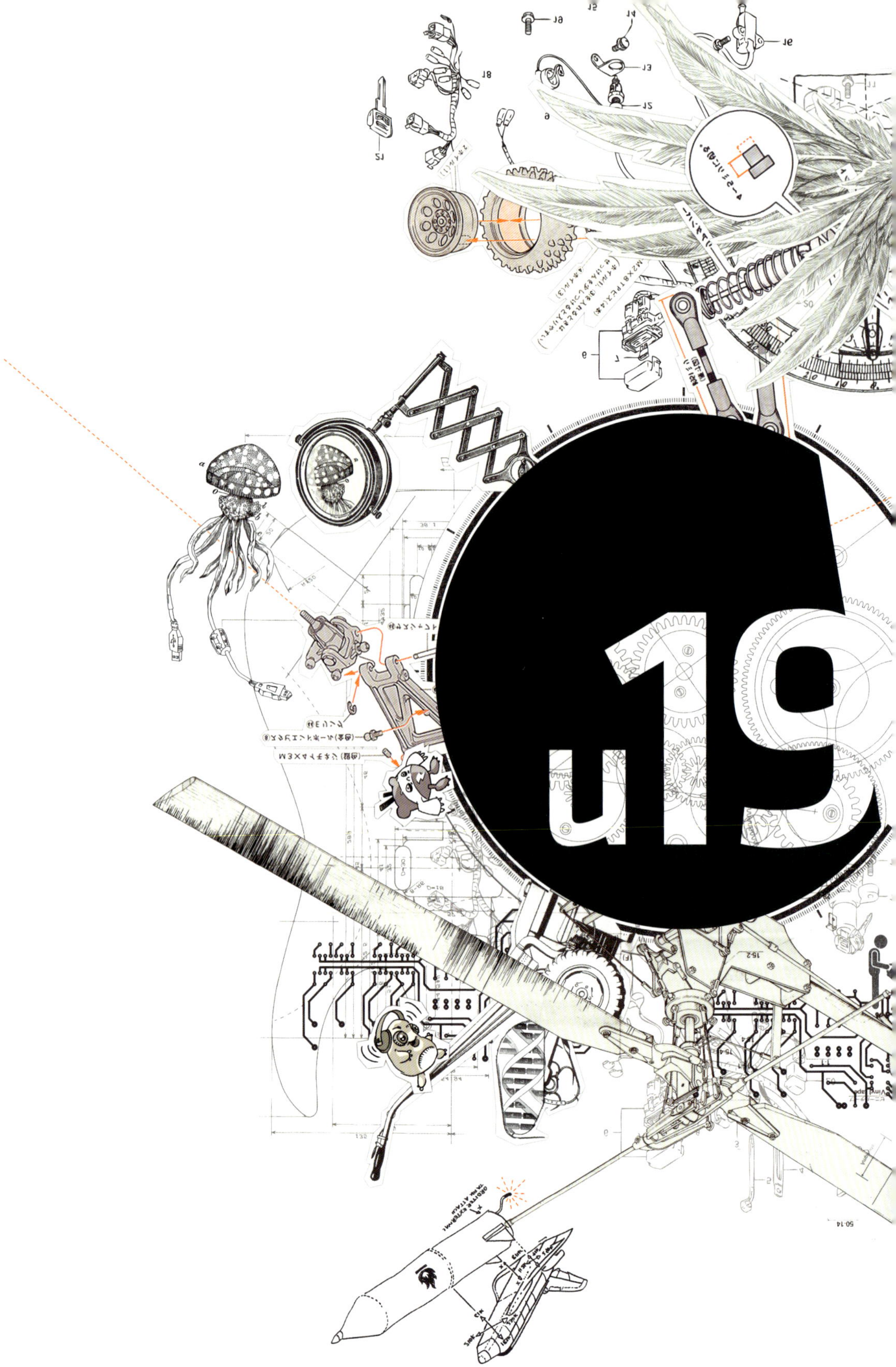

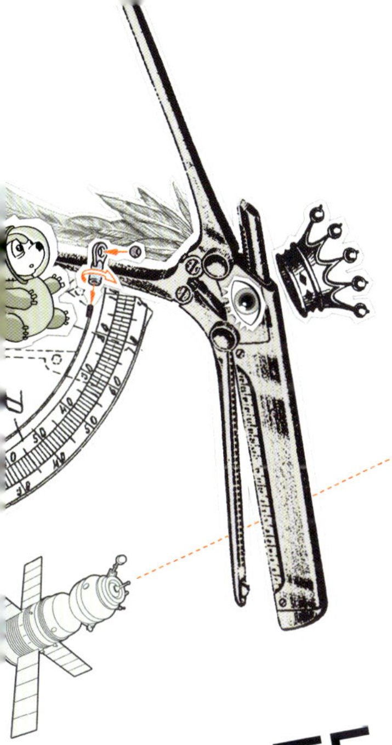

CREATE YOUR WORLD

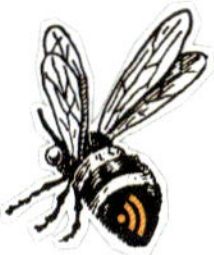

ZUKUNFTSFESTIVAL DER NÄCHSTEN GENERATION

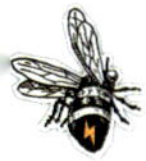

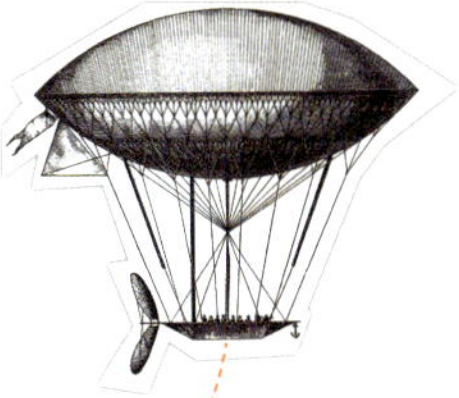

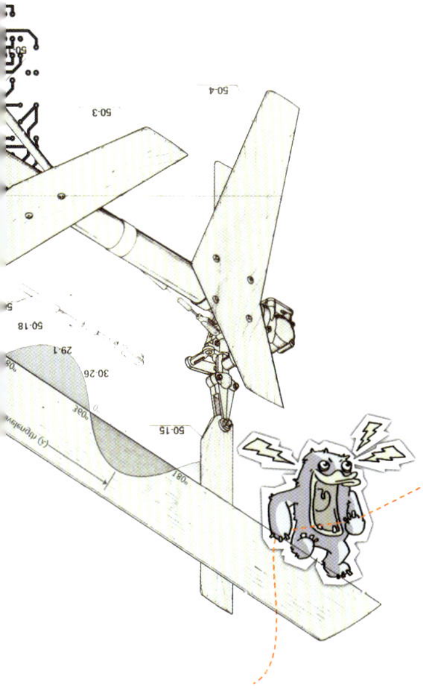

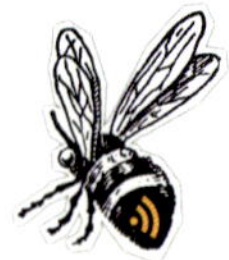

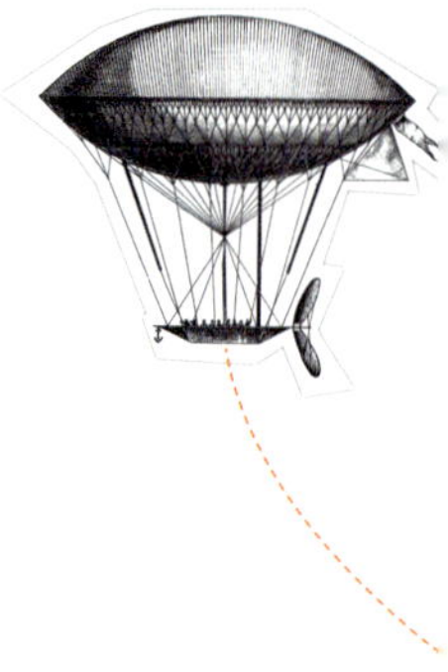

u19 – CREATE YOUR WORLD
Zukunftsfestival der nächsten Generation

The u19 – CREATE YOUR WORLD Festival is being staged for the third time this year. It was launched in 2011 as a spinoff and upgrade of the Prix's u19-freestyle computing category for young people and as the future festival of the next generation. This festival within a festival was reprised in 2012 along with the Prix competition. Now in 2013, u19 – CREATE YOUR WORLD is also establishing an expanded presence in the Ars Electronica Center, the site of a diversified year-'round program dedicated to the world of tomorrow, and the epicenter of the Festival.

Extending out around the Ars Electronica Center's Maindeck is a colorful festival village accommodating a fascinating assortment of sustainable, social, scientific and artistic projects. The u19 – CREATE YOUR WORLD Festival is a playground for dreamers and tinkerers, young people with a thirst for knowledge and a hunger for experience. It's an oasis of effervescent ideas, a forge for creative concepts, and a proving ground for new technologies. An interesting array of exhibitions, open labs and events invite festivalgoers to participate, to acquire hands-on skills and consider current developments and future prospects.

Das *u19 – CREATE YOUR WORLD*-Festival geht dieses Jahr in die dritte Runde. Gegründet 2011, als Spinn-Off und Weiterentwicklung der Kategorie *u19-freestyle computing* des Prix Ars Electronica, wurde es zum Zukunftsfestival der nächsten Generation. Als Festival im Festival präsentierte es sich auch 2012 und erweiterte mit dem Motto auch den Wettbewerb. 2013 ist die Marke „u19 – CREATE YOUR WORLD" nun auch im Ars Electronica Center präsent, wo schon das ganze Jahr über ein vielfältiges Programm für die Welt von morgen gestaltet wird und das stets ein Zentrum des Festivalgeschehens bildet.

Von dort dehnt sich eine bunte Stadt, die nachhaltige, gesellschaftliche, wissenschaftliche, technologische und künstlerische Projekte beherbergt, auf das Maindeck des Ars Electronica Center aus. Das *u19 – CREATE YOUR WORLD*-Festival ist ein Tummelplatz für TräumerInnen, TüftlerInnen, Wissensdurstige und Erlebnishungrige und entpuppt sich als Oase für sprudelnde Ideen, als Schmiede für kreative Gedanken und Versuchsstation für neue Technologien. Verschiedene Ausstellungen, Open Labs und Events laden zum Mitmachen, Ausprobieren und Nachdenken ein – über die Zukunft oder als Weg der Erinnerung, einem *Total Recall* für die Welt von morgen.

Patron / *Ehrenschutz:* Margit Fischer, Vorsitzende des Vereins Science Center Netzwerk / *Chairwoman of the Science Center Network Association*, Dr. Claudia Schmied, Bundesministerin für Unterricht, Kunst und Kultur / *Austrian Federal Minister of Education, Art and Culture*

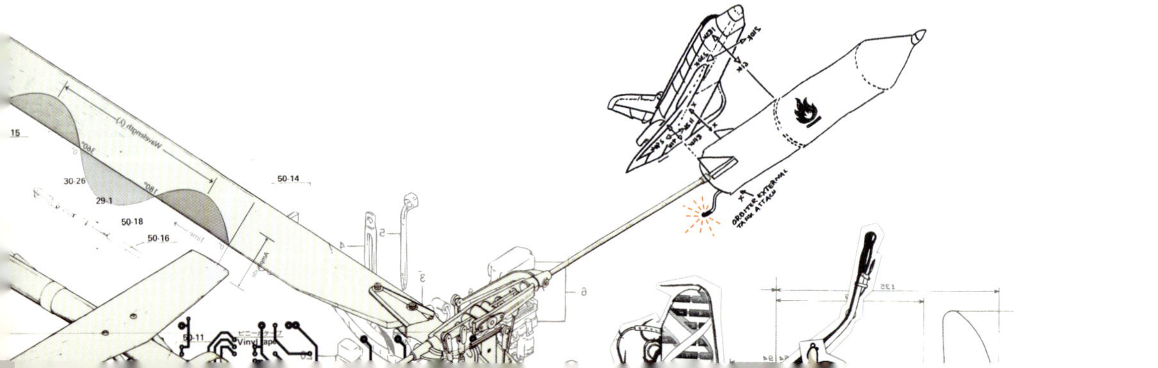

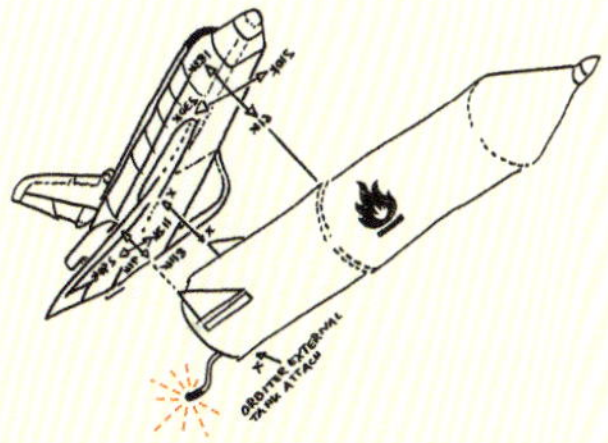

The following projects are being conducted in conjunction with the 2013 u19 – CREATE YOUR WORLD – Future Festival of the Next Generation
Beim diesjährigen u19 CREATE YOUR WORLD – Zukunftsfestival der nächsten Generation sind folgende Projekte beteiligt:

u19 – CREATE YOUR WORLD EXHIBITIONS

Layers of the City
Queensland University of Technology (AU), Ars Electronica Futurelab Academy (AT)

Trail of Traits
Alice Brown (AU), Andy Bates (AU)

Flow[er]
Jeniffer Heng (AU), Vidhi Shah (IN)

Pixel Streets
Michael Hiley (AU), Declan Brincat (AU), Yonghan Ji (CN)

u19 Exhibit

Die *u19 Exhibit* zeigt die 15 ausgezeichneten Projekte der Kinder und Jugendkategorie des Prix Ars Electronica. Das Highlight der Ausstellung ist das Projekt *Visual:Drumset* von Dominik Koller, bei dem Trommelschläge direkt auf dem Fell visualisiert werden.

GewinnerInnen der u19 – CREATE YOUR WORLD Kategorie des Prix Ars Electronica

Goldene Nica

Visual:Drumset
Dominik Koller

Auszeichnungen

Destino/ facebook/ BluCar/ Nur Kreide
Isidor Dietrich

Soilution – Erde mit Zukunft
HLFS Ursprung (25 TeilnehmerInnen)
Magdalena Irnstötter, Magdalena Giessham-mer, Doris Plasser, Elisabeth Winkler, Christina Proßegger, Theresa Eichhorn, Jessica Saria, Iris Rosenstatter, Lukas Schmidbauer, Christoph Unterraßner, Anna Greier, Daniel Groder, Florian Mackinger, Peter Schnitzhofer, Martin Pfaffinger, Sandra Mackner, Christiane Bachmann, Fabian Sanin, Martina Windsperger, Christina Zieher, Johannes Schmitzberger, Simon Kletzl, Philipp Klieber, Sebastian Perschl, Julia Karl

Sachpreis u14

Feldversuche
Florian Bührle

Sachpreis u10

Lernprogramme für die Volkschule
Sasan Hoseini, Arian Hoseini

Anerkennungen

Schulgedächtnis – Eine interaktive Rauminstallation
HBLA für künstlerische Gestaltung Linz, 35 TeilnehmerInnen
Magdalena Barteder, Flora Besenbäck, Marina Burankova, Anna Döcker, Magdalena Gollner-Hollnbuchner, Anna Greifeneder, Andrea Grünstäudl, Martina Gundolf, Fabia Hahn, Luise Heininger, Johanna Hirth, Monika Huber, Thomas Kirchweger, Anja Labner, Valentin Lichtenberger, Orenda Mohan, Carina Oberleitner, Lisa Maria Palasser, Iris Piringer, Sandra Prandstätter, Jasmin Rammerstorfer, Kathrin Schinnerl, Cornelia Schraml, Laura Starsich, Lena Strasser, Bibiana Traxler, Theresa Winter, Birgit Wögerbauer, Sarah Zauner, Eva Zöchbauer, Nina Blaschke, Johanna Doblinger, Jana Katzlberger, Alina Bittner, Simone Hart

Modern Media Guide
Christoph Auer, Kristina Cvetkovska, Melanie Eder, Nicolla Ivanov, Matus Porubsky, Fabian Zechmeister, Jan Kuschel, Raffael Hagleitner
BRG Kandlgasse Wien

KOMPOSITUR
Sabine Bischinger, Barbara Pfaller, Madlen Weingartner, Razila Semic, Melisa Mujcinovic, Ines Tiefenbacher, Karoline-Melpomeni-Hermine Schager
BRG Horn

Gekommen um zu bleiben: Zur falschen Zeit im falschen Land
Kübra Börekci, Chiara Fürpass, Tunahan Harmankaya, Ali Özenir, Ana Protrka, Atilla Kahraman
BRG/ORG Henriettenplatz Wien

Biogas für Burkina Faso
Johannes Egger, Patrick Maier, Dražen Petrović, Simon Zigala, HTL Anichstraße Innsbruck

stop war – start thinking
Michael Dunkel, Nikolaus Müller, Georg Schneider, Philipp Unger, HTL Rennweg Wien

Dictatorship of Perfection
Simon Stix

A Moving Picture
Elisabeth Bloder, BRG Kepler Graz

Konstruktion eines Fortbewegungsmittels nach dem Vorbild einer Ameise
Gabriel Krög, HTL Vöcklabruck

Massageschulranzen
Lena Sophia Wagner

Gamelab Exhibit
u19 – CREATE YOUR WORLD – Prix Ars Electronica, bugnplay (CH), mb21 (DE), C3<19 (HU)

Paseo Project Mini –Cinema in Aragonés
Fundación Zaragoza, Ciudad del Conocimiento

[the next idea] Exhibit
[the next idea] voestalpine Art and Technology Grant, Ars Electronica Futurelab (AT)

Hyperform
Marcelo Coelho (BR), Skylar Tibbits (US), Natan Linder (IL), Yoav Reches (IL)

Global Sounds
Rebecca Gischel (DE)

Bad Trip
Alan Kwan (HK)

What does Souvenir remind you of?
Alias Rosalie (AT/IT), Giovanni Jussi (IT), Michael Schultes (AT), Mario Stadler (AT), Maria Spanring (AT), experimonde (AT)

Young Animations
u19 – CREATE YOUR WORLD – Prix Ars Electronica, bugnplay (CH), mb21 (DE), C3<19 (HU) – kuratiert von Sirikit Amann (AT)

Line up:
Heart Beats

Kompositur
BRG Horn, 14 Jahre; u19

Wenn ich du wäre, würde ich aufpassen
BORG Henriettengasse, 16 Jahre; u19

Amitié sous-marine
Esther Montanbert, 9 Jahre; bugnplay

Dorotea
GRG Draschegasse, 18 Jahre; u19

Create your world

stop war, start thinking
Michael Dunkel, Nikolaus Müller, Georg Schneider, Philipp Unger; HTL Rennweg, 19 Jahre; u19

In the Middle of Nowhere
Zagyva Balázs, 17 Jahre; c3

Create Your World
Victoira Ettl, Astrid Schildberger, 18, 19 Jahre; u19

Hollow
Nadine Mauhart, Verena Claudia Engleder, 19 Jahre; u19

surfwettbewerb
Nico Mangold, Anniina Burgermeister, Nathalie Imfeld, 11 Jahre; bugnplay

Unbekannte Welten

Tit for Tat
Benjamin Lewek, 12 Jahre; mb21

Leo reist durch die verrückte Welt
Nicole Horne, 9 Jahre; bugnplay

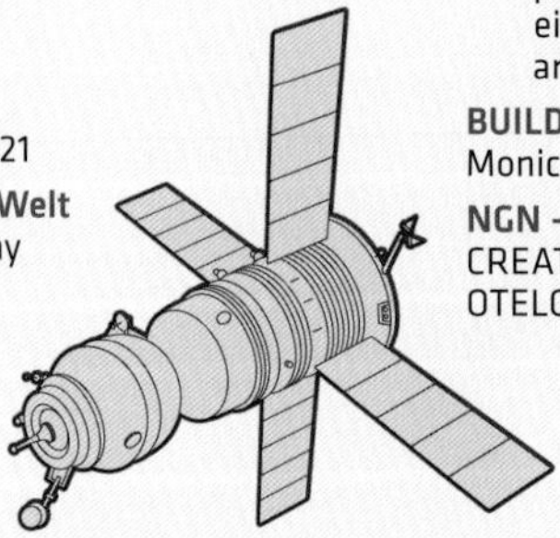

Der Zeichenplanet
Richard Forstmann, Konrad Schoeninger, 14 Jahre; mb21

Mission top secret
Philipp Persano, 13 Jahre; bugnplay

Die größte Erfindung aller Zeiten
Joshua Jacobs, 13 Jahre; mb21

Panel Paranoia
Máté Varga, 18 Jahre; c3

That's life

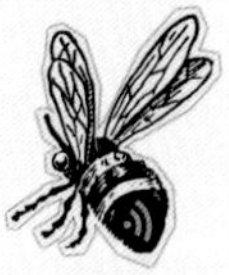

Beautiful Days
Bettina Szremkó, 16 Jahre; c3

Harte Nuss
Leopold Blümel, 13 Jahre; mb21

Hunger
Kolja Tomisch, 10 Jahre; mb21

Urban
Máté Varga, 18 Jahre; c3

Wild Races

Stucked
Attila Almási, Szilárd Enyedi, Richárd Ipacs, Tamás Kiss, 17 Jahre; c3

Shake Ray and Blu
Stiftung Talente| 14 – 19 Jahre; u19

Cubes
Lea Hofer, 17 Jahre; bugnplay

In die Tasche gesteckt
Midas Kempcke|, 11 Jahre; mb21

BluCar
Isidor Dietrich,18 Jahre; u19

Feldversuche
Florian Bührle, 14 Jahre; u19

u19 – CREATE YOUR WORLD – OPEN LABS

Nobody is perfect
Verein FAB – Virtual Office (AT)

Bei diversen Wettkämpfen, wie einem Rollstuhl-Rennen und Rollstuhl-Parcours oder bei Computerspielen mit Augensteuerung wollen die Jugendlichen mit Beeinträchtigung spielerisch soziale und zwischenmenschliche Barrieren abbauen.

Gamelab
u19 – CREATE YOUR WORLD – Prix Ars Electronica, bugnplay (CH), mb21 (DE), C3<19 (HU), eine Jugendbegegnung gefördert von Jugend in Aktion

16 Jugendliche aus Österreich, Deutschland, Ungarn und der Schweiz entwickeln, gestalten und programmieren während des Festivals gemeinsam ein Serious Game, in dem sie die Themen verarbeiten, die ihnen am Herzen liegen.

BUILDASOUND
Monica Rikic (ES)

NGN – NeXt Generation News vom Festival
CREATE YOUR REGION Traunsteinregion, Verein OTELO (AT)

Nachrichten aus der Zukunft
CREATE YOUR REGION Traunsteinregion und Linz Land (AT)

ImproTheater – Erinnern – Vergessen – flüchtige Momente
CREATE YOUR REGION Traunsteinregion und Traunviertler Alpenvorland (AT); Bernadette Laimbauer (AT)

Lehmbackofen – Selbst machen statt abgespeist werden!
CREATE YOUR REGION Traunsteinregion (AT); ZIB Hagenmühle/ Kirchham (AT)

Fly Doo
Lehrlingswerkstatt BRP Powertrain (AT)

Endlich be-greifen – WELTRAUM
Science Center Network (AT)

Marketing für gute Nachrichten
NERONT (AT)

KNIT YOURSELF
Ildiko Sera (CH)

Meinungsvertreter
Ars Electronica (AT)

Vertrete deine Meinung – im wahrsten Sinne des Wortes. Mit Buchstabenstempeln an den Schuhen kann man hier Nachrichten hinterlassen und weitertragen und sich im Festivalgeschehen verewigen.

SOUNDSTICKS
Leo Betinelli (AR)

u19 mobil relaunch
nähküche (AT)

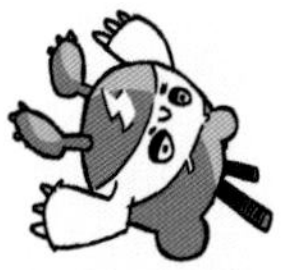

Nähküche – eine Offene Nähwerkstatt
nähküche (AT)

Soilution – Erde mit Zukunft
HLFS Ursprung (AT)

SchülerInnen der HLFS Ursprung vermitteln, wie sie CO_2 in der Erde binden, wodurch diese sehr fruchtbar wird, ähnlich der „Terra Preta", der natürlich vorkommenden Schwarzerde aus dem Amazonasgebiet.

Biogas für Burkina Faso
HTL Anichstraße Innsbruck (AT)

Lichtlabor
Kunstuniversität Linz Bildnerische Erziehung und Mediengestaltung, Philipp Luftensteiner (AT)

DRONE ZONE
OTELO – Offene Technologielabore (AT)

Action Cam Festival
OTELO – Offene Technologielabore (AT)

In diesem Open Lab entstehen ungewöhnliche und actionreiche Blickwinkel auf das Festivalgeschehen. Man erfährt, was es braucht, Videos dieser Art in Szene zu setzen, und integriert gleichzeitig seine persönliche Perspektive ins kollektive Festival-Videogedächtnis.

Utopia – Stadt deiner Zukunft
Kunstuniversität Linz – sustainable architecture & spatial tactics, Franz Koppelstätter (AT), Katharina Weinberger (AT), Matthias Böttger (DE), Hannah Kores (AT)

World Map Archive
Benjamin Pollach (DE)

Jam Session
Zquetschte Zwetschkn (AT)

Die Lebensmittelschule – Wie geht's, was ist's und wo kommts her?
Produktionsschule Wels (AT), Produktionsschule Leonding (AT)

Wo kommt eigentlich mein Essen her? Die Produktionsschulen Wels und Leonding bieten BesucherInnen nicht nur leckeres Mittagessen, sondern auch Informationen zu den verwendeten Lebensmitteln. Man darf in Kochtöpfe schauen, selbst mitkochen und experimentieren.

Espressomobil
espressomobil OG (AT)

TOTAL RESET
Papplab (AT)

Magic Shifter
Florian Bittner (AT), Philipp Tiefenbacher (AT)

u19 – CREATE YOUR WORLD – EVENTS

Das Experiment – Kick Off
Rotes Kreuz OÖ, Pädagogische Hochschule OÖ (AT)

Zum Schulbeginn wird ein neuartiges, gemeinsames Jahresprojekt gestartet, bei dem SchülerInnen und StudentInnen die Möglichkeit haben, mit der Unterstützung und dem Input von erstklassigen Experten, Projekte zu Humanität, Resilienz, Wissensmanagement und Soziale Innovation zu realisieren.

BLINDgehen – SEHENDführen
CREATE YOUR REGION Traunsteinregion, Flora Hollinetz und SchülerInnen der NMS Vorchdorf (AT)

Fly Doo Show
Lehrlingswerkstatt BRP Powertrain (AT)

SOUNDSTICKS Performance
Leo Betinelli (AR)

u19 Ceremony
Prix Ars Electronica (AT)

Prix Forum u19
u19 – CREATE YOUR WORLD – Prix Ars Electronica, bugnplay (CH), mb21 (DE), C3<19 (HU)

Lehrlingstag UBIT @ Ars
Ars Electronica (AT), Wirtschaftskammer OÖ (AT)

u19 – CREATE YOUR WORLD – Warm Up
Ars Electronica (AT)

u19 – CREATE YOUR WORLD – Recall
Ars Electronica (AT)

u19 – CREATE YOUR WORLD wird unterstützt von:

Jugend in Aktion
KulturKontakt Austria
LIFEtool gemeinnützige GmbH.
Pädagogische Hochschule OberÖsterreich
Pro Helvetia
REHA Service GmbH
Sparkasse Oberösterreich
Wirtschaftskammer Oberösterreich

Impressions u19 – CREATE YOUR WORLD – Future Festival of the Next Generation 2012

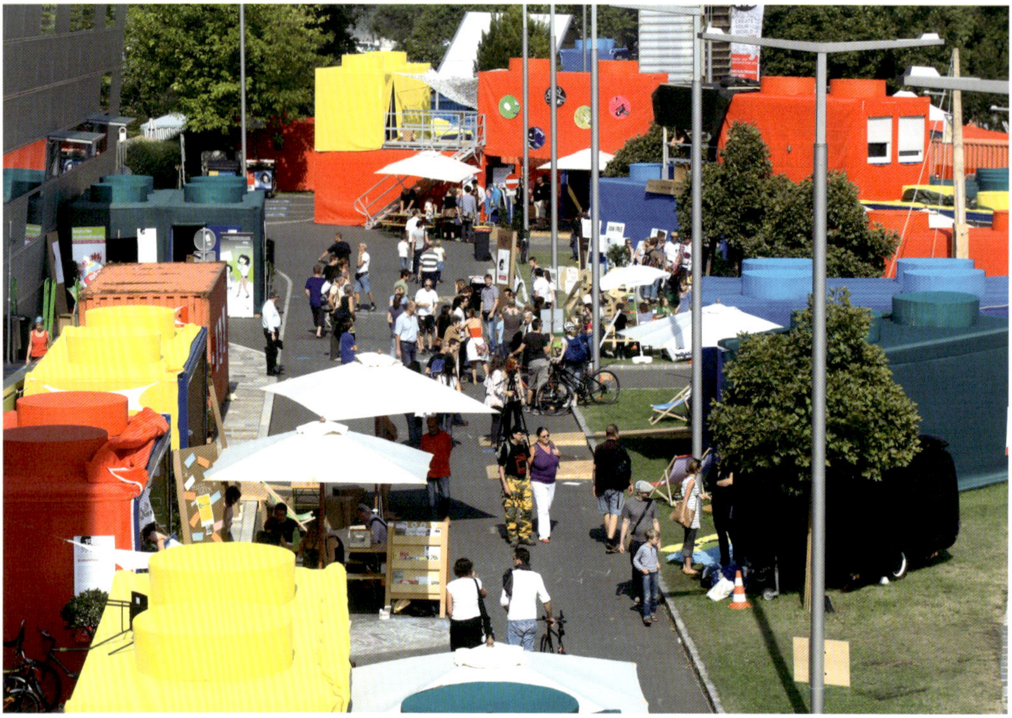

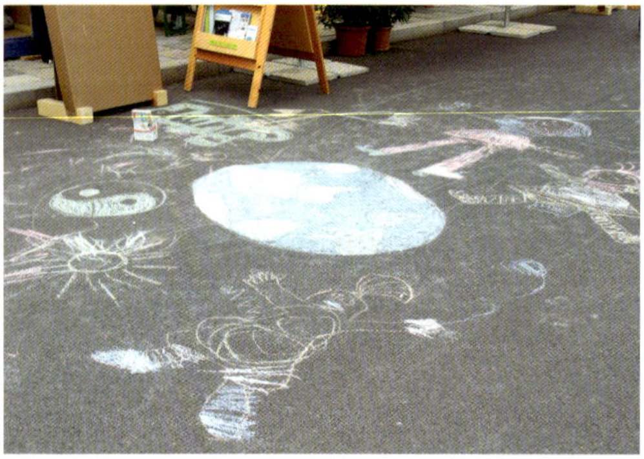

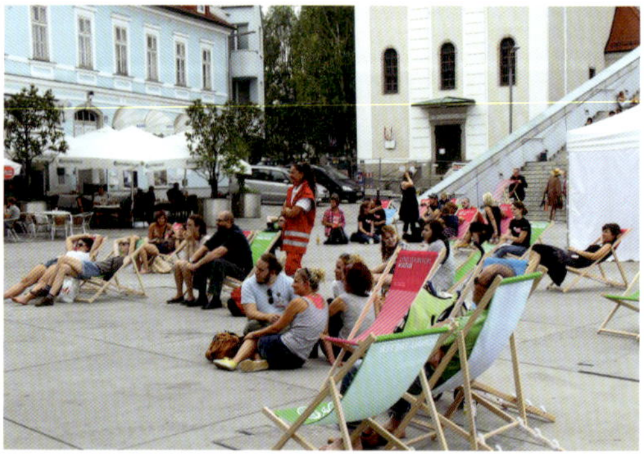

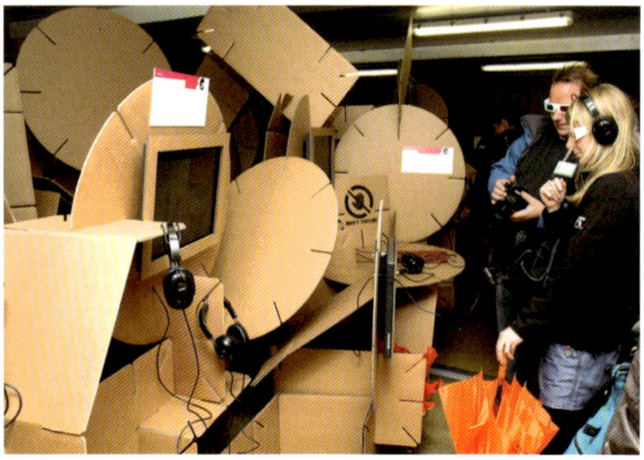

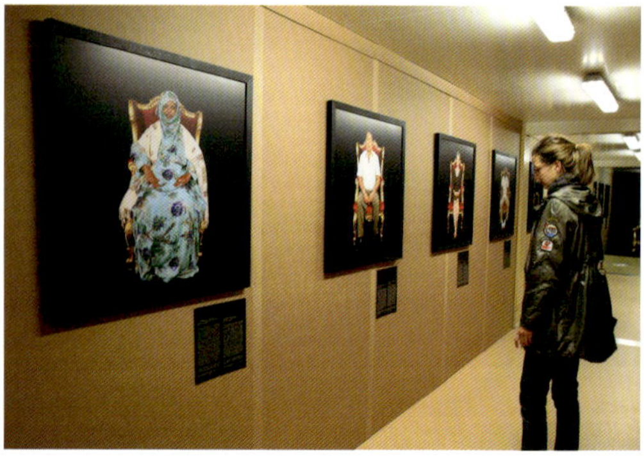

Impressions u19 – CREATE YOUR WORLD – Future Festival of the Next Generation 2012

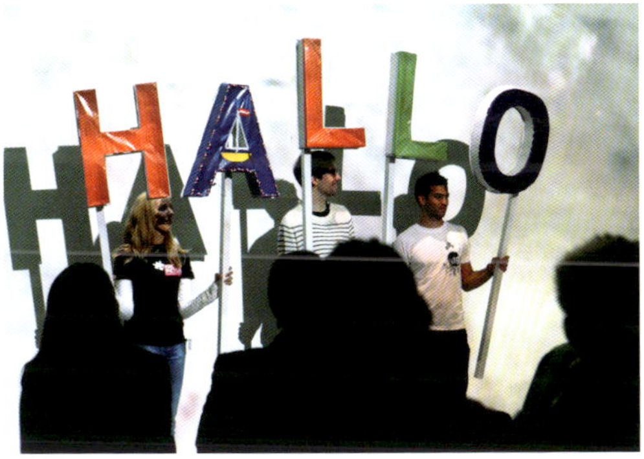

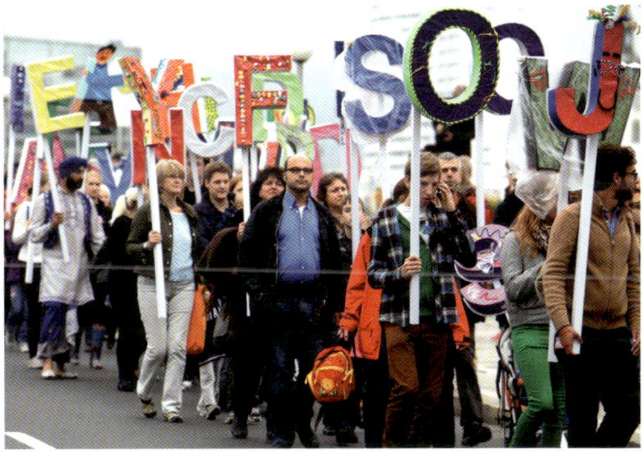

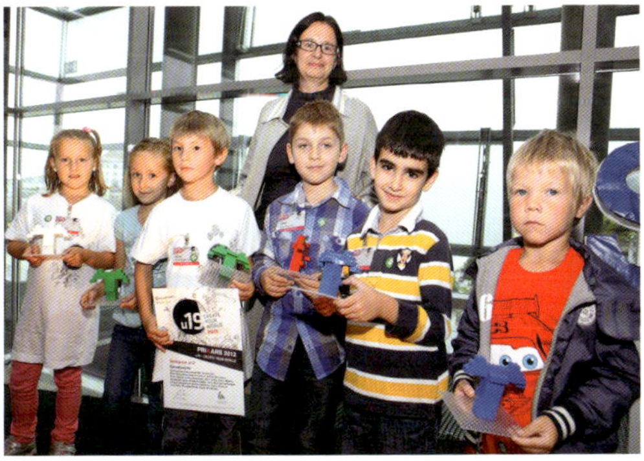

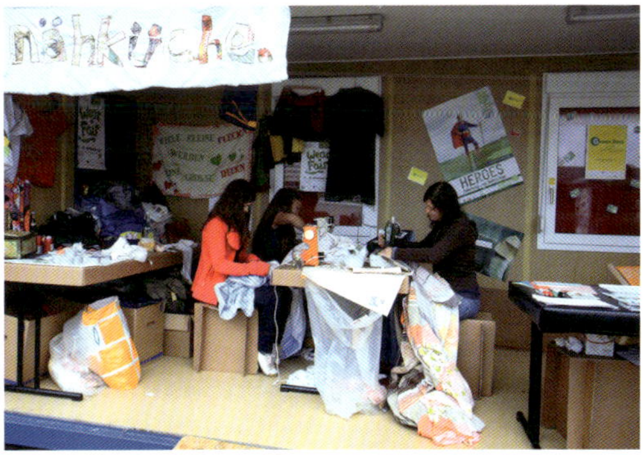

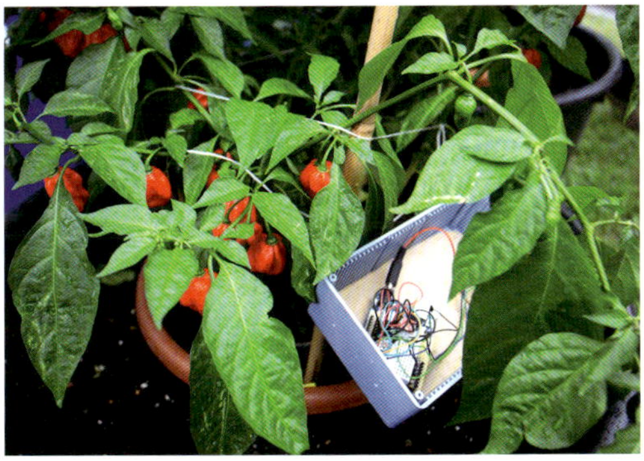

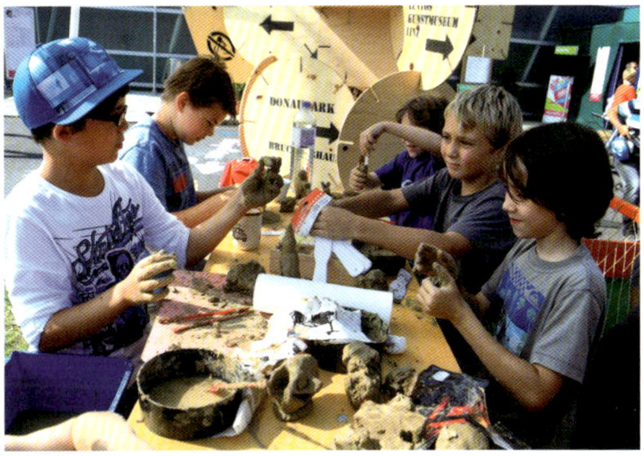

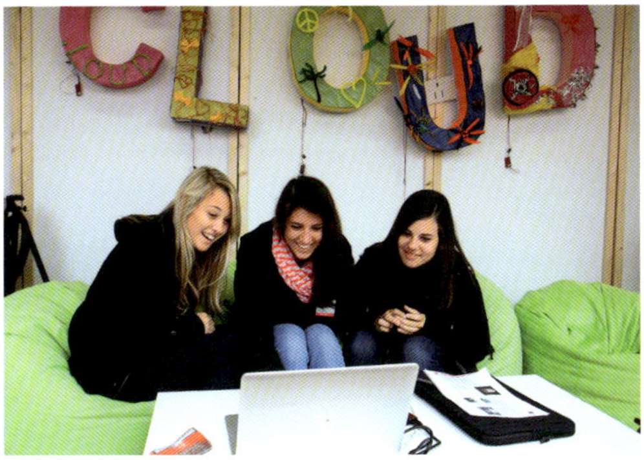

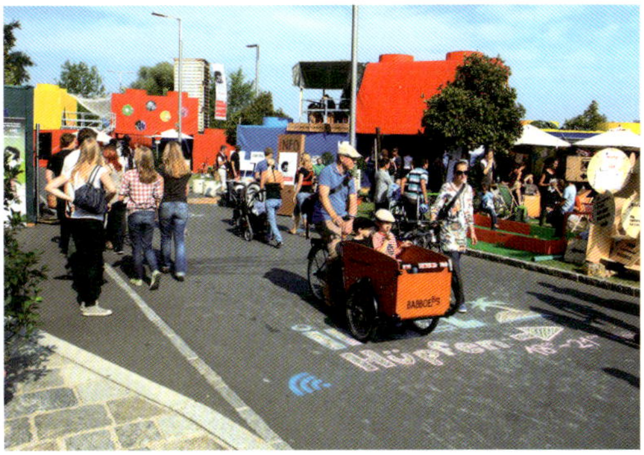

AEC, rubra

Biographies

ArtScience Interfaculty (NL) is an interdisciplinary bachelor and master program that fosters curiosity-driven research as an approach for the making of art. The program considers art and science as a continuum and promotes the development of new art forms and artistic languages. The ArtScience Interfaculty is embedded in both the Royal Conservatoire and The Royal Academy for Fine Arts in The Hague, NL.
http://www.interfaculty.nl/

Austria Game Jam (AT) has been held since 2009 as part of the worldwide Global Game Jam *(http://globalgamejam.org)*. It has grown steadily over the years, and planning for the next Austria Game Jam on January 24-26, 2014 has already begun. The jams are organized by the not-for-profit Verein für Innovative Unterhaltungssoftware. *http://austriagamejam.org*

Oliver Bimber (DE), at the age of 36, Oliver Bimber was appointed as a full university professor (2009) and became Head of the Institute of Computer Graphics at Johannes Kepler University Linz. Bimber's research interests include visual computing, real-time rendering and visualization, computer vision, image analysis and processing, optics, and human visual perception in the context of next-generation display and imaging technologies.

Rica Blunck (DE) is a choreographer, singer and author. Her passion for combining various forms of artistic expression led her to found the COAX Dance Company in 1989. COAX has performed in Scotland, Switzerland and at numerous venues throughout Germany. Her travels are not only of a geographic nature; she also undertakes interdisciplinary excursions that allow her to reconnoiter unexplored artistic territory.

Pierre Bongiovanni (FR) Artistic director of La Maison Laurentine, Managing Director of D'abord les forêts festival, art critic, chief editor of the online magazine *Slunk*, filmmaker and producer. In 1990, Bongiovanni founded the CIVC Pierre Schaeffer (Center of International Video Creation), the first digital and media art center in Europe. He led the CIVC to support a wide range of pioneering projects till 2004 while curating many important European festivals and engaging in-depth exchanges in South America and Asia. *www.laurentine.net*

Sayfan G. Borghini (IT) graduated as a doctor in Physics in Rome in 1997. Her interests in the last ten years have focused on complex systems at the intersection of technological, cultural and artistic forces. She is currently a lecturer in the Master Course in Integrated Design at H.I.T. in Israel, where she is also collaborating on curatorial projects.

Claudius Brodmann (DE) is a director and digital media designer. He was born in Rumania and has lived in Germany since 1983. He studied at the Filmakademie Baden-Württemberg. In 1999, he founded m.a.r.k.13, an animation & post-production studio, which he headed until 2004. Since then, he has worked as a freelance director and specialist in digital & interactive media. He has also taught at Merz Akademie Stuttgart since 1999.

Michael K. Buckland (UK/US) is Emeritus Professor, University of California, Berkeley, School of Information. Born and educated in England, Prof. Buckland studied History at Oxford and Librarianship at Sheffield. After working as a librarian in England and the USA, he was director of the School of Library and Information Studies at Berkeley. He has written extensively about library services, the organization of knowledge, and history documentation.
http://people.ischool.berkeley.edu/~buckland/

Ching-Wen Chang 張晴文 **(TW)** is Assistant Professor at National HsinChu University of Education, former chief editor of *Artist Magazine* (2004–2010) and art critic. Publications include *Emerging Taiwanese Painters* (2013), *Tsong Pu: The World Comes from Existence* (2010), *Playing/ Interaction* (2003). He curated *It Takes Four Sorts: A Cross-Strait Four-Regions Artistic Exchange*, *Crush on EMU* (2012), *Xing-Dian Boys* (2012), *Weak Painting* (2009), *The Empire Strikes Back* (2008) and *Depth of Surface—New Spaces of Contemporary Painting* (2004).

Ina Conradi Chavez (US/SG) is an award-winning digital media artist. Her films have been screened internationally at Ars Electronica Festival, Brooklyn Film Festival, Anima Mundi, Dimension 3 Festival, and Edinburgh International Film Festival. Ina holds an MFA from UCLA. She is a Japan Foundation Fellow and a member of the Union of Slovene Fine Art. Currently she is Assistant Professor at Nanyang Technological University. *www.inaconradi.com*

Lila Chitayat (IL) is an architect, designer, new-media artist and an experimental practitioner of design through computational processes. Lila is a senior lecturer at the Design Faculty of H.I.T (Holon Institute of Technology) teaching in the Masters program and Interior Design departments. Founder of LinC Studio: a trans-disciplinary design environment involving media and technology to produce a wide range of projects in urban installations, space design, exhibit design and digital architecture for virtual environments. Collaborative projects with her brother, Alon, include *Taxilink* (winner of PRIX Ars Electronica 2010), *Ideal Virtual Jerusalem* for MIC, the urban installation *White Tent City* and AR at the Hansen old Hospital. Lila received her M.Arch from Columbia University and B. Arch from Pratt Institute.

Heather Dewey-Hagborg (US) is an information artist who has shown her work internationally at events including the Poland Mediations Biennale, Jaaga art and technology center in Bangalore, and the Monitor Digital Festival in Guadalajara. She has exhibited nationally at PS1 Moma, the New Museum, Eyebeam, Clocktower Gallery, 92Y Tribeca, Issue Project Room, and Splatterpool in New York City. She has a BA in Information Arts from Bennington College and a Masters degree from the Interactive Telecommunications Program at Tisch School of the Arts, New York University. She is currently a PhD student in Electronic Arts at Rensselaer Polytechnic Institute.

Jeremiah Diephuis (US/AT) was born in 1976 and grew up in the great arcades of the American Midwest. He currently works as a lecturer in the Media Technology and Design program at the Hagenberg Campus of the University of Applied Sciences Upper Austria.

Dimension+ (HK/TW), Bi-city New Media Arts Team based in Hong Kong and Taipei, founded by Keith Lam (HK) and Escher Tsai (TW) in 2009. By mixing-and-matching they transform the invisible, digital form into tangible physical and visible experience, creating works that combine digital and analog, linking the digital and the physical. Keith Lam received the Young Artist Award from Hong Kong Arts Development Awards 2008, the "40 under 40" Global Creative Talent by *Perspective Magazine* and a Prix Ars Electronica Honorary Mention in 2008. He has been invited to numerous festivals around the world, lectures at various universities and has a magazine column. *http://www.dimensionplus.co*

Wolfgang "Fadi" Dorninger (AT) Sound is the centerpiece of his artistic work. Wolfgang Dorninger is the proprietor of base, an experimental electronic music label, a performer, composer of theater & film music, sound designer, sound artist and lecturer at Linz Art University. Two diametrically opposed approaches dominate his works, which can be positioned between digital sound production and concrete environmental noises. They range from spatial-tonal installations in a concert setting, multimedia performances and acoustic presentations all the way to techno and music for the theater.
http://dorninger.servus.at

F.M. Einheit (DE) lives in Tittmoning.
http://www.fmeinheit.org/

Ewald Elmecker (AT) was born in 1972. He's one of the proprietors of Off-Space, a nomad encampment in Linz, and a visual artist at the interface of architecture, sound and, at times, botany.

Yael Eylat van-Essen (IL), PhD., is a researcher in the fields of Digital Culture, New-Media Art and Museology. She teaches at Tel Aviv University and in Holon Institute of Technology, where she is the curator of the Research Gallery and she established and directed for many years a pioneering "New-Media" department in Israel. Until recently, she was the Head of the Art Department in Seminar Kibbutzim College and Academic Director of the International Curatorial program. She edited the first anthology on Digital Culture published in Hebrew.

Joaquin Fargas (AR) is a multidisciplinary artist who combines biological material and technological tools in order to break up limits and generate dialogues so as to draw us nearer to nature and life. He is the academic director of San Isidro Interactive Exploratory Museum and professor of Technological Art at the Miamonides University, where he started and directs the Bioart Argentine Laboratory.

Patrick Feaster (US) is a two-time Grammy nominee, co-founder of FirstSounds.org, and author of *Pictures of Sound*. Patrick Feaster has participated in locating, contextualizing, and making audible many of the world's oldest sound recordings. He received his doctorate in folklore and ethnomusicology in 2007 from Indiana University Bloomington, where he is a member of the Media Preservation Initiative and teaches in the Department of Communication and Culture.

Hans-Joachim Frey (DE) was born in 1965. He is the managing director of the Brucknerhaus and the Bruckner Festival. He graduated from Hamburg University of Music and Theater with a triple major: opera singer, director of music theater, and culture manager. 1997-2002, he served as artistic director and 2002-07 as opera director at the Semperoper in Dresden; 2007-11, as general director of Theater Bremen. He has directed numerous opera productions. Since 2011, he has been guest professor at Seoul Institute of the Arts in South Korea.

Matthew Gardiner (AU/AT) is an artist/researcher at the Ars Electronica Futurelab most well known for his work with origami and robotics. Coining the term Oribot (折りボト) spawned a series of art/science works concerned with the aesthetic, biomechanic, and morphological connections between nature, origami and robotics. Recent works include *Oribotics [the future unfold]* 2010, *Shadowgram* 2010–11, *Light is Time, Folds are Space* 2012–13, *Synthetic Memetic* 2013, and made his debut as a curator for *Project Genesis/ Yours Synthetically* at the Ars Electronica Center.

Stephanie Geiger (DE) is an artist and costume designer. She combines modern concepts and approaches with traditional designs. Her work is both timeless and international. Her creations have been in the spotlight at Residenztheater in Munich and on stages in Zurich, Breda, New York and Linz.

Andranik Ghalustians (AT) was born in 1972 in Vienna and studied Political Science and Philosophy at the University of Vienna. In addition to various journalistic activities in the field of retro games, he is also the proprietor of one of the largest video game collections worldwide.

HR Giger (CH) was born in 1940 in Chur, Switzerland. 1962-65: Zurich University of the Arts; *Atomkinder* ink drawings; 1968: props for *Swiss Made 2069* by Fredi M. Murer; 1972: exhibition at Kasseler Kunstverein; 1976: exhibition at Galerie Sydow-Zirkwitz in Frankfurt; 1980: Oscar for *Alien* by Ridley Scott; 1998: opening of the HR Giger Museum in Gruyères, Switzerland; retrospectives in Paris, Prague, Vienna, Frankfurt and Chur; 2012: *Prometheus* by Ridley Scott; lives in Zurich.

Jeremy Goh Jie Xing (SG) co-founded IMBA Interactive, a sound design firm based in Singapore. Jeremy has been a musician and percussionist in set-ups ranging from symphonic orchestras to jazz combos. Since completing his BFA in Interactive Media NTU 2011, he has collaborated with filmmakers, animators, game developers and artists from across the globe. Several of these works have received honorable mentions both locally and internationally. *http://www.imbainteractive.com*

Nick Goldman (UK) works at the European Bioinformatics Institute (EBI) in Hinxton, UK, researching algorithms to study genome evolution. He holds degrees in mathematics and zoology from the University of Cambridge, and has worked at the Natural History Museum and the National Institute for Medical Research, London, and the Departments of Genetics and Zoology, Cambridge, before joining EBI in 2002. He has published approximately 100 scientific papers.
http://www.ebi.ac.uk/research/goldman

Doris Graf (DE) was born in 1968 in Krumbach, Germany. She studied at Villa Arson in Nice, France 1990-95 and 1996-2000 at Stuttgart State Academy of Art and Design. In 1994, she received a grant to study at Goldsmiths College in London. She has lived in Stuttgart and worked as an artist since 1995. She has exhibited widely in Germany and abroad, and been the recipient of numerous prizes and grants. In 2012, her *Eu, Rio* project represented the State of Baden-Württemberg at the CRIO Biennale in Rio de Janeiro.

Jürgen Hagler (AT) is an associate professor in the Digital Media department at the Upper Austria University of Applied Sciences (Hagenberg, Austria) and is in charge of computer animation and animation studies. He became the programme coordinator for the Digital Arts master's degree programme in 2009. Since 2008 he has been actively involved in Prix Ars Electronica and in 2009 he became curator of Ars Electronica Animation Festival.

Frank Hartmann (AT/DE) is full professor at the Faculty of Art & Design, Bauhaus-University Weimar, Germany. He was educated in Austria where he did his doctorate in philosophy at the University of Vienna and received his postdoctoral qualification (Habilitation) in the new interdisciplinary field of Media Philosophy. Work includes graduate teaching at several European Universities, international lectures and guest professorships including the USP - Universidade de São Paulo, Brazil. He has published several books on media theory, media archaeology and visual communication. *www.medienphilosophie.net*

Canan Hastik (DE): doctoral thesis in Digital Humanities and Cultural Analytics, works at the Department of Collaborate and Media, Media Campus of Darmstadt University of Applied Sciences. In 2011, she launched MEGA – Museum of Electronic Games & Art, where she curates themed exhibitions on digital culture.

John-Dylan Haynes (DE/UK) is a psychologist, neuroscientist and Professor of Theory and Analysis of Large-Scale Brain Signals at the Bernstein Center of Charité Berlin. Haynes and his team conduct research on the neuronal basis of consciousness, volition, intentions and free will. They have used MRI technology to show that decision-making is initiated by subconscious brain processes.

Andreas J. Hirsch (AT) was born in 1961 in Vienna. He is a curator, author and photographer. 2004-07: Prix Ars Electronica juror; since 2008, curator at KunstHausWien, retrospectives of works by René Burri, Henri Cartier-Bresson and Linda McCartney; author of books about Pablo Picasso, Tina Modotti and Friedensreich Hundertwasser; 2010: concept of Ars Electronica's "Open Source Life" symposium; 2011: curator of the exhibition *HR Giger—Dreams and Visions* at KunstHausWien.

h.o [hdoto] (JP) is an artist group which was started by Hideaki Ogawa. Each member of the group has a specialized field such as sensor technologies, database system, interaction design, hardware design and robotics, and the group has unique forms of collaboration, changing team members depending on the kind of work. h.o's interest in works has coincided with encounters with new members and collaborators. The artists Hideaki Ogawa and Emiko Ogawa have been in Linz at Ars Electronca since 2007. Based in Tokyo and Linz, they create and exhibit works all over the world. They search for witty new ideas relating to current social contexts, and h.o. realizes artistic expression at the speed of technological progress. *http://www.howeb.org*

Kurt Hörbst (AT) was born in 1972 in the Mühlviertel region north of Linz. Following training as a telecommunications engineer in Graz, he attended the Prague School of Photography 1992-95. Since 1996, he has taught journalism and the history of photography at that institution, and worked on establishing its Austrian campus. Since 2005, he has taught photography at St. Pölten University of Applied Sciences. In recent years, he has focused his interest on multimedia projects with video installations and media performances in Austria and abroad. *http://www.hoerbst.com/*

Horst Hörtner (AT) is a media artist and researcher. He is an expert in the design of human-computer interaction and holds several patents in this field. Hörtner was a founding member of the Ars Electronica Futurelab in 1996 and since then he has been the director of this atelier/laboratory. He started work in the field of media art in the 1980s and co-founded the"media-art group x-space" in Graz, Austria, in 1990. Horst Hörtner works at the nexus of art and science and gives lectures and talks at numerous international conferences and universities.

Brian House (US) is a media artist whose work traverses alternative geographies, experimental music, and a critical data practice. By constructing embodied, participatory systems, he seeks to negotiate between algorithms and the rhythms of everyday life. His work has been shown by MoMA (NYC), MOCA (LA), Eyebeam, and Conflux Festival among others and has been featured in publications including *WIRED, TIME, The New York Times*, and on Univision Sports. *http://brianhouse.net*

Chien-Hung Huang 黃建宏 (TW) Film, contemporary art and performance art critic, associate professor of Taipei National University of Arts, Institute of Trans-disciplinary Art. Specialized in G. Deleuze, J. Baudrillard and J. Rancière's theory. Published *COQ* (2009), *An Independent Discourse* (2010), *Trans-Plex Agenda* (2011), *EMU* (2012). *Curated Exception* (2007), *S-HOMO,* (2009), *Look by the cinema* (2010), *TRANS-PLex* (2011), *Solarium* (2011), *Beautiful World* (2012) and *Crush on EMU* (2012).

Hiroto Ikeuchi (JP), born in 1990. He graduated from Tama Art University, Department of Information Design in 2013, where he studied design and Flash content, and spent most of his free time creating plastic models. He conceived the idea of a computer as a secret base, and has created hybrid dioramas combining plastic models and PC equipment.

ikono is an international media platform that displays and broadcasts visual arts. Through its HDTV channels ikonoMENASA and ikonoTV, ikono showcases a unique program dedicated to the arts of all epochs from antiquity until today—reaching more than 30 countries and from September 2013 on a global audience via livestream on *www.ikono.org*. Without adding any sound or commentary ikono offers a pure visual and emotional art experience.

Hiroshi Ishiguro (JP) received a D. Eng. in Systems Engineering from Osaka University, Japan, in 1991. He has been a Professor in the Department of Systems Innovation, Graduate School of Engineering Science, Osaka University, since 2009 and Group Leader of the Hiroshi Ishiguro Laboratory at the Advanced Telecommunications Research Institute and ATR fellow since 2011. His research interests include sensor networks, interactive robotics, and android science.

Charlotte Jarvis (UK) is an artist and filmmaker who collaborates with scientists. For the past four years Charlotte has also been collaborating with photographer and writer James Read on a series of pop-up restaurants. Charlotte has just completed a year as artist in residence at the Netherlands Proteomics Centre, during which time she created the project *Blighted by Kenning* in which the Universal Declaration of Human Rights was encoded into DNA and used to "contaminate" apples—a realization of "forbidden fruit". The piece was exhibited at The Big Shed in the UK and is due to move to Amsterdam and The Hague in November

Werner Jauk (AT), born 1953. Musicologist/psychologist and scientific media-artist. Professor of Musicology at the University of Graz (KFU), Austria, working on „music + media/art“ with the focus on music as a role model for media arts. Studies in perception, cybernetics and experimental aesthetics led him to try and bridge a gap between science and arts. He has published many scientific papers, exhibited installations as a scientific artist at international festivals such as Ars Electronica, Cynetart, liquid music and Biennale di Venezia.

Ariane Koek (UK/CH) is a writer, producer, cultural policy maker and strategist. She directs the Collide@CERN programme, which she created following a 4-month feasibility study at CERN thanks to the Clore Fellowship—an international award for cultural leadership.

Alan Kwan (HK), born 1990, is a media artist and filmmaker based in Hong Kong. He started making short films at the age of 9, and 10 years later he started to bring invention ideas from film to real life. His research focuses on lifelogging and virtual mindtrip systems, and his latest installation *Bad Trip* was recently showcased at various media art festivals and featured in major media including Discovery Channel, *WIRED, and Popular Science. www.kwanalan.com*

Lois Lammerhuber (AT) was born in 1952 in St. Peter in der Au. Since 1984, this self-taught artist has worked closely together with *GEO* magazine, a collaboration that has strongly influenced his approach to photography. The facts and figures: 2,400 photo essays, 69 books, many magazine covers and, among other honors, three Graphis Phototography Awards for the year's best reportage. Lammerhuber has also been the author of countless radio broadcasts in Germany and Austria. In 1996 he founded the Edition Lammerhuber publishing house, and his books have garnered numerous prizes. Lois Lammerhuber is a member of the Art Directors Club New York.

I-Wei Li 李怡衛 (DE/TW/CA), Artistic Director of SideBySide Studio e.V., CEO of Artout Artist Escort Service, and "contexterin"—a female person who aims to generate new contexts in her creative practice. She works extensively with cross-discipline exchanges in Europe, South America and Asia and gives great importance to critical research situated between art, the economy and crisis. Recent curatorial projects include *Kunst Apotheke Salon, Between Windows—Latin America and Beyond* and *D'abord les forêts. www.sidebysidestudio.net*

Michael Madsen (DK), born 1971, is a film director and conceptual artist. He studied Dramaturgy and Art History at the universities of Aarhus and Copenhagen. Madsen has directed several documentaries including *Celestial Night - A Film on Visibility* (2003) and the prizewinning work *To Damascus - A Film on Interpretation* (2005). *Into Eternity* is a feature documentary film directed by Michael Madsen, released in 2010. It follows the digging and pre-implementation of the Onkalo nuclear waste repository on the island of Olkiluoto, Finland.

Timo Maier (DE) studied German literature, philosophy and history at RWTH Aachen University. He's interested in combining insights from the field of cultural studies with new forms of communication using digital media, whereby he focuses on the question of how interaction and collective processes will be able to reconfigure art, politics and society in the future.

Camillo Meinhart (AT) is a Vienna based filmmaker engaged in science communication. With a background in international TV broadcasting, he documents and features science and technology in many different ways. Together with Markus Schmidt, he co-founded Biofaction. His recent works deal with seed diversity in agriculture, synthetic biology, biodiversity and bio-art. He co-organized the 2011 Biofaction Science, Art and Film Festival. *www.biofaction.com*

Miraikan (JP) The National Museum of Emerging Science and Innovation is a new type of science museum that links people directly with the new wisdom of the 21st century. At the heart of Miraikan's activities is cutting-edge science and technology—"state-of-the-art knowledge and innovation" that Miraikan aims to share with the whole society. Founded in 2001. *www.miraikan.jst.go.jp*

Andy Müller-Maguhn (DE) has been an active member of the CHAOS Computer Club since 1986. In this capacity, he investigates the interplay among new technologies and their effects on social welfare, culture, the economy and politics. He founded the DATA TRAVEL AGENCY in Berlin, where he conducts research on security issues, surveillance technologies and their psychological implications. Since 2012, he has been director of the Wau Holland Foundation that works on behalf of freedom of information and the right to privacy.

Maki Namekawa (JP), pianist, is equally at home in classical and contemporary repertoire. She performs regularly at international venues such as Suntory Hall Tokyo, Ruhr Piano Festival, Musik-Biennale Berlin, Festival Eclat in Stuttgart, ZKM Karlsruhe and Rheingau Music Festival and records frequently for the major German radio networks. Recent engagements include Seattle Symphony Orchestra, Concertgebouw Orkest Amsterdam, Münchner Philharmoniker, Munich Chamber Orchestra, Dresdener Philharmonie, Stuttgart Chamber Orchestra and Bruckner Orchester Linz. In 2012 she performed Arvo Pärt's *Lamentate* at Carnegie Hall New York and Igor Stravinsky's *Concerto for Piano and Wind Instruments* with the Bamberg Symphony Orchestra. Since 2005, Maki Namekawa and Dennis Russell Davies have been performing together as a piano duo in Europe and the US.

Reinhard Nestelbacher (AT) is a molecular biologist, science communicator and bioartist. He has produced numerous projects at the nexus of art and science designed to reach general audiences: *Spermrace* (2000); *GFPixel* (2001); exhibitions at Ars Electronica, Max Planck Forum, ARCO Madrid, Donumenta and Roche; *Hidden Scientific Bodies* (2003 & on permanent display); the cabaret *Mr. Gene* (2004); involved in the setup of the Ars Electronica Center's Biolab; *Cellpainting* (2011); *Eyecatcher* (2013). *www.nestelbacher.com*

Roberto Paci Dalò (IT), a musician, film & theatre director and visual artist who presents his work worldwide in museums, theatres, radio, and the public space. A pioneer in the use of Internet and telecommunication systems in art, he is the artistic director of the Giardini Pensili group. His work has won him international admiration from, among others, John Cage and Aleksandr Sokurov. *robertopacidalo.com*

Benjamin Pollach (DE) is an art director based in Berlin. His passion for maps started at an early age. Instead of reading children's books, he was attracted to world atlases. Years later, while hanging out with friends in a bar, someone asked who's able to draw the world map from memory. After discovering the maps again a few years later, and still fascinated by the results, Benjamin Pollach decided to create the *World Map Archive;* he asked friends, and friends of friends, all over the globe, to draw a map of the world and contribute to his collection. *www.worldmaparchive.com*

Rodrigo Quian Quiroga (AR) holds a research chair and is the director of the Centre for Systems Neuroscience and the head of the Bioengineering Research Group at the University of Leicester. He graduated in Physics at the University of Buenos Aires, Argentina and obtained his PhD in Applied Mathematics at the University of Luebeck, Germany. In 2010, he obtained the Royal Society Wolfson Research Merit Award. His main research interest is on the study of the principles of visual perception and memory. He discovered what has been named "Concept cells" or "Jennifer Aniston neurons"–neurons in the human brain that play a key role in memory formation– a finding that was selected as one of the top 100 scientific stories of 2005 by *Discover* magazine. His work has been published in about 100 research articles and has received worldwide media attention, including articles in the *New York Times*, the *Washington Post*, *Scientific American*, *Daily Mail*, *New Scientist*, the *Independent*, etc. He is the author of the book *Borges and memory,* linking the thoughts of Argentinean writer Jorge Luis Borges with memory research in Neuroscience.

Daniel Reetz (US) is an artist, a camera hacker, and an engineer. He is best known as the founder of the DIY Book Scanner community, a group of thousands who develop Open Source Hardware and Software, exploiting cheap cameras and modern tools to scan books quickly, especially in places where traditional scanning is unaffordable, impossible, or inappropriate.

Helga Rohra (DE) was born in 1953. Originally an interpreter specializing in the natural sciences and medicine, she went on to train herself in the field of dementia. In 2007, she was diagnosed with Lewy Body Dementia. In 2010, she became a member of the board of the Munich Alzheimer Society. Since 2010, she has been the patroness of the Dementia Center of the City of Erlangen. In 2011, Helga Rohra published her bestseller entitled *Aus dem Schatten treten. Warum ich mich für unsere Rechte als Demenzbetroffene einsetze* (Stepping out of the Shadows. Why I am a lobbyist for the rights of Dementia sufferers). Since 2011, she has also been a member of the scientific advisory committee of Alzheimer Ethik and, since 2012, a member of the board of AE (Alzheimer Europa) /Luxembourg as well as first Chairperson of the EU Working Group of People with Dementia.

Dennis Russell Davies (US) studied violin and conducting at the Juilliard School in New York. His activities as opera and concert conductor, pianist and chamber musician are characterized by an extensive repertoire ranging from Baroque to contemporary modern works, by fascinating and brilliantly conceived programs, and by close collaboration with such prominent composers as Luciano Berio, William Bolcom, John Cage, Manfred Trojahn, Philip Glass, Heinz Winbeck, Laurie Anderson, Philippe Manoury, Aaron Copland, Hans Werner Henze, Michael Nyman and Kurt Schwertsik. Since 2002, Dennis Russell Davies has been chief conductor of the Bruckner Orchester Linz and opera director at Landestheater Linz. He will debut at Teatro Real de Madrid in 2013.

Mariano Sardón (AR) is a professor and chair of the Electronic Art Degree at the Universidad Nacional de 3 de Febrero and the academic advisor of the Interactive Art Program at Espacio Fundación Telefónica Argentina. He studied Physics at the Universidad Nacional de Buenos Aires. He was visiting scholar at the University of California Los Angeles. He has had many solo and collective exhibitions. Many of his works belong to museums and private art collections in Argentina and abroad.

Alexander Schellow (DE), is interested in relations of space, perception and action, in an overlapping field of artistic and scientific research practices. Since 1999 he has developed a continuous practice: a process of drawing reconstruction from memory. This serves as the basis for various formats that unfold over long periods of time and that are partly site-specific: drawing series, animations/films, archives, installations, lectures, performances or texts. Most recently he developed an open archive of orientation practices within the context of the fast-growing new areas of Tirana (Albania), reflecting the related local and translocal spatial politics. Alexander Schellow holds a professorship in the Cinema d'animation department at the ERG, Brussels.

Markus Schmidt (AT) is founder of Biofaction, a research, technology assessment, and science communication company in Vienna, Austria. His scientific work focuses on the societal ramifications of new biotechnologies. He also aims to contribute to a better interaction between science and society through public talks, production of scientific documentary films, Science Film Festivals (Bio:fiction) and art-science exhibitions (synth-ethic).
www.markusschmidt.eu

Claudia Schmölders (DE) gained her doctoral degree in philosophy and German language & literature at the Free University of Berlin in 1973. She worked for 20 years as an editor at publishing houses and as a freelance journalist in Zurich, Cologne, Frankfurt and Berlin. In 1991-92, she was a Fellow at the Wissenschaftskolleg zu Berlin. Since 1998, she has been a lecturer at Humboldt University. Her most important works are: *Die Kunst des Gesprächs: Texte zur Geschichte der europäischen Konversationstheorie.* Munich, 1986, *Hitlers Gesicht. Eine physiognomische Biographie,* München, 2000 and Die Stimme des Bösen. Zur Klanggestalt des 3. Reiches, *MERKUR* 581 (1997). *www.claudiaschmoelders.de*

Christine Schöpf (AT), PhD, studied German and Romance Languages. She has worked as a radio and television journalist and was the head of the art and science department at ORF Upper Austria (1981-2008). Recently she was appointed Honorary Professor at the University of Art and Industrial Design in Linz (2009). Since 1979, she has held a number of positions in which she has been able to contribute considerably to the development of Ars Electronica. She was responsible for conceiving and organizing the Prix Ars Electronica from 1987-2003. Together with Gerfried Stocker, she has been the artistic co-director of Ars Electronica since 1996.

Stefan Schraml (AT) was born in 1973 in Vienna and has worked as a Game Producer and User Interface Designer. He is the primary founding member of GameStage, a Linz-based gaming community and presentation platform.

Heribert Schröder (DE/AT) trained as a violinist, pianist and vocalist before studying music, ethnology and Catholic theology at Bonn University. Worked and taught at the Department for Sound Studies, Bonn University. Since 1999, he has taught orchestra & opera management in the Department of Cultural and Media Management at Hamburg University of Music and Theater. Since 2001, he has been artistic director of the Bruckner Orchestra Linz, responsible for the administrative agenda of Chief Conductor Dennis Russell Davies.

Theresa Schubert (DE) is a post-media artist and researcher in everything concerning the intersection of art, science, and its social impact. In her artistic practice she treats nature's phenomena not only as inspiration, but as a material and critical process to better understand the complexity of our lives by combining biological matter with digital art. Currently she is a PhD Candidate in media art at the Bauhaus University Weimar.

Mariano Sigman (AR) obtained a PhD in neuroscience in New York and then moved to Paris. His research is in perception, decision-making and consciousness. In 2006 he founded the Integrative Neuroscience Laboratory at the University of Buenos Aires. He has been awarded with the HFSP Career Award, the young investigator prize of the Collège de France, the IBM award and is a scholar of the James S. McDonnell Foundation.

Social Fabrication Center SFC/SFCSFC (JP), Shonan Fujisawa Campus, Keio University, Tokyo, was founded by Yusuke Tominaka, Shigeki Shimizu, Yusuke Nakamura and Hiroya Tanaka in 2012. It is a research center where tools, machines, and systems for the future Fablab are developed. Our mission is to develop new technologies and methods for solving problems that emerge both within and outside Japan. We focus on social and on personal fabrication—on community, group and collaboration. Via social fabrication, we also carry out social studies on various collaborative platforms, and plans include the creation of a place called "future sessions".

Oliver Spiecker (DE) is an author and event designer. Among his venues are Konzerthaus Berlin and Royal Albert Hall London. His credits include Die Goldene Kamera, World Sports Awards, Cinema for Peace and *Graz fliegt,* the opening event of Graz 2003 European Capital of Culture broadcast by the ORF – Austrian Broadcasting Company. On the occasion of Richard Wagner's 200th birthday, he conceived the TV extravaganza from the Leipzig Opera. He has written lyrics for Peter Maffay and Udo Jürgens. *Look – don't listen!,* his biography of Gottfried Helnwein, was published in 2013. Oliver Spiecker lives and dreams in Berlin, Bali and Mallorca.

STATION ROSE (AT) was founded in 1988 by artist Elisa Rose and composer Gary Danner, pioneers of digital culture in Vienna. 1987: diploma from Vienna University of Applied Arts; since 1988: Gunafa Clubbing; 1988-89: Cairo; 1991-2011: STR in Frankfurt; 1995: Prix Ars Electronica; 1996: Sony Music; since 1996: Social Web; since 1999: webcasting; 2002-04: professorship at Darmstadt University of Applied Sciences; 2002–06: "Best of Webcasting" TV, ARD; 2008: 20 Digital Years; performances and exhibitions worldwide; since 2011: back in Vienna & in MQ; 2012: recipient of the Art Recognition Prize of the City of Linz. *stationrose.com*

Gerfried Stocker (AT) is a media artist and electronic engineer. In 1991, he founded x-space, a team for the realization of interdisciplinary projects. In this framework numerous installations and performance projects have been carried out in the field of interaction, robotics and telecommunication. Since 1995 Gerfried Stocker has been a Managing and Artistic Director of Ars Electronica. 1995/1996 he developed the groundbreaking exhibition strategies of the Ars Electronica Center with a small team of artists and technicians and was responsible for the set-up (and establishment) of Ars Electronica's own R&D facility, the Ars Electronica Futurelab. Since 2004 he has been in charge of developing Ars Electronica's program of international exhibition tours. Since 2005 he has planned the expansion of the Ars Electronica Center and implemented the total substantive makeover of its exhibits.

Synergetica Lab (NL) based in Amsterdam, Synergetica is an art-science laboratory, investigating photonics, fluid dynamics, acoustics, quantum chemistry and psychophysics. In addition to providing a platform for artists working in these domains, Synergetica serves as a curatorial and educational entity, disseminating interdisciplinary art works and art-science research.

Joshua Tan Cheng Quan (SG) is a co-founder and creative director of CraveFX Pte Ltd. He has worked on a wide range of projects, including corporate work, award winning short films and university funded research work. Joshua graduated with a BFA in Digital Animation from Nanyang Technological University and was awarded the Lee Kuan Yew Gold Medal by President S.R Nathan for his achievements.
http://portfolio.joshuatan.net/p/videos.html

Salvatore Vanasco (IT) was born in 1960 in Montalbano, Italy, grew up in Hessen, Germany and now lives in Berlin. 1982: studied literature at La Sapienza University in Rome. 1984-89, studied visual communications at the HFBK-University of Fine Arts in Hamburg. From 1989 to 1998, he was a founding member and director of the European Media Art Lab. In 2006, he cofounded xailabs GmbH in Berlin. He is an artist, software entrepreneur and one of the first German Internet entrepreneurs. He served for many years as professor and dean at Merz Akademie Stuttgart, and is a recipient of the German Media Art Prize.

Eyal Vexler (IL), is a producer and curator of cultural art events and exhibitions, who initiates, organizes and produces a variety of events such as art exhibitions (institutional and independent), mass cultural events, music shows, video art, movies and fashion line productions.

Ei Wada (JP), born in 1987, is a musician and an artist. Ei Wada adapts old-fashioned electronic machines, converting them into computer-controlled devices. He puts on performances with these machines, as well as creating musical work and installations for exhibitions. In 2009, he started the group Open Reel Ensemble, which manipulates and plays reel-to-reel tape recorders. The group is involved in a wide range of activities including concert performances, DVD/CD and book publishing, art installations and providing music for movies and catwalk shows. Recently it has begun an ambitious orchestral project using 20 reel-to-reel tape recorders. Wada also works for the Braun Tube Jazz Band project, which plays CRT monitors as instruments and has performed in various locations around the world.

Cheong Davier Yoon Wai (SG) is a multi-disciplinary artist and animator, co-founder at and creative director at CraveFX Pte. Ltd. His expertise covers a wide gamut of animation techniques. He graduated from Nanyang Technological University with a BFA in Digital Animation in 2010 and joined a stereoscopic research project exhibited in Deep Space in 2011. Together with Ogilvy Singapore, he directed the computer generated imagery of *Tools of Destruction*, which won a Spikes Asia Gold Award. *http://reivad.net/*

Huang Yi (TW) is a choreographer, experimenter, and an inventor. He makes dances through different lens and media, and is actively engaged in video, photography, and installation arts. A two-time winner of the Taipei Digital Art Performance Award, he is known for the mix of rich images and delicate body. Since his 2006 short film *Costume, Dance with Visual Effect*, Huang Yi ventures into dance videography and continuously quests for new technological expressions for dance.

Arie Zinger (IL) lives.

Andre Zogholy (AT) was born in 1975 and lives in Linz. He is engaged in cultural studies, and is a sound researcher and an artist. He works at Linz Art University, at the University of Linz and with the qujOchÖ art collective.

Oren Zuckerman (IL), head of the interactive communications program, and founder of the Media Innovation Lab at the Interdisciplinary Center (IDC) Herzliya, Israel. Zuckerman's research areas are at the interface of interactive technologies & human behavior, focusing on physical-digital interactive experiences. His research projects include sensor-based mobile technologies for wellbeing and tangible interfaces for learning. Zuckerman completed his MSc and PhD at MIT Media Lab, publishes regularly on HCI and CMC related topics, and is a frequent speaker on HCI and interactive media events. In 2001, the World Economic Forum recognized Zuckerman as a "Technology Pioneer" at the annual forum in Davos, Switzerland. In 2012 a group of researchers including Zuckerman received the prestigious Israeli Excellence Center grant in the field of "Education in a New Information Society".